FRENCH ENTRÉE 15

BED and BREAKFAST in FRANCE

A Gatwick Region by Region Guide

FRENCH ENTRÉE 15

BED and BREAKFAST in FRANCE

A Gatwick Region by Region Guide

Patricia Fenn and Rosemary Gower-Jones

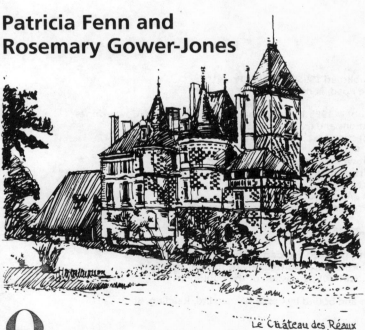

Le Château des Réaux

Quiller Press

Important Note

Readers are encouraged to send in their comments and suggestions but please address these to Patricia Fenn for Normandy, Brittany, the North, Picardy, Champagne, Ardennes, Western Loire, Burgundy, and all the rest to Rosemary Gower-Jones – Both c/o Quiller Press, 46 Lillie Rd, London SW6 1TN.

First published 1995 by Quiller Press Ltd
46 Lillie Road, London SW6 1TN

Copyright © 1995 Text: Patricia Fenn and Rosemary Gower-Jones
Illustrations and maps: © 1995 Quiller Press Ltd
Wine Section text: © John Doxat

Line drawings: Rosemary Gower-Jones
Area maps: John Gower-Jones, Neil Shepherd and Helen Humphreys
Front cover: Tim Jaques
Design and production in association with
Book Production Consultants plc, Cambridge

ISBN 1-899163-01-8

Printed and bound by Cox & Wyman Ltd, Reading, Berks

Contents

Foreword

A unique French experience awaits everyone embarking on a chambres d'hôtes holiday. It could mean a cosy room in a sixteenth-century farmhouse or a stately suite in a magnificent château – the choice is endless and there is something to suit all tastes and budgets.

Daily flights to fourteen of the most popular French holiday destinations from London Gatwick perfectly complements the flexibility of the chambres d'hôtes' accommodation system. Set up by the French Government, travellers can book an inexpensive night in a French home – with private facilities – and even eat home cooked French cuisine with the family. As more and more French families offer the warmth of their hospitality to visitors, this new Entrée guide has been designed to help you make the most of your chambres d'hôtes holiday.

For many people the holiday begins at the airport and at London Gatwick we have invested in a major £100 million redevelopment programme to make sure it's an enjoyable experience, whether you are flying on business or pleasure.

A smooth and efficient service from checking in to boarding the aircraft is complemented by a whole host of tax and duty free shops, including familiar high street and internationally renowned brand names, as well as a selection of bars and restaurants which cater for everyone's tastes. At London Gatwick we have created a truly world class, world beating airport.

We hope that you find this Entrée guide a valuable source of information when planning your trip and that your holiday, from start to finish, is an all round success.

Eric Lomas
Managing Director
Gatwick Airport Limited

The Regions and Départments of France

Tips for Beginners

Maps and guides: Good maps add so much to the enjoyment and success of a holiday that it seems unnecessary to insist that they should be essential companions. I must stress that those in this book are intended only as an indication of where to find the entries. They should be used in conjunction with the appropriate Michelin maps, which are models of clarity and comprehensive cover.

The red Michelin, apart from all its other virtues, has useful town maps. Its cost is justified if it directs you to even one good meal, I believe. In the areas already covered by French Entrées I like to think you won't need any other guidance. That said, chambres d'hôtes landladies are experts on their immediate locality and have regular feedback from their guests, so take their advice.

Currently in print are: FE8 – The Loire, FE9 – Normandy Encore, FE 10 – The South of France, FE11 – Paris, FE 12 – The North of France, FE13 – Provence, FE14 – Brittany Encore, FE16 – The Gardens of France, all published by Quiller Press.

Booking: Sunday lunch is the Meal of the Week, when several generations settle down together to enjoy an orgy of eating, drinking, and conversation that can well last till teatime. You should certainly book then and on fête days. Public holidays are as follows:

New Year's Day
Easter Sunday and Monday,
Labour Day, 1st May
VE Day 8th May
Ascension Day
Whit Sunday and Monday
France's National Day, 14th July
The Assumption, 15th August
All Saints Day (Toussaints) 1st November
Armistice Day, 11th November
Christmas Day

Make good use of the local tourist bureaux, where you should find some English spoken. Let them do the booking for you if you have problems. This is the place to pick up maps and brochures.

Take with you: Depends where you're heading. If it's the S category that interests you pack some soap, and a decent towel if you can't stand the risk of a handkerchief-sized baldie. Shouldn't be necessary in M and L grades. In the latter group you can expect to find free-bies like shampoo, bath oil, hair dryers and even trouser presses, but a total blank when it comes to a bedroom clock, so consider taking a travelling version. A small iron is a precaution, except where we specifically mention laundry facilities.

I would always advocate using the local markets for self-catering but it's worth taking tea if you don't like stale teabags, marmalade (good for presents, too), biscuits and cereals if you have favourites – all of which are either hard to locate, expensive or hor-rible.

Bring Home: The list of Best Buys doesn't change much. Obviously wine – you should be able to buy it for half the price you pay back home if you stick to the cheapos and the medium-priced bottles. There is far less differential on the vintage wines and sometimes they are cheaper here. Be a lager lout by all means, stock up on cof-fee, plain chocolate, ironmongery, kitchen gadgets. Best of all are impulse buys in the markets.

Closing Times: If you can't beat 'em, join 'em. Accept that not a cat stirs between 12 noon and 2.30 p.m. and that if the rest of the pop-ulation is eating then you might as well join them. Even the markets snap abruptly shut – forget impulse picnics after midday. At the other end of the day it's a joy to be able to find shops open until 7 p.m. Mondays are almost as dead as Sundays, so if it's a long week-end you're planning, try and add on the Friday instead. Sunday din-ner and both meals on Monday can be a real problem.

Breakfasts: Usually a strong plus point for chambres d'hôtes. The breakfast that is normally included in the price tends to outclass those served in hotels and should certainly be taken into account when comparing prices. Many a farmer's wife will throw in morn-ing-collected eggs, a slab of home-produced butter, and a selection of home-made preserves. On the other hand don't expect the budget stops to offer expensive pâtisserie and fresh orange juice and if your lodging is excessively remote it may not be possible even to arrange for that French breakfast staple – the fresh baguette. A trend of which I do not approve is that practised by some of the more upmarket chambres d'hôtes – of charging extra for breakfast. This is a sneaky way of upping the charge, since you are hardly likely to drive from your rural château into the nearest town for a cup of coffee and, without the self-catering facilities that tend to be the preserve of the M and S groups, you have little choice but to add another 100f to the bill. They could of course argue that 'chambres d'hôtes', unlike its British so-called equivalent 'bed and breakfast', makes no mention of food, but the ploy just adds fuel to the hotel keepers' claim that chambres d'hôtes are just small hotels with fewer taxes.

Telephoning: Bearing in mind how few rooms are available in each chambres d'hôtes and how much rural navigation is often involved in finding them, it makes sense to telephone ahead – the landlady will switch on the heating if she's sure of a customer – and if you are planning on eating in, a reservation is usually essential. Every chambres d'hôtes owner that I asked reckoned that they could handle a telephone booking, however meagre their English. If you have difficulties, use a bar – inevitably the customers will rally to your aid if you look helpless enough. The public phones in France actually work.

To dial another department dial just eight figures (eg. 21.33.92.92).

To dial Paris – dial 16 and 1 then 4, followed by 7 figures (eg 6/1/4/X XX XX XX).

To dial UK from France, dial 19, 44, then STD code minus 0, then number.

To dial France from UK: 010 33 8-figure number.

Emergencies: Fire 18; Police 17; Operator: 13; Directory Enquiries: 12.

Introduction

Talk about a growth industry. When I started writing French Entrées, fourteen years ago, chambres d'hôtes were a rarity; I included one or two as I came across them, just to gauge the reaction and discovered a long-felt want being satisfied. Readers were enthusiastic about the opportunity to get to know their French opposite numbers, sleep in interesting homes, not bland institutions, and to eat the real French family cooking that they had heard so much about. And the price was right. With families, for extra breaks, or just the budget-conscious b. and bs. proved the answer. 'I would never use a hotel again' was the recurring refrain, which is how this book came to be written.

The French customers were not so sure. They saw no reason to chat to the farmer's wife over breakfast, and preferred to spend their holidays in the way they always had – in a safe hotel, eating the most expensive food they could afford. But slowly, belatedly, even the conservative natives are coming round to the idea and with the Scandinavians and Germans, who are just as keen as the Brits on the concept, they are making the b. and b. business boom. The State thinks it is an excellent idea and helps out with useful conversion grants. Barns that had no roofs a few years ago now shelter a cluster of efficient, modern *en suite* rooms, rustic cottages cash in on their picture book prettiness with entranced townees, widows eke out their pensions and forego their loneliness sharing their empty nests, and aristos who have inherited gorgeous buildings without appropriate fortunes need no longer worry that their children will see the family pile left derelict or part of a chain of hotels.

Everyone, very nearly, is happy while the bandwagon rolls. Perhaps this is no place to point out the hazards, but I must. There are signs that fings might not be wot they used to be. Greediness is creeping in – given a full house one year, Madame sees no reason why she should not raise her prices for the next. The tradition of hospitality is sometimes interpreted loosely, so that the family opt out of eating with the guests; the generosity of home fare can sometimes founder, so foil-wrapped butter pats replace the slab, one shop jam appears for breakfast where there used to be five homemade. On occasions I have felt distinctly processed, usually when the owners have been b. and b.-ing for some years, have a number of rooms to handle which are usually full, and are getting a little blasé.

Paradoxically this is the justification for a book like this one. With so many to choose from, informed selection is ever more vital. Rosemary Gower-Jones or I have personally visited every chambres d'hôtes listed which are not quotes from friends. (We have visited a lot more too, which you will not find here, saving you the grief.) The old French Entrée criteria of comfort, good value and welcome have been applied in our choice. Welcome has always been the aspect that has invoked more enthusiastic letters than ritziness or cheapness. Given a smile and a cuppa no end of shortcomings can be overlooked. In chambres d'hôtes it is particularly important because of the close relationship between host and guest. If you hate your host, can you bear to stay in his house? Looking back it is astonishing how few hates I found. The landlady breed seems to be exceptionally nice.

It would seem that their niceness brings out the niceness in us. The temptations attached to staying in stately homes, surrounded with easily-pocketed valuables, would seem irresistible but no, every chatelaine I asked said that her clients, and especially the British clients, were models of rectitude. If you enjoy meeting folk with similar tastes to your own and making new friends, do not demand smooth service or immaculate taste in decor, can accept wellies in the hall and trikes on the lawn, chambres d'hôtes are for you. Readers' letters frequently relate how they have come to regard their hosts as real friends, too, and that at least one annual visit has to be written into their diaries. It is miraculous how the language barriers seem to collapse, and certainly the evening chat is a perfect way to oil long-rusty French.

But it is essential for first-timers to know exactly what to expect and to have a choice. We try to paint the picture with more detail than the bare facts of prices and addresses and leave it to you to make the decision. You need to know about the style, comfort, character, location, before you can do that successfully. Even your co-authors have their different priorities. Rosemary's *bête noire* is bare floors (except in the South in summer); she places secure parking top of her list of essentials and, influenced by her sociable husband John, who likes to practise his French, will always pick a b. and b. with an evening meal. My priority is a hot bath in which to soak away the cares of the day – showers are just not the same –

and because I already know the regions' restaurants well and am always on the lookout for new ones for future editions of French Entrées, am happy to eat out. As husband Colin, who contributes his subjective judgements.

We have split the country roughly south (Rosemary)/north (me), because these are the regions covered in previous FEs), except that I bagged Burgundy and Rosemary got landed with Normandy when I ran out of time. We have tried to locate at least one option in every *département* in France. In the top tourist areas – Brittany, Normandy, the Loire and Burgundy – they came thick and fast and elimination had to be ruthless; in the less-exploited areas we had to scratch around a bit. Entries within easy reach of the main autoroutes have been a priority, since a b. and b. is ideal for *en route* stops, particularly where cheap family suites are available. Frequently a one-night stand leads to a long-term relationship.

Categories: The French Entrée formula has been retained – 'S' for Simple, 'M' for Medium and 'L' for Luxury. Prices quoted are for a double room with two breakfasts unless stated otherwise. Here's what to expect:

The S group predictably were the hardest to select. One man's simplicity is another's discomfort. Their price range – roughly from 100–250f – generally precludes luxuries but should involve modest comfort. Aware that most couples nowadays expect *en suite* 'facilities', we have ruled out any that involve nocturnal corridor-padding. Most have individual shower and loo attached, though if other considerations look good you may find some where the sanitation is opposite the room and often if there are two family/friends' rooms the bathroom is shared between them.

Many S chambres d'hôtes are on farms. Custom-built conversions of outbuildings usually result in modern rooms, perhaps lacking in character but perfectly acceptable, with reasonable (for the French) lighting and a ban on lumpy mattresses. Dormer windows are common, which is a pity because the (usually) rural outlook is lost. You could get lucky here with breakfast – farm eggs and butter, home-made jams – but you might have to put up with toasted bread and no croissants. Fruit juice sometimes.

The S evening meal can be astonishing value. 50–90f will ensure three main courses, plus salad, and veg, all home-grown, plus cheese, and coffee and often includes wine. *Compris* means all-

inclusive from *apéritif* to *digestif*. The welcome drink on arrival sets
the tone. I have never known this appear on the bill, as it certainly
would in a hotel. Loads of goodwill has to substitute for fluent
English.

The M group, from 250–450f, are a very mixed bag; they
include manors, town houses, ex-monasteries, mills and modern villas, and their owners are just as heterogeneous – single ladies,
entrepreneurs, retired couples, ex-pats, some totally amateur, some
making a business of it. You are more likely here to stay in the
existing rooms of the house, spruced up and put to good use.
Expect *en suite* sanitation here and usually a bath. The rooms are
more likely to vary in character and price, so it pays to specify
whether you prefer double or twin beds, shower or bath, the cheapest or the most expensive. They will have more character, thanks to
family furniture, and Madame is more likely to speak English.

Fewer landladies in this category offer *table d'hôte*. One
friendly widow told me that with only one pair of hands she preferred to devote her time to welcoming her guests and chatting with
them over an *apéritif* rather than disappearing into the kitchen to
cook. They will always be able to recommend local restaurants for
all tastes and pockets. If an evening meal is on offer, it will probably cost between 90 and 180f – excellent value if that includes wine.

The L group are very dear to my heart since I prefer staying in
one of them to any luxury hotel; I have rarely been disappointed
and always come away enriched by this opportunity to live in a
style to which I am definitely not accustomed. They will generally
be châteaux. Inheritance rules in France mean that property and
financial assets are divided equally between the children, leaving
none sufficiently well endowed to support a money-swallowing
pile. Before the prospect of opening their homes to guests became
conceivable it was sad to see these ghosts of past splendour decay-
ing – their gates rusty, their parks overgrown, their roofs in holes.
But now new life has been breathed into them by the combination
of bank manager's backing and owners' dedication. It has been
realised that a lovely historic building and priceless belongings are
not enough to woo customers away from hotels. The plumbing
must be equally conducive to the luxury label....Bathrooms have
been contrived out of surplus adjacent bedrooms and are consequently splendid in size and accoutrements. Towels and carpets are

thick. Bedrooms will be all different and furnished with covetable antiques. Occasionally they can be overpowering (I left out some horrors), but generally these hostesses are sophisticated ladies with excellent taste and they present their lovely spacious rooms with great style.

Dinner is usually available, sometimes prepared by Madame, sometimes by minions, so that you don't feel so guilty. The style is lavish, very good home cooking, usually with wine included for between 150–250f. Breakfasts come on elegant china, with freshly squeezed orange juice, fruit, buttery croissants, a variety of breads, a choice of jams and the option of something more substantial like ham and cheese to please the Scandinavian and German clients who love this group. You could economise on lunch if you take full advantage of what's on offer. The good news is that the owners realise that they personally are part of the attraction of staying here so, however unpromising the guests, they make the effort to join them at the very least for apéritifs and coffee and usually for the entire meal. They have learned how to become suave manipulators of their clients' personalities and skilfully keep the conversation going. English is invariably their second language and the lingua franca round the dinner table. The bad news is that this is the group whose prices, I believe, are getting out of hand and out of reach. True, their accommodation is superior to that of a hotel, true that the inclusion of breakfast in the deal helps to soften the blow, but I still deem the maximum price I have had to pay – 900f – too high for what is essentially an amateur operation. The hotels hate their guts, of course, and charge them with dodging taxes and often breaking the rule of only five rooms to a chambres d'hôtes. Certainly the line between a hotel and a luxury b. and b. with staff is a fine one. But mercifully there are still plenty who do the job for pleasure as much as for gain, setting their prices between 500 and 700f, which I consider good value.

It does pay to book ahead if you can. Basic telephone-English has usually been mastered. With only a few rooms to allocate the more popular beds are grabbed early. Don't even think of turning up on spec on busy weekends and *fêtes* (see list on p. ix). Have the courtesy to phone again if you are delayed – thus strengthening the entente cordiale. Don't bank on an evening meal unless its pre-booked; this is not a hotel with a big freezer, thank God. The ideal hour to arrive is around teatime, giving Madame a chance to go out shopping and do her chores and allowing you to get your bearings and relax.

I cannot claim that the years spent researching this book have offered many opportunities for relaxing. I have discovered that tracking down remote chambres d'hôtes, often with sketchy directions and arriving to find no one at home, is not conducive to low blood pressure and appreciation of the view. But that's the name of the game. 'It's the readers wot gits the pleasure and the writers wot gits the blame.'

Special Recommendations: Arrows ➤ are special recommendations, tried and tested. Criteria for inclusion are one or more of the following virtues: good food, comfort, welcome, situation.

Opening Times: all year round unless stated.

Parking: one of the big pluses with chambres d'hôtes – safe and enclosed, unless stated otherwise.

Directions: we aim to save you the hassle of bumping down the wrong cart track in the dark by giving clear and detailed directions. The maps are mere indications – you would be foolish to travel without the appropriate Michelin.

Payment: cash is preferred. Plastic money occasionally in the L class.

NORD

....

Départements: **Nord**
                           Pas de Calais.

Companion guide to the area: 'French Entree 12 – Calais and the North'.

NORD

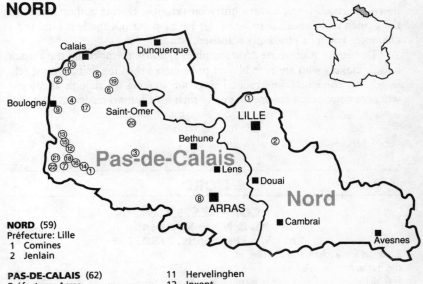

NORD (59)
Préfecture: Lille
1 Comines
2 Jenlain

PAS-DE-CALAIS (62)
Préfecture: Arras
1 Aubin St Vaast
2 Audinghen
3 Azincourt
4 Belle-et-Houllefort
5 Bois-en-Ardres
6 Bonningues-les-Ardres
7 Campigneulles-les-Grandes
8 Duisans
9 Echinghen
10 Escalles

11 Hervelinghen
12 Inxent
13 Longvilliers
14 Marasquel
15 Maresville
16 Marles-sur-Canche
17 Menneville
18 Montreuil-sur-Mer
19 Muncq-Nieurlet
20 Pihem
21 St Josse-sur-Mer
22 Verton

◼ Préfecture

◼ Town

① Chambre d'Hôtes

A much-maligned area. Anyone who still believes that the North of France is all featureless, flat, industrialised and boring, should be dragged to the Boulonais hills, the time-warped villages a few miles inland, the fascinating towns of Arras, Montreuil and St. Omer, the sophistication of Le Touquet, the glorious beaches, the unique canal network and the *hortillonages* (market gardens), and made to repent. Of course there is industrialisation and whole tracts of mining territory that do not contribute to the holiday scene, but even here the biggest city, Lille, is underestimated. It's a prosperous city and destined to become ever more important as the hub of a European multi-transport system. Its art galleries, restaurants and restored mediaeval heart rival those of many a better-loved town.

The autoroute system through this area is superb – fast, efficient and uncrowded. Pick it up at the Calais docks and Arras is just a short hop down the road. Don't always hurry on through. Devote a short break to the French region nearest to home, let FE 12 point out the best bits, and I guarantee you'll be pleasantly surprised.

This is not a great area for chambres d'hotes. Despised by the French holidaymakers who are even blinder to its merits than the Brits, it must rely largely on foreigners for trade. Things are looking up though and some welcome newcomers are opening up in time for Chunnel business.

NORD

COMINES. 59560
M. & Mme Vermes
Chemin du Petit Enfer. 20.39.21.28.

Looking for a chambres d'hotes in the flat industrial land round Lille I was delighted to find a quiet farm just south of Comines, surrounded by fields. Madame Vermes works in Lille all day and returns at 6 p.m. with her two young daughters, to cook the evening meal. Providing you phone ahead and book, Madame Vermes senior will come over from her farmhouse to welcome you with a refreshing cup of

tea, if you arrive before 6 p.m. The three rooms which are spacious and attractively furnished are warm and have very good *en suite* facilities. Double room 180f. There is one family room with bunk beds in an alcove. Dinner taken with the family is excellent with fresh produce from the garden and interesting dishes cooked by Madame. Dinner is 70f, wine *compris* and Monsieur is a jolly young host who speaks some English. Good night kisses from the young Vermes! Monsieur usually serves breakfast with a variety of bread and homemade jams as he is at home working on the farm all day. Comines is a border town half in France and half in Belgium and very handy for visiting Ypres and the many cemeteries from the First World War.

Bypass Lille by the A25 Autoroute leaving at exit 8 (Armentières) and take the D 945 to Comines. Turn right just inside the town on the D 308 to Ste Marguerite. Just before the village turn right and the farm lies 800 yards down a very small road.

JENLAIN. 58144

8 km SE of Valenciennes by N49, direction Maubeuge. Industrialised suburbs, dominated by autoroutes, are not situations where one expects to come across stunning châteaux in lovely gardens. Don't despair when you turn off the *nationale*, following the signs to Jenlain (dreary). Before you turn right into the village you will see discreet gates straight ahead and a half-obscured chambres d'hôtes sign. This is it.

Chateau d'En Haut (M–L)
27.49.71.80. Open all year.

Chambres d'hôtes don't come any more 'L' than this one. Your delighted eyes will alight, after a worrying drive up an overgrown drive, on a large and lovely château, set in well-kept and flowery grounds. Why the patronne, Mme Demarcq, should want to allow plebs like you and me loose amongst her valuable antiques and tread on her Persian carpets and sleep beneath her handworked
quilts is beyond comprehension. Especially when she charges only 300f for a superb double room and breakfast.

Breakfast, a good start to the day, is served in a stunning, yellow room with toile on the walls, at a yellow lacquered table. No evening meal but plenty of recommended nearby restaurants. All the rooms are different, all except one (cheaper at 180f) has its own bathroom, all are furnished not only with valuable antiques, but with great flair.

This is a most unusual b. and b., wonderful value, and would certainly brighten up the northern gloom or provide a sensational first night at the beginning of a holiday. Good, too, for a pampered, weekend break.

PAS-DE-CALAIS

AUBIN ST VAAST. 62140

5 km NW of Hesdin on the N39. Heading towards Hesdin, take the Route de Lambus, a turning on the right in the village, from which La Gentilhommière is well signed.

Hesdin is a delightful little town, familiar perhaps as the setting for the Maigret T.V. series. It lies at the confluence of the rivers Canche and Ternoise whose rivulets crisscross the town. Hump-backed bridges, cobbled streets, nice old houses, the Renaissance Notre Dame church, and above all the vast market square all lend considerable character. The magnificent town hall which dominates the square gives a clue to the town's former importance. Above the porch flies the Imperial Eagle of the Hapsburgs and the royal arms of Spain surmount the balcony. Once the frontier of the old Hapsburg Empire, founded and fortified by Charles V of Austria in 1554, the town fell to the Spanish until Louis X111 regained it for the French in 1639. This mixed pedigree accounts for the charmingly eclectic architecture. On Thursday mornings the farmers from the surrounding countryside set up their stalls in the Grand' Place and contribute to one of the best markets for miles around. Sit and watch the action from a nearby café.

La Gentilhommière (M)
Mme Vezilier. Route de Lambus. 21.86.80.48.66.

A popular FE6 choice and still going strong. A gentilhommière is a nice word for a gentlemen's house and this one, though not very old, looks as though it might have been built originally for someone of style.

Le Gentilhommière

Furniture is a mixture of old and new. The yellow room on the ground floor (bathroom with shower) costs 200f, the Rose room has a bathroom next door (180f) and the two family rooms can take four people for 270f, sharing a bathroom.

AUDINGHEN. 62179

14 km N of Boulogne, 19 km Sw of Calais. Turn off the D940 opposite the turning to Cap Gris Nez, on to the D191, signed 'Onglevert'. The sign for Maison de la Houve faces the other way, so keep eyes skinned for a turning on the left. The landmark is large, white, iron gates outside Mme Danel's latest project 'Jardins des Simples', or herb garden.

➤ Maison de la Houve (S)
21 32 97 06/21 83 29 95.

Maison de la Houve

The act of extreme altruism that led me to share this incomparable b. and b. with FE6 readers has predictably backfired. Now there is no way I can turn up on spec as the mood takes me. 'There is no "season",' says Mme Danel. 'My friends come to see me throughout the year.'

As well they might. To retreat to the pampering of La Houve in a winter depression makes just as much sense as a summer visit. Though I have to say that the ideal season is June, when the roses that are Mme. Danel's emblem are at their magnificent best. Shell pink *Madame Meilland* rampages over two walls of the erstwhile farmhouse. The blooms of *Distinction* are so tightly packed together that the impression is a cerise sea.

Pink, of a Barbara Cartland persuasion, has always been Mme Danel's signature and since my last visit she has got even pinker. Now not only the roses, the petunias, the doors, the shutters, and the table linen are of that hue but, rather more unexpectedly, so is the wheelbarrow, the stepladder and the *deux chevaux* van.

The eight bedrooms, with pink touches of course, are named after roses. Mine, *Distinction*, featured cabbage roses climbing up latticework but I liked *Madame Meilland* even better, partly because of its romantic lace bed canopy and partly because it boasted a bath as well as shower. But it really doesn't matter which you get because all are lovely.

A charming clutter is distributed all over the house. I don't think Mme Danel can bear to throw away anything that has given her pleasure, so in the lounge are piles of books and magazines and photos and cushions and silk flowers, and in the citrus-yellow study the armchairs are occupied with dolls for the amusement of young visitors – 'J'adore les enfants'; in the dining room, with its sensational view of the buttercupped Boulonnais hills dotted with cows, rolling down to the sea which is dotted with boats, the sideboard is loaded with gifts from her British clients – a lamp, a platter, a doll and a vase.

Breakfast, served at a long lace-covered table, making the most of the view that should be required viewing for those who insist that the North of France is all boring, is generous. Four different kinds of jam: 'my friends make it for me and an English lady gave me a pot of her *confiture de citron*'. There are eggs and *pain de campagne* as well as the standard orange juice and bread; copious coffee is served in deep china cups and this is all included in the remarkable price of 170f for two people. Prices are kept low so that young people – students and parents – can afford them.

Mme Danel is a remarkable lady, whose philosophy of enjoyment permeates the establishment. I asked her how on earth she managed to keep the place so pristine (all those ornaments and silk flowers take some dusting). '*Je danse, je danse*' she replied. And dance around she does, cossetting her guests, but never intruding on their privacy.

I drove away reluctantly on a hot, June evening to have dinner in Wimereux. One family were picnicking among the buttercups, another, newly arrived from the ferry, were stretched out in the evening sun on the rose-chintz recliners in the courtyard, unable to believe their luck. I am happy to say FE was much in evidence. It's the only English guide featuring La Houve and Mme Danel intends to keep it that way. 'All the people with your book are so kind and happee.' As well they should be. Arrowed of course.

AZINCOURT. 62310

15 km NE of Hesdin by D928, then right on D71. Fluttering banners, coats of arms in red and gold, and heraldic devices suspended at the roadside ensure that no one can fail to notice that something remarkable must have taken place in this unremarkable village. On these wide open fields it was that Henry V and Charles VI met in the combat that was to lead to 10,000 of the French nobility being slain or captured in 1415. A new museum offers a lively video presentation of the battle. In the village take the Tramecourt road and the house is on the right.

La Gacogne (M)
Mme Marie Jose Fenet. 21.04.45.61.

Not your run-of-the-mill basic chambres d'hôtes. The tall house, once the village school, is set in a tangle of greenery. In the main building where the Fenets live and serve breakfasts, the ceilings are lofty with lots of exposed rafters, and an amazing fireplace is surrounded by a sunken, semi-circular seat. The guest rooms are in an adjoining wing with names to indicate their fantasy decorations –

La Gacogne

Romantique (white drapes over the bed, lots of lace), *Retro, Espace,* and *Voyages* (utilising some of the souvenirs picked up by this much travelled family). They cost 200f with own bathroom (shower) or 180f without. Not everyone's choice for sure, but for those who don't mind a bit of eccentricity so long as the beds are comfortable and the natives friendly, it's certainly the best in the village. Reports would be particularly interesting on this one!

BELLE-ET-HOULLEFORT. 62142

14 km E of Boulogne. Now listen carefully – I shall say this only once – you take the N42 out of Boulogne and after La Capelle turn left onto the D234 to Conteville and just past the turning to Wierre Effroy, look out for a sign to the left to Le Breucq. If you get to what the Michelin map marks as 'Belle' you've gone too far. Then bump for half a mile down a farm track.

And the fact that I have to spell out such instructions is proof enough of the rural nature of the valley of the Wimereux – quite astonishingly near the *nationales* and port.

Le Breucq (S)
Mme de Montigny. 21.83.31.99.
Open year round, in winter by reservation.

If you crave for the Good Life and don't mind a bit of mud on your boots, this is the one. Such value! Such rusticity!

Mme Isabelle de Montigny has five spacious guest rooms in her large, rambling farmhouse. They are all furnished in a delicious time-warp of two generations ago, with the incomparable luxury of real fires in real fireplaces in every bedroom whenever the weather demands.

Fires we have, ensuite bathrooms we do not. Two shared bathrooms, painted in uncomfortably anachronistic bright paint, have showers and plenty of hot water, but as the general atmosphere would indicate heads-under-the-pump-in-the-yard plumbing, these must be considered very mod cons indeed.

The best room – grab it if you can – costs, wait for it – 180f, including two farm house breakfasts – and Madame makes all her own jams and brioches. For the truly impoverished, there are other rooms at 100f. Equally amazing value is the evening meal – 60f for four courses of home-grown produce. This would make a great base for a family of townees, wanting to experience the kind of country living which is fast disappearing. But forget the frills.

I look forward to some reports on this one. Could be a star.

BOIS-EN-ARDRES. 62601

12 km SW of Calais by RN43. House is at entrance to the village on the right.

Ardres, down the road, is an extremely pretty little town, long beloved by the English. It has two centres, a wide shady green square bordered by two little hotels, and the eccentric, triangular Grand' Place, cobbled, with houses awry. There is a fine 15th century Flamboyant Gothic church to admire and nearby a 2½ km lake for fishing, sailing, pedaloing or just walking around. Cafés have terraces overlooking the water, and it's all ideal for kids, near the ports and peaceful.

La Chesnaie (M)
Geneviève and Bernard Leturgie. 21.35.43.98.

An attractive not-very-old house set in a large garden featuring swings and a sandpit. Nice youthful-looking Madame Leturgie has six children and, surprisingly, several grandchildren, so she is used to having a full house. She has obviously realised that children need space (for the adults' sakes as much as their own) and has allocated a large upstairs room as a playroom with dolls, darts, T.V. and lots of games. She proudly showed me the huge salon which is used for breakfasts in inclement weather. Its most striking feature is a full-sized French billiard table (different from ours in that there are no pockets).

She has four rooms, with lots of beige flowered wallpaper; they all have a private bathroom somewhere, opposite or adjoining, with choice of bath or shower. 200f.

BONNINGUES-LES-ARDRES. 62890 TOURNEHEM-SUR-LA-HEM

12 km S of Ardres by N43, then right on to the D217 towards Licques. The house is in the village centre.

Le Manoir (M)
Mme Christiane Dupont. 16 route de Licques. 21.82.69.05.

FE readers have approved of this
nice, old, shuttered manor house,
set back from the road in a lovely
garden. At the rear is a terrace for
breakfast and, surprising views of
hills. It used to be Madame
Dupont's family home and now she
has furnished the six old-fashioned,
high-ceilinged bedrooms as chambres d'hôtes. There are variations of
twins, doubles, private bathroom,
shared bathroom, bath/shower at
prices from 200–220f.

BOULOGNE-SUR-MER. 62200

32 km S of Calais. The withdrawal of the ferries from Boulogne has left it a sadder
and wiser place. I now find it more agreeable than ever, with fewer tourists and
keener competition for those that are still faithful. I have written in more detail
about its attractions in FE12, but I would emphasise that there is much of interest
to admire in the port and in the Haute Ville and that the Wednesday and Saturday
markets are a particularly good reason for a visit.

I didn't think there were any chambres d'hôtes worth recording in the town
itself, but, too late for inspection, I had two recommendations worth passing on. I
should very much like to hear about any personal experiences.

Mme Delabie (M)
26 rue Flahaut. 21.31.88.74.

Described to me as five rooms in an old farmhouse outside the ramparts. One room
has *en suite* facilities, two have modern showers, and I was assured that the welcome was especially warm: 250–350f.

Mme Vanheeckhoet
24–26 rue de Lille. 21.80.41.50.

I don't even have any prices for this one but you can find it in a pedestrian precinct
in the heart of the old town, so it would be worth following up.

CAMPIGNEULLES-LES-GRANDES. 62170

5 km SE of Montreuil by D917. Towards Berck, through Campigneulles-les-Petites, past Rond Point. The Place Verte faces you in the village centre but is poorly marked.

Another of those undiscovered, unspoiled, flowery hamlets that make the triangle between Montreuil, Berck and Etaples so attractive. The perfect location for peaceful enjoyment of beaches and attractive towns where accommodation is busy and expensive.

Chez Smith (M)
1, Place Verte. 21.06.02.76.

No prizes for guessing that mine host here is a Brit. But John Alexander Smith has a French wife, Annie, so there is no danger of blanket chauvinism. They live in a very pretty cottage with an independent wing of two rooms, bath and loo behind the curtain in the bedroom. Its all very pretty indeed, beamed, with old fashioned bed and lace bedspread, for 220f.

DUISANS. 62161

5km W of Arras. Take the N39 direction Le Touquet, then turn left on to the D56. The house is on the left.

Arras would be high on my list for a short break in the North. It is an underappreciated town, full of interest. Its Grand' place, the largest open square in Europe, is lined with arcaded, Flemish-style houses, whose ornamented stepped gables, red brick, old stone and heraldic signs create an intensely satisfying total harmony. Few of them are the 17th and 18th century originals they would seem, but are in fact a cunning reconstruction from the rubble that was left after the devastation of the First World War. The extent of the damage of four years' bombardment can be seen in the photographs in the impressive Town Hall, which forms one side of another glorious square, the Place des Héros. Try and arrange a visit for Saturday or Wednesday, when the best market in the North takes place in the accommodating squares, but on no account miss this beguiling town.

Le Clos Grincourt (M)
Mme Annie Senlis. 18 rue du Chateau. 21.48.68.33.

Arras can do little wrong in my eyes, but I have to admit a shortcoming in the matter of hotels (see FE12 if you want to know which is the best and which restaurants to choose). This makes a good chambres d'hôtes in the vicinity all the more interesting. And Le Clos Grincourt is good. Montgomery chose it as a base in 1944, but he had to be installed in an armoured van outside for security reasons. We can be more fortunate.

Why can't the owners of other lovely old buildings like this one recognize that if money is short and the bedrooms cannot be furnished with valuable antiques, it is far better to keep it all simple. Here the rooms rely on fresh, light decoration to enhance their elegant proportions; furniture is plain, but in good taste. Each has its own bathroom; with shower – 200f or 370f for four – one with bath is 210f.

There was a family wedding there on the day I visited, but even at this busy time I was made welcome and shown all I wanted to see. Because the groom was a farmer, the theme of the wedding was vegetables, so each table in the marquee was named after something he grew – the leek table, the carrot table... Clever arrangements of veggies took the place of usual floral tributes.

I buttonholed a nice English family, the Kirbys, who were just leaving and they confirmed what I had suspected – that the accommodation, welcome and breakfast had all been great. This is one that I really look forward to sampling at first hand.

ECHINGHEN. 62360

4 km S of Boulogne by N1 at St-Leonard at the second traffic lights, take the D234 left, signed Echinghen.

Almost immediately the traffic fret dies away and the atmosphere becomes quiet and rural, making it hard to credit that the port and the Nationale are so near. Not many people know that.

Turn left in the village, following signs in village for:

Chez Boussemaer (M)
2.91.14.34. cl. for Christmas and New Year.

Nice Madame Boussemaer's son farms the surrounding land, growing cereals. The family home, an old farmhouse, has been heavily restored to provide guest accommodation. Rooms, looking out on to the courtyard are modern and pleasant.

The one at 230f, with a shower opposite is particularly agreeable, but for 250f you can have your shower and loo *en suite*, with choice of double or twin beds (four rooms altogether).

If you don't want to get the car out again to eat in Boulogne, there is another indication in the village that the simple life still rules OK in the Boulogne hinterland. *Chez Joelle*, recommended to her guests by Mme Boussemaer, is a village café with a daily menu for 60f.

ESCALLES. 62179

14 km SW of Calais. From the ferry follow the signs to Le Port, bump over the level crossing into the town, turn right over the swing bridge and follow the coast road, the D940 all the way.

Once in Escalles turn left at the bottom of the hill and look for the signs a half km out of the village, on the right.

The coast road will immediately give the lie to the general theory that the Pas-de-Calais has to be flat and boring. The high chalk cliffs at Cap Blanc Nez are of considerable stature and the countryside is spectacularly rolling. There is a pebbly beach in Escalles and a very popular fish restaurant, Restaurant du Cap.

La Grand' Maison (M)
Jacqueline Boutroy. 21.85.27.75.

This is one of the splendid old farm complexes that are such a pleasing feature of this part of France. Rustic buildings on three sides enclose a huge courtyard, big enough for small boys to be playing football where we visited, and an interesting square *pigeonnier* in the centre was soon pinpointed as the source of much contented cooing. The farm has been in Mme Boutroy's family for generations and is now getting the facelift it deserves, thanks to the p.gs.

There was only one room left – the smallest – but it was pretty nice, all white with a blue frieze and garlanded curtains, bath and separate loo, for 200f. The larger rooms, termed 'studios', have less character but are good value for their size and comfort. *Accueil* and breakfast are both irreproachable. An excellent choice for port proximity, amongst many other considerations.

HERVELINGHEN. 62179

20 km SW of Calais by coast road, D940. Turn off at Wissant on to D244 and farm is 1 km on left.

Between the two Caps, Gris Nez and Blanc Nez, in pleasant rolling country-side, with plenty of nearby beaches and fishy restaurants.

Les Rietz Quez (S)
Mme Boutroy Hazalard. 21.85.27.06.

A heavily restored old farm, built round a courtyard that takes the worry out of parking. The rooms are clean and wholesome, if a bit characterless – modern, sloping ceilings under the eves, with showers – 200f. Farm butter and milk for breakfast.

INXENT. 62170 MONTREUIL

7 km N of Montreuil by the D149. This enchantingly pretty little road, which follows the sparkling river Course, has come to be known as La Route des Anglais, since so many Brits have discovered it (partly *mea culpa*) and choose it in preference to the parallel Nationale. Inxent is one of the prettiest villages along its course and the only one to boast a quality restaurant, l'Auberge d'Inxent, which has been installed here as long as I (or anyone else around) can remember.

Coming from Montreuil, turn right just after the Auberge to drive up a leafy lane, crossing the river on the way. The Relais is on the right.

Le Relais Equestre (S)
Henri and Corinne Bourdon. 21.90.70.34. cl. September.

In the days when the virtues of chambres d'hôtes had yet to be generally discovered and before there were many others around I often used to make Le Relais my base for the multi-facetted region around Le Touquet, Montreuil, and the Boulonnais. It was peaceful, comfortable and cheap. Much water has passed under the little bridge over which you must drive (get out, hang over and watch the trout) to reach the cottage. There is a new Madame Bourdon here now and a programme of improvements has been implemented, but the basic deal is much the same.

This is a riding establishment, with six guest rooms, in M. Bourdon's 18th century family home, once a farmhouse. Unlike most riding establishments, however, humans do not come off second best to horses here. The rooms are

appropriately simple, with rough-cast white walls; brass or oak beds have crocheted coverlets, floors are scrubbed, rug scattered and the bathrooms are modern with plenty of hot water (a welcome innovation since my time). Only one room has its *salle de bain particulier*; the rest, which are family rooms, share two more between them. 200f for two, 255f for three.

Breakfast is taken at oak tables in the delightful, beamed dining-room, warmed by a big log fire in winter.

There are all kinds of horsey deals, for children and adults, beginners and experts, with full pension thrown in with the use of the animals, and I should think the prospect of galloping along the sands and rambling through the quiet, surrounding lanes would be most appealing for family holidays.

LONGVILLIERS. 62630 ETAPLES

10 km N of Montreuil by N1 and D146 on left, or D146 all the way from Beutin off the N39. An extremely pretty, extremely rural ride through extremely peaceful villages, whichever way you get there. There is no sign – a deliberate omission – so make sure you turn left just before the church in the village. The house is the first on the left.

Chez Francine and Pierre Desrumaux (M)
1 route de Courteville. 21.90.73.51.

Madame Desremaux has no sign because she does not want to be continually turning would-be lodgers away. With only two rooms to fill (and I would guess no financial necessity to go flat out), she has little need for publicity.

Her English-speaking husband is a most important man – the Mayor of Longvilliers no less. They are a charming friendly couple, who used the 1801 ex-presbytery as a *maison secondaire* for 26 years before they decided to make it their permanent residence. Now, amongst her other activities like selling honey from their bees, she offers two rooms at 250f, or a suite which could accommodate six, with a 60f supplement for each additional body. The rooms have beams, sloped, pine ceilings, small, high windows and showers. A good evening meal is to be had down the road at the *auberge* in Cormont.

1, Rue de Courteville

MARESQUEL. 62990

10 km SE of Montreuil by N39. There is a sign for the château but it faces the wrong way if you are coming from Montreuil, so look out for a *Depot Vente* sign just before the village of Maresquel and turn right here, past the church, up the hill, and the château is at the dead end.

Château de Ricquebourg (S)
Mme Pruvost. 21.90.30.96.

'Château' in French can mean anything from Versailles to a dilapidated large country house. Think in terms of the latter here. High on a hill overlooking the verdant valley of the Canche is this old manor house, potentially stunning, given a good deal more time and money than its owner, Madame Pruvost, has been able to apply. The stone is crumbling, the adjoining barns sag, the roof looks dodgy. So it was with some trepidation I included it in FE6 – one of the pioneer chambres d'hôtes. I did stress that it was atmosphere rather than luxury that counted here and to my delight it invoked nothing but praise from readers who had decided that the warm welcome, country peace and the simple life appealed more than a safe, hygienic, plastic cube.

Indeed there have been changes since then and all for the better. The nice old fashioned high-ceilinged rooms all have access to private bathrooms – 'Chambre Rose' has its own bathroom with shower, as does 'Jaune' albeit next door. 200f.

There is an extensive, sloping garden, children are welcomed, and a special meal laid on for them in the evening. Otherwise its 90f including *apéritif* but with wine extra.

MARESVILLE. 62630

8 km NW of Montreuil. Alternative routes are north on the N1, turn left and follow any sign that says Maresville, or look for the sign on the N39 west of Montreuil, at Beutin, on the D146, and keep going. But whichever way you choose I guarantee astonishment that anything so rustic could lurk so near the coast, so near the Nationale.

Chez Quehen-Ledhuy (M)
38 rue de laDordonne. 21.86.75.73.

Next door to the *ferme auberge* a retired couple have taken up b. and b.ing and are often used by Madame Delianne as a useful overflow. They do not want to have to turn away a stream of potential Gîte de France customers, so it's no use looking for that familiar green and yellow sign here.

It's an attractive modern house, spic and span inside and out, with a large colourful garden. The two bedrooms are charming. Flowery fabrics and wallpaper give them an appropriate country look. Between them is a good, modern bathroom (bath) and because they have to share this the prices are encouragingly low – 150f with two breakfasts, or 130f with none. The lowest prices in the neighbourhood, but with 'M' style comfort.

➤ Ferme Auberge des Chartroux (M)
Mme Delianne Ferme. 21.86.70.68; fax.21.86.70.38.

Restaurant closed Thursday and
Sun. p.m. Rooms by reservation.

Ferme Auberge du Chartroux

'Oh dear,' I said on a wet and windy, prematurely grey Wednesday evening. 'We shall be eating alone tonight'. Who, I thought, would want to drive through the dripping countryside to eat in a resolutely rustic *ferme auberge*? Fifty other diners, that's who. All of 'em French, all of 'em recognizing the value on offer at the Ferme de la Chartroux is worth a muddy boot or two.

So near Le Touquet, so near Montreuil, the auberge typifies the diversity of the region. Leave the main road and you immediately come across hamlets and farmyards that look as though they have never heard of videos, so concerned are they with their cattle and ploughs and painting their cottages white and filling their window-boxes with geraniums.

The approach to les Chartroux, which is M. Delianne's family home, is through an avenue of tall trees and already the clues are there – the verges are well-tended, the fences neat – this is not going to be a rough and ready experience.

Assorted livestock raise their heads at the car's arrival. A plump white mare and her new foal, black-headed sheep, Charolais cows, a friendly donkey, chickens of course and some ornamental fowl.

The *auberge* is ridiculously picturesque – a typical 19th century Picardy farmhouse, low, white walls, brown shutters. You step down into two surprisingly sophisticated dining rooms – Villeroy and Bosch china was not what I expected but the rusticity is happily preserved – rough walls, farm implements, open hearth. Plump and friendly Mme Delianne is there to welcome you. Her husband, daughter and son (very professional, doing a *stage* at La Réserve in Beaulieu) do the waiting while she cooks. And it soon becomes obvious why you have to book well in advance to get a table here.

The speciality is lamb – home-grown – which comes in the shape of leg, fillet or loin. Otherwise it's Charollais beef, so bad luck vegetarians. Before comes soup, *pâté de foie gras* or salmon; after comes salad, cheese and classy desserts, all for 140f. If your appetite is not up to it, pay 80f and skip the *foie gras* and cheese. Gloriously simple and good.

As are the rooms. Ours on the ground floor had pretty, green striped paper, green check curtains and covers on the twin beds, plenty of space and a very un-rustic bathroom with shower. Upstairs three more rooms may have been carved out under the eves – all very pretty, but I like ours best (280f). They share a large sitting-room with a table big enough to spread out maps and books.

Hard to fault this one for charm and situation. Perhaps the breakfast was a little disappointing – I had hoped for home-made jam, fresh bread and perhaps a farm egg, but I can see that nice Madame Delianne and her team have more than enough on their hands.

A real winner, which I know will be top of the pops with FE readers.

MARLES SUR CANCHE. 62170

5 km from Montreuil, on the D113 on the north bank of the Canche, in green and pleasant countryside.

Just past the enormous bulk of La Chartreuse (and another chambres d'hôte) look out for the hand-painted sign on the right-hand side on the bend before the village.

> ### La Manoir (M)
Mme Dominique Leroy. 21.81.38.80; fax 21.81.38.56.

It was an English property developer, a millionaire they say, who was the first to spot the potential of the group of crumbling 18th century farm buildings and seigneurial manor house. His intention was to create a luxury leisure complex, encircling a swimming pool – a nice idea, but one that fell by the wayside after he had invested a fortune converting the old buildings and propping up the tottering structure.

Bad news for him, good news for us, since Madame Leroy, looking for a property in the country, not too far from the sea, to develop for chambres d'hôte, recognized her dream come true as soon as she saw it. Eighteen months later, she has four delightful rooms. The white chalk walls have been left completely natural – bedrooms, bathrooms, corridors, salons, all share this feature and even the ceiling in

Le Manoir

the dining room is carved from the same material, vaulted into neat little arches. Huge brick fireplaces have been retained in the bedrooms, pale beams straddle the ceilings, floors are tiled and furniture antique.

Smart, fleecy, navy towels were in generous supply, along with the freebies that are usually associated with hotels charging three times the cost here. Bathrobes, cotton wool, tissues, bath oil, shampoos all appeared in the large bathroom. Best of all was the kettle and equipment for making tea. Clearly a perk for the Brits.

Breakfast too aimed to please – fruit and yogurt as well as raisin bread and five jams. Friendly, English-speaking Madame was on hand to chat, proffer maps and local advice. In low season she will cook an evening meal (70f) for those loath to leave her roaring log fire. In summer there is no need, since Montreuil has become a *gastro-ville* with several of my favourite restaurants offering meals for under £10 (buy FE12 to find out the best!).

The grounds and gardens are extensive and child-friendly. A pleasant, green and peaceful spot to repose in. You could pick an apple from the tree from our bedroom window.

An excellent choice, with loads of character, in an ideal situation. Outstanding value for 250f and arrowed accordingly.

MENNEVILLE. 62240

2 km N of Desvres. Look for the signs to Mont Éventé

Le Mont Éventé (S)
M. et Mme Desalase. 21.91.77.65.
Open from 1/4–30/9; 1/11–31/3 at weekends only by reservation.
A nice old farmhouse, freshly whitewashed, with dark red shutters and lots of stables built round a courtyard. There are two bedrooms, both with private shower and w.c. Remote and utterly peaceful. 200f a double.

MONTREUIL-SUR-MER. 62170

13 km SE of Le Touquet by N39, 35 km S of Boulogne by N1. No. 1 choice for a weekend break near the ferries. Interesting old town, cobbled streets, Saturday market, wide range of restaurants, rampart walks – you name it. Plenty of chambres d'hôtes in the surrounding countryside, but only one that I liked in the town itself.

Chez Mme Moncomble (S)
Rue de la Tour de Justice. 21.06.07.06.

In a quiet, residential area, the house is modern but not aggressively so, built in low Picardy style, freshly painted white, with green shutters, well kept garden and view of the valley below.

There are two pretty rooms, one up, one down, which share a bathroom: 180f.

MUNCQ-NIEURLET. 62890 TOURNEHEM

25 km SE of Calais. Leave Calais by N43, then D217 to left, signed Ruminghem, through Recques. The farm is 1 km after village on the left.

La Motte Obin (M)
Mme Breton. Rue du Bourg. 21.82.79.63. cl. 1/11–Easter.

The creeper-covered 200-year-old farmhouse is framed in a massive, ancient archway, through which you must drive to arrive in the flowery courtyard. Madame Breton will probably be there to meet you – she likes to know what's going on and never misses an opportunity for a chat. She is one of the few hostesses in the area to provide an evening meal – 80f exclusive of wine, with vegetarians' requirements taken into consideration, if they give her due notice. Otherwise it's pot luck both for ingredients and company, since you eat altogether with Madame presiding.

The two bedrooms are decorated in pastel colours with pretty flowery curtains and integral showers: 190f.

The peace of the place is almost tangible. Not even a cockerel nor a duck is allowed to destroy it. It all seems a very long way from home in space and time.

PIHEM. 62570

7 km SW of St Omer by D928. Look for signs to left shortly after crossing autoroute, leading to the hamlet of Pihem. *Aux Campagnes* is signed from both directions.

St Omer is the first sizeable French town you reach after leaving Calais; the new autoroute makes it quickly accessible. If it's hypermarkets that are your goal, you would do better to use the one here, which caters for real French people than the tourist-geared versions in the port, but I would go for the markets which take place every Wednesday and Saturday in the Grand' Place, when the market gardeners from the *hortillonages* bring in produce that was still growing/squawking/being laid that morning. Take a trip on one of the typical black boats along the 'watergangs', the Flemish name for the complicated network of canals and waterways just east of the town. It's an interesting area that takes more time to appreciate thoroughly than a hasty deviation, so a base in the area would be a good idea.

Aux Campagnes (S)
Mme Nadine Renault. 18 rue du Flot. 21.93.81.53.
It claims to be open all year, but it certainly wasn't on our first attempt to investigate. True the thick ice of that April morning which made the surrounding lanes perilous must have discouraged the casual dropper-in and only your intrepid reporter was abroad. All we could ascertain was that Aux Campagnes, highly recommended to us by several local spies, was a modern, cream building with highly efficient shutters.

We had better luck later in the season when Mme Renault showed us the four guest rooms, each with own bathroom, modern, functional, clean and comfortable.

Her establishment is better known for its restaurant, which is open to the public at weekends only for lunch and dinner. It serves good-value chicken or steak dishes and is very popular with families, especially on Sunday midday. Menus are 78f, 195f, and 148f. She will cook for residents on demand.

ST JOSSE-SUR-MER. 62170

4 km S of Le Touquet by D143 then left on to D144. St Josse is one of the several unexpectedly unspoiled, totally delightful villages that lie in the triangle between Etaples, Berck and Montreuil. It is as peaceful as you could ever wish, which makes its proximity to the busy coast even more agreeable. The choice of FE favourite restaurants all around (see FE12) means that you could choose a different menu every night for a fortnight.

Allée des Peupliers (M)
Chez Leprêtre. 21.94.39.47.

Marie-Jo and Alain Leprêtre live in the house at the entrance to the drive. Their newly-built chambres d'hôtes and gîte accomodation is the block up the hill. I cannot say it is a thing of beauty, but it certainly caters very efficiently for most holiday needs. Below it is a large lake, geared for modest fishing, canoeing, sitting around, and there are swings and slides on the extensive grassy slopes.

On the ground floor are the apartments, which have to be booked weeks ahead (months in high season). They can sleep six, have their individual terraces, and kitchenettes, and cost 1,600f a week, without breakfast. On the first floor are six chambres d'hôtes, functional, clean, comfortable, at 250f for two, including breakfast which is served in a dining room on the same floor, with kitchen for guests to prepare their own snacks and drinks throughout the day.

Very much a commercial enterprise, without much contact with the owners, but a good, safe family choice, with other children around.

VERTON. 62180

5 km E of Berck by D719, 15 km S of Le Touquet by D143. Once the haunt of artists like Manet and Boudin, Berck took on a new role in 1861 when, thanks to the theory that the iodine in the air was particularly powerful, it was decided to set up a centre for the cure of bone disease here. Napoleon III's wife, the Empress Eugenie, opened the hospital and there are still 3,000 beds available for patients. You can see them in beds-on-wheels being pushed along the prom. Apart from this, Berck is a surprising contrast to neighbouring Le Touquet's upmarket image, in being a lively, youthful holiday resort, rather too fond of amusement arcades and discos for my taste, but with a good range of restaurants and a superb, sandy beach.

La Chaumière (M)
Madame Geneviève Terrien. 19 Rue du Bihen. 21.84.27.10.

Not all thatched cottages are old. This one was built 16 years ago and a new wing added to house guests in 1993. Nonetheless it is all very pretty and immaculately presented, under the benign jurisdiction of nice Mme Terrien. She showed me the dining-room first – all white, more contemporary in character than I had expected, with expensive flowery china set out for breakfast, which is above average, including fruit and yoghurt as well as the norm.

She had four bedrooms, all quite different – *Chambre Anglaise* has flowery, rose-patterned Sanderson paper; the yellow room is Laura Ashley-esque with a hand-painted cupboard, and *Le Pigeonnier* has a pitched roof with dramatic, blue stencils around the white walls. There is one more in the house itself, which is definitely different – all black and white. All have good, colour-coordinated bathrooms with showers: 250f. Nice atmosphere, good situation.

PICARDY

....

Départements: **Aisne**
 Oise
 Somme.
Companion guide to the area – 'French Entrée 12 – The North'.

The battlefield of Europe bears many scars and memorials as lasting witness to its tribulations. Its rich and inoffensive farming land is where yeomen archers lined up, where horses were caparisoned for battle, where trenches were cut, where marching boots churned up the mud, where tanks rumbled, where treaties were signed, and where the victims of conflicts fell, body upon body. Its such a short drive and such a long time between Crecy and the Somme. But Picardy is not all negative sadness and monotonous plains.

There is no other region that can rival the Gothic churches and châteaux of the region. In villages, cities, crossroads throughout the departement you can trace the development of Gothic art, from the very first pointed arch at Morienval to the final expression of the Flamboyant. The cathedrals of Senlis, Amiens, Beauvais, the abbeys of St Germer-der-Fly and St. Riquier are individual history lessons of the conception of religious architecture of the times. Some, like Amiens, are constructed with such industry that a young craftsman might live to see its completion; some, like St. Riquier, whose building was interrupted by war, and St. Germer, delayed by additions and reconstructions, explain, as no schoolteacher could, how fashions changed in the intervals.

The little-known area of Aisne receives few tourists, apart from those visiting the miracles of Laon and Soissons cathedrals. St. Quentin is a typical big provincial city, with attractive central square and unusual art galley. Vervins is completely different – ancient, fortified, self-contained, and hinting at the Ardennes next door.

In the south, less than 50 km from Paris in the departement of Oise, lies the incomparable Chantilly, whose château and stables, together with the neighbouring Senlis, alone would merit an excursion to this region.

PICARDY

AISN E (02)
Préfecture: Laon
1 Berzy-le-Sec
2 Chéret
3 Chigny
4 Connigis
5 Missy-sur-Aisne
6 Vic-sur-Aisne
7 Villers Agron

OISE (60)
Préfecture: Beauvais
1 Avilly St. Leonard
2 Bargny
3 Buicourt
4 Chambors
5 Cressonsacq
6 Fontaine-Chaalis
7 Macquelines
8 Pontpoint
9 St Arnoult
10 St Germain La Poterie

SOMME (80)
Préfecture: Amiens
1 Argoules
2 Auchonvilliers
3 Bavelincourt
4 Béhen
5 Creuze
6 Digeon
7 Dury
8 Erondelle
9 Frize
10 Liomer
11 Port le Grand
12 Querrieu
13 St Riquier

■ Préfecture

■ Town

① Chambre d'Hôtes

For those who have already explored the Pas-de-Calais and are looking for a worthwhile extension to their experience of the accessible North of France, I would suggest a drive down to the Somme. The capital, Amiens, well repays a visit; look beyond its wartime devastion to the remarkable restoration in the St. Leu area, take a cruise on the waterways and allot plenty of time for the stunning cathedral. The battlefields of course are an abiding interest and sobering jolt. The lively port of St Valery, with good market, superb walks and lots of fishing activity, would make a good cheerful contrast.

AISNE

BERZY-LE-SEC. 02200

5 km S of Soissons. The house is 2 km S of Berzy, so head for Léchelle, via N2, and then left on to D172, and left again on D177. House is signed at entrance to village.

Ferme Léchelle (M)
Mme Nicole Maurice. 23.74.83.29. In winter by reservation only.

A pretty country house, white-shuttered, creeper-clad, courtyard-fronted. The furniture is family antiques; the floors are polished wood. Bedrooms are mostly decorated with pretty Laura Ashley designs, but there is one more modern with sloping pine ceiling and dormer window. Some have private shower rooms, three share one between them in a suite, and there is a single room at 150f with no private facilities. Otherwise they cost 230f.

Breakfasts are especially good, served on pretty pink china and including extras like cereals and yoghurt. They are served on a big pine table by the open fire in winter. Chic Madame Maurice (who talks so volubly that I only catch half what she says) will sometimes provide an evening meal (on reservation) for 90f, but I sensed that this is offered somewhat reluctantly.

CHÉRET. 02860 BRUYERES ET MONTBERAULT

8 km SE of Laon via D967 and D903. In lovely countryside, well sited for Laon and autoroute.

Le Clos (S)
23.24.80.64. cl. from November–Easter.

Le Clos

M. and Mme. Simmonot's home is a stately 17C 'vendangeoir', whose paint now is sadly peeling but whose dignity is unimpaired.

The rooms likewise – spacious, lovely proportions, old furniture, pleasant aspect over green rolling hills. They have embroidered flower emblems on the door. I liked 'Iris' best, for its size, view and private bathroom, on the far side of which is a smaller room ideal for two children or another couple of intimates. This, at 250f for two including breakfast, is the most expensive of the five rooms – the cheapest is a mere 180f.

Don't miss dinner here. 80f buys apéritif, four courses and wine, taken at a communal table. The multinational atmosphere can be hilarious. As M. Simmonot says, the best teacher of French is the apéritif. And it gets much more fluent as the wine goes down.

CHIGNY. 02120 GUISE

12 km W of Etréaupont by the D31 and D26. Surrounded by fields and approached by narrow winding lanes, there is an atmosphere of deep deep repose about Chigny. Presumably there are births, marriages and deaths in the village, but it is hard to imagine its somnolence disturbed by any great passion. Its red brick flower-bestrewn cottages are typical of the Thiérache; some of them date from past centuries, many of them were built just after the First World War.

➤ ### Mlle Francoise Piette (S)
Place des Maronniers. 23.60.22.04.

One of the most successful recommendations in FE7. The file is full of letters like the following:

"*My daughter and I reached Chigny on spec at about 7 p.m. and were relieved that Mlle Piette was able to accommodate us. When we enquired about eating places, she told us that there were none locally, but on learning we were vegetarians,*

*suggested she would be able to pro-
vide us with supper. From our bedroom window we spotted her in her
excellent vegetable garden selecting
a lettuce which we were later to
enjoy.*

*"Our first course was a deli-
cious vegetable broth served in a
tureen for us to help ourselves. This
was followed by an omelette filled
with sautéed potatoes, home-made
bread and the green salad we knew
was 100 per cent fresh. It subsequently emerged that Mlle Piette and her sister were
both vegetarians – unusual enough in France. They did cook meat for visitors but
preferred their veggie specialities. Our meal concluded with a slice of mousseline
cake and a bowl of garden redcurrants sparkling with a little sugar. Next morning
we shared a table with a German family and feasted on a large selection of home-
made preserves and local butter."* Julie Trier.

This report says it all, but just to reinforce the picture – this is a small red-brick
1765 Thierache farmhouse, white doors and shutters, near the village hall, in a
chestnut-shaded square – les Marroniers. The sisters Piette live in the modern whitewashed house next door. They have converted the upstairs of the old farmhouse,
once a granary, still with exposed beams and rafters and steps up and down, into
five bedrooms, all beautifully decorated and furnished with antiques. One of the
beds has a lovely old white bed-cover, a family hand-me-down.

The garden is obviously the subject of tender loving care. It positively burgeons
with healthy plants, and the revelation that the Mademoiselles are vegetarians
comes as no surprise, having seen the size and content of their *potager*.

The price for two people is 250f; dinner is 75f and requires prior warning. Spe-
cialités include *galette vegetarienne*, *chou farci*, *flamiche poireau* and *terrine de
céreales*, all according to the season naturally.

Arrowed for comfort, good food (especially for the usually deprived vegetarians) and good value.

CONNIGIS. 02330 CONDÉ-EN-BRIE

12 km E of Château Thierry by N3 (Epernay road). Turn right after Crézancy on to
D85 after the bridge, then follow signs. House on left.

The valley of the Marne has fewer tourists than it deserves. Within easy reach
of Epernay and Reims, centring on the historic town of Château Thierry, with
formidable castle, pleasant walks, opportunities for river excursions, convenient for
Eurodisney, very near autoroute, it would make a good choice for a short break.

Chez Leclère (S)
23.71.90.51; fax 23.71.48.57.

Once the farm attached to the
château of the village, the Leclère's
nice old house is part of a complex
around a courtyard, whose centre
is a strange, mossy fountain. Huge,
bleached, crumbling barns form the
other wings. Over the door a sign
says 'Accueil' and it means what it
says. Nice plump Madame gener-
ates friendly welcome, and this is a
real find for those seeking country
peacefulness and genuine rustic
atmosphere, supported by anxiety to please. M. Leclère is an English-speaking *viticulteur*, so you can be assured that the wines with the evening meal (70f) will be
well-chosen and the conversation easy.

There are four spacious bedrooms, including two family rooms. One has a
shower and the others have baths, all modern and efficient; 200f for two people, 60f
for each additional occupant. The furniture is family antiques, the admirable wooden
floors are highly polished and the big windows give pleasing views of the vineyards.

In winter the two, big, old-fashioned salons are agreeably cosy, thanks to big
log fires.

MISSY-SUR-AISNE. 02880

8 km E of Soissons by D925. It's a very watery landscape, between two rivers, Aisne
and Vesle, with numerous lakes. Carp fishing is available on the property.

Just before entering the village look for the house on the right.

Mme Duffie (M)
23.72.83.54; fax 23.72.91.43.

A working farm that has been in
M. Duffie's family for over two
centuries. A barn has been renovated to provide independent
accommodation for p.g.s. One
double room, all blue and pink, has
its own bath, as does the even better room upstairs with twin beds,
250f, with any add-ons at 80f
extra. There is a private garden
space reserved for the guests' exclusive use.

Breakfast and evening meals (100f by reservation) are served by chatty Madame Duffie, who speaks a little English, in a separate dining-room.

VIC-SUR-AISNE. 02290

16 km W of Soissons by N31. A pretty village, well situated for visits to the forest of Laigue; picnics on the river Aisne and the A1 autoroute.

Domaine des Jeannes (M)
rue Dubarle. 25.55.57.33. cl. Oct-May.

Not easy to find, but in fact it is tucked away a few minutes from the centre. Follow the narrow rue Dubarle off the main square beside a greengrocer and the gates of the Domaine are on the right.

It's an imposing 17th century house, built on a prime sight high above the river, with lawns rolling down to the water's edge.

The most impressive room in this unpretentious establishment, well run by M. and Mme Martner, is the dining room, with massive carved fireplace and tall windows making the most of the view. Mme Martner enjoys cooking and her evening meals are served at well-laid tables, with high-quality linen and glass. Dinner is good value at 90f.

All the five bedrooms have views of the river and grounds, and although simple in decor and furnishings they do all have private bathrooms. 'La Verte' is my favourite. 320f for two people, 390f for four.

VILLERS-AGRON. 02130

18 km SE of Fère-en-Tardenois on the D2. Just north of the A4 autoroute and only 23 km SW of Reims but light years away in character. This is deep, deep farming country.

➤ Ferme du Château (M)
23.71.60.67; fax 23.69.36.54.

If Xavier Fery were not still an active agriculteur and his wife Christine an even more active mother of three hyperactive children, one would be tempted to call this a hotel, so well-equipped are the rooms, so well-organised the comfort of the guests. But the sandpit on the terrace (among lots of expensive chairs and recliners), the child's desk, the homework on the piano, the board games on the table, all make it

a home not a hotel and this is what
chambres d'hôtes are all about.

That said, this is a quite exceptional representative of the genre.
The old farmhouse starts off with
enormous advantages – a lovely
stone building, a slope down to the
river, a delightful setting – but
Christine and Xavier have skilfully
capitalised. Their four spacious
rooms are furnished with style; all
have colourful chintzes, and luxury

bathrooms with fittings probably more refined than yours or mine back home. The
salon is huge – raftered, log fire, piano – the dining room extremely elegant.

Christine's cooking is way above average for a farmer's wife. 90f is well spent
on her evening meal. As is 250–350f for any one of the rooms, all of which have
delightful rural aspects. There is even a golf course for the pampered guests.

There is one snag. After a visit *chez* Féry you will be spoiled for any other b.
and b. Arrowed for excellence.

OISE

AVILLY-ST-LEONARD. 60300

4 km W of Senlis by D924 towards Chantilly, then signed left. The gateway to the
house is on the right at the entrance to the village, just before the bridge.

A highly desirable location between two fascinating and very different towns.
Senlis' quiet, cobbled streets and stunning cathedral remain mysteriously unknown
to many British travellers who never think to deviate off the autoroute or Nationale
in order to appreciate them. Chantilly, too, seems to merit few diversions from the
rush to the capital, relying rather on traffic from the other direction – Parisians
seeking escape. It is a unique lively town with plenty of good restaurants and bars
and, of course, the magnificent Renaissance-style château which was the result of
enlisting the finest artists, craftsmen, designers and gardeners that Anne (masculine)
de Montmorency, Grand Constable of France, could assemble in 1528. Make sure
you leave time to visit the stables.

La Maison Rose (M)
Christine Pertus. 44.57.65.39.

Push open the high iron gate to enter the quiet confines of the park of Chantilly. La
Maison Rose was once part of the extensive stables that lie behind it, where visitors
can hire horses on which to cover the vast grounds. It is somewhat crumbling and

faded now, very much a family
home, but in a superb situation.
Residents have the privilege of
walking through the park all the
way to the Château – a superb
opportunity to enjoy the lovely
walks at times when the tourist
hordes are not admitted.

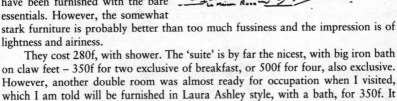

The rooms themselves are spacious with good views – but they
have been furnished with the bare
essentials. However, the somewhat
stark furniture is probably better than too much fussiness and the impression is of
lightness and airiness.

They cost 280f, with shower. The 'suite' is by far the nicest, with big iron bath
on claw feet – 350f for two exclusive of breakfast, or 500f for four, also exclusive.
However, another double room was almost ready for occupation when I visited,
which I am told will be furnished in Laura Ashley style, with a bath, for 350f. It
was certainly large and potentially lovely.

BARGNY. 60620

10 km SE of Crépy-en-Valois by D332 towards Betz. Three km after Lévignen
crossroads, turn left to Bargny village. I had trouble finding the house because it is
deliberately not signed. (The owners say they have only one room and do not want
to be continuously turning people away.)

Chez Triboulet (M–L)
21 rue de la Gruerie. 44.87.23.52.

Jacques Triboulet may be a farmer
but this is no ordinary farmhouse.
Mud on the boots would be
unthinkable in such a luxurious,
well-tended establishment. Its a
lovely old building, substantially
built of old stone, now creeper-covered, with an intriguing corner
tower of zig-zagging red bricks. The
approach is via a huge courtyard,
flanked by barns and an army of
tractors.

Climb up the marble staircase inside the tower to reach the spacious guest
room, with twin beds and the possibility of an extra one, and a sitting area looking

out over the farmland. The bathroom, too, is lavish, with twin washbasins and a luxurious shower compartment and there are numerous extras, like bathrobes, a wake-up radio, clothesbrush and all the minor appendages that you leave behind at home if, like me, you pack in a hurry.

Downstairs there is a *coin privé* – a section of the garden set aside for the guest's use, and a huge salon decorated with stags heads and huge beams, but managing to be light and bright, thanks to the high ceilings and many windows.

Best of all there is a huge swimming pool in the grounds, but Madame Triboulet stresses that this is to be used by invitation only. She has had some unfortunate experiences with unguarded children there.

A truly exciting discovery and, considering the luxury of accommodation and surroundings, good value at 300f for two or 390f for three.

BUICOURT. 60380

This is rolling farming countryside with a forest nearby.

17 km NW of Beauvais by D901, then left on D133 to Songeons. Turn left onto D143. The house is on the left, by the pump, after the church.

Chez Mme Verhoeven (S)
44.82.31.15.

No need to stir from the simple white cottage to search for dinner elsewhere. Mme Verhoeven enjoys cooking a traditional meal based on the fresh produce from her kitchen garden – 85f on reservation.

Guests sleep in a modern extension in two double rooms, each with shower. The breakfast included in the 220f is a good one, with home-made preserves, of course.

CHAMBORS. 60420

4 km SE of Gisors, 72 kms NW of Paris. Take the Paris road out of Gisors. Turn right after 1 km signed Cambors. Follow lane (C9) for 3 km to village. Take second turning right after church, then signed left. Sharp right turn into gate. Gisors has a good Saturday market.

Chez Bernard (M)
4 rue de Gomerfontaine. 44.49.77.28.

Here I run out of superlatives. But I'll try – the prettiest bedroom, the best breakfast, the kindest hosts, the most picturesque village...

4. Rue de Gomerfontaine

Chambors is an enchantingly pretty village on the Normandy border, convenient for visits to Giverny, Rouen and the Seine valley. Roses scramble up the old walls of the sedate little stone houses; the Mayor's manor house beside the sprawling farm buildings is gorgeous, even by mayoral standards, and the ancient church sits exactly where an ancient church should sit – in the hub of the village.

The Bernards' house is a delight; their wing is old with dark beams and weathered stone walls, fronting on to a pleasant terrace surrounded by well-tended flowerbeds. Well-tended is the feeling for the whole house; everything is immaculate and the dust of ages is kept under control. The two guest rooms, at right angles to the hosts' quarters, have a separate entrance; one has twin beds and shower and the other what Madame terms a *lit francais* (double) and a bath. Both bathrooms are roomy and efficiently equipped not only with mod. cons. but with the extras that show somebody cares – the hair dryer, the bath robes, the co-ordinated towels.

Charming wallpaper, curtains and bedspreads give the bedrooms country charm. The cream and rose colours and the flowery patterns hint of Victoriana. '*Anglais*' says Madame proudly.

Breakfast (terrace in summer, little dining room when it's chilly) lacks for nothing – fresh fruit, yoghurt, orange juice squeezed to order, four different breads, apple cake, three home-made jams and honey and delightful china. But best of all is the atmosphere – modest, anxious to help in any way. A charming couple in a charming chambres d'hôtes. At 250f a bargain.

CRESSONSACQ. 60190

27 km NW of Compiègne. A pleasant village to stay in whilst visiting the Compiègne area and the *Wagon-de-l'Armistice* where the Armistice was signed in 1918 and where Hitler insisted that the French surrendered to him in 1940. (Closed 12 to 2 pm and on Tuesdays).

At the junction with the N31 and the N17, 15 km west of Compiègne, take the N31 north to Estrées St Denis then the D36 to Cressonsacq. The chambres d'hôtes is near the crossroads in the centre of the village.

M. & Mme Alexandre (S)
2 rue du Bois. 44.51.72.99.

M. & Mme Alexandre, now retired, are a very creative couple, with many talents. Their 17th century house, once a church academy for girls, has been renovated by them and now has a gîte and a very comfortable guest room built over the granary. There is parking to please the most pernickety here; drive through the gates to an inner garden and two gates are locked behind you! Your first-floor room with two single beds is warm, with every convenience, and overlooks the house and sheltered garden, where there are chairs for fine weather. Three small cats guard the conservatory. Monsieur is a computer buff and madame used to write computer programmes; now retired, they are no mean artists and use their skills to enliven their chambres d'hôtes. There is a map on the ground floor which lights up routes for drives and walks and a mini-computer which gives you information about local places (in French or English)! With such talented hosts conversation at dinner never flags.

Evening meals are excellent value at 60f each, *apéritif* and wine included. Orange juice, toast and multiple jams for breakfast. You're in clover here. Rooms 210f.

FONTAINE–CHAALIS. 60300

8 km SE of Senlis by D33a, direction Nanteuil. Between Borest and Fontaine-Chaalis. A more ideal situation it would be hard to devise – near the delightful Senlis, just 8 km from the autoroute, on the edge of the Forest of Ermenonville and the Abbey of Chaalis and with Paris only half an hour away down the rail-track.

La Bultée (M)
Mme Annie Ancel. 44.54.20.63; fax 44.54.08.28.

An old farmyard approached via a huge courtyard. The guest rooms in an independent farm building were a touch disappointing in view of the external character – modern, with small windows, shower rooms, 300f – but comfortable and well-equipped. Breakfast is eaten in the main salon, with big fire in winter or else outside in the pleasant garden. Madame Ancel is an efficient and helpful hostess.

MACQUELINES. 60620 BETZ

11 km S of Crépy-en-Valois by D332 towards Lévignen. 3 km after the Lévignen crossroads, Macquelines is on the right.

Farming country that may look as though it's in the middle of nowhere, but don't forget that it's only 35 minutes to Paris by train from Crépy and that Euro-Disney is only 40 km away.

Ferme de Macquelines (S)
Mme Hamelin. 44.87.20.21.

You drive into a vast open cobbled courtyard and wonder which way to turn. The Hamelins' quarters are on the right and the guest room, contrived out of farm buildings in 1992, on the left. There is a pleasant garden with swings and a tennis court, so this is altogether a good family halt.

The rooms are modern, two with showers and twin beds, one with bath behind a Wild West swinging door, all at 300f, and a little suite with four beds and shower-room at 420f. I thought it a tad expensive, but the rate goes down to 280f after the first night. Madame Hamelin is a friendly hostess and happy to chat while serving breakfast in the stone-walled dining-room.

PONTPOINT. 60700

14 km N of Senlis by N17, then right at St Maxence on to D123. The neat little village of Pontpoint is hidden away, heavily disguised behind the main road. Turn left after the sign to the Stade into rue du Gaudin and the house is on the right.

An area with too many attractions to pack into a single 24 hours. Stay several days to visit the enchanting old town of Senlis, to see the château, gardens and stables at Chantilly, the abbey of Chaalis, the forests of Compiègne, Halatte and Chantilly. In the village itself are numerous lakes, with the possibility of sailing, fishing, windsurfing and canoeing. Good picnicking. Restaurants, gastronomic and simple, abound. And Paris is a mere 30 minutes away by train, so leave the car safely parked for a day and hit the capital the easy way. It will be a pleasure to return to:-

➤   ### Chez Flochmoan (M)
Rue du Gaudin. 44.70.03.98 and 44.72.52.03.

Despondently we learned from Mme Ancel (see Fontaine Chaalis) that, although it was a Monday night and we had arrived early, all her rooms were taken. Sceptically we listened to her suggestion that friends of hers who had just opened their chambres d'hôtes might be able to accommodate us, and wearily we drove back into Senlis and up to Pontpoint.

One look at the charming cottage that was to be our home for the night (we stayed longer) was enough for spirits to rise. The welcome from the lovely Flochmoans completed the restoration of *joie de vivre*. The *joie* here is a completely independent cottage, which the hosts have converted over a period of seven hard years from an old barn. We still didn't cotton on that all this was for us – a huge living room, luxury kitchen (sauna leading off) two spacious double bedrooms, two large bathrooms, (showers, alas, but good ones) our own garden, two terraces. For 270f.

There were even our own cherry tomato plants from which M. Flochmoan encouraged us to pick the little red globes to eat with our much-needed *apéritif*. Which was a welcoming bottle of wine left in the fridge. 'Can I write that you do this for all your guests?' I asked as the Flochmoans invited us to drink on their terrace, catching the last of the evening sun. 'Only the sympathetic ones, but the wine is there for everyone.' So you will soon know how you are rated.

Their 300-year-old cottage is almost a mirror image of the restored barn. In termtime both the Flochmoans work at the college in Senlis, he as a P.E. instructor, she in administration, but of course their long holidays correspond with the busiest tourist seasons and at other times they are home early enough to welcome their guests. He is a mine of information about the region and endlessly helpful and she is a quiet supportive back-up. They are justifiably proud of what they have achieved, much by their own labour – three separate houses (one for their grown-up children).

Prices will be kept at this level for another year to encourage new customers and then – who knows? Better book that ferry now.

ST ARNOULT. 60220

30 km NE of Beauvais by D901 to Faugquières, then left on D71.
This is the rich farming Bray country near the Normandy border.

Le Prieuré (M)
Mme Nelly Algave. 44.46.07.34.

Listed as a *Monument Historique*, the erstwhile 15th century priory certainly looks archetypal Norman – dramatic dark timbering on cream walls. The hoi polloi must pay to take a look inside, but house guests can drink in the atmosphere for free. Breakfast is in the lovely, beamed dining-room with vast, open fire.

There is only one spacious bedroom, with canopied four-poster bed, bare wooden floor and another fireplace capable of roasting an ox. Adjoining bathroom has a shower and loo. Definitely different. 380f.

ST GERMAIN-LA-POTERIE. 60650

8 km W of Beauvais. Take the N31 out of Beauvais and turn right at Le Becquet on to the D626. House is signed in village, on the edge of the forest; it is hard to imagine a quieter setting. For centuries pots have been made in this area and St Germain is just one of the villages which commemorates this in its name. Potters' *ateliers* and shops are dotted around. In all it makes a restful base from which to visit Beauvais (not a lot to see I must admit) and in the other direction St Germer-de-Fly, a picture-book village on the Normandy border, completely dominated by an amazing abbey.

Chez Mme Legrain (M)
10 rue des Tuileries. 44.82.28.54.

A pretty, old brick cottage, white shutters, white bench, well cared-for garden, with smart yellow striped canopy over white garden table and a swing in the willow tree.

Mme Legrain has two rooms; one has its own kitchenette and salon and own entrance and the other, with big modern shower room and double bed, is all orange and brown – 250f inclusive of breakfasts, which are D.I.Y.

SOMME

ARGOULES. 80120 RUE

7 km from Nampont St Martin on the N1. Follow any of the rivers sloping diagonally across the map from north-west to south-east – the Canche, the Authie or the Somme – for a delightfully rural peaceful ride. Take a picnic to eat at the water's edge in a village like Maintenay, with its giant watermill churning up the Authie, or indeed on the other bank at Argoules, beneath the legendary lime tree on the green. It all seems a long way from the hustle of the N1.

Abbaye de Valloires (M)
22.29.62.33; fax 22.23.91.54.

The old Abbey of Valloires, founded by the Cistercians in the twelfth century, rebuilt in the eighteenth, has had a facelift recently. Its elegant, grey stone was looking neglected and shabby and its gardens run-down, but now all is good news – the gardens are fine enough to be opened to the public and the facade has been scrubbed and painted. Excellent, because the potential was always there for this

Abbaye de Valloires

truly lovely building to be better appreciated. One of the innovations is to restore six rooms and create chambres d'hôtes. Four of them accommodate three people and the other two have beds for two, but all are lovely. They are at the side of the house, with tall windows looking out towards the gardens, wooden floors highly polished, furniture antiques, wallpapers flowery. At 350f for two people, including breakfast, they are a very good buy.

AUCHONVILLERS. 80560

10 km N of Albert by D53, or 27 km NE of Amiens by D919 and D53 right from Mailly-Maillet.

This is in the heart of the war graves area of World War One, and recommended purely as an inexpensive base for those wishing to visit the unforgettable memorials and cemeteries. Take the Beaumont road out of Auchonvillers and the house is on the right.

Les Galets (S)
Julie Renshaw. Route de Beaumont. 22.76.28.79.

A wooden chalet-type building with a conservatory extension. The Renshaws have four rooms available, a twin with shower, a twin with bath, a double with shower, all for 225f, and a four-bedded room – 325f. At least there will be no problem here in discussing which arrangement suits you best and for those who tire of struggling with their French and long for some British cooking, this is the answer.

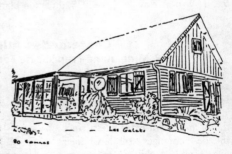

Julie provides a good-value evening meal – 2 courses £5, three for £6.50 and four for £8, with coffee and wine thrown in. Her prematurely-retired husband is an amateur war historian and has a good stock of videos and books to prepare his guests for their war-grave tours. They are a friendly, hospitable couple who enjoy their new lifestyle as b. and b. hosts, and I have a recent testimonial from Doug Goodman who organises tours of the area that they provide an excellent service.

BAVELINCOURT. 80260 VILLIERS-BOCAGE

15 km NE of Amiens by D919 and D115. Signed in village. In deep countryside but useful for visits to both Amiens and Somme battlefields.

M. Noel Valengin (M–S)
22.40.51.51.

Chez Valengin

Although I personally liked this well-preserved manor house very much, I dropped it from later editions of FE6 because reports inexplicably faded away. Now, after a reassessment, I am happy to report that M. et Mme Valengin and their chambres d'hôtes are alive and well. They now have three double rooms, (one on the ground floor) each with own bathroom, and two smaller rooms suitable for children at 190f. I look forward to a new batch of readers' views.

BÉHEN. 80870

9 km SW of Abbeville. Take N28, direction Blangy, turn right at Croisettes and follow arrows.

Château des Alleux (M)
M. & Mme. Réné-François de Fontanges. 22.31.64.88.

Les Alleux

A lovely 17th century manor house rather than château, with faded brick and white shutters. It looks a substantial building, but there is little room here for extra guests since the de Fontanges still have their own brood of children to accommodate. This would be a good place for children generally, with ponies to ride and lambs to pet.

So most of the chambres d'hôtes are in a former, farm-servants' wing, complete with old bread oven. They have a modern bathroom apiece with bath or shower across the corridor, at 280f. I preferred the one room in the main house, in Empire style, with *bateaux* beds and a green bath (also 280f). There is a small kitchen corner that the guests can use for hot drinks and snacks, and a nice, big salon with an open fire in winter.

Evening meals are available on reservation – 110f inclusive of wine. I liked this one very much – particularly the friendly, family atmosphere.

CREUZE. 80480

13 km SW of Amiens by N29 then left on to D162. Signposted from Creuze.

See Dury for Amiens' attractions. The village of Creuze is similarly well-placed and has the added delight of the forest nearby for leafy strolls.

➤ ### Chez Mme Lemaître (M)
26 rue Principale. 22.38.91.50.

Digeon 80590 Morvillers-St-Saturnin (Somme) 4 km E of Aumale by N29. Turn right at Le Coq Gaulois crossroads; house signed in village.

As you turn in from the road under the archway you are liable to be greeted by a selection of residents. Two geese were being very protective about their territory, decorative bantams were pecking about and a shaggy dog lay soaking up the sun. More decorative fowl strutted on the lawns of the delightful garden, but although the 200-year-old building, whitewashed, dark beamed and brown shuttered, was indeed once a working *fermette* it has now been converted into an elegant and highly attractive home, with the stable block serving as chambres d'hôtes accommodation.

Doors lie open, white, wrought iron chairs dot the lawn and there is a charming feeling of outdoor living, under the shady trees, on the well-kept grass. Chic, blonde Madame Lemaître has decorated the four rooms with style, but always kept the rustic character. She loves white and so a light and airy atmosphere predominates, helped by long french windows and in one room by a white gauze canopy over the bed – 280f with bath, same price for another room with shower and small kitchenette.

I was not surprised to learn that Mme Lemaître is a painter – her clever sense of decoration is evident again in her own house, where breakfast is served in winter by a huge log fire.

A lovely place to stay, highly recommended.

DIGEON. 71160

Chateau de Digeon (M)
M. and Mme Goisque. 22.38.07.12.

The château is an enormous red brick pile, whose many windows are softened with geraniummed windowboxes. At the rear, facing on to extensive lawn shaded by

cedars, is a long glassed-in verandah with delicate iron supporting
arches. But the most interesting
aspect of this unusual b. and b. is
the truly gorgeous garden. Open to
the public for 20f a go, its treasures
are freely available to house guests.
Snugly enclosed within stone walls,
as all the best gardens are, it is not
at all like an English version. Jum-
bled together in the same beds are
vegetables, annuals, shrubs, and

Chateau de Digeon

herbaceous plants, all thriving in promiscuous proximity. Because they are all so
well cared for and healthy, the juxtaposition works well and it became a pleasure to
discover an arbutus next to a lettuce and begonias beside a Christmas tree. It's as
though someone has come across a plant he could not resist, bought it and popped
it in wherever there was a space. Once 'real' gardeners have got over the unortho-
doxy they will find many unusual specimens amongst the cottage garden faithfuls.

This is very much a family home – at teatime on Sunday numerous members
were still sitting round the long lunch table – and the whole of the second floor is
still used for childrens' accommodation. The chambres d'hôtes are one up again.
Three not particularly exciting rooms share a bathroom with bath and shower for
220f. Downstairs is a very pleasant dining-room with tall windows overlooking the
garden. The nice owners, the good vibes and the outstanding gardens are the reasons for staying here.

DURY. 80480

Ancient and historic capital of Picardy, home of the largest, most magnificent
Gothic cathedral in France, set in a unique water landscape, Amiens should be a
must on every Northern France itinerary. It does have its traffic problems and a
maze of one-way streets, so obey the Fenn No. 1 city rule which is to head for the
spire of the cathedral and dump the car as soon as possible. From here everything of
interest is within walking distance. The newly restored area of St. Leu is now a
delightful enclave of bars, restaurants and old houses, just behind the canal and
always within sight of the glorious spire. Another good reason for a visit is to take a
trip around the watery wonderland of the *hortillonages*, an hour's meander in a
high-prowed punt that will give you a duck's eye view of the squares of gardens
criss-crossed with mini-canals and the larger navigable canals, all irrigated by the
rivers Somme and Avre. Allow plenty of time to visit the magical cathedral, if possible early or late when the tourist crowds have gone. Good shopping and restaurants
are a cheer-up for a wet day.

4 km S of Amiens by N1. Just before Dury turn left on the St Fuscien road. Signed from there.

Chez Mme Saguez (M)
2 rue Grimaux. 22.95.29.52.

An interesting 19th century house in a quiet, residential area, which would make an excellent base for visiting Amiens, ten minutes away. In the large, shady garden are some of the colourful carriages that M. Saguez restores and in the stables are horses to pull them. Guest bedrooms are in an annexe, with modern pine ceilings and a mixed bag of regional furniture. One on the ground floor, with twin beds and bath, costs 290f, as does another with sloping ceiling and shower, and there is a suite of two rooms, sharing a bathroom, for four people, for 480f.

ERONDELLE. 80580 PONT-RÉMY

12 km SE of Abbeville. Not easy to locate on a dark and dirty night and not in Erondelle at all, so play safe and head for Pont Rémy (on the D12 from Abbeville), cross the river towards Liercourt, then take the D13 towards Huppy, from which the Manoir is signed. The countryside around is truly lovely – deeply forested, hilly enough for good views down the valley of the Somme.

➤ Manoir de la Renardière (M-L)
Mme Helene Thaon d'Arnold. 22.27.13.00. cl. mid Jan–mid Feb.

The quirky Gothick house set at the end of a long lime alley has come a long way (ever onwards and upwards) since I wrote about it nine years ago. What was a somewhat ramshackle eccentricity has now become a romantic folly of enormous charm. Its turrets, towers, balconies in the fashion dubbed by the French *Le style Anglais* are newly painted and scrubbed, the garden slopes have been cleared to reveal a stunning view of the Somme lakes, and expensive white table and chairs are set out on terrace and grass for summer relaxation in perfect serenity.

Mme Thaon, who speaks near-perfect English, is a very unusual, exceptionally hard-working hostess. She has decorated the interior with light bright colours, banishing Victorian gloom. The dining-room is particularly charming – white and green, with high-backed chairs covered, unusually but successfully, in striped mattress ticking.

Our bedroom – the Garden Room – was the smallest (you have to book early here to get the best) decidedly *bijou*, but with every necessity in its place – plenty of towels, good lights, midget bath and shower, Sanderson wallpaper, 350f. Bigger rooms with larger bathrooms, open fires, white mono-grammed pillow-cases and balconies cost 450–500f (350f midweek). A two nights' stay is the minimum in high season.

But it is the atmosphere that makes Le Renardière so special. There is absolutely no feeling of this being a purely commercial enterprise. Madame Thaon gives freely of her time and experience, relishing her guests' company. She was a literature teacher until recently and knows the area, its inhabitants and attractions inside out. Her formal candlelight dinners on Saturdays (other days on request) are much in demand. She specialises in generous seafood platters, but her cooking is way more sophisticated than that normally encountered in chambres d'hôtes – 250f for four courses inclusive of *apéritif* and plenty of good wine and conversation. Elegance may be the word that springs to mind about the whole enterprise, but not so elegant that the guests are disinclined to march into the kitchen and help carry out the croissants or chat there with Madame. With an English painter friend and Jack of all trades, John, she also runs her 'pub' in a cottage in the grounds, where simpler meals are available at 100f. And if, as would be a very good idea, you stay for several days, there would be a superb alternative – the little restaurant at the bottom of the hill, *Le Temps Jadis*, which I consider to be one of the best discoveries of this particular tour.

Classical music lovers should arrange to be there on the third Saturday in the month, when Madame arranges a concert in the elegant salon; tours of local *antiquaires* and especially interesting churches are also organised. In fact – you name it and the lovely Madame Thaon will make sure your wish come true.

FRISE. 80340

10 km W of Peronne. A unique landscape of rivers, canals, lakes, waterlilies, anglers and wildfowl is to be discovered simply by following the course of the river Somme, on either bank, from Amiens eastwards. Along the river are hamlets devoted to the pursuit of fish and game. At weekends French families arrive, father to fish or shoot, mother to unload vast quantities of food from the car and to set up the picnic tables, children to paddle and squeal delightedly at the proximity of so much wetness. It's a watery wonderland, quite different from any other landscape in France, and totally unspoiled.

La Ferme de l'Ecluse (S)
Mme Annick Randijia. 1 Rue Mony. 22.84.59.70.

Overlooking the lock in a picturesque hamlet. Three rooms have private bathrooms, all simply furnished
but perfectly comfortable. A good
choice for those looking for perfect
peace in lovely surroundings, with
the possible diversion of fishing or
meandering round the waterways in
a hired boat.

Double room – 250f, evening
meal 80f per person without wine.

LIOMER. 80430

40 km E of Amiens by D211. In the village centre.

Vieux Rouen (M)
Mme Catherine Ruiz. Place de l'Eglise. 22.90.53.31.

An unusual chambres d'hôtes in that
Catherine Ruiz cooks for outside
customers as well as for her house
guests. Her *table d'hôte* costs 90f
with wine, and consists of a sophisticated presentation of Picardy specialities. She needs a minimum of 24
hours notice though for either lunch
or dinner. You eat at separate tables
in the dining room of her chunky
town house, or on the verandah
fronting the steeply sloping garden.

One of her two horses was happily chomping the roses in the front garden
when I visited, another was stabled behind the house and lots of dogs seem to be
part of the family; this is a very relaxed household. There is a big salon with basket
chairs for guests to relax in too.

Catherine, who speaks perfect English, has many irons in the fire – she organises exhibitions, holds musical soirées, and runs a *salon-de-thé* as well as coping
with her chambres d'hôtes. Comfortably furnished rooms cost 280f for three with
bath, or 210f for two with shower.

PORT-LE-GRAND. 80132 ABBEVILLE

8 km NE of Abbeville by D40. Turn right in Port-le-Grand and follow signs down lane for 2 km. The two chambres d'hôtes are on the right, next door to one another.

Since both the previously recommended chambres d'hôtes in St. Valéry have closed down, these two have become even more valuable as bases from which to visit one of the most delightful towns in the North of France. William the Conqueror set off from here in 1066 for the conquest of England, taking a sword to fight with, wine to fortify him and a bishop to give him absolution – look for the tablet on the quayside by the canal for commemoration.

The little port is sited where the river Somme flows into the wide estuary. Le Crotoy guards the entrance from the other side of the bay. The enticing approach is over the bridge, with yachts lined up in the canal. Fishing boats unload their catch in the port and there are tree-shaded walks by the water's edge to appreciate the vast expanse of water, marsh and sky. The tide recedes for miles, making swimming problematical but the walks over the sea lavender are memorable. Lots of cafés and restaurants and a Saturday market add to the animation.

➤ ### Le Bois Bonance (M)
Jacques and Miriam Maillard. 22.24.11.97.
cl. between Christmas and New Year.

Le Bois Bonance

There is an English feel about this unusual house, probably because of the lovely, (very un-French in that it does not try to look like a public park) garden, with large swimming pool. It is very efficiently run, as indeed it has to be, as one of the most popular and heavily-booked in the area. The three double rooms are elegantly furnished with flowers and Teasmades (380f) and there is a suite capable of sleeping six in an annexe (400f for two, 600f for up to six). The breakfast room is particularly charming, painted spring-green with matching porcelain table settings. Highly recommended all round.

When the house is full, Madame directs the overflow to her son's farmhouse next door (Ferme du Bois de Bonance (M) Benoit Maillard 22.24.44.97.) He has a young family and so the character is quite different – much more informal, with modern furniture in the barn conversion. Guest here have the use of the parents' swimming pool, 300f for two, supplement of 100f for each additional child.

QUERRIEU. 80115

10 km NE of Amiens by D929. Not only is Amiens a fascinating, under-estimated town, a worthwhile destination for a winter break, but it is the gateway to the strange, watery world that extends eastwards along the Somme. Paradise for anglers and walkers, intriguing for photographers and wild-life fanciers, a peaceful antidote to too much driving, too many cities, this is a region that amply repays exploration. Querrieu would make the ideal base to do just this.

➤ ### La Ferme du Bois Galhaut (M)
Château de Querrieu. 22.40.13.42.

The château has been in Mme d'Alcantara's family for 500 years, with one or two hiccups, like World War I when it was taken over by the British to be Haig's headquarters, and then again in the next confrontation when Goering decided he could be very comfortable there. Nowadays the Alcantaras are firmly installed in the dignified, grey stone, bay-windowed château/mansion, but have guests in their erstwhile stables.

These have been converted into five efficient and very comfortable chambres d'hôtes, galleried to provide a little sitting area. The feeling is modern-rustic rather than aristocratic-grand, with cane bedheads, dark beams, space rather than bric-à-brac clutter and good bathrooms. Guests have the use of a kitchenette to prepare breakfasts and snacks during the day, and a washing machine to cut down on the laundry chores.

These b. and b.s have been so well equipped that they verge on hotel standards, but the bad news might be that guests who are looking for the matiness of the usual chambres d'hôtes will be disappointed. There is no sitting round a big table and practising your French on the family. Madame recommends a good little restaurant, le Val d'Ancre, at nearby Bonnay for meals.

Beds for two people cost 360f for three – 430f and four – 480f.

ST. RIQUIER. 80135

9 km E of Abbeville by D925. Just a square full of plane trees, dominated by the abbey, impressive and strikingly beautiful – the centre of what is now a small town, but was once, eleven centuries ago, one of the most formidable strongholds in Picardy. Razed, rebuilt, razed, rebuilt, it never regained its former importance. Today's abbey is mostly 17th century, with only traces of its 13th century origins.

The local white stone has been delicately wrought into icicles of flowers and leaves and animals. Inside, don't miss the statues of the saints and the glorious staircase. The *Centre Culturel*, in the monks refectory and upstairs in their cells, is one of the best of regional museums.

Chez Mme Decayeux (M)
7 Rue du Beffroi. 22.28.93.08.

Couldn't be more central, near the belfry, opposite the abbey, a nice old 18th century house, once a farm, now offering five bedrooms, colour-coded, with bathroom apiece, *Jonquille* has a double bed – 250f, *Marguerite* is smaller again with a double bed for 220f, *Rose* has twins for 270f, *Lavande* is a single for 180f, and *La Primevère* has one double and two singles – 210f for two plus 80f for each extra body. There is a pleasant *salle de séjour* with big, open fire, and TV everywhere – in the salon and in each bedroom. You can park the car in the locked, central court-yard at night so there is no need to unload.

There was a wedding in the abbey at the time I called and not a bed to be had in the town, least of all at Mme Decayeux' central vantage point. So I have to rely on the report of a reader, who wrote to tell me that the beds were comfortable and the evening meal at 80f with wine included good value.

Chez Mme Gence (M)
12 Rue Drugy. 22.28.83.19.

Take the first turning left after leav-ing the square towards the hamlet of Drugy. The house is on the right. It's a spic and span little modern house, painted white, with a nice garden. Mme Gence caters particu-larly for families, with two family suites, each capable of sleeping four, with independent bathrooms. 240f for two people.

NORMANDY

Départements: **Calvados   Orne
                 Eure   Seine-Maritime
                 Manche**

Normandy has a special place in many British affections as their first expe-rience of a real holiday in France. The toe may have been dipped briefly into the waters of Calais and the North on a day trip or in transit, but it is frequently Normandy that proves to be the base for further exploration, leading to long-term addiction. Having no fewer than four ferry ports to choose from all helps, of course.

Dieppe looks set to become a favourite, with a brand-new ferry termi-nal, ever-decreasing crossing time and the shortest distance to Paris. Le Havre has excellent communications and frequent sailings. Ouistreham, right in the heart of the region, leads directly to some of its most appealing aspects of countryside and cultural heritage, and Cherbourg offers a short-ish crossing, the calmer atmosphere of a smaller port and the laid-back atmosphere of the Manche.

The five *départements* that make up the region could not be more dif-ferent; between them they offer an unsurpassed introduction to French scenery, history, coastline, customs, food, drink, and people. There are more chambres d'hôtes here than in any other region, from picturesque Auge farmhouses to impressive châteaux.

The most northern *département*, Seine-Maritime, is dominated by the capital of Upper Normandy, the lovely city of Rouen, set in a bend of the Seine, protected by encircling hills. Recovery from its wartime horrors has been skilfully achieved and the city now offers a rewarding amalgam of mostly old, partly new, urban delights. It's an open-air city, more light-hearted than its rival Caen, with plenty of incentives to linger at a café table in the historic and colourful market place or to drink in the atmosphere by the magnificent cathedral. There is an abundance of good restaurants to choose from.

NORMANDY

CALVADOS (14)
Préfecture: Caen
1 Aignerville
2 Amfréville
3 Bernières d'Ailly
4 Beuvron-en-Auge
5 Bonnebosq and Léaupartie
6 Bourgeauville
7 Bretteville-sur-Laizé
8 Bures-sur-Dives
9 Cahagnes
10 Caumont l'Evente
11 Clarbec and Pierrefite-en-
12 Clécy   Auge
13 Creully
14 Douville-en-Auge
15 Géfosse-Fontenay
16 Gonneville-sur-Mer
17 Maisons
18 Mathieu
19 Nonant
20 Osmanville
21 St Philbert-des-Champs
22 St Remy-sur-Orne
23 St Vigor-le-Grand
24 Tortisambert
25 Vouilly

EURE (27)
Préfecture: Evreux
1 Les-Baux-de-Breteuil
2 Beuzeville
3 Boncourt
4 Conteville
5 La-Croix-St Leufroy
6 Dangu
7 Fourmetot and St Ouen-des-Champs

8 Houlbec-Cocherel
9 Mainneville
10 Reuilly
11 St Clair-d'Arcey

MANCHE (50)
Préfecture: Saint Lô
1 Avranches
2 Bricqueboscq
3 Bolleville
4 Brucheville
5 Canville-la-Roque
6 Ceaux
7 Glatigny
8 Hébécrevon
9 Montfarville
10 Percy
11 Poilley
12 St Georges-de-la-Rivière
13 St Germain-de-Tournebut
14 St Germain-sur-Sèves
15 St James
16 St Sauveur-Lendelin
17 St Senier-sous-Avranches
18 Senoville
19 Sourdeval
20 Teurtheville-Bocage
21 Vergoncey

ORNE (61)
Préfecture: Alençon
1 Argentan-Occagnes
2 Banvou
3 Briouze
4 Courgeon
5 Courtemer
6 Faverolles
7 La-Fresnaye-au-Sauvage
8 Moulicent
9 St Ouen-sur-Maire
10 Le Sap
11 Tanques

SEINE-MARITIME (76)
Préfecture: Rouen
1 Anceaumeville
2 Bacqueville-en-Caux
3 Caudebec-en-Caux
4 Criquebeuf-en-Caux
5 Criquetot-l'Esneval
6 Jumièges (x2)
7 Manneville-la-Goupil
8 Rainfreville
9 Saâne-Saint-Just
10 St Martin-de-Boscherville
11 St Sauveur de L'Emalleville
12 Senneville-sur-Fécamp
13 Sotteville-sur-Mer
14 Les Trois Pierres

Further north are the white cliffs familiar from Post-Impressionist paintings, fronting cobble beaches. Behind them are the chalky plateaux of the Caux area, dedicated mostly to cereal crops. It is a bit bleak sometimes, which makes the discovery of the occasional pretty village and rushing stream all the more pleasing. It is not generally tourist territory, which means more space to go round.

On the other side of the Seine we reach Calvados country, which is where the chambres d'hôtes cluster most thickly. This is Normandy at its most picturebook. The posters do not exaggerate. Guaranteed are half-timbered thatched cottages, hollyhocks round the door, gnarled apple trees, one dog, three sheep and six chickens. Take your pick of signed routes – 'fromage' 'cidre' and just 'touristique' – it really doesn't matter. Wherever you leave the thunder of the autoroute you are bound to stumble upon hard-to-credit, stage-set rusticity.

The coastline will be no less familiar. Honfleur, the favourite of artists for many a generation, is still as picturesque but perhaps threatened with too many tourists, thanks to the new Pont de Normandie. (Go out of season). Deauville, a mere hop and a skip away from deepest countryside, is posh Normandy. Expensive, well-groomed, elegant, humming during the August races, a conference centre for the rest of the year, it adds yet another dimension to the département. Next-door Trouville is altogether earthier and cheaper, with beaches just as fine. Good for families who are looking for sea and sand for the kids alongside plenty of grown-up activity.

Three-quarters of Caen, the capital of Lower Normandy, was tragically destroyed in 1944, but it is still the home of two magnificent abbeys, built for William the Conqueror and his queen Matilda, an imposing castle in the city-centre, some lovely churches and a thriving university. Linked by a canal to its port, Ouistreham, it makes a good winter base for shopping and eating. The Mémorial, a museum of peace, is one of the most moving and impressive museums I have ever visited. Don't miss it and do allocate half a day to its proper appreciation.

Bayeux is another must for any Calvados itinerary. Go early or late in the day to get the best value from the sensitively presented tapestry, and enjoy its ancient narrow streets and massive Gothic cathedral. The nearby Bessin countryside is gentle and pretty, with some attractive fishing ports along the coast, which, after the landing beaches, bends north at the dairy centre of Isigny.

Most of the popular Normandy cheeses – Pont l'Evêque, Camembert, Livarot – come from Calvados, where the black and white eye-patch cows are most prominent. Acres of apple orchards provide the raw material for Calvados cider.

The Cotentin peninsula forms most the the *département* of the Manche, which is, I suppose, my favourite. It is the least sophisticated, the friendliest, the easiest-to-handle. I recommend it for first-timers. Apart from Cherbourg there are no big towns and the pace is correspondingly slower. Inland some of the towns are boringly post-war, but a drive along the coastline is a good way to sample the scenic diversity that defied destruction.

West of Cherbourg one thinks of Cornwall – rugged cliffs, wild seas, granite cottages, fishing villages. The Nez de Joburg feels like the end of the world, not just of France. Further south, and nature mellows considerably. Carteret is ideal for bucket and spade holidays, with lovely sands, rock pools, river estuary, trips to the Channel Islands and a Michelin-starred restaurant/hotel. Granville is a lively fishing port, looking across the bay to the fabled Mont St Michel, rising like a floating mirage from the salt marshes.

Drive east of Cherbourg to Barfleur and St Vaast to find colourful, small fishing harbours and marinas much favoured by British yachties. The seascape here is dotted with islands, the beaches sandy and undeveloped. Unless you are heading for the landing beaches, call it a day – the vast sandy Bessin bay is pretty featureless.

The Orne is an aristocratic *département*, rich in châteaux, manor houses and stud farms. Bagnoles-de-l'Orne, a dignified spa town, typifies the away-from-it-all, elegantly relaxed atmosphere. The lovely river Orne flows through green, unspoiled countryside with attractive little towns like Mortagne, the cathedral at Sées and the stud farms in the Perche area to lend interest.

The mighty river Seine dominates the *département* of Eure. Exploring its looping course is a delightful exercise, revealing charming villages nestling in the escarpments, like Les Andelys. Giverny, the home of Monet, and its gardens are a favourite excursion. Approaching Paris, it all gets busier and more developed, so swing westwards to explore some of the tributaries, like the meandering river from which the *département* gets its name – the Eure.

CALVADOS

AIGNERVILLE. 14710

15 km NW of Bayeux in deepest countryside.

Mme Yves Corpet (L)
31.22.51.79; fax 31.22.75.99. cl. 31/12 to 15/3.

Manoir de l'Hormette

From Bayeux take the N13 for 16 km direction Cherbourg. Look out for the D517 to Formigny on the right and then take the next turning left, signed Aignerville. At the first crossing turn left again and the entry is the second white gate on the right, all well signed.

Madame Corpet has been a pioneer of the château chambres d'hôtes business from the very beginning about ten years ago, acting as secretary to the various groups of owners. She speaks fluent English and is an excellent source of local information of every kind. She is also a very good cook and has the unique distinction among b. and b. châtelaines of appearing in the discriminating Gault-et-Millau guide on the strength of her cuisine. She charges 250f for dinner, eaten with the owners, but this includes wine before, during, and after, and coffee; reservations required.

Inside the immaculate 17th century farmhouse she has three bedrooms with private bath or shower, one of which is split-level to provide a sitting area, 500–550f for two, and in the well-kept grounds are two independent cottages for four or six people for 850 or 875f. Breakfast is extra – another 50f per person – which I personally do not approve of – b. and b. should be just that – but it is exceptionally good, with a selection of home-made jams, so perhaps you could skip lunch.

AMFREVILLE. 14860

12 km NNE of Caen. D514 west from Cabourg; turn on to the D236.

A neat but not exciting village, close to the river Orne and Canal de Caen, not far from the sea at Houlgate, and near Pegasus Bridge.

l'Ecarde (S–M)
M. & Mme Lamotte. 31.78.71.78.

On the fringe of the village is a well-kept farmhouse surrounded by high walls, where two guest rooms in a converted farm building have tiled floors, each with a shower and a wash-basin, but sharing one toilet on the corridor. One room for four with double bed and bunks, is really large, with a fireplace in one corner. The other for two with double bed costs 200f. Nice outlook over a lawned garden, excellent parking, and the added advantage of a free, hard tennis court for guests. Bikes for hire at 50f a day.

L' Escarde

No evening meal, so treat yourself to an omelette at Mme Gondrée's famous café at Pegasus Bridge or visit the floating restaurant moored alongside the canal – very reasonable prices and the fun of eating on board. Rooms 200f.

BERNIERES-D'AILLY. 14170 ST PIERRE SUR DIVES

9 km SW of St Pierre–sur-Dives; 11 km NE of Falaise on D511 and then right on to D242. The farm is 2 km past the village.

Ferme d'Ailly (S)
Arlette & André Vermes. 31.90.73.58. cl. Dec to Easter.

The Vermes have converted another room in their old stone farmhouse since my last visit. They now have five altogether in different styles. You can sleep 'Retro' with fin-de-siècle lamps and beading, 'Romantique' with a small draped four-poster, 'Campagnard' – very Laura Ashley or – oh dear, I forget. But you get the idea. Anyway they're all comfortable, with their own shower-rooms and rea-

Ferme d'Ailly

sonably priced at 180f for two, 220 for three. Evening meal, as yet unsampled, costs 70f.

BEUVRON EN AUGE. 14430 DOZULÉ

30 km E of Caen by N175 to Dozulé, then D85 and D146. If I had to pick one area of Normandy as 'typical' I would pick the Auge region and if I had to pick one village it would be Beuvron. I'm sure it's featured on many a Come-to-Normandy

poster, thanks to its ancient, beamed and crooked market hall, and its ridiculously
picturesque timbered cottages. Various routes are suggested for touring the region –
the *route des fromages*, the *route du cidre*, the *route des douets* (little streams), but
you hardly need guidance – it doesn't matter which way you turn you are bound to
be engulfed by pleasing rusticity, a million miles from the autoroute hustle.

Le Bourg (M)
Chez Mme Hamelin. 31.39.00.62. cl. from Nov to Easter.

La Place de Beuvron

Right in the village and one of its
most attractive buildings, L-shaped
enclosing a flowery courtyard. One
room, with shower, opens directly
on to the garden and the other on
the first floor, with pretty English
wallpaper, has a bathroom. Most
attractive dining room for breakfast
and a warm welcome from the
English-speaking Madame Hamelin
in this outstanding village add up
to an arrow possibility, so more
reports would be particularly welcome.

Reader's Recommendation:

Le Lieu Brunet (M)
Jacques Marie. Route de Gerrots. 31.79.23.01. cl. Nov to Easter.
Turn right off the D146 on to the D146A towards Gerrots and the house is on the
left. Two rooms in a pretty half-timbered house, with showers, for 200f.
   More reports welcome.

BONNEBOSQ. 14340

32 km E of Caen by N175 or autoroute. At La-Haie-Tondue turn right on to the
D16 and 3 km before Bonnebosq look for a sign indicating a right turn. The house
is on the left.
   Right in the heart of some of the loveliest countryside in Normandy – the Pays
d'Auge and all that implies – typical cottages, typical cows, typical cider, typical
cheeses.

Manoir du Champ Versant (M)
M. & Mme Létresor. 31.65.11.07. cl. 1/11 to 1/4.
If you set out to find a typical Manoir Augeron you could not do better than look
at le Manoir. Picturesque cottages abound but manor-houses in good condition,

like this one, are rarer. It has the statutory black and white half-timbering, but above that is a tall steeply pitched red tiled roof with two eye-brow windows and the side of the house is strikingly chequered in red brick and creamy Caen stone. Chickens peck around, apple trees blossom, immaculate white ducks swim on pond, horses pose... film crews, where are you?

Le Champ Versant

Inside is equally photogenic and authentic – huge, open-hearthed stone fireplaces and country antique furniture in salon, dining room and two bedrooms, all with views over countryside totally in keeping with the character of the house. Lovely. 235f for this taste of the real Calvados is a bargain.

BOURGEAUVILLE. 14430

12 km W of Pont-l'Evêque. 12 km NE of Caen. 13 km S of Deauville.

La Belle Epine (S)
M. & Mme Clouet. 31.65.27.26.

A large courtyard here with a modern farmhouse, detached farm buildings and stables on both sides. Over the stables are four rooms entered by wooden stairs at each end. Some are for families; electrically heated. Nothing very spectacular but plain functional rooms in different colours. Young Madame Clouet is very pleasant and gives you breakfast in her large dining room which is warmly heated in winter.

La Belle Epine

These rooms are very popular with Parisians wanting to be near Deauville but not wishing to pay Deauville prices, so booking is necessary at weekends, even in winter. Rooms are 200f for two, and only 280f for four people. No evening meals but the Auberge du Cardinal, nearby, has a good reputation.

BRETTREVILLE-SUR-LAIZE. 14680

10 km S of Caen by the N158 towards Falaise, then right on to the D23 at La Jalousie. Just before Bretteville turn right on to the D125, where the château is signed.

Château des Riffets (M)
Anne Marie and Alain Cantel. 31.23.53.21.

I am delighted with this success story. My first encounter with the Cantel family must have been five years ago now, when I called on impulse at a terrible time – on January 1st, when every French family is clearing up after the St. Sylvestre feast of the night before. The Cantels must have been horrified, but disguised their feelings magnificently, offering refreshment and welcome. They had just started their b. and b. operation and I recorded that the interior did not match up to the impressive first impressions of the approach up the drive, through extensive grounds, to the château. Many changes since then, as Anne Marie, who lived in England and speaks and writes perfect English, tells me. The bedrooms were always lovely, high wide and handsome and filled with light, but now they have their own shower-rooms – two doubles for 400f and two suites for 600f. The public rooms have original period ceilings, but the furniture is modern.

Another new asset is the heated swimming pool – very popular with the Cantel's small daughter as well as the guests.

Dinner is served by a maid, but the family will join you if that is what you wish – 120–200f, with vegetarians catered for.

BURES-SUR-DIVES 14670

15 km E of Caen 15 km SE of Ouistreham. A visit to Pegasus Bridge is an absolute must. It was here that the first British troops of the Sixth Airborne Division landed on the morning of 6th June 1944. They took the vital bridge over the Caen canal and liberated the café right by the bridge, the first house in France to be freed by the invasion. M. & Mme Gondrée were in the café at the time and for three nights no sleep was had by anyone. Madame Arlette Gondrée who was then four years old

has taken over from her parents and maintains the café just as it was; none of the decor has been changed, only enhanced by numerous gifts from visiting old soldiers, their friends and relatives. Open from March to November. With great charm she welcomes her many visitors, offering them drinks and sandwiches and her special Normandy omelettes at any time of the day. It is truly a living memorial to the most exciting day in French and British history this century. In summer you can sit outside on the terrace facing the canal or in winter sit at one of the cafe tables unchanged for fifty years. The original bridge has been dismantled and replaced by a new one.

To finish your exciting day book your room at Bures-sur-Dives. In the village of Troarn take the D95 to Bures, bear right to the church and the manor is down the lane alongside, well signed.

➤ Manoir de Tourpes (M-L)
M. & Mme Landon-Cassady. Rue de l'Eglise. 31.26.63.47.

Manoir de Tourpes

It was Arlette Gondrée who recommended this elegant 17th century manor house. It stands beside the village church with sweeping lawns to the banks of the river Dives, where the water rises with the tide. After persevering in French on the phone we discover that Monsieur is American, but Madam is French. We were given a very warm welcome, Madame switching easily from French to English and back again as she showed us round, but generally the French atmosphere prevails throughout their home. Three first floor bedrooms overlook the garden and river, all so different but each having a special allure, making a choice difficult. The largest is pure honeymoon material, almost a suite, with windows on three sides and the luxury of a real log fire. Thick carpets, fresh flowers by the bed, *en suite* bathroom in delicate peach and blue, thick towels and even a peach towelling gown. If the log fire isn't enough there's also an electric blanket. Next door, a smaller room with the most compelling view of all from the double bed, has a washbasin and a large private bathroom across the corridor with a deep old copper bath tub, but a shower too if you can't face the novelty; not many do, Madam tells me. The third bedroom is *en suite* with shower and toilet, and boasts a balcony. So charming are the rooms I shall not be satisfied until I've stayed in them all. And only 250-350f.

Breakfast in the lounge/dining room, where a cheerful log fire blazes away, is laid on an attractive round table and is not to be hurried over. A wide choice of cereals, fruit juice, yoghurt, fresh fruit, jams, bread, brioche and all the usual drinks.

You won't find such luxury in any hotel at these prices. No evening meals. Logis in Troarn, or your hosts will advise for further afield.

You will need to book ahead. Arrowed for situation and good value.

CAHAGNES. 14240

27 km SW of Caen. Take the N175 out of Villers-Bocage heading south-west. In 12 km after passing the village of Quéry look for the chambres d'hôtes sign on the right up a lane, before Benneville.

Benneville (S)
M. & Mme Guilbert. 31.77.58.05.

It is hard to realise that this sprawling old farmhouse was in the thick of the fighting in Normandy in 1944. M. Guilbert has a very interesting American book written on the Battle of Normandy with pictures of local press cuttings. Now restored, the farmhouse is surrounded by gardens and the farmyard. An ideal place for children. Five comfortable rooms in different buildings, warmly heated for cold weather, are all different; some are on the first floor with independent entry up outside steps, and there is one large family room on the ground floor for five. All have a delightful outlook. M. & Mme Guilbert are a youngish couple with four grown-up children. They are a very interesting family, with lots to talk about. Meals are taken in an enormous salon which opens on to the garden. The whole place grows on one every hour you stay here. Dinner is very good value with cider and wine included at 65f, 35f for children.

On arrival we were greeted with tea and cakes. Madame Guilbert was resting after a hectic holiday week feeding 27 people, but she still managed to give us a very good meal which we ate with all the family. There are not many places like this, so it would be wise to book ahead. Rooms 160f.

CAUMONT-L'EVENTÉ. 14240

38 km SW of Caen on D9 towards Torigni. Turn right at Caumont on D28 towards Balleroy and the house is 300m on the right on the main road.

Balleroy is a unique, little town, like a film set, with one wide main street of grey stone houses, all of a period, leading down to the focal point, the Château de Balleroy, built in the 17th century by Mansart. Nearby is the delightful forest of Cérisy and of course Bayeux is only a short distance away.

> ### Le Relais (M)
Claude & Jeanne-Paule Boullot. 19 rue Thiers. 31.77.47.85.

I can only find one fault with this attractive, well-run hospitable, good value establishment and that is I didn't find it first. It features in every known b. and b. guide and so, if you want a bed, you have to be quick off the mark.

Creepers clamber so abundantly up the walls of this old staging post that you can hardy see the building, apart from the glass conservatory built to overlook the lovely swimming pool. The exuberant hosts are horse breeders and '*equitation*' is one of the optional extras. Jeanne-Paule is a generous hostess and her breakfasts and dinners are all part of an enormous bargain on offer here. A typical evening meal might be a vegetable terrine, chicken Vallée d'Auge, cheeseboard, gooseberry fool, all for 130f, wine and cider included.

Rather feminine, boudoir-ish rooms, furnished with some antiques and lots of personal touches, cost as follows: One double – 270f, one treble – 330f, one double suite – 340, one treble suite – 420f, all with bath or shower.

Arrowed for all-round excellence.

CLARBEC. 14130

45 km E of Caen, 6 km SW of Pont-l'Evêque by N175 and left over the autoroute on D280, then D285 towards St. Hymer. Cross three little bridges, turn right and look for sign.

Another choice in the lovely Auge region, where the silver strands of the river Touques are known as *douets* and tourist routes are marked to follow them through archetypal Norman countryside, well endowed with eye-patch cows, apple orchards, chocolate-box cottages, beamy farmhouses and roses round many a door.

Pressoir Lieu Hubert (S)
Madame Elie. 31.64.90.89.

The half-timbered cottage was originally used to house a cider press. One of the two bedrooms is in the section where the apples were crushed and has a super

bathroom, well equipped with all
the necessaries, like generous towels; mirrors and atypical (for
France) efficient lighting. Breakfast
is eaten outside on the small terrace
in summer or in the Elies' homely
family room, decorated with photographs and bric-à-brac. 200f.

CLÉCY. 14570

37 km S of Caen by D562. Claimed to be the 'Capital of the Suisse Normande', a
particularly attractive area, but one that bears little relation to Switzerland. It does
not even include Normandy's highest peaks, but it does have a distinctive landscape
of green hills and greener valleys. The river Orne winds peacefully through rich
pastureland or dramatically cuts into the rocky escarpment of the Amoricain massif.

Vey is 1 km E of Clecy on the D133A. A lovely old bridge crosses the wide
fast-flowing river.

Le Vey (S)
Mme Leboucher. 31.69.71.02; fax 31.69.69.33.

An old FE favourite. Mme
Leboucher has three comfortable
guest rooms in an independent
building on her husband's farm,
each with its own bathroom, for
190f. Several readers have testified
to the success of their visit; here is
one of the most recent: *'We had
ensuite room, stone walls and
wooden beams, overlooking fields.
Incredibly quiet. They make their
own Cider, Pommeau and Calva-*
dos. *The cider was like dry champagne'* Derek W. Smith.

Not quite so near Clécy as I had hoped and easier to find if you stay on the D562
south of Thury-Harcourt and turn left on to the D1 signposted Falaise; then left
again on to the D168 and you will find it not far down on the right.

La Loterie (S)
M. & Mme Aubry. 31.69.74.38.

A real farm welcome here from elderly owners now retired farmers. They have one large sunny comfortable family room with two double beds on the first floor, centrally heated, warmly carpeted with windows north and south overlooking farm land. The *en suite* bathroom is also large, light and carpeted with a separate toilet off the room. At the moment there is just the one room in the main ivy-covered farmhouse; but two other rooms in an annexe are being prepared, one double-bedded room and one twin, 170f. Breakfast is copious with a good choice of cereals for the grain brigade, not often offered in France. The evening meal entirely of farm produce – 65f. Cider *compris*. A very comfortable budget stop at all times of the year.

CREULLY. 14480

17 km E of Bayeux. From the ring road at Bayeux take the D12 to Creully, then the D22 to Caen. At Le Fresne the chambres d'hôtes is signed on the right down a side road.

Clos Chanteclair (M-L)
Mme Robineau Le Fresne Camilly. 31.80.00.28.

In a pleasant residential area this lovely old manor house has six up-market rooms beautifully furnished with thick carpets; but sadly though all have washbasins only two rooms are *en suite;* the others share bathrooms on the landings. The small tower room is well worth 300f *en suite*. One room in the granary part of the house has a whole tree as a beam across the ceiling. An excellent breakfast is included. No evening meal but the Auberge de la Mue in Thaon looks promising or the Hostellerie St Martin in Creully.

Rooms at 250/380f are a little high for shared facilities but the hostess is charming and the rooms are extremely nice.

DOUVILLE-EN-AUGE. 14430

7 km SE of Houlgate. 28 km ENE of Caen.

Ferme de l'Oraille (S)
M. & Mme Houlet. Chemin d'Eraine. 31.79.25.49.

Searching for somewhere warm and comfortable in November fog in the region of Houlgate, I found this old farm tucked down a lane off the D45. The typical black-beamed Normandy house faces down a pretty valley, with terrace for sitting outside, but is equally suitable for winter use since it is centrally heated with cosy carpeted rooms on the first floor, all furnished in comfortable 1930s style, for 180f. The welcome is warm and thoughtful. No evening meals but the Maison Blanche restaurant on the main road a kilometre away will fix you a meal from 50f. Nothing *gastronomique*, but well cooked country menus or just omelettes and salads if you prefer and a good bowl of fresh fruit. A most attentive *patron*, especially if you come from this chambres d'hôtes. It is a working dairy farm, so your hosts are early to bed, but you may have a key if you come in late. For a budget stop you can't lose here.

GÉFOSSE. 14230

65 km SE of Cherbourg, 30 km NW of Bayeux by N13 west, just past St Germain-du-Pert, then D514 towards Grandcamp Maisy. Turn left on to the D199A to Géfosse-Fontenay. L'Hermerel is the second driveway on the right, but be sure you get the right chambres d'hôtes – there are several other signs around here.

What a fabulous position, set in the vast bay of le Grand Vey, looking north all the way past the landing beach of Utah to St. Vaast. The light around here is unique – enough to tempt you to pack some watercolours. Vast sandy beaches to walk along, and Bayeux within easy reach. More practically – halfway between the two ferry ports, Cherbourg and Caen.

Ferme de l'Hermerel (S)
Agnes & François Lemarie. 31.22.64.12.

Friendly English-speaking Agnes Lemarie says that they are aware of their good fortune to live in such a house – a 17th century fortified manor house, typical of the region. It's a working dairy farm – nearby Isigny is the centre of the dairy industry; the Lemaries have four children to look after as well as their guests and the cows, but still manage to find plenty of time for friendly chat. They are justifiably proud of the gem

of a Gothic chapel which they have
restored, now used as a salon, and
of the old pigeonnier in the courtyard where guests can enjoy picnics
in a unique setting. The guest rooms
are in the wing at right angles to the
main building, where breakfast is
taken in the stone-walled, chequered
floor kitchen with massive fireplace
and copper utensils.

L' Hermarel

Furnishing in the four bedrooms, each with private shower, is
simple and the stone can strike a little chilly at times, so perhaps this is a better
choice for summer than on cold winter nights when the wind can howl across the
bay. Pick fine weather and benefit from the proximity to the sea – only 20 minutes
walk away across the fields.

Accommodation is one twin-bedded room on the ground floor – 190f; one
double on the first floor – 250f; two rooms forming a suite for two couples or a
family – 250f, plus 70f per person extra; another on the second floor with a mezzanine, again for four or five people, again 250 plus 70f supplement.

GONNEVILLE-SUR-MER. 14510

2 km SE of Houlgate. 14 km SW of Deauville.

La Ferme de la Bruyère-Mannet (M)
M. Crochet. Chemin de Dramard. 31.28.04.15.

Situated in a residential lane above
Houlgate this unusual shaped
house has a room on the first floor
sharing a large bathroom on the
landing, with a possibility of
another single room. On the third
floor two more rooms share one
bathroom 220f. A very pleasant
house, neither old nor new, in a
large garden which also has the
advantage of a heated swimming
pool. Within easy distance of the
beach at Houlgate or Cabourg.

La Ferme de la Bruyère Mannet

LÉAUPARTIE. 14340 CAMBREMER

19 km SW of Pont-l'Eveque by the N175, then left on to the D16. The Auge region, either side of the autoroute but far removed from its rush and noise, is deeply rural and full of fascination. It is a countryside of rich pastures and small farms. Many of the farmers' wives have adopted the chambre d'hôtes lifestyle and here is a typical example which has pleased readers over a number of years.

Le Bois Hurey (S)
Mme Guérin. 31.63.01.99.

Le Bois Hurey

Léaupartie. 14

To find the Guérins' pretty slate-clad farmhouse turn left just before the bridge on the side road to Rumesnil.

There are many testimonies to Suzanne Guérin's friendliness and generosity; one cites the weekend when she was up to her eyebrows with Parisians and managed to feed twelve hungry guests by dint of setting up a trestle table outside for a memorable dinner which lasted until midnight.

She has only two rooms (so book), one double on the ground floor for 190f and one on the first floor for four people, sharing a bathroom – 190f.

"*Definitely the success of the trip. Two nights was quite enough – our stomachs couldn't take more! Every dish of the five-course meals was perfection – especially the soufflé de truite sauvage – and bags of all, too. On the last night Mme Guérin had two friends to dinner and I'm sure I spoke more French there than I have in the past ten years. Next morning we left after hugs and kisses (x 4) all round. Mme G. presented us with a litre of her home-brewed Calvados and we reciprocated with a litre of malt whisky.*" Roger Lushingham.

This feast cost 90f.

MAISONS. 14400 BAYEUX

3 km NW of Bayeux. Just a dot on the map, approached from the D100 between Tour-en-Bessin and Port-en-Bessin.

In other words, the best of all worlds. No one should visit this part of Normandy without a visit to Bayeux and its excellently-presented tapestry – a year-round treat in an interesting and lively little town, and no one should miss Port-en-Bessin, the most attractive little fishing port on the Bessin coast, contrasting with the landing beaches on either side. The fishing fleet pull up along the quays of the deep inlet of the harbour, so that you can stroll along the edge peering into the holds and checking the catch. Lots of head-clearing, ozone-packed walks here along the headlands.

➤ ### Manoir du Carel (L)

Monsieur and Madame Jacques Aumond. 31.22.37.00; fax 31.21.57.00.

Last time I wrote about the Manoir the Aumonds were still in the process of converting their superb mediaeval fortified manor-house, part of which is still a working farm, into a luxurious home with rooms for guests. This has now been achieved with a great sense of style and originality. A huge glass door has been let into the sitting room, allowing the natural light to illuminate the lovely galleried room and its grey and honey stone walls.

There are now three double rooms with private bath or shower, from 350–600f and a small, independent house with lounge and kitchen and its own garden for four people for 650f.

Here is a chance to stay in great comfort with delightful, English-speaking hosts in a house steeped in history. FE readers have approved, so the arrow stays.

MATHIEU. 14920

8 km N of Caen. A nice quiet place for visiting Caen, close to the superb *MÉMORIAL* Museum of Peace and also very handy for the Ouistreham ferry.

Take the D7 northwards from Caen (signed Langrune-sur-Mer). Shortly after the village of Epron fork right over the dual carriageway (signed Périers-sur-le-Dan) and you will find Le Londel on your left in about 1 km. Beware there is another chambres d'hôtes at Le Londel, which I haven't yet visited.

Le Londel (M)

M. & Mme Leblanc. 31.44.51.55.

In a flat wooded area this spacious modern house in large grounds has three good-sized, comfortably furnished rooms on the first floor for 210f and 280f for four. This is no cottage and there is a feeling of great space around one. There is a swimming pool and an excellent tennis court behind the house. No evening meals, but restaurants are only five minutes away. Quote:

"Madame is a really lovely person, who got up at the crack of dawn to give us breakfast when we were catching the early ferry."

NONANT. 14400

5 km SE of Bayeux. Ideal for a visit to Caen or Bayeux. From the N13 SE of Bayeux in 6 km turn right following signs to Nonant. At the church in 1 km turn left then right following the signs to La Poulinière on your right.

➤ La Poulinière (M)
Mme Simand. 31.92.51.03. Closed 1st Nov to Easter.

Don't expect to learn French here. Madame Simand delights in entertaining her 80 per cent English guests and has learnt excellent English without setting foot on our soil. Her restored farmhouse in an apple orchard and pretty gardens now has five totally different rooms, some in the main house, others in a converted barn opposite, furnished with great inspiration; the choice is yours – adjoining

rooms for a family with shared bathroom, fresh green and white for two, chic gold with polished black tiled floors, or mouth-watering strawberry and more. Italian tiles in one shower room are delightful. 200f. Breakfast is copious – eggs or ham as well as traditional French, and an excellent evening meal costs 100f including home-made apéritif, wine and coffee. The menu changes every night. Madame adores cooking and her meals are enjoyed by all. Non-smokers preferred. Pretty garden to sit in. Parking well off the road behind the barn.

Unanimous approval from readers of FE3 and FE9 ensures an arrow.

OSMANVILLE. 14230

12 km E of Carentan. 30 WNW of Bayeux. Take the N113 from Carentan to Caen; in about 8 km, at a large roundabout, take the Osmanville road. The hotel 'Les Amies de la Route' will be on your left and right opposite is the turn into Champ Manlay; the main house is on the right past some chalets.

Champ Manlay (M)
M. & Mme Manlay. 31.22.02.91.

If you want to spend a few days in summer exploring the Normandy beaches this is a real find. Some rooms are in the main house, but two very practical rooms on the

first floor of an annexe, overlooking the swimming pool, are *en suite*
with kitchenettes 200f – 250f. M.
& Mme Manlay are natural and
charming hosts. Breakfast is in their
dining room. No evening meals but
use the excellent cheap restaurant
across the road, if you're not into
self-catering. There are also five
chalet-gîtes in the large grounds
and a small flat on the ground floor
of the annexe. All the occupants

have access to the pool, but this does not seem to make it at all crowded. Parking
well away from the main road.

PIERREFITTE EN AUGE. 14130

5 km S of Pont l'Evêque. Turn right off the D48 south of Pont l'Evêque on the
D280A, following the sign 'La Route des Douets'. *Douets* are the streams of the
Pays d'Auge that emanate from the river Touques and add yet more character to the
delightfully rustic countryside, unbelievably just a few km either side of the
autoroute. A visit to Pierrefitte, which must qualify as one of the prettiest villages in
Normandy, is alone good reason enough for a detour from the hectic motorway,
but I found another reason for FE8 – the colourful café/bar/restaurant of Les Deux
Tonneaux. A reader following that one up made another discovery:

Les Trois Ormes (S)
M. Marcel Lebéhot. 31.65.03.67.

'*Situated off the D280, 1 mile from
the village in the direction of St
Hymer. At the top of the hill, turn
left down lane for 1 mile. Three
rooms available in modern villa
180f, including breakfast. Our
room was very large with adjoining
shower/bathroom – other rooms en
suite. M. et Mme Lebéhot very
friendly and keen to be helpful; no
English spoken. Breakfast of fresh
bread, jam and marmalade. The*

*only thing against is the one mile lane, but the Visitors Book seems to suggest plenty
of people find their way there*'. Derek W. Smith.

ST PHILBERT-DES-CHAMPS. 14130

9 km NE of Lisieux, 11 km SE of Pont l'Evêque. Take the D579 from Lisieux to Quilly-le-Vicomte, then the D98 to St Philbert and the farmhouse is on the left just before the village.

La Ferme des Poiriers Roses (M)
M. & Mme Lecorneur. 31.64.72.14; fax 31.64.19.55.

Ridiculously pretty. One of those 18th century black and white farmhouses that are so typical of the lovely Auge region of Calvados. Geraniums tumble from every conceivable aperture, natural and contrived, roses cluster round the door, the lawns are well tended, with green park benches inviting repose and the gravel on the terrace is well-raked. Inside are all the charming clichés – low beams, tiled floors and antique furniture. Until 1950 its function used to be the production of cider and Calvados and the lovely old still is still *in situ*. The land around is used for a dairy herd.

La Ferme des Poiriers Roses

The abundance of flowers continues inside the house – Madame Lecorneur loves them dried as well as fresh and there is an arrangement in every room, including the six bedrooms and one suite, two in the house and five in the erstwhile stables. Cunningly all the inherent rusticity has been retained while large, light-giving windows and luxurious bathrooms have been added.

The Lecorneur's affection for their home is very evident – they have named the rooms after their favourite romantic heroines: Lara, Emilie, Anna, Kalinka... and lavished particularly pretty fabrics and paper on their embellishment. 300-500f for two.

Breakfast is extra, alas, but the 52f buys a good deal more than the normal croissant and coffee. A true *petit déjeuner gourmand*.

SAINT-RÉMY-SUR-ORNE. 14570

2 km from Le Vey-Clécy, 8 km S of Thury-Harcourt. Overlooking the valley of the Orne, close to the well known 'Moulin' at Le Vey this makes a very economical stop.

La Vallée (S)
M. & Mme Dumont. 31.69.78.64.

An excellent welcome waits you from the young owners of this dairy and pig farm. Three rooms warm in winter are on the second floor of their farmhouse situated above the road with glorious views of the valley. A sunny front garden is good to laze in. Warm winter rooms, 'Orchidée' for three, 'Jacinthe' for two, but 'Primavère' for two has only a toilet and washbasin, usually let with one of the others, which are each *en suite*. Madame Dumont, who has a young family, doesn't do evening meals but suggests a good restaurant 1 km away in the village on the D562, or picnic in the sunny garden beside the old cider press. 190f for such nice rooms is good value for this area.

SAINT-VIGOR-LE-GRAND. 14400

1 km E of Bayeux. A handy stop if you wish to spend a day in Bayeux viewing the Tapestry, which of course is the great attraction here, now so well presented in the Cultural Centre. A film explains it all, and there is a photographed copy of the Tapestry also shown as a rehearsal, so by the time you reach the real thing you know something about it and what highlights to look for. There are two versions of the film, one in French, the other in English. Lace making is also exhibited here. Visit the Cathedral built in the 11th century where the Tapestry was originally shown. The streets in the centre of the town are mostly pedestrianised so meandering round the shops and cafés is easy and agreeable.

From the by pass at St-Vigor-le-Grand take the D12 signposted Courseulles, turn first right and the large archway to this chambres d'hôtes is on your left in about 200 metres.

M. & Mme Suzanne (M)
31.92.09.39.

You approach the lovely old farmhouse by an arched gateway into a large courtyard with centre flower beds. So easy for parking and offloading, the car can be left right outside the door of your room.

There is just the one spacious room on the ground floor with windows on both sides, housing a double bed and two singles round the corner for the offspring. A superb family room with shower

and w.c. adjoining, 200f for two, 300f for four. Old beams and furniture contrast with modern beds. The floor is an interesting mixture of wood and tiles. Central heating is laid on for winter and table and chairs for the garden in summer. There is a couch to recline on and a large solid oak table to work on. What more could you ask? Breakfast is taken in Madame's own dining room along the terrace. Such a pleasant hostess who looks after all your needs. Nice for two, lovely for a family. No evening meals, but restaurants in Bayeux.

A second choice for Bayeux:-

M. & Mme Vingtrois (S)
1 Residence de la Rivière. 31.22.03.16.

About a kilometre out of Bayeux in the residential area of Saint-Vigor-le-Grand is a very new, modern house in a large garden with enclosed parking. Madame Vingtrois has two, occasionally three, rooms to offer. One on the first floor has an elaborate bathroom and separate toilet just outside the room.

Sometimes the extra room offered shares these facilities. Another room for two on the ground floor which I haven't seen, has a private bathroom. Judging by the thick carpeting and immaculate decor of the other rooms I am sure this is just as good. No evening meal, but many restaurants in Bayeux. Rooms 200f.

TORTISAMBERT. 14140

5 km S of Livarot. Take the D6 west from Livarot, then left on to the D38 (signed Heurtevent) and La Boursaie is signed in 5 km on the left. Wind down a grassy lane and bear right along an even smaller wooded track for 1 km (mind the ducks and geese) and you will find yourself on a hillside in the heart of the *Pays d'Auge* where there is an isolated collection of typical Norman buildings, gîtes and chambres d'hôtes with wonderful views of the countryside. One gîte still has the cider press incorporated in the salon/kitchen.

La Boursaie (S)
Peter & Anja Davies. 31.63.14.20; fax 31.63.14.28.

A change of ownership here; many will remember this old cider farm which the Wilsons converted, now taken over by Peter (a Yorkshireman) and Anja (his wife from Düsseldorf), who have been in the catering trade for many years – a charming couple who are continuing the good work. Already the gîtes and chambres d'hôtes are thriving. There are two rustic

La Boursaie

rooms, heated, with a shared kitchen where breakfast is laid from 8 a.m. onwards, 230f. Plenty of scope for self catering and 65 acres of land to roam; a very relaxed atmosphere. Anja fetches the bread for the gîtes as well as the chambres d'hôtes each morning and hopes to start evening meals on request for first and last nights (which sounds a good idea). Special weekend courses organised if wished, on cheese and cider making. Bikes for hire. Only 5 km from the town of Livarot, but you feel miles away.

VOUILLY. 14230, ISIGNY-SUR-MER

7½ km S of Isigny. 61 km SE of Cherbourg by N13 to Isigny. Then turn right onto the D5 towards Le Molay, and left near Vouilly church and the château is on the right, 500 metres on.

Isigny is not really *sur-mer* but near the mouth of the river Vire; there is a little quay where colourful fishing boats unload their catch, and sheds of assorted crustaceans and molluscs. This is stomach-country, not only for the wonderfully fresh fish and oysters but for all dairy produce – Isigny is the distribution centre – and for the flavoursome lamb that graze on the surrounding salt marshes.

Château de Vouilley (M)
Marie-José & James Hame.l 31.22.08.59. cl. 1/12 to 1/3.

L' Eleveurs

The château has many charms – it is light and airy, it has five splendid bedrooms all equipped with bathrooms, it is situated in the Parc Régional du Marais du Cotentin et Bessin, it is within easy reach of both Caen and Cherbourg, not to mention Bayeux, it is a mellow old manor house rather than château, built in the 15th and 16th centuries and enlarged in the 18th, and it boasts a moat and a large pond. Its special attraction, however, and pride is its surrounding garden. Until the end of the last century it was a typical formal French garden, but the grandmother of James Hamel instituted an ongoing process of 'anglicisation' (which I take to mean making it less structured, with more herbaceous borders than box hedges). Today it is a riot of colour in summer, with lawns that are certainly better tended than most French versions, masses of roses, lavender and white hibiscus. Wooden benches invite repose and I can think of nothing finer than returning here after a long day in the car.

For ten years now the family have been involved in chambres d'hôtes, with Grandmère, whose portrait surveys the situation from the wall, very much part of the scene.

It must have been a fascinating experience for her to welcome for the 50th anniversary of D-Day celebrations some of the 42 American war correspondents who were stationed at Vouilley, using the dining room, now freshened up with flowery decor, as their press office.

The price for two people is 290f, no doubt including their own dairy produce.

EURE

LES BAUX-DE-BRETEUIL. 27160

27 km E of l'Aigle. 16 km S of Conches-en-Ouche. The house stands down a lane from the D833 between Les Baux-de-Breteuil and Breteuil; well signed.

La Bourganière (M)
Mme Noel. 32.30.68.18.

In the middle of flat, forested country this cereal farm has a very well kept old Normandy house overlooking a neat garden with a large pond. The beamed guest room, luxuriously carpeted and furnished with velvet Louis XV chairs and padded bedhead, has an equally large and luxurious bathroom 210f. Madame Noel drives the school bus, so book ahead and she will arrange for her son to be looking out for you when she isn't there when you arrive. Dinner with the family (65f) Madame, her son and daughter, in a dining room decorated with many beams and memorabilia, all spotless and of such good quality. Covered parking. A good summer stop in pleasant, quiet surroundings.

BEUZEVILLE. 27210

15 km E of Honfleur, 52 km S of Le Havre by A15, and N178. An ideal staging post. We often stop here for breakfast at the Cochon d'Or after staggering red-eyed off the night ferry. The Tuesday market fills the square with colourful animation – you could easily stock up on last-minute take-homes here. Better still book in at:

Les Coutances (S-M)
Mme Régine Bultey. 32.57.75.54.

Look for the signs in the place de la République indicating the way to Les Coutances, which is 1 km from Beuzeville in the direction of St-Pierre-du-Val. There's a youthful cheerfulness about this typically Norman restored farmhouse with statutory white walls and herringbone beams. The garden is well equipped with the standard begonias and geraniums tumbling from barrels, windowboxes and wheel-

Les Coutances

barrow. The flowery theme continues in the interior, decorated with taste and loving care. Three bedrooms are quiet and comfortable, each with its shower or bath, and look out over the countryside and neighbouring Norman cottages. Very pretty indeed. Doubles cost 200f for two or 250f for three. With some arm-twisting, Mme Bultey will provide an evening meal (80f wine exclusive), but there is a choice of restaurants in Beuzeville, so there should be no problem.

BONCOURT. 27120

18 km W of Vernon. This small area of Eure is well supplied with quality resting places. A highly recommended chambres d'hôtes, totally different, but equally luxurious:-

Les Ormes (M)
M. & Mme Beghini. 5 rue Divette. 32.36.92.44 or 32.36.73.01.

In the residential area of this small village, Les Ormes is situated in a large garden of lawns and trees. The main house is old and well restored; across the courtyard is an ancient, beamed stable beautifully rebuilt to make a large salon for guests with a small kitchen area. Pass through this salon out to an enclosed, grassy area and you will find five new bedrooms in an L shaped wooden construction, 270f

Les Ormes

for two. So well insulated, they are suitable for winter use, with electric heating. Madame Beghini has enjoyed furnishing three rooms. All are differently decorated, three have baths for those who prefer to soak away their cares, two have showers. One room is for three, but another small bed for a child can be put in any of the other rooms. Breakfast is on the terrace in summer, in the main house in the winter. Evening meals as such are not served, but Madame has a menu of snack meals to choose from should her guests want only a light supper or salad. Things like *Croque Monsieur* or ice-cream sundaes, all in the region of 30f. I am sure they are most tastefully served.

CONTEVILLE. 27210

9 km SW of Pont-de-Tancarville, by N178, or a 16 km drive eastwards from Honfleur on the coast road, D312 – a pleasant route all the way, very rural with glimpses of the Seine estuary. From here you can rest assured that Le Havre is only 45 minutes away, or even less once the new Pont de Normandie is ready, so a convenient last stop before catching the ferry might be in the village of Conteville.

Ferme du Pressoir (M-S)
Odile & Pierre Anfrey. Les Clos Potier. 32.57.60.79.

There are several chambres d'hôtes in the region, but only one Ferme du Pressoir, so make sure you follow the signs to Le Clos Potier. You will find it tucked away in a lane behind a white fence, a half-timbered archetypal Normal farmhouse, festooned with geraniums from tubs, pots, windowboxes and wheelbarrows. It takes its name from the massive grape press dating from the 17th century which is  still in working order but, says Madame Anfrey sadly, 'We no longer have the horses to pull the crushing stone round the trough'.

The 250 year old farm has been in the family for three generations and nowadays the energetic Madame Anfrey and her husband concentrate on the raising of cows and chickens; this does not hinder her in making guests feel pampered and welcome. Furnishing is family antiques, copper pans, dried flowers, lace cloths, resulting in a pleasantly cluttered homely atmosphere. There are three smallish rooms in the house, with private bath or shower, and one family room with two double beds and bathroom in an annexe. 240f for two.

The evening meal is an excellent 120f worth, with all drinks included and breakfast is charmingly laid out on white Limoges china on a pink tablecloth.

LA CROIX-SAINT-LEUFROY. 27490

100 km SE of Le Havre. 40 km S of Rouen. Much to see in the area; Les Andelys, Monet's garden and the Seine are all close by. Don't miss Les Andelys. Le Petit-Andelys is tucked in by the river under the hill on which the ruined Castle Gaillard stands, a fortress built by Richard the Lionheart to prevent the French king Phillipe-Auguste from reaching Rouen in 1196. For the energetic there is a lane up to it behind the tourist office; otherwise drive three kilometres through le Grand-Andelys and follow the signs. Once high on the car park the view is fabulous, the Seine below like a silver ribbon winds in and out of view, protected by sharp white cliffs on the north-east bank, the barges now steadily make their way to Rouen. Glorious place for a picnic. You won't regret a visit here. The farm is deep in the country on the plain above the small village of La Croix-Saint-Leufroy, just off the D10 but only 3 km from the A13.

Ferme de la Boissiere (M)
M. & Mme Senecal. Hameau de Boissaye. 32.67.70.85.

When we arrived one bitterly cold winter's day Madame showed us to a huge ground-floor room with a dark, red-tiled floor. Ugh! Not another cold, carpetless trip to the loo. Mysteriously the room was quite warm and I looked in vain for the central heating. The equally large salon next door was just as comfortable. Puzzled I asked Madame Senecal, whilst she was making us a cup of tea, how the house was heated – 'Underfloor heating', came the answer by water pipes, masses of them; we were shown all the pictures of the reconstruction of this old stable about five years ago. Every inch of the bathroom floor was warm too. What joy! The old house dates back many hundreds of years when it was once used as a home for the monks at La Croix-Saint-Leufroy. Nothing has been spoilt in the reconstruction. The old beams, and windows now double-glazed, remain. The large salon has windows on both sides and adjoins the main house.

One bedroom on the ground floor and three others beautifully furnished and electrically heated upstairs overlook the enormous front garden where ducks of all varieties were walking on the icy pond, even black swans and a peacock. So definitely an all-year-round stop here and Madame is happy to give you an evening meal even if you arrive late. We had booked only half an hour before and were lucky to get a room in November, and an excellent meal for 87f which we ate by a log fire – *oeufs-en-cocotte au jambon, escalope de veau à la Normande* laced with cream, cheeses of the region and a delicious apple crêpe. Apéritif *Pommeau* (Calvados and apple juice) is to be taken cautiously. Madame shared an aperitif with us and served the meal but Monsieur is too busy on his cereal farm to eat with guests each night. Usually there are other guests to join one for dinner. You will want to stay far longer than one night here. Room 220/240f.

DANGU. 27720

8 km SW of Gisors, preferably by the pleasantly green little D10 (D181 if in a hurry). This is the Vexin region, far enough away from Paris (60kms) and the ports to be untouristy, near to very pleasant countryside, the river Epte that Monet loved to paint, the valley of the Seine and Giverny.

➤ Les Ombelles (M)
Mme Poulain-des-St-Perè. 4, rue de Gue. 22.55.04.95; fax 42.67.29.02
cl. 16/12 to 15/3.

A firm favourite, well deserving an arrow on the strength of many readers' commendation.

The 18th century restored house is in the village, close to the bridge. Look for the distinctive green shutters. They are green at the rear, too, opening out on to a large paved courtyard, with a luxurious tent arrangement for shielding guests from the sun during their repose. The flowery garden slopes down to the banks of the river Epte. It's all so pretty, with petunias and geraniums contributing to the colourful scene. It's pretty nice inside too, with a clever mixture of family antiques, paintings, and cheerful colour schemes. When it's not garden weather, it is in the cosy salon, before the fire, that *apéritifs* are taken before the evening meal. Don't miss it. Invariably it turns out to be a very jolly affair, with plenty of liquid laughter. One guest arrived without a booking and was immediately invited to join the family for a beef barbecue.

The two pretty double rooms, above average in size, are reached by independent staircase; one with shower *en suite* looks out on to the village and the other overlooking the garden has a bathroom and loo next door. Nicole writes that 1995 fees will be 170f for 'friend's room' and 180f for 'Granny's room' (for two people). I haven't quite worked that one out yet because I understood that the price was 260f (it was last year).

Nicole was at school in England, and trained as a translator, so there will be no language problems. She volunteers the information that she has brought up five children and is now divorced. A very popular lady...

24 hours notice needed for dinner (130f for the gastronomic menu, 90f for 'Granny's dinner' (more confusion!)).

FOURMETOT. 27500

4 km NE of Pont Audemer by D139. Turn right at the church past the turning on the right to La Croisée, and l'Aufragère is on the left.

There is such a tangle of autoroutes and nationales, such a hurrying to be in Paris or Honfleur or Rouen, that this corner of Normandy, only a 40-minute drive from Le Havre, often gets neglected. Pont Audemer is an attractive little town, once you penetrate beyond the railway sidings and dusty concrete outskirts and discover its ancient heart. Here rivulets from the river Risle thread their way beneath old bridges and beamy old houses overhang the water. The best market in the district takes place here on Mondays and Fridays, when the main street, the rue de la République, is closed to traffic – priorities correct!

➤ L'Aufragère (M)
Régis & Nicole Dussartre. La Croisée. 32.56.91.92; fax 32.57.75.34.
An 18th century half-timbered house, recently restored by the Dussartres to provide five guest rooms, with attractive different characters but all with private bathroom – 210f for two, 370f for three.

The big attraction here, apart from the friendly welcome from the hosts, is Nicole's culinary skill. She is a professional cordon bleu cook, making good use of the wonderful range of local produce in the market to produce a superb evening meal for 100f. If you want to cook like her, sign up for one of the long weekend or five-day gourmet cookery courses she organises at l'Aufragère. Régis too is involved in matters gastronomic. He is a cheese specialist and will share his expertise in advising which of the tempting display on the market stalls should be purchased to take home. He also makes his own cider in large wooden casks in one of the barns on the premises, so you can sample that, along with the local Calvados, of which he always has a good stock.

A lovely place to stay, arrowed for good value, good company and goodwill.

'Régis and Nicole Dussartre are a quite charming young couple who are in the first year of setting up their business, having restored their Normandy farmhouse to a high standard. They could not be more welcoming and attentive and their five bedrooms are stylishly individual, spotlessly clean and well appointed. Dinner is taken with them around the large kitchen table. In view of the fact that Nicole is English and that Régis spent some sixteen years working in England, you are unlikely to improve your French language over dinner. However our recent visit for three nights developed into lively and animated evenings. The food was very good indeed, including beef and rabbit casseroles, fish kebabs, artichokes, Calvados sorbet, home-produced cheese, excellent pastry ... My strongest recommendation, particularly for the ambience and the warmth and welcome of the Dussartres.' John Simmons.

HOULBEC-COCHEREL. 27120

10 km W of Vernon. The Ferme de la Moinerie is right in the middle of cereal fields, but well signed off the D65 from Houlbec-Cocherel to Menilles (only 5 km from the A13 to Le Havre). This is yet another luxury chambres d'hôtes which would certainly complement a visit to Giverny.

Ferme de la Moinerie (M)
Mme Besnard. 32.26.00.44; fax 32.26.28.49.

On a delightfully well-kept farmstead, this old house was once a stable, given to young M. and Mme Besnard by his parents when they were married. They have renovated it themselves, and what a superb job they have made of it. Madame is an artist and delights in making dried flower arrangements. Now she is bringing up a young family and just to make sure she has enough to do has made three luxu-

rious chambres d'hôtes rooms on the ground floor, all with private facilities, very prettily decorated with everything coordinated.

One room is for three people, the third bed screened by dainty curtains. The other two rooms lead into a private conservatory overlooking the garden, thus affording another entrance, superb for four friends travelling together. 270f. The large salon, where breakfast is taken, is beamed and has a log fire and also a conservatory overlooking a pond. There are excellent restaurants in nearby Pacy to suit all pockets and Madame will give you cards to all of them, with directions.

MAINNEVILLE. 27150

10 km NE of Etrepagny. 23 km E of Rouen. From the D915 halfway between Gisors and Gournay-en-Bray turn west to the village of Mainneville. The church is very large for such a small village; it serves a lot of the hamlets in the rolling countryside around. It houses the only authentic and lifelike statue of St Louis (Louis IX) who was canonised by popular demand in 1297, very soon after his death. The statue dates from the early 14th century. In the southern part of the village take the road signed Le Timbre and the farm is immediately on your left, next to a *maison-de-maître* once owned by the grandson of Victor Hugo. This makes an economical stop for Giverny, only 40 km south.

> ## Ferme Sainte-Geneviève (M)
> ### M. & Mme Marc. 32.55.51.26.

Ferme Ste. Geneviève

A ewe on the front lawn keeps an eye on all approaching visitors to this lovely old farmhouse with central heating, fuelled by straw! A warm welcome awaits from Mme Marc. The back garden is enclosed by the main house and converted barns. Two large rooms are on the first floor of the main house and there is a cosy room on the ground floor. Two others on the first floor of the building opposite share a kitchen, ideal for a family or friends. 200f. Two salons for guests. *'With advance notice Mme Marc will provide dinner of excellent quality and more than adequate quantity. Four courses with a different selection of cheeses each evening, plus all the coffee one can drink and a bottle of wine for each couple, and all for only 80f.'* – Michael Turner.

I agree with everything said by Robin Totton (FE9), and reinforced by Michael Turner. Madame Marc is such a sweet person who thinks of your comfort all the time. Evening meals together are a pleasure to look forward to. The true spirit of a chambres d'hôtes here and arrowed accordingly. Mme Marc's sister (Mme Vrel) keeps a chambres d'hôtes in Ygrande, Allier (see section on Auvergne).

REUILLY. 27930

8 km N of Evreux. A useful base for Monet's garden at Giverny. The gardens are small and laid out in straight lines. The coordinated colours are magnificent, wallflowers, tulips, polyanthus from cream to dark red in great drifts, with lilac and cherry trees shedding their petals in the wind. The water garden, with the renowned bridge, is across the main road, now reached by a subterranean passageway. It is a complete contrast to the rest of the place, and Monet painted here frequently. The house, open to the public (not from 12 to 2 p.m.) is long and narrow and the rather uncomfortable rooms are redeemed by the cheerful yellow dining room. Not a stick of furniture has escaped the yellow paint, but how I enjoyed this room, ancient kitchen in blue and white.

I love my first breakfast in France and always refuse to eat on the boat so that we have an excuse to stop at the first interesting hotel *en route*; with a few miles under one's belt it always tastes better. This time we stopped at Neubourg, a small market town, where we parked in the large square right outside Le Grand St Martin hotel; sitting in the window we could keep an eye on the car. This proved to be a good choice as it was next door to the boulangerie, and they kept nipping in to replenish their stocks of croissants. After a good feast of hot bread and croissants with butter and jam in dishes and unlimited coffee, 52f for two, and having booked a room for the night *chez* Nuttens, we set out for Reuilly first.

Take the D155 from Evreux north through Gravigny and branch right on to the D316 to Reuilly, turning left at the silo on your right. The Ferme de Reuilly is on your left in the middle of the village.

Ferme de Reuilly (M)
M. & Mme Nuttens. 20 rue de l'Eglise. 32.34.70.65.

We were so early that Madame Nuttens was still out shopping, but her son who speaks some English had been briefed about our arrival and showed us to our room. There are three warm, comfortable, homely first-floor rooms with independent entrance at one end of the house, with a small guest kitchen downstairs. 200f.

The dining room with armchairs and TV links the guests' part of the house to the Nuttens, all immaculate. We relaxed over an excellent evening meal with the family. 70f wine not *compris*. She and her husband are very pleasant hosts and keep up lively conversation at dinner.

SAINT-CLAIR-D'ARCEY. 27300

30 km S of Pont-Audemer. 6 km SE of Bernay 3 km from the village on the D42 in the direction of Saint Aubin-le-Vertueux; turn left at the sign.

La Bérnadière (S)
M. et Mme Huet. 32.45.84.57.

A lovely, long, low Normandy house with cows grazing peacefully on both sides. One end is devoted to a chambres d'hôtes, entrance through a private salon with tables and settee. A spacious bedroom takes up the first floor, one double bed and two singles at the other end of the room all with bedside lamps, stairs coming up through the middle and a good large shower and w.c. at one end. The pitched roof in the bedroom has rafters to catch the unwary, but has pretty dormer windows and the room is thickly carpeted. 180f for two, 260f for four.

Madame offered us a light meal with them even though we didn't descend on her until 6 p.m. We ate soup and salad of beans and chicory with paté and a lovely sweet of pears in chocolate and Grand Marnier sauce. Cider and wine was included. Nice, interesting people to talk to, M. Huet is a retired cabinet maker. It would be lovely in summer, with chaises longues in a large garden with lawns, close to the house.

Breakfast was home-made bread, four jams and honey and good coffee served by M. Huet as Madame had to go out. Evening meal 80f, but book ahead if possible.

ST-OUEN-DES-CHAMPS. 27680

5 km N of Pont Audeme. The Marais is a strange other-world region that even the Normans don't seem to know about. And yet it is bounded to the south by an autoroute and to the north by the Tancarville bridge and completely surrounded by major roads. It is a land of low-lying fields, swimming in mist, dotted with lakes and ponds, and with peasant farmhouses straight from a Corot landscape. I heartily recommend investigation for yet another aspect of this fascinating region.

La Vallée (M)
M. & Mme Marcel Blondin. 32.42.17.25.

'Beware, it is not at St Ouen des Champs, which is on the other side of the uncrossable autoroute. As soon as you turn off the D90 down the hill, i.e. first right, the landscape will become breathtakingly beautiful. (Don't try any clever short cuts. Get to it from the D90 – you could get lost very easily any other way. The rooms are on a staircase completely cut off from the Blondins' part of the house and are very comfortable.' Robin Totton.

There are three double rooms with shower and loo – 170f.

Fresh farm produce is used for the excellent breakfast. Madame Blondin gives handicraft classes in the house. More information about these would be welcome.

MANCHE

AVRANCHES. 50300

125 km S of Cherbourg. A lively and colourful town sited on the main approaches
to Brittany and Mont-St-Michel and therefore popular for overnight stops.

On the site of the former cathedral is 'La Plate-Forme' where Henry II knelt to
do penance for the murder of Thomas à Becket. Having viewed the little square,
walk to the end of the terrace for an amazing panorama of the Mount and the surrounding salt marshes, dotted with the fat sheep destined to yield the gourmet-
prized gigôts du pré salé. Good market on Saturdays.

Mme Couëtil (S)
8 place Carnot. 33.68.29.88.

A long-term favourite of FE readers, mainly because of Suzanne Couëtil's 'gentil-
lesse'. Her terraced house is very conveniently situated near the Jardin des Plantes, a
colourful public garden with gorgeous views. Everything is immaculate and the furniture is 'real'. Breakfast is taken in a delightful conservatory looking out on to a
secluded walled garden, a bonus in the centre of the town. The two rooms on the
top floor share a shower-room (so this would work well for friends or a family),
while that on the first floor has to share with Mme Couëtil. Not ideal, but for only
165f (200f for three) you can put up with worse than this.

'The next seven days we spent with Mme Couëtil. She was very kind and helpful, in spite of speaking little English and even gave us one of her home-made tarts,
which was delicious. We were on the top floor and had use of a fridge, very useful
when you have children who constantly want cold drinks.' Sylvia Fenton.

BOLLEVILLE. 50250

17 km SE of Barneville-Carteret. This would make a good holiday base only 7 km
from the sandy beaches south of Portbail, where on a fine day you can see the coast
of the Channel Islands. Not far off the main D903 from Bolleville to Carteret; well
outside the village turn right to La Croûte and you will find it signed up a lane.

La Croûte (S)
M. & Mme Roptin. 33.46.00.58.

An ornamental moulin stands in the forecourt and a real old millstone beside
the house. The Roptins are beef farmers. Three very plain simply furnished
rooms with independent entry, two on the ground floor and one above. All share
a small kitchen if you wish to self-cater, but Madame will give you a meal for

70f with cider, coffee and Calvados *compris*. Very pleasant *accueil*. If you feel like a budget stop, this is just the place. There are not many *en suite* places left charging only 160f for bed and breakfast for two plus the facilities for self-catering.

La Croûte

BRICQUEBOSCQ. 50340

10 km SW of Cherbourg. Leave Cherbourg by the D3 which becomes the D904; in 5 km turn left on to the D22 to Couville. Go through the village and you will pick up the signs to the chambres d'hôtes at La Pistollerie on your right.

La Pistollerie (S-M)
M. Villot. 33.04.40.81.

La Pistollerie

Many moons ago driving up the Cherbourg peninsula in dark, torrential rain, looking for somewhere to stay neither of us would brave the downpour to look at hotel prices. Eventually out of curiosity we followed the signs to a chambres d'hôtes at Bricqueboscq where Madame Villot met us with a welcome suggestion that we parked the car right outside the door of our room. This turned out to be the first chambres d'hôtes we ever visited. In a lovely granite building, on the ground floor, adjoining the Villot's handsome farmhouse are two large rooms separated by a small dining room. Rooms have access to a terrace with tables; one double bed, the other two singles. 175f. M. & Mme Villot are always ready to stop for a chat, but as breakfast is served in the guests' dining room, one does not see a lot of the family. This makes an excellent first or last stop for Cherbourg as it is only 15 mins. from the harbour and Le Continent supermarket for last minute shopping. La Pistollerie is a busy working farm right in the heart of the Normandy countryside.

BRUCHEVILLE. 50480

11 km NE of Carentan by N13. Then right on to D329, through hamlet off Rochefort to Brucheville. The house is 200 yards from the church.

I have a reader to thank for the following report: *'Five rooms spread around farmhouse and outbuildings. All have shower and loo en suite for 165f, including breakfast. Pleasant comfortable rooms, hosts friendly and accompany guests to their cars in fond farewells.'* Derek W. Smith.

CANVILLE-LA-ROQUE. 50580 PORTBAIL

43 km SW of Cherbourg by the D904 and D903 direction La Haye; 9 km after Barneville-Carteret look for the D15 to St Sauveur and take the next left to Canville.

I love this part of the Cotentin. Carteret is the best of all the Manche family resorts, with miles of golden sands, rocks, estuaries, and lovely walks, Portbail is a charming sleepy little town and the beaches in between are near perfect. Canville-La-Rocque is on the little river Ollonde which flows into the Portbail estuary, a charming rural setting, in which I set out to find an unsophisticated inexpensive lodging:

Rocque le Bas (S)
Bernadette Vasselin. 33.04.80.27.

Only 5 km from the beach, in peaceful farmland, stands this 18th century farmhouse. Mme Vasselin, a cheerful sociable hostess, has two double rooms, one on the first floor with bath, and one on the ground floor with shower. 160f.

La Rocque de Bas
Canville — La -Rocque. 50

CÉAUX. 50200

7 km S of Avranches. Just off the coastal road to Mont-St Michel. Turn off the N175 to the D43 to Courtils, then turn right to Céaux at sign to chambres d'hôtes.

Le Mé Provost (S)
M. & Mme Delauny. 33.58.55.63.

Looking for another place, I came
across this dairy farm and decided
it was well worth visiting. Madame
has four/five prettily furnished
country rooms, fitted carpets
throughout. Two in the main house
comprise a suite for a family, a
double and two singles. In an
adjoining building three doubles on
the first floor with sitting room and
kitchen below for general use.
Rooms 180f; a bargain so near

La Méa. Provost

Mont-St. Michel, especially for a family self-catering.

GLATIGNY. 50250

30 km NW of Coutances 7 km W of La Haye-du-Puits.

Le Manoir (S)
Mme Duvernois. 33.07.08.33.

Only a short distance from the
coast, south of Portbail, in the
middle of country lanes, is this
old farmhouse. Enter through the
front door and immediately a
very wide stone staircase takes you
up to the bedrooms above. Two
rooms adjoining for a family sharing bathroom, and one double.
Nothing spectacular, but neither is
the price at 165f. Evening meals at
90f, all drinks *compris*. Downstairs

Glatigny 50　　La Ferme du Manoir

is an old, stone-floored dining room with large fireplace. Possibility of a corner
kitchen here too. Madame is an agent for trips to Jersey and Guernsey from
Granville.

HÉBÉCREVON. 50180

8 km W of St Lô. St Lô, Préfecture of the Manche, was devastated by the last war
and has been totally rebuilt. A very large industrial area skirts the town on the
southern bypass and it is just outside the 'Leclerc' exit that you will find the road to

Hébécrevon, D900. It winds uphill for about two kilometres before running through this immaculately clean, dull village, but take heart and turn off to St Gilles the other side of the village on the D77 and immediately on your right is the long drive up to the Château de la Roque.

Château de la Roque (M-L)
M. & Mme Delisle. 33.57.33.20; fax 33.57.51.20.

Built in the 17th century, the château has passed through many hands before becoming the home of the Delisles. (Monsieur won the Tour de France in 1969.) It is a compact, beautifully restored building with a choice of tastefully decorated rooms, three on the first floor of the main building, three others in a wing down an old stone spiral staircase, very *rustique*, loved by Americans; the floors are tiled but surprisingly warm. All have lush bathrooms, piping hot bath water, large fluffy towels, hair driers, etc. Every comfort thought of down to the last threaded needle for running repairs. Television and direct telephone in each room. Room number 1 is especially pretty and cosy.

Across the extensive gravel forecourt is another old building which suffered a bad fire recently, but has been rebuilt and houses the banqueting hall for evening meals with four very pleasant extra rooms above, all equally luxurious. Candlelit dinners are served at a long oval table, prettily set out with flowery pink cloth and napkins; brass candlesticks and a roaring log fire make this an elegant setting for dinner. Madame Delisle heads the table and her young staff do her bidding. Meals vary each night from simple to more *gastronomique* with cider as an aperitif and wine and Calvados all *compris* at 90–100f. Even in the depth of winter fifteen of us sat down to dinner.

Grounds of about four hectares have sweeping lawns, a lake and tennis court. Some say this is more of a hotel but the fact that M. and Madame eat with you rather sways it to a chambres d'hôtes, but with affordable price – 300f. You certainly get your money's worth here. You will be kneeling at a *prie-dieu* as you fill in the *livre d'or*!

MONTFARVILLE. 50760

27 km E of Cherbourg. 2 km S of Barfleur. Barfleur is a neat little port full of bobbing boats. The light from one of the tallest lighthouses in France at the Raz de Barfleur sweeps the port at night. This chambres d'hôtes is just off the coast road

from Barfleur to St Vaast. Easy to find; leave Barfleur on the D9 and take the second turning right after the town exit sign, it is the next turn left. If you turn earlier you will be in the mess we were, circling the village of Montfarville. Matilda (wife of William the Conqueror) commissioned his ship here for the invasion of 1066 and all that!

Le Manoir (M)
M. & Mme Gabroy. 33.23.14.21.

Le Manoir

Fresh flowers even in December to greet you in your room in this tall, granite manor house, overlooking fields of thriving vegetables and sea views of the English Channel. There are two rooms in the Manoir, large, warm and comfortable, one up a spiral staircase, the other easy for offloading, on the ground floor. 250f. Handy for the ferry from Cherbourg. These large rooms take some heating in winter but Madame had everything on full blast for us after we had booked ahead by phone one wintry day. No evening meal, but a reasonable menu from 65f at the Hotel La Phare in Barfleur or more expensive at Montfarville at a restaurant opposite the church, which looks quite attractive.

Breakfast is served in a dining room/sitting room for guests, all attractively set on a flowery tablecloth.

PERCY. 50410

25 km SSW of St. Lô. In the centre of the Cotentin peninsula this is a delightful sunny house and garden for a long holiday or for just passing through the Manche area of Normandy. Trips to the Channel Islands from Granville, Portbail and Carteret.

La Voisinière (M)
Mme Duchemin. 33.61.18.47.

Gardeners will love this place; on arrival you will probably find Madame deep in the lilies. An outside staircase leads you to a pretty blue room, double bed with cherry wood ends and a third bed slotted into an alcove behind a dainty blue curtain. The low window overlooks a large peaceful garden massed with bushes and flowers for all seasons. Above is a room with twin beds; stairs rather tricky for the elderly. Three other rooms are in a separate cottage, where there is a shared kitchen for guests. Parquet or tiled floors in all rooms. 190f to 230f. Madame Duchemin offers light meals out of season; but self-catering would be a real pleasure here and there are some very good restaurants close by; FE3's hotel of the year, the *Auberge de l'Abbaye* at Hambye just by the ruined Abbey, and the *Auberge* at La Baleine.

ST–GEORGE-DE-LA-RIVIÈRE. 50270

2 km W of Barneville-Carteret, 40 km SW of Cherbourg. Portbail, down the road, is an enchanting village, leading to a stretch of fine beaches, backed by dunes, with enough space for everyone, even in high season. Sandsailing is a popular sport.

➤ ### Manoir de Caillemont (L)
Madame Coupechoux. 33.53.81.16; fax 33.53.25.66.

From Barneville-Carteret take the D903, direction Coutances. At St Georges-de-la - Rivière crossroads turn left towards St. Maurice-en-Cotentin. The manoir is the first on the left, well signed.

A lovely late 18th century building, with two guest suites. Both have sitting rooms; the one at 520f has two double beds (extra bodies at 100f each), wood panelling and fireplace in the sitting room; the other, at 470f, has twin beds, a smaller sitting room and again a fireplace. Very nice indeed, especially as the use of a heated swimming pool is included, the owners are particularly friendly and helpful, and the whole area is so delightful.

The arrow from FE9 remains.

ST GERMAIN-DE-TOURNEBUT. 50700

7 km from Valognes by D902, then right on to D115. Valognes is an important market town for the surrounding agricultural area, with a huge market filling the square on Fridays. A very useful stop, so near Cherbourg.

Château de la Brisette (L)
M. Gentien de-la-Hautière. 33.41.11.78; fax 33.41.22.32.

A vastly imposing first impression as you approach the magnificent iron gates and see the 18th century château, belonging to the same family for over 100 years. It has all the desirable accoutrements – a private chapel, a lake, wooded grounds and charming outbuildings.

Each of the three bedrooms has been furnished and decorated to a different theme – Empire, Gothic and Louis XVI – spacious and light, and house guests have the use of the lovely chandelier-ed salon and high-ceilinged dining room. 500f for two, with an evening meal at 200f inclusive.

SAINT-GERMAIN-SUR-SÈVES. 50190

16 km W of Carentan. 20 km N of Coutances. In a central position on the Cotentin peninsula, within easy reach of beaches on the east and west coasts, I would recommend this place highly for a delightfully comfortable farmhouse holiday. Coming from Périers on the D971 take the third road left on the CD301.

Les Tilleuls (S)
M. & Mme Vautier. Rue de Remeurgues. 33.46.64.34.

Outside the village this old Normandy house is excellently maintained and has five well-furnished rooms. Four on the first floor, some family, have choice of baths or showers. The room downstairs which sleeps three, with a kitchenette, is suitable for the handicapped, with independent entry. A very warm welcome from M. and Mme Vautier, who produce evening meals (by a log fire in winter) at 65f, cider *compris*, wine extra. Rooms 160/180f; only 260f for four.

SAINT-JAMES. 50240

21 km SE of Mont-Saint-Michel. A small town. Surprisingly spelt the English way, a
relict of the Hundred Years War when the English were here. Easy to find this on
the D12 just west of St. James.

La Gautrais (M)
Mme Tiffaine. 33.48.31.86.

A dairy farm with a modern house
overlooking the valley; a lovely terrace for the summer. Rooms have
polished wood floors, some with
baths, some with kitchens but all
self-contained and comfortable:
there is central heating for winter
and the *accueil* to go with it, exceptionally good storage space 175f.
Excellent evening meal for 79f and
the best Calvados I have tasted,
made on the farm.

SAINT-SAUVEUR-LENDELIN. 50490

15 km NE of Coutances. 2 km S of Perriers on the D971 turn left on to the D52 just
after the sawmill. The Château du Perron is on the left up a long drive.

Château du Perron (M)
Mr & Mrs Russell. St. Aubin du Peron. 33.45.33.25; fax 33.47.08.79.

Built in 1860 this château in excellent order is situated in 100 acres of
woodland and fields overlooking a
lake. Super views from all the first
floor windows. Now the preference
is for school parties in term time
sharing the four bunked dormitory
rooms on both floors which are
interspersed with double rooms,
some *en suite*, some sharing. But in
the holidays Mr & Mrs Russell like
families to come and enjoy the won-
derful freedom of the grounds, particularly families who know each other when the
children can share rooms and play together. This doesn't rule out other guests even for
one night if you can't manage longer. Cycling in the grounds is ideal for children.
Evening meals are available if booked ahead. No longer cheap at 350f for two and

demi-pension 300f per person, reductions for children but the situation is superb. Send for the brochure. It's all in it, but you have to pay when you book.

ST SENIER-SOUS-AVRANCHES. 50300

5 km E of Avranches on the D5. Ideally situated for visiting Mont-St-Michel and the pleasant town of Avranches (Market day Saturday). There is an astonishing panorama of the Mount and the surrounding marshes from the dazzling *Jardins Publiques* (lots of French-beloved gaudy cannas and begonias). Avranches escaped the devastation of many Norman towns because the 3rd Army attack which General Patton launched from here in 1944 got off the mark so promptly that the enemy did not have time to hit back. The Patton Memorial was erected in a square whose earth and trees were flown over from the States, so that it stands on American, not French, soil. Plenty of restaurant choices here.

La Champ du Genet (M)
Annette Jouvin. Route de Mortain. 33.60.52.67.

2 km S of the hamlet of St Senier on the D5, well-signed.

An 18th century château, well endowed with towers and pinnacles. Tall white shutters frame the many windows, Madame Jouvin, who speaks and writes good English, has welcomed many FE readers to her home (and looks forward to receiving many more). She has four rooms, two with baths, two with showers, two of which (but I forget which ones) come with the ever-useful kitchenette corner – 210f.

Breakfast is served on the massive oak table in the imposing dining room, furnished with antiques, or on the terrace if the sun shines.

SENOVILLE. 50270

6 km N of Carteret. 27 km SW of Cherbourg. Turn right at the Le Becquet restaurant, off the D904 if travelling north from Carteret, on to the D131, then first left along a tree-lined avenue leading to Senoville church and opposite is Le Manoir.

Le Manoir (S)
M. & Mme Delaroque. 33.04.33.24.

If looking for somewhere to stay near Carteret on the west coast of the Cherbourg peninsula you won't be disappointed with your welcome at Le Manoir, a flower-bedecked house in summer, built in 1772. Madame Delaroque can offer you a large warm room and a bathroom adjoining; if other guests are there the bathroom is shared with one more room, which has a washbasin, and a small bedroom for a child on the same landing. This is fine for a family or if you are the only guests. 200f.

Le Manoir

Such pleasant hosts and a quiet, comfortable home to stay in.

No evening meal but an excellent restaurant at a short distance, Le Becquet, where Madame assures me that the meals are copious at 75–100f. When the French recommend a restaurant they are not very often wrong.

SOURDEVAL. 50150

13 km S of Vire by D977. I cannot claim that Vire is my favourite town – the wartime devastation and subsequent re-building was unfortunate to put it mildly, but the site is attractive enough, high above the rolling Norman countryside, and it is a useful shopping stop, with a Friday market.

There is a very pretty drive from Sourdeval to Avranches and the coast along the valley of the river Sée, so a stay in this region could well be extended beyond the practical consideration of a useful staging post on the way south.

La Maurandière (M-S)
Mme Evelyne Dupart. 33.59.65.44.

A lovely place to stay, with a kind hostess who goes out of her way to ensure her guests feel happy and comfortable. Nine years has not made her blasé about the b. and b. business. 'I hope that my house will be a haven of calm for everyone of my visitors, after the stress of big cities and all the agitation on the roads,' she writes.

La Maurandière

And haven it is, set in a green and peaceful valley, a mellow old farmhouse, dating from 1730, typical of the region, with beams and huge granite fireplace. The garden is a perfect place to recover from the stress and agitation Madame Dupart deplores. Breakfast is served here, on the terrace, whenever feasible. One of the guest rooms is totally independent in a separate cottage, with its own little terrace

– a bargain indeed at 200f. But the other three rooms are lovely too – each with private bath or shower, all furnished with family antiques, 200f well-spent francs. I need just one confirmation to ensure an arrow here. Will someone please oblige?

TEURTHEVILLE BOCAGE. QUETTEHOU 50630

15 km from Cherbourg, 5 km from Quettehou by D602, then left on to D119 direction Teurtheville-Bocage. Keep left at fork and the village of Sainte-Croix and the Presbytère are on a right-angled bend.

I love this part of the Cotentin, so near the port but so utterly remote in character, self-contained, uninfluenced by tourist trade. Le Wast is a particularly pretty village, the coastline is magnificent, and there are the fishing harbours and sailing activity of St Vast and Barfleur for diversion, so I was particularly pleased to have the following suggestion:-

l'Ancien Presbytère (M)
Sainte-Croix. 3.23.90.32.

"*Accommodation is in a picturesque old rectory, where the rooms with en suite bathrooms cost 200f, or in the self-contained Stable Cottage for 275f plus 50f for each additional child. Excellent evening meals, on request, offering local produce with organic vegetables; vegetarian meals available. English spoken.*" Carmel Bardsley.

VERGONCEY. 50240 ST JAMES
5 km S of Pontaubault by D998, then right on to D308. Pleasant countryside, only 18 km from Mont-St-Michel.

➤ ### Ferme de l'Etang (S)
Brigitte and Jean-Paul Gavard. Boucéel. 33.48.34.68.

This creeper-covered farmhouse overlooking the large lake from which it gets its name, has long been a favourite with FE readers. The welcome and helpfulness of dairy-farmer owners, who speak good English, has been particularly applauded, as has the evening meal featuring produce from their farm, served in winter by the huge fireplace.

The good news (and there seems to be only good news about la Ferme de l'Etang) is that the four bedrooms (two twin, two double) now have *en suite* facilities and still are reasonably priced at 180f. Dinner, with copious wine, cider and Calvados costs 80f.

'*The Ferme de l'Etang at Boucéel was absolutely fabulous, as you said, and as the place had the statutory two dogs and a kitten, the children were thrilled. A room for five, with breakfast and dinner was a bargain.*' Tessa Richmond.

Arrowed for sustained good value.

ORNE

ARGENTAN-OCCAGNES. 61200

1 km N of Argentan. An excellent place for visiting the *bocage* area of Orne or just a handy stop to and from the ferries at Ouistreham or Cherbourg. A very peaceful place only a kilometre away from the busy N158 from Caen, but you feel miles away.

Le Mesnil (S)
M. et Mme Laignel. 33.67.11.12.

You will really know you are on a farm here with cows close by the house and chickens at your feet. What a charming little cottage this is, tacked on to one end of the farmhouse. Just two rooms, one up, one down, but they each have a minute kitchen cupboard and their own little lawn with tables and chairs and Madame likely to join you with a tray of coffee at 4 pm.

No evening meals as a general rule; just occasionally possible. It depends, I think, on how much French you speak. One son speaks some English. Rooms 190f.

BANVOU. 61450

12 km S of Flers. Banvou is a small village in the Orne countryside where Sir Lancelot's father once lived. (The remains of his castle are quite near). Within walking distance of the village is a really rustic chambres d'hôtes. Horses and riders welcome.

Le Pont (M)
M. & Mme Jeusset. 33.96.44.02.

Situated above the horse boxes in the old *ecurie* are two heavily beamed rooms, one for four and one for two, warm and carpeted, with baths – probably a necessity if you are having a trekking holiday. A comfortable new sitting area is in the making on the same floor over the rustic dining room which has a huge old fireplace. M. and Mme Jeusset dine with their guests; 65f, all drinks *compris*. Should be quite a jolly evening with such an exuberant host as M. Jeusset. I think this is one of the best chambres d'hôtes I've found for equestrian travellers, but non-riders just as welcome. Rooms 260f.

BRIOUZE. 61220

25 km SW of Falaise. 13 km N of Bagnoles.

M. & Mme Pierrot (S)
Route de Bellou. 33.66.07.98. Closed August.

For those who like to be on their own about a kilometre outside the village Mme Pierrot has just one *en suite* double room in an independent chalet in the garden, having two single beds and a small entrance hall with table and sink handy for washing clothes. No kitchen. A nice lawn outside with chairs, etc. could make this a pleasant summer stop. The main modern house (where breakfast is taken)

stands back from the road with an easy entrance and parking. Electric heating in the chalet, but I should think only for the brave in winter, though it is available all the year except August when it is used by the family. Pleasant country views all around. Within easy reach of Putanges or the lake at Rotours. No evening meal. Room 190f.

COURGEON. 61400

8 km E of Mortagne-au-Perche. The massive Basilique at La Chapelle-Montiligeon is only a short distance away.

Ferme de l'Hotel Neveu (S)
M. & Mme Simoen. 33.25.10.67.

When you arrive in the village of Courgeon, turn left towards the church, then right in the direction of La-Chapelle-Montligeon and you will find directions to a busy farm well off the main road, facing south. Madame Simeon has two rooms for guests on the first floor up steep wooden stairs. One for a family has a double bed, two singles and a cot with still plenty of space. Large skylight windows face north but the room is quite light. The other room for three faces south and is very sunny. Both rooms are pleasantly beamed and carpeted, have electric heating and a little central heating with more being installed. Downstairs a huge inglenook fireplace welcomes you to the sitting/dining room where all meals are served. Sometimes the Simoens eat with their guests, but Monsieur is a busy dairy farmer making yoghurt and cheese and is often away delivering his goods. Evening meal 75f, cider *compris*. Rooms 190f.

COURTEMER. 61390

16 km from Sées. It's a mistake always to take the by-pass around Sées, benefiting only by a tantalising glimpse of the cathedral on its mound. Take time to drive in to the centre of the little town and visit the cathedral square, lined with other ancient buildings. The *Son et Lumière* which floodlights the whole town on summer evenings is inspired by the 14th century pilgrims who used to spend the night of the summer solstice in the cathedral. By any light it's a magnificent example of 13th and 14th century Norman Gothic architecture. Accommodation is limited, however, so it is good to know about:

La Motte (S)
Evelyne & Gilles Bunel. 33.28.40.03.

A *ferme-auberge*, serving meals to non-residents, which is usually good news, since the standard has to be high.

'*As we planned to go to the Son et Lumière in the evening, Mme Bunel made an early meal for us – vegetable soup, chicken in cider, yoghurt with cream, and cottage cheese, all made from their own produce and washed down with home-made cider. We were so impressed with our accommodation – light and airy comfortable bedroom with shower (185f) and the meals (85f) that we stayed for three nights and found Courtemer a very good centre for exploring Normandy. Each night the main course was a different local speciality'* Beryl Welbrook.

FAVEROLLES. 61600

13 km S of Putanges. 10 km N of Bagnoles. Coming south on the D19 to Bagnoles before the village of Faverolles look for the chambres d'hôtes signs on your right.

Le Mont Roti (S)
M. & Mme Fortin. 33.37.34.72.

Not far off the D19 to La-Ferté-Macé, this farmhouse on a dairy and cereal farm has been completely rebuilt in a modern style using much natural wood in ceilings and furnishings. There are three rooms, immaculately kept, with plenty of well-fitted cupboard space, centrally heated and warmly carpeted. Rooms are for two, three or four, reached by a staircase from the very large conservatory in the

main house. The third room has private access from an outside wooden staircase. Excellent meals, taken with the family, are unbeatable value, all drinks *compris* at 70f. Rooms 180f.

LA FRESNAYE-AU-SAUVAGE. 61210

4 km S of Putanges. Only a few kilometres south of Putanges, a pleasant, small town where parking is easy except on Thursday (market-day) and within easy access of the sportive Lac-des-Rabodanges at Les Rotours, a very pleasant place for a picnic or to join in the various boating activities. Café by the lake.

La Fleurière (S)
M. & Mme Gaultier. 33.35.01.47.

Here we had booked ahead, and
arrived one cold dark night after
supper. We drove down a narrow
lane to what I thought was a cluster
of houses. Madame Gaultier welcomed us into a warm room, offering us tea or coffee in this small
spotless farmhouse. The owners are
now retired but still keep a few
cows, while Madame has turned
two ground-floor rooms into chambres d'hôtes, carpeted and centrally

La Fleurière

heated with pretty flowered wallpaper and matching bed linen. They are cosy winter
rooms. One room has double and two good single beds, the other double is smaller.
Each is entered by a vestibule having a toilet and shower room with plenty of space.
180f; breakfast is toast and jam. After a comfortable night I looked out of the window
to find the lane was really a long private drive leading to the house through a delightful garden which I hadn't realised was there in the darkness. The cluster of houses
were farm buildings and a gîte, all overlooking the garden and a small lake complete
with island and summer house with chairs for guests. A very pleasant spot in the summer.

MOULICENT. 61290

26 km S of l'Aigle by D918, then left on to D89. Signed from there. Or, from Alençon,
leave the RN12 at the Ste-Anne roundabout in the direction of Longny-au-Perche.

This is Perche country, dedicated to the horse, and of course in particular to the
sturdy Percheron. It's prosperous, heavily forested, unspoiled, with few towns, but
scattered with dignified manor houses. Within easy reach are the charming little town
of Mortagne, the Haras du Pin, le Château d'O, Alençon, Verneuil and even Chartres.

La Grand Noë (L)
M. & Mme Jacques de Longcamp. 33.73.63.30; fax 33.83.62.92.
cl. 15/11 to 1/4.

The delightful château has been in the same family every since it was built in the
15th century. Originally a hunting lodge for the Dukes of Alençon, it was extended
in the 18th century, and received a new facade at the beginning of the 19th century.
In spite of its antiquity and historic importance it is never intimidating, though the
fine oak panelling in the dining room, the chandeliers and antique furniture inspire,
if not awe, certainly respect.

Its owners are responsible for the unstuffy ambience; speaking near-perfect English, they repeat what pleasure it gives them to talk with guests from all over the world and to share the evening meal (in the superb dining room) with them. They stress that (unlike some château businesses) theirs is not a professional activity 'though we try to take professional care of our guests'. If you are looking for a taste of the best of France *à l'ancienne*, guided by friendly hosts, you have come to the right place.

La Grande Noë

The 'Chambre Empire', with double bed, costs 620f, as does the 'Chambre Ronde' with twin beds; the 'Chambre Verte', with double bed, costs 450f, all with excellent bathrooms. Dinner (48 hours notice required) is 220f, all inclusive. I regret the 40f extra for breakfast.

SAINT-OUEN-SUR-MAIRE. 61150

20 km S of Falaise.

La Cour (M)
Mr & Mrs Smith. 33.36.74.83.

Nicely in the country but within easy reach of many interesting small towns like Alençon and Falaise. Turning down the long drive lined with daffodils in the spring, the large house of La Cour stands out across the fields, almost surrounded by an old, red brick wall. The well laid-out garden feels almost English, which is not surprising really as the owners are British. Having bought the prop-

La Cour

erty about four years ago they have set about restoring it to its former glory, making the outhouses at one end into three superb chambres d'hôtes with a private entry from the garden.

One double room on the ground floor has *en suite* shower and toilet. Upstairs is a room for four and another for two, both with washbasins, but sharing one bathroom with shower and toilet, a suite for six people reached by its own private staircase. All the really charming rooms are centrally heated, thickly carpeted, windows facing south with views of the garden, tastefully decorated with matching fabric and good bedside lamps and tables. 200f. No evening meals as a general rule, but occasionally Mrs Smith will oblige if you give her notice well ahead; then the meal is 150f, all drinks *compris*, a choice of *apéritif* and different wines with each course.

LE SAP. 61470

Near Vimoutiers. Vimoutiers, a regrettably post-war little town, is the centre of the dairy industry. A statue to Marie Harel, who gets the credit for having 'invented' Camembert, a source of much of the area's prosperity, gets pride of place. Another memorial to the farmer's wife who is said to have neglected her cheesemaking one day and found the mixture strangely and deliciously transformed the next, is erected in the actual village of Camembert, three km to the south-west. The *Route des Fromages* is lined with farms offering their version of the local speciality. You could taste enough to dispense with lunch, especially combined with the generous *dégustations* of cider, Calvados and apples freely available in this land of freebies.

Les Roches (M)
Mme Bourgault. 33.39.47.39.

A pretty, half-timbered house on a farm. The pleasant double room has a bathroom and the rooms for three and four have showers. 200f for two, 250f for three and 80f for the evening meal.

'*Everything exceeded our expectations, the spacious well-equipped rooms and especially the meals, with unlimited wine and cider and a Calvados digestif.*'

TANQUES. 61150

7 km SW of Argentan. Not far from the busy N158 at Argentan, this peaceful home would be a very pleasant place to stop on a journey south or for visiting the Haras du Pin or the attractive old town of Sées.

La Noe (M)
M. & Mme Sineux. 33.67.05.51.

Retired farmers own this cosy old farmhouse in which Madame has made a suite for a family. It is a delightful room with a double bed and a crib both elegantly covered in flowery toile with matching curtains. Warm, carpeted, centrally heated, just the job on a wintry day. 250f. Another room for two children is in the making.

Extremely courteous hosts would make your stay here most memorable. A warm, friendly atmosphere strikes you as soon as you enter.

For directions, I confess I've failed; it is in a tangle of country lanes; we were led there by the Mayor, so call at the *Mairie* first, or book ahead and your hosts will advise. Rooms 250f.

SEINE-MARITIME

ANCEAUMEVILLE. 76710

40 km S of Dieppe, 20 km N of Rouen, 1 km off the N27 between Rouen and Dieppe, a farmhouse on the right as you enter the village.

M. & Mme Alexandre (S)
35.32.50.22.

These young farmers have converted their garage into three immaculate little guest rooms with private baths and showers, two carpeted and with electric heaters, one wooden floor and central heating. 200f. In the centre of quiet, flat farming land, the hamlet has a church and telephone, no shops. Madame will produce an evening meal on reservation for 60f.

A perfect stop coming south from Dieppe. Wish they were all as nice and easy to find as this; it would make my job a lot easier!

BACQUEVILLE-EN-CAUX. 76730

12 km S of Dieppe. Only 3 km from the N27, turn right on the D23 signed on your right, then right again to the red brick farmhouse. The small town is further on and

has most amenities and excellent parking in a large square and a restaurant Le Relais.

Le Tilleul (S)
M. & Mme Le Marchand. 35.83.20.14.

You'll be all right here for a night stop and probably want to stay longer if you have the room with the *en suite* bathroom, heated towel rail and the sunniest aspect I've ever met. The other room will be *en suite* by 1995; at present only basin, shower and toilet private on the landing. 180f.

CAUDEBEC EN CAUX. 76490

51 km E of Le Havre 36 km W of Rouen. There are several routes from the ferry to Caudebec. Leave the port by the autoroute and turn off on to the D982; then stay on it all the way or turn off to Norville on the D81, surprisingly high above the Seine for a pleasant drive along the river.

Not much of the old town survived the fire of 1940. Only three mediaeval houses and the very fine 15th century Flamboyant Gothic church, described by Henry IV as 'the most beautiful chapel in the kingdom' remain to drop a hint of how attractive it must once have been. Sad though its concrete reincarnation may be, the setting remains attractive, a good base from which to explore the Seine valley and Rouen. It also has a good Saturday market. From a small roundabout near the quay take the Yvetot road (D131) and the rue de la République is on the right just after the end of town sign. The chambres d'hôtes at no. 68 is well signed on the corner.

Cavée St. Leger (S)
Mme Villamaux. 68 rue de la Republique. 35.96.10.15.

'Television, refrigerator and microwave for use in both rooms. Off-street parking available on site. Nice breakfast with selection of delicious home-made jams. Open all year. Mme Villamaux solicitous and most pleasant.' John Procter.

Easygoing Madame Villamaux now offers a choice of five rooms, all totally different in size, shape and decor, with heating and TV. Three larger rooms have fridge and microwave, others share them in the main salon. No evening meals, small-scale self-catering expected, china supplied. Best of all no washing up, dishes left on a tray are whisked away by Madame. Pleasant upward-sloping garden and terrace behind the house. One locked garage now available and Madame will pick you up from bus or train. Many Brits love this place and it improves all the time. Rooms 220–250f. Exceptionally good value for so many amenities.

CRIQUEBEUF-EN-CAUX. 76111

4 km SW of Fécamp 46 km N of Le Havre. Near to Fécamp where the ornate Gothic Benedictine distillery, once a monastery, is well worth a visit, to see the building and smell the herbs which go into the liqueur. Fécamp is a large fishing port with interesting harbour. For a chambres d'hôtes nearby take the D940 (Fécamp to Etretat road), turn on to the D211 in the direction of Yport and in 200m the Ferme Auberge is on the left.

M. & Mme Basille (S)
190 le Bout de la Ville. 35.28.01.32.

Don't be discouraged by the rather tatty look of the house; on the inside the two rooms on the first floor are very pleasant, especially the south-facing one for a family of four. A room with two single beds faces east. All warmly carpeted and meals on tap in the ferme auberge from 100–145f. Wine not *compris*.

Rooms 190f but demi-pension works out cheaper at 190f each. A handy stop for the Côte d'Albâtre.

CRIQUETOT-L'ESNEVAL. 76280

9 km SW of Etretat. 16 km N of Le Havre. I prefer Gonneville, a more open village, to Criquetot l'Esneval. It has two restaurants sometimes closed out of season, and a church with a rather strange exterior, like a corn exchange, but very beautiful

stations of the cross inside. The farmhouse chambres d'hôtes lies peacefully between the two villages.

M. & Mme Paumelle (S)
Route de Gonneville. 35.27.28.47.

Route de Gonneville
Chambre d'hôtes.

An elegant house at the end of a tree-lined drive well back from the main road. Two family rooms (two double beds) on the ground floor with midget baths make this a good ferry stop on the north side of Le Havre, a lawned terrace outside the rooms for repose. No evening meal; there is a small auberge in Gonneville (closed on Wednesdays) or Etretat, an easy drive, has many restaurants. Rooms 190f for two, 310f for four.

JUMIEGES. 76480

28 km W of Rouen. Famous for the Benedictine Abbey (rebuilt then consecrated in 1067 in the presence of William the Conqueror) now in romantic ruins. Its two imposing towers dominate the village.

La Mare au Coq (S)
M. & Mme Douillet. 3093 Route de Mesnil. 35.37.43.57.

La Mare au Coq

Very popular with locals, this newly built Ferme Auberge is opposite the Abbey towers on ground surrounded by trees and fields. Ducks, geese and chickens wander around and a ferocious turkey guards the door. Three large modern comfortable rooms for two, three or four people on the first floor with independent entrance. Warmly carpeted and heated for winter, 200f. It is truly a charming family who look after their resident guests superbly and even eat with them on rare quiet nights. Opt for a room and special resident's meal of four courses, excellent pâtés, large helpings, *apéritif*, wine or cider and coffee all *compris* at 70f. Alternatively, you can have the 110f or 135f menu. Sound-proof floors take care of the restaurant noises; but double glazing loses the battle with nearby quarry lorries on weekday mornings. Aim for Saturday nights here unless you want an early start!

Relais de l'Abbaye (S)
M. & Mme Chatel. 798 rue de Quesney. 35.37.24.98.

Just 700 m from the main street in a residential area behind the Abbey, this very old Norman farmhouse has been beautifully restored and stands in a prize-winning garden. Patrick and Brigitte have five rooms for 210f, all with toilets and wash-basins, but shared showers. I'm assured that showers will be *en suite* by 1995. Parking in the garden behind closed gates at night. No evening meal, a choice of restaurants in the village. FE9 readers have long approved.

MANNEVILLE-LA-GOUPIL. 76110 GODERVILLE

26 km NE of Le Havre by N15 to St-Romain-de-Coulbosc, then D10 to Manneville. Look for the sign opposite the church; turn left and after 1.5 km the house is on the right.

This is flat, farming country, well placed for visits to the coast (Etretat, Fécamp) and the Seine Valley. There are relatively few chambres d'hôtes in the region, which is a pity because of its proximity to the ferry, so I was particularly pleased to come across:-

➤ ### Nicole & Hubert Loisel (M)
35.27.77.21.

The tall, red brick farmhouse, an 18th century *maison de maître*, is surrounded by a large garden, separating it from the farm where the Loisels raise cattle, sheep, donkeys, chickens, turkeys, geese... anything that moos, baas, honks, crows or cackles. A paradise for animal-deprived children. A paradise, too, for the guests who get to sample the end result at Mme Loisel's dinner parties. 110f buys, for example, home-made terrine or quiche Normande, then Poulet Vallée d'Auge accompanied by 'divers' vegetables, Norman cheeseboard (none better), and fruit tart according to what's in season, or maybe that flossy confection *île flottante*, all accompanied by excellent *cidre bouché* made by Hubert. Breakfast is similarly copious, with homemade jams and gâteaux, farm milk and butter.

Enough of the board – what about the bed? The four lofty double rooms have been recently redecorated in pleasing pastel tones. One has a pretty pink chintz bedcover and drapes over the bed, all have well equipped bath or shower. Bargains at 225f, 240f or 255f. Downstairs the mostly oak furniture was part of Nicole's grandmother's dowry and contributes to the pleasing atmosphere of taken-for-granted continuity.

I'm finding it hard to find any fault with this one, especially as the energetic Nicole is so helpful at guiding her guests around her region – so an arrow.

RAINFREVILLE. 76730

23 km SW of Dieppe. Pretty unspoiled countryside, conveniently near Dieppe, which is probably the most interesting of the Channel ports, good for shopping, Saturday market, and a wide choice of restaurants. It has a surprising shortage of recommendable hotels, so it is particularly good news to find an alternative.
From Dieppe take the D925, direction Fécamp. At Ouville-la-Rive turn left on the D152, then D2 through Brachy, then D270 on the right.

➤ ### Les Clos Cacheu (M)
Angela Stewart and Gilbert Bankual. 35.06.10.99.
cl. 1/9–15/10; Christmas, New Year.

Angela and Gilbert's original plan was to set up a business here advising British prospective purchasers of French property. While they sorted out the tangles of housebuying they were offered the opportunity of staying at Le Clos as p.g.s. Thanks to a Wish You Were Here programme, the p.g. operation developed so fast that it did not matter that the property side faded away.

Le Clos Cacheu

It's not surprising that people should want to stay here – the typical Norman house, all black and white beams, elegant interior decoration with period panelling, fireplaces with roasting spits, landscaped garden.

There are two double rooms in the house and one studio in the successfully renovated old baker's hut in the garden – 350f for two people – all attractive and comfortable with bath or shower.

Gilbert is a wonderful cook, with competition successes behind him, so don't miss dinner here; a bargain at 150f, wine included.

ROUEN. 76000

87 km E of Le Havre. Rouen has to be first choice for a Normandy winter break because of the diversity of treats there. Everyone is aware of the wonderful cathedral – and it looks just as good swathed in soft mist or sharply outlined against a frosty blue sky as it does in sunshine or any of the other twenty aspects that Monet recorded – but there are at least two other churches for essential viewing – St Maclou, all Flamboyant Gothic, and St Ouen, with magnificent organ and stunningly beautiful chancel. The Musée des Beaux Arts is a feast for the eye, the Vieux Marché a feast for both eye and stomach. There are Joan of Arc associations everywhere, the best range of restaurants in Normandy, ancient timbered buildings begging to be photographed, trips down the Seine ... I could go on. And on.

Apart from the usual chains, hotels have been difficult to track down – there is only one arrow allocated for the whole city in FE9 – so finding a recommendable chambre d'hôtes became very desirable indeed:

Annick and Philippe Aulnay (M)
45 rue aux Ours. 35.70.99.68.

Right in the heart of the old quarter is this half-timbered house, part-15th century, part-17th. To find it follow the Seine past Le Théatre des Arts and take the first left. An old alleyway leads to the entrance on the right. The house has been in Philippe Aulnay's family for over a century and he is rightly proud of its charm and history. Furniture is in keeping with the antiquity of the surroundings and there is intriguing

Rouen 76   Rue aux Ours

Norman bric-à-brac to admire, massive beams and tall windows.

The three guest rooms are surprisingly light; the two doubles and one suite for 3/4 each have good modern bathrooms and two of the rooms have cooking facilities, always an asset. 265f.

Philippe is a cheerful host and will supply plenty of local know-how during the excellent breakfast served in the family dining room.

A potential arrow, for convenient location and good value in a delightful city. More reports needed please.

SAANE-SAINT-JUST. 76730

25 km SW of Dieppe. On the D2 to Biville-la-Rivière, north of Saâne near the crossroads with the D149. Very pretty valleys round here and peaceful wooded farmlands.

M. & Mme Fauvel (S)
Route de Biville. 35.83.24.37.

In a separate building friendly Madame Fauvel has everything, five small, warm rooms, salon with log fire and comfortable chairs, and kitchen corner with microwave, fridge and washing-up machine for self-catering or she will cook you an evening meal for 60f, wine and coffee *compris* if you reserve. There are even cots, bath and pram for a baby. Breakfast: orange juice, cereal and croissants in your room if you like; she is very amenable. Very popular; book ahead. A very pally place, and only 170f for two.

SAINT-MARTIN-DE-BOSCHERVILLE. 76840

7 km W of Rouen. On the D982 St. Martin-de-Boscherville has a fine Benedictine Abbey founded by William of Tancarville in 1144. The pale stone walls make this well-kept church very light inside. It has an ornately carved confessional and pretty Lady Chapel. The new organ was consecrated in May 1994 and many concerts are held here in the summer.

Mme Liandier (S)
178 Route de Duclair. 35.32.03.11.

A new house standing well back from the main road only one km from the abbey, with delightful views from the large lounge and smart kitchen. Five modern, double-glazed rooms, for three people with choices of shower or bath, shared toilets or *en suite*, ground floor to second floor, 200f. Large lawned front garden and good parking. Very handy for Rouen. Evening meal 80f.

SAINT SAUVEUR DE L'ÉMALLEVILLE. 76110

12 km N of Le Havre. At last I have found an ideal night stop near le Havre, so good it is worth spending far longer. Take the N925 north from le Havre to Goderville. Turn right at the road after the sign to St Sauveur and the chambres d'hôtes is signed on your right.

M. & Mme Debreville (M)
Route de la Ferme Chevalier. 35.29.50.01.

Route de la Ferme Chevalier

The picturebook, half-timbered thatched house stands in a country lane, surrounded by large hedges. Madame has three very pleasant beamed first-floor rooms with independent entry up an outside staircase, good sized shower rooms for each, One extra room for two in the main house has private facilities on the landing. All have quality carpets and pretty matching decor. A large log fire heats a 'Marmite' central heating system. Monsieur keeps a few sheep and poultry and has a very large garden. Evening meals, mostly home produced, taken *en famille* are very convivial, four or five courses, all drinks *compris* for 80f.

Totally peaceful here yet only twenty minutes from Auchan and Mammouth supermarkets and the ferries. Madame speaks some English. Rooms at 180 to 200f include a good breakfast.

SENNEVILLE-SUR-FÉCAMP. 76400

3 km from Fécamp. 40 km N of Le Havre. Fécamp is France's fourth fishing port and most of the town's interest centres on the quays. However, there are good walks around, high on the chalky cliffs that the Post-Impressionists liked to paint. It was here that the 16th century monk Vincelli found the herbs used to flavour the liqueur Bénédictine; the town's top tourist attraction now is a visit to the distillery. Richard the 1st's church, La Trinité, is a beguiling hotchpotch of architectural styles from the 12th to the 18th centuries.

One of my favourite budget restaurants, Le Grand Banc, is on the Quai Bérigny – not for those who insist on spacious comfort I have to emphasise, but great for fresh and cheap seafood straight from the boats.

Le Val de Mer (M)
Mme Lethuillier. 35.28.41.93. cl. Aug.

Take the D925 and the house is in the village, near the church, a few hundred metres from the sea. It's a modern but well timbered house with three smallish rooms, quiet, comfortable and pretty, with either bath or shower. The one on the ground floor opens directly on to the well-tended garden. 260f. Mme Lethuillier is welcoming and helpful about the local resources.

Le Val de La Mer

SOTTEVILLE-SUR-MER. 76740

24 km SW of Dieppe. Close to Veules les Roses, Sotteville is a small village 200 yards back from the cliffs, where at low tide a tiny beach can be reached by wooden steps. Church, restaurant, boulangerie and two épiceries are all near the village square and a small road from there beside the telephone box, leading to the D925, will take you to the farmhouse home of

Le Bout du Haut (S)
M. & Mme Lefèbvre. 35.97.61.05.

Situated in a pretty orchard garden sideways on to the road, the house is of *colombage* construction, but next door in her mother's modern house Mme Lefèbvre has three first-floor guest rooms, private facilities for each but not all adjoining. One particularly nice room is *en suite* with a balcony; all have good furniture and are warm and comfortable year round. 200f. You trot next door to the farmhouse for meals;

Le Bout du Haut

dinner with your hosts is good value at 80f, all drinks *compris*. You'll love it here, so friendly, the real spirit of a chambres d'hôtes.

LES TROIS-PIERRES. 76430

20 km E of Le Havre. Coming from Le Havre take the N15 towards Bolbec; in about 22 km after St. Romain-de-Colbosc turn left on to the tiny D31 signposted Gommerville and you will find the farm signed on your right. Drive right up to the front door. Despite the address it is not in the village of Les Trois-Pierres.

Manoir de la Froide Rue (S)
Mme Paumelle. 35.20.03.74.

M. & Mme Paumelle are retired farmers who are venturing into chambres d'hôtes, after having had a gîte for eight years. They now offer south-facing, sunny bedrooms for three or four on the first floor. There are plenty of towels and flannels, but no cupboard space for long stays. Children can chase the chickens in the morning. Only 23 km from the ferry. We breakfasted on fresh baguettes and soft rolls, plentiful yellow butter from a neighbour, choice of jams, huge carafes of coffee and-milk, which we drank from pint size *bols*. Prices have increased this year, which is a pity as it is a handy stop just outside Le Havre, right in the country, well off the main roads and very peaceful. Rooms 250f for two, 350f for four.

CHAMPAGNE-ARDENNES

....

Départements: **Ardennes**
            Aube
            Haute-Marne
            Marne.
Companion guide to the area: 'French Entree 12 – The North'

Champagne is a unique area, visited by thousands of tourists every year principally to sample its famous eponymous product. Although grapes are grown throughout the area, the champagne industry centres on Epernay in the Marne département. A visit to the world-renowned cellars here is a must for any itinerary in the area but I would not devote more than a couple of days to the town, which is otherwise without interest. Reims is much more rewarding, with its glorious cathedral, and some memorable restaurants, thanks to the patronage of the wealthy champagne-growers.

The Marne is a mighty river, which ought to be more picturesque than it turns out to be. Little capitalisation, other than that of industry, has been made of its green and pleasant banks.

Much the most appealing département scenically is the Ardennes, with a capital, Charleville-Mézières, that deserves to be better known. A truly delightful town, with vast central market square bordered by delightful old buildings. This is a territory that has been fought over and on for many generations and it has affiliations way beyond its borders. The Ardennes spill over into Belgium and so do the principal rivers, the Meuse and the Semoy, carrying picturesque barges throughout the watery Northern European network. If you are looking for an inexpensive, away-from-it-all, scenically attractive holiday you should certainly consider the Ardennes, but I fear that chambres d'hôtes are few and far between. Any discoveries would therefore be particularly good to know about.

CHAMPAGNE-ARDENNE

ARDENNES (08)
Préfecture: Charleville-Mézière
1   Brienne-sur-Aisne
2   Grandpré
3   Grivy Loisy
4   Thugny-Trugny

AUBE (10)
Préfecture: Troyes
1   Plancy l'Abbaye

HAUTE-MARNE (52)
Préfecture: Chaumont
1   Coiffy le Haut

MARNE (51)
Préfecture: Châlons-sur-Marne
1   Igny Comblizy
2   Maisons en Champagne
3   Matougués

■   Préfecture

■   Town

①   Chambre d'Hôtes

ARDENNES

BRIENNE-SUR-AISNE. 08190

20 km N of Reims. Follow the River Aisne along the N925 from Soissons through quiet little villages to Neufchâtel where the D366 from Reims joins the D925 and round a bend is the nice little village of Brienne-sur-Aisne.

M & Mme Lériche (S)
24.72.94.25.

A warm welcome at this restful farmhouse on the far fringe of the village. Three rooms full of character are on the first floor of the adjoining building, two of which have sitting-rooms and beds on the mezzanine above, accommodating a family of five. So many amenities – indoor games for children, bikes for hire, and a washing machine for 10f, a pleasant garden and country views from the windows. No

evening meals but a shared well-equipped kitchen with microwave (15f extra per day). Very useful if you don't want the expense of eating out, but there is an excellent restaurant *À la Bonne Volonté* at the other end of the village (1 km away). We ate well there; menus at 70f and 96f and wine *en carafe*. Most attentive service.

The Leriche's 10 year old son has made an interesting museum of fragments of shells, cooking utensils etc, remnants of the First World War found in the surrounding battlefields. Good breakfast. A bargain at 180f for two.

GRANDPRÉ. 08250

17 km SE of Vouziers by D946. A sizeable village with a couple of bars, strung out along the main road. Surrounding countryside is typical Argonne Ardenne – flat rolling farmland, both arable and dairy.

Ferme d'Argonne (S)
Dominique and Phillipe Arnould. Rue de Montifix. 24.30.52.87.

On the main road on the right as you enter the village. The very reverse of its nearest chambres d'hôtes neighbour at Givry, the suave M. Creuwels, this is first and foremost a working farm atmosphere. The hardworking Mme Arnould who was trained to look after handicapped children, decided ten years ago that she wanted to continue to earn a salary of her own and, not content with helping her nice husband on the farm and bringing up three un-handicapped children of her own, she maintains four bedrooms and cooks two meals a day on demand, for her clients.

The present rooms are large, each with its own bathroom, but very simply furnished with haphazard hand-me-downs. They cost 180f. On the day of my visit Madame was waiting for the 'iron-man' to fix railings on the little balconies she has contrived overlooking the wide farm courtyard and massive barns housing the 150 Limousin cattle, horses and assorted livestock which M. Arnhould tends, as did generations of his family before him.

All the ingredients for the meals are home-produced. Our lunch was cured Ardennes ham from their own pigs, breast of turkey in a rich brown sauce, a huge platter of roast potatoes and a tureen of strawberries from the garden, accompanied by a home-baked Madeira cake. It cost 60f.

Mme Arnould has recently opened up her attic to make three more bedrooms. They were nearly ready when I inspected in June 1993 and looked good – beams exposed, lofty and full of character. The sanitary fittings, in the strong mottled blues and strawberry beloved by the French, were sitting there wanting to be installed. Madame was confident that they would be up and running by the following month, so I can safely predict that the new rooms will be available by the time this book is read.

GRIVY-LOISY. 08400 VOUZIERS

23 km SE of Rethel via D983 and D21, 6 km NW of Vouziers by D946 and D21. A village larger than most in the Porcien and Champagne Ardenne, a countryside of flat pastures, dedicated almost entirely to farming. It centres round its church and, more surprisingly, a crêperie and a 'pub'.

➤ ### Ferme-Auberge du Pieds des Monts (S)
24.71.92.38.

This is a very smart *ferme auberge*. So smart that it teeters on the fine line between upmarket b. and b. and small hotel. Its farmer owner, Mr. Creuwels, is energetic, resourceful and ambitious and in five years has transformed his old farmhouse into a restaurant capable of serving 42 covers and five bedrooms, each with its own bathroom and TV. The rustic style has been preserved to some extent, with exposed beams

and lovely curving brick wall in the dining-room, but the plumbing and furnishings are modern.

The evening meal, too, is more sophisticated than you might expect. Mr. Creuwels says he cannot get too fancy, partly for reasons of economy and partly because a no-choice menu must please all tastes, so local specialities like game are rarely involved. For us it was stuffed avocados, a tender, roast farm chicken served with chicory in a rich brown sauce, and four, fat profiteroles filled with ice-cream and dripping with glossy chocolate sauce – excellent value for 60f.

The rooms, all but one with sitting area and sleeping balcony, cost a very reasonable 200f. Breakfast is another 20f.

This would suit those doubters not quite ready for the rough and tumble of a farm stay. You miss out on the personal touch – no improving your French over dinner at a communal table – but don't have to suffer other people's plastic ducks in the bath. It merits an arrow for excellent value.

M. Creuwels is already involved with his next project. He has bought a railway station! This one overlooks a lock on the canal 7 km away at Vonck. The plan is to convert it into another larger gîte and restaurant. The pedalos and canoes are already bought and *in situ* on the canal. Monsieur has it all worked out – his field of operations will extend between two well-spaced-out locks and there will also be more adventurous canoeing on the twists and loops of the nearby Aisne. No doubt, before this guide becomes obsolete, it will be operational.

In any case its worth a drive out to the attractive village of Vonck, high on a hill, with a *table d'orientation* over canal, river, wheatfields, forests, villages, and as far as Vouziers.

THUGNY TRUGNY. 08300

5 km SE of Rethel on D983.

Mme Robert Camu (S)

Who could resist staying in a village with a name like this? (Though it does not sound so droll in pronounced French.) To find Mme Camu's rustic hideaway turn right off the main road, following the chambres d'hôtes signs. It is a romantically faded old house, shaded by giant chestnut trees and backed by what the French term 'un parc' and what we would call a normal garden.

The bedrooms have not been tarted up – some might think that a pity since they are very modest – and retain the panelled walls, painted blue in one room – and family furniture. There are showers and shared loos.

Good value at 140f, 19f less if you cancel breakfast, served by the ubiquitous Madame Camu in her everlasting carpet slippers. French Entrée readers have thoroughly approved of the value on offer here.

AUBE

PLANCY L'ABBAYE. 10380

37 km N of Troyes. Exit from autoroute A26 at Arcis-sur-Aube, then N for 1.5 km on N77, turn left on to D56 for 13 km.

Plancy is a pleasant, sleepy village grown up around a large, open square, centring on an old, iron bandstand. Tourists rarely venture in this direction, as prices indicate. On one side of the square is the blank apricot-painted facade of an old presbytery. Looks good but not half so good as the garden side.

➤   **Mme Violette Misswald** (M)
25.73.00.11.

A secret garden, cool, shady, colourful, runs right down to the river Aube. There are tables dotted about the lawns and on a little terrace at the water's edge. The house, facing south, presents a sunny honey-coloured aspect, grey shutters enclosing deep windows, mellow old roof tiles. Utterly charming.

At present there are three good chambres d'hôtes, all with bath or shower and loo and view of garden and river, approached by an outside staircase. A kitchen is available for guest's use, as is the charming salon. Outstanding value at 210f a double, and an evening meal at 70f (on reservation). Madame Misswald and her delightful daughter Madame de Bonade, who helps her mother, would like to convert another room, but they have only been hostessing for three years, and need a few more tourists to discover their gem before they can afford to carry out the work.

Even if you do not intend to stay here (big mistake), at least cross one of the bridges to the opposite bank for a superb picnic. Willows dip into the river, fast-flowing here because of the defunct lock gates which funnel the stream, plenty of shade, and even a little beach. A magical place altogether.

Arrowed for lovely house, kind hosts, superb position, good value.

HAUTE MARNE

COIFFY-LE-HAUT. 52400

54 km ESE of Chaumont. 6 km SW of Bourbonne.

Ferme du Granges du Vol-Adrien (S)
M. et Mme Pelletier. 25.90.06.70. Open all year.

From Chaumont take the D417 to
Bourbonne-les-Bains; in about 40
km after Montigny le Roi take the
D130 right to Laneuville and Coiffy
le Bas. Stay on the D130 and in a
short distance turn right on to the
D26 to Chézeaux. You will find Les
Granges du Val on your right and
Ferme Adrien on the left.

Searching for this farmhouse
deep in the country near Coiffy-le-
Haut on a wet autumn day, we
would have given up if we hadn't already phoned ahead and booked a room; but I
am so glad we didn't, as this proved to be one of the best value-for-money stops.

The farm nestles below the little hill village of Coiffy-le-Haut, surrounded by
fields and lanes. It is a busy working farm but Madame Pelletier has created a
delightful garden in front of the house which is a pleasure to sit in. The five guest
rooms are all on the first floor, reached by an independent outside staircase: all have
en suite facilities and are well furnished in a variety of different ways, some carpeted, with antique furniture, others with polished wood floors and rattan fittings;
there are fresh flowers in the rooms and reading material and a large childrens'
playroom with toys for wet days. If you go for a walk you will be accompanied by a
friendly dog which makes sure you don't get lost.

Dinner with Monsieur and Madame Pelletier is a real treat. Almost all the
ingredients are produced on the farm – even the wine! Madame is very keen to pick
up all the English expressions she can and in return will help you improve your
French. 180f for a double room and 70f each for dinner with all drinks *compris*,
comfort and a warm welcome make this a worthwhile stop.

MARNE

IGNY-COMBLIZY. 51700

20 km SW of Epernay. Take the N3, direction Château-Thierry; turn left at Dormans on the D18, 7 km to go. This is green, pleasant country in the regional park of the Montagne de Reims.

Château du Ru Jacquier (M)
26.57.10.84; fax 26.57.11.85.

Set in a vast and peaceful park whose denizens include rabbits, deer and horses. A long drive leads to the somewhat grim château, nestling among the buttercups. Patron M. Granger, a Brian Blessed look-alike, runs his operation on the knife edge between hotel and chambres d'hôtes. This is a good choice if you do not wish to take the risk of having to chat to uncongenial fellow guests, since the tables are separate in the extremely pretty, chintzy dining-room. Classy dinner has several choices in each of four courses – 150f exclusive. (e.g. *foie gras, coq à la champagne, cheese, creme brûlée*).

Bedrooms, reached by a lovely old wooden staircase, are cheerfully furnished, with either bath or shower in modern bathrooms. The green one has a canopied bed and costs 410f, the other five are 380f.

MAISONS EN CHAMPAGNE. 51300

10 km W of Vitry-le-Francois. 32 km S of Châlons-sur-Marne. From Vitry take the N4 west, direction Fère-en-Champenoise. The house is on the left, just past the village church. Rather dull countryside.

M. et Mme Collot (S)
19 rue de Coole. 26.72.73.91.

Ignore the drab, uninviting entrance through the farmyard, with tractors lined up. This is still very much a working farm. The 17th century house has its back to the road, and once inside the courtyard things perk up considerably. Roses cover the black and white timbered frame, geraniums tumble out of window boxes, the walls of the newly whitewashed barns are decorated with antique farm implements, and there is a nice terrace with inviting tables and chairs for fair weather breakfasting. Each of the simply-furnished double rooms has its own bathroom, 180f.

Madame Collot enjoys her guests and offers an excellent value evening meal at 65f, exclusive, which makes this a fuss-free early-night, economical choice for a stopover.

MATOUGUÉS. 51510

11 km W of Châlons-sur-Marne.

La Grosse Haie (M)
M. & Mme Songy Gaec. Chemin de St. Pierre. 26.70.97.12.
Open all year.

Take the RD3 from Châlons-sur-Marne to Epernay; in 8 km turn left at Saint-Gibrien at the chambres d'hôtes sign; down a small lane and you will find the farm on your right.

Within easy reach of Epernay and Châlons-sur-Marne. If you enjoyed Noel Barber's book 'Farewell to France' you would have fun finding his villages in this area.

A most efficiently run house, of modern design, but with three interesting beamed bedrooms, fully-carpeted with *en suite* facilities tucked into one corner, all on the first floor. This is a tidy farm with the house standing in a lawned and flowery garden in front of the farm buildings. There is a pleasant lounge at one end of the dining room, where guests gather for an aperitif before dinner, served at one long table. M. & Mme Songy join you for coffee or *tisane* at the end of the meal.

Booking advisable all year round. Well off the main road so nice and quiet at night. A very comfortable place to stay and good value for dinner, bed and breakfast.

Room 220f. Dinner 80f.

LORRAINE

Départements: **Meurthe-et-Moselle**
Meuse
Moselle
Vosges.

Often Alsace and Lorraine are clubbed together, presumably because they
are both in the north-east corner of France, and the area around Metz was
part of Alsace after the Franco-Prussian war.

Geographically and culturally they are very different. The natural border of the wooded Vosges mountains stretches from Franche Comté in the
south tailing off into the Parc Régional des Vosges du Nord at the German
border in the north. A thousand small glacial lakes are hidden in the folds
of these mountains, the highest peak being 1,424 metres. These peaks are
rounded and treeless, aptly called *Ballons*. Skiing takes place here in winter
and sheep graze in summer, producing milk for the Munster cheese.

Lying on the western side of the Vosges, Lorraine has four départements. Mountainous Vosges in the south, where Epinal is the préfecture, a
town I found unexpectedly pleasant, spanning both banks of the Moselle
river. Moselle in the north, bordering Bas-Rhin, Germany and Luxemburg,
where Metz with its beautiful Gothic cathedral is the county town, is a
more industrial part. Further south Meurthe-et-Moselle stretching a finger
north to the Belgian border, has Nancy, the capital of all Lorraine, as its
préfecture. Never miss an opportunity to visit the beautiful Place Stanislas
in the centre of the old town. Lastly (or perhaps first if arriving from U.K.),
Meuse, the most westerly departement, borders on the Ardennes and Belgium. Unremarkable Bar-le-Duc is the main town, but further north is
much fought-over Verdun, and close by is the *ossuaire* (war memorial)
overlooking the surrounding countryside where many bloody battles took
place in the 1914–1918 war.

The cultural difference between the two regions is striking, especially
when flitting from one to the other over *cols* or through the one tunnel in

LORRAINE

MEURTHE-et-MOSELLE (54)
Préfecture: Nancy
1 Cirey-sur-Vezouze
2 Hatrize
3 Herbeviller
4 Loromontzey
5 Maizières

MEUSE (55)
Préfecture: Bar-le-Duc
1 Ancemomt
2 Dannevoux
3 Le Claon
4 Les Islettes
5 Maxey-sur-Vaise
6 Saint-Maurice-les-Gussainville
7 Thillombois

MOSELLE (57)
Préfecture: Metz
1 Arry-sur-Moselle
2 Assenoncourt
3 Cuvry
4 Lidrezing
5 Rezonville
6 Rodalbe

VOSGES (88)
Préfecture: Epinal
1 Chaumousey
2 Liezey
3 Nayemont-les-Fosses

■ Préfecture

■ Town

① Chambres d'Hôtes

the Vosges. Whereas Alsace has the affluent busy attitude of a Germanic society, Lorraine is totally French, and resolutely laid back, and only in the north-east is German spoken.

Small farms, with livestock and fruit fields, cover the land. The tasty little mirabelle plum is a great favourite, made into pies, jams, liqueurs etc. – almost a rival speciality to the famous *Quiche Lorraine*. Some light industry near towns supplies work, as do spa towns like Vittel, where you can visit and taste the water.

The Roman remains of an amphitheatre at Grand, in the western Vosges, are being excavated. The region was a Duchy until the death of Stanislas when, under the marriage agreement between his daughter and Louis XV, it reverted back to France.

Joan of Arc was born here, Louis XVI and Marie Antoinette were caught in Lorraine trying to flee the guillotine. History is kept well alive in the various villages.

MEURTHE-ET-MOSELLE

CIREY-SUR-VEZOUZE. 54480

70 km E of Nancy. At the foot of the western edge of the Vosges mountains. Follow the N4 from Nancy east to Blâmont, then turn right on to the D7A (signposted Cirey-sur-Vezouze). The chambres d'hôtes is through the town on the Val-et-Châtillon road.

M. & Mme Bouvery (M)
18 rue du Val. 83.42.58.38.

For those who like to stay in spacious houses, this old *Maison-de-Maître* beside the road has been well restored and has five large guest rooms; a lounge, overlooking the garden, extends into a billiard room. There is a choice of rooms, with baths or showers, for two, three or four. The best rooms, Nos. 1 and 2, overlook the enclosed rear garden. Parking off the road in a side yard. Evening meals 70f, wine not included. Rooms 280f.

18, Rue du Val.

HATRIZE. 54800

25 km NW of Metz. In the northern part of the département, a village with easy access to the A4 has an isolated up-market chambres d'hôtes on the N103 just north of the village.

La Trembloisière (M)
M. & Mme Arizzi. Route de Briey. 82.33.14.30.

La Trembloisière

When the Arizzis were on the point of retiring they visited their first chambres d'hôtes in Brittany and were so impressed they decided to keep their large, well-furnished family home and take in guests. Many are the lucky people who have stayed here and partaken of their excellent evening meals. Expansive double-glazed windows overlooking the countryside and the A4 allow you to watch the traffic glide silently by. A very handy stop, where you will be made most welcome. Three rooms, a choice of double or single beds for 250f. Parking in the garden behind locked gates. Evening meals 110f, wine included.

HERBEVILLER. 54450

50 km SE of Nancy. Situated on the N4 from Nancy to Strasbourg. Leave Nancy by the N4. In 50 km at the end of the village, the house is on the right.

M. & Mme Brégeard (S)
7 Route Nationale. 83.72.24.73.

7 Route Nationale

This old farmhouse, on a corner of the Nationale and a country lane, looks most unpromising as you enter by an old passageway, but it has been restored internally with great taste and now has two of the brightest, sunniest rooms I have ever met, very prettily decorated, with all mod. cons. A small room for two is for one-night stoppers. Stay a few days and qualify for the larger room for three. Both are

220f. Large windows overlook the rear garden and the blue line of the Vosges mountains beyond. Downstairs they have kept the old stone-flagged floor of the kitchen and made a feature of the ancient sink in a charming simple dining room opening on to a terrace. Equally charming is young Madame Brégeard, who will prepare evening meals (wine *compris* for 75–80f on reservation).

Parking is beside the house off the road, with possibility of putting the car inside the garden gates.

LOROMONTZEY. 54290

28 km N of Epinal. 29 km SE of Nancy. Take the N4 east from Nancy; in 8 km turn right on to the D112 to Bayon, then the D22 east; in 4 km turn right to Loromontzey.

Ferme de Loro (S)
M. & Mme Colin. Loromontzey. 54290 Bayon. 83.72.53.73.

Loromontzey is situated close to the Canal de Moselle l'Est, between Nancy and Epinal, and the Ferme Loro is a farm of character, surrounded by a wall. 'M.A.' writes:

'*A lovely, old, oak staircase led to our room on the first floor, both light and airy and with a pleasant* en-suite *bathroom. Our windows overlooked the lovely garden, where we could see a large sign advertising strawberries for sale.*

'*The sitting/dining room was spacious and the meal abundant: soup, followed by chicken and a range of fresh vegetables, a choice of cheeses and strawberries and cream. We were joined at our table by another couple, on a walking holiday in the Vosges, who had brought their own packed meal with them. Not only was this accepted as a matter of course but they were offered strawberries and cream as a dessert – a nice touch from charming hosts.*

'*M. Colin, the proprietor, came up to us and asked, with a twinkle in his eye, if we would like to join him at 6 a.m. the following morning to help with the strawberry picking.*

'*The surrounding countryside is both peaceful and lovely to look at. A very enjoyable stay.*'

Two rooms at 180f for two. One room has an adjoining room (120f for two) with two beds for a family sharing the same en suite facilities. Evening meal 55 to 70f.

MAIZIÈRES. 54500

13 km SSW of Nancy. A perfect place to stay for visiting Nancy, the capital of Lorraine and *Préfecture* of Meurthe-et-Moselle. Though 1000 years old, the city really prospered under the rule of Stanislas Leszczynski, the ex-king of Poland who was given the Dukedom of Lorraine by Louis XV when the king married his daughter, Maria. The previous Duke, François III, had left Nancy to become Holy Roman Emperor after his marriage to Maria-Theresa in 1736.

Stanislas set about making Nancy one of the loveliest cities in France. To this day the Place Stanislas is superb. Beautiful wrought iron gates, railings, balconies and fountains surround the square, painted in black and gold. An *Arc de Triomphe* leads from the square to the Place de la Carrière and the Ducal Palace, now a museum. The rue Maréchaux close by, where Victor Hugo's father was born, has many small restaurants with reasonable prices, but on a first visit you won't be able to resist a table outside one of the larger restaurants facing the square. The Hotel-de-Ville, the Theatre and the Grand Hotel all magnificently overlook the Stanislas statue in the centre. On the other side of the town is the Church of Notre-Dame-de-Bon-Secours. Stanislas and his wife are buried here. The church is almost entirely of marble, floors, walls, statues and altars. Place Stanislas floodlit at night is like fairyland. Wisely Louis XV insisted that the Dukedom went back to France at Stanislas' death. A day in Nancy will be complemented by a stay in the lovely home at Maizières of:

➤ ### M. & Mme Cotel (M)
69 rue Carnot. 83.52.75.57.

Easy to find, on the right hand side of the road coming from Nancy. Large gates lead into the long courtyard of this large, terraced house, once the bishop of Toul's palace.

The three rooms are delightfully furnished, overlooking the quiet green garden behind, ensuring tranquillity. A family room has a charming extra alcove bed. Comfortable armchairs and thick carpets, modern shower rooms, matching drapes and pretty flowered wallpaper complete the picture. Evening meals in front of a log fire are imaginative and beautifully served, while an enormous portrait of M. Cotel's great great-uncle in Napoleonic uniform watches your every mouthful. Your farmer hosts will give you all information about the area, where to park in Nancy and easiest ways of getting there, etc.

Evening meals 70f. Wine not *compris*, but not thrust upon you. Rooms 190f. This really is a charming place; you will want to stay many nights. Arrowed for good value.

MEUSE

ANCEMOMT. 55320

10 km S of Verdun. Close to Verdun. Visit the cathedral which was badly damaged
in the First World War, but fared better in 1939–45. It has a canopied High Altar
held up by four gigantic barley sugar marble pillars and some very good, stained-
glass windows, particularly the rose window above the organ.

North of Verdun is the largest Beer Museum in Europe, at Stenay on the R.
Meuse. The Meuse rises near Domrémy-la-Pucelle and flows north to Verdun and
eventually over the border to Belgium, heading for the North Sea at the Rhine delta
– a restful narrow river, sometimes flowing alongside canals, with small boats cruising peacefully and tying up at villages *en route*.

From Verdun follow the D34 south along the R. Meuse, turn right in the centre of
Ancemomt and the château is on the left.

Château-de-Labessière (M)
M. & Mme Eichenauer. 29.85.70.21; fax 29.87.61.60.

A very impressive château, with
plenty of space for parking in the
forecourt. The pleasant garden at
the side now has an inviting swimming pool. Over the years the village seems to have encroached on
the lovely building, but inside the
château has maintained its former
glory and the large rooms are very
pleasant, one on the ground floor
richly furnished with a luxury
bathroom, others on the first floor
include a suite for six. M. Eichenauer, who speaks perfect English, prefers guests on
demi-pension basis and does a special rate of 300 to 350f per person, all drinks and
wine *compris*. Reduced rates for children. Good value for all the amenities. A very
pleasant place to stay if you want that little extra atmosphere of days gone by.

DANNEVOUX. 55110

25 km NW of Verdun. Crossing the border from the Ardennes to Meuse in Lorraine
the little village of Romagne-sous-Montfaucon appears more prosperous than those
left behind. Leaving the village on the D123 for Verdun you suddenly pass under a
large archway, the road divides into two and you are on American territory. The

beautiful American cemetery of the First World War is all around you. A carpet of emerald green lawn dotted with white crosses in impeccable lines, tiers up the hillside to a small marble church where scrolls on extended walls commemorate the names of the fallen. The church faces down a tree-lined gap in the graveyard sweeping up to a mansion house where the American Director lives, and keeps a record of all the graves. A quiet fountain plays in the centre of the roads and you leave through another archway into another world, still on the D123. Shortly down the road you will come to the village of Dannevoux close to the River Meuse.

M. & Mme Lechaudel (S)
2 rue des Carmes. 29.85.82.00.

Although this must be the least expensive chambres d'hôtes I have found, the two rooms are by no means poor, each entered by a vestibule which has a large shower room and wc. They are large, one having two double beds and the other one double and a single. (Ask for this one, sunny and carpeted overlooking the garden.) No evening meals, but very kind hosts allow you to use their fridge and picnic in the garden or dining room. The nearest restaurant is about 14 km away. The *Relais* at Vacherville looks promising; there are plenty of French cars outside at lunchtime.

Rooms at only 135f make this a very economical stop for visiting memorials of the First World War.

LE CLAON. 55120

54 km NW of Bar-le-Duc. 11 km NW of Clermont-en-Argonne. In the village on the D2, going north, turn right at the crossroads and the house is straight ahead.

Visit Varennes-en-Argônne, 10 km north of this hamlet, where Louis XVI and Marie Antoinette were caught trying to flee the country. They had to pass through a small archway over the road and M. Drouet, a good revolutionary, drummed up support to stop the coach as he felt sure it was the king's. It was near midnight on 20th June 1791 and they held them in the village, while they investigated. Two years later a memorial tower was built on the spot, but in the First World War the whole village was destroyed. The tower has been rebuilt, but no archway over the road. A pleasant village with a large American memorial to the 1914–18 war and a small museum where the arrest is depicted exactly as it happened.

Le Claon (S)
M. & Mme Wender. 29.88.28.74.

This pleasant *Maison de maître*
stands in large grounds in a park
well away from the road. It was
once a tile factory but has been
rebuilt and is immaculately kept.
Madame Wender has two rooms
on the first floor, with showers and
kitchens but sharing a toilet on the
landing. A small unit for three on
the second floor is en suite, nicely
carpeted, and has a kitchen, too.
Excellent parking. Rooms 190/210f.

LES ISLETTES. 55120 CLERMONT-EN-ARGONNE

27 km W of Verdun. 55 km N of Bar-le-Duc. From Bar-le-Duc take the N35 north,
the *Voie Sacré*, so called because it was the road by which all the reinforcements
and supplies were taken up to Verdun in the First World War. Branch off at Erize-
la-Petite on the D998, head for Clermont-en-Argônne and Les Islettes is on the N3,
just on the border with Ardennes. On the right at Les Vignettes the next hamlet,
you will find:

Villa les Roses (M)
M. & Mme Christiaens. 26.60.81.91; fax 26.60.23.09.

Two houses, one 18th century the
other 16th century, furnished in
keeping with the age of the house,
stand in a large park. In the main
house Madame has four rooms, one
double *en suite*. The bathrooms in
the others are being renovated, at
the moment they share facilities. In
the older house is one family room
with kitchen and bathroom and
another *en suite* for two on the
ground floor. A very comfortable

lounge for guests. Ample parking, guarded by two Alsatian dogs.

No evening meals generally; but Madame is a very congenial and relaxed person who will give you a meal if you are stranded. Breakfasts more than adequate –
ham, cheese plus ample jams and home-made bread.

Rooms 180/250f.

MAXEY-SUR-VAISE. 55140

60 km SE of Bar-le-Duc. 10 km N of Domrémy-la-Pucelle. The nearest chambres d'hôtes to Joan of Arc's birthplace at Domrémy-la-Pucelle. The house with flagstone floors stands empty beside the church where she was christened and took her first communion. Next door is a small museum, mostly of old manuscripts (6f entry). On the hill above, a Basilica has been built in her memory on the spot where she first heard the voices of Saint Cathérine and Saint Marguerite telling her to fight for France.

The peaceful Lorraine village of Maxey is quite charming, embellished by the small River Vaise being channelled into a canal dividing the wide street, a shallow stretch of water teaming with trout. It is the trout maternity home of the region, fishing absolutely forbidden! The people are very honest, occasionally feeding the fish. A fascinating place to spend an hour peacefully gazing into the water. Unfortunately there is no restaurant or café in the village.

Mme Cardot (S)
La Grande Rue. Vaucouleurs. 29.90.85.19.

Young Madame has a very large house overlooking the river, and has turned the granary into two pleasant rustic rooms, each *en suite* for three or four. A salon with kitchen facilities for light meals has an ancient *petrin*, a wooden bread-making trough used on the farms in years gone by. Rooms 180f.

SAINT-MAURICE-LES-GUSSAINVILLE. 55400

23 km E of Verdun. For visiting the battlefields of the First World War, this would be one of my first choices. The most interesting areas are round Douaumont which lies off the D913 east of Bras-sur-Meuse. The *Tranchée des Baïonnettes* is a reconstructed trench which forms the graveyard of the men of the French 137th Regiment who were killed here in June, 1916. The *Oussaire-de-Douaumont* is a magnificent memorial to the 130,000 French and German soldiers killed on the battlefields of Verdun in the Great War, whose bodies were never identified. On the first floor is a chapel and two galleries, each 140 metres long, containing 36 sarcophagi. The walls are covered with memorial tablets dedicated to individuals and regiments. In the chapel there are two tombs, that of Monsignor Charles Ginisluy, Bishop of Verdun, and Ferdinand Noël, chaplain to the Ossuaire who ministered to the bereaved. Mass is celebrated daily at 9

a.m. (10.30 on Sundays). The Ossuaire is dominated by the 46 metre high '*Tour des Morts*', and in front is the National Cemetery with the graves of 15,000 French soldiers marked by simple wooden crosses and red rose bushes. On the ground floor is the usual shop and a cinema with an audio-visual presentation of the battles. Shows last about twenty minutes and are given in French, English and German.

At Fort-de-Vaux (5 km north-east) are the remains of an outpost defended to the last by 250 French soldiers under the command of Commandant Reynal, against ferocious gas attacks by the Germans from 1st June 1916 until their surrender seven days later. It was from here that Reynal sent an appeal for help, by carrier pigeon, his only method of communication. Despite the hazards of gas and smoke, the pigeon got through on 4th June, dying on arrival at French HQ. The fort was retaken by the French in November, 1916. To this day there exists a society which commemorates this brave pigeon.

The pleasant drive along the N3 to Etain gives you time to reflect and brings you back to the world today.

This chambres d'hôtes is signed at Etain or can be reached by the autoroute A4 exit Fresnes-en-Woëvre then the D908 north to Etain and the house is 7 km on the right.

Le Ferme des Vales (M)
M. & Mme Valentin. 29.87.12.91; fax 29.87.18.59.

This modernised barn didn't look too promising beside a busy road, but on inspection, it proved to be a charming house with a huge salon and log fire burning merrily in September. The rooms are on each corner of the first floor, reached by a galleried balcony, overlooking the salon. Sunny and light, with double-glazed windows, they are furnished with great taste in different colours. One could be a bridal  suite, with white lace *ciel-au-lit*. Monsieur, an ex-Air Force pilot, has rebuilt the barn himself, keeping all the old character but installing modern conveniences. Evening meals *en famille* with local produce from the farm opposite are 50 to 100f, wine *compris*. Parking at the back of the house. Good value here. Rooms 200f.

THILLOMBOIS. 55260

34 km NNE of Bar-le-Duc. Bar-le-Duc, the *préfecture* of Meuse, is a modern commercial town in the valley of the *Canal de Marne-au-Rhin*. Not very exciting, but drive up to the old town on the hill and look down at it from the *Belvédère*.

Park in the Place Saint-Pierre and visit the well-kept church where there is a sculpture by Lizier of Duc René-de-Chalon (Prince of Orange) as a skeleton. He was killed at the siege of Saint-Dizier in 1544 and his dying words were that he should be immortalised as he would look in three years' time. They certainly took him seriously!

Stay at Thillombois, a peaceful little village in the Meuse valley between Bar-le-Duc and Verdun.

Take the N35 north from Bar-le-Duc, in 26 km turn right on to the D101 and follow signs to Neuville and Courouvre then the D121 to Thillombois. The chambres d'hôte is next to the château in the centre of the village.

Le Clos de Pausa (M)
Mme Dufour. Rue du Château. 29.75.07.85; fax 29.75.00.72.

Madame Dufour has visited England frequently and now has almost the only chambres d'hôtes with coffee-making facilities, a mini-bar and satellite TV in all the guest rooms. Situated in a very pleasant enclosed garden the house was once the stables of the château next door.

Rooms 'La Rose' and 'Le Bluet' are on the ground floor. 'Le Lilas', on the first floor, has the added advantage of a large fridge and a hair drier, and a small double room without bathroom can be let with this one.

Evening meals 100f, wine *compris*. Rooms 260f/300f.

MOSELLE

ARRY-SUR-MOSELLE. 57680

15 km SW of Metz. A small village on a hill above the river Moselle.

Mme Finance (M)
5, Grand' Rue. 87.52.83.95.

A hostess bubbling over with enthusiasm here and a very different sort of chambres d'hôtes – a narrow terraced house, the oldest in the village, bedecked with flowers. It reminds one of an English boarding house at first. Rooms on two floors vary, with baths or showers, well furnished and warm; there is even one for a family of six. Madame likes you down in the small lounge for *apéritifs* (Kir or Monsieur's home-made rhubarb wine) before dinner, where in front of the log fire you can get to know your fellow guests.

Meals, all at one long table, are tasty and copious. Madame cooks and serves and keeps the conversation and wine flowing. Not a place for people who like to dine in solitude. Mixed nationalities make this a very jolly evening. Breakfast is no mean meal – cereal, ham, cheese, yoghurt, as well as many different breads and cakes. All this will set you back 110f. for the evening meal, all drinks included. Rooms 250f. If you don't like street parking, there is a garage available.

ASSENONCOURT. 57810

55 km ENE of Nancy. 73km SE of Metz. In the centre of the Parc Régional de Lorraine in southern Moselle. From Nancy take the N74 direction Château-Salin; in 26 km fork right on the D38 to Drieuze, then the D999 south and turn left in 6 km (signpost Assenoncourt). Turn right in the village and the farm is on your left.

La Foly (S)
M. & Mme Viville. Maizières-les-Vic. 87.03.93.02.

A modernised farmhouse on a dairy farm, with two neatly furnished rooms with modern amenities and warmly carpeted, on the ground floor having independent entry, double bed or two singles. Four-course meals – pâté, ham omelette, salad, cheese and fruit salad – are simple but copious, produced at short notice, even when Madame is away and her teenage daughters are in charge. The dining room above

in the main house has a large balcony for fine weather. Safe parking on the fringe of this quiet village. A really good budget stop. Evening meals 70f (wine *compris*). Rooms 180f.

CUVRY. 57420

7 km S of Metz. There are quite a few good chambres d'hôtes outside Metz and this is one of the nearest, though deep in the country. Don't miss a visit to Metz, where the ornate Gothic Cathedral steals the limelight. The *Portal de Nortre-Dame* is a mass of finely carved figures; inside stained-glass windows tier up into the tremendously high nave, more square metres of stained glass than in any other cathedral in the world. Modern windows in the Chapel of the Blessed Sacrament were created by Jacques Villon in 1957, when he was 82 years old. Don't miss the semi-circular organ perched near the roof of the nave, recently repaired. Unfortunately you can't miss the new organ, a modern monstrosity hiding some nice windows in the south wall; doubtless it is a superb organ when played. The reredos of the High Altar is almost a Gothic church in itself. The large spacious entrance allows one to view the vastness of this lovely building, a close rival to Chartres, I feel. Metz with the river Moselle meandering through is a lovely city.

For Cuvry, take the D5 from Metz to the junction with the D66 and then the D5A left to the village, signposted from here on the other side of the village.

Ferme de la Haute-Rive (M)
M. & Mme Morhain. 87.52.50.08. Closed 1/11 to 31/03.

A 13th century farmhouse, whose gigantic wooden gates open over cobbles to a totally enclosed courtyard. Winding corridors up and down stairs lead you to the four guest rooms in an independent building. Two for a family share a toilet but the others are *en suite*, furnished pleasantly in keeping with the age of the house. Evening meals with farm produce and wine *compris* 90f. Rooms 240f.

LIDREZING. 57340

56 km ESE of Metz. 46 km NE of Nancy. This low-lying area of the Moselle is very peaceful, with small isolated farms and hamlets almost surrounded by water.

Take the D999 from Metz to Morhange, continue to Conthil and turn left on to the D79 and then the D79C.

La Musardière (M)
M. & Mme Mathis. Morhange. 87.86.14.05; fax 87.86.40.16.

A very warm welcome awaits you here, in this cosy home offering three guest rooms with every comfort. One even has a jacuzzi bath; all are decorated artistically; one has independent ground floor access. A chambres d'hôtes well worth a detour, situated in a restful garden.

Evening meals of regional dishes taken together add to the enjoyment of your stay. 100f excluding wine. A popular place. You need to book well ahead. Rooms 295f.

REZONVILLE. 57130

18 km W of Metz. Close to the ancient village of Gorze where the Roman aqueduct once took water from the R. Moselle to Metz. The surrounding area was fiercely fought over in the Franco-Prussian War of 1870, and many monuments dot the countryside. (After this war the Moselle Department was annexed by Prussia, and remained part of Germany until 1918).

Take the D903 from Rezonville to Vionville and turn left at sign to Flavigny in 2 km.

M. & Mme Lambinet (M)
Hameau de Flavigny. 87.31.40.13. cl. 31/10 to 31/3.

A sheep and bee farm where the young owners have made two most attractive rooms (a third on the way). One is for four with two double beds and one for two, heavily beamed, warmly carpeted and originally furnished, all with modern conveniences. There is a pretty sitting-room for meals but sometimes you eat in the kitchen; once a stable, it still has the full-length trough complete with rings. Evening meals 80f, aperitif *compris*. Rooms 250f.

RODALBE. 57340

48 km SE of Metz. In this lake area of Moselle the villages are often rather poor – just one wide street with terraced houses well back from the road. Rodalbe is no exception, so it was a surprise to find a thriving business on a geese and duck farm here, catering for the gourmet market, with a *ferme-auberge* restaurant producing the specialities of the region, and selling their many products. From Metz take the D999 through Morhange to Conthil then the D79 to Rodalbe.

Ferme du Hasenwald (M)
M. Schmitt and Mme Charbonnel. 87.01.56.65.

The enthusiastic owners arrange picnics and fishing trips on the farm and offer guest rooms in the old cottages of unexpected luxury for such humble dwellings. Five rooms accommodate from two to five people in style and comfort, with log fires, luxurious bathrooms, some with circular baths, and even the odd kitchenette. Especially popular at weekends with people from Metz and Nancy.

Not really a true chambres d'hôtes; but not a hotel either.

Demi-pension 348f per person.

VOSGES

CHAUMOUSEY. 88390

8 km W of Epinal. Epinal, the county town of the Vosges, lies on both banks of the Moselle. Attractive bridges cross in the centre, one with glass covered pathway, enabling you to loiter on the bridge in all weathers and watch the *jet d'eau* in the middle of the river. The old cathedral, with sturdy capitals, is worth visiting as is a Museum of Coloured Prints.

On the D460 from Epinal to Darney:-

M. & Mme Mandra (S)
575 rue d'Epinal. 29.66.87.12.

If looking for a bed outside Epinal with dwindling francs, you could do a lot worse than stop at this typical old *maison-de-maître*. A small flowery front garden and larger vegetable patch alongside leaves room for parking behind gates. The Canal de l'Est from the Moselle to the Saône runs straight behind the house in an elevated position. Lots of passing barges carry their wares.

Madame has one room for three, with a large comfortable shower room, two armchairs, a modern bed and desk, flowery wallpaper. Large sunny windows facing south overlook fields across the road, and even though traffic noise may wake you in the morning, the room still has a certain charm and comfort. Two rooms for a family, sharing facilities, at the back, are not so interesting. Madame Mandra is a very easy-going cheerful hostess with a great sense of humour. Evening meals can be quite entertaining, when she produces *raclette* and you cook your own meat and cheese. Genuine kind people, now retired, who really enjoy their guests. Excellent breakfast, very fresh bread and brioche, six different jams and a large slab of butter on the table. Evening meals for 60f, wine included. Rooms 160f. All very good value. Simple, friendly hospitality.

LIEZEY. 88400

8 km W of Gérander. 41 km SE of Epinal. Only a short distance from the delightful holiday town of Gérarder, where the largest lake of the Vosges reflects the forested hillsides – almost a mini Annecy. Plenty of hotels here but good value at a *ferme-auberge* chambres d'hôtes in the hills. Follow signs to the Bout-du-Lac in Gérarder on the D417, then the D50 right to this small hamlet up in the tree-lined slopes of the Vosges.

Ferme-Auberge de Liezey (S)
M. & Mme Girault. 29.63.09.51; fax 29.60.85.08.

A very popular place to eat, judging by the Sunday lunchtime clientele, with cars from a wide area, even a bus load from Germany. Madame has six simple spacious rooms above the restaurant in her chalet-type farmhouse. Three *en suite*, others share facilities. One family room, excellent bedside lights.

Promising menus from 75–110f of local specialities or a choice of four courses on the *demi-pension* which is compulsory if you stay here. Demi-pension 200f each.

NAYEMONT-LES-FOSSES. 88100

50 km NE of Epinal. A hamlet in the hills above Saint Dié, not a very interesting town which lies just west of the Vosges mountains. It can be reached from Alsace by the N59 from Sélestat taking you over the Col-Sainte-Marie-aux-Mines, where on a fine day there are excellent views over the vineyards of the Rhine valley. We sloshed along in a damp cloud in September. The town of Sainte-Marie was once a silver-mining centre, now only enthusiastic mineralogists use it, but it has become a centre for woollen material, particularly tweeds. The small *col* is covered with tall pine trees. As you descend towards Saint-Dié you will be in the Vosges departement of Lorraine, a totally different environment, no German spoken. An alternative route is through the tunnel from Sainte-Marie to Saint Dié, once a railway tunnel now the only road under the Vosges mountains. (Toll 17f.)

The chambres d'hôtes at Nayemont is in Les Hautes-Fosses. Take the C1 from Sainte-Marguerite, a suburb of Saint Dié, and the farmhouse is on your right as you enter the tiny hamlet.

M. & Mme Bodaine (S)
120 Chemin du Giron. les Hautes-Fosses 29.56.19.02.

One of the places where the prices seemed too good to be true, and we nearly didn't visit. What a lovely surprise when we turned the corner and saw this very pleasant house with a well-tended front garden. A family Sunday lunch party of twenty people was in process but still Madame had time to show us her empty rooms without any rush. Such pleasant *accueil*.

Four rooms, three *en suite* with small showers and toilets, one with private facilities on the landing. Simple mixture of 30s style furnishing, flowery wallpaper, large windows and central heating. Evening meals 40f, wine *compris*. A light meal on Sunday nights.

Rooms 160f (supplement of 20f for one night only). Ask for a south-facing room and you won't regret it. Real budget prices and a large safe garage for your car.

ALSACE

Départements: **Bas Rhin**
Haut Rhin.

Situated in the north-east corner of France, this region is separated from Germany by the river Rhine. The German influence is still very strong, noticeably in the architecture, the language, and the food. The houses are more like Swiss chalets, heavily timbered and everyone speaks not only German and French but a tongue of their own, Alsatian.

Since the Franco-Prussian war of 1870, all Alsace and part of Lorraine, the sister region, belonged to Germany until after the 1914/18 war, and again in 1940 Alsace became totally German (not just occupied); this meant the young men had to join the German army or suffer concentration camps.

The Vosges mountains in the west form a natural boundary with Lorraine.

The region is divided into two departments Bas-Rhin and Haut-Rhin. The former, in the north, is on low-lying land, the *préfecture* of Strasbourg, once a tiny island on the river Ill in 800 BC is now a vast city, housing part of the European parliament. Hops are grown in the neighbouring flat lands, and very good beer is produced both here and further north at Hochfelden.

The southern department of Haut-Rhin has the attractive city of Colmar as the county town. The great wealth of Alsace comes from the vineyards covering the eastern slopes of the Vosges. The wine route begins at Marlenheim in Bas-Rhin and extends south, running west of the main roads and railways, to Thann, south of Colmar. Extremely pretty little medieval villages, decked with flowers, line the route, and many happy days can be spent exploring them, and tasting their products. Mostly white wines are produced, a choice of seven different varieties, named after the grapes of their origin. A small amount of Eau-de-Vie and fruit liqueurs are produced in the Dieffenbach valley.

Food-wise, Alsace is famous for copious dishes of *chaucroute*, based on pork sausage and cabbage and *Baeckeoffe*, a stew of beef and lamb with

ALSACE

BAS-RHIN (67)
Préfecture: Strasbourg
1   Betschdorf
2   Breuschwickersheim (2)
3   Coswiller
4   Dambach-la-Ville
5   Dieffenbach-au-Val (3)
6   Itterswiller
7   Mittelbergheim

HAUT-RHIN (68)
Préfecture: Colmar
1   Ammerschwihr
2   Beblenheim (2)
3   Husseren-Wesserling
4   Saint-Bernard
5   Soultzmatt

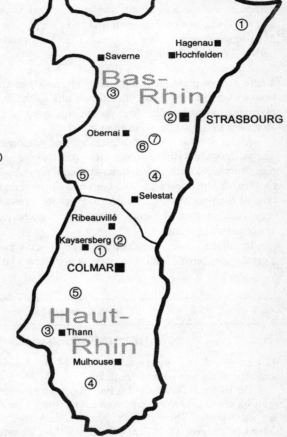

- ■ Préfecture
- ■ Town
- ① Chambres d'Hôtes

potatoes, but the crowning glory is the *Tarte Flambé*, savoury or sweet, with the *Tarte à l'Oignon* a close second. There are rich varieties of *charcuterie*, and of course the *Kugelhopf*, a light yeast cake with a scattering of raisins and almonds, always baked in a fluted mould. The only cheese of note is Munster, common to both regions. The sheep producing this graze on the high slopes of the Vosges.

The emblem of Alsace is the stork. To have one nesting on your roof is a sure sign of good luck. Since they are now becoming scarce, parks have been set up to breed them, one notably at Kintzheim where a little train will take you round for 20f. Many buildings have cart wheels fixed on their chimneys to encourage them to nest.

Alsace is at its best in September and October during the *vendange*. The villages are a riot of colour from the hanging geraniums and the streets pleasantly alive with tourists, mostly Scandinavian, American and German; the British don't seem to have cottoned on to the fact that this is the best time of the year to visit. The Alsatians, though busy with the *vendange*, are very welcoming, unlike some parts of France where chambres d'hôtes close at grape-picking time.

In Alsace hardly any chambres d'hôtes serve evening meals. However, a great many have a kitchen corner, or access to a larger shared kitchen.

BAS-RHIN

BETSCHDORF. 67660

44 km NE of Strasbourg. From Haguenau N of Strasbourg take the D263 northwards; in 10 km turn right to Betschdorf.

The village of Betschdorf has been noted for its pottery since the beginning of the 18th century. The grey pots with strong cobalt blue and highly glazed designs are widely known. There are many potters in the village; the trade has been handed down over the generations. The village, now three kilometres in length, has typical Alsatian houses on either side of the road all half-timbered. Just a drive through the length of the village is quite a feast for the eyes. To add magic to your visit stop off near the beginning of the main street at:-

Christian & Joelle Krumeich (M)
23 rue des Potiers. 88.54.40.56; fax 88.54.47.67.

The house and pottery stand well back from the main road in a garden filled with bushes and flowers. Christian's family goes back through nine generations of potters and they offer not only lessons in pot making but very attractive accommodation.

Three rooms have been tastefully and interestingly furnished, two having a sunny west aspect where you can relax before going out to an evening meal in a local restaurant, one with its own kitchenette. Breakfast is taken in the comfortable salon on the first floor, of course served on their own pottery.

Your hosts are such natural and charming people that even if you arrive with no interest in pottery you will find yourself succumbing to their charm and having a go at 'throwing a pot'. Highly recommended in an area where there are few interesting chambres d'hôtes.

Joelle speaks English, and credit cards are accepted.

Rooms from 200f to 290f, according to size and amenities. 30f extra for use of the kitchenette.

BREUSCHWICKERSHEIM. 67112

10 km W of Strasbourg. These are the nearest chambres d'hôtes to Strasbourg, the main city of Alsace. A visit is essential, however much you dislike cities. The European parliament in modern buildings is on the outskirts.

For *Centre Ville* there is a good underground car park in the Place Gutenberg within easy walking distance of the cathedral, Tourist Office and museums which are all in the same square. Some very old houses here, like the Maison Kammerzell, now a restaurant, and also the oldest chemist in France.

The great crowd-puller is *'l'Horloge Astronomique'* in the cathedral; it chimes daily at 12:30 pm because the clock is half an hour slow. The body of the cathedral closes at 12 noon and admission by ticket only (6f) at side entrance for those wishing to see the clock in action. Figures of the twelve disciples pass the Christ-figure and bow, a cock crows three times at St. Peter's turn, various other things happen, but you need to be six foot tall or take your stilts along, to get a good view – the small area of the cathedral by the clock is jam packed. They weren't joking in the tourist office at a quarter to twelve when they said, 'You had better hurry if you want to see the clock working.' Though only one minute away, the queues were extensive even then.

There are some lovely windows in the cathedral, a very interesting carved pulpit and a sculpture of the Mount of Olives. The high altar was shrouded for repairs when I was there so I can't tell you anything about it. Somehow the noise of so many people talking was more like a cocktail party than a church, and the constant loud speaker reminders to 'watch your handbags and wallets' was most off-putting, (and this wasn't in August). A pity really – it is a lovely cathedral. It was here that Marie Leszczynska married Louis XV by proxy.

Walk down the small streets from Place Gutenberg to La Petite France where the small tributaries of the river criss-cross the tiny streets, and the medieval houses dip into the water. There are plenty of small restaurants to choose from here in the prettiest part of Strasbourg.

It was the Mayor of Strasbourg who suggested to a young officer that he should compose a song for the army of the Rhine in 1792. Rouget de Lisle went away and produced a rousing song which is now the Marseillaise.

Traffic and parking in Strasbourg is always a nightmare, particularly in summer, so the alternative option of leaving your car safely at a chambres d'hôtes and taking the bus is an attractive one – something you can do easily from the following places in the busy village of Breuschwickersheim on the N4.

Mme Diemer (S)
51 rue Principale. 88.96.02.89.

A typical Alsatian farm with large enclosed courtyard and even larger accommodation than usual over an outbuilding. Gîtes and six plain, well-equipped rooms, facing south on the first and second floors, all with kitchenettes. More like an apartment block, but there is a swimming pool in the garden where people meet. Breakfast in a salon across the courtyard. Plenty of parking and the advantage of buses to Strasbourg outside the door. Restaurants in the village. Rooms 220f.

On the eastern fringe of the village, turn left from the main road into a lane just before a large garage and fork right immediately. On your right again a more homely place to stay, *chez*:

M. et Mme Meppiel (S)
Chemin Galgenberg. 88.96.08.19.

Two light, sunny rooms, ground and first floor, in a modern house just 100 metres from the busy main road. Both have kitchenettes; the upstairs with balcony has views over to the mountains. Breakfast in Mme. Meppiel's dining room. Excellent safe parking and the No 22 bus to Strasbourg stops a few yards away. Swimming pool in the making here, it was being dug out the day I visited. Highly recommended. Book ahead – only two rooms. Restaurants close by. Rooms 220f.

COSWILLER. 67310

29 km W of Strasbourg. 11 km S of Saverne. Peacefully hidden in the country, this elegant house could be just the antidote for a hectic day visiting Strasbourg, or complement a quiet day in Saverne close by. Take the N4 to Saverne from Strasbourg and at Wasselonne in 25 km turn off to Coswiller on the D824. Through the small village by the *Au Coq Blanc* you will see a sign to Tirelire on a telephone pole. The house is the second on the right in 800 metres.

Mme Bochart (M)
2 Hameau Tirelire. 88.87.22.49.

Situated in a country garden with roses and lawns, Mme Bochart has four of the most enchanting rooms I have visited. Her taste in furnishing is impeccable. Dainty *Ciel-de-Lit* on every bed, matching covers and curtains. These cosy rooms have large light windows and glorious country views and all have *en suite* facilities with mini baths. Two rooms on the ground floor, 'Rose' and 'Bleu', are adjoining, sharing

one bathroom – useful for a family of three or four. 550f for four. One double bed and two singles. (One can be let on its own when the other remains empty then 350f.) Upstairs both the yellow and blue rooms are adorable, for 325f. Another room on the ground floor is a mixture of green and yellow, TV and telephones in all rooms.

No evening meals but a *Ferme Auberge* next door operates at weekends or daily if you book ahead, or a pleasant restaurant is 3 km away in Romanswiller (*Aux Douceurs Marines*). Breakfast is taken in the dining room reserved for guests, which has an adjoining sitting room. Such a delightful place – you will not be able to resist staying many nights. Madame, who hails from Normandy, likes to make sure that her guests are really comfortable.

Close by is *Saverne*. Don't miss a visit to this lovely little town north-west of Strasbourg. Many locals prefer it to Strasbourg for shopping. The *pietons* (pedestrian precinct) leads down the centre of the town where the *mairie* is flanked by two very old houses. At the foot of the town the Marne-au-Rhine canal runs past the Château-de-Rohan. Once owned by the well known Rohan family, taken over by Napoleon III, the black railings still surmounted by large gilt 'Ns'. Now belonging to the State, you will find the Syndicat-d'Initiatif up in one of the gatehouses. Closed from 12 noon to 2 p.m. but then everyone is having lunch outside the restaurants in the *pietons*, where you can relax peacefully and enjoy a full meal or a light *tarte à l'oignon*. The town is twinned with Leominster and for the homesick a gift of a red British telephone box in working order sits outside the boulangerie/café.

DAMBACH-LA-VILLE. 67650

9 km N of Sélestat. A fortified village in a hollow on the hillside, very much on the wine route, the old town is quite picturesque and still has three gateways and much of the ramparts left. You can stay the night in the centre where all the houses are half-timbered and Madame Nartz's stands out as the oldest.

M. & Mme Nartz (S)
12 Place du Marché. 88.92.41.11.

There's a wine cellar under this lovely old building where light meals are served at weekends and tasting during the day. Madame has five rooms (occupied when I was there, so I didn't see them, I was assured they are well furnished and *en suite*). Exciting to stay so centrally in such a lovely village, but the car would have to be parked in a public car park nearby. If that doesn't worry you, go for it!

Plenty of restaurants around the village and a lot to see within easy walking distance. Rooms 220 to 240f.

DIEFFENBACH-AU-VAL. 67220

48 km SW of Strasbourg. 10 km NW of Sélestat. A quiet village at the foot of the Vosges mountains in the Valley Kirsch where Eau-de-Vie and other liqueurs are distilled, west of the *Route-des-Vins*. Sélestat, nearby, badly damaged in the last war, is now rebuilt; it is a commercial town useful for banks, supermarkets and petrol. Dieffenbach is not the usual pretty flowery village of the *Route-des-Vins* but has some very good chambres d'hôtes which are worth a detour. Take the road from Sélestat to Villé (D424); in 7 km turn left (signposted Neubois) on the D697 and it will lead you to Dieffenbach. Chambres d'hôtes are well signed on the main road, left up a private road where the same family have three different houses.

Mme Collette Geiger (S)
18 rue de Neuve-Eglise. 88.57.60.91.

When Madame Geiger moved from her large house with four chambres d'hôtes into her bijou little green home next door she felt compelled to keep at least one guest room and has created a delightful small room up a private, spiral staircase. It has a kitchenette with microwave on the landing, two single beds, private shower and toilet and the most adorable little balcony for al fresco meals. Madame whisks breakfast up to you on a tray. All this for 250f.

Mme Engel-Dorris (M)
19 rue de Neuve-Eglise. 88.85.60.48.

Having taken over her mother's house, Mme. Engel-Dorris still keeps the guest rooms on the first floor. This large comfortable house overlooks a most attractive garden where mountain streams flow down into little stone troughs – never a shortage of water here. All rooms are well furnished and one shares facilities with a fourth room, making a family suite. A pleasant lounge/dining room overlooks the garden and parking is just under the window. Rooms 210f.

The long private road finishes at the top of the hill at 'La Romance', a son's house.

M. & Mme Serge Geiger (M)
17 rue de Neuve-Eglise. 88.85.69.76; fax 88.85.69.76.

Top-of-the-market chambres d'hôtes here. A beautifully furnished house, with marble floors and staircases and artistic decor to match. All rooms are thickly carpeted with matching shower or bathrooms. On the ground floor 'Bluet' has two single beds 'Lavande' with a double bed overlooking the hills behind. On the first floor 'Rose' has a double bed with a cute little tower sitting room, 'Pine' with a double bed has a mezzanine which can be used either as a sitting room or as an extra family bedroom.

The quality and decor of the house is impressive. Madame is very artistic, designing and painting many of the pictures on the walls. A large, comfortable, marble-floored salon is used for breakfast. (Swings for children and a private lawn for guests.) The Geigers have a young family and provide really good value with such luxury.

The restaurant in the village *le Hühnerstall* is strongly recommended by the whole family as *correct*, which usually means good food at reasonable prices. Closed on Mondays.

Rooms 260/310f for two according to amenities. 500f for four.

ITTERSWILLER. 67140

43 km SW of Strasbourg. One of the prettiest villages on the wine route; situated on the hillside, the timber-framed houses and hotels are a riot of colour. You will meet many tourists strolling down the main street and tasting in the various *dégustations* – worth a visit whether you stay here or not. The best chambres d'hôtes I could find was in a modern house where in the cellars below Monsieur offers *dégustations* from his vineyards beside the house. At the end of the village, within easy walking distance of restaurants, etc.

M. & Mme Hoffmann (S)
1/A Route d'Epfig. 88.85.52.89.

Three rooms on the first floor with their own entrance, plainly furnished but carpeted, each with a private shower and toilet, not adjoining but on the landing, numbered the same as the room. A small, sparsely furnished room for breakfast has a lovely terrace overlooking the village. Budget prices at 175f.

MITTELBERGHEIM. 67140

20 km SW of Strasbourg. A pretty little village, south of Barr, dominated by the wine house of Boekel. Turn right off the main road to:

M. & Mme Dolder (S–M)
4 rue Neuve. 88.08.96.08.

A large house with a wide driveway where over the rear garages are three chambres d'hôtes. Off-putting from the outside, but inside quite different, these are very pleasant simple rooms with fresh green and white decor and pine furniture, carpeted, centrally heated and having excellent lighting. Large windows look south-west over vineyards to the tree-lined slopes of the Vosges

mountains. Tables on the wide landing for breakfast, where there is a mini kitch-enette with fridge. Good parking below windows, and *dégustations* on the spot. Rooms 200f.

There is a choice of three restaurants in Mittelbergheim, or 1 km north in Barr where *La Fleur d'Or* has local specialities at very reasonable prices and a jolly patron.

HAUT-RHIN

AMMERSCHWIHR. 68770

12 km NW of Colmar. At the southern end of the *Route des Vins*, this prosperous wine village was almost destroyed in the German retreat of 1944 but luckily the old part survived to tell the tale. It has been tastefully rebuilt combining old and new. Many *viticulteurs* live here offering upmarket *dégustations*. Just up the road is Kaysersburg, the birthplace of Albert Schweitzer, surprisingly not spoilt by the hordes of tourists seeking his house. There are a fortified bridge and many lovely old houses and shops where prices are reasonable. Return to Ammerschwihr and make for the old part of the town, where a stork nests on the stone gateway, and you will find the home of a *viticulteur* at:-

M. & Mme Thomas (M)
41 Grande Rue. 89.78.23.90; fax 89.47.18.90.

Elegant Mme Thomas is well organised. She has studios, apartments or just plain rooms, for two, three or four people, superbly furnished but facing across the narrow street. Better to ask for one on the first-floor room, which is lighter. (Don't let this put you off, the place is charming.)

A pleasant dining room leads to a sunny terrace and private parking. If you feel like self-catering, choose a studio complete with kitchen. There is a *boulangerie* and an *epicerie* (and in the village, restaurants).

Rooms and studios vary from 230f to 260f.

Colmar, the *préfecture* of Haut-Rhin, is only a short distance away. A busy town with some fine buildings, and open squares, good shopping facilities, some under cover, and best of all the adorable *Quai-de-Poissonerie* where the flower bedecked bridges straddle the canal in the old town, very peaceful after the hubbub of the commercial centre. There are plenty of restaurants beside the water, where small punts are moored. It is possible to tour the town by a little train, but never between 12 and 2pm!

BEBLENHEIM. 68980

13 km N of Colmar. Looking for somewhere central to stay in the southerly part of the Route-des-Vins where the villages come up thick and fast sometimes only a mile apart, presented a problem. The larger towns had no exciting chambres d'hôtes and the prettier villages offered more frills than basic comfort. However busy little Beblenheim, totally absorbed in the *vendange* at the end of September produced a choice. You will be dodging trucks of grapes as you wander through the flower-filled streets. A village not inundated with tourists, but the wine has a good reputation. Turn right by the fountain into the rue Jean Macé and the rue de Raisins, a cul de sac, is immediately on your right.

'Gambrinos' (M)
M. Klein. 4 rue des Raisins. 89.49.02.82.

Hidden behind large gates, this 16th century house has a cosy courtyard. An old wood staircase leads to rooms on the first and second floors, comfortably furnished. Enjoy the window boxes and fresh flowers in your room. Small net curtains screen the surrounding roof tops but let in the sun. An extra bedside lamp was brought at once on request. Well-worn stone steps (for residents, the public have another door) lead to a *Winstub* (wine cellar) an added bonus, where from 6pm, *tartes flambés* cooked in a wood oven, served on a wooden platter and eaten with fingers, are quite the best I have tasted. Local wine by the carafe available. Cheerful Jean-Jean, Jack of all Trades, does everything. The elusive owner M. Klein, an antique dealer, I have yet to meet. A hearty breakfast is served by a *femme de ménage*.

Parking outside the gates in the small cul de sac. Plenty of character here. Rooms 260f. Credit cards accepted.

Another option at the edge of the village, overlooking a vineyard, is in a modern house. Drive through the village in an easterly direction, take the last road right and the rue Riesling is on the left.

M. & Mme Colaianni (S)
17 rue Riesling. 89.49.02.83.

Italian hosts here offer three rooms
under the eaves, pleasantly furnished in different colours with
beds for three in each and light
shower rooms. A kitchen corner for
all is in the little breakfast room.
Guests have independent entry, and
parking is in the garden behind the
house. Rooms 265f.

    Beblenheim is a good place to
stay for visiting Ribeauville, a town
situated at the foot of the Vosges
mountains. Delightful nooks and crannies lead off the main pedestrian precinct in
the centre. Shops and pleasant restaurants line the street. From the 13th century
Tours-des-Bouchers near the *mairie*, there is a good view of the three castles, one a
ruin, ancient homes of the Ribeaupierre family, whose Counts once owned vast
lands round here. The town is noted for its festival of strolling players at the end of
August. Lots of pottery and Alsatian wine glasses selling at reasonable prices; the
shops often stay open from 12 noon to 2pm. The parking is excellent, under shady
trees at the entrance to the town.

Much fighting went on here in the German retreat of 1944. Ostheim nearby, an old
town, was totally destroyed at that time; just one remaining wall in the village
square has a stork's nest on top of it. The town has been rebuilt in modern style,
losing all its character.

    Spare time for peaceful Hunawihr, where the small church still has its sur-
rounding fortified walls commanding a view of the whole valley. (The church is
used by Protestants and Catholics alike.)

    Up the road is Riquewihr, known as the 'pearl' of the wine route. Certainly
there are many very old and colourful houses in blue, red, mustard and green, all
timber framed. The main street leading down from the gate tower, where there is a
museum, is heavily cobbled and thronged with tourists. Although a wine village
there is not much evidence of the *vendange* in *centre ville* – too busy with the tourist
trade, where prices are high in the shops. There are numerous restaurants here and
plenty of *dégustations*. It will cost you 10f to park outside the walls of the village.
Even the loos are 1f.

HUSSEREN-WESSERLING. 68470

34 km NW of Mulhouse. 41 km SW of Colmar. Take the N66 from Mulhouse to
Epinal and in 29 km turn left at Ranspach to the village. The house is on your left
on the road to Mollau, at the foot of the Vosges mountains.

Mme Herrgott (S)
4 rue du Gare. 89.38.79.69.

A long 18th century house standing on the roadside, parking just off the road by the two garages, one for guests.

The bedrooms are on the ground floor just inside the front door. Both have kitchen facilities. The rear one is particularly nice, overlooking a very pleasant garden. Single beds and feather duvets among the many comforts.

Generous breakfast served in a room further along the house – three types of bread, orange juice, cheese, cereal – everything you could want. Rooms 240f, or 200f if you stay a week.

SAINT BERNARD. 68720

53 km S of Colmar. 13 km SW of Mulhouse. Within easy reach of Colmar, dual carriageway on the N83 south to the junction with the D466, then in 9 km at Spechbach-le-Haut turn right. Signed in the village by the restaurant 'Cheval Blanc' in the rue Principale.

Mme Bairet (S)
13 rue de l'Eglise. 89.25.44.71.

A very warm welcome here from accommodating hosts who have built guest rooms over their tobacco drying sheds. Their pleasant house is in a quiet road not far from the church. Of the four simple rooms, only one is *en suite*, with a private fridge; others share facilities and a fridge on the landing.

Quiet and friendly, in an area where the choice of chambres d'hôtes is limited. Rooms 190f for two, 360f for four.

SOULTZMATT. 68370

22 km SSW of Colmar. One of the most southerly wine villages of Alsace and quite a large straggly place, running into the next town, not nearly so pretty as ones further north, but a good budget chambres d'hôtes. In the village turn right at rue Général de Gaulle, then right at the church.

Mme Flesch (S)
1A Route d'Osenbach. 89.47.03.13.

High above the road, with private parking behind the house, this bright modern house overlooks one end of the village. A very secluded lawn is the place for summer breakfasts. Two rooms, one with double bed with a tapestry bedhead and another room with two singles. A kitchen for guests. Rooms 180f for one night, 170f for longer. (Pleasant hosts.)

BRITTANY

....

Départements: **Côtes d'Armor**
Finistère
Ille-et-Vilaine
Morbihan.
Accompanying French Entrée guide – 'French Entrée 14 – Brittany Encore'

One third of France's coastline is to be found in Brittany, and that's a lot of sand, rocks, surf, headlands, fishing villages, bays and beach resorts. The snag here is that, unlike its more sophisticated Paris-fed neighbours – Normandy and the Loire – Brittany tourism dies for the whole winter. Toussaints (November) to Pacques (April) is the normal closure, but October to May is a distinct possibility too. This, after all, is the cold windswept north, and the heating bills make landladies think twice before incurring them. When you reckon that there's rarely an unoccupied bed to be found in this No. 1. bucket and spade region during school holidays, that doesn't leave much of the year to take pot-luck.

It's worth the effort to plan ahead. Brittany, land of myths, ghosts, will-o-the-wisps, legends, is pure magic. You can sense it most powerfully in the central Forest of Brocéliande, the home (so say the Bretons) of the Arthurian legend, and in the far north-west in wild Finistère, where the miracles worked by local saints, many of them monks from Britain, are still revered, and pagan spells are accepted side by side with colourful Christian traditions. This is Brittany at its most Breton – home of the unique *enclos paroissiaux*, astonishing church enclosures crowded with amazingly elaborate carvings of triumphal arches, calvaries and ossuaries, parish vying with parish over several centuries to produce the most glorious combined effect, working with the rough, local granite. At the most famous in Guimiliau are 200 figures depicting Passion stories... It is in the south, in Morbihan, that you are most likely to catch another Breton phenomenon – the *Pardon*, an impressive local religious procession, where the *coiffes*, collars and costumes handed down through the generations are brought out and proudly

BRITTANY

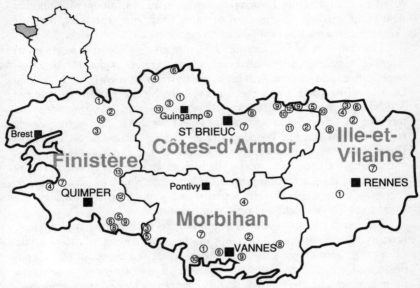

COTES D'ARMOR (22)
Préfecture: Saint-Brieuc
1   Brélidy
2   Dinan
3   Kergueréon
4   Louannec
5   Plélo
6   Plougescrant
7   Pommerit Jaudy
8   St Alban
9   St Cast
10 St Lormel
11 St Michel de Plélan
12 Trégon
13 Trégrum

FINISTERE (29)
Préfecture: Quimper
1   Carantec
2   Coatélan
3   Commana
4   Douarnenez
5   Kerdruc
6   Nevez
7   Plonevez-Porzay
8   Port Manech
9   Riec sur Belon
10 St Martin des Champs
11 St Yvi
12 Scaer
13 Spezet

ILLE ET VILAINE (35)
Préfecture: Rennes
1   Bains sur Oust
2   La Boussac
3   Cherrueix
4   Dol de Bretagne
5   La Richardais
6   Roz-sur-Couesnon
7   St Ouen-la-Rouerie
8   St Pierre de Plesguen
9   St Briac sur Mer
10 St Suliac

MORBIHAN (56)
Préfecture: Vannes
1   Auray
2   Elven
3   Guidel
4   Josselin
5   Larmor Plage
6   Locqueltas
7   Pluvigner
8   Rochefort en Terre
9   Theix
10 La Trinité-sur-Mer

■   Préfecture

■   Town

①   Chambre d'Hôtes

paraded. The principle *Pardons* are listed in FE 14, along with another treat – the markets. In this land of superb fish and vegetables, they are exceptionally attractive to supermarket-weary eyes.

I can never decide which is my favourite area – Côtes d'Armor with its fantastic coastline, marvellous beaches, pink granite rocks, the beguiling river Rance, and two of Brittany's most attractive towns, St. Malo and Dinan, or the south, with the astonishingly Mediterranean-like Gulf of Morbihan with an island for every day of the year. I love the twists and turns of the river Belon and picturesque Pont Aven, I love the seaside resorts of Finistère, like Benodet, and the fishing villages of the west, like Douarnenez and Concarneau; I would not neglect exploring the interior, particularly the canals and towns like Josselin and Dinan. Nowhere is very far from the feature that dominates the landscape and the character of the Bretons – the sea. Nowhere is sophisticated – forget your nightclubs and smart clothes – everywhere is very, very beautiful.

Because this is essentially a region where tourism is a top industry, Brittany has one of the largest crops of chambres d'hôtes to choose from. They range from severe, granite châteaux – there is a cluster of three beauties in the Côtes d'Armor whose owners are exceptionally friendly – to simple farm accommodation. Many a Breton farmer has blessed this supplement to his income in agricultural hard times.

There is so much to see, so many things to do, so many new experiences to savour that I wager the first visit won't be the last.

CÔTES d'ARMOR

BRÉLIDY. 22140

14 km N of Guingamp by D8 and D15. An area of quiet woods and streams.

Château de Brélidy (M)
Mme Yoncourt. 96.95.69.38; fax 96.95.18.03.
An unusual combination of hotel and chambres d'hôtes. The advantage is that it is open year-round and everyone can use the hotel's splendid public rooms and very pleasant grounds.

The Yoncourt family have
(heavily) restored the old château
and are now making good use of
the former attics for b. and bs.
They are cheerful and bright
with excellent bathrooms. 470f a
double.

Château de Bretigny

DINAN. 22100

A gem of a town, probably the most attractive and interesting in the whole region
and not to be rushed through on any account. Penetrate into the heart of the old
town with camera well-loaded, to record the photogenic crooked gables, pillars and
beams of the houses built for 15th century merchants whose trades are echoed in
the street names:- Cordeliers, Merciers, Lainerie, Poissonerie. The rue d'Horloge is
one of the most picturesque, with its strange 15th century clocktower enclosing four
bells, one of them a gift from the ubiquitous Duchesse Anne.

Stallholders used to sell their wares in the shelter of the arcades formed by the
stubby granite pillars supporting overhanging upper stories – as practical today for
keeping off the Breton rain as ever was. Visit the fish market, open every day in the
narrow rue de la Chaux, part of a tangle of little streets round the Old Market. The
main market takes place on Thursday on what used to be a mediaeval fairground,
the Places du Champ and du Guesclin, full of cars on other days.

When the delightful meandering round the old town is complete, take a closer
look at the port, where the pleasure boats take off for a fascinating trip up the
Rance to St. Mâlo in summer, by walking down one of the most beguiling lanes in
Brittany. It leads from the English Garden, via the rues du Rempart and Michel,
into the rue du Jerzual and its extension, the rue du Petit Port, winding through the
500-year-old Jerzual Gate, between the elegant houses now owned and restored by
craftsmen, right down to the water.

Le Logis du Jerzual (M)
25 rue du Petit Fort. 96.85.46.54.

Breaking all the rules, this one remains uninspected and is mentioned only because its
site is so exceptional. When I called all the rooms were taken and Madame was out,
so all I know about it is that it is on the steep hill that connects the port with the

town – one of the most picturesque in all Brittany; it is run by the family that owns a tea room there, and looked most attractive. In this top tourist town, which should be on everyone's 'Must visit' list, this could be a great find. I badly need reports, please.

LOUANNEC. 22700 PERROS-GUIREC

5 km S of Perros-Guirec on D6. Perros is the largest resort along the Pink Granite coast, lively and modern, centring round its marina. Good Friday market. Several beautiful bays edge the point, fringed with pines. From Trestraou you can take a Vedette Blanche on an excursion to the Sept Iles, to view the extraordinary rocks along the coast – the turtle, the scallop shell, the old man, the elephant, formed by the creasing and crumpling of the granite. Wonderful walks along the old coast-guards' paths.

Rosmapamon (M)
Mme A Sillard. 96.23.00.87. cl. Oct-April.

A pale stone house with white shutters on floor-to-ceiling windows, set in a secluded, lush garden where palm trees thrive. Much-travelled Madame Sillard speaks good English. Her four bedrooms all have a private bath or shower, but the one I fancied boasted a splendid tub on claw feet. They are furnished with a mixture of antiques and more modern furniture; flowery fabrics add to the feeling of being in the country, though Rosmapamon is only 300 metres from the port. Breakfast offers freshly squeezed orange juice, and is served on a long wooden table in the drawing room. 280–350f.

PLÉLO. 22170

20 km NE of St. Brieuc by N12, sortie Plélo. Lovely wooded countryside.

➤ Le Char-à-Bancs (M)
The Lamour family. 96.74.13.63.

When we turned up on a Sunday afternoon they had just had a full house for lunch, were expecting two sittings that evening, and had been packed out the previous evening, too, but the welcome was unstinted, to the extent of hugs and kisses all round, with the third generation now participating from her cradle; fresh crêpes were produced, tea and coffee appeared, spaces were cleared at the kitchen

table and we all sat down for a
good gossip.

The Lamours are a remarkable
family, working together in appar-
ent total harmony to run several
projects in one. Their home is an
old mill, whose raftered dining
room overlooks the millstream.
Tables are contrived from rugged
millstones or long, polished oak
boards. They are best-known as a
crêperie, but there is more, much

more. Their famous potée, a thick stew, simmers continuously in a huge iron pot on
the perpetual fire. All its ingredients are home-grown: – vegetables, pork, and I
daren't ask. They also grow much of the cereal, to make the flour, to make the pan-
cakes and galettes. Parisians drive for four hours to spend their weekends here, sampling such rustic fare, walking along the river, leading their children on the ponies,
paying for pedalo rides on the fast-flowing river.

All this made the Char-à-Bancs a highly popular entry in FE5, but now there is
a new attraction. They have recently converted another old building down their
drive, some 500 metres away, into utterly charming chambres d'hôtes. One of the
Lamour daughters is an interior decorator and has skilfully furnished it in country
style; another daughter is responsible for looking after the guests' welfare. 'I am the
femme de ménage' she said. The rooms are far more sophisticated than I would
have guessed, each with a theme:- 'La Chapelière' has straw hats as decoration,
(500f) 'Les Oiseaux' has birdcages, (320f) 'La Musique' simply a music stand (420f)
and 'l'Horloge' must have a clock but I can't actually remember it. You can opt for
bath or shower. I like La Chapelière best, but they are all special.

PLOUBEZRE. 22300

10 km S of Lannion by D11, then D30 towards Ploumillau. The manoir is down the
fourth turning on the left, after the railway crossing. The signs are often hidden in
the trees.

Manoir de Kerguéreon (L)
M and Mme Gérard de Bellefon. 96.38.91.46.
cl. from November to Easter.

There is an astonishing network of 'old' families in Brittany, many of them related,
and indeed Mme de Bellefon is sister to the Comte de Kermel at Kermézen.
They support and encourage one another in this b. and b. business, which they all
seem thoroughly to enjoy. The Manoir de Kerguéreon has been in the de Kermel
family for many generations as a country retreat and farm, but the family had

to flee to England after the Revolution and by the time the present
owners decided to live here it was
in a sorry state. They have renovated and restored it to a typical
Breton manorhouse so successfully
that they won first prize in the
Vieilles Maisons Françaises awards.
Now it is both a stately residence,
with a tower and sculptured friezes
over the doors, and a family home,
with young grand-daughter insist-

ing on her share of attention. The de Bellefon's son runs the adjacent thorough-
bred stud.

Tall, elegant M. de Bellefon's father was in the diplomatic service, appointed
Ambassador to Britain at one stage, so of course he speaks very good English and is
a particularly charming, friendly, interesting and interested host; he and Madame de
Bellefon will do all they can to make your stay here a profitable one. For us a log
fire was lit and tea produced. Although no evening meals are provided, an apéritif is
always offered – a chance to get acquainted. Recent satisfied guests were Sir Leon
Brittan and his wife, who used the manor as a base for a walking holiday. Two
rooms have been adapted to make comfortable guestrooms furnished with family
pieces, and with good modern bathrooms. 500f.

PLOUGESCRANT. 22820

7 km N of Tréguier by D8. The Pink Granite coast is one of the wildest and
probably the most interesting in all Brittany. The tide drops sharply and reveals
another world of jagged rocks, islets and drifts of sand. Hell's Bay to the east is
aptly named; in a deep cleft the sea thrashes and booms alarmingly and one is
always aware around here of the brute force of the powers of Nature. Plougescrant
is a typical Breton village, famous for St Gonery's church, whose 17th centurylead
spire is 'perched awry like an inebriated astrologer's bonnet'. They say it was the
ageing of the rafters and the weight of the lead that made it slope. When it was
rebuilt in 1962, the angle was reduced, but it is certainly a bizarre sight today.

➤   Manoir de Kergrec'h (L)
Vicomte and Vicomtesse de Roquefeuil. 96.92.56.06; fax 96.92.51.27.
Many are the attractions of the 17th century manor, not least among them its pretty
young blonde chatelaine, Martine de Roquefeuil, but quite unique is its situation. At
the end of the world, high above a magnificent stretch of coast, its vast grounds run
right down to the sea. Walking, as you might imagine, is superb.

Martine is the perfect hostess, efficiently combining her role as mother of two children who need to be ferried to the local schools with that of b. and b. organiser. Her breakfasts are famous. I listed croissants, bread, *far Breton, chausson de pommes,* crêpes, Danish pastries, pain de raisin, freshly squeezed orange juice, bananas, apples, pears, plums, and four kinds of jam. No wonder her splendid rooms are usually booked up for weeks ahead (unusually for a

stately home, she stays open year-round). She joins the guests at the long polished beautifully-laid table and advises them on their day's projects. The assembly comprised Italians, Japanese, Americans and us, so, speaking limited English, she did well. (Her husband has worked in Boston and does the difficult bits.)

All the rooms are lovely, from the ground-floor suite with priceless antique furniture and yellow canopy (850f) to the oldest one, decorated in green, with high rafters, a bed on the gallery level and a mediaeval latrine hidden away in a corner. More modern plumbing is evident elsewhere, with super-luxury bathrooms and co-ordinated bathrobes and towels. Bank on being thoroughly spoiled. Rooms: four at 450f, three at 550f and four at 850f.

POMMERIT JAUDY. 22450

9 km S of Tréguier by D8 and D6. The valley of the river Jaudy is a particularly green and pleasant area of northern Brittany. The rugged coast is not far away, but the scenery here bears no relation to its harshness. All is lush and gentle.

➤ Château de Kermézen (L)
Comte and Comtesse de Kermel. 96.91.35.75.

M. Kermel used to be a coffee planter in Africa before he returned to claim his inheritance of the 15th century château that had been in his family for 550 years. The colonial tradition of hospitality is still evident. If you ever felt intimidated at the thought of being entertained by a Count and Countess, forget it. This hostess patently enjoys sharing her gorgeous home with guests, many of whom have become friends. It's hard to not to be friends with the ebullient Madame Kermel, who is the unstuffiest comtesse imaginable. She claims that she was pushed (by the energetic François de Valbray at Les Briottières) into the b. and b. business but, given no option but to get out the paintbrush and start decorating the rooms that had been left empty for the past forty years, she, typically, buckled to and made the best of what has proved to be a very good job.

The bedrooms are all lovely. Mine had twin Directoire beds, rose-covered fabric on walls and at a tall window looking directly down the drive flanked by two solid pigeonniers 450f. Next door was larger, with attractive green toile, panelling painted pale green and a *lit-matrimonial* – 550f. To reach them involved climbing a winding stone staircase, slippery and crooked enough to necessitate hanging on to a rope with unengaged hand, so this one is not for the handicapped.

To reach what is probably the nicest room of all involves another similar flight and, encumbered as always with excess baggage, it seemed an unwise choice for me. More prudent packers should consider this charming yellow room, with bigger bathroom (550f), whose aspect is south down towards the river. Leave time for a walk here. Madame Kermel, who loves nothing better than organising, will distribute maps. It was early spring for me, the banks of the lane that follows the rushing river were covered in bluebells, Ragged Robin, wild garlic, primroses, buttercups, violets, Star of Bethlehem, wild cherry blossom. The willows were at that brief moment before the green takes over, when their flame foliage would indicate autumn rather than spring. This is a lovely place to stay, with the kindest of hosts. You'll want to go back and back. No evening meals but a superb restaurant nearby at la Ville Blanche.

ST ALBAN. 22400

9 km N of Lamballe by D791. At St. Alban take the St. Brieuc road for 2 km. Deep farming country.

La Ferme de Malido (S)
Huguette and Robert Legrand. 96.32.94.74; fax 96.32.92.67.

Good for kids. The Huguettes have three of their own, so all the gear is there – ping-pong, slides, and the farm (pigs) to explore. The rooms, some in a wing of the house, some in a separate building with high open-raftered ceiling, are simple, clean and functional. 200–300 for two, plus a supplement of 70f for each child. No table d'hôte, but there is a cooker and fridge in the new building for the guests' use and barbecues in the gardens.

Ferme de Malido

ST CAST. 22380

20 km NW of Dinan, 30 km W of St Mâlo, along the coast road. The popular resort of St Cast and the village of le Guildo together cover the narrow peninsula pointing to St. Mâlo at the Pointe de St. Cast. All round the promontory are scattered beaches of fine sands and rocks and some spectacular views.

Chateau du Val (L)
M. and Mme de la Blanchardiere. Notre Dame du Guildo. 96.41.07.03; fax 96.41.02.67. cl. 12/11–1/3.

Turn off the D786 half a km after the bridge, following signs on the right. The 16th-18th century château has been in the de la Blanchardière family for 200 years.

The present young incumbents have breathed new life into its old stone walls since I first wrote about it for FE5, and are gradually improving the decorations and facilities. It is magnificently sited in 15 hectares of grounds sloping down on to a private beach, with a tennis court, and golf course and restaurants are nearby. The rooms are all quite different of course, one furnished with blue Toile de Jouy at 420f, the Châteaubriand room –

560f with a particularly good bathroom and twinbeds and other variations of shower or bath, up to a suite for 750f. The young hosts, who speak good English, will do all they can to ensure their guests enjoy the delights of the nearby Emerald Coast.

ST LORMEL. 22130 PLANCOËT

On the banks of the river Arguenon.

La Pastourelle (S)
Mme Lédé. 96.84.03.77. cl. from 15/11-1/3.

2 km N of Plancoët, via D19. On entering the village, just after the name sign, look for La Pastourelle signs and follow them (sometimes obscured) for two km deep into the countryside.

A typical old Breton farmhouse that has been in the family for four generations. Family heirlooms, like those lovely polished armoires that are given to young couples on their wedding day, furnish many of the rooms, flowery country wallpapers brighten up the walls, and chintzy canopies hang over the beds. The vast stone-walled salon had a cheerful fire burning on a cool spring day and a giant leather halter on the staircase was put to good use as a key-holder for the guest rooms. One has a bath, the rest have shower and loo – 220f. Madame Lédé is a very professional hostess, recommended in many guidebooks; she serves excellent breakfasts and dinners (by reservation) at separate tables, and cooks delicious meals on a wood-fired range, using local farm produce – 75f. She is also able to

La Pastourella

arrange special terms for longer stays – 164f per person demi pension for three days.

ST MICHEL-DE-PLÉLAN. 22980

17 km W of Dinan by D176, then right on to D19, direction Plancoët to St Michel, then follow signs on left 1 km after village.

La Corbinais (S)
M. Beaupère. 96.27.64.81; fax 96.27.68.45.

A particularly warm welcome guaranteed here from pig-farmer M. Beaupère and his English-speaking wife. Beaupères have lived in this old Breton granite cottage for four generations. The main room has a huge fireplace, whose cheerful flames were very comforting on a miserably wet day. Guests sit at the long oak table here for excellent breakfasts and dinners composed entirely of farm produce. Five-

La Corbinais

course dinners cost a mere 70f with the Beaupères joining the guests for conversation and advice on local activities. M. Beaupère is very proud of the nine-hole golf course that he has recently constructed round his property, and there are lakes for carp fishing.

The four rooms (with either bath or shower and w.c.) have been contrived out of the attics, which means that they are a bit dark, thanks to sloping wooden ceilings and dormer windows, but comfortable enough, at 240f.

TRÉGON. 22650

10 km W of Dinard. On the main road, just a km or two from the sea and the intriguing peninsula of St. Jacut. This long spit of land between two deep bays boasts an unsurpassed panorama of wild rocks, sands and neighbouring headlands. Around its fringe are no fewer than eleven beaches to choose from.

➤ La Ferme du Breil (M)
Comtesse de Blacas. 96.27.30.55. cl. first fortnight of June and December.

After Ploubalay stay on the D168 for ½ km, then turn left towards Plessix-Balisson, and look for signs. A long low farm building, exquisitely restored, two arms enclosing a courtyard and terrace. The four bedrooms are among the best I have discovered, a splendid advertisement for Laura Ashley; I envied nice Mme de Blacas the fun she must have had in choosing the colour schemes, used with great style. The bathrooms are super, too, justifying the price of 360–410f. If you stay for a week you get the seven days for the price of six. With so much variety in the neighbourhood this would be a very good idea. The vibes of this unusually luxurious b. and b. are great. Highly recommended.

TRÉGROM. 22420 PLOUARET

25 km NW of Guingamp by N12; take the Louargat exit, then D33 to village. Trégrum is a pretty sleepy hamlet of grey stone houses covered in roses. In the centre opposite the church is:-

➤ Le Presbytère (M)
Nicole de Morchoven. 96.47.94.15.

Open the blue wooden door on the village street and discover a magical secret garden. A courtyard, flowery, enclosed and deeply peaceful, fronts the 17th century presbytery, a lovely grey stone building with blue shutters, exuding an extraordinary atmosphere of serenity.

I like every thing about le Presbytère – the warm kitchen with old porcelain stove and bunches of dried flowers hanging from the ceiling, and all the bedrooms –

the peach one with a big bathroom
and tub (300f), the twin bedded
one with beams and blue Toile de
Jouy fabric (280f with shower), the
red Toile de Jouy (ditto). Most of
all I like the atmosphere of a comfortable family house presided over
by nice Madame de Morchoven.
She is well known for her evening
meals (100f – must be reserved)
which include lots of fresh vegetables. A winner.

FINISTÈRE

CARENTAC. 29660

15 km N of Morlaix. Take the coast road, the D73, if you're not in a hurry. It follows the river Frout through Locquénolé to the estuary, up to Carantec, a charming
little seaside resort on a peninsula, with beaches and bays in all directions. Excellent
walks abound, like those to La Chaise du Curé, a promontory overlooking the bay,
the estuary of the Penze, St. Pol-de-Leon and Roscoff. The little town itself is lively
and very busy in summer. Its chief industry, apart from oyster farming, is tourism.

Kervézec (M)
M. and Mme Bohic. 198.67.00.26.

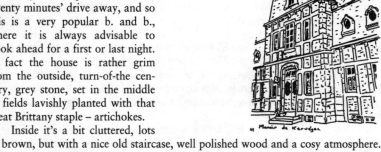

The main attraction here is the
proximity to the port of Roscoff,
twenty minutes' drive away, and so
this is a very popular b. and b.,
where it is always advisable to
book ahead for a first or last night.
In fact the house is rather grim
from the outside, turn-of-the century, grey stone, set in the middle
of fields lavishly planted with that
great Brittany staple – artichokes.

Inside it's a bit cluttered, lots
of brown, but with a nice old staircase, well polished wood and a cosy atmosphere.
The comfortable old-fashioned rooms all have private bathrooms; I liked No. 3 best
(320f) or perhaps No. 6 at 300f. Views of the sea if you peer hard. Other rooms
from 260f.

COATÉLAN. 29640 PLOUGONVEN

7 km SE of Morlaix by D109 direction Plourin-les-Morlaix, then Plougonven, then follow arrows to Coatélan. Totally unspoiled countryside not far from the lovely valley of the river Touffleuch and conveniently near Morlaix.

La Grange de Coatelan (S)
Charlick and Yolande de Ternay. 98.72.60.16.
cl. from November to Easter.

An old grange tastefully converted by a young couple into a b. and b. and crêperie. Strong colours – bright blue paintwork and even the beams painted pink – brings cheerfulness to the old grey stone. Two rooms up in the rafters, modern furniture, baths, for 230f.

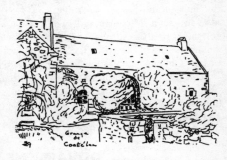

The crêperie is a delight – the long room with good views over the Monts d'Arrée has a huge chimney and open fire over which grills are prepared in the evening, but its most striking feature is the hull of a boat, painted smart blue and white, which serves as a bar.

This would be a good choice for a family, since the de Ternays (who speak English) have young children themselves and because the evening meal could be eaten *in situ*. Two nights minimum.

COMMANA. 29450

25 km SW of Morlaix. Not easy to find – the easiest route is the N 12 to Landivisiau, D764 to Sizun, D30 to St. Cadout, then 2 km on the right, signed Commana. Commana itself is an isolated village in the foothills of the Monts d'Arrée, a strange, wild region of rock and heather, rising abruptly from the surrounding flatness. Roc Travézel offers a rare panorama, somewhat Scottish, somewhat Greek islands, intensely Breton, and the natural home for many legends. Look out for wills o'the wisp. Even more important look out for the fine *enclos paroissial* in the churchyard. The chambres d'hôte in fact is nearer St. Cadout; nearby is a huge reservoir, the Barrage de Drennec, with sailing and wind-surfing. Super picnic-territory.

➤ ### Kerfonedic (M-S)
M. et Mme Le Signor. 98.78.06.26.

A gem. The hamlet is of very old stone walls, lichen-covered, sleepy, intensely quiet, superb views of lovely countryside. You enter Kerfonedic by an ancient stone archway into a courtyard, where everything is crooked – the granite walls, the roof, the windows. Hansel and Gretel could have lived here, or some fairy folk because the air of enchantment is potent. This could only be Brittany.

Inside is just as enchanting – all that a country cottage should be, with thick walls whitewashed, masses of dried flowers and herbs hanging from the kitchen ceiling (the hub of the house), charming salon for petits déjeuners and two extremely pretty bedrooms. Real country furniture, pine, white, cotton, old lace curtains, intrinsic simplicity. Except for the plumbing – good showers in the private bathrooms. 250f.

Nice Mme Le Signor prepares a good breakfast for her guests and then helps them to decide where to eat in the evenings. Lack of any restaurants nearer than 6 km – and then only a crêperie – might be the only disadvantage I can think to this utterly delightful find.

DOUARNENEZ. 29100

24 km NW of Quimper. Powerfully fishy. No doubt that its heart lies around the harbour; the rest of the town is drab and grey but down by the water there are endless diversions. In the commercial harbour you can watch the fishing boats unloading, listen to the gulls screeching, visit the fish market in the morning. To the east of the town, connected to Tréboul by a bridge, is the river mouth, recently developed in a most enterprising way, with a parade of fishing-related boutiques, galleries, museums running alongside old fishing boats, open for public inspection. I heartily recommend a visit.

Manoir de Kervent Pouldavid (M)
Mme Lefloch. 98.92.04.90.

From the roundabout at the entry to Douarnenez take the D765 towards Audierne and keep eyes skinned for a chambres d'hôtes sign on the right soon after the first traffic light. Kervent is 2 kms up this lane.

Easily the best b. and b. option for Douarnenez visits and correspondingly popular. During a spring tour, this was the only chambres d'hôte that could not offer us a room (but I had a good look round all the same). Its situation is ideal, near the town but set in its own grounds and very quiet. Right for children, with swings in the garden.

The four guest rooms all have showers, but are otherwise quite different (240f), furnished with an eclectic selection of antique and modern furniture. Breakfast is taken in a light, airy salon or on the terrace if the weather is kind. Nice Madame Lefloch is an experienced hostess, who will help her guests profit from the local attractions. Not much English, but lots of goodwill.

KERDRUC. 29920

5 km S of Pont-Aven by D783, direction Tregunc, then D77. One of my favourite areas of Brittany, near the delightful Pont-Aven, the enchanting Belon river, and the unspoiled beaches of southern Finistère. In spite of all these obvious attractions the village of Kerdruc is untroubled by many tourists.

Pen Ker Dagorn (M)
Mme Brossier-Publier. 98.06.85.01. cl. 1/11-Easter.

Look for the sign in village (in German unfortunately!) A concrete electricity station on a kind of roundabout is the landmark. The house is down the prettiest, narrowest lane, the overhanging thatch of one house almost blocking the route.

Pen Ker Dagorn

Set in intense verdure, in a generous garden, the house is described in French as *'une belle maison de maître'* – a beautiful gentleman's residence, built for the grandparents of chatty Mme Brossier. It is certainly lovely and each room has its own delightful character, with big beams and lots of space, good bathrooms, all tastefully decorated and furnished.

Madame Brossier deplored the fact that business was so bad (while Kerambris not far away was full). The extra cost (rooms here are 240f and breakfast is an extra 30f) is probably the reason as far as families are concerned, but I would have felt 300f for two people, b. and b. in such an agreeable setting was well worth it, especially as the breakfasts, with freshly squeezed orange juice, yoghurt and homemade jams are way above average.

NEVEZ. 29920

South-west of Port Aven at Nevez take the D77 to Port Manech. Turn right to Raguenès before you go down to the port and almost immediately turn left down a small lane to Kérebris which will be signposted on the main road.

➤ ### Kérabris (S)
Mme Gourlaoen. Port Manech. 98.06.83.82.

This farmhouse is in an excellent
position away from the main road
down a private lane, a short walk
to the cliff paths across Kérabris'
fields. One mile to the nearest
lovely sandy beach. There are garden chairs and tables in a large
orchard. Mme Gourlaoen is a
young charming hostess always on
hand to help you. The six rooms,
with independent entry from an
outside staircase, are very compact

with efficient shower rooms and WC *en suite*. They look out over farm buildings
and fields. Breakfast is a real treat here, not only fresh bread and huge croissants,
but also a local speciality such as *Far Breton*, all served at a long table in Madame's
dining room. This is a wonderfully central place to stay for visiting the coast from
Concarneau to Pont-Aven. There is a super beach for children at Port Manech.
Good restaurants and a crêperie are only a mile away. There are also three large
gîtes at one end of the farmhouse, very safe for children away from the main road.
Double room 180f. Secure parking. Some English spoken.

PLONEVEZ-PORZAY. 29550
Mme Fertil Bélard-Huella (S)
98.92.50.73.

From Douarnenez on the coast take
the D107 to Plonevez-Porzay. Drive
right through the village and after a
roundabout on the other side you
will find a small side road on your
left with a chambres d'hôtes sign
which leads you to the farm Bélard-
Huella. 12 km NE of Douarnenez.
21 km NNW of Quimper.

Only a mile from the beach
this old farmhouse has been turned
into six bedrooms, three up and
three down, all *en suite* with showers and loos. One room especially is very rustic,
with a granite fireplace, as it was the original kitchen. Double room 220f. Breakfast is
taken in the new farmhouse across parking area. Two other rooms not *en suite* in
the main house are 180f. A very comfortable place to stop and not expensive. Plenty

of interesting things happening on this farm; children would have loved the new litter of piglets which were born when we stayed there.

Locranon is close and has excellent restaurants. Try the Grimaldi where a very jolly rotund patron will often join you for a coffee and chat if he has time. A lot of the locals eat here.

RIEC-SUR-BELON. 29340

Riec itself is 4 km E of Pont-Aven (Le Chatel is actually nearer the latter). Both are utterly charming, and very good reasons for finding a base in the area. Riec is a handful of cottages on the banks of the lovely winding river Belon, which reminds me of the Dart in Devon. There are sandy beaches at intervals along the river's course, trees sloping down to the water and so many twists and turns that a new surprise awaits you every few minutes. A big attraction is my favourite restaurant in the area – Chez Jacky, overlooking the water, famous for its shellfish and of course in particular the Belon oyster.

Pont-Aven can be a tourist honeypot in summer, but it is not hard to see why it should be so popular. Apart from its artistic connections with the post-Impressionists and Gauguin especially, resulting in numerous art galleries, it is an enchanting little town, through which rushes the river Aven. A kind benefactor has recently endowed it with a river walk, which involves wooden bridges crossing and re-crossing the tumultuous stream. Hand me a paintbrush someone.

Le Chatel (M)
M. et Mme Gourleöuen. 98.06.00.04.

1 km E of Pont-Aven on D783, signed to the right. A ravishingly pretty ensemble of farm buildings, creeper covered, white-shuttered, set in a colourful garden, tables and chairs all ready. The Gourlaöuens are deer farmers (ask to see the animals if you are interested) and venison terrines are sold in the house, along with other country produce, like honey and wax candles.

Le Chatel

Furnishings are in the simple rustic style that one longs to encounter more often – rough white walls, white cotton bedspreads, lace curtains, polished wooden floors. Rooms are all different, all sizeable, with good bathrooms (choose either bath or shower). One room has a mezzanine, making it suitable for three people (300f). Others cost 240f for two.

Nice Madame Gourlaouen prides herself on her breakfasts, eaten in a lovely room decorated with old country furniture.

ST-MARTIN-DES-CHAMPS. 29600

25 km SE of Roscoff. In a suburb north-west of Morlaix. Coming from Roscoff on the D58, at the first roundabout at Morlaix before going under the N12 motorway take the first exit and at the next roundabout take the third exit signposted to the Chambres d'Hôtes Kéréliza.

Morlaix is set in a steep-sided valley, where the rivers Jarlot and Queffleut join, and dominated by a giant viaduct. It's a pleasant colourful town, with many yachts tied up at its entrance. Traces of antiquity remain in steep cobbled streets and 16th century mansions like Duchesse Anne's house, one of the town's showpieces.

Kéréliza (M)
Mme Abiven. 98.88.27.18.

Situated in large grounds not far from the Morlaix bypass. This makes a very comfortable overnight stop for the Roscoff ferry. The attractive house has been tastefully renovated by the young owners and the five rooms all have very smart new shower rooms with loos. Double rooms 200f. There is a pleasant sitting room and dining room where an excellent breakfast is served. Some English spoken.

ST YVI. 29140

15 km E of Quimper on D765 towards Quimperlé. Well-situated for visits to the lovely southern Finistère coast and Concarneau, but in peaceful, hilly, forested countryside.

Kervren (S)
Odile & Jean LeGal. 98.94.70.34.

Turn left at St. Yvi and follow signs for 2½ km. Don't be misled, as I was, by thinking you've arrived when you come across a chambres d'hôte sign on a modern house on the left. This is where the LeGalls live themselves. The one you are looking for is a completely separate building up the hill on the right; it backs on to a working farm, and has spectacular views over the surrounding countryside. Although the long low building is new, I suspect it may have been built with old stone and certainly blends into the Breton scene very well. The rooms, with flowery curtains and pastel paint, are modern, cheerful and comfortable, with good showers in the

bathrooms and the owners have
made the effort to make them all
individual. 220f. A very pleasant
garden, with children's swings,
would invite breakfasting outside,
but there is also a large salon, with
open fire for less clement days. A
good safe choice.

SCAËR. 29390

32 km E of Quimper by D15 and D50. The village of Scaër, the largest for some
miles around in this sparsely populated area, is famous for the 'Celtic wrestling'
contest in late August, which must go back to time immemorial; The Coadry chapel
was founded in the 12th century by the Knights Templars; the nave is Romanesque,
the chancel 14th century and the west front 17th century.

Kerloai (S)
M. and Mme Penn. 98.59.42.60.

Take the Coray-Briec road, the D50
from Scaër, then turn left at Ty
Ru-Bar and follow arrows down
first turning on the left; 4 kms
altogether from the village.

A very jolly couple, the Penns,
who having had seven children of
their own, know how to make them
feel at home. There are childrens'
games in the garden, where tea is
served (or cider if you prefer); and
although Mme Penn does not serve
an evening meal unless really pressed there is a barbecue which guests are welcome
to use. There is also something I have never encountered before – a kiwi fruit tunnel
– an archway supporting kiwis, which feature in due course on the breakfast table.

You have a choice of room style: two are furnished with old-fashioned family
pieces and have most character, and two others are more modern; all with showers.
240f.

SPÉZET. 29540

6 km E of Châteauneuf-du-Faou by D117 or 13 km SW of Carhaix-Plouguer by D769, N164, and D17. Deep farming country, threaded by the river Aulne. Few tourists disturb the calm. Châteauneuf is a rather disappointing town but it does have a good boulangerie/general store to stock up on picnic basics; the Nantes-Brest canal is particularly picturesque just here and we found the perfect spot on its banks. (turn left before the bridge to discover benches overlooking the water) Alternatively le Relais de Cornouaille in the main street offers an amazingly good value four courses for 60f.

Pendreigne (S)
Madame Lollier. 98.93.80.32.

Turn down the road at the side of La Cremaillère restaurant in the village.

A sweet couple are Madame Lollier and her retired farmer husband. They have contrived to make two guest rooms in the attics of their grey and white stone village house (two flights of stairs must be negotiated to reach them), furnished them simply and charge 180f. The adjoining bathroom

Pendreigne

(shower) is shared, so they might be most suitable for a family. Make no mistake, this is no luxury stop – the floor covering is lino, but it and everything is spanking clean and the goodwill is so evident that a stop here is bound to be a pleasure to spirit as well as wallet.

ILLE-et-VILLAINE

BAINS-SUR-OUST. 35000

4 km from Redon on the road to La Gacilly. Redon is a delightful little town where the Nantes-Brest canal crosses the river Vilaine, making it a natural centre for the Brittany water network. A walk along the quays, especially the quay St. Jacques with its fine 18th century houses, provides the opportunity to be inquisitive about

the boats (and occupants) tied up there. The market place brims over with stalls on Mondays and there are some recommendable restaurants in the town. (see FE5). I had hoped to find a chambres d'hôtes in such an agreeable setting, but failed to do so. Here is a note from someone more fortunate:-

La Picotterie (M)
Mme Soudy rte de Gacilly. 99.71.20.86.

'Two bright cheery rooms open up to a terrace banked with hydrangeas, roses, phlox and cosmos, and lead to extensive gardens. Luxurious (but shared) bath, quiet and privacy and dear Mme Soudy, a warm hostess who took care of us like a mother – 220f. M. Soudy rushes to town at 6 a.m. to pick up fresh croissants and baguettes. We vote an arrow for it in your book!' Lilot S. Moorman.

A few more reports like that and an arrow it may well have!

LA BOUSSAC. 35120

8 km SE of Dol-de-Bretagne, by N176 and D155. Lovely green countryside.

Le Moulin de Brégain (S)
Mme Mary-Anne Briand. 99.80.05.29; fax 99.80.05.22.2.

½ km from Boussac by D155. I have to use that word again – there is no other but idyllic for the setting of this converted watermill set in a deep green valley, sur-rounded by trees, with stream running through the grounds and a lake for fishing (rods supplied). The Briands have young children themselves, so could certainly cope with other people's.

The rooms have slanting wooden roofs, making them a bit dark but they are pleasantly decorated in pastel shades which helps. Two communicating rooms are in blue and pink with bathroom between them. Two others have showers. 230f for two, 360f for four.

CHERRUEIX. 35120

7 km NE of Dol-de-Bretagne, by the D176, D80, D85. Two chambres d'hôtes here, well-signed. Cherrueix 2 km away on the coast in the Bay of Mont-St Michel is dubbed 'the capital of the *char à vents*' (sand yachts). Between the coastal road and the sea sheep, destined to become the famous *gigôt pré-salés* graze on the salt marshes.

La Croix Galliot (S)
Michel & Marie-France Taillebois. 99.48.90.44.

Cereal farmer Michel and his nice wife Marie-France opened their b. and b. in 1993 and are already taking repeat bookings for their five spotless light and bright bedrooms with showers. Leather armchairs in the salon, comforting fire, terrace and a warm welcome. 200f low season, 250f in high.

Le Hamelinais (S)
Jean Glémot. 99.48.95.26.

The renovated stone house was bought by Mme Glémot's parents as a retirement home, with the Glémots running the dairy farm; as rooms became available on her parents' demise Mme Glémot decided to open them as chambres d'hôtes. She has one room with a bath for 250f and four others with showers, from 200f, with varying accommodation to suit families, like the two with mezzanines for extra beds and a separate entrance. Open fields, swings and the farm make this a good family choice, near the sea.

DOL-DE-BRETAGNE. 35120

23 km NE of Dinan 30 km WSW of le Mont-St Michel. An ancient town that has been vastly improved by the semi-pedestrianisation of its main street; now you can stand back and admire some of the mediaeval wooden carving that adorns the buildings. La Grabotais is a highly recommended little restaurant.

Ferme de Beaurégard (S)
Baguer-Morvan. 99.48.03.04.

1 km S of Dol by D119. Nice Mme Bourdais has three spotlessly clean rooms, 1 with three beds, in her rambling 15th century stone manor house, plus a very pleasant salon for the guests' use. A useful overnight stop. 230f.

Manoir de Halouzé (S)
M. Mathias. 99.48.17.16 and 99.48.07.46. cl. 31/11 to mid-Feb.

Leaving Dol de Bretagne by the N176 to Dinan, in about 3 km turn left to Baguer Morvan on the D8. Before the village you will see a sign on the right to the chambres d'hôtes, the Manoir de Halouzé; it is further down the lane on the right.

The Manoir is an old farm house on a working cattle farm, though M. Mathias has now retired, and helps his daughter Myriam to run things. It is well away from the main roads and has extensive, roughish grounds with a large lake for fishing. The five bedrooms are delightfully rustic with old beams and matching shower rooms and loos, simply furnished and all with country views. There is a large salon where all meals are taken *en famille* at a long table. M. Mathias often barbecues in the huge granite fireplace. There are plenty of tables and chairs outside on the terrace for sunny days. The atmosphere is very easy going and homely, and there are usually some English staying. Double rooms 200/220f. Family rooms 250f for three to 370f for five. Evening meals 80f wine *compris*. Some English spoken, bikes for hire and rides in a *barouche*.

Manoir de Launay Blot (M)
99.48.07.48.

2 km out of Baguer-Morvan on the
D119, signed to the left. Built in the
seventeenth century, this was once
an imposing manor house; surrounded by its moat, it still has an
impressive approach and the proportions of the house retain their
elegance, even if the peeling paint
gives a somewhat shabby first
impression.

Inside the rooms are above
expectations – lovely and comfort-
ably furnished. The largest and nicest costs 350f, the others 300f, all with bath.
Nice, shy, young Mme Geneviève Mabile speaks good English and runs the house;
she produces an evening meal (farm produce – 100f including wine) with the help of
her mother, while husband Bernard looks after their diary herd. Pleasant atmosphere – a peaceful rural stay, well placed for ferry and beaches.

LA RICHARDAIS. 35780

5 km SW of St. Malo. Cross over the barrage and turn immediately left to find the
village high above the Rance. There is a little dinghy harbour and sailing school and
the views over the river are quite delightful.

Mme de la Heraudière (S)
26 rue du Manoir de la Motte. 99.88.65.69.

Look out for the signs opposite the
Mairie in the main road and turn
right to follow them for about 1
km.

The manoir is not very grand – just
a pleasant stone house in a residential area, with a flowery garden.
Nice Madame Heraudière has a
bright and light modern room with
shower upstairs and another bigger,
very attractive room downstairs
with two big beds and bathroom.

250 for two, 330f for four. Good atmosphere here and extremely well placed for
access to the port.

ROZ-SUR-COUESNON. 35610

4 km SW of Mont-St Michel. Well signed off D797. The area around the Mount is generally flat marshland, so it is a surprise to find the flowery village of Roz perched on a hill. This gives it a unique viewpoint of 'La Merveille' (and from here it truly is a miracle). Good picnicking possibilities on the hill winding down, with benches thoughtfully provided.

La Bergerie (S)
Mme Jacky Piel. 99.80.29.68.

On the D797. Chosen for the following reasons: situation so near Mont St Michel, easy access for the handicapped to ground-floor rooms, and the evening meals, which include some of La Bergerie's produce – foie gras. This is the Piels' other interest – raising the geese about whose enforced feeding the less said the better.

The rooms are bright and modern and cost 200f. Dinner runs from 90f-200f, including wine and depending on how much expensive foie gras you consume.

Le Val-St Rever (S)
Mme Hélène Gillet. 99.80.27.85.

Madame Gillet is a retired nurse, who says 'I do not run my chambre d'hôte for the money, but for the company'. She loves to chat to her guests and obviously enjoys her new lifestyle.

This was a lovely old family house once, and in spite of some disastrous 'modernisation', vestiges of its former style remain – look at the staircase, for example. The huge bonus is that fantastic view.

Her rooms cost 200f, or 300f for a brand new one that sleeps four, with its own terrace. There is another terrace, from which to boggle at the vista and to consume a 'copieux' breakfast. No objection raised to buying local fish, cooking it yourself and eating it here.

ST BRIAC-SUR-MER. 35800 DINARD

16 km W of St Mâlo by D168 across the barrage, then D603. My favourite seaside
resort in the area happens to have two chambres d'hôtes worthy of it. St Briac is
blessed with a variety of beaches, some just coves, some sizeable stretches of sand,
facing in virtually all directions, so that there is always one sheltered. Whichever
way you look there are vistas of rocks, islands, bays, boats, begging to be painted.
Lovely walks, lovely picnicking, either on the beach or on one of the benches along
the St Brieuc road, with super views over the water.

➤ ### The Laurel Tree (S-M)
Olivier and Helen Martin. 41 Bvd de la Houle. 99.88.01.93.
On the main road (not very main) into the village, on the right.

Looking for La Duchée I
found this one by happy chance.
An English wife with French husband, have transformed the 17 century cottage, once painted by
Signac, into a charming b. and b.
The old stone is covered in roses
and wisteria and there is a lovely,
casual atmosphere about the place,
generated no doubt by its being a
family home. (Children particularly
welcome here.) When I admired all
the cleverly-coordinated wallpapers, fabrics, friezes and bedcovers, Helen told me
that they were from M. and S! Three rooms, all delightful, cost from 225-310f
(the last with mezzanine beds), all with showers. Evening meals on reservation from
65-95f. Another winner.

➤ ### Manoir de la Duchée (M)
Jean-Francois Stenou. 99.88.00.02.

Some 1½ kms from the village. Off
the D3 on to the D5 signed Ploua-
balay, then another 2½ kms, signed
left. Easier to find than these directions would indicate, thanks to
good signing. You end up in deepest
countryside, with only the birds for
company.

Well worth the effort. This one
is a winner. A 300-years-old stable
has been converted by M. and
Madame Stenou, 'Les jeunes' as

their neighbour fondly calls them, into a picture-postcard home, covered in roses. The rooms have been tastefully decorated in country style, coronets of muslin hang over the beds, and bold colours have been cleverly introduced so that the old stone never seems gloomy; good bathrooms come with each of the four double bedrooms and one suite, 350f and worth every sou. The place exudes rural calm, but the comforts are there too. The salon is surprisingly grand.

When I was there in the spring a new breakfast room was being added on and I am confident that that will be as agreeable as the rest of the ensemble created by the talented Stenous.

Riding is available and the hosts are happy to accompany their guests on magical rides along the nearby beaches. This has to be the chambres d'hôtes with everything going for it.

ST-OUEN-LA-ROUERIE. 35460

18 km S of Mont St Michel, 25 km S of Avranches by D40. From Pontorson take the N175 and turn left on to the D97. Signed from there. Set in pleasing, wooded countryside.

Château des Blosses (L)
M. and Mme Jacques Barbier. 99.98.36.16; fax 99.98.319.32.
cl. 15/11 to 1/3.

The 19th century home of the Barbiers was the very first château chambres d'hôtes that I ever sampled. It was the hospitality and interesting experience of staying with such appealing hosts that first led me to investigate many other examples of genre.

I liked its unpretentiousness then – it may be a château but the childrens' muddy boots furnished the hall – and although those children may now be grown up, there is still an informal atmosphere.

The château stands in ten hectares of grounds, with the border of Normandy and Brittany running through, and a six hole 'swing golf' track. There are now seven comfortable bedrooms, spacious, light and elegantly furnished, with bath and loo, costing from 550-800f. Breakfast, featuring home-made conserves, farm butter and fresh eggs, is a *petit déjeuner gourmand* as M. Barbier puts it. Book before 2 p.m. for dinner, costing from 220f depending on the wine, which is included in the deal.

ST PIERRE-DE-PLESGUEN. 35720

13 km E of Dinan by D794 and N137. Take the St Pierre-de-Plesguen exit, turn right towards village, turn left on to D10 for 2 km. Do not get confused by two other chambres d'hôtes signs on the same road. It's a very pretty drive at the edge of a forest.

➤ Le Petit Moulin du Rouvre (M)
Mme Annie Michel-Québriac. 99.73.85.84.

There's no doubt that there's something very romantic about old water mills. The first time I visited Le Petit Moulin for FE5, some eight years ago, there was a honeymoon couple in the next bedroom and now I find a photographer busy taking wedding photographs of another bride and groom. Undoubtedly the setting for the converted 17 century mill is highly photogenic, fronted by a huge lake, with vast millwheel still intact.

The file has been unanimously enthusiastic about the Petit Moulin and Mme Québriac's welcome. She's been doing b. and b. for eighteen years now so she should be pretty good at it. Her evening meals have been particularly well received and I can understand why. She describes her cooking as 'familiale' but that's a bit modest. The menu on my last visit was soup made from her own vegetables, rabbit terrine, fish with beurre blanc sauce and apple tart. For 110f.

The rooms are small, cozy and extremely comfortable, each with a private bathroom. The furniture is mostly antiques, with colourful plates on the stone walls, and a big salon for the guests' use. With a strong track record, Le Petit Moulin comes highly recommended, but make sure you book – it's now in plenty of other guidebooks.

ST SULIAC. 35430

I. et V. 9 1, S of St. Malo by N13i7 and D117. A delightful village of old stone houses tumbling down to the river. On the water's edge is a favourite restaurant, La Grève, facing west, the ideal place for an evening meal.

➤ Les Mouettes (M)
Mme Isabelle Rouvrais. Grande Rue. 99.58.30.41; fax 99.58.39.41.

The Grande Rue is not very grande and no one need worry about traffic fret in this sleepy hamlet. Les Mouettes is one of my favourite chambres d'hôtes, partly because of its extremely pleasant young owner, Mme Rouvrais. She has furnished the old grey blue-shuttered house with cheerful bright colours and modern carefully-chosen furniture that co-habits well with the antiquity.

She has one room suitable for the handicapped with double bed, three more double bedded rooms and one with twins, all with private bathrooms. The standard throughout is high and the atmosphere is excellent. The price of 290f is well justified for this very special b. and b. in a delightful situation.

MORBIHAN

AURAY. 56400

As Auray is a small town it is easier to stop and ask in the town for the rue de Pontneuf, which is on the north-west side of the town. You will find the chambres d'hôtes well signed halfway along the road.

Les Evocelles (?)
M. Muet. 24, rue du Pontneuf. 97.56.42.03.

A pleasant modern house in a residential area of Auray. Five functional rooms, all of which have *en suite* bath, shower, wc, TV and a pleasant suburban outlook. There is a swimming pool in the small garden, which could be a plus in hot weather. A rather impersonal atmosphere, as one rarely meets the owners, a maid receives one on arrival, and serves a very good breakfast in the morning, shared

with other guests. A quiet place to stay, at a reasonable price. Parking can be a little tight if all rooms are occupied. No evening meal. Double room 190f.

ELVEN. 56250

16 km NE of Vannes by N166. Vannes is a delightful town on which to centre a holiday that could combine a lot of water, inland and marine, with unspoiled countryside and urban delights like good restaurants, shops and market (Wed. and Sat.). The canalised waterway from the lovely Gulf of Morbihan drives into the heart of the town, lined with masts and rigging, so that the charm of the place is immediately obvious. It becomes increasingly so as you progress to the main square, full of café tables, and then through the 17th century St. Vincent's Gate into the shade and calm of the mediaeval town. Lots to see here, lots to admire, lots to photograph, all flowery, extremely pretty, easily accessible from Elven.

Kergonan (M)
Francoise and Jacques Parioleau. 97.53.37.59. cl. Feb.
"Kergonan is tucked away at the end of a lane with several acres of woods surrounding a river. What a find! Four rooms, each with own entrance and bathroom. Civilised plumbing and good shower. Breakfast – a pot of coffee each, four different breads, a slab of real butter, plus home made jam. Dinner 77f exclusive of drinks. All the guests eat together at one table, making for fascinating Anglo-French-Italian conversation. Menu:- Artichokes stuffed with crab, magret de canard with honey sauce, poire Belle Hélène and cassis sorbet. Every evening a different free apéritif was offered, from Kir to Pommeau. In the old barn dining room Jacques cooked tuna steaks on an enormous stone fireplace. If this is a rave notice, forgive me, but it was remarkable. One of those places you are tempted to keep to yourself. Françoise (the wife) keeps her three children firmly out of the way so that there is no danger of them intruding on guests' comfort." Sandi Williams.

Not a lot to add to that, except that two double rooms have shower, one double on the ground floor has bathroom, and one room for four to six on the first floor also has a bathroom. Prices are 250f for two, plus 50f for each extra person.

GUIDEL. 56520

11 km SE of Quimperlé. An ideal situation, only a short drive from the coast. The chambres d'hôte is actually four kms N of Guidel, near the Forest of Carnouet.

Ty Horses (M)
M. and Mme Hamon. Route de Locmaria. Le Rouho. 97.65.97.37 or 98.96.11.45
Take the Guidel exit from the Nantes-Brest autoroute, follow signs on right 'Locmaria-Guidel', turn left at T junction, and at 300 metres look for sign on right.

A large luxurious modern house with thatched roof. The horses in the house's name refers to the Hamon's main occupation – a stud farm, with twenty horses when I was there.

The guest rooms, named after Breton islands, are in a separate building from the main house, modern, cheerful and spotless. They are all different, some twin beds, some double, and with individual colour schemes – 250f. Breakfast is taken in a room with big glass windows making the best of the view of the countryside, or indeed outside on the terrace, weather permitting. Scattered under the trees in the garden are plenty of expensive recliners and tables, indicating a real concern for guests' comfort and relaxation. I like this one very much.

JOSSELIN. 56120

56 km N of Vannes by N166. A pleasant little town, dominated by its massive castle, half palace, half fortress, whose turrets reflected in the river Oust far below feature on many a 'Come to Brittany' poster. Wander behind the castle grounds to find old slate-roofed houses, shops and bars or take a walk along the river bank. You can hire a boat from here for a day, a week, a month.

➤ ### La Carrière (M)
M. and Mme Bignon. 8 rue de la Carrière. 97.22.22.62.

From the centre of the town follow the Pleyel signs and then La Carrière is signed up the hill, a luxurious white villa built by M. Bignon, a retired vet. He found the lovely mirror and four carved doors that now embellish the entrance hall in a ruined chateau in Finistère, and designed the lofty galleried hall around them. A grand piano and unique Celtic harp stand there, available for any guest with the nec-

essary talent to play. In the lovely salon, looking down over the extensive sloping garden to the town below is a vociferous orange canary in a white cage.

It's an elegant house, whose rooms are all large and light, with white, chequered floors. The six guest rooms, all with excellent bathrooms, represent good value for 340f with bath, 290f with shower; two children cost an additional 160f. Breakfast, eaten on the extensive terrace or the salon, is something special – fresh squeezed orange juice, home-made jams and croissants from a pâtissier to whom nice M. Bignon drives expressly every morning: 'The croissants in the town are not made with butter'. The Bignons are pioneer chambres d'hôte hosts, chalking up fourteen years' experience and speak good English. Their home is a highly-recommended choice, good value for such comfort in an interesting town.

LARMOR PLAGE. 56260

3 km S of Lorient by D29. The village still has an appealingly unsophisticated air about it, in spite of Larmor's popularity as a dormitory suburb for the Lorientais, and the new development along its southern beaches. This has opened up a new promenade of restaurants and bars, and it is indeed very pleasant to sit here, catching all the sun and dipping into the water whenever feasible. This beach is fine sand, as is the original town bay, curving round to face the fortifications of Port Louis across the estuary. Spare time to visit the Gothic church, with some remarkable 16th century Apostle statues in its side porch.

Villa les Camelias (M)
M. and Mme Allano. 9 rue des Roseaux. 97.65.50.67.
From the town follow the Route de Kerpape, which becomes the rue des Roseaux. The house is on the right.

Les Camelias is well named – when I visited in spring the shrubs surrounding the house were studded with exotic pink and red blooms. It's a lovely garden altogether, ideal for recuperation after a hard day on the beach. The white, modern house is much bigger than it would seem from first impressions – from the road it looks like a bungalow. Two guestrooms have french windows opening directly out on to the lawn – good for the handicapped – and have baths – 240f; those upstairs, slightly smaller, have showers and are more rustic, at 210f or 220f, but all are charming, fresh, and comfortable.

Mme Allano makes every effort to please her guests and I thoroughly recommend a stay here, particularly for a family, who could have the buckets and spades in action within ten minutes.

LOCQUELTAS. 566390 GRANDCHAMP

10 km N of Vannes by D767, then north on D767. Well signed from here deep into the countryside.

Chaumière de Kerizac (M)
M. and Mme Cheillestz-Maignan. 97.66.60.13; fax 97.66.66.73.
The old stone farmhouse with thatched roof forming eyebrows over top windows, garden tumbling with roses, makes as pretty a picture as you could wish. Inside is just as good – a vast salon with massive beams, huge, open fireplace, polished slate floors, rough stone walls, lovely antique furniture, lace cloths on tables loaded with objets d'art, souvenirs of time spent in Morocco and Indo-China.

The two big rooms, approached by an old stone staircase outside the chaumière, are dominated by stretchers of old black beams, old furniture, quite lovely. Not quite so impressive, but still of a high standard, is another with separate entry in an adjoining building. All have good bathrooms.

I didn't find mother and daughter (who helps with the organisation) too friendly. The *chaumière* is already very well known and in all the guidebooks. The three bedrooms are often full and Madame said that she already had enough customers, so that she was going to put prices up 30f (one of the very few who was not holding prices until the recession eased off). But this is not the general view and I should very much like to know what kind of *accueil* is offered to residents.

Chaumière de Kerigac

PLUVIGNER. 56330

11 km from Auray by D768. A hilltop village with 12th century church dedicated to Our Lady of the Nettles (must be a history there).

Chaumière de Kerreo (M)
Nelly and Gérard Grèves. 97.50.90.48 and 97.50.90.69.
At Pluvigner take the D102, direction Languidic, then follow the chambres d'hôtes signs.

I found this one by accident. Quite lost in a maze of country lanes, looking for Le Cosquer Trélécan from what proved to be the most obtuse directions, I came across another sign. A happy chance, because this one is a treasure. Apart from the fact that it is an extremely pretty thatched 16th century cottage, with decorative old beams, big log fire and pleasant garden, the big bonus is that Gérard is a professional cook. He used to be chef at the prestigious Moulin des Ducs and was also an instructor at the hotel school, so you can rely on eating well here, not only at breakfast (nothing plastic – crêpes, eggs, real butter and home-made jams) but also at dinner, when he offers a *repas du marché*, on reservation, for a modest 80f, up to 150f if the guests want expensive fish.

He and Nelly have been in the b. and b. business for only two years, and are still in the first throes of enthusiasm (always a good bet). Their three bedrooms with showers are well fitted and country-pretty. 250f. Gérard was building a new terrace for summer lazing while I was there, which should be ready by now. For the more active he tells me that there are several good golf courses nearby.

Le Cosquer-Trélécan (M)
Bernard and Françoise Menut. 97.24.72.69.
Even deeper countryside, even prettier *chaumière*. Françoise is an antique dealer, so there are plenty of 'Brocante' signs to follow. An old barn on the property is her storeroom and if, like me, you are tempted to buy (gilt mirror, old lamp) this might

not be a cheap stop (but a good-value one nevertheless).

The cottage has a lovely, big-beamed salon with gallery, and three guest-rooms, all naturally enough furnished with well-chosen antiques. 250f for two people or 350f for a suite of two adjoining rooms, sharing bathroom.

Gentle, kindly Bernard, whose hobby is bee-keeping, speaks such slow, perfect French that even beginners should comprehend. Françoise serves excellent breakfasts to the strains of classical music.

ROCHEFORT-EN-TERRE. 56220

33 km NW of Redon by D775, then D774. A candidate for the title of Brittany's prettiest village. Peacefully pedestrianised, steeply cobbled, ancient grey stone houses, boutiques, restaurants and bars, all hung about with flowers. A tourist honeypot perhaps but still a very agreeable one. I recommend the Café Breton, a good crêperie in an old wine cellar.

Château de Talhouët (L)
Jean-Pol Soulaine. 97.43.35.04.

Take the D774, direction Malestroit, from Rochefort and the château is signed after 4 kms on the left. Drive down a long alley of pine and beech trees to find this severe, granite, Breton chateau, which Jean-Pol rescued from dereliction and restored to a new life as a chambres d'hôte/hotel. When I asked him which hat he preferred to wear, he said 'Both'. Certainly his restaurant is highly professional and well-known in the area for its fine cooking and elegant place settings in the lovely, blue dining room.

The bedrooms are all very different, from 550-950f, including an excellent breakfast. Their tall windows are hung with bright chintzes, relieving the sombre grey and the bathrooms are definitely de luxe. The vast salon has painted beams, pink walls and Breton figures carved on the oak mantel. Piles of international glossy mags on the coffee tables.

Lovely walks, deep peaceful countryside – an elegant retreat.

THEIX. 56450

Take the D7 from Theix across the N165 (the Berric road). As soon as you have crossed the N165, turn first left and the lane will take you to Le Petit Clerigo on your left.

Le Petit Clerigo (S)
M. & Mme Le Gruyère. 97.43.03.66.

Situated just off the Theix by-pass, on the opposite side of the road from Theix, surrounded by fields. In a modern farmhouse with independent entry at the rear of the house. Five rooms are very large with ample wardrobe space, and large shower rooms *en suite*, but are rather dull, as most face North East. Some rooms are on the first floor and the rest on the ground floor where there is also an excellent kitchen for guests use, with all amenities. Breakfast is pleasantly served in Mme. Le Gruyère's dining room. Good value at 160f, considering all the amenities offered.

LA TRINITÉ-SUR-MER. 56470

30 km W of Vannes on the Quiberon peninsula. The wide estuary of the river Krac'h, reminiscent of Salcombe in Devon, is a yachtie's heaven. Hundreds of masts align themselves in the marina, transatlantic maxis are dressed overall, and it is an intriguing pastime to stroll up and down the jetties peering down on the boats' occupants and guessing their nationalities. The town itself is new and fairly boring, with its rows of souvenir shops and bars, none of them with the benefit of afternoon sun (drive a few kms west to Carnac Plage for that), but all round are wonderful sandy bays, waiting to be discovered. On no account miss the walk around the headland from the yacht club to the point – half an hour's pure delight, with aspects of sand, rocks, river and, ultimately, sea. Le Latz is a grey stone hamlet on a finger of the river. To one side are unattractive mud flats but around the corner, where stands the Maison de Latz, there is always deep water to accommodate the bobbing boats.

La Maison du Latz (M)
Mme Nicole Le Rouzic. 97.55.80.91.

3 kms from La Trinité, very well
signed from the town. Try and beat
this one – combine an idyllic setting on the water's edge with an
extremely comfortable bedroom, a
charming, intelligent hostess in one
of the most interesting parts of the
coastline and you have La Maison
du Latz.

La Maison du Latz

Nicole is both efficient – the
modern house is spotless, the
chambre d'hôte business well run –
industrious – the almond cake for breakfast is baked before she goes to bed – and
thoughtful – nothing is too much trouble to help her guests enjoy their holidays.

Little touches abound. As well as lots of thick towels in the bathroom, there is
a dumb valet to tidy overnight clothes, the lights work and the windows open (on to
a view of river, boats and utter calm). Classical music wafts. Tea is automatically
offered if guests arrived looking in need. My downstairs room had white cane bedheads, white covers, pastel curtains and plenty of space, with adjoining bathroom.
300f. Upstairs is a suite, highly desirable for a family at 400f and two other bedrooms at 250f.

A glass verandah runs round the side of the house, and breakfast here is a treat
well worth getting up for. Apart from the excellent almond cake and the usual
croissants and bread, there are yoghurt, ham and eggs and five kinds of home-made
jam – mirabelle, fig, apricot, sweet orange and green tomato.

Nicole's evening meals are not to be missed (reserve ahead because everything
is fresh). It changes every day, but for me it was *bisque de crevettes, brochettes of
lotte and pâtisserie*. Sometimes there is a spectacular *plâteau de fruits de mer*, or
oysters. For 80f! Understandably popular and you should book weeks ahead.

WESTERN LOIRE

Départements: **Loire-Atlantique** **Sarthe**
Maine-et-Loire **Vendée.**
Mayenne
Companion guide to the area: 'French Entree 8 – The Loire'.

It is a highly confusing piece of administrative bureaucracy that half the
Loire valley should be in the region of 'Centre Val de Loire' and the other
half 'Western Loire'; just to make matters worse the latter is sometimes
referred to as 'Pays de la Loire'. Go to the tourist office in Chinon and they
cannot help you with any information on neighbouring Saumur, and vice
versa. The 'Centre' gets most tourists because of proximity to Paris and
because many of the famous châteaux are here, but in many ways I prefer
the Western Loire. The river here is more interesting. As if sensing that the
end of its journey is near, it hurries along, rather than dawdling around
sandbanks. There are islands, some inhabited, like charming Béhuard, and
small fishing villages right up to the Nantes agglomeration. The pace is
slower here, the crowds thin out, beds and meals cost significantly less. The
roads following the river are quieter, with more space, better views, fewer
lorries. Particularly attractive it the stretch between Saumur and Les
Rosiers on the south bank, and so is the Corniche Angevin, high above the
water, with lovely views down to the river and the vineyards.

If I had to pick just one base along the whole Loire it would be
Saumur, if I had to pick just one city it would be Nantes, both in this
region. The former has multiple interests – a fine château overlooking the
river, famous sparkling wine, the prestigious Cadre Noir riding establishment and the mushroom caves, to name but a few. The pedestrianisation
and restoration of the mediaeval section has been a great success, and
Saumur is now a good town, of manageable size, to cover on foot. Nantes,
again with a fine château and fascinating history, is elegant and underestimated.

The *département* of the Loire-Atlantique is still considered by many (myself included) as part of Brittany. Historically and culturally yes, admin- istratively no. Nantes certainly leans towards the Loire, but the rest is so distinctly Breton in character that I have included (the very few) chambres d'hôtes that I was able to find in the Brittany section.

The northernmost *département*, Mayenne, deserves to be better-known. It suffers from an identity problem – associated neither with Normandy nor the Loire Valley, so that many people have difficulty in placing it geograph- ically. I was surprised to find how few guidebooks even bother to mention it. However it is a pity to consider it purely as a transit area since it encom- passes some lovely green, unspoiled countryside and the river from which it takes its name flows swiftly through lush meadows. The two main towns, Laval and Château-Gontier, both on the Mayenne, are well worth a visit. The old part of Laval has some picturesque 16th century houses clustered around a rather grim 12th century château and Chateau-Gontier offers a fine Romanesque church and a pleasant walk through the old priory gardens (*le Bout du Monde*) to the narrow streets around the riverside.

Maine-et-Loire is the *département* most closely associated with the Loire, with most of the tourist attractions (and chambres d'hôtes) within its confines. The préfecture, Angers, is actually 8 kms north of the Loire, on the banks of a very short river indeed, the Maine, formed by the confluence of the rivers Sarthe and Mayenne. From the château, one of the most inter- esting in the entire region thanks not only to its position and antiquity but to the miraculous Tapestry of the Apocalypse it houses, is a magnificent view of all the watery configuration below. There are good shops and restaurants to visit on gloomy days and as this is a university town, plenty of café-activity. Angers prides itself on being the cultural centre of the region, so you can also bank on a variety of concerts and exhibitions for further interest. Saumur comes within this *département* and the final resting place of the Plantagenets – Fontevraud – both of them top priorities on any tourist's list. North of Angers the tourists fade away and the prices tumble, but there is plenty of attraction still in the rivers that flow towards the Loire – this is the best area for a boating holiday.

Sarthe too has its share of tributaries; notably in the pleasant bustling country town of Sablé-sur-Sarthe, famous for its buttery biscuits – 'sablés' – where streams of the Sarthe, the Erve and the Vaige crop up all over the place. Neighbouring Solesmes is famous for the Gregorian chant that can be heard in its elephantine abbey, where many recordings of the newly- popular plainsong have been recorded. The main city of the *département*, Le Mans, is of course most famous for the 24-hour motor race which brings droves of enthusiasts into the area for one brief frenzy, filling the

WESTERN LOIRE

■ Préfecture

■ Town

① Chambre d'Hôtes

LOIRE ATLANTIQUE (44)
Préfecture: Nantes
1 La Chapelle St Sauveur
2 La Turballe
3 Varades

MAINE ET LOIRE (49)
Préfecture: Angers
1 Andard
2 Baracé
3 Blaison
4 Champigny
5 Chaze-sur-Argos
6 Cunault
7 Durtal
8 Grez Neuville
9 La Jaille Yvonne
10 Le Lion d'Angers
11 Le Longeron
12 Montreuil-Bellay

13 Parnay
14 Fontevraud
15 La Possonière
16 Le Puy Notre Dame
17 St Lambert
18 St Lambert des Levées
19 St Mathurin-sur-Loire
20 St Remy-la-Varenne
21 Le Vieil Bauge

MAYENNE (53)
Préfecture: Laval
1 Belgeard
2 Chammes
3 Ernée
4 Gennes-sur-Glaize
5 Lassay-les-Chateaux
6 Ruillé Froid Fronds
7 St Denis d'Anjou

SARTHE (72)
Préfecture: Le Mans
1 Champfleur
2 Lavenay
3 Mareil-sur-Loir
4 Moncé-en-Belin
5 Monhoudou
6 Oizé
7 Poncé-sur-Loir
8 Pontvallain
9 St Leonard des Bois
10 Solesmes
11 St Paterne

VENDEE (85)
Préfecture: La Roche-sur-Yon
1 Chaillé-les-Marais
2 La Gaubretière
3 Les Herbiers
4 Manoir de Ponsay
5 Moreilles
6 Saint-Pierre-le-Vieux

hotel beds for miles around. I wonder how many bother to explore the mediaeval city, let alone the cathedral where Geoffrey Plantagenet married Matilda of England, the granddaughter of William the Conqueror. Their son, Henry, later to become King, was born here.

The Vendée is an area that often surprises those who believe they know all there is to know about France. Inland lies a unique watery network where the residents go about their daily business by flat-bottomed boat and the light filters eerily green through the overhanging leaves. The coast is one long sweeping sandbank, ideal for family holidays. It is a region more appreciated by the French than the British and tends to die outside their holiday periods. Consequently few chambres d'hôtes.

LOIRE-ATLANTIQUE

`LA CHAPELLE ST SAUVEUR. 44370

24 km W of Angers, exit by autoroute A11, exit Ancenis, or N23, as far as Varades. Then take D30 to La-Chapelle-St-Sauveur, then direction St Sigismond on D102. Signed on left. I love this part of the Loire Valley. The tourists all seem to turn back at Angers, leaving the little fishing villages on the river banks and green islands in mid-stream unexplored. Nantes, that vastly underestimated, fashionable, historic, lovely city, is within easy reach. The only deficiency is of chambres d'hôtes.

Château de la Jaillière (M)
Comtesse d'Anthenaise. 40.98.62.54. cl. 15/10 to 15/5.

The red-brick 19th century château was built on the site of a mediaeval *forteresse* destroyed during the Revolution. The vast grounds, family chapel and surrounding farmland are now cared for by Madame's son, diligently raking the leaves during my autumn visit.

Château de la Jaillière

The family furniture remains *in situ* and very lovely it is too – covetable carved gilt mirrors, ormulu clocks and candlesticks, stunning Louis Philippe chairs and tables; the ceiling mouldings are exquisite, the fireplaces are carved marble, the panelled doors are marvels of craftsmanship. All this rich heritage on the ground floor – salons and dining room – is there to be enjoyed by the fortunate guests, but what is more the guestrooms are just as lovely, and not at all intimidating. The wallpapers and fabrics are charming and cheerful, the bathrooms are efficient and luxurious The countess has obviously a great sense of style, so that the impression is never stuffy; one of her super bathrooms is enlivened by orange-tree tiles. Grey haired and motherly, she does all the cooking herself (dinner for more than four people, 220f all inclusive) and speaks perfect English during the cocktail hour get-together. You have only to mention her name to fellow châteaux-owners to discover how loved and respected she is. Rooms 650f, suite 850f.

LA TURBALLE. 44420

6 km W of Guérande by D99. A busy fishing port, whose harbour is always full of determined little boats. The fish market (*la Crée*) on the quay makes interesting viewing. An area full of variety: take the coast road, the D92, to discover the weird world of the salt flats, where egrets pose on white, moon-like surfaces. Roadside stalls invite you to buy bags of rough sea salt. Do so. It will revitalise the tastebuds. A few miles further and another worlds-apart option opens up. La Baule is a sophisticated oasis of luxury in the middle of a natural protected environment. Makes a change to have a drink in a lively bar or go extravagantly shopping. Beaches all round and the National Park of La Guérande, with its medieval walled town, the delightful fishing village of Le Croisic and excursions to Belle-Île are other options to consider.

There is a cluster of chambres d'hôte in Turballe with colour-coded signs to help you find the one you want. My first choice would be:

Les Rochesses (M)
Colette and Michel Elain. 58 rue de Bellevue. 40.23.31.29.

A substantial modern house standing in a large pleasant garden, with the considerable advantage of a new swimming pool. The house is sparkling clean, and the bedrooms have good bathrooms with showers 240-280f depending on season, 400-450f for a family duplex. A good south-facing terrace is ideal for breakfasts.

Nine kms north at St Molf is a newcomer to the b. and b. scene:

Kervenel (M)
M. and Mme Brasselet. 40.42.50.38.

A large, modern house, set in a
pleasant garden in a residential
area. The house is furnished with
light, cheerful colours and the three
bedrooms have good bathrooms
with showers, though I find them a
little dark because of the all-too-
common mansard windows. The
salon is well supplied with TV and
books. Could be a useful address
when the coast is full. B & B 300f.

Kervenel

VARADES. 44370

45 km WSW of Angers.

Château du Grand Patis (M)
M. & Mme Roy. 40.83.42.28. Open week ends and school holidays.

From the town of Varades take the
N23 in the direction of Ancenis; in
about 2 km you will see a chambres
d'hôtes sign to the Château du
Grand Patis on your left down a
long drive.

Le Grand Patis

The Le Roys have renovated
this lovely old château and now
have five large chambres d'hôte
rooms with very good shower
rooms. One room has an adjoining
room, sharing facilities, which is
super for children; it even has two school desks for them to scribble at. 300f for
three, 400f for a family of five. There is a double room *en suite* 250f and two rooms
with twin beds, each with a private shower and toilet on the landing–220f for two.
A very quiet night is assured well away from traffic and the extensive grounds are
ideal for small children to explore accompanied by the château chickens. Breakfast
is nicely served in the dining room or on the terrace. Evening meals 75f. Excellent

parking, English spoken, a splendid place for children and good value for the Loire. Reservation advisable.

MAINE-et-LOIRE

ANDARD. 49800 TRÉLAZE

7 km E of Angers. The address is misleading. This is not in the village of Andard but on the other side of the N147. Heading east from Angers follow the U-turn directions signed Sarrigne; after the crossroads the house is signed on the left. There is very little of interest in the immediate region, since it is hemmed in by the main road, so it is not a good choice if walking is important, but excellent for Angers and other châteaux.

Le Grand Talon (M)
Mme Annie Guervilly. 41.80.42.85.

Light years away from the busy traffic, so near and yet so far in spirit; I cannot swear that you cannot hear it if you try, but it certainly didn't worry me, so soothing was the atmosphere of rural calm in Mme Guervilly's nice 18th century creeper-covered house. She is a keen gardener and keeps the borders filled with brilliant geraniums and the lawns well mowed. Breakfast is served on the south-facing terrace whenever possible.

Le Grand Talon

The three rooms are quite different – the two up a short staircase in a wing off the main building are small and dim but very cosy, attractively furnished with antiques (Mme G. used to be an antique dealer). They have a bath/shower apiece but share a loo. I would have been very happy in either, but because we had so much luggage with us we settled for the slightly more expensive ground floor room, with an abundance of space. It is light and airy, with big floor length windows, furnished very simply, mostly in white, with two double beds.

The breakfast room, with old beams, massive stone fireplace and tiled floor is similarly spacious.

A recommended stop with particularly friendly and helpful hostess (little English but lots of goodwill). 2 doubles at 230f, one family room at 280f.

BARACÉ. 49430

8 km SW of Durtal by D68.

Château de la Motte (M)
Michel and Lucia Francois. 41.76.93.75.

The 18th century (mostly) château is set in an estate of 300 acres, handed down to Michel François from his mother's family. He finds it a full-time job maintaining the property and helping his Peruvian wife Lucia look after the p.g.s

The atmosphere is of faded grandeur – one feels the château is begging for a lot of money to be spent on it – but the rooms are comfortable, with good bathrooms and a choice of shower or bath. 3 double rooms at 400f, one family suite 550f. Dinner 120f, exclusive of wine.

BLAISON GOHIER. 49320

15 km SE of Angers. Cross the river, take the D791, turn left on to the D132 through St Sulpice and follow the signs to the village, which is only a kilometre or so from the river. It's a delightful rural ride through vineyards and sleepy hamlets.

Le Château de Chéman (M)
Mme Antoine. 41.57.17.60.

The approach to the 15th century château is through a cobbled courtyard encircled with barns and enlivened with a few scratching hens. All round are the slopes of the vineyards from whose grapes is made the excellent and unique Cabernet d'Anjou wine named after the château. It's an extraordinary colour: a very pale golden rose is as near as I can get to describing it – *ambre gris*. Quite delicious, fresh and fruity. Take some home with you as a souvenir of a most unusual chambres d'hôtes.

Château is a bit of a misnomer; this is part farm, part country house, full of old beams, steps up, steps down, winding stone staircases, massive worm-eaten oak doors, crumbling stone facade, impossible to photograph, impossible to pigeonhole.

I wrote in FE8 that I found it hard to believe that Madame Antoine was 80 years old, and I now find it even harder to believe that she is five years older now. She is still so sprightly, climbing all those winding stairs, and enthusiastic about her rooms and knowledgeable about her wines.

She accomodates her guests in three spacious suites, with bedroom, sitting room and bathroom apiece; there are brass bedsteads and washstands, but modern bathrooms with efficient showers; there is a kitchen corner, too, so knocking up your own lunch would save a bit. Downstairs guests are welcome to make use of the salon, over-furnished perhaps in the old style, but with a wonderful old white porcelain stove throwing out lots of comforting warmth.

Certainly an intriguing stop for those who want absolute peace and quiet, with the interest of a working wine château, very near the tourist belt, with comfortable rooms, presided over by a kindly hostess.

3 apartments 450f each, with breakfasts, or 1,500f a week without linen or breakfast. 1 double room with child's bed in alcove 400f.

CHAMPIGNY. 49330

32 km N of Angers, by N162 and D768. Go through the village of Champigny and take the road for Sablé. The château is signed on left after approx 3½ km. This is unspoiled farming country between the rivers Mayenne and Sarthe, relatively undiscovered by tourists, with plenty of interest – boating, châteaux, Angers, Sablé, Solesmes – all within easy reach.

➤ Château des Briottières (L)
François and Hedwige de Valbray. 41.42.00.02; fax 41.42.01.55.

Ask anyone in the château b. and b. business 'Do you know François de Valbray?' and the answer comes: 'Mais très bien, he is my friend'. François is everybody's friend, especially his guests'. A pioneer of the stately-home chambres d'hôtes he shares his acquired experience (some of it bitter, mostly lyrical) generously. His is a typical riches to rags story – the scion of an old family well endowed with châteaux, he

Château des Briottières

now cheerfully carries suitcases, lays bricks, drives a tractor, pours out drinks, writes out bills, trouble-shoots. He inherited the stunningly beautiful 17th century Les Briottières fifteen years ago and took on the daunting task of restoring its fading beauty, subsidised by p.gs. It's a never-ending mission. One year it's the stables that get the treatment, now used for wedding receptions, then the lovely *orangerie*, now converted into a charming villa and let to an English family, then the doll-sized chapel where the increasing brood of de Valbrays (five at the most recent count) get baptised, then the swimming pool, much appreciated by his guests in the long, hot summer of '94. Some welcome extra income accumulated from letting out the whole château to the film crew making *Impromptu*, the story of Georges Sand and Chopin, who made two most attractive innovations – they painted the lovely glassed-in promenade panelling in Chinese yellow and added a trellis to the verandah.

I had Emma Thompson's bedroom, 'La Chambre de Ma Grandmère', decorated since my last visit in dusky pink and almond green, with chintz canopy and curtains, pink moiré walls and pink bathroom tiles. Lovely, and along with 'La Chambre de Mon Grandpère', the most expensive room, at 900f. Another, with twin beds, decorated in pink Toile de Jouy, with marble bathroom costs 750f, as does 'La Petite Chambre Rose', where François has resurrected an old, green, claw-footed bath and lined the walls with old door panels, and there is another smaller but perfectly good version at 550f. Eight rooms altogether, all charming.

It must be hard for Hedwige to spend her evenings alone, bathing and bedding their lively children, then cooking the guests' dinner, but it is certainly true that the success of these evening meals owes as much to François' ebullient presence as to her excellent cooking. He is a natural host, whose gusts of laughter soon break down the shyest guest's inhibitions. Fourteen frequently sit round the long *faux-marbre* table and often continue the party in the salon long after François retreats, thankfully I should imagine, around midnight. 250f includes copious alcohol.

An acerbic article written by an American journalist commented on faded fabrics, cracked paint and an 'odour of cow', which I certainly didn't detect, but in common with many of the other *châteaux privés*, it is no use going to Les Briottières in search of bland luxury hotel perfection. Go rather for appreciation of a charming French family, living in a lovely building, good company and the *joie de vivre* of your host who can truthfully say, 'I'm the King of the castles.'

CHAZE-SUR-ARGOS. 49500

13 km W of Le Lion d'Angers. Take the Candé road, the D770, and the turning is on the right 3 km after Vern d'Anjou, well marked.

This is fertile watery countryside, with several rivers speeding through to join the mighty Loire. Lots of opportunities to explore them by boats hired from Le Lion d'Angers and other pleasant bases.

La Chaufournaie (M-S)
Susan and Peter Scarboro. Fax and phone 41.61.49.05.
'*We stayed here in June 1994 for five days, when they were first opened. Run by an English couple, who have converted the loft of an old farmhouse to provide comfortable accommodation, suitable for all year use. There are six double rooms with*

en suite shower-rooms and a delightful view over the surrounding countryside. The farmhouse is in a quiet spot but convenient either as a centre for exploring Angers and the Loire Valley or as an overnight stop when travelling south from the Channel ports. The price for the room and a substantial Continental breakfast was 200f, with a small supplement for guests wishing to have a cooked English breakfast. I can highly recommend this accommodation to be included in your book'. Jill Geliot.

So I went to see for myself:

The Scarboros (No, not Yorkshire but from Sevenoaks) first visited the region when their home village was twinned with Vern d'Anjou, and liked it so much that they resolved to buy something suitable for b. and b.s. Word of mouth from satisfied customers like Jill Geliot has ensured that even in their first year, without the assistance of any guidebooks, thank you very much, they have welcomed many guests from England and elsewhere, and are settling down into their new lifestyle, and enjoying it very much. The rooms are well equipped with thoughtful extras like Teasmades, and although the windows are set in the roof, there is plenty of light and space. I counted five rooms altogether, but perhaps Ms Geliot knows better. Certainly there was one larger one, at the end of the corridor, with twin beds, so I should bag that if you get in early enough. All cost 220f now, with 90f for additional beds. The English fry-up breakfast costs a mere 25f supplement, and nice, comfortable Susan Scarboro also provides a further taste of home cooking. 'Nothing fancy', she modestly disclaims, at dinner-time – 80f for four courses including *apéritif* and wine. Susan looks forward to joining her guests at the table and sorting out their excursions for the next day.

CUNAULT. 49350 CHÊNEHUTTE-LES-TUFFEAUX

6 km NW of Saumur on the south bank of the Loire. The stretch of river road between Gennes and Saumur is one of my favourite Loire rides. It is a pleasant and peaceful drive, with little mediaeval villages, like Chênehutte-les-Tuffeaux, strung along the way. Then suddenly you come across the magnificent abbey of Cunault, claimed to be 'the most majestic and most beautiful of the churches of Anjou'. I agree. It was built in the 11th and 13th centuries with massive 11th century bell-tower and 15th century tower. Thanks to the gleaming tufa stone with which it is built, its great height and wide side aisles, the interior radiates brightness and banishes gloom. Another Romanesque gem awaits a mile or so further east, at Trêves.

Beaurégard (M)
Mme François Tonnelier. 41.67.92.93. cl. 1/11 to Easter.

Beauregard

One of the very few chambres d'hôtes actually to overlook the Loire, this old manor house, built from the local pale tufa stone makes the best of the view by being built on a spur. The spacious guest rooms get the benefit of the same view. Furniture is a mix of old and new in the suite consisting of two rooms separated by a shared bathroom. 330f for two, 450f for three and 550f for four. English spoken.

DURTAL. 49430

12 km SW of La Flêche, 39 km NE of Angers. A pleasant town on the banks of the Loir, with a good view down to the river from the terrace of the 15th century château. Apple and pear orchards abound in the vicinity and the forest of Chambiers is just to the south, so this is altogether an agreeable place to halt awhile.

Château de Gouis (M)
Mme Monigue Linossier. Grande Rue. 41.76.03.04.

In the centre of the village of Gouis, virtually a suburb of Durtal, well-signposted.

A red brick 19th century château, whose grounds overlook the river. The autoroute runs very near but there is no noticeable traffic noise within the château grounds and this would provide an inexpensive, quiet base. Apart from the poodle and Alsation that is, who give plenty of warning of any possible intruders. Ring the bell and wait for Madame Linossier to come and open the big, iron gate.

Inside there are lots of plastic flowers, gilt, stained wood, red plush and space. Breakfast is served on the terrace in summer, in the over-furnished salon otherwise. Bedrooms are huge and comfortable, with river views. The bathrooms are modern with good efficient showers. None of them has a bath, but if you are allergic to showers – '*Pas de problème*' says accommodating Mme Lionissier. You use hers. Rooms 280-380f. No evening meal but there is an excellent, little restaurant, the Boule d'Or, in Durtal.

FONTEVRAUD. 49590

16 km SE of Saumur, 21 km W of Chinon. A few introductory lines is no way to describe even a small part of the treasures of Fontevraud. Buy a guidebook (or even better French Entrée 8 on the Loire!) and fill in the gaps on what should be an essential stop on every tourist's Loire itinerary. Particularly every British itinerary, since in the abbey here, dubbed the Westminster of the Plantagenets, lie four effigies that belong to our heritage – Henry II of England, his wife Eleanor of Aquitaine, their son Richard Coeur de Lion, and Isabelle of Angoulème, second wife of their son John Lackland. All most moving, especially if you get there early or late and can view them without the distraction of other tourists. Painted in faded blue and red, all individuals, Isabelle carved in wood and the others in tufa stone.

Their resting place is the largest and virtually complete ensemble of mediaeval monastic buildings in France. A whole village, in fact, within a village. Take a tour, but leave time to visit the Romanesque parish church of St Michel.

The pleasant little town has plenty of comfort stops – a well-known family hotel, a Michelin-starred restaurant, several bars and a good *salon de thé*, so a visit here can be rewarding gastronomically as well as spiritually.

More comfort is at hand if you turn off the D947 some 3 km before Fontevraud and follow the signs to:

➤ ### Le Domaine de Mestre (M)
M. et Mme Dauge. 41.51.75.87.

The monks of Fontevraud used the Domaine as an agricultural complex, and some of the weathered stone buildings round the courtyard date from the 12th century; traces of a Roman road indicate that there has been a settlement here since time immemorial. Good use has been put to the assorted outbuildings: one is now a shop selling tempting take-home souvenirs – fragrant soaps and toilet desiderata made from pure,

Le Domaine de Mestre

natural ingredients, perfuming the whole room. In another building are four rooms, smaller than those in the main building and used in winter because they are easier to heat. A 12th century chapel is now a lovely dining room, with dark, wormy beams straddling the lofty ceiling and a massive oak *armoire* presiding over all. This is where dinner is served, with lots of home-grown vegetables served as first course, along with meat or fowl, then cheese and home-made desserts. Rosine Dauge does all the cooking, farmer husband Dominique serves and daughter Marie-Amélie helps out here and in the shop. It is very much a family affair and always has been – the Domaine has been in the same family since the 18th century.

The late Laura Ashley would have been delighted to see the good use that her fabrics have been put to here. I recognized my own yellow cabbage rose pattern in the dining room and our bedroom in the annexe exploited a familiar blue and beige bird design, but it is in the main building that Rosine has had most fun, using different colour schemes in every room (with co-ordinating bathrooms), every-one a winner, spacious and gracious, furnished with antiques.

There are extensive grounds attached to the Domaine and breakfast in summer is served on the terrace looking down to the green valley. All this is very good news indeed, at a reasonable price, with all the joys of Fontevraud thrown in; the bad news is that the word has got around and it is not easy to get a reservation in high season. So be sure to book early and don't miss out on this one whatever you do. Twelve rooms: 350f. Dinner: 130f, exclusive of wine.

GREZ-NEUVILLE. 49220

16 km NE of Château-Gontier by D28. 20 km N of Angers. One of those time-warped villages, utterly delightful, with grey, sun-bleached stone houses, that one sometimes stumbles upon in France. In this case the big attraction is the river Mayenne that flows fast and wide here, over a weir. Boats are for hire, there are walks along the bank, the activity of a lock to contemplate, and a crêperie and bar make sitting, sipping, supping, watching the water, a leisurely delight. What an added bonus then to find next to the church:-

➤ La Croix d'Etain (M)
Mme Jacqueline Bahuard. 41.95.68.49.

An immaculate Directoire period house, very French, all grey and white and proving to be much bigger than one might guess from first sight. The yellow salon, embellished with an amazingly ornate grandfather clock, is huge, and a very pleasant place to sit if the weather does not suggest a seat in the garden (where breakfast is served in summer). The grounds too are surprisingly extensive – 1½ hectares, much of it river frontage.

La Croix d'Etain

Bedrooms, each with individual character, are lovely, spacious, pleasantly furnished, and like the rest of the house, look as though they had just been painted. Two have splendid river views.

I rate this one very highly as an agreeable, comfortable place to stay, in a particularly attractive village. Four rooms – 350f. Dinner 120f, excluding wine. Officially closed Nov-Easter, but Mme Bahuard is in residence throughout the year and welcomes guests in winter if they phone ahead.

LA JAILLE-YVONNE. 49220

39 km N of Angers. Turn off N162 to D189 and then D187 signed Chambellay. The château is well-signed.

An excellent location, not only for an *en route* stopover, but as a base from which to explore this gentle watery territory, where a river is never far away. At Le Lion d'Angers, 9 km south, or at Chenille-Changé even nearer, you can take a soothing excursion on the meandering Mayenne. In total contrast, the urban attractions of Angers and many of the lesser-known châteaux are within easy reach.

➤ ### Château Le Plessis (L)
M. et Mme. Benoist. 41.95.12.75; fax 41.95.14.41. cl. 1 Nov.–1 Mar.

M. Benoist is now President of Chateau Accueil, a group of château-owners who were pioneers in the aristocratic b. and b. business. Their rule is that the château must have been in the family for at least two generations. 16th century Le Plessis certainly qualifies since it has been in Mme Benoist's family since well before the Revolution, when in 1793 all the furniture except one treasured table was

burned by the rebels. However, to be able to say that the replacements date from the time of your great-great-great-grandfather is more then most of us can claim.

This continuity and the feeling that the furniture and house are there to serve the family, not to be regarded as 'antiques' permeates the atmosphere. This is a home that happens to be in a very beautiful and historic building; all is friendly and relaxed. Venerable trees and sweeping lawns, studded with primroses and daffodils whenever I've been there, surround the house and contribute to the calm. Tea on the lawn, *à l'anglais*, is a nice touch.

M. Benoist used to work for Mobil Oil, so his English is fluent and Mme Benoist is an unusually good cook, so that dinner round their large oval table, served with carefully-chosen Anjou wines is bound to be a rewarding experience. Eight rooms, all with bath, 700f. Dinner 270f.

LE LION D'ANGERS. 49220

27 km NW of Angers, by N162. The house is 2 km W of Lion d'Angers by D770, direction Candé. After the roundabout take first road on the left, past the wooden cross, then turn right after 500 metres and the farm is at the end of the road on the right.

The river Oudon flows into the Mayenne at Le Lion, so there is plenty of watery activity in the pleasant surrounding countryside, which remains largely unspoiled.

Le Petit Carqueron (M)
Mme Carcaillet. 41.95.62.65. cl. 31/10 to 15/4.

Madame Carcaillet wrote to me at the suggestion of some FE8 readers who were staying with her, and as I already had their testimony that a night under her hospitable roof would be very well spent, I was pretty sure that my visit would not be wasted.

Le Petit Carqueron

Le Lion D'Angers

The 200 year old farmhouse has been sympathetically converted to provide four bedrooms – two doubles, two twins – each with shower-room and two loos between them. Because of the shared loos Madame Carcaillet has been denied the coveted *trois epées* rating in the *Gîtes de France* categorisation and so her prices are correspondingly low – 200f. If you can live with this, (and certainly a family would have no problems) this is remarkably good value, especially as the evening meals are said to be especially good (90f, all included). What is more, there is a swimming pool at the disposal of the guests, and a pleasant garden in which to take breakfast, so it all sounds like a very good deal. More reports welcome.

LE LONGERON. 49710

18 km SW of Cholet.

La Rouillère (M)
M. et Mme Leroux. 41.46.54.20.

Almost on the border of the Vendée, Le Longeron is only 24 km from the Puy du Fou. About 800 metres from the small village of Le Longeron is the farm La Rouillère, in a lovely position with garden tumbling down to the river Sèvres Nantaise, where you will find a rowing boat at your disposal.

Hidden well off the main road this pleasant, modern farmhouse has two guest rooms (really studios) with excellent amenities, on the ground floor facing south, with independent entry through patio doors. One with single beds has an adjoining shower and toilet, and a kitchen and dining area with full essentials for self-catering. The bedroom has TV and a phone with an outside line. On the patio your own garden table and chairs. Room 210f for two.

The second room has a double bed with an alcove cupboard large enough for a child's bed, small shower and loo and a smaller kitchen alcove, patio furniture for 200f. The view across country is very pleasant.

Evening meals available at 65f all drinks *compris* with home-made aperitif, should you want a change from self-catering. Best of both worlds here.

Swings for children, free fishing in the river from the boat, even use of Madame's washing machine. A really attractive, sunny couple of rooms with so many amenities. Booking necessary here at all times. Three gîtes also on the premises.

MONTREUIL-BELLAY. 49260

18 km S of Saumur by N147. A most interesting small town, thanks to its site high above the river Thouet, almost surrounded by 13th century fortifications, and the imposing castle that reflects its turrets in the water far below. Montreuil refers to the town itself and Bellay to the belligerent family who originally owned the castle.

Demeure des Petits Augustins (M)
M. et Mme Guezenec. Place des Augustin. 41.52.33.88. cl. 1/11–1/3.
A lovely 17th century *hotel particulier* tucked away in the centre of the town behind an old square. It's all a little shabby nowadays, but the bones are still as elegant as ever. Nice, plump Mme Guezenec and her husband bought it in a totally dilapidated state in 1991 and are slowly restoring it – a formidable exercise, helped by the income from the chambres d'hôtes. Its structure forms three sides of a square, courtyard enclosed, small garden beyond. Very French – grey slate roof, white shutters, grey stone walls. Access to three of the guest rooms is by a magnificent, curving, white stone staircase, one in each wing. Not for the infirm. Decoration is a bit hit and miss, with some rather fierce colours, but the rooms themselves are lovely, with beams and some antique furniture, like the 'bâteau' beds. The nicest is 'La Grande', available only after Easter (used by the family until then).

No evening meal, but the Relais St. Jean in the town is within walking distance. Mme Guezenec makes up the deficiency by supplying particularly good breakfasts, served in the family's nice old dining-room, or in the courtyard. Three double rooms, one ground-floor double with kitchenette, 250f for two people, 60f for each additional bed.

PARNAY. 49400 SAUMUR

6 km SE of Saumur on the south bank, D947. I generally prefer taking the south bank route along the river and between Saumur and Montsoreau it is particularly pleasant and uncrowded, with views of the water unimpeded by high banks or incessant *camions*. The cliffs are the white tufa stone of the region, riddled with caves, put to practical good use by the wine merchants, who find the constant temperature ideal for storing their produce. One such is:

➤ ### Domaine du Marconnay (M)
Mme Goumain. 41.67.60.46; fax 41.50.23.04. cl. 15/11–1/3.
'*Dans un cadre troglodytique*', says Mme Goumain's card. And certainly just behind the Domaine are the caves, cool in summer, warm in winter, where families have lived for generations. M. Goumain uses those on his property to store his wine, *dégustations* of which are available to the public. Naturally enough, these are the wines that are offered at the dinners that Mme Goumain serves to her guests.

There is a cool, green garden behind the property and an unexpected swimming pool, so, what with the pleasant breakfast-room and the bright and cheerful bedrooms with luxurious bathrooms, a husband who speaks fluent English, ideal situation, and a reasonable price tag, I call this one a winner. Two double rooms, one room for three and one for four, at 360f for two people, plus 30f each for breakfast. Dinner 80f exclusive of (very reasonably priced) wine.

LA POSSONIÈRE. 49170

On the North Bank of the Loire, 15 km SW of Angers. On the D11. The easiest way to find La Possonnière, coming from Angers, is to take the N23 (direction Nantes) to St Georges-sur-Loire, then follow the directions to Chalonnes, turn left to Possonière, then left again for 1.5 km.

This is a lovely un-touristy section of the Loire, where the river senses that its destination is near and starts flowing fast and free, round numerous islands, some inhabited, some mere sandbanks. There is a sad deficiency of chambres d'hôtes (chicken and egg situation – no tourists, no beds), so I was pleased to find:

La Rousselière (M)
Mme Jeanne Charpentière. 41.39.13.21. cl. Nov.
Set in ten acres of the family estate (plenty of space for a good swimming pool) is this 19th century manor house. Four good bedrooms, all with bath and loo, cost

290–400f. There are plenty of gourmet restaurants around, but the temptation would be stay put and enjoy Madame Charpentier's presentation of a 90f dinner, served by the pool, on the terrace or in the pleasant dining room. More reports needed, please.

La Possonnière   La Rousselière

LE PUY-NOTRE-DAME. 49260

4 km W of Montreuil Bellay, 20 km S of Saumur. From Montreuil Bellay take the Thouars road, the D938, and after 4 km turn right on to the D158, direction Passay; the mill is signed from here. The drive is through pleasant wine country.

Le Moulin de Couche (M)
M. et Mme Bergerolle. 41.38.87.11; fax 41.38.86.99.

The river Thouet divides the *départements* of Sèvres and that of Maine-et-Loire. The old flour mill stands on the banks of the latter. In 1993 Anny and Jean Bergerolle started the conversion into a comfortable chambres d'hôte in the actual mill and a restaurant in the old stables. The rooms have lovely views over the tranquil river, flowing to join the Loire near Saumur. The rooms are freshly decorated with flower themes like *Hortensia*, *Violettes* and *Bleuets*, with a mixture of old and new furniture, some with showers, some with old-fashioned baths, some with large, new ones, some adjoining to form suites.

The situation is perfect – especially for breakfast on the sunny terrace or under the willow tree – and there are relaxing walks along the river banks, far from any sound more disturbing than birdsong and bubbling water.

The restaurant, *La Ponote*, is very pretty indeed, decorated in lilac blue and white with a mezzanine floor looking down on the activity below, and a huge, raised fire, where grills are cooked in winter. Four doubles at 190f, suites at 340 and 400f. Breakfast 30f. The restaurant has menus from 90f-165f.

ST LAMBERT. 49400 SAUMUR

1½ km from Saumur. Take the N147 towards Angers, cross the Loire and the railway and turn left (Ave. des Maraîchers). 300 m from railway station you will find the house on the right.

This is really a suburb of Saumur, extremely useful for visiting that most delightful of Loire towns. Readers of FE8 will known it is my No. 1 favourite and

first choice to stay and explore in both directions. In fact on every visit I like it more
and find new attractions. The pedestrianisation has been a great success, the castle
is superb, the Cadre Noir and mushroom-caves remain prime excursions and now
the town's one shortcoming – lack of good restaurants – has been remedied. So
finding a chambres d'hôtes with good access to the joys across the water became a
priority.

La Bouère Salée (M)
Catherine and Emmanuel Bastid. Ave des Maraîchers. 41.67.38.85.

The young, extremely pleasant
Catherine and Emmanuel run a
wholefood shop in town and
Catherine is a naturopath, so you
can be sure of getting a healthy
breakfast here, consumed in the
sprawling family kitchen. They
have four attractive energetic children, so don't go expecting the
house to be either immaculate or
particularly tidy. Go rather for a
friendly, intelligent, helpful atmo-
sphere, probably best suited to families; there is a large garden and numerous
assorted creatures, feathered and furred, to be petted and stroked in the plot next
door.

There are two suites with showers for 250f for two, or 320f for three.

ST LAMBERT-DES-LEVÉES. 49400

Saumur 3 km W of Saumur on the north bank of the Loire. From Saumur cross the
river, but don't turn immediately left on to the river road. Take the next turning,
past the railway station, the D229. 3 km further on look for the chambres d'hôtes
sign on the right.

➤ La Croix de la Voute (M)
Helga and Jean-Pierre Minder. 41.38.46.6.6. cl. Nov-Easter.

Look no further if you seek a chambres d'hôtes with enthusiastic English-speaking
hosts, stylish comfortable rooms, within easy reach of the Loire and Saumur, with a
swimming pool thrown in, and all for a reasonable price.

German Helga, married for 25 years to French Jean-Pierre, opened the four
rooms in the 15th century wing of this mostly 17th century house in 1990. Since
then the Minders have continuously renovated and improved the property. Not only
is the comfort exceptional but the taste is irreproachable – the character of the old
manor house respected but with colourful touches to enliven the old stones. The

rooms are all quite different and it is obvious that Helga has had great pleasure in choosing the decor for each one. The largest boasts a four-poster bed, massive stone fireplace and old *armoire*. Antique furniture throughout and low beamed fire-places contribute to the atmosphere of times gone by (but with modern plumbing). The Minders like noth-ing better than to see their guests stretch out on smart recliners by

their pool. They also like to see them mellow. So in each room is a *seau à champagne* – an icebucket, so that the guests can buy the local fizzy wine (who could resist?) and bring it chilled to drink by the poolside. Conviviality guaranteed. This is just one of the personal touches that make staying here such a pleasure. Jean-Pierre, who works in Paris three days a week, supports his nice, smiling wife for the rest of the time and sees to it that the garden is full of flowers and a pleasant place to sit for breakfast. He is readily available to help plan the guests' day and advise on itineraries. Four rooms: 500f with bath, 400f with shower. Breakfast 35f. No dinner offered because there are so many restaurants in nearby Saumur or Les Rosiers to choose from.

ST MATHURIN-SUR-LOIRE. 49250

11 km SE of Angers, 22 km NW of Saumur, on the north bank of the Loire.

Verger de la Bouguetterie (S)
Claudine and Christian Pinier. 118 rue du Roi René. 41.57.02.00; fax 41.57.31.90.

1 km from St Mathurin heading west.

There must be some initial doubts about traffic noise since the Pinier's pleasant 19th century house is right on the road, but nice young Claudine assured me that there is little movement at night, definitely no lorries, and that the double glazing is most effective. That worry overcome, the advantages of actually overlooking the river prevail. There are surprisingly few establishments in this book that can actually claim to be within view of the mighty Loire.

The house is pristine, with pleasant, faded, old-fashioned furniture of the brown and beige persuasion, with several attractive original features, like the moulding on the salon ceiling and its marble fireplace. In spite of coping with two young children, Christine runs an efficient operation and finds time for the extra touches like home-made jam and apple juice for her guests' breakfasts, and serving copious evening meals, supplemented by fresh veg. from a pleasant garden at the rear. Behind this again are extensive apple and pear orchards, tended by Christian.

All the bedrooms are spacious and light; You have the choice of overlooking the river or the guaranteed calm of one at the back. Four rooms, 240-300f. Dinner 90f including wine.

ST RÉMY-LA-VARENNE. 49250

23 km NW of Saumur, 18 km SE of Angers On the south bank. Take D952 to the village, where the chambres d'hôtes is signed.

This is a lovely unspoiled stretch of river, certainly to be preferred to the opposite north bank. St. Rémy is one of the many quiet villages that gets on with its daily business undeterred by tourists.

Château des Granges (M)
M. Jean du Réau. 41.57.02.13.

In winter open by reservation only. The château was actually built in the early 19th century, but looks older with its classical lines and weathered stone. Its drive slopes down to extensive grounds, spattered with celandines and daffodils when I was there, with the iris just beginning to show and evidence of last month's snowdrop patches. A spectacular magnolia was promising great things. It's all very peaceful with views of a stretch of water and a stream flowing through the grounds. 'Bring your fishing rod next time', said M. du Réau, 'plenty of pike and eels'.

He was born in this château and his family have been in residence ever since it was built, so it's not surprising that he welcomed the chance to restore and redecorate it to welcome guests. His taste is unerring, with the advantage of plenty of priceless family antiques to supplement the furnishing. Lovely, polished Empire-style *bâteau* beds are the centrepiece of one room; polished chests and *armoires* are practical as well as highly decorative. This may be a bachelor household, but there is no shortage of 'little touches'. There are bibelots and family photographs and lots of flowers.

Breakfast is eaten informally, sitting at a long wooden table in a kitchen that looks as if it has been designed for a glossy magazine as the ideal 'country kitchen look'. Copper pans glow decoratively and there are definitely no plastic cupboards. An out-of-the-ordinary b. and b. but one that is very much to my taste.

Two double rooms with shower; one double with bath, shared loo: 380f.

LE VIEIL BAUGE. 49150

18 km S of La Flêche by D938. At Bauge take the D61, signed Angers, to Le Vieil Bauge. The house is signed after 2 km. Deep farming country.

La Chalopinière (S)
John and Vanessa Kitchen. 41.89.04.38.

If you like the idea of sharing in a family's life in France but find the French hard going, stop trying too hard and stay with English folks, like the Kitchens, from

Southsea. John is a sailing man, who finds no problem combining his duties here on the small farm with delivering the occasional boat anywhere in the world. He and Vanessa and their daughter wouldn't swap their life here with a more conventional one back home, and thoroughly enjoy making new friends among their guests. When I visited in the spring the lambs were just making their appearance, the

pond was well populated with geese and ducks and there are pigs and chickens too, so this would be an appealing stop for a family.

The flavour of their chambres d'hôtes is simplicity and friendly homeliness. Breakfast is eaten at the scrubbed kitchen table; their living room, with plenty of English books, is available for guests' use and the country-style bedrooms have white-painted beams and washbasins. The bathroom is shared. Three rooms at 180f for two. Dinner 55f, featuring home-grown produce.

MAYENNE

BELGEARD. 53440

8 km SE of Mayenne.

Le Closeau de Brive (S)
Mme Le Lièvre. Ancien Bourg. 43.04.14.11.

Right in the country outside Mayenne; from Belgeard take the direction of Ancien Bourg and (down a side lane) you will pick up a sign to this chambres d'hôtes, a very pretty little cottage sideways on to the road overlooking a pleasant garden of lawns and trees, with swings for children.

Mme Le Lièvre is so kind and creates such a homely atmosphere; it is the ideal place for a lone traveller to stay.

There are three rooms in all, two reached by a staircase inside the cottage. One is carpeted having two large single beds and a large bathroom. The other room has a lino floor, double bed and shower cubicle but the loo is on the landing. However, this second room can interconnect with a most attractive single room which has it all – shower, toilet and a kitchenette and delightful views over the countryside. It is reached by an outside wooden staircase. Rooms are 170/180f. Evening meals with your hosts are possible, at 65f, wine *compris*; but Madame likes advance warning. Advisable to book ahead here in any case – it is a popular stop.

CHAMMES. 53270 STE SUZANNE

35 km W of Laval towards Le Mans. Take the Vaiges exit from the autoroute A81. Chammes is 2 km from the village of Vaiges.

The medieval village of Sainte-Suzanne, besieged unsuccessfully by William the Conqueror in 1083 is only 5 km away and the whole of the Coëvrons area of the Western Loire is on your doorstep for horse trekking or rambling with a guide.

Le Chêne Vert (S)
M. and Mme Morize. 43.01.41.12.

A useful stop just off the autoroute.

Somewhat startlingly new buildings built round a courtyard in flat farming country. The Morizes are cereal farmers, now relishing their new role as hosts. Their swimming pool, an unusual feature in a rustic b. and b, was only built in 1993; guests are welcome to use it. A maid, cleaning rooms, told us they were *complet* except for the dormitory which we

Le Chêne Vert

could have if we like. Rather expecting to have to sleep with others, like a *Gîte d'Étape*, we were pleasantly surprised to find we could have the eight-bedded room to ourselves, complete with excellent shower and w.c. Both room and bathroom are thickly carpeted and fitted with wall moquette. I think we hit the jackpot. All the rooms are very modern and extremely functional with large bath towels, flannels and soap, in fact all the best hotel amenities with a chambres d'hôtes setting. Evening meal is taken at a long table 70f each, cider *compris* but aperitifs and wine charged. The local aperitif is 'Kir Duchesse' (Cassis with cider) at 10f a glass, and a bottle of Bordeaux is 25f. Rooms 200f. Demi-pension available at 160f per person per night if you stay longer than three days.

Another good reason for staying here would be to sample the astonishing value at a little restaurant in Ste Suzanne, the Restaurant de l'Erve. Their four-course 55f menu, including wine, is unbeatable in the region (few tourists explains the price).

ERNÉE. 53500
La Gasselinais
Catherine et Florent Gendron. 43.05.70.80.

Recommended by François de Valbry, (See Les Briottières p. 119), than whom there can be no greater expert on chambres d'hôtes.

Three rooms in a farmhouse in the Haute-Maine, with independent access, each with private shower-room. One family room has mezzanine and kitchenette. François writes that it is ideal for families, on a working farm, with comfortable rooms and charming welcome.

GENNES-SUR-GLAIZE. 53200

8 km NE of Château-Gontier by D28. An unspectacular stretch of farming country, peaceful and unspoiled; an inexpensive, calming break on the way further south perhaps.

Les Marandes (S)
Mme Mourin. 43.70.90.81. cl. last two weeks in September.

Les Marandes

Once a row of stables, now converted into the Mourins' home and chambres d'hôtes. The character has not been lost – the old stone walls and red brick window surrounds are still there and the surrounding fields are as rural as you could hope for. Bedrooms are simple, but spotless and Mme Mourin makes good use of farm produce in her evening meals and breakfasts.

Four rooms: one large room for four with two singles, one double, private bathroom and loo; two rooms for three with one double and one single with private bathroom; one room for four with two doubles with private bathroom; shared loo for the last three. 170f for two, 260f for four people. Dinner 70f.

LASSAY-LES-CHATEAUX. 53118

16 km N of Mayenne. From Mayenne take the D23 north to Ambrières le Grand. Turn right on to the D33 (to Lassay), then almost immediately left on to the D214. Follow this road almost to Mallery la Vallée. La Rajellerie is on the left just after Torcé.

La Rajellerie (S)
M. et Mme Maignan. Mallery la Vallée. Lassay-les-Châteaux.
43.04.73.43. Open all year.

La Rajellerie

Deep in the country of Mayenne is this really quiet, small farmhouse, with one end dedicated to guest rooms with excellent facilities – _en suite_ shower or bath, and a nice outlook over fields from the windows. There is a dining room and a little sitting room with TV. Outside there is a table and chairs on a pleasant, shady lawn overlooking the farm courtyard. Dinner is plentiful – four courses, 80f, but wine or cider are _compris_. Afternoon tea is charged for. Madame Maignan comes from Martinique and will produce a Créole meal given notice. M. Maignan is a farmer and rarely seen. Double room good value at 185f.

LAVAL. 53000

146 kms S of Caen, 249 kms SE of Le Havre.

An under-appreciated town, generally conceived as merely a staging post on the way between port and the Loire Valley. In fact there is much to value, particularly in the old town which clusters round the castle on the sloping west bank of the picturesque river Mayenne. The modern town centres on the huge square named after Marshal Foch, from which the main shopping streets radiate. Climb up to the courtyard of the Vieux Château, enclosed by ramparts from which there is a good view of the multi-coloured, multi-centred roofs of the old town. The bulk of the castle dates from the 13th and 15th centuries, but the windows, whose white tufa stone is carved with Italianiate scrolls, were added in the 16th century. The crypt and the keep are the oldest parts (12th and 13C). The most interesting feature of the keep is the extraordinary timber roof built in 1100 in an ingenious circular design, incorporating great beams radiating from the centre and projecting beyond the 6ft thick walls.

Take a walk along the quays on the east bank for the best overall views of Laval, across the now canalized waters of the river. The hump-backed Pont Vieux dating from the 13C also offers good views of the slate roofs, the narrow streets of half-timbered houses and the keep of the castle. Lovely walks in La Perrine Gardens, with rose garden, ponds and waterfalls.

➤ ## Le Bas du Gast (L)
M. & Mme François Williot. 6 rue de la Halle aux Toiles.
43.49.22.79; fax 43.56.44.71. cl. 1/2–30/11.

This one is special, on several counts. Although it is a rare city chambres d'hôtes, it is country-quiet by virtue of its setting in a sleepy square of dignified old grey houses and because of its surprising garden. The garden is typically 18C French, very formal and graced with no less than 85 box pyramids which the energetic M. Williot prunes himself every year. You can imagine yourself an elegantly

dressed aristocrat as you play a gentle game of croquet, or settle for more plebian boules.

Hard to choose between the four lovely bedrooms, each decorated with style and excellent taste. I like the double-bedded Chambre Jaune (550f), but the Toile de Jouy version with twin beds, at 650f, is pretty nice too. Then there's the very imposing Chambre Napoléon with three beds (supplement 250f for third incumbent) or the suite of Chambres Bleu and Verte which can be opened up for one luxurious ensemble for 1100f, or booked separately. All have outstanding bathrooms with every conceivable freebie. M. Williot is the friendliest, most accommodating, English-speaking host, who will go to endless trouble to point you in all kinds of right directions. Arrowed for all-round excellence.

RUILLÉ FROID FONDS. 53170

11 km NE of Château-Gontier by D28 and D15 or 20 km SE of Laval by N162 and D109. Take the C4 out of Ruillé, signed Bignon, and the farm is 1 km on the right.

Villeprouve (S)
Mme Davene. 43.07.71.62.

As rustic as they come (and that's pretty rustic). This is a working cattle farm, so you must expect a bit of mud around. The farmhouse is 17th century, creeper-covered, long and low. Set in 50 hectares of green and pleasant countryside. Bikes are available for exploring.

Mme Davenel has smartened up the four bedrooms with trendy innovations like coronets over the bed, but they still retain much of their country charm and

are large and comfortable. So is
the dinner she cooks, composed
entirely of home-grown ingredients.

One family room, one triple,
two doubles, all with showers;
300f for 4, 260 for 3, 220 for 2.
Dinner 70f.

Ville Prouvée

ST DENIS D'ANJOU. 53290

9 km SW of Sablé by D27 direction Champigné. Just before the village, signed on
the left. Lots of attractions in the area – Gregorian chant at Solesmes, boating on
the river Sarthe, and the agreeable little town of Sablé. St Denis itself is a flowery
mediaeval village with 16th century market halls and ancient church.

Le Logis du Ray (M)
Martine and Jacques Lefèbvre. 43.70.64.10; fax 43.70.65.53.

In the game of tracking down
chambres d'hôtes there are some
good days and some bad ones but
I've never suffered one as totally
frustrating as this. It was early
November, the last tour before
Delivery Day and the last chance to
tidy up loose ends. I targeted seven
likelies and set off in increasing
drizzle and fog, buoyed up by the
hope of adding seven amazingly
exciting new finds to the book. It

Le Logis du Ray

took all day and 170 miles and as darkness fell the tally was six visited and six
blanks. What I had overlooked was that the November school holidays often over-
ruled the landlady's assertion that she was *ouverte toute l'année*; and whereas some
were just out – shopping with the kids, leaving aggressive dogs to do the accueil bit
– others had packed up altogether and gone to see Grandmère for the week. Cyni-
cally I rang the doorbell of the seventh, Le Logis du Ray, wearily I asked if I might
see a room, unbelievingly I heard nice plump Mme Lefèbvre offering me a cup of

tea before showing me three rooms that I knew would rate very highly indeed. So if you detect a shade of prejudice here, please make allowances.

It's an old creeper-covered farmhouse, furnished with antiques (M. Lefèbvre is a man of many roles, among them that of *antiquaire* and *ebeniste*). Mme Lefèbvre has done her bit admirably, choosing cheerful stylish decorations. One room has blue and white mattress ticking fabric very successfully used on beds and sidetables, coordinating with blue paint. With good shower-room, it costs 350f for two or 480f for three. Another with four-poster and old *armoire* is decidedly Laura Ashley-esque, decorated in navy blue and white tiny flower pattern. Only the yellow shower-room is assertively modern. 350f again. The third, smaller but still recommendable, is blue again, with navy shower and suite, for 300f.

I like this one very much, but is does have one shortcoming – no salon. However, there is a dining room and a garden and the Lefèbvre's smiles make up for a lot. Another house attraction is the horse and carriage rides that Monsieur organises to discover the area at an appropriate pace. Madame provides the picnic lunch. Arrowed for friendly comfort.

SARTHE

CHAMPFLEUR. 72610

6 km SE of Alençon. Drive over to the little village of St. Céneri-le-Gérei just across the main road south. This is a pretty village, almost an island with the river circling round it. Locals will be sitting outside the café chatting. The church has interesting paintings on the walls, and there is another small chapel, which stands isolated in a field past the church.

La Garencière (S)
Mme. Langlais. 33.31.75.84.

Leave Alençon by the N138 heading south. In 3 km turn left to Champfleur on the D55. Go through the village and immediately after crossing the railway for the second time, turn left, then shortly left again and you will see the farm on a small hill above you.

Tucked away on a hill side off the Alençon-Le Mans road, just south of Alençon, is this rustic cluster of farm buildings. Most rooms are in the main farmhouse, some on the ground floor, with independent entry, but one is in a delightful little cottage facing the farm courtyard. Rooms are large, cool in summer with well-provided individual showers and loos. Two upstairs rooms are communicating, useful for a family and one room has an independent entry up an outside wooden staircase. There is a TV/sitting area on the landing in the main house, and a telephone in the dining room for guests' use. Double room 220f.

Mme Langlais was most welcoming giving us tea at 3 p.m. and sitting down to chat, not minding that we were a little early. There are small patches of lawn around the house with plenty of tables and chairs for sitting out on sunny days. M. Langlais is a cheerful, busy farmer who hosted us well at dinner while his wife produced a copious meal of many local dishes, with excellent sweets, joining us when she could. Wines and aperitifs are included, at 90f. There was plenty of lively conversation as all the rooms were occupied. All this adds up to real value for money. The Langlais are used to children as they have three of their own. Covered parking available.

LAVENAY. 72310

8 km E of La Chartre-sur-le-Loir on the D305. Unspoiled and very green, with the interest of the Loir river not far away.

Le Patis du Vergas (S)
Mme Monique Deage. 43.35.38.18. cl. Dec-Mar.

The big feature here is the 1 hectare lake, fringed with willows, backed with woods. Together with the swings, ducks, croquet, boules and barbecue, it would help to make this a great place to bring the kids.

The five smallish rooms, each with shower, are in a separate building from nice Mme Deage's modern house, and decorated in powerful colours. Simple, clean and cheap at 300f for a family, including breakfast that offers home-made cake, cheese, rillettes, as well as the usual. The evening meal is similarly generous. Five guest rooms: 300f. Dinner 80f including wine.

MAREIL-SUR-LOIR. 72200

8 km NE of La Flèche. Take the N23 towards Le Mans, then turn right on the D13 at Clermont-Créans to Mareil. In the village, just before the church, look for the hand-painted sign on the left pointing to the road opposite. Hard to spot because a No Entry sign has been stuck in front of it. It's the rue de la Gare that you want, on the right. Bump along here for another km or so, then take a left down a track and the house is the last on the left, about 2 km from the village.

➤   **Ateliers Josy-Here** (M)
                Michel Partemben. Ferme de Semur. 43.45.44.24.

Not hard to guess that the owners
are artists/interior decorators. Their
home is colourful, imaginative,
stylish. They picked a delightful old
farmhouse, 14th century, weathered, warm, to start with, and its
setting is idyllic, complete with very
pretty garden and lake. To this they
have added a terrace with lots of
recliners and tables for alfresco
breakfasts.

French windows from the two
bedrooms look out on to all this verdure and each room has its private mini-terrace
for sunbathing. Both rooms are lovely, lace curtains, painted cupboards and
Provençal yellow paper. A dolls house and a piano lend character to the double-
bedded one. Both have good shower-rooms – 320f. At the side of the house beyond
the pretty kitchen is a splendid verandah with fresh striped green curtains and a big
fire for warmth in winter and barbies at other times.

A one-off hidden treasure, as individual as they come. Arrowed for originality.

MONCÉ-EN-BELIN. 72230

8 km S of Le Mans.

M. & Mme Brou (M)
            3 rue du Petit Pont. 43.42.03.32.

Just south of Le Mans at Arnage
fork left on to the D307 to Moncé
en Belin, signposted Lude. Drive
through the village to the church,
turn right then left and immediately
right again and No. 3 rue de Petit
Pont will be on your left with a
chambres d'hôtes sign outside.

Tucked away on the edge of a
small village is this lovely old farmhouse, on a working farm. One
guest room is in the house, the oth-
ers are in a restored outbuilding nearby, all *en suite* with independent entry, and all
furnished tastefully in different colours. Meals are taken in the pleasant main house

with beautifully furnished lounge/dining room. The garden in front of the house has a large tree-shaded lawn where guests can sit in fine weather. M. & Mme Brou are very caring hosts who go out of their way to accommodate guests. When we arrived every room was occupied. First Mme Brou rang through to another chambres d'hôtes, but they were also full; then she decided we could use her niece's house in the village, as she was away. At the same time she was preparing dinner for twenty-five people! Mme Brou sat us in her dining room with tea and biscuits until she could spare a moment to take us round to the niece's house. We joined the party of twenty-five for dinner at 8 p.m. in the main house, and came round for a leisurely breakfast at 9.30 a.m., when both M. & Mme Brou had time to sit and chat to us and share a coffee. For kindness and welcome I cannot recommend this chambres d'hôtes too highly. Beware of arriving when there is a big race on in Le Mans without booking first; Mme. Brou's niece may not always be so conveniently away!

Double room 220f. Evening meal 80f, wine *compris*. Good parking.

MONHOUDOU. 72260

40 km NE of Le Mans, 38 km SE of Alençon by D311 to Mamers, then D300 to Courgains, then D32 to Monhoudou.

Château de Monhoudou (M-L)

Vicomte de Monhoudou. 43.97.40.05; fax 43.33.11.58. cl. 15/10 to 15/4.

An affordable luxury, well situated for a stop *en route* south. Rooms in this 1625 bijou château cost only 450f; we are not talking châteaux-belt here. It is set, reflected in its lake, in 20 hectares of grounds, with walking trails, outing by horse-drawn carriage and even hunting laid on for those suitably equipped.

The four rooms, each with modern bathroom, are furnished as one might expect – with family antiques. Candlelit dinners can be booked ahead, with the chance to hobnob with a friendly Vicomte, who will be delighted to share his enthusiasm for the region.

OIZÉ. 72330

15 km SW of Le Mans. Take the N232 towards La Flèche to Cerans-Foulletourte, then D31 to Oizé; turn left on D32 and the house is signed on the right. A useful *en route* stopover, very near the *nationale*.

Château de Montaupin (M)
M. and Mme David Dubois. 43.87.81.70.

Said to be open all year apart from the last two weeks in July, but was certainly bolted and barred when I paid my visit. Grrrr! So apart from opining that this is more house than château, that it is covered in Virginia creeper, looks out on to woods and farmland, is down a short track not far from the village, I shall have to rely on a reader's report: Make sure you telephone before arrival!

This château is not at all intimidating. More like a family home, with enormous rooms and nice views. The two suites each have their own bathroom and sleep up to six people, but we were just two so we paid 250f, and 85f for a very jolly evening meal.

PONCÉ-SUR-LOIR. 72340

7 km E of La Chartre-sur-le-Loir on D304 towards Le Grand Lucé. Turn right at La Maladrerie on D305 towards Montoir and after 6 km turn left to Poncé; signed.

Poncé is an attractive craftsmen's village, well placed for *en route* stopovers.

Château de la Volonnière (M)
Brigitte and Claude Bécqueline. 43.79.68.16.

An unusual château, older than most in the region, built mainly in the 14th century, on the site of a Roman fortification. Its pale cream stone banishes any tendency to grimness, and its aspect is towards gentle green slopes and three hectares of wooded grounds. The rooms, one double and one triple, are themed:- 'Louis III' and '1001 Nights' and this romantic and artistic approach is evidenced again in the art exhibitions held in the château. Price 400-450f for two.

PONTVALLAIN. 72510

17 km NE of La Flêche. 30 km S of Le Mans on the D147, then the D307 from Aruage. Signposted in town centre.

Chez Mme Vieillet (M)
43.46.36.70.

Firmly closed when I visited in November in spite of conflicting information received so I shall have to rely on bare facts. It scrapes in because it is a useful overnighter on the way south and because it is in a town, unlike so many chambres d'hôtes down muddy lanes. In winter and especially for one night stands one does not always have the time and patience to navigate into deep rusticity, and since Mme Viellet offers reasonably priced evening meals (40-85f) it should be possible to put the car away and call it a day without any further hassle.

I was able to view the exterior – pleasant, said to be 14th century, weathered, creeper covered, bang in the small town centre. Traffic noise should not be a problem because the accommodation is in restored buildings at the rear of a pleasant back garden. Accommodation consists of one double room with bathroom, and a family suite with small kitchen; 240f for two. More reports welcome.

ST LÉONARD-DES-BOIS. 72590

19 km SW of Alençon by D315, then at Moulins-le-Carbonel turn left to St Léonard. Drive through the village and the mill is signed on the right.

If for nothing else (and in fact there's a lot) I would be grateful to this entry for the chance to discover the gorgeous countryside in the area. I had never visited Les Alpes Mancelles before, and now I find it a region of, if not alps as we know them, sizeable hills, beech forests, deep valleys, rushing rivers, lush green vegetation. Yes, now I come to think of it, it is a bit like lowland Switzerland without the cuckoo clocks. What is more, it is a perfect *en route* stop from the ferry ports on the way south.

➤ Le Moulin de l'Inthe (M)
Mme Claude Rollini. 43.33.79.22.

Even if this were in a factory belt I would still give it an arrow. It was the very last chambres d'hôtes I checked out on my way home from the very last tour of the year and I think it is one of the best. The building and its site are, yes it's that word again, idyllic. The river rushes by, around and through the property, its gigantic old wooden wheel cleverly incorporated into a glassed-in appendage to the lovely sitting room. Mesmerising. Hills slope down to water, picnic spots abound, there are walks galore, swimming in the river and riding nearby.

The old mill has been perfectly converted to retain its rusticity – rough brick walls, beams and tiles – while insisting on comfort – huge log fire burning (and it was morning and they didn't know I was coming), a piano, deep chintzy armchairs.

Similarly the five bedrooms, with French windows opening on to the garden, have cheerful colours, and a mix of old and new furniture, with very modern bathrooms apiece. A bargain at 300-350f.

Nice Madame Rollini who speaks English has only just started b. and b.ing, but I bet it won't be long before the word gets around about this one, so book soon and write and thank me. Arrowed of course.

ST PATERNE. 72610

3 km SE of Alençon. On the Chartres road, the D311; since the new autoroute has been built, the village of St Paterne is now very well signed from all directions, and the château is in the centre.

➤ Château de St Paterne (L)
Charles-Henry de Valbray. 33.27.54.71; fax 33.29.16.17. cl. 1/1–1/3.

It is hard to believe that the experienced patron here, Charles-Henry de Valbry, is still not thirty. He runs his empire with enthusiasm, style and confidence, born of finding out the tough way over five years what can and cannot be done on a small budget, a lot of unbelievably hard work and total dedication. He inherited the potentially lovely 15th century château, crumbling and sad, from his grandmother, and, often with his own hands, has restored it to something of its former glory, helped by p.g. finance. The work goes on – there are many more rooms begging to have the magic wand waved over them.

FE3 readers loved what they found here, tentatively booking for one night first time and for a week subsequently.

Charles-Henry was able to pick up plenty of tips from his brother, François, who successfully runs Les Briottières (see p. 199) but the furnishing schemes are all his own. I love best the yellow room with pleated canopy over the bed, grey panelled doors, grey trompe l'oeil columns and antique furniture. I can sit at the table in the little tower to write up notes, looking out on to the daffodils in the park. Down three steps is the bathroom with blue iron bath on claw feet, three steps down again to the loo (not advisable for the night-incontinent).

New since my last visit is the beginning of the restoration of the top floor, with one beamed room already functioning, decorated with oriental trophies collected from C.H's eastern travels. New, too, is a delightful conversion of the 12th century *pigeonnier* into a comfortable suite of salon/kitchen and upstairs bedroom. Provençal style this time, all white tiles and simplicity, harking back to the de Valbray childhood in the South.

With the help of the admirable Mari-Louise – 'My creme brûlée went wrong so Marie-Louise has whipped up a tarte Tatin' – the tireless Charles-Henry cooks the evening meal, served by candlelight in the peach and green dining-room, warmed by a massive white porcelain stove. And very good it was too, with salmon trout and haddock on a bed of leeks sprinkled with red peppercorns, preceding roast pork and the tart.

Another new feature is the arrangement made with a band of Laotian refugees based in the town; in exchange for some land on which to cultivate their own delicacies and keep chickens, they keep the château totally provided with fresh veg. and flowers. So don't think you're going mad when you see the kitchen garden transformed into a slice of Asia, with coolies in cone-shaped hats tending their crops. Rooms 450-750f, breakfast 40f. Pigeonnier (four people) 450f or 1,800f a week.

Conveniently placed on the route south, this is a lovely place to stay with a charming host as a bonus. Arrowed as exceptional.

SOLESMES. 72300

3 km E of Sablé, 44 km SW of Le Mans. The river Sarthe rushes through lovely countryside around Solesmes, bordered to the south by the deep Pincé forest. From Sablé, a pretty flowery little town, with pedestrianised heart, you can take a delightful boat trip, incorporating, if you wish, lunch on board, from Easter to November. Or hire a fishing boat, or even a pedalo. Solesme's main claim to fame is its monumental Benedictine abbey, founded in the 11th century (though most of the existing buildings go back only 100 years or so. Do try and contrive a visit in the morning to hear the Gregorian chant movingly sung by the monks. Mass at 10 a.m. on Sundays, 9.45 a.m. on weekdays.

La Fresne (S)
Marie-Armelle and Pascal Lelièvre. 43.95.92.55.

Follow the river as closely as possible on the Parcé road. 3 km out of Solesmes take the C5 to Beaucé, well signed on the left. The farm is signed on the right.

I never saw so many chickens in one field. Should be no problem over fresh eggs for breakfast here. Kids will love it and there are swings as well as animals to amuse them. The Lelièvres have converted a barn (or perhaps it was a stable) to the

right of their own home into three
comfortable guest rooms, offering a
choice of facilities, one with two
singles and one double bed and
bath, one with twins and shower
and another with one double and
twins on a mezzanine floor, with
shower, all with independent entry.
230f for two people. Evening meal
by arrangement.

Le Fresne

VENDÉE

The Vendée is in the southern part of the Western Loire Region, stretching from the
Atlantic coast, where many Brits take their camping holidays, to near Niort in Deux
Sèvres. There is a lesser known area in the south and east called the Marais Poitevin
which is always depicted in brochures by an idyllic cottage with *Volets Bleus* (blue
shutters), right beside a peaceful waterway.

This is an extremely well hidden area. I've passed through Niort many a time
and never known I was a stone's throw away. I think the French really do want to
keep it to themselves. You can imagine my delight when heading south west from
Niort I found Coulon, not really in the Vendée but just over the border in Deux-
Sèvres. This small village seems to be the tourist centre of the Marais Poitevin, and
when driving along beside the Sèvres-Niortaise river just on the outskirts there was
the cottage with the *Volets Bleus* looking better than in any brochure. *Barques
Volets Bleus* for hire by the bank. I felt I really had found the Vendée's secret.

Generally the name *marais* applies to land which was flooded in winter from
the rivers Sèvres-Niortaise and Vendée. The monks got so fed up with their
churches under water in the 11th century that they began to dig out canals to drain
the land and the good work has been going on ever since.

This particular area consists of two parts, the Marais Mouillé or Venise Verte,
wooded and very damp, and the Marais Desséché, a drier, windy area in the west.
By far the more attractive of the two is the Venise Verte which lies partly in Deux-
Sèvres, Coulon being the most popular village with Arçais a close second. Strangely
Coulon, with all its tourist buses, little trains, and landing stages for trips on the
river and canals, remains unspoilt. It is a lively little village well worth visiting with
a good choice of restaurants and cafés. Prices for small, flat-bottomed boats with or
without guides are not extortionate and the Sèvres-Niortaise at Coulon, which is the
base for all excursions, is very well maintained. So many canals lead off the river

every few yards, 12,000 km in all; it is amazing the guide-less ever find their way back to base. You can take a picnic on a boat for as long as you like; some firms even have their own picnic fields among the canals where you tie up your boat, a nautical *Aire de pique-nique*. A few even have hutted loos. Maps are issued to boat trippers without guides. Large flat paddles are issued with the boats; quite hard work if you get stuck on the muddy banks.

Robust Madame Fichet at Coulon has had her fleet of boats for 45 years and I think is queen of them all. (Parking in the high season may be difficult; but there is a huge car park by the river just at the edge of the village. In September you can be lucky enough to park alongside your boat departure point outside a pleasant crêperie overlooking the river.) Boats with a guide cost approximately 125f for one hour. Never mind if you get lost – the boatmen who have been paddling the canals almost from birth will soon find you. Lazing in a boat with overhanging branches dipping into the water as you glide along is a very pleasant way to spend a hot summer's day. Cows and sheep marooned on islands step down the banks to drink; no need for hedges to keep them on their grazing patch. I am told even *ragondin* (coypus) can be seen, if you are lucky. Every house bordering on the canal has its own boat tied to a pole. There are pockets of methane under the canal beds, and on a guided tour the guide will stop in a shallow place, stir up the mud at the bottom and set alight to the canal! Luckily you are in a metal boat! Motorboat trips are allowed only on the rivers so peace and quiet is assured in the backwaters. The lesser used canals tend to get overgrown with green weeds and algae and at Arçais there is one part that looks like an attractive emerald green lawn.

A minibus excursion in the season drives round the small lanes bordering the canals for 170f each including lunch and a boat trip. A large boat in July and August does trips on the river for 60f, or better still a lunch trip on the boat Tuesdays, Thursdays and Sundays for 180f each. The same price for the evening run with dinner on board (wine not *compris*) on Saturday nights, from 8.30 to 11.30 p.m. could be quite fun, especially if staying close by.

Over the border in the Vendée dèpartement, Damvix has its own boat stations also at Maillé and Maillezais, where there is an enormous ancient abbey worth visiting. The rivers Sèvres-Niortaise and Vendée join just before Marans and flow into the Anse de l'Aiguillon north of la Rochelle. These quiet, flat lanes besides the canals are ideal for cycling.

The whole Marais-Poitevin stretches from Maillezais in the north to Mauzé in the south and from Bessines near Niort in the east to Marans in the west. If time is short, head for Coulon and Maillée. A totally different and peaceful holiday for all. Some chambres d'hôtes have their own boat which you can take out for picnics or you can be taken out by the owner.

Fontenay-le-Comte is the largest town of the Marais, in the more northern part, a wide open town with a good parking square near most of the banks and an interesting old part near the Abbey Church of Notre Dame, which has some attractive stained-glass windows, with royal blue predominating, and an ornate pulpit.

Fontenay-le-Comte was always Royalist and suffered badly in the Revolution. Walk down the many side streets leading to the river Vendée. Plenty of cafés for coffee before wandering through the *Pietons* shopping area.

On the edge of the town the Château Terre-Neuve is worth a visit; it is still a family home, but the great hall is open to the public with its unique collection of arms and many paintings. In May from 2 to 6.30 p.m., June to September 9 to 12 noon and from 2 to 6.30 p.m.

The wine of the Vendée is not famous outside France, although it was well known to Rabelais and also to Richelieu. The vineyards are in four *Fiefs* on the limestone plateau above Fontenay-le-Comte:- Bream, Mareuil, Pisotte and Vix, and wine has been produced there since the ninth century. The local association of viticulteurs has now achieved the V.D.Q.S. standard (Vin Delimité de Qualité Supérieur) and is hoping soon to be awarded the treasured A.O.C. (Appellation d'Origine Contrôlée), which is the highest standard in the world of French wine. It is interesting that the famous champagne house 'Mercier' is now taking an interest in Vendée wine and has acquired a vineyard in the area.

CHAILLÉ-LES-MARAIS. 85450

20 km SW of Fontenay-le-Comte. 6.5 km N of Marans.

Le Paradis (M)
M. & Mme Pizon. Le Sableau. 51.56.72.15. Open all year.

Not actually in the town of Chaillé les Marais but in the village of Sableau 4 km south on the N137. The long drive up to the house ensures you are well away from the main road and there is no noise at night. Madame Pizon is a very accommodating hostess; not only does she have five rooms, but a kitchen especially for guests where they can cook their own meals or do their washing. All rooms are *en suite* with a small shower and toilet. Some on the first floor and some on the ground floor. Ample parking and best of all a pristine clean swimming pool with plenty of plastic loungers, so in hot weather this is a real respite from the hot sticky drive along the N137 to or from La Rochelle. Excellent breakfast included for 230f. Evening meals are served normally for 60f, but not with an impending *Mariage*, as there was when we were there. There are two restaurants within five minutes' walk, one a *Routiers*. Good value all round here.

LA GAUBRETIÈRE. 85130

22 km SW of Cholet.

Soudelache (S)
M. & Mme You. La Gaubretière. 51.67.24.41. Open all year.

Soudelache

This 14th century farm house lies on the D27, east of La Gaubretière, just after the turning to La Châtaigneraie. The ancient tower can be seen from the road. Young M. & Mme You will give you a great welcome. The house has been completely restored, keeping all the old features such as the stone staircase to the bedrooms and the very tiny windows in one room. The whole place is a wealth of antiquity from beams to stone walls, but the kitchen is skilfully modernised; you enjoy your meals here, which are totally of home produce from the farm, even the wine.

Two rooms, one double, with modern shower and toilet, but rather dark with its 14th century slit window through which many an arrow must have been shot. The other had a pleasantly large window overlooking the courtyard and has a double and single bed, and equally modernised toilet facilities. Floors are tiled but there is good heating for chilly months.

The large, beamed sitting room has an ancient wooded contraption for shelling haricot beans, quite a museum piece. The garden is delightful with lawns sloping down to the duck pond, and a lake, used both for fishing and swimming, looked a bit murky. I think I would stick to catching trout, or walking round the perimeter, a very necessary exercise after one of Madame You's dinners, which are 70f all drinks from aperitifs to digestifs *compris*. Rooms are 200f.

LES HERBIERS. 85500

15 km SW of Cholet. 5 km from the Puy du Fou.

L'Abri des Alouettes (M)
M. & Mme Pineau. La Cassonerie. 51.67.11.42.

Probably the nearest chambres d'hôtes to the Puy du Fou; the spectacular *Son-et-Lumière* is held during the summer months depicting life in France as experienced by a humble peasant after the revolution.

On arrival we found a large *panneau* (notice) announcing that all the family were in the *Secheur*, whereupon we duly walked across to the large shed where we heard voices and could smell the scent of tobacco. Sure enough the whole family were in there sorting the tobacco leaves and preparing them into blocks like hay for the heated drying containers. We were instructed exactly how to sort the leaves into three different qualities and shown the ones already drying. M. Pineau hopefully suggested that we should be on duty next day to add to the labour force!

Madame soon stopped work and took us over to the house, where one wing has recently been converted into four chambres d'hôtes rooms on the first floor, having independent entry up a steep flight of indoor stairs. They have sloping wooden ceilings and huge exposed rafters. Our choice was a sunny room with large dormer skylight, a modern shower and loo, one double bed and a single, plainly furnished, two bedside lamps, simple but adequate. There is also a small kitchen with fridge and stove on the landing, really just for drinks and baby feeds. Rooms are 210f for two. Evening meal, taken all together at a long table, was a jolly affair with a very jovial M. Pineau. Excellent mixed salad, turnkey casserole with second helpings all round, followed by Camembert cheese and a sweet of apple purée. Potent aperitif is home-made orange juice, eau-de-vie and a mixture of medicinal herbs bought from the chemist. This is an organic farm and the medicinal additions in the apéritif are all health-giving, I am assured. Dinner is 70 to 80f each, all drinks *compris*, from apéritif to digestif. After dinner we were shown an interesting video of life on the farm, from young turkey chicks, Limousin cows, to the tobacco-growing and reaping.

A very happy easy-going place to stay and conversation flowed easily at dinner with all rooms *complet* by then. Quite a large party including family. An added attraction in the basement was a very large playroom and adjoining kitchen for families who wish to self-cater, as the evening meal is not obligatory. At breakfast we ate *pain complet* made in the *boulangerie* with flour from the farm. There are many windmills in this region still used for milling the flour. During the Vendée wars the sails were left at certain angles signalling danger or danger passed.

MANOIR DE PONSAY. 85110

24 km SW of Les Herbiers.

Manoir de Ponsay (L)
M. & Mme Ponsay. Saint-Mars-des-Prés. 51.46.96.71; fax 51.94.56.12.
Credit cards accepted.

Two kilometres from the nearest village; entry to the grounds is beside an old, round tower.

Treat yourself to undiluted luxury in a château that feels like a real home. It has been in the same family since 1644; destroyed by fire in the Vendée war, it was rebuilt after the revolution.

Manar de Ponsay

The stone entrance hall is surprisingly homely as are the high-ceilinged salons which lead off on either side, yet nothing has been done to destroy the feeling that you are staying in a really old château.

Four rooms all face south, with large windows to take in the splendid views of the valley and undulating countryside. Large, carpeted rooms with luxury bathrooms have fluffy towels, soap and shampoo, and a tray with *Evian* water and chocolates in each room.

Price varies from 450f for two people to 580f for a family in the Louis XV suite for three plus a cot for a baby. This room is in the round tower. One room has a *baldaquin* in the Polonaise style brought to France by Louis XV's wife. Other rooms are less ornate but sunny, large and luxuriously furnished. In the converted granary are four lesser rooms named after the colour of their bathrooms at 350f. Three with twin beds and one with a double. These rooms are a little smaller, but have the same amenities. The rooms can all be reached through the house by a circular stone staircase, but there is direct access from the rear courtyard up an outside flight of stairs to the granary corridor which leads to the main house.

Breakfast (40f extra), with freshly squeezed orange juice, is taken in the salon which has the tallest grandfather clock I have ever seen. A cosy dinner is also served here if only a few people are staying, otherwise the large dining room is used and candle-lit dinners are in order. Regional Cordon Bleu dishes are served for dinner, which is 170f each, 60f for small children; but apéritifs, wine and coffee are all *compris*. The speciality sweet is an iced coffee desert made with the Vendée liqueur *Kamok*. There is a very comfortable lounge with a huge fireplace. With such very pleasant friendly hosts, it would be a real pleasure staying here. Madame Ponsay speaks English fluently. There are replicas of the old fisherwomen's sardine baskets for sale containing local wine, honey and small liqueur bottles.

If you wish, seats can be booked for you at the Puy du Fou festival, 25 km away.

MOREILLES. 85450

22 km W of Fontenay-le-Comte.

'Le Château' (M)
M. & Mme Renard. 51.56.17.56; fax 51.56.30.30.
Open all year. (Oct-Mar on request only).

On the western side of the Marais Poitevin right beside the N137 on the outskirts of the village of Moreilles is a very pleasant manor house dating from the 17th century. Part of the house, beautifully furnished with many antiques, is the remains of an abbey to which Richelieu was once appointed. Great care has been taken in furnishing the bedrooms to make them interesting; some beds have very pretty *ciel de lits* (testers). The Madame Otéro room is the most fascinating, with an ornate bed which really did belong to this lady of rather doubtful virtue. Her lifestyle did her no harm as she lived to be ninety-five, but she fell on hard times and her picturesque bed landed up in an antique shop and is now installed in a bedroom here, none the worse for wear.

There are eight rooms in all, giving plenty of choice, double and twin bedded and a delightful small room for one person, all *en suite*, most with baths, one more like a swimming pool it is so large. A family room with adjoining double room for children on the ground floor has access to the garden.

Madame Rendard collects porcelain cocks and has a fantastic collection decorating the dining-room. There are two salons, both adjoining this room. Doors to the lawned garden with chairs and table tennis, which is well hidden from the road by trees, and a swimming pool surrounded by bushes. Rooms vary from 350f single to 650f for the family rooms. Direct telephone line in all rooms. Breakfast is 45f extra. Evening meals 185f, but children up to six years free. Wine is not *compris*.

You will receive a warm welcome from Madame Renard, an accomplished hostess who has spent many years entertaining guests. If you are looking for a luxurious spot to be pampered, you've found it here. Good English spoken. Gîte also on premises.

SAINT-PIERRE-LE-VIEUX. 85420

4 km NW of Maillezais.

Ferme des Ecluseaux Les Bas (S)
M. & Mme Pepin. St. Pierre-le-Vieux. 51.00.76.14.

Not far from the old Benedictine Abbey of St Pierre de Maillezais is a very pleasant, modernised farmhouse with excellent rooms *en suite*, one for four people with two bunks and one for three persons. A salon with kitchen is being added so that guests may prepare their own evening meals. Extremely clean and nicely furnished rooms. The owners will take you on a trip on the Marais canals adjoining their land and there is even a horse at your disposal. Very quiet and deep in the country but only a short distance from the small town of Maillezais. Rooms 180f.

ILE DE PARIS

LE CHATELET EN BRIE. 77820

12 km E of Melun. 16 km NE of Fontainebleau.

'Labordière' (S-M)
M. et Mme Gureif. 16 Grande Rue. La Borde. Le Châtelet en Brie.
(1) 60.66.60.54. Open all year.

A quiet little hamlet just a few kms from the Seine and Fontainebleau. The road by the Seine is quite pretty between Chartrettes and Fontaine-le-Port. (Fontainebleau Château is open 9.30 to 12.30 and 2.30 to 5 p.m.) Parking at Bois-le-Roi station is free and the train to Paris takes only thirty minutes. Come back to an evening meal prepared by Monsieur, who has retired from his charcuterie in Paris and enjoys cooking. Madame still commutes daily to Paris. No 16 is next to the mairie, where you park; it's a pleasant old house, restored by the owner two years ago and has west-facing sunny bedrooms, one with a shower-room as big as the bedroom, featuring two arched entrances. You could put a family through in record time in one way and out the other. There is also a central dual vanity unit so no ablutionary fights in the morning here. Two other rooms united by a sitting area, make a good family unit. Nice sitting room downstairs opens on to a shady enclosed back garden. Double rooms are 220f and evening meal 90f each (reserve ahead). Worth it, with all drinks *compris*. Alternatively, there is a small restaurant a few doors away.

VAL DE LOIRE

Départements: **Cher**   **Indre-et-Loire**
        Eure-et-Loir   **Loir-et-Cher**
        Indre   **Loiret.**

Accompanying French Entrée guide – 'French Entrée 8 – The Loire'

One of the most popular of all French tourist destinations. For many good reasons. With autoroutes and TGV linking the main cities, Parisians can, and do, nip down for the weekend. This means sophisticated hotels and restaurants and sophisticated prices. It's handy for the Brits too – a halfway stop on their way to the Med. and accessible after a fast three–four hour drive, making it ideal for the first or last night from and to the ferry.

The area offers great variety – wine production, university cities, cathedrals, abbeys and river attractions. But, of course, its unique attraction is the châteaux. There are legions of them, strategically sited to defend, enhance, and profit by the mighty river that used to be the main highway through the land. To come to this area and not visit some of them would be unthinkable, but do resist the temptation to tackle too many too quickly. Ration the daily allowance. One or two will do nicely. And be selective. Some, like gargantuan Chambord, lovely Chenonçeau and verdant Villandry should be on every list. Others, like Loches and Valençay are for connoisseurs. Thirty one are described in FE8 with a (highly subjective) rating system. The Loire is the big name but some of its many tributaries are even more attractive than this shallow, sandbanked, often silted giant. Follow their courses, picnic by their willow-fringed banks and take a boat ride upon them, getting acquainted with areas other than the tourist-ridden Loire banks.

All this potential is good news for bed-providers. There are hundreds of chambres d'hôtes to choose from here and elimination was particularly hard. There are more in the 'L' bracket than in any other area for obvious reasons – the super-abundance of châteaux begging to be converted being one. Some were just too good to leave out, their standards being just as high as luxury hotels and, price for price, far superior. I did manage to find

VAL-DE-LOIRE

■ Préfecture

■ Town

① Chambre d'Hôtes

CHER (18)
Préfecture: Bourges
1 Berry Bouy
2 Le Briou
3 Le Chatelet-en-Berry
4 La Reculée Montigny
5 Sancérre
6 Saint Germain-des-Bois

EURE-ET-LOIRE (28)
Préfecture: Chartres
1 Pré-Saint-Martin
2 St Luperce

INDRE (36)
Préfecture: Châteauroux
1 Le Blanc
2 Buzançais
3 Rivarennes
4 Tranzault

INDRE-ET-LOIRE (37)
Préfecture: Tours
1 Azay-sur-Indre
2 Beaumont-en-Veron
3 Berthenay
4 Bourgueil
5 Chambourg-sur-Indre
6 Cheille
7 Cinais
8 Cinq-Mars-Pile
9 Continvoir
10 Cormery
11 Cravant les Côteaux
12 Ferrières-sur-Beaulieu
13 Fondettes
14 Francueil
15 Huismes
16 L'Île-Bouchard
17 Langeais
18 Lussault-sur-Loire
19 Luynes
20 Mosnes
21 Nazelles
22 Neuil-Sache
23 Neuille-le-Lierre
24 Panzoult
25 Port Boulet
26 Pussigny
27 Richelieu
28 Rochecorbon
29 Saché
30 St Branchs
31 St Jean-St-Germain
32 St Michel-sur-Loire
33 St Nicolas de Bourgueil
34 Savonnières
35 Sepmes
36 Truyes
37 Vernou-sur-Brenne
38 Villeloin-Coulange

LOIR-ET-CHER (41)
Préfecture: Blois
1 Bourre
2 Chaumont-sur-Tharonne
3 Contres
4 Danzé
5 Mer
6 Mesland
7 Monteaux
8 Mont Près Chambord
9 Muides -sur-Loire
10 Onzain
11 St Aignan-sur-Cher
12 Troo

LOIRET (45)
Préfecture: Orléans
1 Châtillon-sur-Loire
2 Donnery
3 Jouy-le-Potier
4 St Benoît-sur-Loire
5 Vrigny

a few under 200f away from the main tourist areas. Those on a really tight budget should look elsewhere. In whatever category the availability of chambres d'hôtes hosts for discussions scores highly here – they will advise on how best to allocate the time between so many fascinating diversions.

Here is a brief run along the river, from east to west:

Sancerre-Orléans: some of the finest scenery of the whole route. Sancerre is unique, with sizeable hills covered with vines contrasting with the general flatness of the region. The river here is fast-running and island dotted. The first important château is at Gien, famous for its porcelain, then Sully, where the river banks are sandy and the countryside somewhat dull. Châteauneuf is a pleasant, underestimated town and the river here is impressive. Further north the Forest of Orléans, peppered with lakes, is delightfully unspoiled.

Orléans-Blois: Orléans is the administrative capital of the region, mostly new but well laid out, with good shops.

South of Orléans lies the little-known region of the Sologne, wooded hunting country, spilling over into three departements, mostly Loir-et-Cher, Loiret in the north and the rest in Cher. Very pretty villages. Chambord and Cheverney are the principal châteaux.

Along the river the châteaux now come thick and fast and the roads along the banks can become uncomfortably busy at weekends. Meung and Beaugency are both worth a visit.

Blois-Tours: Blois is the first big château-town actually on the river and consequently congested. Amboise is best out of season; then it has much to offer. A diversion from Tours following the river Cher leads to the jewel in the crown, Chenonçeau. Montrichard is a narrow strip of a town between river and escarpment. St Aignan is infinitely more attractive.

Tours-Saumur: Tours is a lively university town, with some attractive restoration in its old quarters, good restaurants, outdoor cafés and markets. Cross to the southern bank and don't miss Villandry, Azay-le-Rideau and the fairy-tale Ussé. Chinon on the river Vienne has probably the most historically important château of them all.

CHER

BERRY-BOUY. 18500

8 km W of Bourges. What a pleasant drive it is down the N76 beside the Canal du Berry close to the river Cher, passing small villages on the left overlooking the canal between Villefranche and Vierzon. The nearby A71 has exits at Vierzon (6) and Bourges (7), so a handy stop whichever way you are going.

From Mehun-sur-Yèvre south of Vierzon on the N76 take the D60 to Berry-Bouy. The farm is 1 km on the right on the other side of the village.

L'Ermitage (M)
Mme De La Forge. 48.26.87.46; fax 48.26.03.28.

Berry-Bouy 18

L'Hermitage

An old manor house on a working farm. The spiral wood staircase in the tower leads to two very old rooms, tastefully modernised with every comfort, one for a family with double and two single beds with attached shower room is really large. *Attention Les Pieds* here, a beam runs right across the room at floor level to trip the unwary. The other room for a couple with twin beds has a bath. Dining room equally old but an elegantly served breakfast (orange juice and croissants) by Madame who is an equally elegant farmer's wife. We were offered Earl Grey tea on arrival, even at 6 p.m. There are two restaurants within 3 km, one upmarket, in the village, menus from 140f, and the other at Marmagne only 2 km further on, where, opposite the church at Les Trois Amis, Madame dispenses no-choice evening meals of five courses, each left on the table to help yourself and a litre bottle of red wine, all of which will cost you 60f each, including Madame's friendly chat between courses. Full of locals playing cards and eating, and you rarely pass a car as you drive back to the farm. Rooms 210/230f.

LE BRIOU. 18300 CRÉZANCY EN SANCERRE

7 km SW of Sancerre by D955 and D86, then signed left. In the heart of the Sancerre vineyards.

➤ ### Manoir de Vauvredon (M)
M. & Mme Cirotte. 48.79.00.29.

The atmosphere is firstly a farm, then a manor house, so there is nothing grand about Vauvredon. There is something special about the ambience, however; hard to define; magical. The 15th century turretted tower contributes, and the mellow, old stones and the worn, spiral staircase, trodden by generations of feet. The owners too are an important factor in making this one of my favourites – a plump, kindly couple Raymond and Simone, who enjoy their guests.

Manoir de Vauvredon

The three rooms (two more next year) are all lovely – spacious, beamed, high, light, airy, with good bathrooms, for 300f. One has two old *bâteau* beds, another is in the tower via a huge oak door. There is also a very pleasant gîte available with open fire, cooker, etc. for 1,000f a week, sleeping up to four.

With all the attractions of Sancerre so near, yet in peaceful countryside, this one is a winner.

LE CHATELET-EN-BERRY. 18170 ARDENAIS

22 kms SW of St Amand Montrond via the D951, direction Culan. Turn right at Fosse Nouvelle, through Loye and take the D38 from Ardenais, from where the Domaine is signposted.

We are talking deep, unspoiled, untouristy, unappreciated France here, the heart of the country. The Berry region gets scant publicity because it lacks exaggeration. It is a countryside of gentle hills, very green valleys, very green woods; there are a few towns but many flowery villages. Bourges makes up for any possible shortcoming.

Domaine de Vilotte (M-L)
Jacques Champenier. 48.96.04.96; fax 48.96.04.96. cl. 26/9–2/4.

I feel that the word idyllic coming on again. How else to describe the roses round the white shutters, climbing the old stone walls, the wide gravel terrace opening out onto the lush Berry countryside? The house breathes serenity, continuity, as well it might since it has been cherished and meticulously conserved by the Champenier family for generations. There's been a lodging here since Roman times,

Domaine de Vilotte

when the local governors used it as a base from which to administer their territory and to entertain their guests.

Entertaining guests is a tradition that the present 'governor', Jacques Champenier, likes to continue. He lives in Paris during the week (when you may miss the perk of meeting the host personally but will be greeted and looked after by his caretakers), but drives down to La Vilotte every weekend to share his enthusiasm for the region, dispensing wine from his 1,000 bottle cellars for the candlelit dinners (90–120f excluding wine).

The rooms are all furnished with family pieces and each has a distinctive character – 'Les Chênes', 'Les Sapins', 'Les Marguérites', 'La Côte Rôtie' (translated as 'the sunny hill room') and 'La Vigne des Terres Rouges' (Vines from the red earth). All have good bathrooms and cost a very reasonable 390f. Six rooms altogether, one twin, the rest double.

LA RECULÉE MONTIGNY. 18250 HENRICHMONT

15 km SW of Sancerre by D955 and D449 through Montigny. Signed after 5 km. Still wine country, though now mixed with cereals; so near Sancerre, yet so rural.

➤   Elisabeth and Jean-Louis Oressin (M)
48.69.59.18.

An absolute favourite, arrowed on all counts – welcome, comfort, position, good value and good food.

Jean-Louis is a farmer and his nice wife Elizabeth has turned some of the farm buildings into chambres d'hôtes with great style and imagination. The rooms are named after flowers and coloured accordingly – I like *Bleuet* best (forget-me-not) with twin beds, fresh blue and

white covers and curtains and a blue bath – 250f. *Liseron* (bindweed) is pink and green, *Primevere* is naturally enough primrose and *Bouton d'Or* (buttercup) is a deeper yellow. *Cocquelicot* (poppy) is the most striking, all red and white with high ceiling and a shower 250f a double.

Lots of blond wood has been used to give a Scandinavian feel and dispel the gloom that sometimes attaches to old buildings. The salon and kitchen (guests may use) follow the theme. Elisabeth cooks light, fresh evening meals for 80f exclusive of wine, using their own farm produce. A gem.

SAINT-GERMAIN-DES-BOIS. 18340

26 km N St Amand-Montrond. Off the busy N144, halfway between Bourges and
St Amand-Montrond

Madame Chambrin Bannay (S-M)
48.25.31.03.

The little village of St Germain-des-
Bois is right in the middle of the flat
grain fields of the Loire. Outside the
village is Bannay, a typical long low
Loire farmhouse with the large
courtyard surrounded by farm
buildings. Madame Chambrin will
welcome you with a cup of tea. Her
bedrooms on the first floor are very
warm and comfortable, with a surprisingly un-French flair for shaded,
strong lighting. There are smart *en-
suite* showers and toilets in each room. Windows are half-dormer, half-skylight but
low enough to see the view. On the same floor there is a very comfortable large
lounge with television and deep armchairs. At 200f for two, this really is a find.

Bannay

  I thought our mattress was a bit lumpy, but my husband refused to acknowl-
edge this, as he had thoroughly enjoyed his evening in a deep armchair watching the
results of the first round of the French General Election and wouldn't have a word
said against the place!

SANCÉRRE. 18300

42 km NE of Bourges, 90 km SW of Auxerre. A unique little town – one of the most
attractive of any in the Loire valley. Perched high above the rolling vineyards, it
offers an astonishing panorama of the slopes that produce the crisp, dedicatedly
scented wine particularly appreciated by the British. Sit in the square (vandalised,
alas, by the excruciating tourist office, only half-disguised below street level, where
the old market hall used to stand) and sip a glass or two from the vantage point outside wine-merchant Joseph Mellot. His cousin Alphonse has a rival establishment
across the road. Don't hurry away. There is so much to see and admire in the region.

La Belle Epoque (M)
31 rue St André. 48.78.00.04.

A delightful surprise awaited me on my last visit. On the corner of one of the old
roads leading up to the Place is a recently-contrived chambres d'hôtes, with a side

entrance in what is soon to be a cul-de-sac. In the heart of the town, it opens on to a unsuspected garden – one of Sancerre's best-kept secrets. The large bedroom is very private. Breakfast can be served on the round table here, if not in the garden – and what a breakfast – forget lunch. The theme is *temps perdu* – lots of white lace – curtains, coverlet, canopy of the bed and on the table. Utterly

charming. But the bathroom and shower are definitely 1990s. 285f.

EURE-et-LOIRE

PRÉ-SAINT-MARTIN. 28800

30 km S of Chartres.

M. & Mme Violette (S)
8 rue St. Martin. La Carcottage Beauceron. 37.47.27.21.

Any opportunity to visit the miraculous Chartres cathedral should not be missed. If the sun is shining through the glorious indigos and crimsons of the rose windows, the experience will be unforgettable. Try and tag on to a guide talking through the stories they portray. Chartres is the kind of place that inspires men to devote their lives to extolling its unique treasures.

Only 10 km from the N10, south of Chartres, in a small village among the huge grain fields of the Eastern Loire you will find a warm welcome from M. & Mme Violette.

Although the house is right on the village street the entrance is through a large gateway to a courtyard and garden surrounded by farm buildings. M. Violette is a cereal farmer – no surprise in this part of the country, in the vast open lands of La Beauce, as the local area is known. Carcottage is the local dialect for a farmhouse. There are four rooms, one in the warm farmhouse up a private staircase to the first floor. My choice for winter, it has a pitched cork-lined ceiling which made it even warmer, a comfortable bed with attractively carved oak ends, thick carpets and two bedside lamps. Soft toys and teddies to keep you company at night! Large *en-suite* shower and toilet just outside the door. 195f a double.

An independent entry from the large courtyard up a few steps to the granary part of the original, old house leads to two more, very pleasant rooms. One room for two has a wood floor, and wash basin *en suite*. W.c. just outside on the small landing down a couple of steps – a little treacherous for night-time padding. The other room, for a family, with a double bed and two good single beds and still ample room; *en suite* shower and w.c. The beamed ceiling is festooned with lethal, old farm implements. Definitely not a room to stay in if you are intent on a matrimonial row! Yet another room has been added since I visited, I believe on the ground floor.

The house is full of ornaments, dolls, china, lace bonnets, you name it, collected over the years. I don't think the French throw anything away but can find an artistic use for the simplest article.

Our dinner at 75f consisted of soup, grapefruit, *boeuf-mode* with carrots, salad, cheese and cake. Wine, coffee and *digestif* included. Beware the *prune digestif* – it is pretty potent. Both Monsieur and Madame take great delight in entertaining their guests.

The lawned garden with *chaises-longues,* swings for the children and a shady arbour of vines is a pleasant place to spend a few hours' autoroute respite.

ST LUPERCE. 28190 COURVILLE

10 km W of Chartres; take the N23 out of Chartres, direction Nogent, turn right on D125A to Loulappe, where the château is signed on the right.

Château de Blainville (L)
37.26.77.36; fax 37.26.78.02.

One of the many attractions of staying in an aristocratic French home is to talk to the (in my experience uniformly) friendly owners. Spend enough time, ask enough questions and amazing stories will emerge. References to glorious achievements, beheaded ancestors, famous names, the Revolution, fortunes made and lost, beautiful foreign fortune-seekers, all drop casually into the conversation. The

Château de Blainville

very stones and fabric of these glorious buildings ooze drama. At 17th and 18th century Blainville (which survived the Revolution because its incumbent refused to run away and was on such harmonious terms with the locals that they saw no point in destroying her home) the latest fairy tale is that of its young châtelaine, Comtesse

Lisa de Cossé-Brissac, who arrived from Brisbane to cook for and chaperone a party of rich American tourists and stayed on to marry son and heir Emmanuel. Emmanuel's spry father, Comte Charles-Louis, is the present owner of the château, but Emmanuel and Lisa are very much in charge of the b. and b. operation, aided and abbetted by Clémence, four, Hugo, two and a half and Gabrielle, rising one. Thanks to them the atmosphere is unstuffy and relaxed.

Their home is a glorious edifice, fittingly approached by a long avenue of beech, a bridge over a grassed-in moat and then an elaborate, immaculately manicured, knee-high box maze.

The five guestrooms, furnished with antiques, vary in size and style, but all have handsome bathrooms with the original claw-feet bath and the kind of basin you can slop around in – 800f. In for a penny in for several pounds, go for the suite, 'La Marquise', decorated in fashionable Laura Ashley paper. Three lovely salons are at the guests' disposal, so no one is obliged to be sociable if they don't feel like it (but they usually do); there is a swimming pool, 300 acres of surrounding woodland, and all the glories of Chartres cathedral just down the road.

The star turn at Blainville is the cooking. Lisa is a professional Paris cordon-bleu-trained cook and you can rely on a superb candlelit dinner here for 250f all inclusive.

INDRE

LE BLANC. 36300

29 km W of Argenton-sur-Creuze by N151 (direction 'Poitiers'). Signed east of Le Blanc on D151.

Good walking country near the Brenne Regional Park, an area peppered with lakes.

Les Chézeaux (M)
Alain Jubard. 54.37.32.17.

Just two bedrooms in this manor house, dating from the 17th century furnished with 1960's furniture. One, at 280f, has a red wallpaper and a blue bathroom, with nice long windows, the other is black and red with a modern green bathroom for 260f, 60f extra for additional beds. M. Jubard is a professional photographer and very proud of his home. No smokers.

BUZANÇAIS. 36500

25 km NW of Châteauroux, by N143, direction 'Tours'. In the rather dull village of Buzançais turn right towards Vierzon on D926 and the château is signed on the right.

Château du Boisrenault (M)
54.84.03.01; fax 54.84.10.57. cl. Jan.

Boisrenault would be at home in Scotland. Its gloomy 19th century exterior presents rather forbidding first impressions, enhanced by the bloodthirsty trophies on the walls inside – antlers, horn chandeliers and swords. But penetrate a little further and the atmosphere changes utterly, considerably helped by the agreeable owners, Sylvie and Yves du Manoir, who speak good English and make their guests feel at home, with much help and information on excursion options in the lush Berry countryside.

Madame du Manoir is also a picture framer and her artistic eye has obviously helped her decorate her six guestrooms, one with bold red and blue decor. When I used the word 'bold' to M. du Manoir he looked it up in the dictionary and laughed at the French interpretation – 'courageux'. Another is more traditional, with a *baldequin* over the bed, and others are perhaps more soothing in pastel tones. They all have in common superb bathrooms, with luxury baths and/or showers. Excellent value at 370f–400f, or 770 for a suite for four, especially when the swimming pool, billiard room, library and extensive grounds are thrown in. This is not the fashionable Loire.

The evening meal, at 145f a head, is served only in summer, by prior request.

RIVARENNES. 36800 ST GAULTIER

76 km of Poitiers, 31 km SW of Châteauroux. By N20 and N151, through St Gaultier, then left on D927. Follow right-hand lane down to the mill.

In the heart of the little-visited Berry country, lush and green.

➤ Le Moulin des Chézeaux (M)
Ren Rijpstra and Willem Prinsloo. 54.47.01.84; fax 54.47.10.93.
cl. two weeks at Christmas. No dogs, no smokers, no children.

Only an interior decorator could own such a ridiculously picturesque edifice. Ren's influence (he used to have a business in Cobham) extends to the exterior of the 14th

century flour mill. The colour
scheme of white paint and Delft
blue shutters is sparked with crim-
son geraniums tumbling from every
window box, and the placing of
duck pond, immaculately white
ducks, and rippling stream seems
more by art than nature. The pro-
fessionalism continues. Ren has
personally sewn all the magnificent
curtains, contrived out of such
unlikely materials as old linen

Rivarennes   Le Moulin de Chezeaux

sheets, but conceived and executed with such flair that one can only be envious. The
furniture has a more aristocratic provenance – covetable antiques for the most part.

The six rooms, including one single, are of course all different in size and
character. One has a huge circular blue-tiled bath, another has the bath actually in
the bedroom, all have sitting areas and commendable plumbing, as you would
expect from a Dutch enterprise that often caters for Americans. The towels are
changed every day and the bed linen is just that. Prices are 350, 400 and 450f,
which includes particularly good breakfasts with freshly squeezed orange juice and
some of Ren's home-made jams.

If you do manage to get a booking here – and in November they were already
full for the following summer months, after a rave article in Country Living, make
sure you book for dinner, too, since Ren is a talented, imaginative cook and his
160f five-courser is bound to be memorable (wine extra). On the night of our visit it
included a carrot soufflé, stuffed baby chicken, and an elaborate chocolate mousse,
but confit and pâté of their home-grown ducks are often on the menu, too, and all
the vegetables come from their *potager*. Ren and Willem, who of course speak perfect English, take an *apéritif* with their guests and leave them to enjoy their meal.

'*Ron and Willem are particularly helpful and friendly people, for whom nothing is too much trouble. The decorations in the cottage are unbelievably attractive
and stylish. We dined on the little terrace better than a 250f meal at the Carlton in
Cannes. In the end we changed our ferry booking and stayed another day. We have
already booked for a return visit next summer.*' Victor Peel.

This is a very unusual stop, arrowed for the loftiest of standards.

TRANZAULT. 36230

16 km NW of La Châtre 8 km W of Nohant. Right in the country about 8 km from
Nohant. Follow the small roads to Tranzault from the D940 and you will find it
easily.

M. & Mme Michot Coutin (S)
54.30.88.42.

The château where Georges Sand
spent most of her life, stands
between the main road and the village church, open to the public
from 10–12 and 2–6 p.m. in the
summer. The entrance fee is 25f,
and a guide will take you round
(but good commentaries in English
are handed out.) Georges Sand's
granddaughter Aurora lived here
until her death in 1967 and the
château is left much as it was in her

grandmother's day. The table in the dining-room is laid with place cards, handwrit-
ten by Aurora, for famous guests such as Chopin and Alfred de Musset. After dinner they used to retire to the little theatre, set up in another room in the house, to
act out Georges Sand's new play or sometimes to watch the puppets which had all
been made by her son, Baron Dudevant. Both theatres can still be visited with all
the puppets preserved in glass cases, and the theatre is still set out with scenery
intact.

The same blue wallpaper is on the wall of the bedroom in which Georges Sand
died. Nowadays looking out of the windows you can hear the swish of traffic on the
main road, but in 1803–1876 it would only have been horses and carriages. Her
first book *Indiana* (1832) was written in one of the salons in a small niche like a
wardrobe. The old kitchen is just as it was in the 19th century, bells above the door
giving a different note for each room. The family graveyard in the château grounds
adjoining the village cemetery is dominated by Georges Sand.

If you feel like staying a night in the area there are quite a few chambres
d'hôtes, but you won't find a better value than at M. et Mme Michot's at Tranzault.
Just outside this village, passing the cemetery on your right, you will see the signs to
their restored farmhouse. A beautiful English garden awaits you, with shady trees
and lawns extending to a massive vegetable garden, orchard and fields beyond.
There are two rooms for guests, one on the first floor with an adjoining shower and
loo and with an outside staircase giving independent entry and the other, newly
built behind the house has a bedroom, loo and a salon, with an attractive corner
kitchen complete with washing machine. The upstairs room is 200f for two and the
ground floor baby gîte is 250f or 1100f per week. Breakfast is taken in Madame's
kitchen or outside in fine weather. For 150f Madame will offer you a caravan in the
orchard, if all else is full. These are very pleasant hosts, who have a son and two
daughters.

INDRE et LOIRE

AZAY-SUR-INDRE. 37310

20 km SE of Tours by N143, D17 and D58. The river Indre is probably the most attractive of the Loire's tributaries – more attractive, I believe, than the mother river itself. Follow its banks for as long as you need to absorb the atmosphere of green tranquillity. Good picnicking here.

Epaud La Bihourderie (M-S)
Mignes and Phillippe. 47.92.58.58.

Not in the village of Azay at all, and quite complicated to locate, in the middle of nowhere. From Azay take the VO1, signed Dolus-le-Sec, past château on left; turn right and follow chambres d'hôtes sign on left. The house is 2 km further on, past the railway line. It's a Hansel-and-Gretel cottage, long, low, white-shuttered, with '1950' inexplicably picked out in tiles on its steeply pitched roof. I must remember to ask why. Flowers tumble profusely in the courtyard – from stone troughs, and old pump, pots and tubs, all well-tended and disciplined.

The entrance to the guestrooms is via a separate door from the rest of the house; each room is named after a Van Gogh painting, with appropriate prints on the walls, and modern furniture. Come the warm weather and breakfast and dinner (both excellent, with lots of local produce) are served on tables set on the lawn behind the house, surrounded by neighbouring fields. Four rooms, each with private bathroom, from 220–240f. Dinner 90f including wine.

BEAUMONT-EN-VERON. 37420

5 km N of Chinon. Take the D749 from Chinon towards Bourgueil, then first left to Montour. The impressive gates of the house are hard to miss. Well-placed near an attractive stretch of the Loire, the forest of Chinon and many châteaux.

Manoir de Montour (M)
Madame Marion Krebs. 47.58.43.76. cl. from 1st Nov to Easter.

The French magazine *Marie-Claire Maison* thought the Manoir de Montour sufficiently interesting to write a feature around it, and I can see why. The building itself, a lovely 17th and 18th century pale grey manor house, has an unusual history, being once a silkworm farm. It's not very farm-like now, furnished with admirable restraint in soft, natural fabrics and gentle pastel colours, antiques providing  further interest. Bedrooms are spacious and restful, two doubles and one twin at a very reasonable 360f.

The garden is as romantic as the house – apparently natural, with unobtrusive artifice, particularly appealing in June when the old-fashioned roses are at their best.

Madame is a friendly, helpful hostess, who speaks some English. She also has some apartments in the outbuildings to let in the summer months, prices on request.

BERTHENAY. 37510 JOUÉ-LES-TOURS

16 km W of Tours. 5 km SW of Villandry. Villandry, the last of the great Renaissance châteaux built along the Loire Valley, should be in the top half-dozen of essential visits. All that remains of its 14th century origins is the keep and the interior does not match the interest of many others but of course it is for the gardens that one should make a detour. The finest in France they say. The formal French garden is designed on three levels: the water garden, the ornamental garden and the vegetable garden, all neatly encompassed by trimmed box hedges and yews. The vegetable garden is particularly fascinating, with its astonishingly vivid displays of purple cabbages, emerald leeks and lime green lettuces, all disciplined into intricate geometric patterns.

The present owner, has made an inspiring video of the garden in all its glory over the various seasons, shown of course to the accompaniment of Vivaldi. Whatever time of year you happen to be in the district, you are assured of a special treat here. Allow plenty of time to enjoy it.

La Grange Aux Moines (M)
Mme Millet. 47.50.06.91.

From Villandry take the D7 to Savonnières. Turn immediately left across the bridge as you enter the village then right on to the D288 over the bridge and continue to a T junction. Turn left to Berthenay and you will pick up signs to the chambres d'hôtes. Six charming rooms double 300F. Evening meal 110F (wine not included). Swimming pool and parking.

BOURGUEIL. 37140

21 km E of Saumur. 5 km north of the Loire by the D749. Famous for its full-bodied red wines, of high quality, relatively low-priced and said to taste of raspberries. Sure enough, if you hear this claim often enough you can readily believe it. It's a charming, friendly, little town, at whose eastern end stands an imposing collection of monastic buildings on the site of a 10th century Benedictine abbey. Aim to be there on a Tuesday to catch the weekly market, when the whole town becomes a pleasing jumble of stalls selling local produce and hideous clothes. The Moulin in fact is not really in Bourgueil at all, but some four km further north, set on a hill and a landmark as soon as you get out of the town. It is actually marked on the Michelin map. Turn off the N147 on to the D142, from which the distinctive blue mill is clearly visible.

Le Moulin Bleu (M-S)
Mme Francoise Breton. 47.97.71.41.

There is a fine view of the vineyards below, towards the river, where the aspect is unfortunately ruined by an obtrusive power station, but sit on the pleasant terrace, avert your eyes from that particular sector and appreciate the wooded seclusion.

This is more of a commercial enterprise than most chambres d'hôtes since Mme Breton also runs a simple restaurant in one windmill, next door to another which is her home.

The main purpose is *dégustations* of local wines, which are served here with simple meals – pâtés and cheeses, and breakfasts for the guests. The restaurant is charming, with the original vaulted ceiling and beams; the bedroom building is perhaps not quite so appealing and the rooms are very simple (but clean, quiet, with individual showers and inexpensive) 2 twin rooms, 1 double 200f. Dinner 60f, exclusive of wine.

CHAMBOURG-SUR-INDRE. 37310

4 km N of Loches on N143, 1½ km after Chambourg, signed on the right.

Very convenient for visiting one of the most interesting and often-missed châteaux in a highly attractive mediaeval town. Even if you are not into châteaux-bashing do climb through the cobbled streets up to the magnificent site of the castle for a fine view over the river. Plenty of bars, shops and restaurants to liven up the scene.

Le Petit Marray (M)
Jacques and Rose-Marie Mésure. 47.92.50.58.

Particularly recommended because of its kind and helpful owners and usefulness for families and those who need ground-floor accommodation. It was originally an early 19th century Tourangelle farmhouse, whose beams and fireplaces have been retained to give a warm and cosy atmosphere. There are swings and recliners in the large landscaped garden which opens out on to the forest.

A big covered verandah is used for breakfasts and dinners, served three nights a week for 90f, wine inclusive. There is one suite which would be ideal for a family, two bedrooms, a good bathroom and a nice little salon for 420f for four people; upstairs the big room with double bed and shower has exposed rafters, at 350f and there is another room downstairs, with french windows, for the same price.

CHEILLE. 37190 AZAY LE RIDEAU

4 km W of Azay on the D17. A most attractive part of the Loire Valley, very different from the north bank opposite. Cheille is a quiet little village, with picturesque old church, where nothing much ever happens. It would be so nice to come home to after a hard day's culture at the conveniently-near châteaux.

Les Ecureuils (S)
Francoise Menoret. 47.45.39.74.

I did wonder if it was worth including a one-bedroom chambre d'hôte,
but this one crept in by virtue of its
simple country charm and nice
English-speaking hostess.

The house is the kind you find
in every French village – grey, 18th
century, tall windows letting in lots
of light, iron railings and slate roof.
The guest room is on the ground
floor, making it suitable for the
elderly and infirm, with its own
shower and loo, and is big enough to have extra beds added for a family. Good garden and tolerance of children – two small daughters live there. 1 room, 240f, dis-
count 10% for four nights.

Evening meal 100f, including wine.

Still officially in Cheille, but some distance away in the country (and it's really best
to ask in the village because there are several ways of getting there) is another very
different-style chambres d'hôtes:

Le Vaujoint (S-M)
Dominique Obligis-Jolit. 47.45.48.819 or 47.48.37.13; fax 47.58.68.11.

Two friends run this charming conversion of an outbuilding to a
country house; it was nice,
cropped-blond Dominique that
showed me round and I never did
quite make out if she was Obligis
or Jolit or both. Anyhow she was
very proud of what they have
achieved, and I don't blame her.
Someone here obviously has a good
deal of taste and confidence – the
rooms are bright and cheerful with
good modern bathrooms, but the character of the old building has been retained –
stone walls, flagged floors, beams, a wood-burning stove, big open fireplace in
lounge, good furniture and lots of flowers, and there's a pleasant garden and terrace. 3 double rooms, 250–280f.

CINAIS. 37500

4 km from Chinon. Follow the river on the D749, direction Saumur. After 3 km turn left on D759 across Vienne. After another 3 km at roundabout turn right on to D751. The mill is 100 yards on the left, signed.

Le Moulin de la Voie (M)
Mme Daniele Cottereau. 47.95.82.90.

A more than life size figure sculpted in metal greets the visitor to the heavily restored 17th century mill. Don Quixote? Could have been, but it was raining so hard that I lacked the inclination to stop and work him out. His creator is M. Cottereau, who accepts commissions!

Even on such a foul day I could appreciate the setting – overlooking the river Negron, tables on the terrace, a pretty garden. The rooms are pretty too – one with yellow Provencal print fabrics for 300f, another with green painted furniture and a double bed covered in flowery cotton for the same price and the smallest for 250f, all very light, bright and cheerful with good shower-rooms. There's one more with bath and double bed which I particularly fancied. A pleasant sitting room with breakfast bar and a modern kitchenette is reserved for guests' use. Because it is near a busy road there must be some traffic noise I suppose, but it certainly didn't worry me.

More reports please – this could be an arrow.

CINQ-MARS-PILE. 37130

22 km W of Tours on the north bank. Not my favourite stretch of the river by any means but the green countryside is only a few km north of the traffic-infested Nationale and all the principal châteaux and Tours itself are within easy reach.

Look for the house right opposite the station, but apart from the occasional train there is little traffic noise in this quiet cul-de-sac.

La Meulière (S)
M. & Mme Bruère. 47.96.53.63; fax 47.48.37.13.

A tall, narrow, typically French house, grey slate roof, beige stone, nice, white, iron balconies and a four-pronged central turret. Behind it is a little garden for relaxing in.

I found Mme Bruère ironing and that will remain my image of her – a homely kind of person who will look after her guests as well as she did the five children who have now left home and enabled her to take in p.g.s. in their bedrooms. These are like Mme Bruère herself – old fashioned in the nicest way, simple, clean and comfortable. Their best feature is the tall windows that allow every room to fill with light. 'The sun moves all round the house,' says Mme Bruère. The family room has windows on no fewer than three sides.

Five rooms, three with private bathrooms; other rooms share bath and loo. Double 200f, triple 260f.

CONTINVOIR. 37340

12 km NE of Bourgueil by D749 and D5 at the church turn left on D64 and after 1 km the Butte is signed on your left. Pretty farming country.

La Butte de l'Epine (M)
Claudette and Michel Bodet. 47.96.62.25.

A cheat – the picturebook-pretty house is not all it would seem. You would bet that, with its beams and old tiles, it had been standing there for centuries, but not so. Michel Bodet was its architect and builder, using old materials and achieving a convincing pastiche. The vertical beams in the salon are particularly distinctive, giving the vast room enormous character. Madame Bodet's contribution to the gener-

ally very pleasing effect has been to furnish it tastefully with country antiques and to set arrangements of flowers from her large garden on many a polished surface.

The guest rooms, set up in the eaves, with private entrance, are pretty and comfortable, with a shower apiece.

Two doubles at 270f or 290f with extra bed.

CORMERY. 37320

15 km SE of Tours by the N143. A pleasant little town, famous for its almond macaroons and dominated by the ruins of the Benedictine abbey, founded in the 8th century.

➤ **Le Logis du Sacriste** (M)

Mme Susanna McGrath. 3 rue Alcuin. 47.43.08.23; fax 47.43.05.48.

I should never have found this one without some local advice; it is tucked away in a quiet street, sharing a small courtyard garden with the actual abbey. As her name might indicate, Susanna McGrath hails from Scotland – from Edinburgh to be precise – and decided to carry not only her own country's banner into foreign territory but those of Ireland and England, too, with bedrooms decorated in appropriate themes. The Scottish room is tartanised, the Irish is shamrock-green, the English red and blue. There is also an American room, I think, but I've forgotten the colour scheme. Anyway they are all quite delightful, furnished with pieces painted by the redoubtable Sue Hutton from Le Moulin (see p. 275) and equipped with good modern shower-rooms; I particularly liked the one with four-poster (250f for two, 310f for three, 370f for four), but the others at 260f and 290f are all to be recommended. The surprisingly large salon is particularly lovely, with comforting log fire burning away when I was there, warming the 15th century stone walls; the kitchen, where breakfast is eaten, is pretty nice, too. On three nights a week, Susanna serves dinner here, too. 90f, including wine, on reservation.

This is a very special b. and b., well situated for the culture bit, in a pleasant town centre but protected from traffic and with an English-(sorry Scottish)-speaking, friendly and efficient hostess. An arrow for all these virtues.

CRAVANT-LES-COTEAUX. 37500 CHINON

8 km E of Chinon. Take the D21 through Cravant towards Panzoult for 2 km. The house is on the right, marked *Antiquaire* and chambres d'hôtes.

Vines, vines and little but the vines; vines to the left of 'em, vines to the right of 'em… and very pretty it all is. Hills slope softly south, there is little traffic to disturb the calm and an evening here after a hard day's culture would be very well spent.

Domaine de Pallus (M)

Barbara and Bernard Chauveau. 47.93.08.94; fax 47.98.43.00.

Combining the businesses of antique dealer and b. and b. hosting must make life very simple – you furnish the rooms with stock and if it sells you replace it. Whatever the arrangement, there is plenty of evidence of an eye for an interesting piece here, with dramatic swings from art nouveau glass to 18th century gilded mirrors, with the odd crocodile skin thrown in. All achieved in perfect taste mind you. The quality throughout is exceptionally high, so it comes as no surprise when breakfast is served on gold-rimmed china set on linen cloths.

The three guestrooms have obviously been furnished with great enthusiasm, all very different. Two have balconies and floor-length windows to make the best of the view over vineyards, garden and swimming pool. Purple touches in the art deco room are softened with mauve and green flowery curtains; the suite has a lovely, black, flowery hand-stitched rug, and the third is a charming attic room with exposed beams. All have truly spectacular bathrooms, equipped with armfuls of fluffy towels in co-ordinating colours. In short no expense has been spared to make this a pampered stay. The price of 450–500f for two is fully justified. Madame Chauveau speaks perfect English.

FONDETTES. 37320 LUYNES

5 km W of Tours on the north bank, N152. Look for the sign after the BP Bellerive petrol station (coming from Tours) or the Total station at Vallières from Langeais. It's a pleasant surprise to find village atmosphere so near the Tours agglomeration.

➤ Manoir du Grand Martigny (L)
M. et Mme Desmarai. 47.42.29.87; fax 47.42.24.44. cl. 1/11–1/4.

When I last stayed in le Grand Martigny in 1988 my feelings for the Desmarais were a mixture of admiration and pity. The admiration was for the improvements already made to the erstwhile crumbling 16th century manor house and the pity for the enormity of the task still in hand. The blue and white *Toile de Jouy* bedroom I occupied then was so pretty, so comfortable that I had no doubt of

the end result of the improvements, but the state of the salon and dining room – plasterwork in shreds, paint peeling, mirrors scarred, damp prevailing – gave cause for doubt as to just when M. Desmarais' dreams could all be achieved. They still haven't – on an estate this size there is always room for more and the aim is a new roof (it was the *pigeonnier's* turn this year) every twelve months. However, the two derelict rooms have indeed been restored, and more bedrooms transformed. I still like the blue and white one best, but it's now difficult to choose, since they are all so attractively decorated and equipped with super bathrooms. The four-acre grounds are lovely – a peaceful retreat and yet so near Tours. A walk round the lake works wonders after a busy day, though breakfast served on the terrace makes you never want to get up and go anywhere.

Best of all are the friendly, English-speaking hosts. They live in Mauritius in the winter and return each spring, revitalised, to start another stage of renovation and to welcome their guests. Five rooms, 690f twin, 620 double-bed.

FRANCUEIL. 37150

3 km SE of Chenonçeau on D80. Ideally placed for a visit to that most exquisite of all châteaux.

La Villa Polumnia (M)
Mme Christiane Sansonetti. Le Moulin Neuf. 47.23.93.44.

Not easy to find, but look for the signs after the village, coming from Chenonçeau on the right.

Le Moulin Neuf
Francueil 37

Monsieur and Madame Sansonetti bought this immaculately restored old farmhouse for their retirement, but there seems to be no sign of that happening yet, with husband still working in Paris during the week. It's a charming place, with white walls, dark timbers, raked gravel and dark shutters. Most striking features are the two huge lakes, with plenty of fish waiting to be caught, and the covered swimming pool and sauna complex (guests pay for the latter).

The two rooms I saw were not particularly large, but comfortably furnished in pastel shades. Another much bigger room at the other end of the house was about to be converted and will, I think, be much more interesting, with beamed ceiling and its own terrace for breakfast.

The main salon is hung with bizarre modern paintings; Madame is gradually accumulating antique furniture more in keeping with the character of the place, but of course this all takes time and she has only been functioning as a chambres d'hôtes since November 1993. Two rooms 400f; the new room will be 500f, all with private bathroom.

HUISMES. 37420 AVOINE

6 kms N of Chinon, 3 km S of Huismes village, on the right, well signed. An ideal situation from which to visit not only Chinon, but the fairy-tale castle of Ussé, Perrault's setting for the Sleeping Beauty.

La Poitevinière (L)
47.95.58.40. by reservation only in winter.

An 18th century château, not too big, not too grand, not too intimate, not at all French. Owned by American Dianne Barnes, which adds up to trans-Atlantic comforts – huge beds, brilliant lighting, soft carpets, showers that spurt not sputter, substantial breakfasts – with French château style – lovely building, tall windows, park with stream-fed lake, and a *temps-perdu* elegance.

Dianne and her husband completely renovated it ten years ago and started b. and b. by word of mouth four years later.

Our huge bedroom was all powder-blue – walls, curtains, carpet – enlivened by striped yellow and blue bedspread. Furniture is antique French, by courtesy of local *antiquaires* and much scouring of auction sales. Our gleaming white bathroom boasted a film-star battery of bulbs round the mirror – great for the evening *maquillage*, not so good for the morning after. Nowhere were there those chilly, bare boards and tiles over which we had become resigned to hopping. Deep carpets cossetted grateful toes.

Breakfast was The Best, served on blue and white Gien china – freshly squeezed orange juice, fruit dried and fresh, cereal, croissants and a kind of hot bread and butter pudding served with raspberry sauce which Dianne said was typically American; eggs and bacon were on offer, too. I had feared that the coffee might be typically American, but no, this was Gallic, dark and strong.

Comfort and luxury do not come cheap, alas, and this breakfast cost 980f for two, room included. For a base, bang in the middle of château territory, I'm afraid this is the going rate and for those who do not wish to struggle with inadequate French, yet are in need of lots of helpful local guidance, Poitevinière could be the answer.

Dianne's next-door neighbour, down the D16 towards Huismes is another b. and b.:

La Piletrie (M)
Marie Claire Prunière. 47.95.58.07.

It's four years now since nice, smiling Madame Prunière decided to convert some of the stables of her 19th century farmhouse for guests. She has two attractive rooms here, with mole-coloured suede carpet in the luxurious bathroom, forming a self-contained suite. In the house itself, which has enormous character – tiled floors, open fire, grandfather clock, old furniture – there are two more, one particularly pretty with blue and white toile on the walls, and the other with a canopied bed and independent entry via French windows. Another room is planned for 1995, up in the loft, with exposed beams, which I am sure will be as pleasant as the others.

Thoughtful extra touches include a fully equipped kitchenette for guests' use – an enormous money-saving bonus for preparing snacks and drinks, and there is a covered terrace, garden and lots of well-behaved animals in adjoining fields. Doubles cost 350f in the stable wing or 280f in the house. Four people sharing the two-bedroom, one bathroom suite pay 600f.

I really like this one – the vibes are all right. Reports please for an arrow.

L'ILE-BOUCHARD. 37220

40 km SW of Tours. L'Ile-Bouchard used to be an important river port but now is a somewhat disappointing town apart from a pleasant, wide bridge which spans the river Vienne.

Moulin de Saussaie (M)
M. et Mme Meunier. 47.58.50.44.

On the fringe of the town is an old mill house standing in 150 hectares of land. M. Meunier breeds mohair goats for wool and cheese and mohair goods are on sale. The old flour mill has been converted into a *ferme auberge* and now has four very pleasant chambres d'hôtes rooms. Two are for four people, double bed and shower and toilet on the ground floor, with a couple of single beds on a mezzanine. One

of these rooms has a private kitchen/sitting room attached; economical if you don't want to eat at the Auberge. A double room on its own is 200f with kitchen 250f. Tiled floors can make bedrooms a little chilly. A nice surprise is to find a good sized fridge in each room. Gardens are pleasant, with grassy islands in the river Manse and plenty of garden furniture.

The mill wheel is still working, but the old flour basin is now incorporated in the dining room of the *auberge*, a very impressive and attractive feature. Parking is within the courtyard, well away from any main roads. Dinner is 85f each, posted on the black-board each night, aperitif *compris* but not wine. Goats cheese creeps into quite a few dishes, and trout or eel are often offered.

LANGEAIS. 37130

22 km W of Samur on the north bank of the Loire. Turn north towards Hommes on the D57 for two km, to find sign on right.

A busy, dusty stretch of the Nationale passes through the town immediately beneath the castle and there is little to persuade one to linger, but don't be put off by the rather grim outward appearance of the château – inside it proves to be one of the most interesting in the region.

You don't have to drive very far away from the river to find that the country-side has reverted to its natural state, free from man-made horrors, as is evident at:

La Ferme de l'Epeigne (S)
Martine and Jean-Pierre Halopé. 96.54.23 or 47.96.37.13.

Turn right at Epeigne sign and continue right on to the end of the drive to find the restored farmhouse that is the Halopés' home. Staying in a working farm can have its drawbacks; all too often the farmer's wife has her hands too full with farm duties to have time to care for her guests. Mucking-in is all very well, but a little cossetting does not go amiss. Somehow this is the exception. It's a very tidy farm for a start, which is most unusual. You feel that the cows, chickens, geese, goats and horses have all been freshly scrubbed and put in place for your inspection. The house, too, is notably free from mud and manure. Martine manages to look after her two young daughters, cope with farm problems and still offer a comfortable b. and b.

The rooms are simple, with sloping ceilings, all fresh and clean, pastel-decorated, two with private loos, all with showers. Breakfasts and dinner are served at the long, wooden table in the dining room, featuring super-fresh ingredients straight from the field, coop and sty.

Good for a family holiday, with three horses to ride and all the fun of the farm. Five rooms, 220–260f. Dinner 95f four courses including wine.

LUSSAULT-SUR-LOIRE. 37400

5 km W of Amboise, 6 km E of Tours by the south bank of the Loire on D751 through Montlouis. In Lussault, near the church, take the D283 (direction St Martin-Le-Beau) for 2 km; château signed, via a potholed drive lined with plane trees. This is wine growing territory, and could not be more conveniently situated for visits to vineyards, châteaux and Tours.

Château de Pintray (M)
M. et Mme Marius Rault. 47.23.22.84; fax 47.57.64.27.

The surrounding vineyards are Pintray property and Montlouis wine is produced on the estate. Samples available for purchase.

The château is neither large nor particularly grand, part 16th century part 19th century, with the distinctive blue shutters that are a common feature on the Isle de Ré, the owners' *pays*. The ground-floor blue and yellow suite with twin beds and independent entrance costs 520f for two and 620f for four, there is one room with double *bateau* bed and a good bathroom for 450f and another, rather grander version with wine-coloured *tissu* on the walls for 520f. The grounds immediately around the house are pleasantly shaded and feature a delightful little 17th century chapel.

Breakfast is eaten outside whenever feasible or in one of the salons, and indoor exercise may be taken at the magnificent 19th century billiard table.

LUYNES. 37320

9 km W of Tours on D76, north bank. Rather boring, flat countryside.

The house is actually 4 km N of Luynes; there are several signs indicating 'Le Quart' in the village and along the route, but they are not the usual green and yellow chambres d'hôte signs and are easily missed. Take the D49 towards Pernay, then the D6, keeping eyes skinned for a small sign, 'Le Maupas'. Take next right and then first drive on right.

Le Moulin Hodoux (M)
Mme Jocelyne Vacher. 47.55.76.27.

From Luynes take the St Etienne road, the D76, for 2½ km. The mill is down a quiet lane, on the left.

It never ceases to surprise me just how rural the aspect becomes so quickly after leaving the *nationales* and autoroutes that border the Loire. A load of heavy traffic thunders through Luynes but here you could be in the depths of Somerset, say. The rivers fit the scale. The little Bresme, a tributary of the mighty waterway down the road, flows through the garden and used to power the 18th century watermill, converted a century ago.

There are four bedrooms, with rather hectic decorations, red and white striped flocked wallpaper much in evidence. Plastic showers are yellow or green, but all cons are mod and efficient. 300f.

I see this as a summer stop, when the terrace, swimming pool, river, garden and prevailing peacefulness can best be appreciated.

Le Quart (M)
M. et Mme Michel Descorps. 47.55.51.70 or 47.48.37.13.

It's a long formal drive, as immaculately kept as the rest of the property. This is one where I would not care to arrive with a car-load of scruffy kids.

Le Quart

The long, low, grey, creeper-covered building has a stable look to it, which is entirely fitting, since M. Descorps was a former four-in-hand champion. He still keeps horses, but they are most definitely not for the guests to ride.

The bedrooms are not particularly large, but tastefully furnished and their *en suite* bathrooms are distinctly luxurious. Although the house is not old, rustic beams have been added to give it added character. Breakfast is taken in the adjoining dining-room, where a kitchen corner has been arranged for the guests' use. Four doubles, 450–850f. Table d'hôte by prior arrangement, price variable.

MOSNES. 37530 AMBOISE

10 km E of Amboise by D751 (south bank of the Loire). In the centre of Mosnes take the D123 for the hamlet of Les Hauts Noyers, which lives up to its name; this is a flat, wine-growing plateau surprisingly high above the Loire.

Château de la Barre (M)
Mme Patricia Marlière. 47.57.33.40.

This one has to rely on a reader's recommendation because on the occasions of both personal visits the château has been so firmly bolted and barred that I couldn't get close enough to take a photo, let alone speak to the owners. Peering through the iron gates all I could see was a stately building, more manor house than château, but reports are good enough to warrant an entry and the photo might come in the next edition:

'The Marlières have three bedrooms, two in an outbuilding, and
one suite, all with private bathroom
and loo, simply furnished but comfortable. Michel Marlière prides
himself on this cooking, so don't
miss the evening meal (150f). Even
the bread is home-made.'

Chez Mme Jeanne Berkovicz (S)
Les Hauts Noyers. 47.30.40.23.

With only two bedrooms, Mme
Saltron is often full, but no need to
look far for alternative accommodation. Just opposite, on the right,
is another option, not so smart, but
not so expensive either and perfectly clean and recommendable.
Mme Berkovicz also has two
rooms, one for three people, with
large bathroom, at 280f (or 210f
for two) and another with shower
for 210f. The house is typical of
many modern French houses, with tall windows and brown shutters, with a well-
tended large garden in which to breakfast (kitchen when cold).

Also in Mosnes, but this time down by the river, on the D751, about 1 km E of the
village of Mosnes.

➤ Les Hauts Noyers (M)
Simone Saltron. 47.57.19.73.

Once a group of farm buildings on a wine estate, with the ancient *pressoire* still in
evidence, the renovation and decoration has been achieved with style and considerable flair. The charming white and blue room has a filmy canopy over the white-
covered bed, with a luxury blue bathroom and a separate entrance into the flowery
garden, a bargain at 250f. A kitchenette is attached, so that picnic meals and hot
drinks can be prepared wherever the fancy takes you. The suite is all yellow and
grey, with fabric-covered walls, white painted beams, yellow cane chairs in the sitting area – again super value – 270f for two plus 100f for each additional member
of the party – ideal for a family.

Madame Saltron's own quarters are quite spectacular – a vast galleried salon, with jungly plants tumbling from the balcony.

This is one of my favourites, hard to beat, so strategically placed, yet so peacefully sited, with luxurious accommodation at a price that Madame is often urged to increase (she is the cheapest entry in the Chambres d'Hôtes de Prestige guide). So go soon.

NAZELLES. 37530

17 km NW of Amboise, 25 km E of Tours. From Tours take the pleasant little D1 through Vouvray and Vernou; just after the village of Nazelles turn left on to the D79 signed 'Chancy'. Continue climbing through the valley in particularly green and pleasant countryside for about 2 km. There is no chambres d'hôtes sign but La Huberdière is on the left, and left again.

From Amboise cross bridge, turn left and follow signs to Nazelles-Bourg (not Nazelles-Negron), then turn right and continue as above.

La Huberdière (M)
Mme Beatrice Sandrier. Vallée de Vaugadelan.
47.57.319.32; fax 47.23.15.79.

A faded, grey stone ex-hunting lodge set in 20 acres of woodland, its wide terrace facing a great lake. Silence broken only by birdsong, lots of wild flowers, ducks on the water. Bliss.

It's a strange feeling returning to a room that was briefly yours some years back. There was a six year gap between my visits to La Huberdière and I half expected it all to be different – better or worse, but different. In a way it was; I still like 'my' room, set on a corner of the house, although it now has apricot hangings, not blue Toile de Jouy; the atmosphere is the same however – spacious, lovely old furniture, lots of light, old-fashioned bath. There is another large room next door now, with green trellis paper, two beds, beams and four more doubles, rather cheaper.

Madame Sandrier was always game to take on twice as much as most of us could handle – it used to be foreign students (she speaks perfect English); now it is gastronomic tours of the Loire. Evening meals are a good bet here. Her house is not smart and a bit bare in places, but the bones are good and most readers have enjoyed the informality and unpretentiousness; however there have been one or two grumbles about 'scruffiness', so don't go expecting château-grandeur.

Four double rooms, three triple rooms from 315f–560f. Dinner 150f including wine.

NEUILLE-LE-LIERRE. 37380

25 km NE of Tours, 12 km NW of Amboise. From Tours take the D46 through Vernou, a particularly pretty road, following the valley of the river Brenne, then turn right onto the D75. From the village it is signed toward 'Reugny' behind the church.

We were actually looking for another chambres d'hôtes said to be in the village, the Château le Goupillon; we asked three people in the village, we asked in a restaurant, we asked in the boulangerie, but no one had ever heard of it. (Any enlightenment welcomed.) So we headed off towards Amboise and decided to investigate the chambres d'. sign on the right. The road passed a strange vast apparently new château and then right next door was the gate for:

La Roche (M)
M. et Mme Rameau. 47.52.98.10.

Set in deep pine woods, a modern building in rustic style, looking somewhat Scandinavian rather than French. All Scandinavian-clean anyway, with a new kitchenette for clients' use and comfortable bedrooms, some with bath, some with shower. Good value. 4 rooms from 220-250f a double.

NEUIL-SACHÉ. 37190

16 km SE of Azay-le-Rideau. 12 km NW of Ste Maure-de-Touraine.

Les Hautes Mougonnières (M)
Mme Soline Mestivier. 47.26.87.71.

From Ste Maure de Touraine take the D760 to L'Ile-Bouchard; in 2 km turn right at Noyant on to the D57 to St Epain. From St Epain take the D8 to Saché. In about 5 km turn left when you see the sign to Les Hautes Mougonnières:

Half-way between Neuil and Saché, Les Hautes Mougonnières an old farmhouse is deep in the country, surrounded by flat fields. Mme Mestivier is a most efficient hostess and an excellent cook – don't miss the evening meal here. The four comfortable, beamed rooms are all with shower and w.c. and there are two adjoining rooms, sharing one bathroom, suitable for a family. 220f for a double. There is a nice lawn in the garden and plenty of garden furniture. Meals are taken with the family, three sons speak some English. We arrived with only an hour's warning on a Bank Holiday and enjoyed soup, charcuterie and salad, followed by enormous helpings of new season's asparagus with Hollandaise sauce; by this time we were getting worried about the next course and were very thankful to see the cheese arrive; even this was followed by fresh strawberries and cream. And Mme Mestivier hadn't been expecting guests when she went shopping that morning, so expect even more for your 90f (including half a bottle of wine) if you have booked, children 50f. Demi-pension 190f for three nights, 120f for children.

Les Hautes Mougonnières

PANZOULT. 37220 ILE BOUCHARD

12 km E of Chinon. To drive along the little D21, parallel with the river Vienne, out of Chinon is to experience another world from that of the tourist-dominated Châteauland. It's a straight, flat road, with glimpses of the river to the south and, suddenly, the entire northern verge is covered in vines. The vineyards slope up as far as the eye can see. Even if a night here is not being contemplated, the stretch brings another dimension to the area's attraction.

➤ ### Domaine de Beauséjour (M-L)
Gérard and Marie-Claire Chauveau. 47.58.64.64; fax 49.95.27.13.
The modern, stone-built house is set high in the middle of the Domaine's vineyards, with glorious views in all directions. Gérard will show you round his vast caves if you ask him nicely and no doubt offer a *dégustation* of the deliciously fruity wine he produces.

I wrote in FE3 that this was possibly the most comfortable and luxurious of any of the chambres d'hôtes that I sampled along the Loire and nothing has changed. A charming little guest cottage has been built in local stone by the side of the swimming pool, and is furnished to a very high standard, in smart rustic style. There are two bedrooms, bathroom and small kitchen. A superb breakfast arrives on a tray next morning, which you can eat in bed or by the pool as you choose. It is very agreeable to be part of the ménage and yet as independent as you choose. The Cheveaus are delightful, friendly hosts and enjoy inviting their guest-house occupants into their own luxurious home for a chat in English. There are two more rooms in the house, furnished with antiques and old paintings, with their own terrace.

Four rooms, two with private bath and loo. 400f a double.

PORT BOULET. 37140 BOURGUEIL

5 km S of Bourgueil, 16 km N of Chinon. The countryside around is dull, but the situation is ideal for château-bashing, and Bourgueil is a delightful little wine town.

Château des Réaux (L)
Mme Florence Goupil de Bouillé. 47.95.14.40; fax 47.95.18.34.

Wedding photos of Florence's great grandmother hang in the magnificent billiard room with its museum-piece table. It was she who bought the 15th century château. Her daughter in her wedding finery and Florence in hers hang alongside and after July 1994 there will be that of the fourth generation – Angélique, daughter of Florence and Jean-Luc. Angélique is to marry Henri, son of the owner of Villandry, so two châteaux families will be satisfactorily united.

The red-painted beams of the billiard room were discovered when the Goupils started renovating the castle, as were those next door in the salon, previously covered in plaster. It is here that the guests assemble for convivial apéritifs before dinner. In the last century this huge room was split up into several smaller ones that could be more easily heated, and the ceiling lowered, but now the original proportions can be appreciated again.

Nothing about Réaux is exactly petite. Our bedroom was the size of a ballroom, with a vast bed on a platform. Blue and yellow, Florence's favourite colours have been very successfully used for covers, curtains and chairs. In the superb bathroom even the loo seat is covered in the same fabric and if that sounds naff I apologise because the reality is not.

What could easily have been a grim fortress inside and out has had the Florence magic worked on it and become colourfully cheerful, like the hostess herself.

She was one of the pioneers of the château-b. and bs. For 14 years now she has been sharing her gorgeous home with multi-national visitors. She and Jean-Luc leave the guests to enjoy their four-course dinner, cooked by a *cuisinier*, in the dining room (blue and yellow stripes) and join them later for coffee back in the salon. At breakfast they are on hand again to answer the 'Where-do-we-go-today' queries.

The exterior of the château has recently been cleaned so that the pale stone gleams creamily again and the red chequered bricks of the tower stand out. There is a gravelled walk around the surrounding moat, willows and chestnut trees for birds to chirp in and plenty of rural serenity. Only the rush of a passing train jolts one back to the 20th century.

Seventeen rooms with private bathrooms from 550–1050f. Dinner 250f.

PUSSIGNY. 37800

45 km S of Tours. Take the N10 to Port-de-Pile, then the D5. Cross the river Vienne and take the D18 on left for Pussigny.

There must be something in the water here in this otherwise unremarkable village at the confluence of the rivers Vienne and Creuse, where the Touraine blends with the Poitou, since there are no less than three chambres d'hôtes within its very pleasant, wine-growing boundaries:

Le Clos St. Clair (M)
Anne-Marie Liné. 47.65.01.27; fax 47.65.04.21.

Easy to find opposite the *Mairie*.

A difficult house to photograph, so you will have to take my word for it that it is far nicer than you might imagine, 150 years old, stone, recently restored; unfortunately the glassed-in verandah makes the most obvious aspect, from the well-tended garden, look bland and new. In fact the glass slides back in fine weather, so that (good) breakfasts can be enjoyed al fresco, and is a highly agreeable feature. There are two rooms in the house, one for two people, with shower-room, for 250f, one for four, 360f, and a double-bedded suite in the attractive annexe with little kitchenette, also 250f plus 60f for extra beds, all decorated in country style, furnished with antiques, pretty fabrics and personal touches.

All good news, but perhaps the best is that Anne-Marie and Henri Liné are particularly kind hosts and will make sure you enjoy your stay with them.

Le Logis du Moulin Berteau (M)
Yves and Marie Beaudet. 47.65.06.77; fax 47.65.67.18.

Signed 200 m after the D5/D18 crossroads. The lovely river Vienne winds its lush green way at the bottom of the garden of this nicely weathered 19th century manor house. Its owners, youngish, with a family to look after as well as their guests, have furnished and decorated it with style. The impression is of cheerful colours and lots of light. The suite, with lavish bathroom, costs 360f for two, with an 80f supplement for further bodies and there are two other bedrooms with showers, also for 360f.

Table d'hôte evening meals are a particular strong feature, with everything home-made, including foie gras. Breakfasts feature home-made jams, and there are 'Truffle and Foie Gras Discovery' weekends which might be worth investigating.

This, I suspect, is arrow-worthy, but I chose a particularly busy time to visit, when Mme Beaudet was closeted with the washing machine man and the two bedrooms were occupied, so I saw only the suite (very nice) and never had a chance to sum the house and hostess up. The price is right, the setting superb, and there is the bonus of a swimming pool, so send me some favourable reports, please.

When I discovered there was a third possibility to investigate I was first pleased because it sounded great, then cross because I ran out of time. Local opinion was that the other two should be considered first, so all I can do is to record the bare facts and hope that some kind reader can flesh them out:

Moulin de Grizay (M)
Françoise Mathias. 47.65.10.11.

Another restored watermill, this time with seven guestrooms in outbuildings, plus a suite for four with its own terrace and garden and independent access. Swimming pool. 350f for two, 500f for three. Sounds good, doesn't it.

RICHELIEU. 37120

19 km SE of Chinon. La Fontaine called Richelieu the finest village in the universe and I can see why. Cardinal Richelieu's dream, the town was conceived in 1621 as an accessory to the extravagant palace he built there and filled with great works of

art. The approach, via pedimented gatehouses, the Grande Rue, is still lined exclusively with dignified Louis XIII – style houses, in white tufa stone. They lead through two wide squares to the gates of the park. Alas, the château has been demolished but the park is still a joy, particularly at weekends when local families stroll along the many walks, beside the canals, through avenues of chestnuts and plane trees, admiring the well-disciplined roses. Just inside the gate a statue of the Cardinal welcomes his guests.

Les Religieuses (M)
Mme Marie Le-Plâtre. 24 Place des Religieuses. 47.58.10.42. cl. 1/1–1/2

The name refers to the house's 17th century origins as a convent. Its entrance is round the corner from the square in the rue Jarry. Mme Le Plâtre is an old hand at the b. and b. game and FE8 readers have been well pleased with the hospitality she offers in her dignified old house. At the rear is a peaceful courtyard, where she is happy to serve breakfast in summer. Furniture is well-polished antiques and the whole house is pristine. I like the *chambre Violettes* best, with a double bed and a square bath, but on the top floor is a slightly cheaper room with the eccentricity of finding the shower hidden inside a cupboard.

Any excuse to stay in Richelieu will do for me, and Mme Le Plâtre, who will fill in any gaps in knowledge of French history in general and that of Richelieu in particular, makes a very rewarding hostess. Two doubles and one twin each with own bathroom, one double and one twin sharing a bathroom. 250–300f.

ROCHECORBON. 37210

2 km NE of Tours by N152 and D77. Virtually a suburb of Tours, but light years away in character.

Château de Montgouverne (L)
Christine and Jacques Desvignes. 47.52.84.59; fax 47.52.84.61.

There could hardly be more aptly named chatelains since the château is surrounded by vines. Nor could there be a bigger contrast than its setting and that of the city just below the escarpment. You bowl along the D77 convinced that you have gone wrong somewhere when the château appears on the right, set in trees and quite removed from any other signs of construction. It's a magical place, 18th century, wondrously converted by the present young incumbents, who took over in 1992 and did much of the conversion themselves.

I would find it difficult to choose between the lovely rooms – each one is so full of character. Perhaps the Lilac suite – two rooms, tiny dressing room in the tower and a marble room, but then I love *Toile de Jouy*, and there is another room draped with red and white toile, coronet over Empire *bateau* bed, or yet the blue and white version, which has the biggest and best bathroom of all. Fleecy bath-robes hang on every bathroom door. This is luxury. All the rooms, including the stunning salons downstairs, are furnished with polished antiques and bright with flowers.

Outside is parkland, a sizeable swimming pool, expensive recliners, and another building which will soon offer another 17 rooms. A lovely place to stay, with every possible asset – elegant château, perfect situation, tasteful rooms and friendly hosts. Four rooms, two suites, 660f for two, 750f or 990f for three. Dinner 200f, including wine. Demi-pension, 2 days minimum 425–625f per person.

SACHÉ. 37190 AZAY-LE-RIDEAU

7 km E of Azay. The north bank of the Indre, on the D84, is a delightful green ride past orchards and watermills; it's worth making a slight detour, crossing the bridge to the village of Saché, to visit Balzac's favourite retreat, the house of dear friends, which became more of a home to him than his birthplace in Tours. One of the more interesting literary shrines in France, the house has become a little museum, where you can browse, un-fussed by guides, among his simple belongings and manuscripts, proofs and first editions. There is also a very good restaurant in the village here.

➤ ### La Sablonnière (M)
Mme Balitran. 47.26.86.96.

Cross back over the bridge and turn back towards Azay to find this favourite chambres d'hôtes, a modern house, built in local stone, with immaculate garden, which I discovered by chance some five years ago, when Madame Belitran had just started operating. The file shows steady approval since then of the hospitality she offers.

Then she had only one delightful small suite on offer on the ground floor, with comfortable bedroom, small room off (suitable for two children perhaps), bathroom and individual entrance via a glassed-in terrace, where breakfast is served year-round, under cover in winter, alfresco when warmer weather prevails.

The good news is that there is now another room available on the first floor, light and bright, with shower, and room for a third bed if needs be.

The salon, available for guests, is larger than you might imagine from the outside appearance of the house, with a comforting open fire. Madame Balatron does not do evening meals (cross the bridge for these), but she says her breakfasts, with home-made preserves, set her guests up for the day!

Two rooms, one with shower at 280f or 310f for three people, one suite at 320f

SAVONNIERES. 37510

14 km W of Tours. Autoroute exit 'Tours/St Avertin', then D7 to Savonnières, then direction Villandry.

Climb up the hill above Savonnières, looking down on the village on the banks of the Cher, and you are leagues removed from the fuss of Tours, just ten minutes drive away. An ideal situation in fact, especially as the lovely Villandry gardens are so near.

La Martinière (S)
Françoise Bonetat. 47.50.04.46; fax 47.50.11.57.

Signed on the right from the village. Check opening times. I did try to visit this one in the spring, but their guestrooms were not ready to receive visitors. By dint of much persuasion I did manage to see the rooms, in an ex-stable building of the old farmhouse, but when I found that this was also a *centre equestre* decided to give the whole operation a miss, since I generally find that where horses and humans

La Martinière

are lodged under the same management, it is the humans who usually come off worse. Another minus factor was that here there are only two rooms with private showers and the other four have to share a shower and loo. The price of 230–330f seemed a trifle high.

However, a reader has had firsthand experience and thinks differently:

'The bedrooms are all extremely comfortable, newly built in a pretty converted barn. Excellent dinner in the farmhouse. Stayed twice and recommend it highly.' John Howard-Jones.

The riding aspect could prove a great attraction. Trails are organised and weekly packages available, with special tours for young riders from 12 to 20 years old during the school holidays. The evening meals, prepared by a cordon blue cook tend to be very jolly, convivial affairs, eaten al fresco whenever feasible. A chambres d'hôtes with speciality appeal.

➤ ## Le Prieuré des Granges (M)
Philippe Dufresne. 47.50.09.67; fax 47.50.06.43. cl. Jan-April.

Philippe Dufresne has combined his antique business with chambres d'hôtes in his lovely 17th and 19th century residence for four years now and enjoys wearing both hats. The house is unusual, long and low, elegant, local stone, Renaissance in character, furnished of course with antiques, set in seven hectacres of grounds, with swimming pool. The dining room (for breakfasts in winter) is particularly attractive, dra-

Le Prieuré des Granges

matically decorated with professional skill in blue and white Toile de Jouy.

Hard to say which of the five bedrooms in an adjoining wing are the nicest – those on the ground floor have independent terraces with little gardens for sunbathing, but some of those on the first floor have spacious balconies for the same purpose. They cost 450f with shower or 500f for bath.

Breakfasts are excellent, but there are no evening meals. No need you might say, but there is another good reason for staying here and saving on meals rather than bed. Just up the road, deeply rural, is the best *ferme-auberge* I have discovered in the Loire, La Giraudière in Villandry. Quite unique, quite delightful, ridiculously cheap. Ask Phillippe to book as soon as you arrive.

Arrowed for a very comfortable stay in elegant surroundings in a strategic position, with English-speaking, friendly host.

SEPMES. 37800

27 km S of Tours. 22 km WSW of Loches. Take D59 through Sepmes

La Ferme des Berthiers (M)
Mme Vergnaud. 47.65.50.61.

The large gates of the Ferme des Berthiers stand well back from the main road just outside the village of Sepmes on the road to Loches. Inside is a square courtyard surrounded by the tall farmhouse and other farm buildings. Our room was one of three on the first floor, very large and artistically decorated, using natural stone walls and warm floor tiles, with a new, pristine shower room to match the bedroom, yellow in our case; the other rooms are blue and red, with even loo seats co-ordinating. Our very pleasant room with bowl of fresh flowers had an extra bed and two comfortable armchairs in the sunny window, and there was still plenty of room to move about. We had arrived unexpectedly, and as Madame was out we could not sample an evening meal, but I am sure they are a real treat, judging by the breakfast we had next day. Mme Vergnaud who speaks some English is a perfectionist, and a stay in this lovely house very handy for visiting the Loire châteaux (or a night stop on route south) is not to be missed. Double room 220f/240f/280f for three. Evening meal on reservation only 80f, wine *compris*.

ST BRANCHS. 37320

8 km S of Montbazon, 9 km SW of Cormery by RN143, direction Loches towards St Branchs, then after 4 km look for the marker PR3 and turn left; after 1 km the house is the fourth on the right. Couldn't be better placed for Loire investigation, yet away from the main drag.

La Paqueraie (M)
Mme Binet. 47.26.31.51; fax 47.26.39.15. Closing times not conveyed.

The elegant Monique Binet had just opened up her similarly elegant home (new but looks mature) to visitors when I investigated. She has three delightful double rooms, one with a canopy over the double bed and a bath, the other two with luxury shower-rooms, all white and beige, for 320f. The dining-room is particularly charming, striped white and blue, looking out on to the well-kept grounds. Monique serves

dinner there for 110f. The grounds are well kept, the swimming pool beckons.

I wouldn't suggest this one for family occupation, but it would make a very comfortable base for those without sticky fingers and a tendency to yell.

ST JEAN-ST GERMAIN. LOCHES 37600

7 km S of Loches on the N143. The village is signed on the left of the *nationale*. Follow the D992 over the first bridge and prepare to swing immediately left, continuing over the second narrow bridge. The Moulin is on an island in the river Indre.

➤ ## Le Moulin (M)
Sue Hutton & Andrew Page. 47.94.70.12; fax 47.94.77.98.

Oh dear, I shall have to use that word. There is no other than 'idyllic' to describe the setting. The Indre is a lovely river – far prettier than its parent Loire – and here a wide curving weir tumbles and splashes in a chocolate-box kind of way. There's even a small, sandy beach from which to swim. English Sue Hutton, *patronne* of the Moulin, who thinks of everything, provides two fibreglass dinghies from which to explore the waterways, do some fishing and even whitewater down the weir. (Sue's done it!) It is all deliciously green and rural and peaceful; wonderful for picnicking.

Sue's territory occupies the whole boat-shaped island, mill amidships, prow in the form of terrace pointing to the weir and stern occupied by pretty flowery garden, leading down to launching jetty for fishing expeditions, organised by Sue's partner, chef, Jacques-of-all-trades, the youthful Andrew Page. It's a real home from home, where guests are pampered and mothered by kindly Sue. Too kind and too motherly sometimes, since she was born to be taken advantage of. An elderly couple stayed for three weeks and demanded two meals every day. During our visit, Parisians with four children turned up at 9.30 p.m. and expected dinner. 'No problem,' says Sue brightly. 'No problem,' says Andrew resignedly, retreating to his kitchen. So FE readers – don't let me down. This one is a winner. Don't kill the goose that lays a very golden egg. Be nice to Sue because she's certainly going to be nice to you.

She's been pretty nice to the mill too, transforming it from a wreck into an utterly charming home. The main room, where guests tend to gather at all hours, overlooks the water, and is full of artistic touches – lovely flower arrangements, paintings, drag-painted walls. Sue has stencilled the walls and painted much of the furniture herself (you can commission items if you like) and hung cheerful yellow and blue curtains. In summer the action moves to the terrace overlooking the river. Bedrooms are small but perfectly formed, mostly looking out over the millstream and the river beyond. Bathrooms are modern, two with showers, three with baths, and prettified again with Sue's stencils. 280f.

The evening meal is the highspot of the day, either in the cosy rough-walled, peach-curtained dining room on a long pine table, or on the terrace. Guests are offered an *apéritif* (not your usual small glass of wine but, in typically generous style, a gin, whisky, pastis – you name it). Conversation is flowing by the time Andrew brings in the first course. Having eaten one dinner there (110f inclusive and I mean inclusive), I broke my rule of one-night stands and booked a second night.

Smoked haddock in cream/duck/salmon/trout/strawberry *sablé* all featured. When Sue asked us three couples what kind of wine we would like, one said white, one red and one rosé. She didn't turn a hair and repeat bottles of each colour followed on. A real treasure and arrowed of course.

ST MICHEL-SUR-LOIRE. 37130

4 km SW of Langeais on the north bank of the Loire. Take the D125 and the château is well signed. This stretch of the Loire on the main coast road is busy and dusty-grey, but once inland the land rises sharply, and there is little evidence of the commerce down below and there are fine views of the river, particularly from:

➤ Château de Montbrun (L)
Ray and Michelle Gentes. 47.96.57.13; fax 47.96.57.13.

There are surprisingly few châteaux that have unimpeded views down to the Loire, but there is no doubt that this one could hardly have been better designed. Below the wide terrace the grounds slope steeply down, threaded by little winding paths among the trees and in spring between daffodils and celandines. Roses take over more formally a month or so later. There are no ugly factories or power stations to blot the landscape – just foliage, fields and river.

The next award goes to that very important aspect of hospitality – the welcome. That of the owners of Montbrun is unsurpassed. Perhaps the fact that their original calling was showbiz – Ray was a singer, Michelle a dancer – may account for the warm-heartedness. Luxury castle this may be, but it's their home (since 1992) and what's theirs is yours. We turned up without warning on a Monday, when all the shops were closed, and so missed what I am sure would have been the star turn – Michelle's evening meal. Judging by the visitors' book no-one ever wants to eat out once they've sampled her presentation; no-one wants to go to bed either – those evenings run and run. She asks the guests what they want to eat, insisting on general agreement, and then charges them (very modestly) according to whether its lobster or chops.

Ray and Michelle met while performing in Las Vegas. They have lived in America so their English is fluent. They decided that a family was more important than their careers, so came back to France to settle down. Now, with son grown up, they are embarking on another career, for which I believe they were born to succeed. Nothing is too much trouble, no detail is overlooked.

The Château is furnished with a mixture of antiques and modern furniture like the huge, black leather sofas that make relaxing in the salon so hard to stop. The bedrooms are all different and cheerfully decorated, named after French novelists. Ours, Balzac, had a rose-patterned wallpaper and fabrics and a powerful shower in luxurious bathroom, complete with towelling robes and fluffiest towels. Lamartine was my favourite, with bath in the tower. The bathrobes come in particularly useful in the summer, when the large swimming pool is functioning. To toddle down there, after a hard day's châteaux-bashing, swim and recline in one of their expensive loungers, with the prospect of Michelle's dinner still to come, must be certain bliss. Highly recommended for comfort, welcome, and good value – especially if you can persuade Ray to sing. Five double rooms, (no children under 12), 550–770f. Dinner from 80–240f, including good wine, *apéritifs*, coffee, digestifs.

ST NICOLAS-DE-BOURGUEIL. 37140

13 km NE of Saumur, on the north bank of the Loire. From Tours take the N152 and then turn right on to the D35. The Manoir is on the outskirts of the village of Port Guyet, a left-hand turn from Bourgeuil.

The pleasant little town of Bourgueil is famous for its full-bodied red wines, generally said to taste of raspberries. An annual wine exhibition is held in the elegant stone-arcaded market place at Easter. Tuesday is market-day throughout the year and the whole town gets taken over by a jumble of stalls selling everything from local cheeses to pink cotton brassieres.

Manoir du Port-Guyet (M-L)
Madame Valluet. 47.97.82.20. cl. 15/10 to Easter.

The blond tufa-stone 15th century building was once a hunting lodge used by the Abbaye de Bourgueil. It stands in peaceful grounds, overlooking a private lake. Ronsard, the great 16th century French poet was inspired to write some of his best poetry here, dedicated to his great love Marie.

Manoir du Port-Guyet

Châtelaine Genevieve Valluet, who speaks perfect English, lives in Paris for the winter but looks forward to cossetting her guests for the rest of the year. Her three bedrooms have their original fireplaces, beams, doors and terracotta floors and are furnished perhaps a little sparsely, with antiques of the period. Bathrooms may have an old-fashioned decor but are 20th century when it comes to plumbing. 450–600f plus 50f per breakfast. Dinner 200f inclusive.

TRUYES. 37320

13 km SE of Tours by N143. Hard to believe that Tours and all the commercialism of the château-country is so near. The river Indre weaves its peaceful way south and it is well worth following it beyond Truyes for a willow-fringed photogenic drive.

Le Manoir de Chaix (M)
Suzanne Fillon. 47.43.42.73.

From Truyes turn east on D45, turn right at chambres d'hôtes sign, then left.

Le Manoir de Chaix

Pale bleached stone and tower approached by a winding stone staircase are evidence of the Manoir's age – 16th century. It has been in the Fillon family for four generations. The feeling is more farmhouse-simple than manor-grand, and very nice, too. The rooms are named after local regions 'Touraine' is for the area, 'Varidaine' is for the old road outside (and is the nicest I feel, with beams, bath, and a child's bed in the cupboard.) All have peaceful outlooks over the countryside.

There are variations on the theme, so specify when you book – an apartment for four with bathroom, one with shower, etc. Madame Fillon herself speaks no English but her son and daughter are happy to practise theirs. Their swimming pool and tennis court are at the guest's disposal, which is very generous, considering the modest price of the rooms. Breakfast is a good one, including fresh orange juice home-made jam and honey from the estate. Four rooms, all with private bathrooms, 270–400f. Dinner 95f including wine.

A nearby barn was being converted while I was at Le Manoir. It was hard to believe that the rubble and shell of a building could possibly be ready in a couple of months time i.e. May 1994, but Madame Fillon assured me that by then it would comprise one very comfortable room and a kitchenette, costing 390f for three people and 460f for four. Seeing what she has achieved in the rest of the house I an ready to believe that this would make a most agreeable base for a well-sited holiday.

VERNOU-SUR-BRENNE. 37210

8 km NE of Tours by N152 and D46. Vouvray is just down the road, and this is pleasant vine and farming country. The Valley of the Cousse is even prettier, and that is the way to head for:

La Ferme des Landes (M-S)
Netty Bellanger. 47.52.10.93.

5 km from Vernou, in the middle
of nowhere, but well signed off the
D46. M. Bellanger's farm covers 80
hectares.

Les Landes

The 15th century ivy-covered,
stone farmhouse reminds me of the
Cotswolds, with more flowers on
its pleasant, wide terrace than is
common on French working farms.
There is an ivy-covered well with
hyacinths planted round its perimeter, annuals in troughs and lilies in
the border. Indoors is an orange tree, so it is obvious that Madame Bellanger finds
tine for other occupations than just her b. and bs. She is in fact an old hand at looking after guests, having been a pioneer chambres d'hôte hostess, with fifteen years to
her credit and still going strong. All very efficient.

Her salon is a delightful room, huge, with powerful old beams supporting the
roof and a raised fireplace at each end. Look at the mantelpiece over the smaller
one; the carving is most unusual – bows carved into the dark wood.

There is a wide choice of rooms here – in the house they are old and full of
character, with brass beds and family armoires, flowery wallpapers, and in one case
a square 'sabot' bath. In the left wing is a newer conversion into four rooms, with
excellent bathrooms and a communal kitchen and small sitting area.

On the other side of the courtyard is another conversion – a splendid new
house is being contrived for the Ballangers' *antiquaire* son. There will be a swimming pool, too, but at present not for the guests' use, alas.

Farmhouse breakfasts and dinners are served at tables outside whenever possible and of course local wine is freely available. Six rooms, 260f a double; 320f for
three; 370f for four. Dinner June-September only: 90f. Wine 30f extra.

VILLELOIN-COULANGE. 37460

2.5 km SE of Montrésor, 36 km S of Montrichard. Between Montresor and Nouans
on the D760. A lovely spot of green country, following the valley of the Indrois.

Château les Gênets (M)
Rosemary and Peter Farley. 47.92.61.

A unanimous chorus of approval for this entry in FE8. Readers have particularly
liked the friendly atmosphere in the 19th century run by an ex-Somerset farmer
and his wife. He is still a farmer, coping with 800 acres and a dairy herd. This

is good news for kids, because
the farm, the 35-acre lake, the
woods and the grounds are there
for them to explore. Riding also
available.

Rosemary now copes with six
bedrooms for guests, speaking
English or French as required, and
will cook an English breakfast if
requested.

Alas, there was no one at
home when I called in March, so I
have not re-inspected the rooms. Nobody has complained though and I am sure
they are even better than when the venture first started six years ago. Six rooms:
240–320f for two people; 310–390f for three.

La Pension de l'Abbaye (M)
Odile Rousseau Wood. Rue de l'Abbaye. 47.92.77.77. cl. 1/11–1/16.

From the village turn left opposite
the church down the hill towards
the abbey, currently being restored.
The pension is on the right. It's one
of those shabby, paint-peeling,
stone-crumbling old houses that no
longer exist in England – someone
has 'done them up'. No danger of
that here – the simplicity has been
cherished, and no doubt Odile's
husband's artistic eye has helped.
In the winter the pair live in New
York; in the summer they return to Villeloin, where he paints and she looks after
her guests.

The walls are thick, white-washed, the beams are substantial, the wood has a
just-scrubbed look and the flowers are fresh. Curtains are embroidered linen. It
could feature in a glossy magazine as the perfect 'country look'. Don't miss the
evening meal here – Odile is an excellent cook. Two rooms with private bathrooms,
295f.

LOIR et CHER

BOURRE. 41400 MONTRICHARD

42 km SE of Tours. 35 km SW of Blois. I am always disappointed by Montrichard. It has everything going for it – a prime position on the north bank of the river Cher, some nice old timbered houses, two squares – and yet it remains without a heart and soul. There are few towns of this size in France without a centre full of lively cafés and brasseries, but Montrichard is one of them; its pedestrianisation hasn't worked – the main street is still traffic-ridden, and it certainly hasn't capitalised on the river aspect – not a single bar or restaurant apart from those of the hotels, in which to sit and sip and look out over the water. That said, you don't have to go very far to find more rewards – the forest of Montrichard lies immediately behind and the road that follows the river along its north bank in both directions is pleasant and not too busy. Bourée lies 2 km E of the town.

Manoir de la Salle du Roc (M-L)
M. et Mme Boussard. 60 route de Vierzon. 54.32.73.54.

Pity about the railway line. which spoils so many views in the Loire valley, but there is enough distance and height between it and the Manoir to blur the blot on the landscape and any traffic noise. The gardens are lovingly cared for by M. Boussard and his gardener. 450 rose buses contribute to the colourful scene. Winding down the slope is an enticing path, with many a tucked-away corner shaded from public view where tables and benches have been thoughtfully provided for shady repose. A water-course and fountains lend even more interest to the scene and there are galleries of chalk caves to explore and a tennis court on which to work off some residual steam. The grounds actually extend to the river, where there is a private island, reached by a little motorboat; a great spot for picnics.

The building is half 15th century manoir, half 18th century château, and, because of the slope, it is very hard to do justice to it in a photograph. Two families share the responsibilities of running it, Patricia and Patrick helping out Patrick's father and mother. There are guest rooms in both the tower and the main building, all furnished with antiques, including in one suite a 'sabot' bath (i.e. square). Others have more conventional sanitary ware, but boast canopies over the beds and family treasures like an 18th century lady's pink shoe and lace baby clothes. Live fires in the rooms are the biggest possible treat.

Situated so near Chenonceaux (10 km) and Amboise (20 km) this would make an excellent, superbly comfortable base.

Four doubles, all with private baths 500–700f. Evening meal by arrangement.

CHAUMONT-SUR-THARONNE. 41600

35 km S of Orléans. From Chaumont take the C2, direction 'Vouzan'. La Farge is 4 km, signed *Centre Equestre* on the right. Conveniently sited near the autoroute and *nationale*, yet right in the heart of the peaceful Sologne countryside, deeply forested and dotted with lakes.

La Farge (M)
Mme Grangeneuve. 54.88.52.06.

The chambres d'hôtes are the first group of buildings you come to after driving up the approach road in the woods. It is Mme Grangeneuve's daughter who runs the equestrian centre and small shop further on.

The 19th century buildings, cream with black crossbeams, are set around a courtyard, featuring an attractive swimming pool. The whole ensemble would make an excellent family stop, especially the little suite (450f for 2, 50f per person extra) which has an excellent kitchen and sitting room with welcoming fireplace, as well as the spacious bathroom and pleasantly furnished bedroom common to all the rooms. There are two more at 300f.

Breakfast is taken in a surprisingly vast room in Madame Granveneuve's quarters, with high beams and fierce trophies of *la chasse* glaring down from the walls. Unless its summer-time of course, when full use is made of the terrace.

CONTRES. 41700

21 km S of Blois by D956. Very near Cheverny, one of the most elegant and popular of all the châteaux on the Loire. From the village take the D102 towards Geverny. Follow signs on the right to La Robouillère.

La Rabouillère (M)
Mme Martine Thimonnier. 54.79.05.14. cl. 1/12–1/3.

Reminds me of Normandy, with its long, low lines, old beams and attic windows, but all is not what it seems. This is in fact a reconstruction of a typical Solognot cot-

tage and although the beams and
bricks are old, the building itself
is not. It was actually erected by
M. Thimmonier himself, and a very
good job of it he has made.
Madame Thimmonier has played
her part too because it is not only
the exterior that oozes with picture-
book charm. She has furnished the
bedrooms (sloping roofs, rafters)
with entirely appropriate Laura
Ashley fabrics and seen to it that

La Roberillière

there are modern conveniences like hair dryers with multi-national sockets.
The bedrooms are charming and comfortable but on the small side – a charge that
could not be applied to the lovely salon, featuring old materials again, tiled floor,
old bricks and beams, antique furniture and a huge fire for the guests to gather
round.

Everything is as well-groomed as the elegant Madame Thimmonier, who does
everything she can to make her guests enjoy their stay. Five rooms with private
bathrooms; 370-double, 550f a suite.

DANZÉ. 41160

15 km N of Vendôme by D36 to Danzé, then the D24 towards La Ville-aux Clercs.
Lovely unspoiled rolling countryside. Vendôme itself is an enchanting little town,
built over several branches of the river Loire.

➤ ### La Borde (M)
Madame Kamette. 54.80.68.42

From Danzé take the second chambres d'hôtes sign, down a made-up
road, rather than the first which
leads very bumpily through the forest. This one is a real find, one of
the best bargains in the book. It's a
1930s house set in ten hectares of
green and pleasant land in pleas-
ingly hilly countryside. The rooms
are all large and well-furnished
with modern bathrooms (shower or
bath). One has its own terrace, two

La Borde

others (forming a suite) have floor length windows looking over the garden; all are
miles away from traffic fret. All good news.

Even better and more unusual is that there is a new covered swimming pool in the garden. And there's nice Mme Kamette, who is an English teacher, so conversation will flow. But best of all are the prices; Mme knows that she cannot compete with accommodation along the Loire as far as site is concerned, but she certainly beats them hollow in value-for-money terms.

A very good restaurant, Le Marmiton, is in the village.

190f for a double, 400f for four, or 450f for five in the suite.

MER. 41500

16km N of Blois on the RN152. Follow signs to town centre.

Mer is one of those forgotten towns on the Loire that no one (including *moi*) has ever heard of. No château, no great river views. It came as a pleasant surprise, with a quiet pedestrianised heart, on which stands:

➤ ### Chez Mormiche (M)
9 rue Dutems. 54.81.17.36.

We had no trouble finding the house, which is well-signed: '*chambres d'hôtes centre ville*', once we had overcome our law-abiding English scruples about driving over a pedestrian area. But if this had not been France, I doubt if we would have proceeded further. The house, bang on the road, is grey and undistinguished from this aspect, with Claude's framing shop attached to it. It is not until you penetrate to the rear that all its 16th century charms can be appreciated, especially the unexpected garden.

There are more pleasant surprises in store; the rooms are all light and airy, with good, white bathrooms. One is delicate pale blue and white, overlooking the garden – 350f – another with grey paint, has two white-covered beds, with the possibility of two more squeezed in – 500f for four – and there is a choice of baths or showers. The rooms that overlook the pedestrianised road have double glazing and cost 300f and all five rooms cost 50f less in winter.

Breakfast is taken in a nice beamed room or outside in the garden, which is a real bonus in the heart of a town, and there is covered parking space. Both Claude and her farmer husband Joelle, are exceptionally friendly and pleasant, but speak no English. However, 17-year-old daughter (Claude doesn't look old enough!) is around to help out.

I really like this one – atmosphere, situation, rooms and hosts, so an arrow comes with it.

MESLAND. 41150

28 km NE of Tours, 32 km SW of Blois, on the crossroads of the D1 and D43. This is wine country and no mistake. There are *Routes Touristique des Vins* all over the place, so it might take a little while to settle down, eschew the *dégustations* and find:-

Domaine du Prieuré (M)
Sylvie and Michel Chrétien. 54.70.21.23.

Turn left up a narrow drive immediately before the Domaine building. This is an unexpected cottage-like building tucked away behind. The whole village, steeply pitched, with nice old church, is dedicated to the making and enjoying of wine.

Michel Chrétien and his family are wine merchants, who have two rooms, with nice old furniture, and private bathrooms available for guests. 250f a double.

MONTEAUX. 41150

27 km NE of Tours 32 km SW of Blois, on the crossroads of the D1, which runs parallel with the main north bank nationale and the D65. This is wine country, but not boringly, uniformly so. The countryside is green and threaded with streams, one of which turns the mill-wheel for:

Moulin de Pasnel (M)
M. and Mme Paul Pelletier. 54.70.22.39.

1½ km W of the village, where it is well signed.

The word idyllic is one to be used sparingly. I shall squander it here. The stream gurgles, the willows weep, the swans swan, the peacocks strut, the birds are vociferous and the wheel of the 17th century mill churns around. Bathed in sunshine on a March day, with spring flowers beginning to add their contribution, it was, well... idyllic.

The big room used for breakfasts is stunning, featuring another gigantic millwheel, but I suspect the temptation to carry the tray into the garden and soak up the watery ambience there will be strong.

Nice, young Madame Pelletier told me that she and her husband were fishmongers as well as hosts for p.g.s. An unusual combination. She has a suite for six people, with own bathroom, another for four people, also with bath, and two more doubles sharing bathroom, comfortable and clean with some antique furniture.

Four rooms: 320f a double, plus 50f for each extra person.

MONT-PRES-CHAMBORD. 41250

9 km SE of Blois by D765 toward Cheverny. Turn left at Clénord, following sign for the Manoir.

A perfect situation, right in the heart of châteaux-country, with lovely scenery, woods and rivers nearby, and the virtue of easy accessibility.

Manoir de Clénord (L)
Mme Christiane Renauld. 54.70.41.62; fax 54.70.33.99.

La Maison de Clénord   Mont-près-Chambord 91

Not as grand as a château, not as simple as a bourgeois house, the white 18th century château has the advantages of both; it lacks the grandeur of a château, with can be overpowering, but the building is impressive enough to make one conscious of staying somewhere special. It is set in 25 hectares of woodland (lovely walks through the *allées*), with a hard tennis court and swimming pool, beside which breakfast and snacks are eaten whenever the weather allows.

Christiane, a widow, and her widower brother Serge Catala are relaxed, experienced hosts who don't fuss over their guests, but just make sure they have everything they need. In winter Christiane fills some of the empty rooms with foreign students who wish to improve their French. For three months she gives them grammar lessons and takes them around the numerous cultural wonders of the area. There were sixteen of us sitting round the long, polished oak table, six different nationalities, but the lingua franca had to be French. Very good for me, too.

On Wednesdays the students have courses on French cooking, and we ate the excellent results for dinner.

The rooms follow the pattern of elegant informality, good proportions, pleasantly decorated. Ours was in blue and yellow with a little sitting room and a good bathroom, furnished with a mixture of antique and repro. In fact, just the kind of atmosphere one might, with luck, aspire to at home.

Christiane's personality does much to ensure that everyone loves staying at Clénord, but the reasonable prices might also have something to do with it. The 380f room may not have an *en suite* loo, but its not often you get the chance to stay in a manor for £20 a head. Other rooms with good bathrooms from 550–950f.

MUIDES SUR LOIRE. 41500

15 km NE of Blois on the south bank of the Loire. The château is set back from the main road, the D951, just before the town of Muides.

➤ ## Château des Colliers (L)
Marie-France and Christian de Gélis. 54.87.50.75; fax 54.87.03.64.
cl. 1/12–1/3

Most of the châteaux of the Loire lack any view of the wide shallow river that was their *raison d'être*. Many others, especially on the north bank, have offensive *'Nationales'* and main railway lines running between them and the water, ruining both the view and the night's repose. The Château de Colliers suffers from neither disadvantage and is probably the best-situated of any entry in this book.

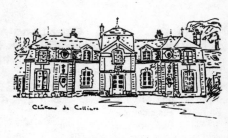

The floor-to-ceiling windows of every room look directly out over a grassy terrace to the fast flowing water and reedy islands, unimpeded on this quiet stretch by man-made views. There is a lovely walk along the river bank, which I thoroughly recommend after a day's car cramp, heading west directly into the evening sun duplicating its effect on the water.

The 1750 château, bought in 1779 from the Chevalier de Beba, has been in Christian's family for eight generations. He was born and raised here. Portraits of his dignified ancestors look down from their gilt frames in reading room, salon, and dining room, where they have to compete with Sistine Chapel-esque murals and ceiling paintings. Over the main door is the family crest and motto in Basque, which, translated, reads. 'If you are happy here, stay awhile.' Advice that I wish I could follow, because I was certainly very happy indeed to be staying here.

In spite of the elegance of the building, with gravel courtyard raked every morning, the lovely panelling, antique furniture (I didn't see a single piece I did not covet) the atmosphere is far from intimidating. How could it be – this is after all a family home in which modest Marie-France has raised five children. Now they have fled their enviable nest, she cooks for even larger numbers – twelve guests often sit round her dining table and eat her delectable dinners.

The rooms, of course, are all different. Mine was ground floor, blue toile walls, flowery curtains and spread, magnificent Directoire beds, walnut chest and armoire and, best of all, a fire in the marble grate. The bathroom is unrepentantly luxurious. The room next door is the oldest, with gorgeous ceiling mouldings and double bed, another upstairs has a secret winding staircase leading to an unexpected large terrace where sun-worshippers can tan privately while taking in the view.

A lovely place to stay, stunning building, charming hosts, comfort and style. And very well-situated. Five rooms with private bathrooms 600–700f. Dinner 200f including wine.

ONZAIN. 41150

15 km SW of Blois on N152, direction Tours. In Onzain take the road for Monteaux; after 3 km look for a Citroen garage on the right and the house is opposite.

➤ Chez Langlais (M)
Martine Langlais. 46 rue de Meuves. 54.20.78.82; fax 54.20.78.82.
cl. December to April.

I probably have more letters of commendation on this one than any other chambres d'hôtes in the Loire. Here is a sample:-

*'The bedrooms are better than many in top class hotels, beautifully furnished and decorated, all with en-suite facilities of the highest standard, and the house itself is beautifully quiet and peaceful, with a garden stretching down to the river. The host and hostess discov-*ered that it was my birthday so immediately opened a bottle of Vouvray, which we all enjoyed in their lovely garden.'* Marilyn Weston.

Truth to tell, after all this praise, first impressions of the little house on the main road are somewhat disappointing and it is not until you push open the big iron gate that you begin to see what all the fuss is about. The rear aspect is entirely different, ivy-covered, cottagey, and the long garden does indeed extend to the river (but not the Loire, just a very minor tributary). M. Langlais proudly showed us his garden and pointed out the private parking slot in the front, off the road. Madame Langlais met us in her delightful salon, with yellow painted beams, matching chairs and curtains. Her good English makes conversation easy. Breakfast is taken in the garden or in the little sitting-room with french windows exclusively for the guests' use. The five rooms are all extremely pretty with attractive country fabrics, a green flowery version with twin beds for 330f and a pink Toile de Jouy fabric on the walls of another. Five altogether, all with excellent bathrooms.

A totally charming place, in which I am so certain that readers will be happy that an arrow follows.

ST AIGNAN-SUR-CHER. 41110

39 km S of Blois, 61 km E of Tours on N76. A delightful little town with lots of character, tumbling down via cobbled streets to the river Cher. Pleasant

walks along the banks, good picnicking and a little beach. The church dates
from the 11th and 12th centuries, with Romanesque porch and crypt. Opposite is
a wide flight of steps leading up to the 16th century castle which is inhabited and
unvisitable. You can stroll round the courtyard though and admire the views down
to the river.

Madame Geneviève Besson (M)
66 rue Maurice Berteaux. 54.75.24.35.

Very conveniently placed, in the
centre of the town, but looking
back towards the castle and church
across a most surprising garden. It
is Madame's pride and joy, a copy
of an old French formal garden,
with parterres and clipped hedges
and paths between the roses. Guests
eat breakfast in the courtyard, prof-
iting from the extraordinary view.

The front of the early 19th
century white stone house is com-
pletely covered with green lattice, to support yet more roses, and very pretty it
looks, too. Inside the rooms a lot of thought has obviously gone into the individual
colour schemes – each one different, one red, one blue (these two form a suite and
share a bathroom from which there is a superb view of the château), another pink
with white beams and a pink bathroom, a dark red room overlooking the road, but
with double glazing and a smaller yellow room. Treasured antique furniture
throughout. There is a library and a lovely yellow salon, all very *raffinée*, as is
Madame herself. No sticky fingers welcome in her house. She makes her own preserves for breakfast served in the nice, blue dining-room and there is a private parking arrangement nearby. A good town base, excellent value, but not for children, I
feel. Four rooms at 250f.

TRÔO. 41800

54 km N of Tours, 62 km SE of Le Mans on the D917. An intriguing little town
perched on a steep slope, famous for its troglodyte dwellings which are still inhabited. The tiered houses are linked by alleys, stairways and creepy passages. Beneath
them a labyrinth of galleries has been cut in the white tufa stone. Climb up to La
Butte, an ancient mound, providing a splendid panorama (helped by viewing table
and telescope), of the course of the Loire, and the little church of St. Jacques-des-
Gérets, and its Byzantine 11th century murals.

Château de La Voute (L)
Monsieur Clays and Monsieur Venon. 54.72.52.52.

Backed by tufa caves, overlooking the Loire, stands the elegant 17th century château. Elegance is the keynote throughout, with the impeccable taste of *antiquaire* M. Clays ensuring that every room is furnished not only with valuable antiques but also with a professional eye for style and colour. Several have canopied beds; one in red *Toile de Jouy* has twin Empire beds, one is brown and turquoise (with matching bath towels) one is red and blue with a coronet over the bed, all have huge luxurious bathrooms and gorgeous views from their tall windows. No hardship to find that the substantial breakfast is served here in these lovely bedrooms if the weather does not favour eating on the terrace.

The prices for one of the most stylish of all the châteaux I visited reflect the fact that Trôo is not on the tourist beat – most reasonable. Next door however is the antique shop, full of desirable objects, so this might turn out to be an expensive stop. No evening meal, but one of the best little restaurants in the district is in the village.

Five rooms, all with bath or shower, mostly at 470f, but the *Toile de Jouy* is 370f and the red and blue 550f.

LOIRET

CHATILLON-SUR-LOIRE. 45360

15 km S of Gien on the south bank, via D951, crossing the river either at Gien or at Chatillon. (I prefer the former). It's a nice old town, famous for its antique shops; there is a choice of water – the canal de Briare or the river itself. A superb picnic spot is at the Ecluse de Chatillon, a lock on the canal by a large lake; there are tables and benches here under the shade, or you can walk on to the river where there are more perfect situations for DIY refreshment and repose.

La Giloutière (M)
Nicole and Gilbert Lefranc. 13 rue du Port. 38.31.10.61.
Just a jolly little bar between the cream stone, white-shuttered house and the canal embankment. It is actually on the main approach to the town, but set back in a cul-de-sac far enough to escape the traffic buzz.

The two double rooms, each with own shower room, are pleasantly furnished and cost 250f, with plenty of room for another bed (360f for three). Nice Madame Lefranc lays on an evening meal for 250f inclusive of wine, but there are nearby restaurant alternatives. She also has a gîte in the garden with two rooms, costing 1,000f a week.

DONNERY. 45450

18 km NE of Orléans.

Les Charmettes (S-M)
Mme Sicot. 38.59.22.50; fax 38.59.26.96.

Les Charmettes in the small village of Fay-aux-Loges just outside Donnery is a large house situated between the canal and the main road. Steps sweep up to the house from the garden. On the other side there is a courtyard with ample room for parking. The evening meal was excellent and beautifully served, as was breakfast. The bedroom on the second floor is *en suite*, the other rooms share a toilet on the first floor. Rooms are now 250f for two persons. Possible noise from traffic if you sleep with windows open. Evening meal on reservation 100f Mme Sicot is a very charming and helpful hostess.

JOUY-LE-POTIER. 45370

20 km S of Orléans. 10 km from Bellefontaine.

M. et Mme Becchi (M)
778 rue de Chevenelles. 38.45.83.07.

Just outside the neat village of Jouy-le-Potier, off the La Ferté-St. Aubin road, is this immaculate modern chambres d'hôtes, well signed in a road with large houses in

spacious grounds. A very restful
stop after a fast drive from the
Channel ports, and easy to find but
book ahead as virtually only one
room here.

You will receive a warm welcome here and be entertained to an
excellent meal as real guests of the
Becchi's. The well furnished main
guest room is on the first floor and
has two single beds, thick carpets
and huge built-in wardrobe. It over-
looks the back garden and fields beyond. There is a very spacious shower and toilet
adjoining it and on the landing a cosy sitting area with TV. Plenty of books provided on the Loire region. There is another room on the ground floor which has an
adjacent toilet, but no washing facilities, suitable for an extra member of the family
sharing the upstairs shower room.

Madame Becchi speaks good English, and has decorated her house with some
striking dried flower arrangements. An elegant stop in the Loire valley where your
hosts will be delighted to give you any information about the area. Room 240f for
two. Evening meal 80f each, apéritif, wine and coffee included.

ST-BENOIT-SUR-LOIRE. 45730

38 km SE of Orléans. 10 km SE of Châteauneuf by D60. Certainly a very grey, drab
little village but for the Basilica in the centre of the village at the end of a wide cul-
de-sac lined with heavily pollarded plane trees.

The Abbaye de Fleury has had a varied life. The monastic community was
founded in 650 by Benedictine monks. Spend a minute in the belfry-porch, whose
delicately carved, golden Nivernais stone is a particularly graphic example of
mediaeval art, and discover the bizarre animals, luxuriant foliage, Bible scenes...
and the story of St. Benoît.

Founder of the Benedictine order, he died in the 6th century, and was buried in
the monastery at Monte Cassino. The abbot of what was then the Abbaye de Fleury
sent off a raiding part of monks 700 perilous miles to rifle the sepulchre, steal the
saint's bones and bring them back on horseback. The monks must have got carried
away for they added the relics of St Scolastica (Benoît's sister) to their loot and gave
them to the monks of Le Mans who had helped them in their journey. Pilgrims flooded
in, bringing gifts and endowments and the abbey became one of the most esteemed centres of learning in Christendom. It was burnt down in 1026 and its successor, as we see
today, became the finest abbey-church in all the Loire Valley. The monks, dispersed
after the Revolution, returned in 1944 and now their Gregorian chant is world-
renowned. Vespers in the crypt at 6.10 p.m. is a memorable experience.

Madame Bouin (S)
6 Chemin de la Borde. 38.35.70.53.

A tiny chapel dedicated to Ste Scholastica stands on the corner of the Chemin de la Borde on the fringe of the town, and is very useful as a landmark, because it is exactly here that a left turn will bring you to La Borde, where you will be welcomed by M. & Mme Bouin and their three children. It is a really warm, modern house, suitable for winter visits. Three carpeted bedrooms nicely decorated without undue fussiness, have large *en suite* shower and w.c. Two ground-floor rooms with tiled floors, with the same facilities, are better in summer and easy for unloading the car. Double rooms are 210f with extra beds in some rooms. Rooms with private shower and w.c. not adjoining 195f.

Dinner with the family is 75f each, e.g. soup, excellent *pâté lapin, poulet bresse*, cheese and baked apples stuffed with blackcurrants. Not exactly cordon blue, but throw in the free red wine from Cheverny (just south of Blois) and you have a very fair meal for the price.

I simply loved the warm conservatory across the front of the house, whose gigantic table can seat thirty for summer evenings. It is here you may eat if you wish to self-cater, as through the garage/office is a small kitchen for guests.

M. Bouin is a beetroot farmer, with 75 hectares in the vicinity. I enjoyed my visit here and it would be a stop where children would be welcomed and relish the company of the Bouin's young family.

VRIGNY. 45300

9 km S of Pithiviers by D921. Driving south to the Rhône valley from Le Havre, a night stop on the Loire is always useful. The Loire turns north to Orléans so isn't so many miles from Le Havre at this point.

La Croix Allard (M)
Mme Pener. 38.34.13.10.

I was surprised to find this house situated right beside the road. It is a converted staging post for the grooms while their élite passengers stayed at the *Relais* down the road about 200 years ago. The courtyard is enclosed by buildings on three sides and has a large gate locked at night, and a nice lawned garden at the back.

An interesting house with beams galore. Four rooms, two in the old hay loft with smart *en suite* shower rooms, for three and for four. Tiled floors are a bit chilly for winter, even with central heating. Windows are right on the road. Two other rooms (would be very pleasant in summer) are in a stable across the delightful court-yard. These are double rooms but have a cot. 240f.

M. Pener runs this chambres d'hôtes *tout seul* as his wife is away working during the week. Evening meals are nicely served at 80f each, but not for robust eaters.

La Croix Allard

RECOMMENDATIONS FROM READERS: these arrived too late for investigation, or didn't fit in with my itinerary, or lacked precise directions. Further reports most welcome.

ST MARTIN DES BOIS. 41800

La Ferme des Pignons. 54.72.57.43.

'*Rural farm, warm welcome. Superb accommodation in converted barn. Enjoyable meal in the evening. 200f b. and b. 75f dinner inc. wine.*' Hugh Coe

PARCAY LES PINS. 49390

La Croix Joreau. 0203 347836.

'*Run by two enthusiastic English couples and just getting established. A warm welcome in a comfortably converted farm. Conveniently situated on the edge of the village, it is only a short walk to the local bar/restaurant where the hostess provides the best value set meal in France at 50f inc. wine. 250f b. and b.*' Hugh Coe

NEUIL SUR LAYON. 49560

Bonne Esperance. Peter Thornton. 41.59.58.40.

'*It is eminently suited to Brits of a certain age who require peace, good books (English and French), a log fire and a five-course dinner including apéritif and wine for 75f. Bonne Esperance is run by Judy and Peter Thornton, a charming English couple who have settled in the French countryside. Their backgrounds, which I will not reveal, ensure there is an abundance of civilised conversation. B. and b. cost 235f for two and dinner is available every night except Wednesdays.*'
Mr and Mrs Stockley and Mr and Mrs Grantham.

BURGUNDY

Départements: **Côte d'Or**
Nievre
Saône-et-Loire
Yonne

The very name suggests good living, good wine, richness, generosity and mellow fruitfulness. Like the Burgundian hills, there is a rounded dignified quality implicit – nothing hurried – sleepy villages, slow-flowing water, time-honoured traditions, centuries of history sun-baked in old roofs and placid squares, and everywhere the cult of the grape.

Viticulture now may be highly scientific – has to be – but the views over those vine-covered hills can't have changed much since Roman times. The Romans knew a thing or two about wine and lost no time in planting the south-facing gravelly slopes with the vines that would keep them well supplied. Names like Vosne-Romané commemorate their dedication. They found the result greatly to their liking.

As did the monks in the Middle Ages, who continued the tradition. They created vineyards like Le Clos de Vougeot eight centuries ago. Pope Gregory XI accepted thirty barrels from this vineyard and was so impressed that he made the abbot a cardinal in recognition of his talents temporal if not spiritual.

The Kings of France preferred Burgundy wine to any in their realm. Madame de Pompadour's favourite tipple was Romanée Conti, while Napoleon preferred Chambertin. By the eighteenth century the superiority of the wine was recognized throughout the civilised world, new markets opened up abroad, and Beaune became the first trading centre for Burgundy wine, followed by Nuits St. Georges and Dijon.

Today, mercifully recovered from the 19th century ravages of phylloxera, thanks to the clean American vines grafted on to French stock, benefiting from the latest oeneological research, the wines have never been finer, and the opportunity to taste the (often) superb results and to buy some to take

BURGUNDY

COTE D'OR (21)
Préfecture: Dijon
1   Aignay le Duc
2   Buffon
3   Chamboeuf
4   Chorey les Beaune
5   Ecutigny
6   Epernay sous Gevrey
7   Gevrey Chambertin
8   Longecourt-en-Plaine
9   Magny les Villers
10   Meuilley
11   Santenay
12   Vosne-Romanée

NIEVRE (58)
Préfecture: Nevers
1   Champlemy
2   Fleury la Tour
3   Guipy
4   Mont et Marré
5   Onlay
6   Oulon
7   Pouilly-sur-Loire
8   St Loup
9   St Reverien
10   Semelay

SAONE-ET-LOIRE (71)
Préfecture: Mâcon
1   Baudrières
2   Bissy-sous-Uxelles
3   Céron
4   Charolles
5   Chassagny-sous-Dun
6   Châtenay
7   Clermain
8   Lournand
9   Fontaines
10   la Guiche
11   Mancey
12   Marcigny
13   Mussy-sous-Dun
14   Poisson
15   La Roche-Vineuse
16   Sennecy-le-Grand
17   Tournus
18   Uchizy

YONNE (89)
Préfecture: Auxerre
1   Escolives-Ste-Camille
2   Lavau
3   Mont St Sulpice
4   Perreux
5   Poilly-sur-Serein
6   Venoy
7   Vézélay

■   Préfecture

■   Town

①   Chambre d'Hôtes

home should not be resisted. To drive through unassuming villages with great names like Nuits St Georges, Pouilly, Mercurey, Vosne-Romanée... is like opening a wine catalogue.

Even without the vines it would be attractive countryside, rolling, wooded, expansive, and dotted with the distinctive, white Charollais cattle that for me are as good as a sign saying You have arrived in Burgundy. It is threaded with rivers – the Saône, the Seille, the Yonne, the Loire – and canals, particularly the Burgundy and the Nivernais, providing plenty of variety for cruising. The tempo of a barge holiday seems exactly right to view this region.

Burgundy's appeal as a tourist area does not stop with its wine. As a medieval and Renaissance art and architecture centre it is unrivalled in France. Since Roman times the duchy has been a crossroads for travellers, who brought their skills and knowledge to Burgundy, and the enlightend Dukes of the 15th century encouraged artists and sculptors from Paris and Flanders to live and work there, leaving behind unique examples of their talents. The Romanesque buildings of the 11th and 12th centuries alone would merit a journey – Tournus, Cluny, Paray-le-Monial, La Charité sur-Loire, Autun are prime examples, but hundreds of small villages have stunning Romanesque churches as their hearts – don't miss any opportunity to dive inside and marvel at the length of time that has passed since their builders laboured to affirm their faith.

A century later Vezelay was the beginning of a new look, known as the Burgundy Romanesque school, more elaborate, leading on to the Gothic, like Notre Dame in Dijon, and subsequently to the Renaissance classical revival – look at St Michael in the same city.

Burdgundy was a bit slow to realise the potential of the b. and b. market but it is fast catching up and there is no shortage of choice now. As the two major autoroutes used by the holidaying Brits pass through the area, and as it is a comfortable drive back to the ports to catch an afternoon ferry, a lodging here makes good sense. It may only be one night the first time, but it would certainly be a shame not to spend longer and taste more of the delights of the region on the next occasion.

CÔTE-D'OR

AIGNAY LE DUC. 21510

28 km S of Châttillon-sur-Seine by N71 and D32, east, which becomes the D954 for the last 5 km after Cosne. Tarperon is well signed on this road, 3 km W of Aignay before Beaumotte. Nearest A 26 exit is at Til-Chatel. This is lovely, wooded countryside in the centre of several substantial forests, providing an idyllic setting for the château. Aignay is a pretty little town with 13th century church and rivulets of the river Coquille running through, providing good picnic opportunities (unless the school is out to play, in which case peacefulness is not in evidence).

Manoir de Tarperon (M)
Mme Soisick de Champsavin. 80.93.83.74.

Set in wooded parkland, interrupted by streams, the well-restored château's white turrets provide a splendid first impression. The good news continues – the five rooms have been cleverly decorated with strong, bright colours and stylishly furnished. The period atmosphere has been preserved – polished wooden boards, family heirlooms, but cheerfulness prevails. I like the blue room best because of the bath, but there is another with bath and two with shower and a pretty yellow and blue room in the tower for a child. Prices are good too – 330f a double or 500f for three or four. Dinner, served in the family dining room, is way above average – 160f including wine, *apéritif* and coffee. Good fishing available on the property. Recommended for comfort, charm and good value.

BUFFON. 21500

36 km SE of Tonnerre. Pick up the D905 near Floretin, just east of Sens for a lovely drive down to Dijon along the Canal d'Armançon, which somehow becomes the Canal de Bourgogne. It keeps reappearing beside the road and one is spoilt for choice of picnic spots beside it. The road is flat and quiet, sometimes dead straight, sometimes weaving in and out with the canal, in rolling countryside with cattle and sheep on the hillsides. The occasional château appears, but not a vineyard in sight – they are all further south.

Mme Busson (S)
80.92.46.00.

As you approach the small village of Buffon, the chambres d'hôtes is a high house built into the hillside, with only a garden separating it from the busy D905. The super views over the canal and field compensate for the possibility of any traffic at night (certainly none out of season).

The three wooden-floored rooms are nicely decorated in country style, with shower and toilet in a sort of moulded plastic capsule. Access is by a steepish outside stairway. Take a break half-way up on the pretty, little lawned terrace.

Rooms 250f. No evening meal but restaurants on either side within easy walking distance; one belonging to young Mme Busson's parents.

CHAMBOEUF. 21220

8 km SW of Dijon. Take the N74 to Gevrey-Chambertin, turn right in the village on to the D31, a pretty, winding drive through an atypical landscape in this green, gently sloping wine country, of high, grey cliffs, following a little river. In the village of Chamboeuf head for the church and turn left to private car park.

Le Relais de Chasse (M)
M. et Mme Girard. 80.51.81.60; fax 80.34.15.96.

As its name would suggest, this is an old hunting lodge; about 1700, surrounded by stately pines and cedars. The garden is truly lovely, shaded, flowery, terraced, and the house is equally well maintained. Either side of the dining room are comfortable, big bedrooms on the ground floor, looking out over the garden, with a bathroom apiece (baths); there is another double room with bath, one with shower

and three singles with shower – 400f for one night or 340f if you stay longer. Furniture tends to be ponderous, but there are some nice touches, like good soap, efficient bedside lights and flowery sheets. A reliable, peaceful, well-situated stop.

CHOREY-LES-BEAUNE. 21200

3 km N of Beaune by N74. The village of Chorey is on the left and the château is well marked.

If you can make only one stop in Burgundy (and that would indeed be a shame) it should be in Beaune. At the heart of the viticulture industry, its name synonymous with good wine, good living, good company, it is also a highly attractive town, easily explored on foot since the interesting parts are encircled by ancient ramparts and the centre is pedestrianised. Strolling along the high-class shopping area, sitting in the sun at one of the many bars in the squares, sipping a glass of local wine in a wine bar (Beaune is unusual in France in accepting the role of *bars à vin*), dining in one of the many good restaurants, one feels in the very centre of Burgundian life and culture.

No one will want to miss a visit to the Hotel-Dieu, the marvel of Burgundian Flemish art, founded as a hospital in 1443, whose magnificent, glazed tile roofs and turrets will be familiar from many a poster.

The third Saturday, Sunday and Monday in November are dubbed 'Three Glorious Days'; rightly so since this is the time when the year's work in the vineyards comes to a climax and the wine is auctioned in Nuits St George, Beaune and Mêursault. By far the most famous of these is the sale in the covered market of the Beaune. If you are lucky enough to be in the area at that time you are in for a colourful, historic, memorable treat.

Château-lès-Beaune (L)
M. et Mme François German. Rue Jacques German.
80.22.06.05; fax 80.24.03.93.

A bit expensive, but I include this one because of two redeeming features – proximity to the most delightful of wine towns and for its interest as a wine-producer. The 17th century château is surrounded by vines and agreeable M. German cultivates 16 hectares of land producing top-quality wines. You can taste, learn and buy. It has been 100 years in his family and was restored by his father after the war. The house itself is like many an old French aristocrat, crumbling and shabby, but with good bones.

The five bedrooms, two flights up a winding staircase in the tower, all with good bathrooms and furnished with dignity, cost from 570–590f and there is a suite for three people at 790f. Breakfast is served on the terrace, looking through a gate on to a formal garden, whose box hedges enclose yet more vines; there is a cool if overgrown garden, murky moat and somewhat dark sitting room.

ECUTIGNY. 21360 BLIGNY-SUR-OUCHE

19 km NW of Beaune by D970. At Bligny take the D33 towards Pont d'Ouche. The château is well signposted on the D33E 1½ km from village. Very pretty countryside, wooded, hilly, threaded by streams and extremely peaceful, but within easy reach of Beaune. 25 km from the Beaune autoroute exit and 18 km from that at Pouilly-en-Auxois.

Château d'Ecutigny (L)
Patrick and Francoise Rochet. 80.20.19.14; fax 80.20.19.15.

Château d' Ecutigny

We were running late and the photo of the château looked so grim that I was all for forgetting that one, but our hostess insisted that we should pay a visit. 'Something special' she said. And something special is certainly what the Rochets have achieved in this reconstruction of a completely derelict château, origin 12th century. It is two years now since they have been able to receive p.g.s. but before that they spent another two rebuilding a ruin with no roof, no windows and sheep grazing in what is now the salon. 'My husband likes a challenge,' said Francoise. There is still plenty to achieve here – the wonderful cellars (with the original fixtures and fittings) – are virtually untouched – and there are tremendous plans for the future, but Francoise hopes that it will be a long time before they run out of scope because she fears that Patrick, a *constructeur* by trade, will be off looking for another challenge. Just ask to see the photos of 'before' and 'after' to appreciate the sale of the work involved.

Patrick may have worked wonders on the exterior but Francoise has had fun transforming the huge bedrooms which could have been unwelcoming, into colourful and comfortable retreats. Each one is different of course; the honeymoon suite in the tower has a four poster – 600f, another yellow room has big windows, an amazing cast-iron stove and an antique cradle – 500f, another has a brown velvet coronet, another is all blue. They all have real fireplaces with real fires in winter – the ultimate luxury. The bathrooms are all to scale, big enough to hold a family, and complete with marble washstands, old weighing scales, baths on painted feet and many other treasures that Francoise, starting from scratch, has discovered in local *antiquaires*.

EPERNAY SOUS GEVERY. 21220 GEVREY CHAMBERTIN

12 km from A31, exit Nuits St George, 22 km S of Dijon. From Dijon take the D996, turn right onto the D25 at Corcelles-les-Citeaux and Epernay is 6 km, near the Route du Grand Cru. Ideally situated in fact for visits to all the great wine villages, and Dijon and Beaune. It's a quiet little village, in whose tree-lined square is to be found:

La Vieille Auberge (M)
Jules and Jane Plimmer. 80.36.61.76; fax 80.36.64.68.

It may have been *vieille* once, but the Plimmers have completely restored the old farmhouse, re-surfaced the crumbling walls, installed new, brown shutters, put on a new roof and generally spruced the place up inside and out, so that you might be forgiven for thinking it was brand new. Jules hails from Dartmoor and Jane from Folkestone, so those nervous of airing their school French should feel quite at home here.

I admire their courage and enterprise – Jennifer aged 5 is now bilingual, and when I visited, a new baby was expected shortly, but Jane still manages to look after five rooms (functional, clean, all with bathrooms, one with bath, two family rooms: 280f a double, 340f for three), welcome their guests and cook an excellent 100f dinner six nights a week. For us it was French onion soup, roast lamb, and almond baskets with strawberries from the garden.

There are swings, a paddling pool and Jennifer to play with, so this would make an ideal family holiday.

GEVREY-CHAMBERTIN. 21220

12 km S of Dijon. Nearest autoroute exist Nuits St Georges 8 km. Take the N74 toward Nuits-St Georges and turn right into Gevrey Chambertin. Well signed from there.

Another unassuming Burgundian village, humble in everything except name. In the heart of the Cote d'Or, and ideal therefore for visiting vineyards and Beaune.

Mme Sylvain (S)
14 rue de l'Eglise. 80.51.86.39.

The house, sideways on to the road, is in the village centre, but there is little traffic and calm prevails. Once inside the high gate the calm is even more impressive, in an unexpected secret garden, where Mme Sylvain grows the materials for her primary occupation – dried flowers. The temptation of her garden shed should be avoided by the impecunious, since the bunches and arrangements there are truly lovely but not cheap.

She has three guest rooms in her house, airy and spacious, one with an ancient porcelain stove. With bath, they cost 220f, sharing a loo between two rooms; 250 with private 'facilities'. Very pleasant atmosphere and good value.

LONGECOURT-EN-PLAINE. 21110 GENLIS

15 km SE of Dijon by D968, which runs along the Burgundy canal. Longecourt is signed to the right.

Plaine indeed. This area is surprisingly flat (and rather boring), compared with the dramatic vine-covered hills west of the autoroute.

Château de Longecourt (L)
Comtesse de St Seine. 80.39.88.76.

A caricature of a château. Vast, its area the size of a small village, with every conceivable château feature added throughout its long life, from 13th century fortification, 16th century manor house and 18th century embellishment. There are towers topped with slate witches hat roofs, terraces, balconies, courtyards, moats, round windows, long windows, slit windows, you name it. The materials are mostly red brick

with fanciful Italianate mouldings, plaques and friezes, now sadly crumbling. The thought of maintaining that pile would make one yearn for a semi-detached.

The rooms are equally gargantuan. The salon, where guests assemble for *apéritifs* has white-tiled floor and chunky pillars supporting the roof. All the rooms have lovely floor-length shuttered windows. In one of the towers is a private chapel, but the jewel in the crown is the first-floor salon, where guests are allowed to sit carefully but not touch, since this is listed as a *monument historique* and is truly stunning.

Gold leaf abounds on glorious mirrors, carvings, pillars and frames; the ceiling is painted with bosomy ladies and plumb cherubim. Furniture has been inherited during the three centuries that the same family has lived here, and is priceless.

Nice Comtesse de Saint Seine, a widow, speaks little English, but her son Roland is at hand to help out. An artist, he had introduced a lighter touch to the dining-room by painting a daisy frieze around the walls. In our bedroom, too, he has been at work, painting colourful birds round the windows and a cheeky intruder (avian) in the bathroom. The four guest rooms differ wildly, some much bigger than others, some in the towers; all have good bathrooms and are furnished with antiques and *objets d'art*: 650f.

Dinner, at 250f, is a sociable occasion, with good food, and breakfast is copious and elegantly served on fine china.

MAGNY-LES-VILLERS. 21700

8 km from Nuits St Georges, exit 1 from A31, then N74 south and D115.

To the west of the autoroute in this area lie villages with names so familiar – Aloxe Corton, Gevrey Chambertin – that it is hard to believe you are actually *there*. This is Premier Cru country and the appellations listed on the boards at the roadsides are proud ones indeed. The territory, as one would expect to produce prime grapes, is gently sloping, with typical Burgundian landscapes in all directions. Pernand-Vergelesses is a particularly pretty, sleepy, rose-covered hilltop village producing wonderfully fruity wine that it would be a shame not to sample. Magny, equally involved in viticulture, with every other house inviting you to stop and sip, is next door.

M. et Mme Robert Dumay (S)
80.62.91.16.

From the church take the Corgoloin road and the house is signed on the right, tucked away at the end of a short track between aged stone houses covered in Danse de Feu roses.

Nice, shy Madame Dumay apologised for her rooms being 'simple'; I assured her that I infinitely preferred their rusticity to flock paper and purple bathrooms. Of the two suites – each has double

and two singles sharing bathroom (showers) – I prefer the older one, with stone flagged floors and a piano, but all is delightful, clean and wholesome and wonderfully quiet enclosed in the courtyard with a terrace for sunny breakfasts and a nice, little salon for inclement weather. A kitchen is available for the guests' use. 200f for double. A super, calm stop with a kind hostess.

MEUILLEY. 21700 NUITS ST GEORGES

6 km from A31, exit Nuits St Georges, then D25 west. Signed from village.
    Lush countryside, with vines, wheat and Charolais cattle on lovely rounded hills.

Roland and Annie Troisgros (M)
Open all year but by reservation only from 1/11–31/4.

This is the kind of chambres d'hôtes that justifies this kind of guidebook. Precise understanding is essential. It would be an excellent choice for a particular kind of person and not at all suitable for others. The Troisgros are exceptionally houseproud of their delightful little detached cottage and would certainly not welcome children or pets. Formal and correct, they are not the kind of hosts who would chum up with their guests. Fair enough – no good for the happy-go-luckys, but excellent for travellers who like extremely comfortable, self-contained accommodation and total privacy. The owners' house faces on to the village street and gives no clue as to what to expect behind the big, iron gate (secure locked parking). Across the courtyard is a pretty cottage with its own garden sloping up behind, terrace and garden furniture complete, with no chance of being overlooked. For 330f it offers a surprisingly vast beamed salon, with TV and two convertible sofas (for adult guests or a husband who snores), a well-equipped kitchen, a pretty double bedroom with flowery paper and covers and a luxurious bathroom, stylishly pink and grey, equipped with all mod. cons. like a hairdryer and multi-voltage plugholes. Everything is pristine, as it should be since daily cleaning is included in the price.
    Unique in this area in offering this standard of comfort at this price, this would be a good choice for anyone wishing to stay more than an odd night and wishing to self-cater (but there are restaurants just 2 km away).

SANTENAY. 21590

4 km E of Chalon-sur-Sâone. From A6 exit at Beaune take N74 then D974 (17 km), signed to Les-Hauts-de-Santenay in village. From Chalon-Nord exit take N6 to Chagny then D974 (21 km). In other words, conveniently placed.

Château de la Crée (L)
Yves-Eric and Rolande Remy-Thévenin. 80.20.62.66; fax 80.20.66.50. cl. 1/12–1/4.

The 19th century manor house, attractively restored and in immaculate condition, is set on a famous family-owned wine estate. The decision to take in p.g's is a recent one and there are great plans to extend the present three rooms, and to add a swimming pool (ready in 1995). The whole operation is very efficiently run and decidedly upmarket.

Yves-Eric is a *viticulteur* and wine buff, who will show guests his amazing cellars beneath the house and offer them a *dégustation* of the estate wines. Evening *apéritifs* are sometimes taken here (or in the large shady garden on expensive garden furniture), and the candle-lit cellars are used for local functions. Very smart cellars, too.

Two communicating rooms share a lavish bathroom with blue and white tiles and his-and-hers basins (650f a double) and the third room at 750f has a dark canopied bed and somewhat-hectic pink luxurious bathroom.

The main decor theme of the salons and library downstairs is military. Father-in-law collected hats, swords, guns, paintings, and memorabilia from many wars. Three rooms have their walls entirely lined with colourful souvenirs, imaginatively displayed.

There are numerous restaurants nearby, but the meals at the chateau are sophisticated and of professional standard (200f plus), as is everything about this luxurious stop.

VOSNE-ROMANÉE. 21700

2½ km from Nuits-St-Georges. From autoroute exit take the N174 through the village of Vosne-Romanée, turn left and the house is well signed. One feels that such a prestigious name should be engraved on gold plate, that there should be flags flying, but no, this village is no grander than any other in the region, where world renown sits lightly. Vineyards, of course, as far as the eye can see, and all around La Closerie.

La Closerie des Ormes (M)
Jean-Paul and Claude Grimm. 21 rue de la Grande Velle. 80.61.20.24; fax 80.61.19.63. cl. 1/11–1/4.

A substantial creeper-covered house, far more spacious and elegant inside than first impressions would suggest. Everywhere is pristine, Laura-Ashley-ed and extremely comfortable. In the large dining-room the window frames spectacular views of the vines that crowd to the very door. The three double and two triple rooms are very nice indeed and reasonably priced at 350f–400f depending on bath or shower, but sadly next year they will be 100f more. Nice Mme Grim related a horrifying tale – that the local luxury chambres d'hôtes were ganging up on her because the com-

Yvonne La Closerie des Ormes

fort she offered was cheaper and better than theirs and she had to agree to bring her prices in line. Even at 450f and 550f the rooms are still good news, with a copious and elegant breakfast, but I don't like the principle. We shall have to keep an eye on this one.

NIÈVRE

CHAMPLEMY. 58210 VARZY

16 km SW of Clamecy by N51 and D977. A sleepy little village, with a couple of bars and one indifferent restaurant. In the square is:-

Steve and Marie-Noelle Taylor (S)
86.60.15.08. cl. Nov-May.

No language problems here – Steve is English, married to French Noelle, and they both, together with their two elder children and soon no doubt the baby, are bilingual. Their home is a typically French town house – steep roof, white shutters, grey stone, geraniums in window boxes, and they have one double room with private loo and washbasin and shower next door for 190f, another with

Chez MacTaylor

three beds and private bathroom for 240f or 310f for three. Nice house, nice rooms, nice couple.

FLEURY-LA-TOUR. 58110 TINTURY

35 km E of Nevers by D975 to Rouy then D132 to Tintury, and D112 to Fleury. Take the first turning right after the village.

Mme Marie France Guény (S)
86.84.12.42.

A substantial beige, stone, three-storeyed farmhouse, white shuttered windows reaching down to the courtyard. Its most striking feature is the enormous lake at the rear, where fishing is free for guests. The whole atmosphere exudes rural tranquility. Mme Guény came to the door cradling her grandson, but was not too busy to show us round the four comfortable rooms, with assorted beds and sanitary arrangements, from 160–230f, all looking out over the lake. 40f supplement for extra beds. Excellent breakfast.

With tennis court and kitchenette for guests' use, this would make a good-value base for a family.

GUIPY. 58420 BRINÇON-SUR-BEUVRON

7 km SW of Corbigny on D977–bis. Way off the tourists' beat but in pleasant countryside, dotted with lakes, like the Etang de Vaux and Etang de Baye nearby, plus the interest of the Nivernais canal.

Château de Chanteloup (M)
M. and Mme Boulanger. 86.29.01.26.

An imposing towered château, 16th and 18th centuries, with extensive grounds and a riding school. This one would make a surprisingly luxurious (and not expensive) base for horsey families, since the three rooms, one with four-poster, all with baths cost only 260f. There is an impressive salon, a bit over-stuffed with artificial flowers, which bloom in every possible container including a cradle, and a music room in the tower with piano and other instruments available for anyone sufficiently talented to play. A kitchen is available for guests' use, too.

MONT-ET-MARRÉ. 58110 CHATILLON-EN-BAZOIS

5 km N of Chatillon by D945 and D259. Miles from anywhere.

Ferme Semelin (S)
Paul and Nicole Deltour. 86.84.13.94.

Well indicated from the approach roads in all directions.

Paul Deltour, a kind gentle man, showed me round the three double rooms, each with its own bathroom. Our double with bath costs 240f and two others with showers are 210f. I liked their country-fresh simplicity very much, as I appreciated the thoughtfulness behind supplying a good kitchenette for the guests' use – almost essential out here in the deepest countryside, far from restaurants.

There is a lovely, long dining-room for un-sunny breakfasts, and a big fire in winter, furnished with family furniture, including an antique cradle. Lovely atmosphere.

ONLAY. 58370

5 km S of Château Chinon by D27 and D157 in the Morvan National Park.

Chateau de Lesvault (M)
Mme Lee. 86.84.32.91; fax 86.84.35.78.

So far away from hassle and dazzle that it is a natural attraction to artists and writers, all of whom are made most welcome by Norwegian Bibi Lee and her artist/sculptor husband. She has been b. and b.ing now for ten years, in order to help with the upkeep of the 19th century château. She has ten rooms, six with private bathrooms. The smaller rooms share bathrooms but cost only 250f, which is good going

for a château. I particularly liked one of the top rooms with old beams and extensive views down the valley, one double and one single bed and a large bathroom for 450f; others are 350f, so there is something for all pockets, which is a deliberate policy.

Bibi is a good cook and serves excellent meals at 125f including *apéritif* and coffee, but exclusive of wine, in a lovely dining-room with huge, central table. You can be assured of lively conversation here, mostly in English. Fly fishing on the lake, walking in the 2½ acres of parkland.

OULON. 58700 PRÉMERY

5 km NE of Prémery by D977 and D129. In un-tourist-ridden Nivernais countryside, with lakes, canal and forests all near by.

Ferme Auberge du Vieux Chateau (M)
Mme Fayolle. 86.68.06.77.

A good bet for a family, with a room for four with big bathroom costing 450f; I thought the double rooms too expensive at 250f since they are small, have a tiny shower cabinet and share one loo between three. The plus points are the romantic atmosphere of the complex of ancient farm buildings and medieval tower, the swimming pool, the farm produce used in the evening meals (menus at 75f, 100f, and 150f), the lovely beamed dining room, the home-made jams served at breakfast, and nice young Mme Fayolle. Not a bad list.

POUILLY-SUR-LOIRE. 58150

15 km S of Cosne-sur-Loire by N7. Not my favourite stretch of the Loire and Cosne is to be avoided at all costs, but here we are in wine country and the whole town is dedicated to the grape. The main street is lined with caves offering *dégustations*, so it would be a pity not to take advantage. The hotels here are spoiled with too easy custom, so a chambres d'hôtes is an especially good idea.

La Reverie (M)
Paul and Maoudo Lapeyrade. 6 rue Joyeuse. 86.39.07.87.

With typical French insouciance turn right off the high street up a road marked No Entry to find La Reverie (actually the house is before the start of the restriction, so it's all perfectly legal). Tucked away behind high dark red railings is a 19th century bourgeois house that has recently been completely refurbished in '*le style Empire*'. Each of the five rooms is decorated in different co-ordinated colours, with their own luxurious bathroom – 410–490f. Excellent breakfasts cost another 35f and are served in a gallery exhibiting modern paintings, to the strains of classical

music. *Raffineé* is the rather offputting way they describe this one, but the welcome is warm, as is the big, open fire in winter. A touch expensive perhaps, but good for those who like their comfort assured.

ST LOUP. 58200

6 km NE of Cosne-sur-Loire by D114 through Cours. Hard to imagine that the industrialisation of Cosne is so near. Here is deep, unspoiled rustic tranquility.

➤ ## Chauffour (M)
Mme Elvire Duchet. 86.26.20.22. cl. 1/11–1/3.

Three km out of the village on the St. Amand road D114. you can hardly see the lovely old 19th century farmhouse for flowers. Daisies and lambstails and wild geraniums vie with roses for a space in the deep flower beds around it and creamy elder flowers rampage alongside. The Duchets have completely re-built the house from a virtual ruin, and now it is picture-book pretty, with original mate-

rials re-cycled – old beams, flagged floors. The breakfast room is particularly charming – galleried, stone walled, heavily beamed, a collection of straw hats on the wall.

The two double rooms are both good news – one blue and white with shower and the other with a good bath, 270f for two, 370 for three, 470f for four. Three more rooms soon available.

Dinner is eaten in the garden when fine – 90f exclusive of wine; sometimes it's a barbecue. Highly recommended for a stylish, inexpensive stay with kind hosts.

ST RÉVERIEN. 58420

On the D977 between Cormery (15 km) and Corbigny (17 km). A little Nirvernais village with an important Romanesque church. Spare a moment to appreciate its lovely 12th century ambulatory and the 16th century frescoes. Nearby the Etang de Vaux is a popular excursion, the Vaux lake for fishing and the Baye lake for sailing.

La Villa des Près (M)
Mme Bernadette Burgi. 86.29.04.57.

'This is not a chambres d'hôtes – it is a maison d'hôte,' says friendly Mme Burgi. In other words the whole house is open for guests' use. And a very nice house, too – very French, white shutters, iron balconies, in the village, but quiet, with a lovely garden sloping down to an unexpectedly dramatic view of the surrounding countryside.

Madame Burgi, who speaks some English, stresses that this is a house of quality, pointing out that the sheets are linen and hand-embroidered and that the mattresses are new and not cheap ones, thus justifying the price of 300f for a very pleasant double room with shower. There are actually six rooms in all, but the three more modern ones on the top floor are only used in the summer, because of high heating costs.

The breakfast room has a splendid view, the terrace even better. There will soon be a *cuisine* (Mme emphasised that I should not call it a *cuisinette*) for the guests to self-cater, and a barbecue, too, as easy alternatives to eating at the restaurant in the village.

I think this one is a good safe bet and if you stay six days you get the seventh thrown in for free.

SEMELAY. 58360
Domaine de la Chaume (M)
Mme Pierre D'Ete. 86.30.91.23.

The Domaine de la Chaume is a restored farm building with much character. It is next door to the Château Bussière, the family home of Madame D'Ete senior. In the old granary, entered by stairs in the farmhouse, are four rooms all facing south, carpeted with original beams. One room has bunk beds and stairs up to an open mezzanine with a double bed, another has the same double bed accommodation up a flight of stairs, but in place of bunk beds a little kitchenette. If you don't like slipping up and down stairs in the middle of the night choose one of the other, normal double-bedded rooms.

Young Mme d'Ete does evening meals (not Sundays) and she is just as charming as her *belle-mère*. It is a nice place for children well off the main road, with plenty of space to play and a small copse behind the house. Lovely views over rolling countryside. Rooms 240f for two people. Evening meal 70f.

Back at the château Madame had assigned us a suite of five rooms, which were really ready for her family arriving at the weekend. She asked if we would like to eat a light meal with them that night, though she never does evening meals. An invitation we were delighted to accept and very delicious it was, too! The hospitality of the French is quite amazing sometimes.

Mme D'Ete has one other gîte a mile or so away.

SAÔNE-et-LOIRE

BAUDRIÈRES. 71370

17 km SE of Chalon-sur-Saône. via D978, D933 and D160. The Tournus exit is 21 km S. Baudrières is a pleasant, sleepy village in the heart of the rich Bresse farming territory.

➤ ### Le Bourg (M)
Mme Yvonne Perrusson. 85.47.31.90.

I think Mme Perrusson's little house in the village centre must be the prettiest in the book. Hard to describe, since it is like no other. The main part is white, shuttered, geraniumed and set back behind a charming garden, and a big chestnut tree. Alongside is a lace-curtained annexe whose verandah gives it a Deep South look, totally un-French. Mme Perrusson is a widow, who has recently taken to b. and b.ing

on the success of her daughter's operation in the same village (see below). She has adapted two charming rooms, between which I find it hard to choose, one blue and white in the front for 300f and one red and green with coronet over bed, looking out at a pretty rear garden, sharing a bathroom with bath. Both 300f or 450f for four.

Breakfast in the kitchen is a delight – another exceptionally pretty room, decorated with straw hats and bunches of lavender, lace curtains framing the garden. Furniture is old and full of character, the table in the salon is a huge bellows, floors are flagged and an old manger serves as a receptacle for table linen.

I am not doing justice to this one – go and see for yourselves. An arrow to lend conviction.

Mme Vachet (M)
85.47.32.18. cl. 15/11–1/4.

Mme Perrusson's daughter, Arlette Vachet, has been hostessing guests in her picturebook village cottage for six years now. She is an artist by profession, as one might guess by the original (some might say bizarre) decoration of her home. The ambiance is cosily cluttered, with big fires burning in the open hearths whenever the temperature drops. Any signs of the 20th century are hidden away, like the TV buried in

an old oak chest, and although the house is in fact not very old, the impression is of centuries of affectionate care. The two bedrooms are smallish, attractively rustic, the downstairs one opening out directly into the pretty garden. The adjoining pink bathroom is a bit hectic in colour but efficient in sanitation. Upstairs the other room has low sloping ceiling covered in flowered wallpaper and another bathroom, 300f each.

Mme Vachet is obviously a very practical lady – she was building a stone wall in her garden when I called and proudly showed me the small swimming pool that she and her husband have recently installed. Former careers include that of antique dealer, so it is not surprising that the house is a treasure-trove of bric-à-brac.

BISSY-SOUS-UXELLES. 71460

10 km W of Tournus. A6 exit. From Tournus take the D215 towards this particularly pretty flowery village sleeping peacefully in rural calm.

La Ferme (S)
Pascale and Dominique de la Bussière. 85.50.15.03.

A lovely old farmyard, part 15th century, built round a courtyard cheerful with geraniums. It has been in the same family for a staggering 500 years. For the past ten of them the present generation have been b. and b.ing, having converted two suites into simple, but comfortable guest accommodation. Approached by an outside staircase two rooms have double beds, a basin and a loo outside, and the other two, at 230f, have their own shower and loo (390f for four). Pascale and Dominique are friendly, caring hosts, who give a little bit extra to their guests in

terms of attention to detail and their time to discuss local attractions. They have delightful children themselves, so this would make an ideal family stay, with the attraction of a herd of goats to admire. No evening meal is provided, but two of the rooms do have self-catering facilities.

CERON. 71110 MARCIGNY

8 km W of Marcigny by D990 and D202. Follow signs to 'Golf'. Not really very near anywhere, and all the better for that.

Le Chateau de la Frédière (L)
Mme Edith Charlier. 85.25.27.40.

Perfect of course for golfers – 18 holes and putting green, but pretty good too for non-practitioners. The rooms are very attractive – Les Tilleuls in the tower for example, has a wonderful bathroom (430f), the Chambre des Oiseaux is the most expensive – 520f with twin beds and another luxurious bathroom. The smallest costs a mere 240f, with shower *en suite* but loo outside; it really doesn't

matter, all six rooms are delightful, except perhaps the 900f suite which I found a bit dark.

The prices are fair for the amenities – swimming pool, lovely building, park, but breakfast, albeit a very elegant one served in your room if you wish, does cost another 55f per person. There is a choice of menus served in the very pleasant golf club restaurant from 95f. You get a special deal if you play golf and stay. English spoken, of course.

CHAROLLES. 71120

13 km E of Paray-le-Monial by N79, 49 km W of Macon. A pleasant little town, which gave its name to the distinctive white cattle which, for me are a sign that I have arrived in Burgundy. On Wednesdays from April to December a lively market is held in the town, when the handsome Charollais are sold, having been rounded up from the rich surrounding pastures.

The town is dominated by the ruins of the former château of the Counts of Charollais, whose surviving building now serves as the Town Hall. Take a walk along the terrace of the public gardens for a pleasant view of the Charollais countryside. The river Arconce flows through the town centre, providing an excuse to hang colourful baskets of flowers on the bridge.

Mme Simone Laugerette (M)
3 rue de la Madeleine. 85.88.35.78.

Right in the town centre. Make for the church on the rue de Champagny, then take the turning opposite, signed *Sous-Prefecture*, then first turning right. The house is on the left, tucked away behind a high, iron gate. Ring the bell and Madame Laugerette will open up and reveal a pleasant, secluded garden, with secure parking. Miraculously quiet, which few people can believe, here is an excellent town base which, as Madame ruefully explains, often has rooms when others are full. Through no fault of hers. It's a nice substantial 18th century town house, grey-slate roof, white shutters, furnished with handsome old family hand-me-downs, unpretentious and comfortable and a very attractive room for breakfasts when it's too cold for the terrace. Our bedroom cost 250f with bath and lots of individual touches like hand-embroidered towels. There is also one single and double, adjoining and sharing a bathroom, for 200f a double. Recommended for a good value town stop.

CHASSAGNY-SOUS-DUN. 71170

19 km S of Charolles by D985 and D308. Nearest autoroute exit Macon. Pleasant farming country.

Aux Chizelles (M-S)
Mme Simone Boujot. 85. 46.43.18.

I nearly missed this one. Having had difficulty in tearing ourselves away from the delectable rose garden at Mussy (see p. 324) we had strayed into penalty time – that sacred hour devoted to *le déjeuner* when every self-respecting French-man and his wife have knees under and napkins tucked. To intrude upon them at this time is (a) selfish and (b) usually non-productive, so we started to look for a picnic spot for our own modest feast. 'May as well head in that direction,' I said. No picnic spot materialised and we were at the Boujot's gate. There was Monsieur settling down for his

Les Chizelles

post lunch nap in the sunny garden, there was Madame wondering what on earth a very dusty English car was doing in these parts. I began to apologise and explain. 'You must eat your picnic by our lake then,' she said—and so it was. We carried the paraphernalia through the pretty garden and down to the sizeable lake, planted with flower beds, little hut for shelter, jetty for fishing, and enjoyed our respite.

By which time Monsieur had finished off his snooze and Madame was ready to show us round two very pleasant rooms with French windows opening into the garden, one with twin beds and one with a double, both with baths. Madame's thoughtfulness continued to be in evidence with the provision of a kitchenette for self-catering, use of a barbecue, and two quite separate lawns assigned to each room for occupants' private sunbathing. 260f for two, 500f for four. Bistros in village, gastronomic restaurants 5 km.

CHATENAY. 71800

27 km SE of Charolles by D985 and D987 east, or 55 km SW of Macon (nearest autoroute exit). This is typical Charollais country where the rich green hills are dotted with the distinctive white cattle and cities seem very far away.

Ferme Auberge de Lavaux (M)
Mme Paulette and M. Paul Gélin. 85.28.08.48. cl. 15/11 Easter.
Well marked off the D987 on to the D500; 1½ km from the village. A very well organised and efficient set-up, in lovely country setting. Superb for kids, with horses, fifty Charollais cattle, chickens, fishing in the lakes, riding and a deer park. As at all *ferme auberges,* Madame Lavaux produces meals for non-residents as well as house guests. And very good meals they are, too. You have a choice of several menus, from 58f to 89f, all based on farm produce. An old stable (complete with beams and rustic accoutrements serves as the restaurant.

The whole farm complex is 150 odd years old and very picturesque, immaculately restored and enlivened by lots of flowers. Bedrooms are in an annexe, fresh, clean, repro. furniture, modern bathrooms with showers, two at 260f, or 290f for three. Madame showed me with great (justifiable) pride the new room, almost ready for occupation, much larger than the others, with a small sitting area and a good bathroom with bath, which will be 300f for two and 60f for any extra child.

A highly recommended country stay, with good choice of accommodation and food, and all the fun of the farm.

Ferme Auberge Lavaux

La Ferme Lavaux is very popular and often fully booked. There is a new alternative in the village, which would provide beds, with meals being taken at the farm: Bernadette and Bernard Jolive have converted two very simple rooms with showers for the use of guests, not particularly cheap at 250f, but comfortable and clean, with pleasant hosts. Les Bassets, 85.28.19.51; fax 85.26.82.10.

CLERMAIN. 71520

10 km SW of Cluny by D980 and N79, then follow signs to Montvaillant, over bridge south of Nationale. Nearest autoroute exit is Macon, 25 km away.

Very attractive countryside, with river Grosne flowing through. Cluny used to be an essential tourist stop. Still is, I suppose, when one remembers that the order from which it takes its name exercised an unprecedented influence on the religious, intellectual, political and artistic influence of the West some eight or nine centuries ago. It was, quite simply, the centre of western civilisation, with over 10,000 monks under its authority, and an abbot more powerful than the Pope himself, influencing the decisions of monarchs and potentates. The youth of Europe congregated here to listen and learn and argue and then return to their own countries to be spread by the teaching. I can remember on a previous visit being bowled over by the ambiance which seemed to permeate the very stones of the place. But this time there seemed to be more construction work, more holes in the ground, more tourists, more souvenirs than signs of spirituality. I was disenchanted.

The huge stables of the National Haras are a joy to visit: you can wander freely and stay as long or as short at a time as you like admiring the beautifully groomed riding horses, small Connemara pones and Arab steeds. A most interesting visit to a very fine stud farm; don't miss it.

Cluny is undoubtedly a very important centre of pilgrimage, and for those wishing to experience what it still has to offer, a convenient bed might be found at:

Montvaillant (M)
Mme Florence de Witte. 85.50.41.34. cl. 15/10–1/5.

A château with two faces. The one that can be spotted from afar is elegant, 18C, grey stone, set on rising ground with views over the river to the wooded hills beyond. Unfortunately the entrance is on the other much older side, blankfaced in a grim courtyard, stucco peeling. Don't be too put off.

The lovely high ceilinged rooms are minimally furnished, but then rooms of this size take some furnishing. The young owner, in whose family the château has been for several generations, with help from her husband, is courageously redecorating the entire building (which is why it is closed for the winter). Those lofty ceilings, those elaborate mouldings, those miles of wallpaper, those acres of curtains – I wish them well. They certainly cannot afford to buy the kind of furniture that would look right, so are acquiring accessories gradually, as and when the guests pay up. One feature, which must be worth a fortune nowadays are the 70-year-old posters which paper the staircase and corridor.

Our room had good *armoire*, repro. bed, usual beside accoutrements and was attractively painted in peach; the adjoining bathroom was fine but rugs on the polished boards and pictures on the walls would have helped.

I cannot say this was the most warm and welcoming château and breakfast was a disappointment, but youthful Mme de Witte was very friendly and I admire her guts. Borderline for inclusion, but the scales are weighed in favour by the un-châteàu like price – 300f for a double – and the position.

FONTAINES. 71150

12 km NW of Chalon-sur-Saône. *10 km from the Chalon-sur-Saône* autoroute exit. Take N6 towards Chagny, then D155 left towards the pleasant village of Fontaines, then well signed.

➤
Les Buissonets (M)
Jacotte and Michel Chignac. 85.91.48.49.

An attractive, old village house with honey-coloured stone and white shutters, built round three sides of a courtyard. The central part is approached by two stone staircases on either side of a wrought-iron balcony. Very nice indeed.

It gets even better inside; Jacotte has furnished the three bedrooms (with bath and loo – 370f) in cleverly co-ordinating fabrics and papers, some Laura Ashley, (which is much more highly respected in France than on home ground). The furniture is mostly antiques – not grand but just looking right for the house.

I particularly commend this one for the *accueil* and friendly atmosphere. An *apéritif* or cuppa is always offered on arrival, and guests are free to use the library and the extensive garden.

Dinner, at independent tables, costs 150f, inclusive or regional wine, so altogether this is a highly recommended stop.

If you plan on staying longer than the odd night, there is also an apartment with salon, two bedrooms and kitchen from 1200f a week for four people (1,800f in July and August).

LA GUICHE. 71220

15 km NE of Charolles by N79, D983 and D27. Truly in the middle of nowhere, high on a rocky plateau, La Guiche is the only sizeable village for miles around.

La Roseraie (M)
John and Roslyn Binns. 85.24.67.82; fax 85.24.61.03.

Through the village, signed on the right. No language problems here. Since John Binns, an airline pilot, is away from home so often, his nice wife Roslyn finds her guests keep her company. I met an English couple staying in their gîte, alongside the main house, who couldn't speak highly enough of her kindness.

The house is an elegant, bourgois residence, cream walls, white shutters, flowery garden, lime tree approach, all immaculate, all very nice indeed. Fresh, frilly, white curtains flutter at the windows. Four bedrooms are decorated in Laura Ashley style, each with its own bathroom, some with their own terraces for private sunbathing, a bargain at 295f. The evening meal is good value too, at 120f.

I was sorry not to be able to stay overnight in this peaceful spot; a personal recommendation from someone who has would ensure an arrow.

LOURNAND. 71250

20 km NW of Macon.

La Ronsière Collonges (M)
Mme Blanc. 85.59.14.80.

Lournand is halfway between Cluny and Taizé. Leaving Cluny on the D981 north turn left in about 5 km, just after Chevagny, to Collonges under a railway bridge and in 1 km you will see the farm well signed on your left.

Cluny, tucked away in a valley, is famous for its old Abbey, which was built in the 11th and 12th centuries, and was a thriving community until the revolution when it was systematically destroyed, taking nearly as long to dismantle it as it did to build! Now in the ruins is a college for engineers. In 1806 Napoléon decided to revive the National Haras (stud farms) and one was built here of stones recovered from the old abbey. The church of Notre Dame is an imposing building in the centre of the town, and has a rather puzzling second world war memorial along side it. Little remains of the abbey but the old pillars of the narthex and a flight of steps. The shopping precinct appears to be pedestrianised, but beware it is only half so and constantly there is a flow of fast cars along the narrow pavements, making sure of their half of the right to use it; no give and take here, the cars win.

The huge stables of the National Haras are a joy to visit. You can wander freely and stay as long or as short a time as you like. Most of the horses are in loose boxes, well filled with clean straw. The large stud draught horses were in different stalls open at one end and luckily well tethered as they were kicking impatiently as the groom brought round their oats, but instantly quiet when he tipped in their feed at midday. Beautifully groomed riding horses, small Connemara ponies and Arab steeds all looking wonderfully healthy. The riding horses are particularly friendly and seemed to enjoy being peered at. See also page 319.

Taizé is a tiny hill village north of Cluny now world renowned since Brother Roger Schutz started a small ecumenical religious community there in 1940. The community is self-supporting and concentrates it spiritual work on young people. The movement has grown every year and is now known in about twenty countries world-wide. An ultra modern church has been built and there is hutted accommodation for all who come to join in the worship and companionship. The original tiny village church is still there and is delightfully simple with a reminder of the real presence in the reserved sacrament on a side altar.

I've yet to meet a Mme Blanc running a chambre d'hôtes who isn't charming! Here the rooms are in a converted farm building, in a truly delightful position, facing south, with views over the countryside, no traffic noise; an occasional train in the distance is all there is to compete with the birds. Two rooms at present, more on the way. One double with *en suite* shower and toilet and one family room, with a double bed and two singles and still plenty of room to swing the cat round. This room designed especially for handicapped in wheel chairs has wide doors and a very large shower and toilet room. Both rooms are prettily decorated. Also included is a large sitting/dining room with kitchen alcove for self-catering, gas rings, sink, fridge, dishes-everything you need. Open all year, but book ahead in winter and the heating will be on before you arrive. Mme Blanc speaks some English and wants to learn more so would welcome English guests. She has a young family; her husband is a farmer. Double rooms 220f, an evening meal in summer only at 60f each. I was most impressed with this chambres d'hôtes especially with the self-catering facilities.

MANCEY. 71240 SENNECEY-LE-GRAND

6 km W of Tournus by D215, a very pretty drive through green and hilly countryside. A visit to Tournus' urban attractions provides a contrast to the wine scene. See p. 327.

Dulphey (S)
Mme Françoise Dérépas. 85.51.10.22.

Not in the village itself but well marked before arriving at the centre. A run-down old manor house marks the entrance to the property, but have courage and continue down the hill to the lovely building that used to be the home farm. Two ancient ruined towers lend considerable character to an already charming setting. Breakfast on the sunny terrace includes a panoramic view of the surrounding countryside. Very nice indeed.

Dulphey

As is hardworking young Madame Dérépas, whose English is good enough to help the conversation along. Her five rooms are uncompromisingly functional, all with simple shower cabinets, sharing two loos, 180f.

An inexpensive stop in a lovely setting, very near the autoroute.

MARCIGNY. 71110

25 km S of Digoin by D982 or 30 km north of Roanne via D482 and D982. Here we are on the western extremity of Burgundy, on the slopes of the Brionnais, just a few km from the Loire. Marcigny is an attractive little town with a cluster of half-timbered houses near the church. Visit the Mill Tower Museum, a 15th century mill that used to belong to a Benedictine priory, with a magnificent wooden roof and unusual cannon-ball decoration on the wall.

This is gastro-land. Some of France's most famous restaurants are within easy reach – *Troisgrois* at Roanne and *Lameloise* at Chagny ... St Christophe-en-Brionnais is the most important market (Thursdays) in France for cattle, especially the Charollais.

Les Recollets (M)
Mme Josette Badin. 85.25.03.34; fax 85.25.06.91.

In the centre of town but facing west towards the valley of the Loire, with a big, sloping garden, the 17th century former convent has a prime position. Clever Mme Badin has made sure that there is no suggestion of austerity nowadays – she has stamped the whole lovely honey-coloured, white-shuttered building, which has been in her husband's family for generations, with her warm personality.

Her decorating touch is assured, particularly in the stunning kitchen where meals are taken. Cupboards and wood panelling painted bright blue, with red and yellow tree motifs; rush-seated chairs, long wooden table, huge open fire, candle-lit, ensure that dinner here will be a meal to remember (200f).

Madame actually lives in the house across the courtyard and has converted the convent itself into a variety of guest rooms – four twin, two doubles, one room for four and two suites for four, all with private bathroom, from 450-600f. They are all different – those in the roof are a bit dark, the twin room has beds tented in gold fabric, one is covered in roses, one double-bedded room is very pretty white, yellow and green, with a hectic pink bath, one is suitable for handicapped ... so specify when you book. I would say go for the most expensive if you can.

'Yes,' we said, at lunchtime. 'It's a bit early, but this is so attractive, we'll stay.'
'Bad luck,' said Madame Badin, 'I'm full.' As she so often is. Les Recollets is in
every imaginable guidebook and Madame also works with Air France holidays, so
you'll have to be quick off the mark to get in here. Persevere.

MUSSY-SOUS-DUN. 71170

7 km NE of Chaufailles by D316, or 33 km SE of Charolles by D985. (Left at Chas-
signy, then D316. Gorgeous, unspoiled rolling countryside, dominated by a vast
viaduct. One presumes it carries the speedy TGVs but certainly no sound of anything more disturbing than birds and bees filtered down the valley.

➤ ### Le Fournay (M)
Mme Josiane Baizet. 85.26.06.47. cl. 1/11–1/4.

I must try very hard not to let my
passion for old roses influence my
judgment on Le Fournay. O.K.
done that – it's simply the chambres d'hôtes where I would choose
to stay in the whole of Burgundy.
You can't ignore the roses though.
Le Fournay is also known as
Jardin Floral du Viaduc and its
garden is open to the public every
day except Tues. from June to
September from 3-7 p.m. Even if
you don't plan to stay (you should, you should) try to arrange a soothing hour here,
walking through the bowers of shrub roses, old and new. If, like me, you are a rose
fanatic, take a notebook because you will discover many species little-known in
England. Some familiars have different names in France. Madame Baizet and I spent
a blissful time showing off our knowledge to one another. I certainly learned a lot
and blessed the providence that sent me there on a lovely June day when the roses
were at their best.

Right, even if you detest roses, this one is worth a detour. The suite on offer
for 300f (40f less if you prepare your own breakfast in the well-equipped kitchen
corner) is unfaultable. It is approached via a white staircase adjacent to the main
house. Big picture windows frame the rose-covered slopes. Here is the living/dining
area, charmingly furnished; next door is the bedroom, all country flowers, canopy
over bed, blue and white bathroom (bath). Beats many a château for quality. But
what I really liked most was the thoughtful and generous little extras – the shoe-
cleaning equipment, the sewing kit, the fridge full of basic necessities so that tired
guests can make themselves a simple meal on arrival. Even a fly swat!

Can't wait to go back to this one. In June.

POISSON. 71600 PARAY-LE-MONIAL

8 km S of Paray-le-Monial by D34. In the village follow signs to Charolles (D458). Paray-le-Monial has become one of the great centres of Christianity, the home of the communities of many religious orders. In 1873 30,000 people made the first pilgrimage to the town and dedicated France to the Sacred Heart, a policy advocated by Sister Margaret-Mary, a 17th century nun, who received many visitations here. A vow was made in 1870 to build a church dedicated to the Sacred Heart – the realisation of which can be seen by visitors to Paris on the hill in Montmartre. In Paray the lofty Basilique du Sacré Coeur stands on the right bank of the river Bourbince, approached by a promenade lined with weeping willows.

> ### Château de Martigny (M)
> #### Mme Edith Dor. 85.81.53.21. cl. from Nov-Easter.

Perhaps some of the sanctity and devotion has spilled over from Paray to Poisson. There is certainly an indescribable atmosphere, intangible yet powerful, that permeates the old house. Martigny is more house than château, more home than just a house. Madame Dor has filled it with lovely possessions, decorated the bedrooms with perfect taste, and welcomes, really welcomes, her friends to share her treasure. She is the kind of lady that naturally assembles friends around her – the sort of gathering that used to be called a salon. They stay for weeks on end – artists, musicians, actors arrive and practise their arts in her converted bar.

Stay here and you too will be in no hurry to leave. I for one certainly count an early morning swim in the pool, with a view over the valley swirling in mist, doves, peacocks and swallows providing the company, as my fondest Burgundian memory.

The choice of room was difficult. Not the twin-bedded Laura Ashley blue room, pretty though it is, because I prefer bath to shower, not the pink suite because while I was dithering a Swiss couple quickly bagged it, not the Chambre d'Honneur, although it is the largest and most impressive (550f) and the bathroom most sybaritic, because I was a bit over-awed by twin baths (I should have thought one big one would be more fun). But I could not fault 'Rubans' named after the enchanting green and pink ribboned wallpaper, the green picked out in the paintwork, double and single beds (500f). It felt as though the lady of the house had actually slept here herself in order to decide where the lights should be (most effective bathroom ever), dressing table, hangers... quite perfect. All the rooms have an extra single bed and there is no extra charge for three people.

Dinner (160 inclusive) is eaten at one big table and was the best sampled in a chambre d'hôtes. Charolais melon, home made terrine, Bresse farm chicken, vegetables organically grown in the potager, salad, cheese, strawberries, home-made ice cream, apricot flan and coffee and lots of wine for 160f. A very special place.

LA ROCHE-VENEUSE. 71960

8 km W of Macon, east off the D79. Some of the loveliest Burgundian countryside is to be found in this area, vines in the foreground, views of distant mountains, and a series of old villages with pink stone houses covered in roses.

➤ La Tinailler d'Aléane (M)
Mme Eliane Heinen. Somméré. 85.37.80.68.

The hamlet of Somméré is about 2 km from the pretty wine village of La Roche-Vineuse, well signed. The road climbs up a hill, and the chambres d'hôtes is on the left; you have to ring the bell on the high iron gate, not knowing what might lie behind it.

La Roche Vineuse

Nice Madame Heinen swings open the gate and reveals a very pleasant surprise. Inside is a charming courtyard, fountain playing and a big colourful garden; the ancient L-shaped stone house, is covered in roses and creepers. To the left is the old bakery, now used as a breakfast room, in which there is a kitchenette for the guests' use, and room for them to picnic – typical of Mme Heinen's concern for their well-being. There is a stunning view from the garden of the highest mountain, La Grange du Bois, on the distant horizon.

The nicest room is on the ground floor, with old furniture, including a four-poster (newly vacated by a honeymoon couple when I was there) and a good bathroom (bath) for a very reasonable 280f. The two other double rooms, one with twin *bateaux* beds and one with a double share bathroom (shower) for 260f, and there is one more with a shower for 240f. Madame speaks good English, so there is the possibility of discussing the options when telephoning.

She offers an evening meal only in winter, by special request, observing very understandably that she prefers to welcome her guests, offer them an *apéritif* and chat a while, rather than absenting herself in the kitchen.

This is one of my favourites, with a well-earned arrow.

SENNECY-LE-GRAND. 71240

14 km S of Chalon-sur-Seine, by N6; 8 km N of Tournus, each with A6 exits. Quite an important, little town, with an imposing, moated castle, now partly in ruins or occupied by the Town Hall.

➤ ### Le Clos de Tourelles (M–L)
Mme Derudder. 85.44.83.95.

The history of the ensemble of buildings, just behind the castle and so virtually in the centre of town, goes back to the 12th century. The Rour de Vellaufant, now used as an intriguing dining room, is the oldest part, encircled by a 17-hectare park. The stables and the barns are old too, but the turreted, château-like building in which the six guestrooms are situated is 19th century.

I would find it hard to choose between the rooms, since each one is so pretty; *Eleanore* perhaps, with yellow curtains and a good bathroom, or *Josephine*, the biggest, with its own terrace. Not *Mata Hari* for my taste, since I don't like four-posters. On balance I think I would either go for the most expensive, at 650f, or the smallest, at 350f (in between are 450f).

Young, pretty Mme Derudder runs the whole enterprise with charm and efficiency, finding time to look after her children as well as cooking quite sophisticated meals (140f exclusive of wine). In winter, when the château is not full, she and her family eat with the guests; she speaks little English herself but her husband is fluent. This is a lovely place to stay, managing to combine a historic setting, superb rooms and efficient management with a cosy family feel. Next year it will be even better, with the addition of a new swimming pool. Arrowed for all these virtues.

TOURNUS. 71700

21 km S of Chalon, 27 km N of Macon on A6. Exit leads directly into the town.

The pedestrianisation of the centre of Tournus provides a chance to catch up on some basic shopping and sit in a square for a sunny drink without being mown down, as was previously the case in this ancient town with narrow streets and even narrower pavements. Walks along the embankment of the Saône provide an agreeable leg-stretcher and there is a variety of boat excursions from here, with or without dining opportunities. The famous abbey of St Philibert dates from the 10th century.

Mme Bouret (M)
33 Quai du Midi. 85.51.78.65; fax 85.40.02.67.

Sometimes it is a good idea to choose a town for an overnight stop. There are several good reasons to do so – if the weather turns nasty it is somehow comforting to look at fellow human beings rather than sodden cows and to sit in a fuggy bar rather than solitarily in a small *salon*; this is the time for a 'treat' meal out, with a choice of restaurants. In the case of Tournus, the distance between

33 Quai de Midi.

autoroute and destination is short so that no time is wasted *en route*. Another tip applies at the weekends and fêtes when towns empty and the country accommodation fills up – you have more chance of finding an empty urban bed. So it was with us – the dilemma of booking ahead and at first glance wishing you hadn't, or leaving it too late to get in anywhere left us tired and homeless, after being rejected by three promising chambres d'hôtes. Accepting that it might have to be a hotel, we headed for Tournus and discovered that Mme Bouret's three rooms were all available.

The choice was between two lovely spacious rooms, one with bath, 320f, one with shower and four-poster (360f) or a smaller room with bath across the corridor for 280f. There is also an apartment for four at 650f. All are well furnished, comfortable, and miraculously quiet.

The elegant substantial townhouse is right on the quay, but the rooms are set well back behind a courtyard (locked, good parking). Breakfast is in Madame's stylish sitting-room, overlooking the river or on the terrace in fine weather. All is very well organised. This is not for those who are looking for matiness; it is clearly (and who can blame her) a business with no frills (like soap or home-made jam) attached, but I heartily recommend it as a first-class overnight stop, particularly as it included the best dinner of the week at the Hotel les Terraces.

UCHIZY. 71700

6 km S of Tournus. From N6, south of Tournus, take the D163 west. This is the 'Route de Chardonnay', though no-one seems to know whether it was this unassuming little village that gave its name to the grape or vice versa. There are numerous other wine routes nearby. Drive through the vineyards to find:-

Mme Sallet (S)
Rue du Puit. 85.40.50.46.

No great surprise to find that
Gérard Sallet and his son Raphael
are *viticulteurs*. The extremely good
news was that the glass of wine he
offered us was so utterly delicious
that we knew we had to look no
further for our take-home treats.

His old stone farmhouse has
been restored (over-restored?) so
that it looks like new! Inside are a
few remaining old beams and a lot
of new pine, plum carpets on the
walls and blue satin bedspreads. All is spotless but not perhaps as rustic in character
as one might have hoped. Plumbing excellent and good value at 260f a double or
330f for three in a charming, quiet setting with friendly hosts.

YONNE

ESCOLIVES-STE-CAMILLE. 89290

14 km S of Auxerre by N6 and D503. Nearest autoroute exit Auxerre Sud, 10 km.
Typical Burgundian countryside – vines, cherry trees, astonishing hillsides blood-red
with poppies, contrasting with misty flax. Particularly pretty villages are Irançy,
with spectacular views pointed out by a *table d'orientation*, and Vincelottes, down
by the river, with an excellent restaurant and hotel. It's hard to believe that Escolives is so near the *Nationale*.

M. et Mme Borgnat (S-M)
86.53.35.28; fax 86.53.65.00.

The Borgnat family are *viticulteurs*
and beneath their home, the 17th
century Château of Escolives, are
magnificent caves where their wines
are matured and stored. Take the
opportunity to taste them. The
building is typically Burgundian, set
round a courtyard, with double-
roofed staircase leading to the
chambres d'hôtes. Lovely atmosphere of mellowness and warmth.

Bedrooms are simple, modern, some with twin beds, 240f with shower, 260f with bath. Next year there will be a swimming pool (expect the price to rise accordingly).

The evening meal is a big attraction here, featuring regional specialities, like *coq au vin* (Burgundian vin naturally), *andouillettes, confit of duck* – 75f. Don't eat lunch that day.

LAVAU. 89170 ST FARGEAU

8 km SW of St Fargeau by D965, 52 km SW of Auxerre by D965. Wooded country-side, flattish, peppered with lakes, un-touristy.

➤   **La Chasseuserie** (M)
Mme Anne-Marie Marty. 86.74.16.09.

Take the Bléneau road, D74 for three km out of the village. Then well signed.

I liked this one immediately. Perhaps it was the welcome of nice Mme Marty (who speaks English) or the sight of the sparkling new swimming pool on a very hot day after a long car drive, or the peace of the garden, or the well-furnished rooms, each with bath. Or perhaps the knowledge that we were getting a bargain – an upmarket room for 250f with an excellent breakfast reducing to 210f if we stayed a second night. It would be tempting to do so, either to enjoy the pool or to appreciate the big log fire in winter. Arrowed on all counts.

MONT ST SULPICE. 89250

12 km E of Joigny, by D91 and D43 or 16 km N of Auxerre by D84 and D43.

Very watery country. St Sulpice is between the rivers Armançon and Serein, not far from the Yonne and very near the Nivernais and Burgundy canals.
See notes on Auxerre on p. 333.

➤   **Domaine des Morillons** (M)
Françoise and Didier Brunot. 86.56.18.87; fax 86.43.05.07.

Easier to find from Brienon. Heading for Auxerre on the D84 cross first the Bur-gundy canal, then the river, then after 200 metres take first left, opposite the Restaurant d'Armançon. The Domaine is not signed (deliberately) so look for the name on the gate.

If there is a more friendly, more entertaining couple in the b. and b. biz than Françoise and Didier I have yet to meet them. The fact that Didier is a wine lover helps. Whatever other mistakes you make, do not fail to have dinner Chez Brunot. The first splendid bottle of Aligoté arrives on the table on the lawn for apéritifs, and then another. 'Come and see my cellars,' says Didier and, after a highly educative tour, it is time for another *petit verre*.

Dinner is both copious and simply delicious – for us a salad of smoked duck, salmon with leeks, salad, two superb local cheeses, raspberries and strawberries picked from the garden. Between courses Didier will disappear and return bearing yet another prize bottle, culminating with a Ratafia for *digestif*. 160f inclusive! Thanks to the Brunots' fluent English, the conversation flows as liberally as the wine.

After midnight we managed to stagger across the gravelled courtyard to our comfortable beds in a converted granary. For 380f we got a large, luxurious bathroom, supplied with all manner of desirable extras like hair dryer, good soap, thick new towels, his and her loos and washbasins and the kind of shower you can turn around in while directing a torrent not a trickle.

There are three other good rooms in the old house, where Brunots have lived for 300 years. I liked the one with rose-patterned paper and a balcony best.

Didier will arrange all manner of activities in this area which he knows so well. You can cruise the canals on a barge for a day or a week, you can take a wine tour in the very best vineyards, you can be guided through the region's most interesting Romanesque churches. You can leave your car safely in his courtyard while you swan off or be met at Paris airport and be transported wherever thereafter. He is yours to command. But best of all, just stay and eat at Les Morillons.

Not hard to see this is one of my absolute favourites. Arrowed of course.

PERREUX. 89120

15 km from Joigny by A6 direction Montargis, then D3 towards Toucy as far as Sommeçaise, then D57 towards Perreux. A sleepy, little, northern Burgundian village, with a lovely old church, conveniently near the autoroute.

Le Coudre (M)
Patrice and Laurence Lysardum. 86.91.61.42.

1 km from the village on the Sommeçaise road. A very upmarket chambres d'hôtes in a restored farmhouse. The salon is huge, retaining its tiled floor and beamed ceiling but now elegantly furnished, as are the three bedrooms. They are each named

after their colour schemes: *Brune*, with bath – 430f, *Mauve* with a particularly good bathroom – 520f and *Bleue* 436f.

Dinner is a sophisticated affair, eaten with the pleasant hosts – 180f with wine.

I like this one very much and consider that the prices are justified in view of the particularly high standards of comfort and style.

Mme and M. Latapy (M)
Route de St Martin/Ouanne. 86.91.62.56.

A very pretty timbered house in the village, with new wing built in character to house four chambres d'hôtes. Tables and chairs, hammock and fountain in the courtyard and lots of flowers welcome their guests, as does nice Nicole Laptapy. The rooms are modern, of the carpet-up-the wall persuasion, all with showers, for 330f a double, a touch on the expensive side perhaps.

POILLY SUR SEREIN. 89310

11 km SE of Chablis by D45. Nearest autoroute exit Nitry, 15 km by D944 and D45 or Auxerre Sud, 20 km, via Chablis.

The town of Chablis, known as the Golden Gateway to Burgundy, is surprisingly modest, in view of its prestige as the wine capital of Lower Burgundy. There have been vineyards here since the 16th century. The light, dry, white wines with delicate taste and bouquet are much prized and retain their freshness for a comparatively long time. The vine is the Chardonnay and the best wines come from both banks of the Serein, The most famous grouped on the steep hillsides of the east bank. The Chablis wine festival is held on the fourth Sunday in November and the Feast of St Vincent, the patron saint of vine-growers, is in late January.

The river Serein threads its way through the vine-covered hills and is particularly picturesque here. In the village centre by the bridge its sandy banks offer perfect picnicking.

➤ ## Le Moulin (M)
Pascale and Hester Moreau. 86.75.92.46; fax 86.75.95.21.
cl. 1/11–Easter.

Pouilly sur Serein   Yonne – Le Moulin

I shan't even try to avoid the purple prose. The old mill, framed by willow trees, stands behind the wide mill pond, with stream flowing beneath its stones and swans posing obligingly. A more peaceful spot it would be hard to find. Pascal and his Dutch wife Hesther have converted the building into a lovely home with five chambres d'hôtes. Hesther is a potter and her artistic eye grasped the fact that the building must be allowed to speak for itself without too much distracting decoration. She has kept the colour scheme light – white walls, white curtains, blond wood, to contrast with the original dark beams and to allow the view to dominate. The overriding impression is of space. The salon, where meals are taken in winter by a log fire, is vast. Bedrooms are light and simple, with efficient shower, mostly modern furniture, lots of pine, 300–360f. Both Hesther and her *viticulteur* husband, a charming couple, speak English and are delighted to point out the amenities of the neighbourhood – canoeing from the door, walks along the river and all that Chablis wine to taste. Arrowed as a very special place.

VENOY. 89290

10 km E of Auxerre by N65, direction Chablis. Nearest autoroute 4 km, Auxerre Sud; follow directions to Chablis, then well signed on the right.

Auxerre (pronounced Auzerre) is the capital of Lower Burgundy, situated on the hillside beside the river Yonne. Although it is not a large town (and all the better for that since it is easily covered on foot) there is much to see and admire. Its steep and busy streets, lined with old buildings, have been partly pedestrianised and there are plenty of pavement cafés at which to sit and sip.

Attraction No. 1 is the glorious Cathédrale St Etienne, a fine Gothic church built between 13th and 16th centuries. The Flamboyant west front, four storeys high, arcaded and gabled, is much to be admired, as is the Romanesque crypt, decorated with 11th century frescoes, unique in France in their depiction of Christ on a white horse surrounded by four angels on horseback, but for me the main reason for spending a quiet hour here is the glorious 13th century stained glass, whose rubies and sapphires defy description.

➤ ## Domaine de Montpierreux (M)
François and Françoise Chone. 86.40.20.91.

What bliss to leave the glare and rumpus of the autoroute and in only four km to be transported into a shady grove, dappled in sunshine, around an old farmhouse, now a family home and base for five delightful guestrooms. Hard to believe that any road, let alone a motorway is anywhere near this haven, down a bumpy track, surrounded by vineyards. François Chone is a cereal farmer who has
recently converted to wine-making; his first vintages have been successes and he is now able to sell some of his produce to his guests. An interesting sideline is the cultivation of truffles in his woodland. He discovered by accident that the conditions were ideal for this finicky fungus and, with the help of a well-trained dog, now regularly harvests a profitable crop.

This is no rough and ready farmhouse – there is evidence of importance in the turreted tour in one corner and the worn, winding stone staircase up which the guests must climb to reach the bedrooms (so not advisable for the infirm). The tall windows have Gothic arches, with appropriate white shutters, a very distinctive feature that I noticed repeatedly in this area. But there is nothing grand about the atmosphere – the rooms are comfortable, with modern bath or shower, but totally unpretentious. Named after their colours – *Blanche, Verts, Rose, Bleue*, it was hard to chose, so we plumped for multi-floral *Fleurie*. At 240–280f they were all bargains.

Unpretentiousness is the essence here. Friendly hospitality is all, with the nice Chones anxious to help in any way. It could not be more conveniently placed, near autoroute and between two interesting towns, Auxerre and Chablis—and the price is right. Arrowed.

VÉZÉLAY. 89450

40 km S of Auxerre by N6 and D951. Vézélay gets three stars in the green Michelin guide and they are well deserved. The setting is perfection – the steep, cobbled street lined with old houses leading up to its apogée, the basilica of St Mary Magdalene. Prime time was in the 12th century, when St Bernard preached here for the Second Crusade. For over a century before that the church had sheltered the relics of Mary Magdalene, and Vézélay was one of the great centres of pilgrimage, the start of one of four routes that led pilgrims to the end of the world – Santiago de Compostella. Restored after centuries of neglect, the church is once more the scene of pilgramages, in particular on 22 July, the fête of St Mary Magdalene.

All this means that thousands of tourists make the pilgrimage to visit the charismatic little town; in order to appreciate its atmosphere to the full and to have the glorious basilica all to yourself, it's an excellent idea to stay overnight and take out your camera in the early morning or late evening. No hotels worth speaking of, so:

La Tour Gaillon (S)
Mme Ginisty. 86.33.25.74.

La Tour Gaillon

Easily located by virtue of its distinctive 15th century tower, familiar from many a Vézélay postcard. Right in the main street, with good view of the basilica – what more could you ask?

The more popular of the two rooms has its own private terrace for sunbathing, double bed – 260f; the other has twin beds for 240f and they share a bathroom with shower. Nice Madame Ginisty serves breakfast in her own dining room. With only two rooms she is often full, and sends would-be customers over the road to her friend: at 80 rue St Pierre, 86.33.32.16; easy to locate again because this is a sculpture gallery.

Here are two rooms (240f), looking out on to the main road, which is not very main and has little traffic at all at night. You can sit at your bedroom window and watch the world go by. Bathroom, with bath, is shared. It is situated outside, by a glassed in terrace full of greenery – very pleasant for breakfast.

FRANCHE-COMTÉ

Départements: **Doubs**
Haute Saône
Jura
Territoire de Belfort

A region lying east of Burgundy, nestling against the Swiss border. There are four *départements*. Haute Saône and Territoire de Belfort to the north, Doubs in the east and Jura in the south west.

Haute-Saône is low, agricultural land and not quite so interesting as the other departments though it is trying to promote itself as a holiday area and many lakes and holiday sites have been constructed. Vesoul, the *Préfecture*, lies at the foot of La Motte, a hill dominating the valley of Durgeon. So damp was this valley that it was only in 1854 that the church of Notre-Dame was built on top of the hill in thanks to God for having rid the town of cholera. It is possible to drive to within 200 metres of the top, then it is shank's pony to the church from which there is an excellent view of the surrounding country.

A very small part of Haute-Saône, bordering Burgundy, produces wine at Champlitte from mostly Chardonnay and Pinot grapes, the white being the most renowned. In the north at Fourgerolles is the centre of the wild cherry growing, the source of Les Griottines, cherries soaked in kirsch and eau-de-vie. A striking feature of the small villages is the number of large arched windows and doorways a relic of the Spanish occupation of this part of France in the 17th century; there is hardly a house without two or three.

Doubs is altogether a different more sophisticated *département*, having the old Roman town of Besançon as its *Préfecture*, a town well worth visiting with large bridges spanning the surrounding river Doubs. Park in the large, shady car park by the Pont de Bregille and you will be within walking distance of the fascinating old town. In the Square Castan is the remains of an old Roman theatre among surrounding trees. Victor Hugo

FRANCHE-COMTE

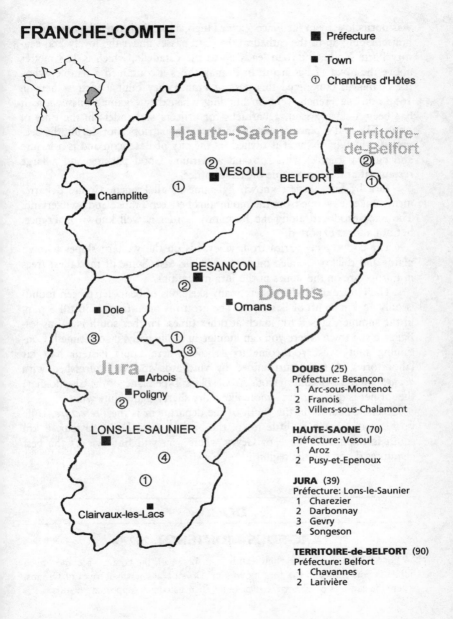

- ■ Préfecture
- ■ Town
- ① Chambres d'Hôtes

Haute-Saône

Territoire-de-Belfort

② VESOUL
BELFORT
① Champlitte
①

② ②
①

BESANÇON
②
Doubs
Omans
■ Dole
③
① ③
Jura
■ Arbois
② Poligny
LONS-LE-SAUNIER
④
①
Clairvaux-les-Lacs

DOUBS (25)
Préfecture: Besançon
1 Arc-sous-Montenot
2 Franois
3 Villers-sous-Chalamont

HAUTE-SAONE (70)
Préfecture: Vesoul
1 Aroz
2 Pusy-et-Epenoux

JURA (39)
Préfecture: Lons-le-Saunier
1 Charezier
2 Darbonnay
3 Gevry
4 Songeson

TERRITOIRE-de-BELFORT (90)
Préfecture: Belfort
1 Chavannes
2 Larivière

was born close by in the Place Victor Hugo; a plaque is over the door of the house. Going up to the cathedral the road passes under the lovely 2nd century Porte Noire; the road leads up to the Citadelle, which is 118 metres above the town of Besançon. In Roman times it contained a temple, when the Spaniards conquered this part of France they built a fortress here in 1688 and the French went on building when they regained possession. It has been a state prison, a barracks for officers and cadets in the time of Louis XIV and a place of execution for many patriots shot during the Second World War. Now it is owned by the city of Besançon and is a leisure and cultural centre, with zoo and aquarium. Good parking and a large restaurant at the top outside the ticket office.

Jura by far the best known by name of all Franche-Comté departements, takes its name from the mountains between France and Switzerland. The wine produced along the Burgundy border is well known in France, but not a lot is exported.

The countryside varies from vineyards on the western slopes to high plains and thickly-wooded mountains in the east. Some of the tallest trees in Europe are on the slopes of the Jura mountains.

The Grotte d'Osselle (where many skeletons of bears have been found) is only 15 km south of Besançon. The grotto is open from 8.30 till 5 p.m. in the summer, closed for lunch at other times. Further south is Salins-les-Bains, a spa town where you can indulge in saline baths if so inclined. Continuing south-west you come to Arbois, where Louis Pasteur had his laboratories. A town surrounded by vineyards and well furnished with *dégustations*. Try Jacques Tillot's Arbois Blanc Type Blanc, or the Chardonnay; the former is quite strong – more like a dry sherry than white wine.

Lons-le-Saunier in the south of the department is the *Préfecture*. Dôle in the north is a busy little town, the birthplace of Louis Pasteur. 6 km south is the small village of Gévry where you will find one of the best chambres d'hôtes in the region.

DOUBS

ARC-SOUS-MONTENOT. 25270

34 km S of Besançon. Travelling south from Besançon the country becomes much hillier as you approach the Jura mountains. Do stop at the small town of Ornans, where the cottages overhang the river Loue, their balconies supported on stilts.

Mme Perrot-Minot (S)
3, Ave Anatole Maillard. 81.49.30.16 or 81.49.37.27.

South of here is a chambres d'hôtes in a modern chalet-type house perched between two roads in the small village of Arc-sous-Montenot, with one nice, new room on the first floor, but private shower and toilet on the landing. Parking below the house a bit exposed. Room et 180f is good value. No evening meal; the nearest restaurant is four kilometres away.

FRANOIS. 25770

1 km W of Besançon.

M. et Mme Garcia (S)
Chemin du Clousey. 81.59.03.84.

Very handy for a visit to Besançon on the outskirts, in a quiet residential area. One room on the ground floor comes complete with kitchen corner, fridge and T.V., shower and toilet, window overlooking garden and your own private garage through which you enter the little flatlet. You can almost take the car to bed with you! The garden has a midget plunge pool (to cool off) in summer. I was hoping to stay here but Americans beat me to it. Very good value, self-catering for evening meal and such nice hosts. Room 200f.

VILLERS-SOUS-CHALAMONT. 25270

36 km S of Besançon. From Besançon take the N83 to Beure, then left on to the D473 to Levier and continue on this road south to Villers-sous-Chalamont.

There is a cooperative *fromagerie* in the village making the famous Comté cheese and all the milk from about a dozen surrounding farms goes into it. It takes

500 litres of milk to make one cheese. No additives at all, just milk. The milk is put into copper vats and is heated and stirred until it thickens. It is then pumped into another container to cool and eventually comes out looking like cheese and is pressed into a large circle, stored and turned frequently. The crust is made by rubbing with salt. The whole process from milking to finished cheese takes about three months. Each cheese weighs 45 kg, slices are enormous and we had one on the table for dinner. The best cheese has the name *Comté* printed round it in green, the less perfect has a burgundy Comté and is sold in the local market. Only two people work in the *fromagerie*, a husband and wife team.

Mme Jeunet (S)
81.49.37.51.

An interesting stop is this farm in the village, where the house stands back from the road, facing sideways overlooking an attractive small garden and field of cows. We arrived unexpectedly, were welcomed with coffee and installed in our room in the main house before Madame arrived back from shopping, to be greeted with the news that she had guests for the night, who had been promised an evening meal! She took it very well and found masses of literature for us about the region. A comfortable sitting-room and super modern kitchen for meals. Two other rooms in a separate house share a kitchen. 180f. Self-catering easy, an *Alimentation* next door. Evening meals 50 to 60f.

HAUTE-SAÔNE

AROZ. 70360

15 km W of Vesoul.

Mme François (S)
84.78.86.19.

Not a lot of chambres d'hôtes in this area, but I found one in this small village. The old presbytery has been made into three very pleasant rooms with a pitched ceiling of original beams. Rooms on the second floor are thickly carpeted and furnished well, but the only washing facility is a very smart bathroom on the landing shared by all three. There is a lawned garden with plenty of chairs and a pleasant country

outlook. A budget stop at 170f for
two people, if the lack of individual
ablutions doesn't put you off. (No
problem if you are the only people
staying.) Restaurant 6 km away or
in Vesoul. Breakfast is nicely laid,
fresh orange juice, bread, hard fruit
rolls, three sorts of jam and honey.
Madame is most attentive. An
interesting standing stone with a
circular hole is in a field almost
adjoining the chambres d'hôtes.

PUSY-ET-EPENOUX. 70000

4 km N of Vesoul. This more than compensates for the lack of other chambres
d'hôtes in the department. As you enter the village of Epenoux from Vesoul, the
château is on the left.

Château d'Epenoux (L)
Mme Gautier. Route de Saint-Loup. 84.75.19.60.

This compact little château is situated in three hectares of parkland
where the oldest weeping beach tree
in Europe stands supreme. Some
well worn shutters at the back are
misleading – the rooms are charming, centrally heated, polished
wood floors with marble fireplaces
in each. Modern beds, pretty
drapes, some *Ciel-de-Lits*, the comfort of huge, carpeted, modernised
bathrooms. Four rooms, one a suite

of two rooms for a family, on the second floor, where on the way up to you will
pass a very old etching of Paris in the 19th century, spanning the wall.

A lounge, furnished with antiques, but with comfortable modern armchairs, is
a delightful place in which to meet your fellow guests before dining together.
Madame does all the cooking.

A tiny chapel stands in the front garden, it even has a small balcony (perhaps
for the servants?) and an old dalmatic hanging by the altar. The château was once
used as a leave centre for Army officers serving abroad. Demi-pension only, 750f
for two people, but wine is extra. Should be worth a detour to stay here. Unfortunately, I had to visit in the morning and was miles away by nightfall!

JURA

CHAREZIER. 39130

20 km SE of Lons-le-Saunier. The lovely, open aspect of the village is delightful; tucked up in a lane off the main D27 from Doucier to Clairvaux-les-Lacs which is 5 km away and has all shops.

➤ ### Mme Devenat (S-M)
84.48.35.79.

Charezier is a really super little hamlet, and this is an excellent chambres d'hôtes, with one room on the first floor of a really spacious house. The room is warm and carpeted with a private shower and toilet across the wide landing. Two other rooms are across a little field in a new purpose-built chalet, one for four with two bunks and one for three. These have tiled floors and no heating, so they are only let from May to September. They are south-facing with an excellent patio overlooking fields and your car outside. Great for children.

Madame Devenat is a delightful, young housewife who keeps everything immaculate. Breakfast is in her kitchen. Room only 160f for two. The evening meal for 55f. Sounds good value.

There is also a *ferme auberge* only one minute away down the lane, and prices there are remarkably low, with à la carte dishes from 20f. Top menu only 85f, not *gastronomique*, but very good value. So you are spoilt for choice. A special recommendation here, especially for *accueil* and situation.

DARBONNAY. 39230

11 km WSW of Poligny. From Poligny take the N83 to Lons, in 8 km turn left to Darbonnay. You will find Les Tilleuis on your right at the edge of the village as you enter, just after the *dégustation* on the left.

Les Tilleuls (S)
M. et Mme Fougère. 84.85.58.27.

Madame Fougère was the first person to start a chambres d'hôtes in this area, in 1987. The house at the end of a tiny village with nice views over rolling countryside is modern chalet-type and the rooms are on the ground floor, making it wonderfully easy for off-loading as the car is parked right outside the french windows. The family rooms have tiled floors, double bed and bunk beds. The en-suite shower room is very large and there is plenty of good hanging space. One room has a loo in the hallway. 210f.

Main rooms are pleasantly cluttered with the family's activities. Monsieur is a design teacher and their young children will entertain you with piano recitals from time to time. The dinner table was well laid with interesting linen, china and cutlery and an equally interesting and satisfying meal was produced by Madame for 75f each, wine not *compris!* There is a *dégustation* in the tiny village selling local Jura wine.

This is a good place for children, as they would soon make friends with the two young Fougéres who are not at all shy.

GÉVRY. 39100

6 km S of Dôle.

➤ M. et Mme Picard (M)
3, Rue du Puits. 84.71.05.93.

A pretty little village just off the N5 to Poligny. No. 3 Rue du Puits is a charming old farmhouse, 250 years old, with old beamed rooms all with showers, loos and thick bath towels. Walls are a mixture of natural stone and rough plaster. Dark beams with hessian-covered ceiling between them made our room pretty dark – romantic maybe but not good for writing or reading. I gather changes are afoot. Our window was floor level but 3 foot high with a very attractive view of the garden from the bed. Lighting apart, the rooms are good value, as they are nicely carpeted, warm and large.

The four other rooms are delightful, especially one on the ground floor with doors opening on to the garden – 200f. Dinner at 90f was excellent: ham and salad, shrimp soufflé, pork in curry sauce with *pommes dauphines* and stuffed tomatoes, good local cheese, rhubarb tart, with *apéritifs*, red and white wine and coffee *compris*. Charming jolly hosts and another guest made it a meal to remember. Breakfast was equally good.

Parking outside or by the church round the corner, probably the only snag, but it is a tiny village well off the main road so I am sure quite safe. Definite arrow here.

SONGESON. 39130

26 km E of Lons-le-Saunier. In the lake region of the Jura there are quite a few chambres d'hôtes. Mountains in the east and forests galore surround them. Trees seem particularly massive in this part of France. Songeson is a tiny village, a turning off from Doucier on the D27.

Mme Moro (S–M)
84.25.72.81.

A restored farmhouse near the church with an excellent patio looking over other houses and fields. Four first-floor rooms, one for four people, one for three, and two for two people, have tiled floors but are well furnished and there is a useful fridge for guests on the landing. The rooms for two have large skylight windows which makes them light but no great view, 200f. Nice modern kitchen/dining room for breakfast and dinner. Parking outside the house on grass in open grounds. All very efficiently run by your hostess Madame Moro. Evening meal 80f, wine not *compris*.

TERRITOIRE-de-BELFORT

CHAVANNES-LES-GRANDS. 90100

18 km SE of Belfort. Territoire-de-Belfort, originally part of Alsace, is a comparative newcomer to Franche Comté. The only part returned to France after the Franco-Prussian war in 1871, it has remained a department of this region. Belfort, the county town, manufactures everything for the railway, from high speed trains to track.

The area is not a very popular holiday region and there are few chambres d'hôtes. One small one I found near the Rhône au Rhine canal. On the D149, east of Belfort.

M. et Mme Mattin (S)
3 rue des Vosges. 84.23.37.13. cl. Oct to May.

In a residential area of the village, very kind hosts who can offer you one enormous room on the first floor, so large that the bed is almost lost in one corner. The room has two windows, one leading on to a balcony. Private shower and loo just outside on the landing. 180f. No evening meals, but a good breakfast chatting to your hosts.

LARIVIERE. 90150

12 km NE of Belfort. Another lucky find in this area at Larivière is within easy access of the lower Alsace vineyards, Colmar and the Vosges mountains. Easy to find in the village, right beside the church.

M. & Mme Ligier (M)
4 rue du Margrabant. 84.23.80.46.

A truly charming house immaculately kept, in a tranquil garden, parking by the garage. M. Ligier teaches German and speaks a little English. Good chambres d'hôtes run in the family; M. Ligier's sister has equally nice guest rooms at Rezonville near Metz.

The three guest rooms, for three or four, are all thickly carpeted, as are their private bathrooms. It is well worth a detour to stay here. No evening meals but restaurants in the vicinity and rooms are very reasonably priced at 180f for two, only 270f for four. Book well ahead, to avoid disappointment. Possible arrow for the future.

Rhone Valley

Départements: **Ain** **Loire**
Ardèche **Rhône**
Drôme

To most people the Rhône Valley just seems one giant passageway from Lyon to Marseille carrying roads and railways and dominated by the large river Rhône, but there is more to it. The river rises in the Rhône Glacier in the mountains of Switzerland; it flows through Lac Léman and out again. Bolstered by the river Arve it continues through the departement of Ain in a south-westerly direction.

Though the region is called the Rhône Valley after the river, there are five very different departments: the Ain, Rhône, and the Loire in the north, the Drôme and the Ardèche in the south.

Ain lies west of Switzerland, only one kilometre from Geneva, and is separated from the Rhône departement by the river Saône. The sudden change of landscape over the border of the river is remarkable, the one side tremendously hilly, sheltering the Beaujolais vineyards, the other in Ain suddenly flat as a pancake with masses of tiny lakes in all directions. Not a decent grape to be seen! In summer the villages are bedecked with flowers, mostly geraniums, tier upon tier almost burying the cottages. Bourg-en-Bresse, the *Préfecture,* which gives its name to the cheese *Bresse Bleu* and the succulent dish *Poulet Bresse*, has a compact shopping centre, but is especially noted for a famous monastery at Brou on the edge of the town (see Montcet). In the middle of the Department the Gorge-de-l'Ain leads to higher ground where there is skiing in winter.

Continuing west the river Rhône passes through Lyon, the second largest town in France, and flows on through the **Rhône** departement. The whole of this *département* is given over to the wine trade, notably the Beaujolais in the north and the Côtes-du-Rhône in the south.

The '*Autoroute du Soleil*' the main route south from Paris to Marseille comes through this valley with vineyards on every available slope. At Con-

RHONE VALLEY

AIN (01)
Préfecture: Bourg-en-Bresse
1 Châtillon-la-Palud
2 Montcet
3 Romans
4 Sandrans
5 Sergy
6 Villars-les-Dombes

ARDECHE (07)
Préfecture: Privas
1 Alba-la-Romaine
2 Pourchères
3 Saint-Cierge-la-Serre
4 Saint-Julien-du-Gua
5 Saint-Martial
6 Villeneuve-de-Berg

DROME (26)
Préfecture: Valence
1 Etoile-sur-Rhône
2 Piegros-la-Clastre
3 Pont-de-Barret
4 La Roche-sur-Grane
5 Tulette

LOIRE (42)
Préfecture: Saint Etienne
1 Civens
2 Saint-Symphorien-de-Ley
3 Vendranges

■ Préfecture

■ Town

① Chambres d'Hôtes

RHONE (69)
Préfecture: Lyon
1 Condrieu
2 Grandris
3 Lantignie
4 Lucenay

drieu the Rhône is a magnificent sight viewed from the top of the hill, a wide navigable river where the pleasure boats and barges ply their trade. The climate is mild in winter except when the *Mistral* funnels down the valley, but in summer it can be very hot. It is here that the river forms the boundary between the departements of Isère and Rhône. West again is the departement of Loire, taking its name from the river flowing north. Attractive hilly farming countryside. Use this alternative route for that long journey south, not so busy as the A6/A7 round Lyon and a much more pleasant run from Nevers round Roanne to St Etienne on the N82, until further south the road joins the river Rhône, where railways run parallel on both banks.

The southerly departments of this region are totally different. The **Drôme** in the east, still fairly high from the descending Alps has lovely mountain roads occasionally running into small, hidden villages in the valleys. One interesting part of the department is at Valréas where a small area belongs to the Vaucluse. In 1317 the Papacy was at Avignon in the Vaucluse and Pope John XXII bought the land round Vairéas to extend his territory. Later he bought Richerenches (now a big truffle market) and Grillons; but at the end of the 18th century when all new boundaries were established the people of Valréas were offered the choice of living in the Drôme or staying with the Vancluse. They opted for the latter and to this day a small piece of land surrounded by the Drôme still belongs to the Vaucluse.

The other departement of the region on the right bank of the Rhône is the **Ardèche**. Turn up into the high rugged cliffs and you will be in a different world. I think it must be the wildest area of France. Isolated farmsteads crop up in most unexpected places; no town planners around here! The main roads are good, but the smaller ones can be very narrow. Occasionally you run into high, flat areas in the south with rather pleasant little villages, giving strong reminders of the Roman occupation. The small hilly town of Privas is in the centre and a road runs across the *département* from here, the D102 on a high ridge; marvellous views on both sides and many small lanes lead off to hidden hamlets where there is often a chambres d'hôtes with very rustic rooms, but modern amenities. A lovely place for getting away from it all. Gorges and rivers, plenty of scope for canoeists and many holiday campsites round the little town of Theuyts, which also has an excellent market on Fridays.

Right on top of the Ardèche on the D102 is the watershed for the Atlantic and the Mediterranean, and close by the source of the Loire. Wild flowers abound; in May the *genêt* (broom) covers all the hillsides, interspersed with tiny daffodils and narcissus. A walker's paradise. If you like it rough, rugged and rural choose the Ardèche; it has it all.

AIN

CHATILLON-LA-PALUD. 01320

30 km S of Bourg-en-Bresse. Difficult to find if you miss the sign on the road to
Châtillon. We landed up in a village and a lady took us to a friend's house to get
correct directions. She said they rarely saw English people in this area even in summer
so we felt we really were in foreign lands. We found it by taking a turning off the
D904 to Chalamont about two kilometres out of Châtillon-la-Palud.

Le Mollard (M)
MM Decre Frères. 74.35.66.09. cl. Oct–April.
Winter weekends by reservation.

This modernised house is totally
isolated in large parkland, where
horses quietly graze beside the
lakes. Gracious living here, a huge
paved courtyard is overlooked by
the chambres d'hôtes rooms in a
separate building. They are more
like a large gîte, with a tiled ground
floor sitting-room and kitchen;
upstairs, are four carpeted bedrooms, very well furnished but all
sharing one luxury bathroom and

Le Mollard

separate toilet, so really only for a family and friends. Evening meal 80f, all drinks
compris. Your hosts are two brothers. 400f for two people.

MONTCET. 01310

10 km W of Bourg-en-Bresse. Bourg-en-Bresse, the *préfecture* of Ain, is well worth
visiting, if only to see the Flamboyant Gothic monastery church at Brou, on the
edge of the town, the only monastery in France with three cloisters. Founded by
Marguerite of Austria early in the sixteenth century in memory of her husband
Philibert Le Beau, the Duke of Savoy. No sooner had she commissioned the church,
than her brother died and she became Regent of Holland and had to leave Bresse.
The building went ahead as planned, but unfortunately she died in 1530, six years
before completion, and her body was brought to Bresse two years later to be buried
at Brou. Back in the town, after wandering round the shopping precincts, stop for a
bite at le Français, Avenue Alsace-Lorraine, crowded at lunchtime; the decor and
fast service will remind you of Paris.

Leave by the D936 west then turn right on to the D45 for:

Les Vignes (M)
M. et Mme Gayet. 74.24.23.13.

Les Vignes

Something for everyone here. Situated on the edge of a small village, a typical Bresse house with huge, sweeping eaves overlooks a large garden with lawns reaching down to a small fishing lake and enticing swimming pool. Abandon the car and use the free bikes for all the family. Four rooms on the first floor are reached by an outside wooden staircase. Chintzy covers and curtains and full bookcases make these both interesting and homely; the windows are sometimes skylights with glimpses, under the eaves, of the garden.

M. Gayet is a psychotherapist and has his own work-cabin in the garden. Evening meals are taken with the family and Madame Gayet produces good four-course meals, diets or *gastronomique* to suite all tastes, from 65f to 110f. A charming, energetic hostess who speaks some English. Recommended for situation, facilities and food. Rooms 260f.

ROMANS. 01400

20 km W of Bourg-en-Bresse. The town of Châtillon-sur-Chalaronne, noted for its floral displays, has a pleasant open square where a lively market is held on Saturdays.

Take the D17 to Romans, in 2 km turn off at the chambres d'hôtes sign and you will find a true Dombes farmhouse with a wooden balcony smothered in boxes of geraniums, so typical of this area.

Le Grand Janan (S)
M. et Mme Montrade. 74.55.00.90.

Le Grand Janan

The Montrades have two family rooms with independent entry, one with Louis XV furniture. All rooms have central heating and are very comfortable. M. Montrade is a cereal farmer. No evening meal, but plenty of eateries in Châtillon–sur–Chalaronne. Rooms 150/200f.

SANDRANS. 01400

30 km SW of Bourg-en-Bresse. Next door to the round-towered château in the village. It is easy to find on the main D2 to Châtillon-sur-Charlaronne.

La Ferme du Château (S)
M. et Mme Berthaud. 74.24.51.35.

La Ferme du Château

Enter the courtyard through an old archway; your young hosts have a farm with Charolais cattle for beef. Group tastings arranged of local specialities, as well as accommodation here.

Three rooms are in a separate building, two on the first floor and one on the ground floor with tiled floors, but electric heating. Meals are taken in a dining-room in the farmhouse where large windows overlook the countryside. Excellent parking in the large courtyard. Evening meals 65f, wine *compris*. Rooms 175f. A budget stop.

SERGY. 01630

10 km W of Geneva. Just west of Geneva under the Mont Jura is the peaceful little backwater of Sergy, one of the many tiny villages which dot the D89. It's a straggly village with old and new houses and farms all mixed up. Little vegetable gardens come right up to the roadside.

Mme Moine (S)
Chemin de la Charrière. 50.42.18.03.

Sergy

No shops, just a little Logis opposite the *mairie* and a few yards further on, the modern house where the Mme Moine has her chambres d'hôtes. Make for the Chemin de la Charrière just behind the Logis and beware of running over ducks; it is more of a farmyard than a through road. Mme Moine's house is the second on the right. If you have booked ahead she will be looking out for you and rather than explain where your rooms are she hops on a bike and leads you round the corner to them. On the ground floor is a *gîte*, and on the first floor two identical studio rooms with the most compact kitchen corner I have ever seen. Automatic washing machine and ironing facilities in the garage. Garden at the back to sit in and views up to the Jura mountains behind. Central heating. Mme Moine, though a busy farmer's wife, is so obliging and friendly. No evening meal, self-cater, or walk to the Logis.

All this for 200f for two or even three people a night if you get your own breakfast. *Boulangerie* 1 mile away in St Genis-Pouilly – if you really can't face that Madame can sometimes make breakfast for you for 20f extra.

VILLARS-LES-DOMBES. 01330

21 km SW of Bourg-en-Bresse. On the N83 from Lyon to Bourg-en-Bresse

Travelling from the Rhône Department to Ain we came into Liergues, a small town outside Villefranche-sur-Saône, at midday and dashed into the Cave des Vignerons hoping to buy some Beaujolais before it closed. We hadn't realised it was the third Thursday in November and the first bottle of the Beaujolais Nouveau had been opened at midnight and everyone was in a very merry mood. American Thanksgiving Day is also on the third Thursday in November. I wonder if there is any connection? We crossed the Saône at Villefranche and made for our destination at Villars-les-Dombes. The little town is in the centre of the lake district of Ain, which is suddenly very flat, contrasting with the hilly region of the Rhône Department where the slopes are full of vineyards producing Beaujolais. The small reedy lakes are on all sides and the whole area is one ornithological and piscatorial paradise. Nearby the Abbaye de Notre-Dame-des-Dombes is occupied by Cistercian monks and the church is open to the public every day until after the night office. The monks grow all their own food, and supply the shop with their handiwork. This order has connections with the Cistercian establishment at Tenby in South Wales.

The joy of 'Le Primeur' had spread into Villars-les-Dombes and at Madame Tribolet's charcuterie 'Open all hours' we were invited to taste not only the Beaujolais but also the Nouveau Côtes-du-Rhône which came in on the act in 1992.

Les Petits Communaux (M)
M. et Mme George. 74.98.05.44.

Turn right at the pharmacy on the N83 and you will find this chambres d'hôtes about half a kilometre along the road on the right, well signed. Mme George has two very smart rooms with a shared bathroom, suitable for a family, or friends. An excellent lounge/dining-room and kitchen corner for light meals. All thickly carpeted and centrally heated, ideal for winter and so spacious. Access from flowery wooden balcony. Parking in the enclosed garden. Breakfast brought up to you by Madame George. Orange juice, baguettes and croissants, etc.

No evening meal, but there are
four restaurants in the village or
self-catering with Madame Tribolet's charcuterie to fall back on is
no problem, her *apéritifs* of the
Beaujolais Nouveau added to the
fun of shopping for two days while
we were there.

Les Petit Communaux

ARDÈCHE

ALBA-LA-ROMAINE. 07400

15 km W of Montélimar. Turn off the N86 at le Teil near Montélimar on to the
N102.

Climbing up into the Ardèche mountains the scene changes dramatically;
the old houses made of small round stones are dotted sporadically around the
countryside. Good, fast, winding roads bring you to Alba-la-Romaine just off the
N102. An attractive little village, surprisingly lively and sporting many old Roman
ruins including a well preserved little theatre only 1 km from the village. No turn-
stiles here; you can park beside it and even picnic on the theatre seats. The village
has shops, restaurants and is not far from the much photographed Gorges
de l'Ardèche.

Le Jeu du Mail (S–M)
M. et Mme Arlaud. 75.52.41.59.

Down a cul de sac leading to the
cemetary only 100 yds from the village centre is a large old house
which has three rooms for two and
a couple of adjoining rooms for a
family. No evening meal, a kitchen
for guests' use in summer.

Ex-air hostess Mme Arlaud
speaks perfect English and knows
how to pamper her guests. The garden is still under construction, but
a new swimming pool is in working

Le Jeu du Mail

order. You will want to stay here more than one night; so many places to visit. M. Arlaud makes his own wine, calling it 'Le Jeu de Mail', like their house after a ball game played in the Middle Ages. Rooms 200/270f.

POURCHERES. 07000

16 km W of Privas. If you like it rough and rugged and hardly a car in sight, north-west of Privas in the Ardèche is the place to make for. A twisting N304 west of Privas will take you to the Roc de Gourdon where you turn on to the D122, a smaller road which winds up and down dale across the region. 2 km along this road turn right on to the D260 to Pourchères – not a chance of passing or being passed by another car so narrow is this road. The beautiful scenery will not be appreciated by the driver, as the bends are continuous. After 5 km you will reach the village of Pourchères, just a few houses and a very squat church in local stone.

M. et Mme Goetz (M)
75.66.80.22. cl. 1/1 to 31/3.

The chambres d'hôtes is past the church and well-signed. Six rooms are all extremely rustic with beams, stone walls, niches and windows of all shapes and sizes, family and otherwise.

Rugged scenery all round, and flowery terraces and small lawns to laze on. An attractive old dining room has kitchen attached where you can see your meals being prepared.

Plenty of good bracing walks with wonderful views straight from the door make this a delightful place to stay a week or so; but it is too out of the way for just one night. Evening meal 90f, wine *compris*. Rooms 190/270f.

SAINT-JULIEN-DU-GUA. 07190

24 km W of Privas. Take the N104 west from Privas. In 11 km turn right on to the D122 and right again in 8 km to St-Julien-du-Gua and follow signs to La Folastère and Intres. The village of St-Julien-du-Gua is 2½ km away. Just a wee cluster of houses at Intres.

La Folastère (M)
M. Lambert. Hameau de Intres. 75.66.85.04.

Yet another 5 km stretch of single lane from a turn off on the D122 to La Folastère, winding and sometimes wooded, sometimes with spectacular views: you are just about to give up when another sign eggs you on and you arrive at M. Lambert's home. Situated on top of a hill overlooking miles of valleys and mountains, it is a lovely place. The one rustic room is in the main house, a veritable suite with a large double bedroom, entered by a real Louis XIII door, bought in an antique shop, a comfortable private lounge plus shower and toilet just for two people. Another very nice lounge and dining room downstairs has a patio for meals in the summer. Also in the grounds is a small campsite, a few caravans and two gîtes in part of the house, and best of all a very nicely situated swimming pool. In summer you would have no need to go out except for walks in the local mountains. Not really a place to stay if you are bent on sightseeing by car.

Evening meals taken with M. Lambert are with *apéritif*, wine and *digestif compris* from 80–100f. No question of driving anywhere after all that! I think I could settle here comfortably for a week, given good weather and plenty of reading material. Room 300f.

SAINT-MARTIAL. 07310

30 km NNW of Aubenas. Following the D122 westwards from Privas you come to the watershed of the Ardèche at a height of 1,404 metres near Bourlatier (Rocher des Baux), where all rivers decide which way they want to flow. Those rising east of this point flow into the Mediterranean and those rising in the west flow into the Atlantic. There is a sign on the road pointing to the Atlantic! Just after this sign is a turn to Gerbier-de-Jonc where the source of the Loire is found beside a small farmhouse. Nothing small about the parking here, the very wide road is full of cars and buses filling it in the season. There are the usual stalls of *crêpes* and knick-knacks which occupy such tourist attractions. From here take the D237 to St Martial which leads downhill, ears popping, to a real village with all shops. I was beginning to think there were none in this part of the Ardèche. A small lake is on your right; fork back on the road to Arcens beside the lake and in a short while you will see the sign to a chambres d'hôtes on your right 'Chez Claire'. If you arrive at La Chazotte you have gone too far. Perhaps a little more accessible than the other chambres d'hôtes in the area, or was I becoming hardened to narrow, winding roads by the time we got here?

Chez Claire (S)
M. et Mme Gelibert. Cros-la-Planche. 75.29.27.60.

A welcome cup of tea awaits you once you have wound down yet another minute track past a few houses. Chez Claire is a restored stone house built of basalt and granite and dating from 1709, sprawling along the hillside with the sound of the river below. Three rustic rooms, carpeted and comfortable. Easy to lose yourself in this house. Bedrooms are on all levels, with diverse ways of reaching them. Stairs and beams are tricky for the elderly. *Apéritifs* on the terrace before dinner; the menu varies every night. Breakfast is whenever you wish and one of the family will produce hot coffee and milk. Everything else is on the table, help yourself style. Some brave ones took theirs outside in spring. A very friendly place, real guests of the family; you join in everything except the washing up! *Demi-pension* 175f each; not compulsory, but most people do eat in. Rooms 210f.

VILLENEUVE-DE-BERG. 07170

26 km W of Montélimar. On the N102 between Montélimar and Aubenas this village is only 30 km north of the much photographed *Pont d'Arc* in the Gorges de l'Ardéche. Tournon is a kilometre south on the D558.

Le Petit Tournon (M)
M. et Mme Loyrion. 75.90.70.33. (Office) and 75.94.83.03. (Home).

The nice little Auberge-de-Loudon is beside the road with the owners' old house standing behind it; the guest rooms are in a restored building way back from the main road. Five spacious rooms in all, some on the ground floor, very tastefully decorated, though the tiled floors might be a bit chilly in winter, but the large sitting/dining-room with inviting armchairs has a log fire. No evening meal, but menus in the restaurant from 70f. I think Madame would fix you a demi-pension rate if you stayed over three days. Worth asking for. Otherwise 200f.

DRÔME

ETOILE-SUR-RHONE. 26800

9 km SE of Valence. Take the Valence (Sud) exit of the A7 and the D111 to Etoile, then the D111a to Montmeyron and the farm is about 3 km along the road.

To find a place like this so near the Autoroute du Soleil is a real treat. Even the little town of Etoile with its round tower, with typical sloping roof, is a pleasure to walk round.

La Mare (S)
M et Mme Chaix. 75.59.33.79.

M. Chaix is a grain farmer, and he and his family have the knack of making their guests feel at home at once.

Rooms for everyone here; the best are the two on the ground floor with their own terrace, natural stone walls with wood ceilings and light pine furniture, electric heating, pretty duvets on the beds. Sorting out the car, catching up on the washing, a large, blowy line available, everything is so easy. Rooms 165–195f.

Other rooms are in another building. A delightful old plane tree outside the dining room makes a pleasant spot for excellent evening meals (70f *vin compris*) eaten with your hosts. Good value.

PIEGROS-LA-CLASTRE. 26400

7 km E of Crest. 40 km SE of Valence. The Drôme valley is a very large wine-growing area, home of the slightly sparkling white *Clairette de Die*.

South of Valence turn off at Loriol-sur-Drôme for Crest (D104), and a little further east you will find the turn off to Piegros off the D164. The chambres d'hôtes is well signposted; go up the hill, bearing left.

Le Pigeonnier (M)
M. et Mme Bouvat. Quartier les Bordes. 75.25.46.00.

Well off the main road, up on a hillside overlooking the town of Crest. Six rooms. One for a family, on the ground floor with two bunks, has shower and toilet a march across the large hallway. A sweeping tiled staircase leads you to the others, nicely furnished, a fridge for guests' use on the landing. Very pleasant lounge/dining room gives a vast view of the surrounding countryside. About 5 km away at Blacons is a reasonable restaurant, so Madame tells me.

Prices seem very fair for such smart modern rooms: 220f for two, 260f for three and still only 260f for four. So really a budget stop for a family.

PONT-DE-BARRET. 26160

18 km NE of Montélimar. Montélimar is a busy town beside the Rhône, best known for its nougat.

Take the D6 from Montélimar; at Cléon-d'Andran turn on to the D9 and soon left to Manas. After the village Les Tuilleries is signed before Pont-de-Barret.

Les Tuilieries (M)
Mr & Mrs Williams. 75.90.43.91.

Surrounded by open countryside this three-storey Provençale house has recently been restored and now has a choice of six light, airy rooms for couples or a family. An interesting entrance, once a *cave*, still has the curved roof, and a large comfortable lounge extends across the house. Two black cockerels patrol the sunny terrace, where you may indulge in a full English breakfast.

Most guests come to take advantage of the photographic courses under the guidance of Mr Williams, your English host, but others who just wish to laze by the pool are equally welcome. Even in March it is warm enough to sit on the terrace. Rooms 390f. Demi-pension 350f each.

LA ROCHE-SUR-GRANE. 26400

35 km SSE of Valence. From Crest take the D104 to Grane, turn left on to the D113 to La Roche sur Grane. The little hill village is interesting to visit, but there are no shops – just many old buildings being restored, mostly as second homes.

La Magerie (M)
M. et Mme Servant-Déjean. 75.62.71.77. cl. 1/11 to 31/3.

At the foot of the hill, La Magerie encompasses chambres d'hotes, campsite and swimming pool and a gîte d'étape where the horses' accommodation is as large as the guests; at least they don't join you for the evening meal in the attractively converted dining room, once a cowshed. M. excels at all the cooking while Madame looks after the guests.

We enjoyed an excellent evening meal, for 75f, wine included, and lively conversation, battling in three languages with our hosts and other guests. The Servants-Déjean prefer people to book ahead and not arrive unexpectedly. 5 small rooms, ensuite 220f for 2.

TULETTE. 26790

16 km NW of Vaison-la-Romaine. On the D94 between Bollène and Nyons. A very pleasant Côtes du Rhône, 'Celliers des Dauphines' comes from Tulette.

La Papeterie (M)
M. et Mme Cibert. 75.98.35.51.

Get clear directions from your hosts before you attempt this one! This chambres d'hôtes is not signposted, as the owners prefer you to book in advance and will then give you directions.

It is not easy trying to find an unsigned homestead in the middle of a vineyard in the Rhône valley. Marital discord was mounting as we bumped along rough tracks of the vineyards, hot and hungry; just before lunch is no time to be looking for this type of house! Madame Cibert was very pleasant and happily showed me over her home. Two bedrooms were large and airy and tastefully furnished. Bathroom *en suite* but one shared toilet on the landing. A delightful terrace for breakfast overlooks an inviting blue pool, which is shared by the *gîte* on the premises. No evening meals, restaurants in Tulette only 1 km away, give or take a few bumps! Rooms 250 to 350f.

LOIRE

CIVENS. 42110

34 km N of Saint-Etienne. Turn at Feurs on to the D113.

Confusingly this is called the Loire departement, where the young river flows through from south to north. A good alternative route south via St Etienne takes you past Feurs; if you are looking for a night stop try the following farm:

Les Rivières (S)
M. et Mme Palais. 77.26.11.93.

Mme Palais will welcome you with a drink. She has two comfortable rooms on the first floor, one with a balcony, for 200f and is happy to give you an exceptionally good meal with very little notice for 55f, wine included. Eating with the family the conversation is relaxed and entertaining.

Les Rivières

SAINT-SYMPHORIEN-DE-LAY. 42270

13 km SE of Roanne. Three kilometres from the N7 between Roanne and Lyon in the direction of the village of Lay.

La Marthorey (S-M)
M. et Mme Bréchignac. 77.64.73.65.

Signs will lead you to the home of M. & Mme Bréchignac, isolated high on a hill above the village. Their fifteenth century house now has a suite of rooms for family or friends. A sitting room with TV and dining-room is on the ground floor and up a steep staircase are three bedrooms sharing a bathroom and a separate toilet. Double beds, single beds, even a single room 225f. I liked the south-facing windows and

La Marthorey

views over the garden. (Monsieur is very knowledgable about the Department of the Loire and will direct you to all places of interest. Don't miss the *barrage* on the Loire at Villerest.) This is an excellent quiet stop on the way to Lyon, or for a longer holiday. No evening meals. St Symphorien is the nearest village and has shops and restaurants.

VENDRANGES. 42590

14 km S of Roanne. The Loire Department, not to be confused with the Loire Valley Region, is part of the Rhône Valley. It lies, a narrow wedge south of Burgundy and east of the Auvergne, so called as the River Loire flows north right through the middle, wending its way from its source in the Ardéche. As soon as you enter this Department, skirting the large town of Roanne in the north, the landscape changes: really high hills and pitched valleys make it quite picturesque. Vineyards on the more southern slopes produce the well known Vin du Forez. This part of the Loire has its own elegant Château-de-la-Roche, almost an island, dating from the 13th century; it has passed through many hands and was finally restored at the beginning of this century – a great tourist attraction. Wonderful sightseeing tours and walks, ancient villages and churches, without having to drive too far each day. It is such an attractive area it really needs a week or more to get to know it well.

From the N82, south of Roanne, turn right at Vendranges on to the D42 to Saint-Priest-la-Roche, and in 1 km you will see a delightful farmhouse on the right in a dip with its own lakes. (There is another chambres d'hôtes in the vicinity, so make sure it is the 'Ferme de Montissut'.)

➤   ### Ferme de Montissut (S)
M. et Mme Deloire. 77.64.90.96.

A dairy farm where on the first floor are two rooms each with an adjoining room for two children, cosy and prettily furnished with duvets and fresh flowery wallpaper for 160f. A charming welcome from Madame, a busy farmer's wife. The whole house has warm central heating in winter and is immaculately kept. Evening meal not obligatory but is well presented country fare with all drinks *compris* for 65f. You may picnic in  the garden in summer if you have a family and need to budget more tightly.

A really delightful place. Even at the end of November I found this a most comfortable refuge. Children will enjoy watching the milking in the pristine parlour beside the house. Arrowed for all round comfort.

RHÔNE

CONDRIEU. 69420

40 km S of Lyon. On the N86 13 km S of Vienne.

    South of Lyon you have plenty of chambres d'hôtes choices, most of them worth far more than a night stop. At le Rosay, high up above Condrieu on the west bank of the Rhône there are two. I liked them both. To find them take the Rosay road out of Condrieu by the Mairie, climb the winding hill and in about 2 km they are well signed at the top on the left.

Les Grillons (M)
Mme Besson. 74.87.87.67.

Here I called unexpectedly and young M. Besson opened the door and said his mother had only just returned from Brazil. On hearing that I wanted to see the rooms but not necessarily stay the night, Madame graciously appeared in her pyjamas and conducted us all round her guest rooms; she was quite charming considering we had dragged her from her bed with jet lag. Full marks for courtesy, Mme Besson.

    Les Grillons is lodged on a hillside and has spectacular views of the winding river Rhône; it is a large modern house with a delightful swimming pool on the patio, and smallish garden. Don't be put off by the short, rough track leading down to the house; it means you are well away from traffic in a residential area. Two rooms share a shower, for a family. One single and a double share a bathroom. The bad news – all share one toilet on the landing. A very smart kitchen with sitting/dining room opens on to a balcony with a fabulous view. What a great place for a family who want to stay some time and self-cater for dinner. Rooms 220f.

Côte de Châtilion (M)
Mme Font. 74.87.88.27.

Better news on the en-suite front here just along the road. Three rooms on the first floor. Two adjoining have superb views and are well heated for winter months – 220f. Hospitable little Mme Font will serve you breakfast on the

lovely terrace in summer. No
evening meals or kitchen here, so
you would be eating out in Condrieu. Difficult to choose between
these two; it depends whether the
pool or the private bathroom pulls
most.

Côte de Châtillon

GRANDRIS. 69870

24 km W of Villefranche sur Saône. The D485 between the N6 and N7 makes a
nice change from busy *Nationales*; it is a wide road winding through pleasant country. For a night stop before Lyon try Grandris. Not a very interesting hill village,
but the chambres d'hôtes is right opposite the *mairie*.

Les Godillots (S–M)
M. et Mme Bibos Route de Goutel. 74.03.11.35.

A tall old house, behind iron gates.
Room for two cars here at a push.
A pair of *godillots* (boots) beside
the front door. Ignore the poor
entrance hall and race up to the first
floor where it all happens. A long,
wide central corridor leads to two
very pretty guest rooms, really
warm in winter, for 220f. A friendly
welcome from M. & Mme Bibos
who produce a copious meal for
70f, wine included, even if you
arrive unexpectedly. Such nice people, a temptation to sit up till late, talking. Surprisingly no noise from church bells or traffic. M. Bibos has done all the conversions of this hundred-year-old house himself, with Madame's good taste right
behind him!

LANTIGNIE. 69430

25 km SW of Macon. Driving south from Macon through Beaujolais country on the N6 one passes signs to villages whose names are more common on dining tables in England, such as Pouilly Fuissé and Fleurie. Visit Beaujeu, a small town steeped in the wine trade, then climb the hill to Lantignie with vineyards on either side, cropped tight in March. Hard to miss as there is an enormous sign Beaujolais Lantignie written across one of the fields in straw, clearly visible from the other side of the valley.

Les Vergers (S)
M. et Mme Nesmie. 74.04.85.80. cl. during the vendage (Sept).

A typical *viticulteur's* old house to stay in and, if Beaujolais is your tipple, learn all about it, watch the grapes grow, drink it and even sleep on it, as the rooms here are on the second floor above the *caves*, where all the wine is stored, old and new. Reached by what must once have been the servant's oak staircase, there are four rooms in all, two *en suite* and two sharing a shower and toilet on the landing. All rooms are carpeted, basically furnished, but spacious. 180–220f. A garden with a swimming pool is behind the house, which would be a pleasant respite from a hot drive. Staying here would mean eating in Beaujeu 3 km down the hill, with plenty of choice. The *caves* under the house are well worth visiting even if you don't stay. The wine is in huge oak vats; tasting all day, but avoid 12 to 2 p.m. No frills here but peaceful safe parking and good views over the hills.

LUCENAY. 69480

20 km N of Lyon.

La Fontaine (M)
Mme Torret. 74.67.05.42.
cl. during the vendange and midweek in winter.

For a stop off the A6 (or N6) just north of Lyon you couldn't do better than branch off at Anse and take the D40 to Luçenay. On your right before the village is a beautifully restored old house on a vineyard. On the first floor of an adjacent wing is one very smart fully-carpeted room, (twin beds) (250f) overlooking a sheltered swimming pool. Evening meal 65f on reservation only, so book ahead to avoid disappointment.

RHONE-ALPES

....

Départements: **Haute-Savoie**
                 Isère
                 Savoie

Bordering on Switzerland in the East of France this is the region with the highest mountains of France, the Alps, towered over by Mont Blanc (4807 metres). There are two seasons of tourism here; the longest is the winter ski season followed by a short spring in May, leading to the summer season.

The Haute-Savoie lies along the southern bank of Lac Léman and extends southwards into the mountains; Geneva in Switzerland takes nearly all the air traffic for this region.

Drive down to Annecy and take the road to such places as Thônes and la Clusaz, then over the Col des Aravis to Megève, one of the oldest and most unspoilt ski resorts. There is a delightful little chapel at the top of the Col, and many tourist shops; when you post your card, as undoubtedly you will, one foot will be in the Haute Savoie and the other in Savoie. Further east is Chamonix, the most famous name of all, a ski resort at the foot of Mont Blanc, pretty, crowded and expensive. In this direction further south are many purpose-built ski resorts such as La Plagne, packed and practical in winter; but utterly lacking in beauty in summer.

Stay a while in Annecy; nothing ever spoils this lovely old town situated on probably the most attractive lake in France – a chocolate box picture at all times of the year.

Continue south to Savoie, still mountainous; these two departments merge into each other. Visit the old Roman town of Aix-les-Bains on the longest lake in France, the Lac de Bourget. Further south Chambéry is the *préfecture*.

South again is Isère, another mountainous department with skiing on high ground. Chartreuse, the liqueur, is produced in the mountains above Grenoble, which lies in a wide valley. This large university city, the *préfecture* of Isère, is bursting with commerce and traffic. Not easy to avoid if

RHONE ALPES

Thonon-les-Bains■ ■

Geneva ■

① Haute-Savoie

Chamonix■

ANNECY■ la Clusaz■ ⑤ Megève
② ⑥ ④ Mont Blanc
③

St. Prim ③

② ③

Albertville■

La Tour-du-Pin■

Isère CHAMBERY■
①

La Plagne■
Moûtiers■

Savoie

② Saint-Jean-
de-Maurienne■

GRENOBLE■

Villard-
de-Lans■ L'Alpe-■
① d'Huez

La Mure■

④

HAUTE SAVOIE (74)
Préfecture: Annecy
1 Bellevaux
2 Chapeiry
3 Les Clefs
4 La Clusaz
5 Megève
6 Thônes

■ Préfecture

■ Town

① Chambres d'Hôtes

ISERE (38)
Préfecture: Grenoble
1 Saint-Honoré
2 Sant-Pierre-Chartreuse
3 Saint-Prim
4 La Salle-en-Beaumont

SAVOIE (73)
Préfecture: Chambéry
1 Apremont
2 Trevignin
3 Viviers-du-Lac

you wish to drive south, as the mountains are so high round it, but you can skirt the town and take the Route Napoléon N85 which takes you all the way, to the Côte d'Azur, small villages and friendly chambres d'hôtes *en route*. West through the town for Lyon.

HAUTE-SAVOIE

BELLEVAUX. 74470

20 km S of Thonon-les-Bains on Lac Léman. From the D26 between Bellevaux and St Jéoire turn on to the D236 to La Clusaz. Bellevaux is a simple mountain village with a school, post office, shop and the *mairie*. Just up the road is La Clusaz, not to be confused with the larger town further south.

M. Pasquier (S)
La Clusaz. 50.73.71.92.

In a little valley high in the French Alps you will be woken by an orchestra of cowbells. This chalet-farmhouse has six cosy rooms, a choice of double or single beds, or a family suite, all with mountain views. The blend of two-tone trees in spring is only surpassed by their autumnal colours. Mme Pasquier is a highly organised lady who runs her chambres d'hôtes most efficiently. All guests dine together at the same table, but Madame rarely has time to join them. *Demi-pension* only 160f, wine *compris*, is extremely good value.

CHAPEIRY. 74540

10 km S of Annecy. Turn off the D201 at Vraisy south of Annecy on to the D38.

Annecy is the *préfecture* of Haute-Savoie, a well known watering place since Roman times. South of Geneva it is situated on one of the most beautiful lakes in France. A wide lake surrounded by snow-capped mountains most of the year, villages dotted around the circumference, small jetties with boats tied up at frequent intervals and lovely grass verges where people picnic and sunbathe. It seems to be unspoilable and always looks very prosperous with the rich having their houses right beside the water. Parking can be a problem in the town, but it is worth spending a day or two walking round and enjoying the relaxed atmosphere.

Chef-Lieu (S)
Mme Fillard. 50.68.28.28.

You will have to drive only 10 km to this peaceful little farm at Chapeiry where friendly Madame Fillard will take you up an outside staircase, to a simple family room, where with roses climbing round your window you can enjoy a view of the farm and countryside 180f. An evening meal, too, of farm produce for 65f.

LES CLEFS. 74230

40 km E of Annecy. On the Manigod road from Thônes – is a well established town, busy at all seasons.

Belchamps (S)
Mme Donzei-Gargand. 50.02.97.56.

Looking for somewhere else, I stumbled on this pretty little chalet where Madame is only too pleased to have guests. High above the Serraval road, your room will have a sunny balcony overlooking the mountains and a bathroom across the corridor. You will be well looked after at breakfast. No evening meals, but Thônes is only 5 km away. There are plans for a further room and even a small kitchen for snacks. A charming room for 168f, and Madame is equally nice.

LA CLUSAZ. 74220

29 km E of Annecy. On the D909 from Annecy. La Clusaz is in a very wide open valley surrounded by high mountains. The original village has grown into a vast ski station with plenty of restaurants, and modern shops in the centre; tennis courts and swimming pool on the outskirts.

Les Groseillers (S)
Mme Thovex. Le Plattuy. 50.02.63.29.

Les Groseillers

Not a chambres d'hôtes for anyone suffering from vertigo. High on the mountain above the town in a residential area served by the ski bus twice a day, this chalet has one carpeted room with balcony with superb views, private bathroom, but not adjoining. A second room, tiled, is *en suite*, kitchenette, too, and has outside access up 'ski' stairs from the parking. (These are metal stairs with holes for the snow dropping off your boots, but hell for high heels in the summer!) Breakfast taken in Madame Thovex's dining room with views over the valley. No evening meal. Rooms 180/250f in the summer, to 270f in winter i.e. high season.

MEGEVE. 74120

28 km W of Chamonix. 15 km from the Col d'Aravis. On the N212 between Albertville and St. Gervais.

What a lovely town Megève is, situated in a valley with Mont Blanc always watching over it. A truly romantic sight with the sun setting over the top turning the snow pink even in summer. The old town of Megève has been there since Roman times, none of your modern man-made ski resorts here. Baron de Rothschild discovered that the waters of Megève were medicinal in 1919 and since 1930 it has gradually grown into a large ski resort with chalets and roads spreading up the mountain side, but no very large apartment blocks as in purpose-built resorts.

Chalet les Oyats (S)
M. et Mme Tissot. 771 Chemin de Lady. 50.21.11.56

Chalet les Oyats

If you climb the winding Chemin de Lady, so called because an English lady had a farm right at the top many years ago, you will cone to a simple chalet house perched on the side of the narrow lane, the mountain stretching behind; in spring a carpet of flowers up to the tree line. One room for four on the ground floor has breathtaking views of the valley below. A *gîte* covers the top floor, where you may be offered a room, if the chambre d'hôtes is full. A simple evening meal can be taken with the family, but there are plenty of restaurants in Megève. The lane is always kept open in winter, but safer to take the bus then. Demi-pension 290f for two, is good value. Room 220f.

THONES. 74230

21 km E of Annecy. Just outside Thônes on the D909 to La Clusaz.

La Cour (M)
Mme Josserand. 50.02.12.22.

Easy to miss this place; in fact I was quite happy to miss it as it seemed to be so near the noisy main road, and some of the rooms are, the best by far being three compact little studio rooms at the back on the ground floor with really good kitchenettes and terraces facing south. I was pleasantly surprised how well furnished and spacious these rooms were. Self-catering but breakfast is in Madame Josserand's house which is in the same garden.

La Cour

Studio rooms 200f per night for two out of season, 175f if staying three nights or more. The season being school holidays, studios are let only by the week then. Other rooms with shower, but shared toilets, are from 160f b and b. for two. Go for studios here; quite the best.

Another possibility the other side of Thônes.

Le Frazier (M)
Mme Ruffon. 50.02.07.99.

Just off the Maingod road to Serraval, the D16, south of Thônes situated on the hillside surrounded by mountains is this flowery chalet with seven rooms, with showers, four nicely carpeted upstairs, some for families, two for two people. There are a few balcony rooms upstairs. The dining room on the first floor has separate tables. Evening meal 60f, wine not *compris*. Rooms are named after

Le Frazier

mountain flowers. The price varies with the season. Here again the season means school holidays.

Rooms for two people are 200f out of season, 300f from 3rd July to 3rd Sept. The largest room will take six people, 390f out of season, 550f in season. You pay the same price however many people you have in the room as it is more crowded with a full complement. The price includes breakfast. Lovely position, excellent for parking, almost more of a small guesthouse than a b. and b.

ISÈRE

SAINT HONORE. 38350

35 km S of Grenoble. Turn by the Intermarché at Pierre-Châtel on the N86.

The N86 is called the Route Napoléon because Napoleon marched to Paris this way from Golfe-Juan, after escaping from Elba in 1815, gathering support on the way. Many are the hotels, restaurants, stone seats and monuments named after him. The Relais de l'Empereur at Pierre-Châtel is good value, meals from 63f and *pichets* of house wine from 12f.

If you are staying in the area, there is a narrow gauge train which runs from La Mure (10 km) northwards to St Georges-de-Commiers (6 km SW of Vizille) along the Corniche Du Drac passing the Lac du Drac. The journey takes two hours and passes through 18 tunnels and over 6 viaducts. There are three trains a day and the fares are 75f single and 90f return, with reductions for children and OAPs.

A little further away are the Caves-de-Chartreuse at Voiron (22 km NW of Grenoble). The Caves and Distillery are open daily from Easter to All Saints Day.

La Dent du Loup (S)
Mme Boulineau. Tors. 76.30.92.42.

La Dent du Loup

Tors is a tiny hamlet before you reach St. Honoré, a sharp fork left into a small cluster of houses and you will find La Dent du Loup clearly marked in a terrace of cottages. It has a lovely little cottage garden on different levels, a veritable suntrap facing mountains snow-capped most of the year. Kind, sympathetic young Madame Boulineau was waiting for us one evening just after we had had a nasty experience of having a tyre slashed and while changing the wheel my handbag snatched from the car. Having spent two hours in a police station in Grenoble cancelling credit cards etc. and giving statements, we were thankful to arrive at the quiet comfort of the house, where Madame swept us straight into her locked garage. Even greater relief to find her husband was a policeman. The Gendarmerie were most helpful and would have directed us to a hotel, but the human contact of a chambres d'hôtes was just what we needed.

There are two comfortable rooms one for a family, a copious breakfast – orange juice, fruit salad, yoghurt, even eggs if you want them, and an equally satisfying evening meal; plenty of fresh fish when Monsieur has been fishing in the lakes. Dinner 75f, wine *compris*. Rooms 230f.

ST PIERRE-DE-CHARTREUSE. 38380

26 km N of Grenoble. A small but smart ski resort in winter, situated in the mountains north of Grenoble on the D512, with plenty of new shops and restaurants.

La Cartannaz (S)
Mme Cartannaz. La Coche. 76.88.64.26.

One km outside the village in the wee hamlet of La Coche, a real mountain chalet with both the well furnished rooms opening on to a balcony with south-facing Alpine views. 170f. A family lounge has log fires on chilly nights. We had an excellent welcome from Madame who is Belgian; her husband is French. Most of the houses in the hamlet belong to their relatives! Dinner with plentiful, regional food,

is *en famille* for 85f, wine *compris* and there are home-made jams for breakfast; Monsieur was making some while we were there. Book early; busy all the year here.

ST PRIM. 38370

40 km S of Lyon. Just across the bridge from Condrieu on the opposite side of the Rhône is St Prim. Over the bridge turn immediately left and halfway up the hill is Pré Margot.

Le Pré Margot (M)
M. et Mme Briot. Les Roches de Condrieu. 74.56.44.27.

At the closed gates we obeyed the sign to *sonnez la cloche* and miraculously the gates slowly opened; we drove into the short driveway and Monsieur was there to marshal us into a parking space. Only then when he had got us where he wanted did introductions begin and we asked if he had a room for the night. Not only one but five! So we had a conducted tour of all the rooms, all very modern, TV, parquet floors and air conditioning. Pristine clean, sanitized to suit the most fanatical. Flannels in sealed packets, to say nothing of plastic loo seat covers that move on at the touch of a button, always great fun for children!

Strictly no smoking here. To emphasise this there is a large ashtray fixed to the outside wall at the entrance. Had I been a smoker I should have felt compelled to empty all my packets of cigarettes in it!

The *pièce de résistance* was the enormous glassed-in verandah which enveloped two sides of the house, all 80 feet of it, with a view of the busy river (very pleasant and full of tropical plants and gentle musak).

The evening meal was perfectly served and cooked, but we ate alone. The food could not be faulted. Everything, even the bread, as Madame expressly told us, was made by her. So why did I begin to long for Madame in her jet-lagged pyjamas, even if her one loo wasn't sanitised! (See Condrieu, Rhône p.362.) Many people from all over the world stay here and clients come back regularly for their summer holidays so Madame tells me. Good value for money, but just a little too much like a smart, well run hotel, with Monsieur and Madame Briot as very pleasant patrons.

Demi-pension 200f includes *apéritifs* but not wine. Rooms from 220f.

LA SALLE-EN-BEAUMONT. 38350

8 km S of La Mure. On the N85 at the northern end of the village

Les Allaures (M)
M. et Mme Grand. 76.30.42.04.

A busy little place this; Madame says they have a lot of people stopping for one night only, hardly surprising on the well used Route Napoléon. Four nice rooms, even one with a balcony if you are lucky. Double glazing combats any noise from the road. Easy to find, easy to park, no evening meals. Good breakfast and away again seems to the the order of the day. Pity, it deserves more. Rooms 200f.

SAVOIE

APREMONT. 73190

10 km south of Chambéry. From Chambéry take the D201 to Apremont; 300 km past the post office, turn right up the Route du Col du Granier.

Apremont is a wine-growing area on the sides of Mont Granier, producing some excellent white wine *Vin-de-Savoie-Cruet*. In the 13th century a large slice of Mont Granier fell on the village, killing 600 hundred people. Looking up, one can still see the straight side where it was sliced off. No movement since then, so no need to worry!

Maison d'Apremont (M)
Mme Joly Lachat. Route de Granier. 79.28.34.78.

Up towards the Col de Granier, and I mean 'up', a winding tiny lane with bend after everlasting bend, one suddenly comes to a delightful house set into the hillside, with a large, south-facing terrace and lawned gardens – a chambres d'hôtes mixed up with a centre of *détente* (relaxation). A very calm atmosphere prevails, created by Madame Joly, who has a serene approach to everything; she is a psychologist and astrologer. Treatment rooms are on the first floor; classes of yoga relaxation and discussions on astrology are taken by Madame whose husband is the masseur. Not a lot of hotels offer these services!

Two rooms for chambres d'hôtes guests on the ground floor share a bathroom. 250f. Madame prefers to let these as a suite to a party of four. You don't have to take part in anything.

Meals are vegetarian without wine but you can have meat and fish for 19f extra and bring your own wine. Simple rooms in the eaves are cheaper, but facilities are shared. Absolutely NO smoking. Evening meal from 67f, all drinks charged.

TREVIGNIN. 73100

7 km E of Aix-les-Bains. Take the D913 from Aix-les-Bains to Trevignin and continue up the hill to St Victor and La Revardière is well signed.

La Revardière (M)
Mme Rocagel. Hameau de St Victor. 79.61.59.12.

The views from this pretty chalet home, perched on a hillside, are magnificent. The house and garden are immaculate and a riot of colour in summer. Two small well furnished bedrooms on the first floor have showers but share a toilet. One larger on the ground floor has patio access and is *en suite*.

There is a little cellar bar for *apéritifs*, which also has a fridge for guests. Evening meals are taken with your hosts; Madame prefers you to eat here and *demi-pension* varies according to the season; 177/259f for the upstairs rooms and 224/342f for the garden room. Bookings must be for at least two days. A more luxurious chambres d'hôtes than most and this is reflected in the price.

VIVIERS-DU-LAC. 73420

2 km S of Aix-les Bains. On the D201 south. Aix-les-Bains is a spa town on the longest lake in France; it was a favourite watering place of the Romans and is still a popular health resort in the modern world. Many people come to take the waters which are said to cure rheumatism. The town, lying a little back from the lake, is busy and prosperous, with a good shopping arcade. The mountains tower above one side of the lake but there is a road right round. Mont Revard is to the east, and 2 km south is Viviers-du-Lac.

Mme Montagnole (S)
516 Chemin De Boissy. Côteau de Boissy. 79.35.31.26.

A homely little chambres d'hôtes above the village, on a ridge between the Lac du Bourget and the N201. The Chemin de Boissy, is a cul-de-sac on the north side of the village, not far from the church; stop and ask if you can't find it. No. 516 is just opposite a vineyard on top of the ridge. Excellent views to Mont Revard, but only two minutes from the southern end of the Lac du Bourget.

The modern house is built into the hillside, with just one room in the basement, facing south with patio doors on to a terrace, and two single beds for only 170f.

Monsieur is a physiotherapist in Aix-les-Bains. Excellent *accueil*, drinks on the terrace on arrival.

AUVERGNE

Départements: **Allier**
            Cantal
            Haute-Loire
            Puy-de-Dome

The Auvergne derives its name from the 'Averni', a Gallic tribe who, under the leadership of Vercingetorix, strongly resisted Roman control. Julius Caesar finally conquered the area and executed the valiant Gallic chief in 46 B.C. The region then became a flourishing Roman province, and evidence of this period of the region's history remains in such sites as the Temple of Mercury at the summit of the Puy-de-Dôme. The local place names ending in –ac, and –at (Aurillac, Carlat, Mauriac, etc.) indicate their origins as Roman settlements dating from this period. After the collapse of the Roman Empire the Auvergne passed through a troubled time politically, being fought over by the Merovingians, the Carolingians and the Dukes of Aquitaine, who finally gained control. The line of defensive 11th and 12th century châteaux along the eastern edge of the Puy-de-Dôme marks the border between Aquitaine and Burgundy. After the marriage of Eleanor of Aquitaine to Henry 11 of England in the twelfth century the Auvergne was part of England, and was the scene of many battles in the Hundred Years War (13th/14th centuries). The Bourbon family, which ruled France from 1589 until the revolution, originated from Allier, and this part of the region is still known as *Le Bourbonnais*.

The area often referred to as the Massif Central is dotted with extinct volcanoes. It is mainly agricultural – wheat, cattle, cheese, grapes and of course wine, with industry concentrated round the central capital Clermont-Ferrand.

Allier in the north is fairly flat farming land, cold in winter but often dry and hot in summer. It is dotted with Limousin cows, small châteaux and villages. Three large towns are Bourges to the north-east, Montluçon south-west and in the east Vichy, which was the seat of the French government after the fall of France in the Second World War.

AUVERGNE

■ Préfecture
■ Town
① Chambres d'Hôtes

ALLIER (03)
Préfecture: Moulins
1 La Chapelaude
2 Lurcy-Lévis
3 Villefranche-d'Allier
4 Ygrande

CANTAL (15)
Préfecture: Aurillac
1 Giou-de-Mamou
2 Parlan
3 Pers
4 Salers

HAUTE-LOIRE (43)
Préfecture: Le-Puy-en-Velay
1 Bains
2 La Chaise-Dieu
3 Mazeyrat-d'Allier
4 St Privat-du-Dragon
5 Vergezac
6 Vieille-Brioude

PUY-de-DOME (63)
Préfecture: Clermont-Ferrand
1 Collanges
2 Courpière
3 Egliseneuve-près-Billom
4 Jose
5 Montpeyroux
6 Perrier
7 Saint-Gervazy
8 Sermentizon
9 Château-de-Vaulx

Driving south, one enters the real volcanic area of the **Puy-de-Dôme** department, with distinctive rounded peaks, a typical dip in the middle, and plateaux with many good roads spanning out from the *Préfecture*, Clermont-Ferrand, which is overlooked by the Puy-de-Dôme peak, 1465 metres high; it has a toll road almost to the top, and on a clear day one can see for miles in all directions, a great tourist attraction; parking, restaurants '*table d'orientation*' – it's all at the top.

For up-market chambres d'hôtes in old family houses you are spoilt for choice in this area.

The Mont Doré and Bourboule area further west is totally geared to the tourist trade, with many lakes, hotels, campsites and purpose-built flats, etc. but very few chambres d'hôtes. Have fun looking for the source of the Dordogne at the Puy-de-Sancy (1886 metres), reached from Mont Doré by *téléférique* in fine weather. Do visit Orcival, a delightful, little village nestling in the hills west of the Puy-de-Dôme. It has a fine Romanesque church, a real picture floodlit at night. Saint-Nectaire also boasts a lovely Romanesque church as well as producing the famous cheese. Visit Ambert where an old paper mill is still producing paper by the same method used at the end of the 16th century.

Haute-Loire to the south-east is a gentle, undulating department, with fields of the lovely wild narcissus in May. Some of the best farm chambres d'hôtes in the whole of France are hidden here, excellent value for a holiday or en route, as they are never far from main roads.

The church of Saint-Paulien in Le Puy-en-Velay was built in the fifth century and is one of the official starting points for the annual pilgrimage to Santiago-de-Compostella in Spain; but the largest Romanesque church in the Auvergne is the Basilica of Saint-Julien in Brioude, dating from the fourth century; it was completely rebuilt with many different stones in the eleventh and twelfth centuries. The Cantal to the south-west of the region does feel less populated, with its sweeping hills and less wooded country-side. It has its own extinct volcanoes. The Puy-Mary (1787 metres) and the Plomb de Cantal (1858 metres) can be visited during most months of the year when there is no snow. Some lovely old houses with the Lauzes tiled roofs make the villages most attractive, notably Salers.

The river Allier crops up all over the region; rising in the Lozère it joins the Loire near Nevers in Nièvre; but not before its salmon and trout have been tickled and caught by ardent Auvergne anglers. Panning for gold is also a possibility in parts of the river. The Loire (known as the Royal River in France), also passes through the region, rising at the foot of the Gerbier-de-Jonc in the Ardèche then flowing through valleys in the Haute-Loire and the Puy-de-Dôme. The mineral waters of the Auvergne such as 'Volvic' and 'Vichy' need no introduction. *Bleu d'Auvergne* is probably the most famous cheese of this region.

Locals have their own vineyards and wine is made and consumed on the premises. Not a lot of Auvergne wine sells outside the region, and there are not many *dégustations*.

ALLIER

LA CHAPELAUDE. 03380

12 Km NW of Montluçon. Take the D943 SW from La Châtre to Montluçon and in the village of La Chapelaude turn left to Montroir. In about 2 km Madame Petit's cottage is signposted.

Montroir (S)
Mme Petit. 70.06.45.57.

In a tiny hamlet this very small cottage, enveloped in greenery, has three to four guest rooms, delightfully rustic, with low beams to catch the unwary upstairs and one room downstairs. Mme Petit is a really caring hostess who remembers to put fresh flowers in the room even though rushed off her feet because all her family were staying. On arrival we were given tea and cakes by a log fire and a son-in-law was sent to talk to us. The bedrooms were warm and cosy, bathrooms small, but with plenty of hooks and shelves.

Excellent evening meal *en famille* for 50f, wine and coffee *compris*. Next morning we woke up to the smell of fresh bread baking. Breakfast of fresh baked bread, fruit and yoghurt was laid on a round table by a log fire as it was a dull day. If this is how she copes with an overflowing house I should love to visit when all is quiet. Perhaps it would not be so interesting. There is a small patio garden behind the house for meals in summer. New covered terrace in the offing. Double room 180f.

LURCY-LEVIS. 03320

28 km NW of Moulins. 12 km south of Sançoins on the D40, which becomes the D1 in Allier.

I wish I felt more enthusiastic about Allier as a Department. It has the lovely Forêt-de-Tronçais in the north-west, but the slightly undulating lands are not spectacular, mostly quiet farming country. There are even coal mines which can be found in the east. In the south at Néris-les-Bains is a spa many people visit, hoping to recover from the stress of modern life and the large town of Montluçon has a well laid-out shopping centre. It is always useful to know some overnight stops, and the chambres d'hôtes I have found are all very welcoming and not expensive.

La Platrière (S)
Mme Vanneau. Grand Veau. 70.67.83.95.

A few kilometres into the department is the little village of Lurcy-Lévis. Take the D64 west to Grand Veau and you will find the Vanneaus' wheat farm signed down a side track, well away from main roads.

Grand Veau

The old, low farmhouse looks as if it's worse for wear, but don't be put off; on the first floor are three newly decorated, beamed bedrooms. The front room would be my choice, facing south, sunny and warm and with a private entry up an outside staircase into the adjoining bathroom. There is a little sitting area on the landing for breakfast but dinner is taken with the family downstairs. A very warm welcome from both your hosts.

Evening meals of farm produce at 70f, wine and coffee *compris*. Rooms 200f for two and only 40f extra for a third person make this a worthwhile stop.

VILLEFRANCHE D'ALLIER. 03430

21 km E of Montluçon. On the D16 between Cosne d'Allier and Montmarault.

Madame Siwiec (S)
23 rue Pasteur. 70.07.46.62.

This small market town has a well restored 19th century tavern in the centre, with two cosy chambres d'hôtes rooms on the first floor at the front, so there is the possibility of traffic noise. Parking is in the open courtyard behind. Mme Siezicz welcomed us with tea in front of her log fire.

Evening meals (65f) are good value, with local specialities. Croissants for breakfast with new bread. Rooms 210f.

Ville-farm d'Allier.

YGRANDE. 03160

38 km NE of Montluçon. 14 km NE of Cosne d'Allier. From the village of Ygrande, which is north of Cosne d'Allier, take a small road left by the school. You will find the chambres d'hôtes Les Ferrons well signed from here, about 2 km away.

This is the centre of France, not far from Montluçon. The true centre of France is in the small village of Vesdun about 20 miles west of Ygrande, where there is a large circular plaque in the centre of the village giving directions and distances to all the capital cities of the world.

Les Ferrons (M)
Mme Vrel. 70.66.31.67.

Hidden in the country, about 200 yards from the main farmhouse stands this lovely old *Maison de Maître* in its own spacious wooded grounds. Four large carpeted rooms, pleasantly decorated, have views over the countryside. 200–210f. The house is entered through a porch into a long narrow room. At one end is a cheerful log fire, arm chairs and TV; at the other are dining table and kitchen facilities.

Les Ferrons

Mme Vrel is there in the morning to serve a very nice breakfast consisting of orange juice, cereal and cheese as well as the normal fresh bread and various jams. She will now provide an evening meal on reservation. All this is excellent value for money with plenty of freedom and very quiet, as is her sister's chambres d'hôtes at Mainneville in Normandy.

CANTAL

GIOU-DE-MAMOU. 15130

7 km E of Aurillac. Just off the N 122.

Barathe (S-M)
Mme Breton. 71.64.61.72.

Overlooking the little village of Giou-de-Mamou is a rustic chambres d'hôtes to suit the most dedicated beam lover. This old, narrow house, built in 1777, has all its bedrooms facing south over the terrace. Very old, wide, wooden stairs lead to a nice first-floor room with a balcony (double bed and bunks). On the second floor are four more rooms equally old and beamed. Warm carpeted floors in all. All *en suite*.

The lovely old dining room has a natural stone floor and a fine stone archway leads to what was the scullery of the original kitchen. An enormous chimney breast towers over the room.

Young Madame Breton insists you eat here if you have a room, and at 170f demi-pension per person it is no deprivation. Meals on the terrace in summer would be most pleasant. A superb situation.

PARLAN. 15630

28 km SW of Aurillac. Driving north from Figeac to the Cantal the winding road (N122) to Aurillac leads through fertile country with the river Célé on one side, but the river branches off just before Maurs, where there is a busy market on Thursdays. Taking care not to mow down the population bent on bargains you soon come to a left turn off to Parlan. Follow this lane (direction Parlan) and you will find the chambres d'hôtes about a kilometre south of the village.

La Vabre (S-M)
Madame Segurel. 71.46.12.84.

La Vabre is a modern house in a
large garden with a separate house
built for guests. Cheerful Mme
Segurel has everything sorted out for
comfort inside and out. Four differently coloured rooms have baths not
showers. There are swings for children and many stone circular tables
for eating outside and a kitchen and
barbecue for self-catering; evening
meals are available for 70f (wine not
compris), I have a feeling this is a

popular place for week-long holidays in summer. Double room only 160f.

PERS. 15290

23 km SW of Aurillac. Further up the N122 from Parlan turn left for Omps on the
little D32 and it will lead you into the tiny village of Pers.

Madame Lacaze (S)
71.62.25.14.

You will find here a large complex
of camping, caravanning, gîtes and
studios on the farm, but a converted barn has been made into a
unit for chambres d'hôtes. The rustic, arched doorway leads into a
dining room with a large corner
kitchen with two fridges. Stairs lead
to a mezzanine sitting area with TV
and along a separate corridor on
the first floor are five very pretty
rustic bedrooms with skylight win-

dows giving good country views. Some beds have pretty canopies over them and all
floors have fitted carpets. 190f.

   Breakfast is in Madame Lacaze's old farmhouse a few steps away. I should
imagine it would be a hive of activity here in summer. Madame Lacaze strikes me as
a very efficient lady who has been running this complex for some years and has
everything under control. The village with a few shops is within easy walking distance, and Aurillac is only 23 km away.

   No evening meal; scope for self catering.

SALERS. 15410

47 km N of Aurillac. Built on a layer of basalt, this medieval village was founded by the Baron de Salers in 1069 and in 1428 Charles VII authorised its fortification against the English and the *Routiers* (roving bands of highwaymen, not today's lorry drivers). Under Henry II in 1550 the town became the seat of government of the Royal Bailiwick of the High Mountains of the Auvergne (*Bailiage Royale des Hautes Montagnes de l'Auvergne*). The Knights Templar had close connections with Salers and the museum in the Maison des Templiers is worth a visit. Little remains of the really old town apart from the church door, parts of the walls and some street staircases but there are lots of cottages and artisan shops in the village. 1 km outside the village on the Route de Puy Mary you will find:

➤ Mme Vantal (M)
71.40.74.02.

Route de Puy Mary, Salers

M. and Mme Vantal, dairy farmers, have given up the first floor of their house to five of the smartest guest rooms I have seen for a long time. Nothing fancy about them, in fact not an ornament in sight, which comes as a relief if you have just suffered from an overdose of bric-à-brac. A choice of rooms with baths or showers, single or double beds, one family room for four. All prettily papered and painted, with good central heating, plentiful hot water and nice views. Lovely white cotton sheets and at least four fluffy white towels and flannels. 210–250f.

You can be spoilt by having breakfast brought to your room, or you can opt for it downstairs or outside in summer. Orange juice, a huge slab of farm butter with fresh bread and croissants and a selection of jams and honey, all beautifully served. Parking off the road at the side of the garage.

There is a good choice of restaurants in Salers. I can recommend the *Restaurant des Templiers* where the 59f menu will give you *Pounti* (a local speciality – a leek soufflé), *poulet volaille* with a selection of vegetables, and cheese or sweet. Menus at 89f and 120f just give you more food, not better. As Madame Vantal said the next morning 'All our regional specialities are calorific!' I really loved this one. The welcome was so friendly and young Madame Vantal is such an animated hostess who thinks of everything. A nice situation too *en route* to one of the highest peaks in the Auvergne.

HAUTE-LOIRE

BAINS. 43370

10 km SW of Le Puy. From the D906 turn off on to the D272 (Bains)

Jalasset (S)
Mme Pelisse. 71.57.52.72.

Tucked away in the tiny hamlet of Jalasset south-west of Le Puy, only a kilometre away from the busy D906. The tall farmhouse has four, fresh, countrified rooms on the first floor with pine floors and lace bed-spreads, overlooking a sunny garden with swings for children.

Meals are served in the large dining-room where there is an ornate, carved sideboard and grand-father clock. From a very modern adjoining kitchen Madame Pelisse produced her own charcuterie, jams and butter; she is justly proud that nearly all her food is home-produced. Evening meals *en famille* make this a homely place to stay, where guests are well looked after by Madame and her daughter. Evening meal 55f, all drinks *compris*, half price for children under nine. Double room 190f.

LE CHAISE-DIEU. 43160

40 km N of Le Puy. On the D 906 between Ambert and Le Puy. The very large Basilica stands out for miles around. Clement VI founded this church, before he was elected to the papacy in 1342. He died in 1352 and is buried here. There are often concerts in the church in the summer. The Moscow State Symphony Orchestra has performed here.

Mme Communal (S)
Rue St. Martin. 71.00.01.77.

Right on the village street these rooms are quite adequate for a night stop, probably not even noisy at night. Parking is behind the adjoining grill restaurant to which it is attached. You enter into a dining room with a nice, modern kitchen attached, so you have an option of cooking your own evening meal or going to one of the six other restaurants or cafés within walking distance. Not a lot of contact with the family except at breakfast or if you eat in their grill.

Four rooms in all, two for three people and two doubles, lino floors. At 170f for two with kitchen facilities this is a good budget stop for a family.

Rue St. Martin   La Chaise-Dieu

MAZEYRAT-D'ALLIER. 43300

46 km NW of Le Puy. Leave the N102 26 km S of Brioude, signposted St Eble, but before you get to the village look out for a cup and saucer sign on your left to Chamalières.

M & Mme Sdei (M)
71.77.12.26.

If you feel like a bit of pampering, head for this chambres d'hôtes, so hidden in the country you can easily miss it, to find excellent up-market rooms not spoilt by excessive prices. Three thickly carpeted rooms are assigned to guests, with a separate entrance from a raised terrace, have very high vaulted ceilings, and a mezzanine platform on which are two other single beds, making three rooms

Chamalières

for four people if needed. They open on to a sitting area with comfortable armchairs and TV. 175f.

The garden is prettily terraced with lawns and flowers, all very private. M. Sdei conducts tours of panning for gold in the nearby R. Allier. Worth a try, you might be lucky! He is really knowledgeable on the subject. A most attractive chambres d'hôtes and full of character.

Meals are taken in your hosts' old farm dining room. Evening meal 55f all drinks *compris*.

ST PRIVAT-DU-DRAGON. 43380

16 km south of Brioude. Cerzat du Dragon is a tiny hamlet at a dead end with farming land all round. Winding lanes take you there if you are lucky enough to find the right lane. French signs have a habit of disappearing at the crucial moment at a cross road. Best to approach from the small village of St. Ilpise which you will find on the D585 between Lavoûte-Chilhac and Vieille Brioude. From St. Ilpise climb the hill signposted Cerzat du Dragon and then follow the sign to the chambres d'hôtes. The lane peters out in what seems like one long farmyard; it is actually the hamlet, with more geese, chickens, dogs and cats than any other form of life. Young Mme Sabatiers' farmhouse is on your right just up the hill.

In the height of civilisation there used to be fifteen families in the hamlet, but now reduced to five. All five families own about three houses each; you haven't a cat in hell's chance of buying a house here however much you fancy it.

Cerzat du Dragon (S)
Mme Sabatier. 71.76.67.71.

Cerzat du Dragon

Mme Sabatier's rooms are in a restored barn just opposite her house. They are just simple little rooms, one for a family, but all have private facilities, showers and toilets. Two rooms have country views but the others are rather dark. Mme Sabatier will cook an evening meal entirely of farm produce for you; she says she never buys meat as they have cows, sheep, pigs even calves for veal as well as all poultry. A large vegetable garden had strawberries coming into season when I was there, so you will not go hungry. There are lovely walks up the lane and a whole field of wild narcissus nearby was gathered for a scent factory the previous day.

At 160f for two and 60f for a four course meal with wine *compris*, children under ten years 30f, you can't really complain. Haute Loire seems to know how to give value for money in their chambres d'hôtes, perhaps because most of them are on farms, and use nothing but their own produce. Nearly all the ones I visited are easily accessible from the N102 between Brioude and Le Puy.

VERGEZAC. 43320

10 km W of Le Puy. From the D906 west of Le Puy take the D27 just south of St Rémy.

Le Puy is the lace-making town of France. The shops are full of it, but it is quite pricey. A spectacular town viewed from the hills above, as volcanic eruptions have thrown up three odd peaks; on one stands a church and on another an enormous crucifix. I was rather disappointed with the town when I visited – it seemed a bit unkempt; but seen from above it is most inviting.

Madame Jourdain (M)
Alientin. 71.08.66.10.

Near Le Puy, another worthwhile stop just off the D906 is at Allentin. Don't go looking for it in Vergezac – that is just the postal address; take a turn to this one just south of St Rémy. Allentin is a small hamlet lying on a road parallel with the D906. Here you will find a very large old farmhouse, set in a walled garden, with ample room for children to play. Good parking behind the house on a

slightly higher level means you haven't quite so far to walk to your rooms which are on the second floor with independent entry. The three rooms all have tiled floors with exceptionally original showers, toilets and vanitory units. At 165–175f, very good value. On the ground floor is a large room housing a washing machine for guests' use and good drying lines in the garden. A large, pleasant, shady lawn is a lovely place to relax in after a hard day's driving, while you wait to be called to the evening meal which is only 60f, wine *compris*, children under ten 30f.

The Jourdains are sheep farmers and keep horses for riding.

VIEILLE-BRIOUDE. 43100

4 km S of Brioude. Just off the N102 at the northern entrance of Vieille-Brioude, on your left near the sports stadium.

La Coustade (M)
Mme Chantel. Chemin du Stade. 71.50.25.21.

On the outskirts of the lovely old village of Vieille-Brioude, in flat country surrounded by hills, is the modern farmhouse home of young M. and Mme Chantel.

Purpose-built at the back are five smart rooms named after flowers, each with different coloured wallpaper, matching bedspreads, etc. Meals are taken with the family in their large modern dining-room overlooking a terrace and there is a comfortable sitting-room for guests and play area for children. Here are the amenities of a motel with the friendly atmosphere of a chambres d'hôtes. Rooms 180f.

La Coustade

Evening meal 60f with four courses and wine *compris*. You wouldn't get that in a motel!

PUY-DE-DÔME

COLLANGES. 63340

15 km S of Issoire. 45 km S of Clermont-Ferrand. Very near the A75 (exit 15 or 17) south of Issoire.

Château de Collanges (L)
M. Huillet. 73.96.47.30.

Château de Collanges

Collanges is rather a poor-looking village, but this large château offers you three very up-market rooms overlooking vast parkland. Two rooms have telephones and canopied beds; thick carpets cover most of the natural wood floors. All have luxurious private bathrooms, spoiling you with towelling dressing gowns and plenty of good towels. One has an exceptionally pretty, circular, flowered wash-basin.

A wide stone staircase leads to this suite of rooms. A large vaulted dining-room for breakfast, and a high ceilinged sitting-room with french windows on to the garden has tables laid ready for bridge and chess and a grand piano waiting for a pianist for your own soirée. Riding and tennis can be arranged and there are antiques for sale in a shop in the outbuildings. Evening meals on reservation cost

130f, wine not *compris;* it will be a candlelit dinner in a romantic setting, but your hosts don't dine with you. Book ahead and you will be given full directions. Rooms 420f for two, 500f for three.

COURPIÈRE. 63120

15 km S of Thiers. 3 km from Courpière; a turning off the D223 to Lezoux leads to the farm of Bonencontre.

Bonencontre (S–M)
Mme Constancias. 73.53.10.51.

Easy to find, situated on a side road. Madame Constancias has made four very pleasant rooms on the first and second floors, brightly decorated, ceilings and walls completely covered in *moquette murale.* Each one is a different colour with matching towels and bedspreads. Downstairs are a large dining room, kitchen corner with washing machine and a small TV room and in the garden a new swimming pool. When word gets around this will be a much sought after place on a hot summer's day, so book to avoid disappointment.

No evening meals, but plenty of restaurants in Courpière. Rooms 200f for two. Very good value. Highly recommended.

ÉGLISENEUVE-PRES-BILLOM. 63160

23 km E of Clermont-Ferrand.

Mme Grimard (S)
Le Mas. 73.68.44.17.

In the small hamlet of Le Mas, Mme Grimard has two chambres d'hôtes rooms, very clean and nicely furnished, sharing a smart bathroom. Also a very good kitchen for guests to cook and eat their own meals. Breakfast is served in Madame's dining room. Entrance is through a little room downstairs where guests may relax and watch TV. Really like a *gîte* for four people, with breakfast served by Madame. An excellent stop for a family or for four friends sharing the bathroom. Rooms 180f.

JOZE. 63350

20 km NE of Clermont-Ferrand. On the D1093 only a short distance from the A71 and the A72.

Loursse (M)
M. Masson. 73.70.20.63.

This beautiful *Maison-de-Maître*, which has been in the family for years, would make a wonderful relaxing stop on the way south; but arrive early, or better still stay a few days and enjoy the exceptional ambience of the house and parkland, with sweeping lawns to the river Allier, a salmon fisherman's delight. One large double bedroom with a modern, comfortable bed, overlooks the garden. The adjoining bathroom leads to a smaller room, probably once a dressing room, now with one or two extra beds for children – a family suite or just a room for two. Fishing permits can be bought in the village of Joze, which also has a couple of restaurants. A lovely, relaxing spot for visiting the northern part of the Auvergne. Do book well ahead. With only one room you haven't much chance of arriving on spec. M. Masson prefers a reservation and will then give you full instructions how to find the house. Room 260f for two. Good value.

MONTPEYROUX. 63114

11 km N of Issoire. 20 km S of Clermont-Ferrand. Exit 7 from A75, then follow signs to the village.

Montpeyroux is a medieval village whose name comes from the ground on which it was built – 'Stony mountains'. Topped by a round tower, which is the central point of the fortress, this hill village (500m) can be seen from a long way off. The village is well worth exploring even if you don't stay here. Drive up to the church to park and go through an old fortress gate. All the old houses were built within the walls. There is a crêperie in the village and another restaurant open in summer. It is only a small village but almost every house cries out to be photographed. Better still make this your resting place as you drive south.

Les Pradets (S-M)
Mme Grenot. 73.96.63.40.

Madame Grenot offers you a charming room in her dear little stone house, which was originally three cottages, with lovely views from the delightful sheltered

garden perched on a hill. It's a very
feminine room with brass bed
decorated with pretty pink bows,
everything else dainty and matching. The room has a wash basin,
but you share a bathroom and toilet with Madame. Better news is
that she is planning two other *en
suite* rooms. Parking is in a small
lay-by just above the house. A very
charming and lively hostess who
will treat you as her private guests.
Madame likes you to book ahead. Rooms 250f.

PERRIER. 63500

3 km W of Issoire. At Issoire leave the A75 at junction 12 and take the D996 to Perrier. Troglodyte caves in this village.

M. Gebrillat (M)
Chemin de Siorac. 73.89.15.02. cl. 1/11 to 31/3 except for weekends.

Whether just travelling south and
needing a night stop or wanting a
quiet relaxed holiday this is just the
place to visit. Your kind and
thoughtful host will give you
enough information about the
region to keep you going for a
month. He has spent many years in
Africa and the house is full of interesting mementoes. The house is situated off the main road in the
village of Perrier but has a two-acre

park, bordered by the river Couze-de-Pavin. It is a fascinating place, with three luxurious rooms on the second floor of the main house, Two doubles and one single.
You don't often find single rooms *en suite*. Another room in an annex with lovely
views of the village has a private luxury bathroom on the landing, which leads to a
vast dormitory playroom where a very large family could sleep. Below this room is
a dining room and fully equipped kitchen for self catering. There are plenty of
restaurants in Issoire and one or two in the village of Perrier.

Madame speaks English. Excellent breakfast with fruit juice and cereals as well
as the usual breads etc. Rooms 250f. Reduced in winter months.

SAINT-GERVAZY. 63340

17 km S of Issoire. 47 km From Clermont-Ferrand. Leave the A75 at Junction 18, then take the D35 to the pleasant little village of Saint-Gervazy.

Ferme de Séjour du Montcelet (S)
M et Mme Trouiller. 73.96.44.51.

For anyone who likes a riding holiday this is ideal. Young M. & Mme Trouiller run this *Ferme Auberge* which also has stables with thirty horses. M. Trouiller has converted an old farm building into four good chambres d'hôtes rooms decorated in different colours. Good rural views from all windows, a sitting-room and small kitchenette for guests' use. Evening meals and breakfast taken in the *Ferme Auberge*, a step across the courtyard. Home-made goat's cheese a speciality.

Demi-pension 160f for one and 300f for two. Wine is *compris* with the evening meal. Very good value.

SERMENTIZON. 63120

35 km E of Clermont-Ferrand. From the D906 south of Thiers take the D223 to Lezoux and turn left on to the D44 To Sermentizon.

Sermentizon is a small village, but it does have a bar restaurant. *Alimentation*, post office and phone box are all in an open square by the church. Many of the old houses are built in the *Pisé* style, which was standard building practice in this region of Livradois until a few years ago – just earth moistened with water and packed in between wooden beams put in vertically and horizontally to support it. The beams leave holes in the walls and in the outhouses the holes are left open for ventilation; but in inhabited houses they are plugged with cement and the wall plastered over. It is interesting to look round and spot the many outhouses built in this way.

Madame Grolet (S)
73.53.03.14.

Retired *viticulteurs* M. and Mme Grolet still live in their old farmhouse in the centre of the village. Large fields and gardens are attached to the property and the courtyard extends round three sides of the house. A stay with the Grolets is very pleasant. They are full of knowledge of the area and while chatting with them on a summer's evening you may be invited to a private *dégustation*. M. Grolet still makes his own

wine on the premises. If you visit during the *vendange* in October you could even get roped in to help.

Madame has four, carpeted chambres d'hôtes rooms, on the first and second floors. Two have private bath and w.c. and others have showers, but share a toilet. 160–190f. There is a little bar across the road where we were lucky enough to get a reasonable four-course meal with wine included for 50f each. There are other restaurants in Courpière nearby. There is a little summer kitchen outside and tables on the lawn behind the house. Breakfast is taken here in fine weather.

CHÂTEAU-DE-VAULX. 63120

14 km SE of Thiers. I am inclined to agree with Georges Sand that Thiers is a black town. Sprawling up a hill, it is divided by the narrow, relentless N89 with shopping precincts on either side and certainly as you leave the town on the east side the tall houses look ill-kept and pretty miserable. But park in the covered car park (payant) near the Mairie and descend down narrow streets to the *Vieille Ville* and you will find much more of interest. (There is a free car park by St Genis church, but a bit difficult to find in the maze of narrow streets.) Almost every other shop is a *couterie*. At nearby Monnerie knives in all shapes and sizes are produced in profusion. The Sabatier factory is here. There is also a museum of knives in the old town. So don't dismiss Thiers with first impressions. It has more to offer.

9 km east of Thiers on the N89 turn right on the D7 to Celles-sur-Durolles, past the village, still on the D7 towards Sainte-Agathe you will pick up a discreet sign to the Château on your right.

➤ ### Château de Vaulx (M)
M. et Mme Dumas de Vaulx. Ste-Agathe. Courpière.
73.51.50.55; fax 73.51.54.47.

Such a gem of a château, with four towers and a moat, looking like a fairy-tale castle yet still a real family home with every room in use. Originally built in the 13th century it has had its ups and downs but remained in the same family. Such sensible use of all the tower rooms, kitchen, butler's pantry, bathroom but best surprise of all through the library is a charming circular chapel licensed by Pope Leo XIII for mass and all the other sacraments, with a really ornate altar and even a child's prie-dieu.

Your charming hosts will gather you in for a cup of tea in the kitchen as though they had known you all their lives. Two rooms are in the château, one enor-

mous with modern bed and mono-
grammed white sheets which
belonged to Madame's grandmother and still going strong. The
bathroom attached to this room is
in a tower and the bath stands
regally on clawed feet. Excellent
lighting and hot water.

Château de Vaulx

The other room is in one of
the front towers. The circular room
is entered by a dressing-room with
wash-basin and the private shower
and toilet is adjacent. Fun sleeping in a tower.

Sometimes an evening meal is available in the kitchen with the family – no pre-
tensions, just real hospitality. Before dinner you may be invited to inspect the cellars,
where the family hid a priest during the Revolution. Down here Monsieur has made
a little bar where *apéritifs* are sometimes taken. Huge parkland round the castle to
explore. Before you complain about lack of luxury carpets remember that you are
going up to bed up the same stone stairs the family have used for hundreds of years
and looking out at the same view down the valley from a château where the English
defended Aquitane from the Duke of Burgundy. All this and the charming *accueil*
will make you think about staying much longer.

No high château prices, just 250f for bed and breakfast for two and evening
meal from 50f each, all drinks *compris*. Arrowed for good value.

POITOU-CHARENTES

Départements: **Charente**
Charente-Maritime
Deux-Sèvres
Vienne

South of the Loire, north of Bordeaux, this western region of France stretches from the Atlantic to the Limousin. Poitou-Charentes is divided into four departments; in the north Deux-Sèvres and Vienne lie side by side, as do Charente and Charente Maritime further south, the latter on the Atlantic coast.

Deux-Sèvres is so called because there are two river Sèvres flowing through the department, the Sèvre Nantaise heading for the Loire at Nantes on its way to the Atlantic at St Nazaire in the north, and the Sèvre Niortaise in the south which has given birth to the delightful little canals of the Marais Poitevin west of Niort. This area is usually attributed to the Vendée, but some of the prettiest parts actually lie in Deux Sèvres. Do visit these quiet waterways and small villages; you will be amazed at what you have been missing. Niort, the *préfecture*, has a large central parking area in the Place de la Brèche, and a colourful indoor market. Only on Saturdays when the large market takes up the main square is parking a problem. Vienne again takes its name from the river, one of the prettiest in France. The large town of Poitiers is the *préfecture*, once the home of the English King, Henry II, and his wife, Eleanor of Aquitaine. Steeped in history and historic buildings, the town is well worth visiting. A few kilometres north to Jaunay Clan (exit 18 off the A10) is the *Futurescope*, a large theme park, which is a must for all visitors passing this way. It comprises a wonderful exhibition of cinemas and commerce of the future with ample entertainment for children. (See Avanton-Martigny.)

Travel down to Charente, named after another river, a lovely, tranquil, country area where the old town of Angoulême rules the department, but the really famous name here is Cognac, where all the grapes grown in the

POITOU-CHARENTES

CHARENTE (16)
Préfecture: Angoulême
1   Bioussac
2   Garat
3   Lignières-Sonneville
4   Luxé

CHARENTE MARITIME (17)
Préfecture: La Rochelle
1   Dompierre-sur-Mer
2   Fouras
3   Loix-en-Ré
4   Thaire-d'Aunis

DEUX-SEVRES (79)
Préfecture: Niort
1   Argenton-l'Eglise
2   Coulon
3   Frontenay-Rohan-Rohan
4   Germond-Rouvre
5   Nanteuil
6   Nueil-sur-Argent

VIENNE (86)
Préfecture: Poitiers
1   Arçay
2   Avanton-Martigny
3   Berthegon
4   Beuxes
5   Château de Vaumoret
6   Leigné-sur-Usseau
7   Mouterre-Silly
8   Pouant (x2)
9   Roiffé
10 St Leger-de-Montbrillais
11 La Trimouille

■   Préfecture

■   Town

①   Chambre d'Hôtes

warm countryside are turned into brandy. Such names as Hine, Courvoisier and Rémy Martin flash by as you drive along (see Lignières-Sonneville). Make sure you taste the *apéritif* of the region, Pineau, made from grape juice and brandy.

La Rochelle is the busy port of the Charente-Maritime where the river Charente finally finds its way to the sea. A very attractive town with the fortress and the harbour always coming into view as you wander through the main streets. This is a strong Protestant region and many Huguenot churches are still here. A wonderful indoor market every day sells the fruit and vegetables of the countryside as well as the *produits de la mer*.

From here you take the toll bridge (110f return for a car in summer, 60f return in October to May) to the attractive island of Ile de Ré where the tiny ports are bursting with small craft in season and the tall lighthouse towers over the island.

About 10 km south of Rochefort is the unexpected isolated village of Brouage, known to many Canadians, as it was the birthplace in 1597 of Samuel de Champlain, the founder of Quebec. The small village is totally surrounded by a star-shaped wall. You can walk round the high ramparts and have an excellent view of the flat salt pans stretching along the Havre de Brouage to the sea. As the salt pans have declined, they are now used for storing shellfish. Enter the village by the old stone archway on the north side and wander round the quiet streets with just a few restaurants serving really fresh fish menus, and the odd shop. The church has a reredos looking like a piece of fine Wedgewood blue and white china, but it actually is wooden and was restored by the Canadians who have also put up the memorial to Samuel de Champlain. The most striking view of the village is from the air, so buy a card from the Tourist Office and see what I mean.

Further south visit the old Roman town of *Saintes* where the large Arc de Triomphe still stands by the riverside and remains of old Roman baths are just outside the town. Visit the pottery at La Chapelle-des-Pots, just north of Saintes, where you will find many old French designs on reproduction pottery, the only place that makes the two-handled Charentais serving dish used in the farms in the last century.

COGNAC

Brandy has been distilled in the Cognac area since the early part of the eighteenth century, the oldest house being Martell (1715), followed by Rémy Martin (1724). Brandy is essentially a double distillation. The process starts with wine made from the Ugny Blanc grapes which grow exceptionally well here owing to the climate and the limestone soil. (The Champagne vineyards round Epernay in the north have the same type of terrain, and the title 'Champagne' is also used here.) The wine comes to the distilleries from their own vineyards and from the surrounding areas. The area which forms a semi-circle extending about 12 km east, south and west of Cognac, produces 'Grande Champagne'. A semi-circle of the same width extending another 12 km further out produces 'Petite Champagne'. The not quite so grand wine known as 'Borderies' comes from the area just round Burie (12 km NW of Cognac), and the even lesser wines known as 'Fins Bois', 'Bons Bois' and 'Bois Ordinaires' come from other parts of the Charente.

On arrival at the distillery the wine is placed in an onion-shaped, swan-necked container, heated and the vapour is passed through lengthy cooling pipes. The resulting liquor, known as *broillié* is then put through the same process once more; this is now *Eau-de-Vie* (brandy) and is stored in large oak vats to mature. The end result is obtained by blending various brandies of different vintages and areas selected by the skill of the blender. To quality for the title 'Fine Champagne Cognac' at least 50 per cent must come from Grande Champagne and the rest from Petite Champagne. The *vendange* starts at the end of September and distillation starts about a month later. To qualify for the title Cognac the distillation must be complete by the end of the following March.

Brandy ages and matures in the cask and not in the bottle. The casks are made of Limousin oak which has been seasoned for four to six years, and the art of the *tonnelier* (cooper) is most esteemed. The brandy can breathe through the wood and a very small proportion, known as 'the Angel's Share', is lost this way through evaporation. One can smell this on a visit through the storehouses (*chais*) where the barrels are stacked whilst maturing. The brandies are selected for ageing by the blender and are kept for a minimum of five years before bottling. The youngest are known as Very Special Old Pale, progressing through Napoleon (9 years old) to other specials such as Louis XIII, in the case of Rémy Martin. The latter is blended from brandies with a minimum average of fifty years, and is sold in crystal bottles individually numbered.

CHARENTE

BIOUSSAC. 16700

62 km S of Poitiers. 6 km E of Ruffec. From N 10 at Ruffec take the D740 to Confolens. In about 5 km, just after Codac, turn left on to the D197 to Bioussac; take the first left to d'Oyer and you will find La Grande Métairie on your left.

La Grande Métairie (S)
M. et Mme Moy. d'Oyer. 45.31.15.67. cl. 1/11 to 1/4.

La Grande Métairie

M. et Mme Moy and their three children are a delightful young family, who work this organic farm, deep in the Charente countryside. The river Charente runs past the end of their lane. The farmhouse is very old, and the large rooms cool in summer, with all mod cons., have kept their original style – old flagstone floors and stone walls in the family room on the ground floor. The other room is upstairs. 200f.

Meals in the summer are taken outside with the family under an old lime tree in the very rural garden. Mme Moy is an excellent cook and uses local produce from the farm. Dinner 65f, wine *compris*.

A swimming pool behind the house overlooking fields and woods, bikes for hire, canoes on the river and use of a fully equipped kitchen make this an attractive place for a holiday, especially for children.

There is also a small *gîte* attached to the farmhouse, whose occupants share the garden and pool. Mme Moy speaks English.

GARAT. 16410

7 km ESE of Angoulême. Leave Angoulême by the D939 signposted Brantôme. In 2 km after a supermarket on the left and the zoo on the right is a chambres d'hôtes sign on your left (easy to miss), where a small road will lead you to La Penotte, 100m down the Route de Bassac on the left.

La Penotte (S)
M. et Mme Liagre. Route de Bassac. 45.60.63.46.

A few wrong turns brought us to this most attractive home of the Liagres, far enough off the main road to be quiet. There are five rooms, not all *en suite*; some have their own terrace. 190–250f. The gardens are a delight, with the added attraction of a large swimming pool, sand pit and games for children. The hosts are very attentive and do all they can to make your stay a happy one. Breakfast on the terrace or in a conservatory is one of the best I have ever been offered in France – fruit compote, orange juice, cereal, fresh bread, croissants, a variety of jams, eggs, as well as the usual choice of coffee, tea or chocolate. You name it, they'll produce it!

Le Panette

There is a fully equipped kitchen, but Mme Liagre now serves evening meals on reservation only (50–70f wine not *compris*), and I am quite sure there will be a candelabrum on the table.

LIGNIERES-SONNEVILLE. 16130

21 km S of Cognac. From Cognac take the D24 to Ségonzac, then the D1 to the crossroads with the D699. Turn left here and the house is on your left.

M. Matignon has vast vineyards all around growing Ugny Blanc grapes and sells all his produce to Rémy Martin, just up the road. First the grapes are pressed on the premises then left to ferment for one month before being collected by the Rémy Martin tanker as Grande Champagne wine for distillation. Most distilleries charge for their visits, but Mme Matignon will give you free vouchers for a visit to Rémy Martin.

Les Collinauds (S)
M. et. Mme Matignon. 45.80.51.23.

This huge three-storey house in the heart of the Grande Champagne region of Cognac is in very large walled gardens. Perhaps it is now a shadow of its former glory but it still has plenty of charm, overlooking an extensive view of hilly vineyards and offering a peaceful retreat. The house, built in 1825, has housed fifteen generations of this family. Now the young owners are restoring it slowly.

Les Collinauds

There is a super sunny grass terrace the length of the house with steps down to the lawns.

There are three rooms on the first floor, but as there is only one bathroom Mme Matignon prefers to let just one room unless it is for friends or a family, so you never share the bathroom with strangers. The main room has a very old boxed double bed, polished wooden floor, an old fireplace laid with logs and a marble washstand with basin and jug, which gave it an authentic touch. The other two are carpeted, one twin and one single.

The dining room has an enormous Charentaise sideboard dwarfing the small round table where you eat breakfast. Avert your gaze from the peeling wallpaper and look out to the garden and the hills beyond as you enjoy an excellent breakfast with orange juice, fresh croissants and baguettes.

A nicely equipped kitchen for self-catering is situated right by the entrance, in a converted coach house. Children welcome; an extensive enclosed garden to play in. Rooms 230f for two, only 20f extra for a child.

LUXE. 16230

28 km N of Angouléme. From Mansle on the N10, south of Poitiers, take the D739 to Luxé Gare. Turn right to Luxé and you will find the Ferme des Vignauds the other side of the village.

Angoulême is near and well worth a visit, Cognac is a little further south-west and has a good shopping precinct; but if you like French pottery do visit the tiny village of La-Chapelle-des-Pots just north east of Saintes, where there is a factory and large showroom with an enormous range of products. English spoken.

Les Vignauds (M)
M. et Mme Richard. Luxé-Bourg. 45.39.01.47.

Four luxurious rooms occupy the first floor of this beautifully restored farmhouse. There is a terrace and large swimming pool, with pool-side barbecue and kitchen facilities. Mme Richard is an excellent cook and really copious meals are taken with the family in her well furnished dining-room. Double room 275f. Treble 310f. Demi-pension 200f each.

CHARENTE-MARITIME

DOMPIERRE-SUR-MER. 17139

2 km E of La Rochelle. Leave La Rochelle by the N11 (direction Niort) and in about 2 km turn right into the village of Chagnolet. Go through the village and Le Baobab is on the right past the school.

La Rochelle is a fascinating town with a modern shopping precinct as well as an excellent indoor market, many interesting churches and of course the busy harbour.

Le Baobab (M)
Mme Diagne. 17–21 Grande Rue. Chagnolet. 46.44.88.16.

Mme Diagne has moved from Paris to this quiet village of Chagnolet, outside La Rochelle, and converted a farm building into very smart rooms with independent entry. The five rooms are pristine clean and are enhanced with pretty matching curtains and covers. Two on the first floor are for families. Mme Diagne speaks perfect English; breakfast is taken in her modern farmhouse kitchen or outside if the weather is good. You can have your morning paper if so desired, bought back with the fresh baguettes (*Le Figaro* not the *Telegraph*!). Nicely situated for visiting La Rochelle and Ile de Ré. Double room 260f. Family rooms 310/360.

FOURAS. 17450

22 km S of La Rochell. In 16 km S of La Rochelle turn on to the D937 for Fouras.

Right on the coast the peninsula at Fouras extends like a nose into the sea. I was pleasantly surprised with this select little seaside resort. No crowds in September. A wide tree-lined promenade leads to Fort Vauban, housing the Tourist Office. It was at the tiny harbour of Port Sud that on 8th July 1815 Napoleon last stepped on French soil on his way to exile in St Helena. No huge hotels on the front here, mostly three-storey apartments overlooking the sea. The usual selection of cafés, restaurants and pizzerias.

Mme Lefèbvre (M)
4 rue des Courtineurs. 46.84.02.87. cl. 1/10 to 30/4.

The rue des Courtineurs, a cul-de-sac on the fringe of the town, leads straight on to the beach, only 150 metres from this chambres d'hôtes, so there is no traffic noise. This particular stretch of beach has many wooden fishing piers where the fishermen hang their nets to be filled by the incoming tide.

This modern house has a wing on the ground floor with superb carpeted rooms, each with brand new facilities; every convenience is thought of.

The excellent breakfast, outside in fine weather, or brought to your room, is elegantly served. No evening meal, so take a trip out to the Pointe-de-la-Fumée where there are fish restaurants and you have views in all directions, or better still make for the front where the choice is wider. We ate at the Chianti, with views of the setting sun, and *moules marinières* at 40f on the menu. We must have made a good choice because by 9 p.m. the tables were all full while other places were almost empty.

M. Lefèbvre is an architect; two new rooms, and a separate salon for guests are in the offing. Parking is in the garden with gate locked at midnight, so all is very safe.

Rooms 302f with a double bed and 322f for twin beds. The odd 2f on the price is the *taxe-de-sejour*, often found in seaside resorts in France.

LOIX-EN-RÉ. 17111

20 km from the bridge. From La Rochelle take the N257 over the toll bridge (110f for cars) to Ile de Ré; keep on the D735 past St Martin and La Couarde, then turn right at La Passe signposted Loix. You will find signs to the chambres d'hôtes on your left before you reach Loix.

The Ile de Ré is a delightful island, rather flat but with many dear little villages to shop in, not to mention the numerous harbours stacked with small boats in August.

La Prise à Vinet (M)
M. et Mme Lucas. 46.09.11.66.

Probably the only chambres d'hôtes on the island, so book early for the summer months. It is well tucked away across a field surrounded by bushes, quite a bird sanctuary, but only 2 km from a sandy beach. The rooms are *en suite* in concrete single storey buildings on the ground floor, but open on to small sheltered lawns. There is a large kitchen for guests with individual fridges and two cooking stoves, so self-catering is expected here, but restaurants 1 km away. A really safe place for children away from the main road. A private tennis court, too. Double room 220f. No evening meal. Plenty of shady parking.

Le Prise à Vinet

THAIRE-D'AUNIS. 17290

17 km S of La Rochelle. From Rochefort take the N137 north and in 11 km fork right on to the D110.

The local *apéritif* is Pineau Charente made from one-third brandy and two-thirds grape juice from *Colonbal* grapes. Pineau matures in the bottle as the grape juice is not fermented before bottling. Most producers prefer not to market their Pineau until it has been two years in bottle.

➤   Mme Fontenay (S-M)
2 rue de Dirac. 46.56.17.29 or 46.56.24.21.

Tucked away in the little village of Thaire-d'Aunis, this really is a very charming place, with equally charming hosts and only 6 km from the beach at Châtelaillon. Ivy-covered and in a pleasant garden, this is almost two chambres d'hôtes as half the house belongs to M. Fontenay's mother and she lets three rooms, one very pleasant on the ground floor with direct access to the garden.

2. Rue de Dirac

Mme Fontenay has four extremely pretty rooms on the first floor, two at one end of the house, and up a private staircase two other rooms share one bathroom. The Monet room has wallpaper appropriately flowery; a very nice couple of rooms have a double bed in one and two singles in the other. 400f for a family of four, but Madame will let it to two people and the second room will remain empty – then only 210f as are the others. Extra third bed 50f, including breakfast.

Evening meals 70f *en famille* are taken in her mother-in-law's house, as she has the larger table. Wine *compris*. A real winner here and arrowed for good value.

DEUX SEVRES

ARGENTON-L'EGLISE. 79290

13 km SW of Montreuil-Bellay, 9 km NW of Thouars. Take the D938 from
Montreuil-Bellay, then D 162 at Brion-pres-Thoet towards Taison; turn left into
village. A pleasant rural area in the Argenton valley. Thouars is a particularly
attractive medieval town, set on a rocky promontory above the river Thouet.

Château de la Roche (M)
Mme Keufer. 49.67.02.38; fax 49.67.02.20.

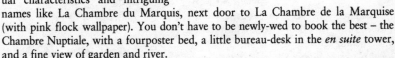

A substantial 19th century château,
with terraces overlooking the river
– good for summer breakfasts and
evening apéritifs. The Keufers
started their b. and b. operation
five years ago and have become
very experienced hosts, thanks to a
regular influx of guests from Brittany Ferries. Expect to find compa-
triots at the dinner table.

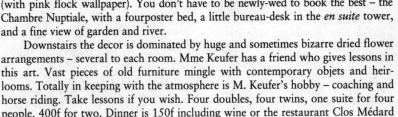

The bedrooms all have individual characteristics and intriguing
names like La Chambre du Marquis, next door to La Chambre de la Marquise
(with pink flock wallpaper). You don't have to be newly-wed to book the best – the
Chambre Nuptiale, with a fourposter bed, a little bureau-desk in the *en suite* tower,
and a fine view of garden and river.

Downstairs the decor is dominated by huge and sometimes bizarre dried flower
arrangements – several to each room. Mme Keufer has a friend who gives lessons in
this art. Vast pieces of old furniture mingle with contemporary objets and heirlooms. Totally in keeping with the atmosphere is M. Keufer's hobby – coaching and
horse riding. Take lessons if you wish. Four doubles, four twins, one suite for four
people. 400f for two. Dinner is 150f including wine or the restaurant Clos Médard
in Thouars is a good alternative.

COULON. 79510

11 km W of Niort. Leave Coulon on the Vanneau road beside the river and turn
right in 1 km at the sign to La Rigole.

➤ ### La Rigole (M)
Mme Fabien. 49.35.97.90.

Close to one of the prettiest villages in the Marais Poitevin this lovely modernised
cottage, well off the main road and right beside the canal, would be my choice for a

holiday exploring the hidden waterways. Boats for hire at Coulon, or
take a ride on the little train round
the canals or even a river trip with
inclusive lunch or dinner, down the
Sèvres Niortaise.

La Rigole

Mme Fabien has three delightful beamed rooms, for four (two
double beds), for three and for two
with even a *ciel de lit*. 200–250f.
She will give you a very large
breakfast, but no evening meal;
plenty of options in Coulon. Bikes for hire. Arrowed as the best introduction to an
under-appreciated area.

FRONTENAY-ROHAN-ROHAN. 79270

3 km S of Niort. About 3 km south of Niort on the N11 turn west on to the D3 and
you will find Clairlas on your left (not in the village of F-R-R.).

Close to Bessines, another good centre for exploring the Marais Poitevin.

Clairias (S)
M. et Mme Calmel. 49.04.58.42.

M. Calmel is a very enthusiastic
host who is a fund of information
and encourages you to visit all the
local places of interest. In this rambling old farmhouse the stables are
now converted into five practical
rooms. There are four on the first
floor up a quiet carpeted staircase,
some for two, some for five, one
downstairs. 240f. A sitting-room
and a simple kitchen for guests on
the ground floor. Across the court-

Clairias

yard in the main house meals are taken at a Henry II table (Monsieur assures me),
seating eighteen. A stuffed *ragondin* (coypu) watches you eat; there are still some
living in the canals of the Marais.

There's a little *barque* tied up across the garden, on a tiny backwater of the
canals, which you may use. You could spend a whole day exploring the waterways
and getting lost. Take a map with you or you won't be back in time for dinner, a
hearty meal with all drinks *compris* for 90f. The *digestif* is distilled from angelica
grown in fields close by.

GERMOND-ROUVRE. 79220

23 km SW of Parthenay. 2 km west of the D743 between Parthenay and Niort. Just off the route to La Rochelle and only 20 km from the *Marais Poitevin*.

Breilbron (M)
M. et Mme Blanchard. 49.04.05.01.

This is one of those lovely little places I would like to keep quiet about, but fear it is already well known. The owners have diligently restored the lovely old house, at the end of the hamlet of Germond-Rouvre, where peace and quiet is assured. Madame has two rooms bordering on luxury class. One on the ground floor has a separate private toilet, the upstairs one is totally *en suite*. A delightful, sunny, sheltered patio ensures meals outside early in the year. A large garden mostly lawn and vegetables with not only an old working well, but an ancient *four* (baker's oven) by the gate. There are two bikes for guests too. Rooms at 180f and meals at 60f with all drinks *compris* make this exceptionally good value for a night stop or longer. Nearly an arrow.

NANTEUIL. 79400

28 km S of Parthenay. Turn off the N11 at St Maixent on to the D737. In 1 km signed to La Berlière on your left.

La Berlière (S)
M. et Mme Memeteau. 49.05.60.71.

Oddly tucked away on a quiet hillside this ancient farmhouse is only 6 km from the A10, with views over the valley and stream below. One pretty blue room with warm carpeting, fluffy white towels and good reading lamps is very comfortable. The second room, a suite, is totally independent, comprising two rooms with beds for four and kitchen area. A bargain stop for a family of four at 300f includes breakfast. A five course dinner, all drinks *compris*, included *farcie-en-pot*, a local speciality of lettuce, spinach, onion and ham all puréed together and cooked in cabbage leaves, and finished with strawberries and cream and liqueur chocolates. At 75f it was excellent. Such a pleasant family; M. Memeteau used to be in the French Air Force and his son still is. Room for two – 200f.

NEUIL-SUR-ARGENT. 79250

22 km SE of Cholet. From Mauléon take the N149 to Bressuire turning left in about 8 km on the D33 to Nueil sur Argent. You will find the farmhouse Montourneau on your right.

Montourneau (S)
M. Gabard. 49.81.08.70.

M. Gabard is justly proud of his goat farm and likes to show his guests round at milking time. Four large rooms on the first floor of his house, with independent entry, have excellent showers, but only one shared toilet on the landing. M. Gabard is an entertaining host at dinner when the fare is simple but copious, finishing with his own cheeses. 50f including wine. No 'plastic' butter on this breakfast table; more likely a kilo! A useful low budget stop on the way south. Rooms 150f.

VIENNE

ARCAY. 86200 LOUDUN

7 km SW of Loudun by D759 and D19; 25 kms SE of Montreuil-Bellay. Loudun is a medieval town of considerable interest, with tortuous old streets and prosperous private houses dating from the 17th and 18th centuries. Surrounding it nowadays are shady boulevards, where once stood massive ramparts. Take an evening stroll along the Promenade du Château, an esplanade with fine views over the countryside, to gain a vignette of French provincial life – families promenading along the sandy *allées*, townsfolk listening to the music from the bandstand, and lovers happily loitering.

Château de Puy d'Arcay (M)
Mme Hilaire Leroux-de-Lens. 49.98.29.11. cl. 1/12 to 1/3.

A 15th century château set in a lovely garden in the village centre. Beamed rooms are furnished with lovingly polished family pieces – oak *armoires*, Persian carpets and *Toile de Jouy* curtains. An ancient stone staircase winds up to the three spotless bedrooms. They are good value at 180f, and the longer you stay the cheaper the deal becomes. Dinner 70f exclusive of wine.

Mme Leroux-de-Lens prides herself on the cultural associations of her family, and is pleased to help guests with their French, giving lessons (for an extra charge of course). Her husband speaks only a little English, but there is obviously no problem here because they are used to entertaining British visitors – the excellent Futurescope is nearby.

AVANTON-MARTIGNY. 86170

12 km N of Poitiers. 5 km west from exit 18 on the A10.

Avanton-Martigny is an excellent place to say for those wishing to visit the Futuroscope, which is a very large theme park just outside Poitiers with entertainment for all the family. The large futuristic buildings can be seen for miles around. You need stamina to spend a whole day looking at all the cinemas and the exhibitions. The inclusive entry fee is 120f for adults and 90f for children (5–16); entrance is free for the under fives. This fee covers one day, but there is a two-day option at 200f (adults) and 150f (children). Just inside the entrance at the Vienne Tourist Office you can obtain free headsets which can be set to translate the French commentaries into English. You have to leave something like a driving licence as a deposit.

There are plenty of activities for children. 76 separate entertainments, of which only six carry an extra charge.

Take a picnic. Food in the numerous cafés and restaurants can be expensive for a family, and there are long queues at peak times. The grounds are ideal for al fresco eating with lovely lawns and lakes. A change of clothing or a swimsuit is useful for children; they won't be able to resist trying the water maze, tempting on a hot day. Don't miss the Magic Carpet cinema, it is superb. Nor the 3D cinema nor even the 360° one. Avoid the Simulator unless you adore the horrors of a roller coaster. Funnily enough it attracted the largest queue of the day, parties of schoolchildren and the *Troisieme Age*. I can't believe they knew what they were letting themselves in for, seven minutes of shuddering big dipper type film with the floor and your seat moving, synchronised with it. Afterwards calm yourself by taking a peaceful boat ride through the rural landscapes of Europe, or take the lift up the revolving tower for an aerial view of the whole of the park. There were some very weary people making their way to their cars and coaches after a full and happy day, so perhaps one should take advantage of the two-day option.

At the time of writing the park closes in the winter, but there are plans afoot to keep it open all year.

➤   **Ferme du Château** (M)
        Mme Arrondeau. Martigny. 49.51.04.57. cl. 1/12 to 14/3.

In a main street of the village you
will find this delightful old house in
a walled garden, once part of the
château, where the stables have
been modernized for comfort but
keep all their old character. Two
rooms on the first floor can each
take an extra bed – 250f. Below is a
really comfortable sitting-room
with dining alcove, a smart kitchen
area and all facilities, even a
microwave. Coffee, tea and cold

drinks are all provided free and there's a nice patio in fine weather. Definitely my
choice near the Futuroscope, but book; always busy in holidays and at weekends.
Parking in the garden beside the house. I couldn't fault this one; excellent *accueil*.

BERTHEGON. 86420

43 km N of Poitiers. On the D14 24 km NW of Châtellerault.
        An alternative stop for the Futuroscope.

➤   **La Chaume** (M)
            M. Kosyk. 49.22.86.69. cl. 1/11 to Easter.

Five years ago young M. Kosyk
bought this old *maison-de-maître*,
once belonging to a *viticulteur*, a
square, three-storey building of
the lovely tufa local stone, and
has renovated it all since then. Now
he runs this chambres d'hôtes
almost single-handed while Madame
goes out to work, and keeps it
immaculate.
        Polished wood floors sweep
through the extended lounge and

dining-room with a table to seat fourteen. There are high ceilings and the same type
of floors in the three first floor bedrooms, one for a family, with bunks. On the second floor, spacious, beamed and fully carpeted rooms are well worth the extra
flight of stairs. Here, too, is another family room and a double, 200f.
        Simple four course meals with wine *compris*, 85f, cooked by him, are well
worth staying in for. Stay a week and you will have a different menu every night.

Book well ahead, I had three attempts before I succeeded. Although 28 km from the Futuroscope it is a straight run down the quiet D757. Consistently good.

BEUXES. 86120

6.5 km S of Chinon.

M. et Mme Lecomte (M)
49.98.70.55.

On the main road south of Chinon (D957) is a very pleasant *maison-de-maître* attached to farm buildings. A stone gateway leads off the road into an enclosed courtyard with lawns and flower beds. The chambres d'hôtes rooms are in an old stable building on the right of the gate. There is independent entry to a pleasant, ground floor tiled room with double bed. Two other rooms, one with cool tiled floor, the other carpeted, are on the first floor. In fact a very pleasant place to stop and an extremely friendly host and hostess. The Lecomtes own the farm, but have a tenant farmer. Evening meal 80f, wine *compris*. Room 220f.

CHATEAU DE VAUMORET. 86000

A turning 8 km E of Poitiers on the D6.

Château de Vaumoret (M)
Mme Vaucamp. Le Breuil Mingot. 49.61.32.11 cl. 1/11 to Easter.

On the edge of Poitiers and handy for the Futuroscope, this elegant château, well off the main road, is approached by an avenue of pollarded trees, ensuring a calm and peaceful atmosphere. Well furnished luxury rooms are in a ground floor arm of the château. 350f. Each has a private bathroom with all amenities; but dressing gown and slippers are needed as they are across a tiled corridor. No evening meals are provided, but there is an excellent modern kitchen, where guests are encouraged to prepare their own meals. Microwave for fast food fans. The rooms overlook the château and courtyard. Double and triple rooms.

Breakfast is served by Mme Vaucamp in the chambres d'hôtes wing so you are not really family guests as in some châteaux.

LEIGNE-SUR-USSEAU. 86230

8 km NNW of Châtellerault. Signposted off the main D749 Richelieu to Châtellerault road:

La Costonnerie (S)
Mme Blandin. 49.86.09.74.

Amongst fields is a farmhouse hidden away where Mme Blandin offers two rooms on the ground floor, opening on to a sunny terrace with your own tables etc. One room is for four people with bunks, and one double has a private kitchen, but both rooms can be joined together for a family. There is a salon/games room for wet days which has an indoor barbecue and more kitchen facilities.  Madame does an evening meal for 55f, but is equally happy to cook you a pizza or something you can heat up in your own kitchen. Very flexible. It could be very hot in summer with a lot of south-facing concrete patios; but that is taken care of by a pleasant swimming pool in front of the house surrounded by lawns. The pool should be warm early in the year as besides the normal cover it has a domed plastic cover to keep the heat in on cold days. The rooms at 200f are a little old fashioned, but perfectly adequate.

MOUTERRE-SILLY. 86200

36 km SSE of Saumur. From the D759 west of Loudon turn left to Mouterre-Silly. Silly is 1 km further on.

M. et Mme Pouit (S)
Silly. 49.22.46.41.

The tiny hamlet of Silly has no commerce, nor even a church; but the Pouit's large farmhouse, once visited by Cardinal Richelieu, dominates the village with its two

towers and extensive gardens of
lawns and vegetables. If you have
been châteaux bashing all day you
will think you are still at it as you
climb the stone staircase in the
tower to the one room here, and
even more so as you open the very
old door with a latch and an enormous 8 inch key. The room is fully
carpeted and warm, two tall
armoires and a huge fireplace dwarf
the double bed and small single in

the corner. There are excellent modern shower and toilet facilities in the adjoining
round tower with bars at the window. 200f. Antique cartwheels decorate the large
enclosed courtyard, outbuildings on all sides; a collection of fossils found in a neighbouring field is displayed on one wall.

Having been given the menu for dinner on arrival we were invited to *apéritifs*
with the grandparents in their adjoining house. Soup, asparagus soufflé, roast duck,
cheese and fresh strawberries, everything but the cheese from the garden. 'Is that all
right?' asked Madame. At 70f it was a feast, with *apéritifs*, wine and coffee all *compris*, especially as we had booked the room by phone only half an hour before we
arrived! Their youngest daughter speaks quite good English, and Madame Pouit
understands more than she admits.

Breakfast included fresh strawberries.

POUANT. 86200

4 km W of Richelieu on the D61. 19 km S of Chinon. The small town of Richelieu,
where the Cardinal once lived, is unique, still completely walled with great arched
gateways. It really is a fascinating place to visit; plenty of shops and restaurants. A
pity the Cardinal's old castle was destroyed in the Revolution; the lovely grounds
remain, but not a stone is left; the citizens took them all to build their own houses.
A case of tit for tat as Cardinal Richelieu had dismantled Loudun castle nearby to
build his palace in the first place.

Le Bois Goulu (S)
M et Mme Picard. 49.22.52.05.

Drive down the avenue of trees like a mini Chenonçeaux and through the towered
gates into the courtyard of the Picard's old ivy-covered house with wisteria rampant
over the doorway. Three rooms are up a well polished wooden stairway and have
equally old well-polished floors. A room with two single beds has a bathroom and
toilet on the landing. There is a garden at the side of the house with shady lawns
and places to sit. Your hosts are a pleasant elderly couple whose family have owned

the house for many years. This is still a working farm. Rooms 160–240f.

No evening meals, but there are two restaurants in Pouant offering meals at reasonable prices of 55f and 70f.

A second choice in this village is:

La Bois Goulu

Le Pin (M)
Mr & Mrs Lawrence. 49.22.55.76.

This restored house, within walking distance of the small village, is a peaceful haven for guests wanting to get away from it all. A lovely shaded courtyard and attractive gardens are at the side of the house, and a plunge pool helps those unbearably hot days in August. Natural stone walls and beams give this large house a pleasant cottagey feel. Three rooms, two upstairs and one downstairs with wheelchair access, all very prettily and comfortably furnished with shower rooms. A very comfort-

Le Pin

able lounge for guests off an equally pleasant old dining room leads through french windows to a vine-covered terrace where candlelit dinners are taken *en famille* in summer. The meal at 90f is a feast prepared by Mrs Lawrence. All drinks are available but not *compris*. Christmas and Easter are celebrated in traditional English fashion. Book early as Madame has her regular guests. There is now a gîte at Le Pin, which can be used as an extra bedroom out of season. You've guessed! your hosts are English. Rooms 240f.

ROIFFÉ. 86120

4 km S of Fontevraud on the D147, on the way to Loudon. In other words very conveniently situated for a variety of fascinating excursions. The château, high on its hill above the vineyards, is hard to miss.

Château de la Roche-Marteau (M)
Mme Jacqueline Moreau. 49.98.77.54; fax 49.98.98.30.

'We dined at Château de la Roche-Marteau and I really can recommend it as a very comfortable place and Jacqueline Moreau and her husband Jacques are the most genial and warm of hosts.' Neil Roland.

So of course I had to go and see for myself. It's certainly an impressive pile, originating from 1047, with strong Plantagenet connections. One of Eleanor of Aquitaine's sons is buried in the little chapel, now in ruins, in the grounds. The vast salon, over furnished with lots of plush and red and gold patterns everywhere, has dozens of chairs arranged round its edges, presumably waiting for the guests to sit down and assimilate the history of the house, readily recounted in minute detail by Jacques Moreau.

If you long to stay in a historic castle, whose very stones are soaked in drama, without paying a fortune, this might well be the one for you. There are five rooms, four with baths (big ones) and one with shower, double bed or twins, costing a mere 340f. The view from the terrace outside is magnificent.

ST-LÉGER-DE MONTBRILLAIS. 86120 LES TROIS MOUTIERS

12 km NW of Loudon, 12 km SE of Montreuil-Bellay via the N 147. St. Leger is a turning to the right, clearly marked.

A very convenient situation, just off the *nationale* but in peaceful countryside, and ideally placed for visiting Saumur, Fontevraud, Chinon...

Le Verger (S)
John Hall and David Kaye. 49.22.93.06.

Messrs Hall and Kaye bought this old cottage, bordered by vines, on the edge of the village only a few years ago and have only two rooms to let, so there is never a crowded feeling. The rooms are surprisingly large, each with one double and one single bed and a washbasin apiece. The loo is shared between them but there is another one downstairs and a bathroom. The price of 190f for two or 220f for three reflects the lack of *en suite* facilities.

The big attraction here is the cooking, a house speciality. 'Cooking is our favourite hobby and we do pride ourselves on providing good food at a reasonable price.' So don't forget to reserve ahead for dinner at a bargain 85f.

A deposit of £10 is requested and final payment may be made in sterling, francs or by cheque.

LA-TRIMOUILLE. 86290

44 km SE of Poitiers. A very pretty alternative route from Blois on the Loire to Limoges down the D675 where the roadside is lined with poppies in spring.

Take the D975 south from Le Blanc to La Trimouille (24 km). The road number changes to D675 just north of La Trimouille. Leave La Trimouille on the D675 and in about half a mile take the first fork right and follow the signs to Toël which will be on your left.

➤ Toël (M)
M. et Mme Vouhé. 49.91.67.59. cl. 31/10 to 30/4.

As we drove down a small country lane just off the main road from Trimouille we soon found Toël, a long low farmhouse well back from the road, surrounded by fields and outbuildings. Toël is another superb up-market farmhouse chambres d'hôtes, a goat farm this time. It was a Sunday afternoon when we broke in on the peaceful scene of a small child riding a pony, with grandparents in attendance. As we

hadn't booked a room we were delighted with our reception. Madame had one room left, and yes, we could dine there. So after stowing our gear we came down and joined M. and Madame Vouhé for tea. Three comfortable bedrooms are on the first floor with shower 200f; with bath 220f. Never miss dinner here. Madame is a true French cook and the meals are excellent and delightfully served on Limoges china. There is a real dinner party atmosphere with many laughs and the conversation never flags – *apéritifs*, wine and *digestifs* are all *compris* for 80f.

Leave time for a tour of the goat farm after breakfast with the Vouhé's small grandson, who is a budding French guide. A perfect example of a chambres d'hôtes, with Monsieur and Madame both participating in the pleasure of entertaining guests.

LIMOUSIN

Départements: **Corrèze**
Creuse
Haute-Vienne

An agricultural region, west of the Auvergne, with three departments. Frequent travellers to France have shot through it without ever knowing they have visited the area. At one time the Route Nationale 20 was the main road from Paris to Bourg-Madame en route for Andorra and Spain. Now with all the new motorways it is much more peaceful and the lovely old villages, *auberges*, *routiers* and small cafés lining its route can be enjoyed by travellers who have time to spare. Limoges, the *Préfecture* of **Haute Vienne**, is a large town famous for the manufacture of porcelain. Every American is determined to return with a piece of 'Limoges'. The city is large and busy, with rather attractive open squares and has an excellent porcelain exhibition from July to September. There is no need to brave the traffic looking for your purchases; as you approach Limoges the roads have many small wayside shops with a selection of china to choose from, and the owners can direct you to the factory/shop in Limoges if you wish to place larger orders.

North-west of Limoges is the martyred village of Oradour-sur-Glane, well worth visiting; but be prepared for the sombre reminder of the horrors of Nazi occupation. The whole village was wiped out by fire on 10th June 1944 and to this day they are not sure why. A completely new village has been built nearby and the original Oradour left in ruins as a memorial to the 642 people who lost their lives.

In the east the **Creuse** department is purely agricultural with the *préfecture* of Guéret hugging the hillside overlooking orchards of apples and pears which line the roads. On the whole the region is undulating farm land, especially in the north-east. In the south-east you will discover Abusson, the Axminster of France with a very fine Museum of Carpets and Tapestries. There is an interesting old Roman church at Moutier-d'Ahun

LIMOUSIN

CORREZE (19)
Préfecture: Tulle
1 Arnac-Pompadour
2 Benayes
3 Saint-Julien-de-Vendômois

CREUSE (23)
Préfecture: Guéret
1 La Chapelle-Saint-Martial
2 Le Grand-Bourg
3 Saint-Pardoux-le-Neuf

HAUTE-VIENNE (87)
Préfecture: Limoges
1 Boisseuil
2 Bosmie-sur-l'Aiguille
3 Isle
4 Peyrat-de-Bellac
5 Peyrat-le-Château

■ Préfecture
■ Town
① Chambres d'Hôtes

just north of Aubusson where the road in the village narrows to cross a most attractive old Roman bridge with parapet wings for pedestrians. The southerly department of the Limousin is **Corrèze**, which is still very agricultural, still with the N20 ploughing relentlessly through its midst, passing through Uzerche, the county town. At Pompadour the *haras*, a branch of the National Stud, is noted for breeding Anglo/Arab horses. There is a fine turreted castle here in this attractive little town, which is within easy reach of the N20. Many of the small villages off the road offer excellent accommodation for night stops or longer, in chambres d'hôtes varying from château to *ferme auberge*.

A little further south is Turenne, a small hill village with narrow, flower-bedecked winding streets up to the old castle. Park by the church and you will be half-way up! The Counts of Turenne often took their family holidays at the neighbouring village of Collonges-la-Rouge, so called because all the houses have been built in red brick. A very pretty little place to visit, but unfortunately it is a popular stop for all the tour coaches. It becomes packed in the high season, but is well worth a detour at other times.

CORRÈZE

ARNAC-POMPADOUR. 19230

16 km W of Uzerche. The château at Pompadour must have more towers than any in France. Only the terrace is open to the public now, as the officers and staff of the *haras* occupy all the rooms. The National Stud here is the cradle of the Anglo-Arabian breed, but the stables are closed from March to July while they get on with it. The small town is lively even in March with a few coach-loads of *Troisième Age* visiting.

Mme le Hech (M)
2 avenue du Midi. 55.73.30.22.

Only 16 km from the N20, worth a detour for a bit of luxury. A little note on the door says 'Apply at the charcuterie next door', which I duly did. Whereupon, when Madame realised it was a bed not meat we were after, she came out, leapt into her car to direct us to her house just out of town and we were swept into a French road race of follow my leader. Arriving at a very large modern house in a nice residential area, Madame gave us a choice of five rooms, with beamed ceilings and dormer windows all warmly heated, with two excellent bedside lamps and many amenities, such as fridge with cold drinks (payable), television and telephone, not to mention luxury bathrooms for 300 to 330f.

No evening meal, but a suggestion that we go to La Grange in the little village of St Sornin, five minutes away. At this dear little rustic restaurant the six course meal cost 68f. Soup left on the table, *crudités* of asparagus, avocado, eggs and tomato, delicious veal with sauté potatoes, selection of cheese and a choice of sweets, none of your 'either or' here. Local wine 4.50f for a quarter carafe.

Pavillon Halte de Pompadour

Cooking was splendid. Should you wish to eat in, Mme le Hech will send round a *plat cuisiné* of your choice costing about 65f. Breakfast was beautifully served in the little dining room overlooking the garden with freshly squeezed orange juice, four varieties of jam and honey, fresh bread and croissants. So *cherchez la charcuterie* for a very comfortable quiet room with safe parking, eat at La Grange and you will have a most pleasant visit to Pompadour.

BENAYES. 19510

40 km SSE of Limoges. Just off the N20 between Limoges and Brive, turn at Masserat on to the D20 to Benayes; you will find Château Forsac signposted up a long winding drive on your left in 4 km.

Château Forsac (M)
Mme Demontbron. 55.73.47.78.

If you feel like a night in a real château which has been in the family for over a hundred years and is steeped in history, then come to Forsac. Four plane trees in front of the house were brought from Marie Antoinette's garden at Le Petit Trianon by a captain of the king's guard, who was a regular visitor. When the château was first built in feudal times it had four towers; one of the originals is still

Château Forsac

standing and is part of the house; the only other one has been rebuilt to preserve it. Situated in 200 hectares of wooded land this is a paradise for early morning walkers and children. In spring drifts of scillas and daffodils light up the lawn opposite the arched door which has the family motto 'Moins Dire Que Faire' (Actions speak louder than words) above it.

Madame is a charming young Countess (de Cheradede Montbron) who speaks perfect English and will be delighted to give you a room. They are in the process of restoring the château internally and have a long way to go, so don't expect anything wonderful. The wide staircase leads to three large bedrooms, one with a crested bedhead! Two rooms can be inter-communicating for a family. The electric heating is not really suitable for cold winter weather, but the château is open all the year if you want to brave it. There is a sunny sitting-room for guests adjoining the three rooms.

Breakfast is taken in the family sitting-room, panelled with enormous rural paintings. No evening meals on a regular basis, but should you arrive tired and late Madame will take pity on you and knock up a light meal of omelette, salad and fruit. So ignore the peeling walls and settle for the charming *acceuil*, the tranquility and improving your history. At 200f for bed and breakfast for two, it is a bargain. Feel you are contributing to the château's restoration!

SAINT-JULIEN-LE-VENDOMOIS. 19210

24 km WNW of Uzerche. Take the D126 out of Arnac-Pompadour and follow the signs for about 5 km. Although the castle was given to Madame Pompadour, she never visited it and Louis XV repossessed it on her death.

Domaine de la Roche (S)
Marquise de la Roche. 55.98.72.87.

A stay here at the Domaine, once the property of the King and Queen of Navarre, would enhance your visit to Pompadour. The young owners are farmers and have a delightful small restaurant in a 15th century cottage. They make and tin all their own produce such as *confits* and *foie-gras*.

Madame does all the cooking and Monsieur waits at table as well as running the farm. Bedrooms, in

St. Julien - le - Vendomois
Domaine de la Roche

another building, are pleasantly rustic rooms entered by an independent staircase. One room can accommodate up to five people with a double bed and bunks, and there are two doubles, for 220–250f. 70f each extra bed. Breakfast is served in your room. Bed and breakfast terms are available only out of season. In season you must stay on *demi-pension* terms, but this is no hardship at 390/420f for two people, with dinner in the *ferme auberge*. If you stay for two weeks you get one night free.

CREUSE

LA CHAPELLE-SAINT-MARTIAL. 23250

22 km S of Guéret. A few miles south of the *préfecture* of Guéret in Creuse, the department of rolling countryside, of cattle farms and apple orchards is a small village called La Chapelle-Saint-Martial.

Le Bourg (M)
Mme Couturier. 55.64.54.12.

Near the church is this very fine house right on the roadside, extremely well maintained with parking through a locked gate in the small courtyard.

There are three superbly furnished bedrooms in the house itself and one in a chalet in the little garden overlooking the small swimming pool, one particularly ornate with canopied bed all with smart *en suite* facilities, on first and second floors. The fourth room in the garden has tiled floors and one wall is completely mirrored. While making the room look twice as large it has the odd effect of making it feel full of many people! Not a room for sleeping late in, as it is only a few feet from the pool and if the other guests are early swimmers you will know all about it. Not really a place for small children; but for guests who appreciate quality furnishing. Rooms are from 240–320f.

LE GRAND-BOURG. 23240

19 km W of Guéret. Turn right about 5 km on the D4 from Le Grand-Bourg to Guéret.

Montenon (S)
M. et Mme Limousin. 55.81.30.00.

Situated on a hill this *ferme auberge* has superb views; unfortunately the four chambres d'hôtes rooms are in the attics on the second floor, a long haul up. Very sparsely furnished though carpeted throughout. All have good skylight windows which are tantalizing as one can enjoy the view only by standing on the bed.

The accent is on the *ferme auberge*; rooms are purely a sideline. The restaurant has a completely glassed-in verandah to take in the glorious view, and has a nice wood fire on cold nights. Very popular with the locals. Menus from the *Leger* at

68f to *Gastronomique* with nine
choices of main dish at 135f. *Demi-
pension* would be your best bet
here as this always includes dishes
on the more pricey menus. Out of
season we chose the 68f menu and
did very well. Little touches like
fromage ou dessert being overlooked and both offered, and
Madame didn't charge for a carafe
of house wine and she didn't know
who we were. I felt the entrées were
a little too rigid, but main courses were good.

Madame Limousin is a kindly hostess and although busy looks after her house
guests well. A very pleasantly situated place and the amenities of an excellent swimming pool and children's play area. Such basic rooms seem rather pricey for 245f
although they are *en suite*.

SAINT-PARDOUX-LE-NEUF. 23200

4 km E of Aubusson on the D941 to Clermont Ferrand turn right to Les Vergnes.

Les Vergnes (M)
M. et Mme Dumontant. 55.66.23.74. cl. 1/11 to Easter.

This really is a delightful spot for a
restful holiday. Situated in open
countryside, the rooms are in a
restored farmhouse near the main
house. Downstairs are a dining
room and lounge for guests, and six
well furnished bedrooms, up and
down, two adjoining, 260f. There
are glorious views of the small private lake and wooded countryside
from the lawns outside and a smart
new swimming pool, solar heated,

so you can swim sometimes as early as April or May. Free fishing in the lake. When
we were there, an Englishman had just caught twelve trout in one day; no prizes for
guessing what was on the menu that night. Guests meet for a complimentary *apéritif* before an interesting evening meal which is cooked and served by your hosts.
90f. Wine works out at about 30/40f a bottle.

HAUTE-VIENNE

BOISSEUIL. 87220

8 km SE of Limoges. Take the N20 south from Limoges turning left at the first sign-post to Boisseuil; in the village turn down by the church and the school forking right at next fork, carry on along lanes between fields bearing right then left where signs lead you to Moulinard farm.

Moulinard (S)
Mme Brigitte Ziegler. 55.06.91.22.

A useful place to stay for a visit to Limoges, only ten minutes from the centre of the town, but a world away from all the noise and traffic. The farm is situated on a promontory between two valleys and guest rooms are in an old *Maison-de-Maître* nearby. Picnic or sit in the walled garden under the trees. You enter the house through the kitchen which has an amazing old floor tiled with moulds from the porcelain factories in Limoges. Four large rooms, on the first floor, have polished wood floors and antique furniture. 200 to 210f. Good radiators for cold weather in the bedroom. Breakfast in Mme Ziegler's own farmhouse is beautifully served in her kitchen with sunny views of her garden where wild rabbits play. Fresh baguettes, home-made jams and the usual plentiful coffee, tea or chocolate with fresh flowers on the table make this a really enjoyable start to the day. There is no evening meal, but there are two *logis* quite near at Solignac. Madame speaks a little English. Rooms are 200/210f.

BOSMIE-SUR-L'AIGUILLE. 87110

8 km SSW of Limoges. Leave Limoges by the N 21, turn left in about 5 km at L'Aiguille on to the D32. Turn right in 2 km to Charroux on the D11, continue on this road to Bosmie-sur-l'Aiguille, a tiny village where you will find signs for the chambres d'hôtes on the rue de Breuil.

M. et Mme Faye (S)
8 rue de Breuil. Charroux. 55.39.07.04.

This nice new house on a hill at the end of the village is another option in the Limoges area.

The rooms open on to a terrace by the swimming pool, with a westerly view over the countryside. The *en suite* facilities are separated only by a screen from the rest of the room 220f. Your hosts, with a young family, will give you a charming welcome and a delicious, generous dinner and breakfast. Evening meals 70f, all drinks included.

ISLE. 87170

8 km W of Limoges. Leave Limoges on the N21 south and in about 3 km, just after the turn to L'Aiguille, there will be a chambres d'hôtes sign on the right and a fork right which will take you up a country lane to the Brunier's house on your right.

➤ Pic de L'Aiguille (M-L)
Mme Brunier. Verthamont. 55.36.12.89.

A real find. A beautiful, new, sprawling house on a hillside outside Limoges with lovely, peaceful views and a swimming pool. The three rooms are extremely pretty, carpeted, with patio doors to one's own terrace with tables and chairs. The Bruniers are a lovely family with two teenage children and receive one as a real friend of the family. Nothing is too much trouble. Drinks offered on arrival. Dinner on the terrace when fine. A typical menu is fish mayonnaise served attractively in lemon halves, followed by a *boeuf daube* with new potatoes, salad, cheese and fresh peaches in *crème anglaise* decorated with sprigs of cherries. Other specialities include *Rôti de veau à la crème des champignons, Tartes Salées et Sucrées,* and *Gâteau au Chocolat.* Vegetables are from the garden and vegetarian diets are available if wanted. Reserve your meal in advance and you won't be disappointed.

Evening meal 80f, wine *compris*. Room 220f, so an arrow. All round value here. Some English spoken.

PEYRAT-DE-BELLAC. 87300

8 km W of Bellac. Tricky to find this one; it lies 3 km S of the N147 between the D951 to Confolens and the D675 to Saint-Junien.

La Lande (S)
M. et Mme Quesnel 55.68.00.24. cl. 1/11 to Easter.

The Quesnels have a sheep farm and their home is tucked away in lanes, but only a few kilometres from the busy N147 (Poitiers to Limoges road), so a good place to stop off for a quiet night and enjoy the pool and evening meal with the family and other guests. Quite near Oradour-sur-Glane.

I caught sight of this farm a year ago but couldn't stop, so I was particularly pleased to visit it. Every bit as nice as it seemed, with two rooms overlooking the garden and swimming pool in front, one room at the back. 210f. A homely dining area opens on to the front terrace for meals in warm weather. Evening meals 80f, wine *compris*.

PEYRAT-LE-CHATEAU. 87470

50 km E of Limoges. The Lac de Vassivière, (1000 hectares in area) is a real holiday centre with beaches, sailing and many cafés etc and trips round the lake.

Quenouille (S)
M. et Mme Perin. 55.69.25.76.

Deep in the country 2 km on foot from the lake (but 5 km by road) is a small sheep farm offering three chambres d'hôtes rooms. The farmhouse is situated on the hillside facing south overlooking the small village of Quenouille. One room on the ground floor has *en suite* facilities, but the two above have showers, sharing a toilet on the landing. Very plain, simple rooms. There is a large sitting/dining-room for meals and access to accommodation is independent. There are some pleasant, sunny terraces in front of the house.

Evening meals are 70f (wine not *compris*). Madame tells me that her cooking is very good and she doesn't like people drinking cheap wine with her food! I can't vouch for it as I haven't eaten here.

I think this chambres d'hôtes has its regular holiday families as it is rather out of the way for a night stop. Rooms 180/210f.

AQUITAINE

Départements: **Dordogne**   **Lot et Garonne**
             Gironde   **Pyrénées Atlantiques**
             Les Landes

From Bordeaux on the Atlantic coast to the Pyrénées on the Spanish border lies the region of Aquitaine, stretching inland to Gascony in the east and the Dordogne in the north. Here you are truly in the south of France. The Romans first conquered this region and gave it the name of Aquitaine in 28 BC. The area has borne several names – Gascony, Guyenne, Armagnac and the Pays Basque – but they are all virtually synonymous and reflect different aspects of history. Of all these names Gascony was the most common.

However some centuries later the Romans could not hold back the invading armies, and Aquitaine became part of the Visigoth Empire. The decisive Battle of Vouillé in AD 570 drove the Visigoths south into Spain and parts of the Languedoc, and Aquitaine became part of the Frankish Empire, and eventually a Duchy owing allegiance to the Kings of France. By the 7th century Gascony had its own language, a combination of the old Latin-based *langue d'oc* with a touch of Basque.

The leading light in this area is undoubtedly Eleanor of Aquitaine. She inherited the whole Duchy in the early part of the 12th century. At that time the Duchy extended as far north and east as Périgord, Limousin and Poitou. Such an inheritance meant that she was courted by many. She eventually married Louis VII of France and had two daughters by him. However her light-hearted manner and conduct did not endear her to the French court and Louis was persuaded to divorce her in 1152. Her dowry, the Duchy, was returned to her and she promptly married an old boyfriend, Henry Plantagenet of Anjou, who became King of England (Henry II) two years later. The Duchy renounced its allegiance to the French and together they ruled the whole of England and Wales and all of Western France. They made their home at Poitiers and rarely visited the British Isles. When Henry died in 1189 his son Richard (the Lionheart) succeeded, and he too spent only a few months of his reign in our country. The English control of Aquitaine was fairly weak, which lead them to follow the example of their Languedoc neighbours in building fortified towns called *bastides* whose inhabitants were granted several privileges to ensure their loyalty.

The French were not happy with this state of affairs, especially when Edward III claimed the French throne on the death of Charles IV in 1328. This led to the Hundred Years War and the English were finally defeated at Castillon-la-Bataille in 1453.

Nowadays Aquitaine has five *départements*:

The **Gironde**, with the large port of Bordeaux, in the west is the heart of a wine-growing country. The vineyards are situated in many areas producing different types of wine, determined by the soil and vines. Despite their differences they are all known as Bordeaux, whether red or white. The reds are often called 'Claret' by the British.

On the north bank of the Dordogne the well known village of St Emilion is geared to tourists, having a *Maison du Vin* with the largest selection of wines in the vicinity. St. Emilion produces the best vintages, many of them *Grands Crus*.

Entre-deux-Mers is the land between two rivers, the Dordogne and the Garonne, before they flow into the Gironde estuary. This area produces a good, well known, dry white wine.

South of the Garonne we come to Langon where the old vineyards of Sauternes steal the limelight, with a sweet white wine. Further north, going up the left bank of the Garonne, both south and north of Bordeaux city are the vineyards of Médoc and Graves. You will find famous names like Château-Lafite, Château-Margaux, and Mouton-Rothschild here. All these areas have slightly different soils and the variety of grape is varied to suit these conditions, producing wines of infinite variety.

Les Landes, once a long sandy coastal strip stretching from Arcachon to Bayonne with a marshy hinterland, has now been rescued from the encroaching Atlantic sand by draining the land and planting huge forests of pine trees. Now the coast from Biscarrosse Plage to Bayonne is two hundred kilometres of glorious sand backed by dunes and pines. In clearings inland a few small villages quietly go about their business. Roads are straight and quiet at all times. The villages near the coast have access roads to the beaches where you often find wooden steps over the dunes. The Atlantic breakers roll relentlessly, so this is no place for sailing or timid bathers. There are campsites in August but otherwise very few people share the beach. Further south nearer Bayonne there are purpose-built holiday villages at Vieux-Boucau and Capbreton, the latter being at the mouth of

AQUITAINE

Préfecture
■ Town
① Chambres d'Hôtes

LANDES (40)
Préfecture: Mont-de-Marsan
1 Biaudos
2 Lévignacq
3 Magescq
4 Port-de-Lanne
5 Soustons

DORDOGNE (24)
Préfecture: Périgueux
1 Le Buisson-de-Cadouin
2 Campagne
3 Cornille
4 Domme
5 Marquay
6 Mauzens Miremont
7 Montipon-Menestrol
8 Proissans & Ste Nathalene
9 St Front-d'Alemps
10 Salignac-Eyvigues
11 Tamnies
12 Vezac

GIRONDE (33)
Préfecture: Bordeaux
1 Coutras
2 Lamothe-Landerron
3 Monsegur
4 Pujols-sur-Ciron
5 Saint-Emilion
6 Saint-Martin-de-Laye
7 Sauternes

LOT-et-GARONNE (47)
Préfecture: Agen
1 Cancon
2 Douzains
3 Montflanquin
4 Penne-d'Agenais
5 Saint-Antoine-de-Ficalba

PYRENEES-ATLANTIQUES (64)
Préfecture: Pau
1 Feas (2)
2 Ger
3 Haut-de-Bosdarros
4 Ossès

the river Adour until the 16th century when shifting sands and a little help from man diverted the river to Bayonne.

In the south are the **Pyrénées Atlantiques**, the Basque country bordering Spain. The Spanish influence is strong here; all town names are in French and Basque. The old coastal resorts so loved by the Victorians grace the coast – Biarritz, St Jean de Luz and Bayonne on the estuary of the River Adour. The Pyrénées and the foothills to the north had been left very much to their own devices when France regained Aquitaine. The area around Pau was ruled by Henri d'Albret who married Marguerite of Angoulême, the sister of the French king François I, in 1527. Both were keen Protestants and influenced the once strong Catholic region. Their grandson, Henry of Navarre, brought up as a Protestant, later married Marguerite de Valois, and when the French king died without an heir he inherited the French throne, but as a Protestant this was unacceptable. At this point Henry decided Paris was worth a mass, and was received into the Roman Catholic Church in 1589. A very good king he was, being particularly lenient with the Protestants. The Roman Catholics didn't really approve of this and in 1610 poor Henry was assassinated, but not forgotten; many of the statues, streets and squares in the region are dedicated to him.

The green velvety tree-covered slopes of the western end of the Pyrénées are in this region. Valleys run towards Spain climbing up into the mountains at the last moment. The Basque houses resemble the chalets of the Alps a little, but many have brick-red roofs contrasting vividly with the white stone, a riot of colour in the summer with flower-bedecked baskets and boxes hanging from every conceivable place. The weather is mild here even in winter. Much favoured by campers in the school holidays, September is the best month to visit. Pau the high town in the Béarnais area of the north, the *préfecture* of the department, was very popular with British settlers at the beginning of the century. A few still remain. The best view of the Pyrénées is from the Boulevard-des-Pyrénées at Pau. The other departments of Aquitaine lie inland.

To the north is the **Dordogne**, so well beloved by the British tourist, dominated by the river Dordogne running through its very pretty undulating country. Périgueux in the centre, with its many-towered cathedral and modern squares, is the administrative town. There are still Roman remains around the old town.

The ancient name Périgord dominates the whole department dividing it into four sections. The Périgord Vert caps the northern part where towns like Nontron and Riberac ring a bell for many and the river Dronne flows through the lovely town of Brantôme making it almost an island. Huge limestone rocks overhang the roads round here.

Périgueux itself lies in Périgord Blanc in the middle of the region where the river Isle cuts through the town. Colourful fields of sunflowers dominate the surrounding landscape.

Périgord Noir in the south, has the interesting old town of Sarlat as its centre. When by-passes were being built Sarlat missed out and the traffic congestion is particularly bad in July and August. Truffles are found in this part and walnut trees are everywhere. Do visit the oil mill at Ste Nathalène, where walnut oil is made. This area has the rivers Vézère and Dordogne flowing through it; but the main attractions are the many prehistoric caves and archaeological sites, notably at Les Eyzies.

Périgord Pourpre in the west is cut by the Dordogne and with Bergerac and Monbazillac in the centre is very much part of the wine-growing area with tobacco plantations a close second.

The last but not the least department of Aquitaine is **Lot-et-Garonne**, south of the River Dordogne, it is also a large vine-growing area. Some of the best *bastides* can be found here; the hill top village of Montflanquin is one of the nicest. Agen in the south is the *préfecture* of this department, a large and uninspiring town. The western area is mostly flat, with pine forests – a continuation of Les Landes.

DORDOGNE

LE BUISSON. 24480

29 km W of Sarlat. 10 km S of Le Bugue. Often linked with Cadouin just up the road, where there are remnants of the Holy Shroud in the abbey. For years this brought great wealth to the abbey, but modern science has cast doubts on its authenticity. The abbey is open mornings and afternoons from Feb. to Dec. Le Buisson lies along the Dordogne just before it is joined by the River Vézère.

Leaving it rather late to book a room at 5 p.m. we looked for the Office de Tourisme and found it closed. On advice from the *boulangerie* we landed up in a little dress shop where two charming ladies joined in the search by ringing round likely chambres d'hôtes. After the first choice was *complet*, we were delighted to find a room at La Coste, a tiny hamlet outside Le Buisson and the promise of an evening meal. The ladies duly directed us to take the D25, direction Cadouin, turn left just as we left the town where there was a double signpost to La Coste; go straight up the hill past a left turn to La Coste and we would find La Feuilliantine on the left.

➤ ### La Feuillantine (M)
M. et Mme Donval. 53.23.95.37.

A very smart, newly built Périgord house with vast views over the countryside. Three well furnished ground-floor rooms; patio access through double-glazed doors. Every comfort thought of.

We shared dinner with two other guests, Monsieur and Madame both beavering away in the kitchen and producing a really fabulous meal. Soup, *mousse de saumon*, *brochettes-de-boeuf* with *pommes noisettes*, cheese and ice cream *chantilly* with meringue. Bergerac wine not *compris* but shared with other guests. One of the best meals I have had in a chambres d'hôtes, and beautifully served. M. Donval, brought up in a *patisserie*, is a very keen chef and takes great delight in producing good food. He and his wife joined us over coffee.

Rooms 250f. Evening meal 100f. Good value both for quality of room, food and *accueil*.

CAMPAGNE. 24260

7 km SW of Les Eyzies on the D706. Campagne is right in the centre of all the places one should visit along the Dordogne: Les Eyzies caves, châteaux at Beynac and Castelnau, and of course La Roque-Gageac and Domme. Restaurants and all shops 4 km away at Le Bugue. There is no noticeable village, but on the right side of the road you will come upon this huge garden sloping down to a modern Périgord house with well kept lawns and double entrances.

'Chez Lucette' (S)
Mme Rieupeyroux. 53.07.41.68.

Rooms to suit all purses; facilities range from shared shower and toilet, to rooms *en suite* plus fridge, even an apartment for four, with modern kitchen area. One other exciting option is a square *borie* across the garden near the river Vézère, also *en suite* with fridge. Parking alongside. Heating in all rooms, so suitable for out of season visits.

No breakfast is offered with any of the rooms, but china and coffee making facilities are provided in all, so bring your own baguettes and you will be all set. Rooms from 170/270f, according to facilities.

CORNILLE. 24750

10 km NE of Périgueux. Take the Ave. Georges Pompidou out of Périgueux, the D8. In 12 km at Les Piles, take the D69 signposted 'Agognac' and Le Grand Pognac is signed immediately on your left.

Le Grand Pognac (S)
Mme Flourez. 53.04.60.05.

Le Grand Pognac

Your hostess, Mme Flourez, will look after you well on this farm in the Périgord Vert specialising in foie-gras. It's a small *ferme auberge*, but I got the impression that her chambres d'hôtes guests take priority. For the evening meal they share one table in a very pleasant glazed terrace at the entrance to the house, where a parakeet keeps his beady eye on them.

Five simple rooms are warmly carpeted; one has an *en suite* shower and w.c. others share two toilets on the corridor but have showers. Two family rooms share a private bathroom and w.c. on the corridor. 180f.

There is a pleasant outlook over the fields and just below the house a private lake provides guests with free fishing, trout and carp if you are lucky.

If you stay three days *demi-pension* is 300f for two people, which sounds good to me. It is possible to have the *Menu Gastronomique* but you will be seated at a separate table from the other chambres d'hôtes guests. To prevent them drooling I gather!

DOMME. 24250

8 km south of Sarlat. Domme is an absolute must when visiting the Dordogne – a most attractive *bastide* built on a rocky crag during the Hundred Years War to keep the English out. They may have succeeded then, but not today. In summer there are more British cars here than French! Approach from Vitrac and you will enter by one of the three old gates; the Porte des Tours is the best preserved, where prisoners were once kept in the tower. Their graffiti are still on the interior walls. Follow the signs to large car-parks on the Belvédère de la Barre (*payant*). A new viewing plat-

form on the terrace gives a panoramic view of the valley below where the River Dordogne flows towards Beynac. Wander round the many little streets with pretty limestone houses bedecked with flowers. Finish up in the Place de la Halle, beside the covered market. Built in the 17th century, it has a very pretty wooden balcony and deep caves underneath where the people hid in times of trouble. Shops, restaurants, cafés to suite all tastes. Sit outside and watch the world go by; if possible avoid July and August when it does!

Leave Domme by the D46e (signposted Vitrac) and Les Quatre Vents is 1 km on the right.

'Les Quatre Vents' (S)
Mme Delord. 53.28.20.33. cl. 1/11 to 30/4.

Shady in the trees above the road is a hotel, and just alongside a b. and b. belonging to the same people. Six functional rooms are designed for warmer weather, all having independent entry to a terrace near a small dining-room open only for breakfast. Nicely situated swimming pool high among the trees well away from the road is just for chambres d'hôtes guests (the hotel has its own pool).

Rooms 200/300f. Breakfast 25f extra each. No evening meals but the hotel is handy, or pop up the hill to Domme.

MARQUAY. 24620

17 km NW of Sarlat. It is not easy to find this place from Marquay. Instead take the D47 from Les Eyzies-de-Tayac to Sarlat, turn left on to the D48 to Bardenat where you will find a sign to the Ferme Veyret on your left.

If you are interested in prehistoric man, Les Eyzies is just the place to visit – lively tourist village with museums and caves galore.

Ferme Veyret (M)
Mme Veyret. 53.29.68.44.

Having found *fermes-auberges* in the past sometimes poor value for money I was rather loath to try this one, but I'm glad I did. Mme Veyret has quite restored my faith. The three, new carpeted rooms are very modern, with heaters in the bedrooms. Parking is right outside, just like a motel. The older rooms are not quite so convenient. Good open views from an enormous terrace overlooking the swimming pool.

Dinner is excellent, consisting of five courses with large helpings and *apéritifs* wine and *digestifs compris*. A typical menu was: soup (tureen left on the table), charcuterie, roast duck with potatoes and fried apple rings, cheese, a choice of about six sweets and coffee or tisane. A buffet-style breakfast is served with four varieties of jam, paté and cheese on offer as well as the usual coffee and toast. A large new dining-room with terrace has just been built.

Ferme Veyret Audrix

This *ferme-auberge* is good value for a stay in a beautiful part of the Dordogne. Good English is spoken by one of the staff. Mme Veyret is a very busy person but she is always at dinner which is open to non-residents, to dispense *apéritifs* and to chat to guests. With so many rooms the intimate atmosphere of a small b. and b. is missing, making this more like a small, very friendly hotel, but you do share tables with other guests. Demi-pension only. 450f for two people.

MAUZENS-ET-MIREMONT. 24260

11 km N of Les Eyzies.

Les Granges (M)
M. et Mme Urvoy. Mauzens-Miremont. Le Bugue. 53.03.25.71.

North of Le Bugue on the D32 between Mauzens and Miremont you will find the signs to Les Granges. Hidden away among trees this modern house has seven rooms on the first floor, all with wooden ceilings and walls making them a little dull, but each with adjoining shower and toilet. There is a delightful terrace for meals in fine weather overlooking a swimming pool which has good views over

Les Granges

the countryside. A quiet tucked away place, but close to the many attractions of Les Eyzies.

Some rooms have entry from a staircase at one end of the house, others through the hall in the main house. Good parking. Evening meal 70f with wine *compris* seems very reasonable. Perhaps rooms at 250f are a little pricey; but with good weather and use of the pool I don't think anyone would have anything to quibble about, especially in such a popular part of the Dordogne. It may be rather crowded in the high season with seven rooms occupied.

MONTPON-MENESTEROL. 24700

23 km N of Ste-Foy-la-Grande. At the junction of the N89 and the D708 turn west to Ménésterol and follow the signs *'Bienvenue à la Ferme'*. From a reader:

La Gravette (S)
Mme Massart. 53.80.44.29.

'We arrived here in the early evening, unannounced and soaking wet and passed one of the best nights of our French holiday.

The rooms have been converted from old tobacco drying sheds and are comfortably and tastefully arranged. At the evening meal, Madame served custard-squash with fresh herbs as starters, while M. François barbecued slices of tender local duck. Home-made apéritifs and wine compris at 70f. Breakfast included a sponge cake made that morning and a wide variety of home-made jams.

'Fruit and vegetable farmers, 1993 was the Massart's first season offering chambre d'hôtes. Rooms 200f.' Helen Gilbert

PROISSANS. 24200

8 km N of Sarlat. 17 km SE of Montignac. A super place to stay for visiting Sarlat, one of the most attractive towns in the Dordogne, and ideal for visiting the *Grotte-de-Lascaux* where the prehistoric paintings of animals were discovered in a cave in 1940.

Going north on the D704 north from Sarlat, turn right in 4 km (signpost La Val d'Ussé); in 2 km turn right again (signpost Les Chanets). L'Arche is 1.2 km on the right on this road. If you book ahead, you will receive a card with exact instructions from all directions.

➤ ### L'Arche (M)
Mme Jeannette Deleplace. 53.29.08.48.

This old house, completely restored in 1992, is now a brand new chambres d'hôtes overlooking rolling countryside, in a hamlet of only three houses. The six rooms, one for a family, are all most attractive, with beamed ceilings, tiled floors in the two ground-floor rooms, fitted carpets upstairs, electric heaters in all rooms and independent entry. Really interesting meals, beautifully served, are taken in owners' lounge/dining-room with log fires on cold nights. Excellent breakfast; fresh bread and croissants, homemade jams, no plastic packets of butter here.

One is treated as a true guest of the family in this really charming home. We were only their second guests, and I wish them luck in their new venture. Some English spoken. Evening meal 70f, wine not *compris*, but litre *pichets* of local wine at 18f or a choice of others at a reasonable price. Rooms 180f. Real value here. After a second visit an arrow for all round value.

SAINT-FRONT-D'ALEMPS. 24009

18 km NE of Périgueux. 12 km SE of Brantôme.

Ferme Auberge de Bost-Vert (S)
Mme Montagut. 53.06.38.83.

Well signed from Saint-Front-d'Alemps near the church, this unpretentious *ferme auberge* has five very simple carpeted rooms in an adjoining building, all with an *en suite* bathroom. The rooms on the first floor, open on to a verandah, plastic chairs provided. Rooms are identical except for colour where care has been taken to make each one different. Rural views from the windows. The main, large, stone house was built in 1875; not a lot done to it since. The dining room is very basic, but you will be made most welcome and perhaps tea will be offered on arrival. Madame slaves in the kitchen, her daughter serves at table and her son complete with baseball cap is always around to chat. Dinner was: soup, omelette, roast duck leg, salad, cheese made from their own milk and *clafouti*. *Apéritif* (walnut or Pineau) and wine *compris*. Good solid farmhouse fare 75f. Quite a few people staying here, including two English artists who seemed to be quite happy in this bucolic setting.

Rooms are 190f for two; but like most Dordogne places this does not include breakfast so add another 40f and you have your b. & b. for 230f. *Demi-pension* 190f each. No charge for extra beds for children under five years. Half price for older children makes this a good family stop, well off the main roads, ample fields to roam about in and safe parking. Just a simple unmodernised farmhouse that has five rooms over the storehouses, and not really budget prices for such simplicity, but excellent *accueil*.

SAINTE-NATHALENE. 24200

3 km ENE of Sarlat. Sarlat is an absolute 'must'. Lovely old buildings, the Boétie house by the tourist office, the Cathedral the *Lantern des Morts* and many others will fill a whole day and more. It is quite my favourite town of the Dordogne. The different squares and cafés are a delight, large parking in the largest. One could spend two or three days just exploring the town. Just north of Sarlat is Ste. Nathelène where the Moulin de la Tour built in the 16th century is still making oil from walnuts in exactly the same way as it did four hundred years ago. You can watch the whole procedure and buy the finished product. Usually I find this sort of thing intolerably boring, but here it is fascinating and doesn't take long. The oil is sold in tins, safe for the homeward journey.

Take the D47 northwards from Sarlat and in 2 km at La Croix d'Allon turn right to Ste-Nathalène. In 1 km, just before the village turn right and Aux Trois Sources is 500m on your left.

Aux Trois Sources (M)
Mme. Mathieu. Pech-Lafaille. 53.59.08.19.

From the moment I saw this old house with its rambling gardens I wanted to stay here, but it was not to be, something to look forward to in the future. Monsieur Mathieu is a talented cabinetmaker who has made many of the 'antiques' you will see around you. The six rooms are all different mostly beamed nicely decorated, some on the ground floor with independent entry, others upstairs in the main

Aux Trois Sources

house. Two of the upstairs ones share a bathroom making them suitable for a family. The dining room is in a separate building where M. & Mme. Mathieu join their guests for dinner. When I called in May all the rooms were full, but M. Mathieu went to great trouble to phone a friend who was just starting a new chambres d'hôtes nearby and got us a room there (see Proissans) – his friend had kindly offered to come and fetch us and direct us there. While we were waiting for him I was shown all the rooms. From 164/194f, and demi-pension 172/272f. Wine is *not* included with the evening meal, but is reasonably priced. Definitely a need to book well ahead here.

SALIGNAC-EYVIGUES. 24590

6 km NW of Souillac. On the D62 from Souillac to Salignac-Eyvigues; 1 km before Borrèze

'Moulin de La Garrigou' (M)
M. et Mme Vallée 53.28.84.88

A turreted 19th century mill house tucked into the hillside on this valley road has now been restored and in a separate building there are four first floor beamed, carpeted rooms, exceptionally well furnished; each has a mezzanine with two single beds, suitable for families. Phone, duvets, every comfort for all seasons. Breakfast, served in your room or by the mill stream in fine weather, is undisturbed at weekends, but during the week a rather noisy sawmill along the road adds background buzz.

An excellent swimming pool tantalises passing traffic on the road above. No evening meals, so little contact with the family. Rather like a tiny hotel, but much nicer. Well worth the 260f for a room, especially in hot summer weather. A *ferme auberge* close by has heavily regional dishes, goose dominating. Best to stick to the 70f menu (wine *compris*) or try the restaurant in Borrèze, where the selection is more varied, from 75f upwards.

TAMNIES. 24620

16 km NW of Sarlat. 12.5 km NE of Les Eyzies by the D47. The easiest approach to Tamnies is from the D706 Montignac to Sarlat road. Turn right at the junction with the D60, leading to the D48. Tamnies is signed off this road. Once in the hamlet pass the hotel and take the second left.

L'Amérique (S)
Mme Passerieux. 53.29.68.30.

This is a lovely place, with a swimming pool in the garden, for a really relaxed holiday. Built about 18 years in the Périgord style with towers at either end, the house overlooks a sheltered garden, completely surrounded by fields. Three first floor rooms with dormer windows have shower and washbasin, but share one toilet on the landing; one room made *en suite* in 1995. Breakfast on the terrace in the summer.

L'Amérique

No evening meals but there is a large *Logis* five minutes away. Madame, a charming hostess, doesn't mind guests picnicking beside the pool. Rooms 220f for two.

VEZAC. 24220

7 km SW of Sarlat on D57. On the D57 just outside Vezac. The Manoir is easily recognizable from the road.

Manoir de Rochecourbe (M-L)
Mme Roger. 53.29.50.79. cl. 16/9 to 31/5.

One of the most sympathetically furnished manor houses I have met. A central round tower dominates the front of the house. Originally built in the reign of Henry IV it has been in the same family for the last three generations and elderly M. & Mme Roger have maintained their home with great care. I find the name 'Manoir' misleading. Climbing the tower and looking into the different rooms I wouldn't have

Manoir de Rochecourbe

been surprised to find the Sleeping Beauty in one. It really does have the feel of an old castle inside. Entry is by a large oak door on the ground floor of the tower. Climb the wide stone stairs to the first floor for your first encounter with Mme

Roger where you step out of the tower into the main part of the house. Here you have a huge sitting-room with a vast stone fireplace, painted designs on the beams incorporating a picture of the manor, furnished with good quality antiques. Across the passage is a prettily arranged dining-room with separate tables. Fresh flowers everywhere.

Back to the tower, climb to the next floor and a large room opens up right off the tower. This one with a large fireplace, is one of the most expensive rooms at 410f. Another room at the rear is delightfully furnished with delicate Louis XVI furniture in perfect condition. Smaller rooms on the third floor are equally nicely furnished with antique beds etc., all in excellent condition, and some rooms have good views of Beynac Castle in the distance. Just one small room has the toilet opposite. Six rooms in all, 280/410f including breakfast.

No real garden – just grassy areas, not really encouraging for sitting outside.

GIRONDE

LA DUNE DE PILAT

Slipping across the quiet roads of southern Gironde from Sauternes to Arcachon one passes through the sleepy little villages which never seem to change. Pyla-sur-Mer is a holiday resort with sandy beaches spreading into Pilat-Plage where the road becomes a very pleasant residential avenue flanked by some lovely old houses, some backing on the sea. All with shady pine trees in the gardens.

The road suddenly turns inland and heads for the Dune de Pilat, or Pyla as the postcards call it. The highest sandbank in Europe, 117m high, stretching for 2.7 km along the coast and 500 metres wide. It has been forming since the 18th century with a little help from man to prevent the sand slipping down into the forests. Well worth a visit although now capitalized as a tourist attraction with large car-park, little shops and cáfes lining the route to the wooden *escalier* which takes you nearly to the top. It is worth the climb of 187 steps, in sets of twelve, with a small platform between. Even the *Troisième Age* were making it. Once on the last step it is wise to take off shoes and trudge up the remaining rise of sand to enjoy the aerial view of the surrounding wooded countryside, Arcachon with the Atlantic on one side and the whole width and breadth of the sandbank around one. If the wind is blowing the sand sometimes stings the legs.

The *escalier pour descendre* as it is euphemistically called is non-existent, just a quick easy run down the bank, sinking in up to the ankles.

Not a b. and b. in sight, so head south to Lévignacq or Magescq.

LAMOTHE-LANDERRON. 33190

10 km NW of Marmande. La Réole lying just north of the River Garonne in the Entre-deux-Mers region, is an interesting old town with a good Saturday market. There are many other hill villages all round including St Emilion. Leave La Réole by the N113 to Marmande and in 8 km the Domaine de Massiots is signed on the left.

Domaine des Massiots (M)
Mme Bareille. 56.61.71.76.

This is a lovely, ivy-clad, old house set well back from the road with safe parking, and an excellent swimming pool in the garden behind the house. All four rooms are on the first floor, reached by a steep, wooden outside staircase. Beamed, but with every comfort, even a small fridge, and all are different. Cosy little sitting-room with TV in the tower. 200–245f. Reduction of 5% for eight days.

Madame's breakfasts are not to everyone's liking; biscuits, cheese, sponge fingers, jam, etc. and coffee in a thermos, are all left on a tray the night before in the guests' well equipped kitchen with 23f extra to pay, but you don't need to have this; it is quite easy to self-cater for breakfast as for other meals, with a *boulangerie* just down the road. Two people in a small gîte share the garden and pool with you.

MONSÉGUR. 33580

14 km from La Réole. 9 km from Duras. Take the D668 from la Réole to Duras; leave it to climb the hill to Monségur and just at the top outside the centre of the town you will find the château entrance. The *bastide* of Monségur has strong English connections, as it received its first charter from Eleanor of Provence, wife of Henry III of England.

Château de la Buche (M)
M. et Mme Lédru. 56.61.80.22. cl. 1/11 to Easter.

If you are feeling like staying in a château but can't afford the astronomical prices, this 19th century edifice is just the place. M. Lédru has been doing it up from scratch over the last two years.

Two square towers at either end, one housing a bedroom, and a round, central tower which was originally a hunting lodge and now has an attractive stone staircase. M. Lédru has thought of everything, four rooms for two or three, one of which has been adapted for the handicapped. On the second floor is a suite with two rooms

for a family, up its own private
stairway. Lovely view from most
rooms over the valley of the river
Dropt. There is a lounge to gather
in before you join your hosts for
dinner. Evening meal 80f, with
apéritif, wine and coffee or tisane
compris. Rooms from 270f for two
to 400f for the suite.

Château de La Bruhe

PUJOLS-SUR-CIRON. 33210

3 km N of Sauternes. 11 km W of Longon. The D116 going north-west from Longon passes Château Yqem; then, in the village of Pujols, take the road past the
church and bear left. You will come to the road called les Tauzins and about three
houses along, on the right, you will find the house.

This quiet little village of Pujols, deep in the heart of the Sauternes vineyards,
doesn't seem to have moved with the times. Until five years ago the large church
bell was rung to disperse the clouds of any approaching hailstorm which could have
damaged the crop; now the *viticulteurs* fire cannon into the sky!

Mme Colon (M)
6 les Tauzins Est. 56.76.60.13.

M. et Mme Colon have created
four new rooms in an old storehouse alongside their own house,
which once belonged to a *viticulteur*. Two rooms on the first floor
with beamed ceilings and two
below. All have tiled floors, double
beds and independent entry and are
furnished superbly.

6. Les Tauzins et.

Pleasant terraced garden is a
mass of flowers in summer and the
excellent covered patio is used for
breakfast on fine days. There are new bikes for hire at 50f per day. M. Colon will
advise on the best routes there are near and around. Really charming hosts, and
prices that won't make a hole in your pocket. No evening meals but a new kitchen
for guests imminent, also a salon with TV etc. Book early; I think this a winner.
Rooms are 190f.

SAINT-EMILION. 33330

35 km E of Bordeaux. The village of St Emilion is charming – sloping down a hill-side, it is seen best from the large bell tower in a small square. Huge car parking by the Collegiate Church accommodates the hordes of tourists at all times of the year. The Maison-du-Vin, a large modern building, is where everyone congregates; all St. Emilion wines on sale here and a museum, too. Beware: it is firmly closed from 12.30 to 2 pm.

3 km from St Emilion off the D243 to Libourne take the D245 to Pomerol and in 300 metres you will find the Château Millaud-Montalabert.

Mme Brieux (M)
57.24.71.85.

An excellent place to drink the wine and absorb the atmosphere. Vine-yards to the right, vineyards to the left as far as the eye can see, all growing the *merlot* grapes, with roses at the end of each row, right up to the front door of this large, old house, the home of a *viticulteur*. Mme Brieux can offer you a choice of four different rooms, with a nice country decor, all warmly carpeted. Evening meal 85f, but surprisingly

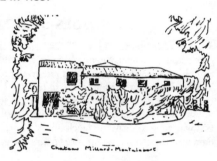

Château Millaud-Montalabert

wine not *compris*. The local wine being a *Grande Cru St Emilion*. I suppose it would be difficult to offer a lesser *Vin de Pays*. Rooms at 280f reflect their nearness to St Emilion, but worth it for the atmosphere, especially during the *vendange*.

SAINT-MARTIN-DE-LAYE. 33910

12 km NE of Libourne. 46 km NE of Bordeaux. Up a track from the D22 between St. Martin-de-Laye and Bonzac.

➤ Gaudard (M)
Mme Garret. 57.49.41.37. cl. 31/10 to Easter.

On the northern fringe of the wine-growing area of Bordeaux is this very comfort-able home, not far from Pomerol and St Emilion. We rang ahead to ask if it was convenient to arrive early one Sunday afternoon and found comfortable loungers and sunshades ready for a siesta in the hot September sun. I felt sorry for the other guests who arrived just in time for dinner.

Situated in large, grassy lands with a perimeter of trees, this restored farm-house of honey-coloured blocks looks very plain from the outside, but don't be mis-led. The large high-ceilinged rooms have beams and independent entry through french windows. Our room faced south and had a palatial bathroom. A second room in a detached building is carpeted and spacious. Sitting on the terrace in the setting sun we enjoyed an excellent dinner with M. & Mme Garret and other guests. Shrimp salad, roast guinea fowl with repeated helpings of chips, a good selection of cheese and the local sweet called *millas* rather like *far Breton*.

The delightful salon, where breakfast is served, has many lovely pieces of antique furniture, collected over the years. Good shady parking and M. Garret helps you with your luggage. Very attentive hosts, who are retired farmers. Evening meal 80f, apéritif and wine *compris*. Rooms 175/230f. Good value, so an arrow.

SAUTERNES. 33210

7 km W of Langon on the D8. Sauternes is a small, smart village totally absorbed in the sale of the wine which bears its name. The sweetness is obtained by using over-ripe grapes, which have a vastly increased sugar content. The famous Château Yquem is close by and their wine, made from 100 per cent *sémillon* grapes, can cost up to 1004f a bottle. In the village square are the Maison de Sauternes and

the Auberge du Vin, where the poor can taste and the rich can buy. The cheapest on sale is 120f a bottle.

A chambres d'hôtes two kilometres away on the D8 from Langon to Villandraut at Brouquet:-

M. & Mme Peringuey (S)
56.76.62.17.

Three simple rooms with very small en suite facilities on the first floor are 220f. for two, there is a pleasant swimming pool in the garden. No evening meal, but restaurants nearby. Another choice at Langon is the Château Malromé, once owned by the Comtesse de Toulouse-Lautrec. Rooms there 300/650f, but I know nothing about them.

LANDES

LEVIGNACQ. 40170

26 km SE of Mimizan. With chambres d'hôtes rather scanty on the ground in Les
Landes, I was particularly glad to find this one. Take the D652 south from
Mimizan; in about 22 km at Lit-et-Mixe turn left on to the D66 to Uza, then the D5
to Narboude crossroads and you will find Estounotte signed on your right.

Estounotte (M)
Mme Lalanne. 58.42.75.97.

Situated in a clearing of pine trees,
this elegant, square house overlooks a large garden and swimming
pool, only 10 km from the Atlantic
beaches. The three different rooms
have showers or baths, but there
are only two shared toilets on the
landing. There is a lounge with TV
for guests. Dinner was not very
exciting the night we stayed here,
but we did arrive unexpectedly, so
that could account for it. Breakfast
however was beautifully served, with fresh baguettes, good coffee and jams. This is
the sort of place one could stay in without going out for a few days – it feels right
off the beaten track, but is actually only a few miles from the nearest small village
and the Lac de Léon, where there is sailing and a nice little holiday town. Straight
roads round here are traffic-free even in August.

Evening meal 90f, wine *compris*. Rooms 280f. (240f out of season).

MAGESCQ. 40140

14 km NW of Dax. A nice little town within easy reach of all the Basque towns like
Biarritz and Saint-Jean-de-Luz which are just over the department border. Leave the
village by the D150 to Herm, which crosses over the N10 and in about 300 metres
la Cassouat is on the right.

le Cassouat (M)
Mme Desbieys. 58.47.71.55.

Ringing up late one evening we were delighted to find a room in this ultra-modern
house, situated in a large park of pine trees, complete with lake. I have often seen

pictures of this place, but nothing
I have read about it really does it
justice. A very warm welcome
awaited us. Two well furnished
rooms upstairs share a luxurious
bathroom, nice for four friends or a
family as they are up a private staircase. One has pleasant views from
the enormous ceiling-to-floor window looking over the back garden
and lake. Two ground-floor rooms
have their own small balcony with
tables and chairs. 190–230f.

An excellent breakfast started with the 'house' speciality, a mixture of fruit
juices and honey, all beautifully served at one table but every couple having their
own special tray of butter, jam, coffee, etc. The village with choice of four restaurants is under a kilometre away, so no problem there.

PORT-DE-LANNE. 40300

20 km E of Bayonne. Turn off the N117 6 km west of Peyrehorade.

Mme Duret (S)
Le Port. 58.89.14.57.

Port-le-Lanne is hardly a port – just
a pleasant landing stage on the
River Adour, where pleasure cruis-
ers land their passengers to eat at
the little *auberge*. Round the corner
is an oldish house in a pretty garden where Mme Duret has a conglomeration of rooms, not all *en
suite*. There is something peculiarly
attractive about this place, garden,
situation; perhaps the 1930s decor
accounts for it. Parking outside the
gate in a side lane.

No evening meals but the little *auberge* (meals from 65f) a pleasant evening
stroll away. Rooms 180/200f.

SOUSTONS. 44140

33 km N of Bayonne.

Cante Grouille (S)
M. et Mme Benoît. Quartier Philip. 58.41.16.10.

Not a lot of chambres d'hôtes in the northern part of Landes, driving south between large lakes at Biscarrosse to Parentis-en-Born. Turn off here to Lévignacq where there is an excellent chambres d'hôtes, but should you want to cover more mileage head further south via Léon to Soustons.

This chambres d'hôtes is in a complex just south of the town, a modern large house with three rooms two of which are *en suite* and the other with private ¬facilities just outside the room. Clean and nicely furnished. Rooms 200/250f. No evening meals. Although this is a farmhouse there are other private houses in the complex. Good parking beside the house. Near a lake but not on the coastal road. You go almost through Soustons before turning right to Quartier Phillip. Better to ask in Soustons.

LOT-ET-GARONNE

CANCON. 47290

19 km N of Villeneuve-sur-Lot. From Cancon take the D145, direction Monbahus, and in 300m turn left. Chanteclair is well signed from here.

Chanteclair (M-L)
Mme Larribeau. 63.01.63.34.

For a handy stop off the N21 at Cancon this 19th century mansion in a large park covered in drifts of tiny mauve cyclamen in September is well worth trying. Swimming pool and many other amenities. A great feeling of space here as you approach up a tree lined drive. Four rooms including a family room, have polished wood floors and are pleasantly furnished. 305/345f. Evening meal 85f. 10% reduction for three or more nights.

Chanteclair

DOUZAINS. 47330

3 km SW of Castillon. 30 km S of Bergerac. From Castillon take the D254 to Douzains. Le Capi is on the right just before the village.

Le Capi (S)
Mme Jacquot. 53.36.83.68.

The small village of Douzains is very quiet – just a church and a few houses. Close to the N21 at Castillon, it is an easy run to Bergerac and Monbazillac. Approaching this large old farmhouse, which has seen better days, we were reassured by a welcoming wave from a man in the front garden, who turned out to be Mme Jacquot's son.

Motherly Mme Jacquot was at the door to show us to our room, one of many off the 27 metre long corridor, well furnished in keeping with the age of the house, 1850. French windows to the garden and flowers by the bed. An adjoining bathroom must once have been another bedroom, marble washstand still in place, generous towels and cupboards. There are two other rooms, one for a family. Son and family live at one end of the house and run the farm. This must have been a very palatial house when it was built, now showing wear and tear, but repairs are slowly taking place. Terraces run the length of the house on both sides. Fun for children exploring the garden. A homely place. 180f.

We joined Mme Jacquot, a widow, for dinner in the dining-room with views to the bastide town of Castillon. Real farmhouse cooking here. Soup, mixed vegetable salad, hot cheese and tomato tart, followed by pork chops, courgettes and spaghetti, then a choice of local cheese and a *clafouti*. Some of us didn't make the *clafouti*! A litre bottle of wine on the table, coffee all *compris* for 62f.

MONFLANQUIN. 47150

17 km NE of Villeneuve-sur-Lot. One of my favourite *bastides*, rising high above the surrounding flat countryside. Small roads approach from all directions, entering through arches to the central square. There is some dispute by locals whether Monflanquin is the best preserved *bastide* in the country, with Monpazier coming second. I have heard the reverse in Monpazier! But do visit them both. The central arcades are not quite flat but the area for *boules* has been carefully levelled. Views from the top are glorious and you can drive all the way up and park free. Take the D676 north from Monflanquin and in 3 km turn left to Roquefère.

Domaine de Roquefere (M)
Mme Sémelier. 53.36.43.74.

In a tiny hamlet with church and a few well restored houses, Mme Semelier offers four identical rooms in her modern *ferme auberge*, all in different colours on the ground floor with their own private terrace, some overlooking the swimming pool. Curtains, bedspreads, lampshades and even the bedside tables are in matching material. Locked garages available but ample parking in grounds. Evening meal 100f in

the attached dining-room but drinks are not *compris*. Rooms 300f; not the cheapest in the area, but certainly the smartest.

PENNE-D'AGENAIS. 47140

8 km E of Villeneuve-sur-Lot. A hill village well worth a detour. The little square is only on the fringe of it. Penetrate further through the old archways, part of the original fortifications, and numerous passages and flights of stone staircases will lead you past pretty flowery gardens to the *table d'orientation* at the top.

L'Air du Temps (M)
Mme Gazottes. 55.41.41.34.

Drive down to the roundabout below the hill and you will find the *Auberge L'Air du Temps*, where Mme Gazottes has two Habitat-style rooms on the ground floor for guests. It is not really an *auberge* in the true sense but a very smart restaurant spreading over two rooms, white tablecloths, old monogrammed damask napkins, etc. Pleasant views over the garden. Parking in car park near the road.

Evening meal 90f, but a choice of à la carte as well. All major Credit Cards accepted. Rooms 230/240f, breakfast included.

SAINT ANTOINE-DE-FICALBA. 47340

18 km N of Agen. 10 km S of Villeneuve-sur-Lot. The unusual name means Saint Antoine of the White Figs. A community of monks founded here cared for people suffering from gangrene caused by a germ in the wheat. From the village on the N21 turn down beside the post office, left at a T junction and the house is about 4 km on the right, well signed.

Pechon (M)
Mme Delaneuville. 53.41.71.59.

Rugs on carpets make an exceptionally warm and pleasant room on the first floor, with windows on three sides and a private terrace. In the spacious salon a welcome cup of tea was ready for us. A second couple of rooms share a bathroom and salon in an independent building in the large garden. Monsieur is an heraldic artist who has designed a crest for the village recalling the village history by using a T-shaped crutch as its motif. Their daughter is a noted wood sculptress, and the carved bedhead and pelmets in our room were all her work. This very intellectual family will furnish you with much local history.

Rooms at 200f and a delicious evening meal with wine at 75f make this exceptional value.

PYRÉNÉES ATLANTIQUES

FÉAS. 64570

8 km SW of Oleron-Ste-Marie on the D919. A very good stop for visiting the peaks and valleys of the Pyrénées, particularly the Vallée d'Aspe which takes you up to the Col du Somport on the Spanish border where the Hotel des Voyageurs still has the flowery terrace which Hilaire Belloc wrote about in 1908. Visit the Vallée d'Osseau in the shadow of that Pic. Many walks in these parts, on the fringe of the Pyrénées National Park, where much wild life survives, even bears. Drive from Eaux-Bonnes and Gourette, (a ski resort) over the Col d'Aubisque for really exciting views, hair-raising bends, but a good road in summer. The quietest and prettiest drive is along

the D117/D417 from Tardets-Sorholus via Ahusqui to St Jean-Pied-de-Port. Hell for the driver some of the way, but fascinating for the passengers.

Oléron-Sainte-Marie is an ever growing town (where the Gave d'Aspe and the Gave d'Osseau meet). A *Gave* is a Pyrénées mountain stream.

Château de Boues (M)
Mme Dornon. 59.39.95.49.

Two km before the village, drive in beside the lovely old arch and you will find good parking outside the stables. There is a pleasant lawned garden with swimming pool and open views of the surrounding countryside.

Mme Dornon has four very comfortable rooms, nicely furnished with matching carved wood bed heads and wardrobes, warmly carpeted, armchairs and TV. Rooms have access from a steep outside staircase. Fridge and phone for guests' use is on the landing. Breakfast is taken in a dining-room like a baronial hall with huge fireplace, a very pleasant room. Good, reasonable restaurants just down the road. A very attractive château well worth a visit. Rooms 300f.

Quartier du Bas (S)
Mme Paris. 59.39.01.10.

Turn off the D919 beside the *Aire de Pique-nique* at Féas and follow the signs to this newly-built chambres d'hôtes which is a place for keen fisherman as M. Paris is a fly fisherman guide who will take you fishing in the nearby rivers. Specially built for guests the three rooms, furnished with spanking new pine, have tiled floors. Choice of rooms for two, three or four with bunks. Very clean and simple place to stay where young Mme Paris will look after you well. The only noise you will hear will be cowbells and possible the stream nearby. Evening meal is 70f. wine *compris*. Rooms are 235f for two but children up to 6 years free.

GER. 64530

12 km W of Tarbes. 5 km from Tarbes on the Pau road (the N117) after the large bend you will see the right turn to Ger village; ignore this and look for a small road on the left between maize fields a little further on; turn left here and left again at the next road and the chambres d'hôtes is on your left.

Maitechu (M)
Mme Clede. 7 chemin La Hourcade. 62.31.57.10.

Tarbes airport, Lourdes and the Pyrénées all close by. This modern house in large shrubbed garden, with pristine clean swimming pool, is only 1 km west of the Greenwich Meridian. It has two large adjoining rooms upstairs with three double beds and a double downstairs. There is also a fridge with cool drinks, hair dryer, bathroom scales, etc. You will be treated as truly personal guests of the family. Madame does not always provide evening meals, but if you do eat here it will be excellent value with fresh garden produce, local specialities and best Bordeaux wine.

M. Clede can tell you the temperature and Ph level of his pool at any time of the day; you will not be flavour of the month if you go jumping in without first taking a shower, but you will find the pool-side shower nicely warm, so use it! Rooms 230f for two, 290f for four.

HAUT DE BOSDARROS. 64800

16 km S of Pau. From Nay south of Pau take the D37 to Bourdettes where you turn left on to the D936; then take the next left turn to Haut de Bosdarros (D388). In about 3 km bear left through the village and further on you will see the signs to the Ferme Loutares, which will be on your right.

Ferme Loutares (M)
Mme de Monteverde-Pucheu. 59.71.20.60.

A few years ago we stayed here knowing full well that it was a health farm with chambres d'hôtes rooms run by Madame Pucheu and her daughter. Then it was vegetarian and no wine. Things have since changed and chambres d'hôtes guests now eat meat and wine flows freely. Deep in the country, south of Pau, with super views of the Pyrénées. You can wander round the fields and woods, hide away in the garden with a good book, chickens and peacocks pecking round you or just laze by the pool. An unwritten rule of silence hangs in the air from 2 to 4 p.m! Mme Pucheu twitters about, always happy to see you relaxing and enjoying yourselves. I think she would prefer to see you all working out in the treatment rooms, but to give her credit she never mentions it. Only the price list behind the bedroom door reminds one.

Seven guest rooms are in a separate rustic house in the grounds, with modern treatment rooms on the ground floor. Rooms of varying shapes and sizes from ancient to modern but there are always fresh flowers by the bed even if the towels have been overlooked! The lounge has comfortable armchairs by the inglenook fireplace. Plastic loungers by the pool. Riding ponies for children.

In July and August meals outside can get a bit hectic, but out of season candlelit dinners are in the main house. Food, though healthy and adequate doesn't always inspire. Parking is opposite the main gates in a clearing of the woods, but you can bring the car in for unloading. Many places offering better value for money, but few with such a relaxed atmosphere in such a lovely setting. Evening meals 80f, wine *compris*.

Rooms 295f. 5% off for second visit and 10% off for subsequent visits.

OSSES. 64780

12 km NW of St Jean-Pied-de-Port. Just before Ossès on the D918, Mendilsau is on the right.

Right in the heart of the Basque country, near Spain, Saint-Jean-Pied-de-Port is the town where pilgrims' passports are stamped on the way to Compostella. St Etienne-de-Baigorry nearby has a church with three wooden balconies dizzily tiered up. In Ossès village the church has a large, gold scallop shell on the reredos, a sign of the pilgrim route.

Mendilsau (S)
Mme Lukumberry. 59.37.70.29.

No frills in these efficiently run rooms in a purpose-built house, with nice views of the Pyrénées. The five well furnished rooms on the first floor have showers and large washbasins, two shared toilets on the landings. Over a nicely served breakfast Mme Lekumberry, who lives next door, chats to her guests. Extra facilities include dining-room, kitchen with gas stove and fridge/freezer and a small, secluded garden. No evening meal, but there is a pleasant hotel within walking distance, where one can eat outside on a cute little terrace. The hotel belongs to Mme Lukumberry's cousin; extra attention guaranteed if you say where you've come from. This is extremely good value whether you self-cater or not. Rooms 160f for a night stop, 140f if you stay longer.

MIDI-PYRÉNÉES

Départements:	Ariège	Hautes-Pyrénées
	Aveyron	Lot
	Gers	Tarn
	Haute-Garonne	Tarn-et-Garonne

The Midi-Pyrénées stretches from the Lot in the north to the Pyrénées and is bounded by Aquitaine on the west and Languedoc-Roussillon in the east, a vast area incorporating eight Departments, three of which lie along the Spanish border. Haute-Garonne just touches the border, Ariège and Hautes-Pyrénées have their share of the mountains. Further north are the Gers, Tarn, Tarn-et-Garonne and Aveyron, and furthest north of all, the Lot. Altogether a very large slice of south-west France. Starting in the west with the **Haute-Pyrénées**, Tarbes, the *préfecture*, is a rather ordinary indus-trial town with the main rail terminal from Paris and an airport with flights direct from Gatwick. The name most people associate with this department is Lourdes, a Mecca for the sick (see Loubajac). More secular medical cures are to be found at Cauteret, a holiday town in the mountains further south, packed to uncomfortable capacity in July and August and very noisy. Better by far take the D921 up to Luz-St-Sauveur at the foot of the Col de Tour-malet. This quiet little town is a much more refined holiday place which seems to have missed the razzmatazz of camp sites etc.

Take a drive across the Col du Tourmalet passing Barèges, a winter sports station. Decide at the top, if the weather is good, to take the rougher road (*payant*) up to the Pic du Midi de Bigorre, to the Observatory where, at 2865 metres, on a clear day you will see one of the most striking panora-mas of the Pyrénées; on other days you may wonder where you are, while sitting on a damp cloud! The Observatory was founded in 1881, and is open to visitors in summer in the afternoons. There you will find the largest telescope in France (two metres in diameter).

Great walking, riding and touring country in summer and skiing in winter. Visit the little town of Ste Marie-de-Campan where two streams

MIDI-PYRENEES

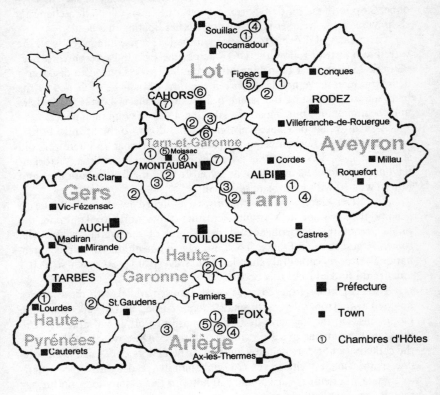

ARIEGE (09)
Préfecture: Foix
1 Cos
2 Ganac
3 Oust
4 Saint-Paul-de-Jarrat
5 Serres-sur-Arget

AVEYRON (12)
Préfecture: Rodez
1 Asprières
2 Salles-Courbatiers

HAUTE-GARONNE (31)
Préfecture: Toulouse
1 Cintegabelle
2 Gaillac-Toulza

GERS (32)
Préfecture: Auch
1 Auterive
2 Tournecoupe

LOT (46)
Préfecture: Cahors
1 Autoire
2 Castelnau-Montratier
3 Lalbenque
4 Loubressac
5 Marcilhac-sur-Célé
6 Saint-Pierre-Lafeuille
7 Saux

TARN (81)
Préfecture: Albi
1 Bellegarde
2 Mezens
3 Roquemaure

TARN-et-GARONNE (82)
Préfecture: Montauban
1 Castelsagrat
2 Castelsarrasin
3 Fajolles
4 Lafrançaise
5 Montesqui
6 Montpezat-de-Quercy
7 Nègrepelisse

HAUTES-PYRENEES (65)
Préfecture: Tarbes
1 Loubajac
2 Pinas

converge to form the river Adour which eventually wends its way to Bayonne. Stop in Bagnères-de-Bigorre, a quiet little town where in a chemist's shop window the weather is forecast by leeches floating in a bottle.

Cross the Col d'Aspin to Arreau, on the D929; mountain bends all the way. From Arreau follow the D618 across the Col de Peyresourd to Bagnères-de-Luchon, first branching off up the Vallée de Louron to discover a delightful man-made holiday resort at the tiny, old village of Génos by the lake, not at all spoiling the serene beauty of the place. Lovely walks here into the mountains, boating on the lake and a public swimming pool.

A small wedge of **Haute-Garonne** reaches down to the Spanish border with Bagnères-de-Luchon being the main town and what an interesting old spa town it is. It seems miles away from civilisation, a little Victorian-flavoured world of its own, a great favourite with the British both then and now. Twinned with Harrogate says it all!

The River Garona rises in Spain and is joined by the river Pique to become the Garonne at Marignac and then flows north to Toulouse, the *préfecture* of the department and the capital of the whole region. The fourth largest town in France. Toulouse has all amenities – hospitals, international airport, cathedral, churches it has everything. So much so that I am afraid I funked it for this book.

The N117 runs from coast to coast almost parallel with the Pyrénées but well away from them, with smaller roads cutting up the valleys into the mountains. On the Bagnères-de-Luchon spur, turn off at Valcabrère where there are the remains of a Roman city and towering above on the hilltop is the cathedral of St Bertrand-de-Comminges behind its city walls; it must be one of the smallest cities ever (217 inhabitants), a delightful place, definitely worth a detour. For chambres d'hôtes in the vicinity look no further than Pinas, near Lannemezan.

St Gaudens on the N117 is a *sub-préfecture* of the department, an industrial town with a pleasant raised parking area where a large market is held on Thursdays. Carry along the main highway eastwards and the next department is Ariège, very mountainous and with many hidden villages just waiting to be discovered. The first town on the route is St Girons, a busy administrative town. Perhaps I saw it through rose-coloured spectacles on my first visit, but I always think of it as an open sunny town with interesting shops and helpful people. Just the sort of place one would want to linger in while having a meal sitting out in the sun.

On to Foix, the *Préfecture* of **Ariège**, a very different town squashed in between high mountains, guarded by its old castle with three distinctive towers high above the main streets, a veritable bottleneck for traffic with the

N20 trunk road rushing past to Spain along the bank of the river Ariège. Help is on the way – there are signs of a new by-pass appearing. I can't imagine Foix without traffic congestion. The surrounding area is dotted with *Pogs*, the local name for *pain de sucre* or sugar-loaf hills, notably one on the left as you drive south from Foix on the N20. Montségur château, one of the last bastions of the Cathars, is built on one. There are many delightful villages with good chambres d'hôtes to choose from in this truly fascinating department, one of the best areas of the Pyrénées for a more rural holiday. Riding, walking, canoeing, it is all there, even the gateway to Andorra.

Gers, sometimes known as Gascony, lies north of the Hautes-Pyrénées and life there can best be summed up by the old Gascon prayer, 'Lord, give me good health, light work, fine meals frequently, a little love from time to time, but above all my daily ration of Armagnac'! The local brandy was already on sale in the fifteenth century, two hundred years before Cognac (a dirty word in this area!). Armagnac is distilled only once, as opposed to the double distillation of its rival, and must age for at least two years in oak casks to be *Appellation*. Three stars indicates an Armagnac three years old, VSOP at least four, Napoleon at least five, and for *Vieille Armagnac* the age is indicated on the bottle.

The **Gers** is a totally agricultural department with rolling hills of sunflowers, corn and vineyards, beside the quiet roads. Some farmers produce vast quantities of *foie-gras*; there are duck and geese farms everywhere. Auch, the *Préfecture*, sits regally on a hill in the middle, with all the roads converging on it. Because it is the only large town in the area it attracts all the tourists. On one side of the hill is the magnificent *Escalier Monumental*, a great stone staircase sweeping up to the cathedral above. A statue of D'Artagnan stands majestically near the top. The 370 steps have shallow risers – it isn't the stiff climb it looks. The Tourist Office is housed in the *Maison Fedel*, a fifteenth century building. The Cathedral of Ste Marie has eighteen beautiful, glass windows painted by Arnaud de Moles at the beginning of the sixteenth century. As he was a Gascon you will find other churches in the Gers with his handiwork. Parking by the Cathedral, but also a large shady car-park near the Place de la Liberation.

Bastides of all shapes and sizes abound in the Gers, even a completely round one at Fourcès in the north, where the Mayor and a great deal of the population are Dutch. There are many Dutch settlers in the Gers now and the Brits are steadily competing. There are lively markets in all the towns. At the garlic fair at Saint-Clar in August everyone is treated to a plate of garlic soup! Some farms grow nothing but garlic around here. A favourite village of mine is tiny Larresingle. Built in the 13th century as a fortress for the Bishop of Condom; it now has a ruined church and castle and just a couple of restaurants. You approach by a bridge over the moat.

The rich local *apéritif* served in chambres d'hôtes is Floc; a mixture of Armagnac and grape juice, either white or red.

The smallest department of the Midi Pyrénées is **Tarn-et-Garonne**, but it certainly packs a lot into a small space. Montauban the *préfecture*, built in the red brick so typical of the Toulouse area, was originally built as a bastide. It suffered during the Albigensian crusade and is now strongly Protestant. Moissac further west is famous for the 11th century cloisters at the Abbey. Close by, the Tarn joins the Garonne, and at Boulou on a hill a few kilometres west there is a lookout which gives a wonderful view of the converging rivers. The rest of the department is mostly agricultural with pleasant, small villages, but I did find some splendid *fermes auberges* with rooms and sometimes a swimming pool, and they all had excellent regional food at very reasonable prices. In fact if you particularly want to stay in a *ferme auberge* head for Tarn-et-Garonne.

Tarn further east is north of Toulouse. Albi is the *préfecture*. Its dreary red brick cathedral, Ste Cécile is nothing to look at from outside, but inside the contrast is magical; here is one of the loveliest cathedrals in France; the red, blue and gold painted walls contrasting with the white carved stonework giving off such warmth it affects all who enter – not a miserable face in sight. There are twenty-nine side-chapels flanking the nave, all different, but in the same colours. Beautiful oak choir stalls lead to the high altar. The vaulted ceiling is superb. So much to see, impossible to describe, far better to go and look for yourself.

Behind the cathedral beside the Tarn is the museum of Toulouse-Lautrec, open every day 10–12 and 2–5 p.m. (closed on Tuesdays); many of his paintings are here, among those of other artists. It is an old bishop's palace, so the rooms are interesting in themselves. It is also possible to visit the house where he was born, in a corner of the rue de Toulouse-Lautrec. Good pedestrian shopping precincts where an antiques fair is held on occasional Saturdays. Nicer views of the Cathedral are to be had from the bridges over the Tarn.

There are many other places to visit such as the hill villages of Cordes to the north of Albi and Lautrec to the south. West are the vineyards of Gaillac, both red and white wines in the many *dégustations*. The *appellation contrôlée* is one of the oldest in France, dating from the twelfth century. The vineyards stretch from as far north as Cordes down to the left bank of the Tarn, and the wines, as in Bordeaux, are classified by regions. *Mauzac* is the main grape; but others add their own quality and taste to the Gaillac wine. You can visit the *Cave de Labastide de Levis* between 10 a.m. and 4 p.m. in July and August. Many of the chambres d'hôtes in the area have coupons which entitle you to two free bottles when you visit the *dégustations*. The Tarn flows through the centre of the department; rising in the Lozère in the east, it flows through the **Aveyron**, a large less known and less populous department; its barren plains and gorges lie west of the Lozère and Gard. The ancient cheese of Roquefort comes from a small village of that name on the plain south of Millau where the limestone caves have just the right atmosphere for maturing it. Fable has it that a shepherd boy in the twelfth century left some sheep's milk and bread in a cave where mushrooms grew while he went off to visit a girlfriend. Three weeks later he returned to find the bread, milk and mushrooms had integrated into a mass of cheese. To this day the cheese is made in the same way using the same caves to store it. A very special type of mushroom is used, grown only in this area, and the milk is collected from sheep farmers for miles around.

Rodez, up on the plain in the Rouergue is the *préfecture*. The large cathedral of Notre-Dame is in the centre. I have never found this city, nor the agricultural land around it very interesting; but Aveyron cheers up a bit east of Rodez at Millau on the Tarn, an attractive town famous for making gloves. On the Causse-Noir above Millau is the interesting *Montpellier-le-Vieux*, weird rock formations which look like the ruins of an old town. The Causse-Noir can be very bleak at times, but in June it is a mass of wild flowers and small shrubs, making it an extremely pleasant drive on a fine day. The tiny village of Lanuéjols is like a desert oasis up here, just over the border of Lozère.

Villefranche-la-Rouergue in the west has more to offer with the pretty bridge over the river and the bastide market square where everyone brings their wares on Saturdays. Look out for Najac a hill village south of Villefranche. But best by far in Aveyron is the valley of the River Lot, which runs along its western border. Delightful, old villages like Saint-Cirque-Lapopie and Cénevières perch along the river to Cajarc, a neat little town once the home of M. Pompidou. As the river winds off to Figéac the road, still in Aveyron, veers off to Capendac and on to Conques which is almost a rival of Rocamadour in the popularity polls and not such an uphill walk from the car park.

The **Lot** to most people means the river and Cahors, which isn't a bad start as both are equally important. Cahors is the *préfecture* and is situated on a bend of the river. It is in the southern part of the department, known as the *Quercy*. The city housed a university in the middle ages and has many old houses and relics of the past. It goes back to Gallo-Roman times.

The interesting boulevard cutting straight through the town from north to south is the N20, lined with shops and cafés, it crosses the river by the Pont Louis-Philippe and goes on its way to Toulouse. The Pont Valentré has a more historical past. Built as a fortified bridge at the beginning of the fourteenth century, it has three square towers each 40 metres high and proved an adequate deterrent to the English. The centre tower is open to the public in July and August from 9 a.m. to 7 p.m. The vineyards outside Cahors have long been known for their dark rich red wine, which in pre-revolutionary times in Russia was the wine always used at the eucharist in the Russian Orthodox Church.

Head north from Cahors to Rocamadour, the hill village of all hill villages, which Henry 'Short Coat', the eldest son of Henry II, pillaged. He caught a fever and died later in Martel asking for his father's pardon. At Padirac, near Autoire are large underground limestone caves through which a river flows. Caves also at Pech-Merle near the Celé river outside Cahors. These have paintings and carvings made by prehistoric man.

The land is rich in the valleys and much fruit is grown, strawberries, plums, etc. Walnut trees and tobacco grow well here, with vines on the western slopes.

ARIÈGE

COS. 09000

5 km WNW of Foix. A fraction off the D117 from St Girons to Foix just before Foix.

Caussou (M)
Mme. Portet. 61.65.24.42. cl. 1/1 to 31.3.

Mme Portet is young and highly organised; she has decorated six rooms immaculately, all in matching colours. In fact you may change your towels whenever you like in her spotless laundry room, but woe betide you if you take the wrong colour for your room. Even the toilet paper has to match! Madame will do your washing for you in her machine. They don't offer that service in hotels.

Caussou

Vast dining-room on the ground floor, and a comfortably furnished lounge which leads to a large terrace with glorious views over the Pyrénées. Even Foix castle can be seen clearly. A veritable sun trap here. Evening meal 80f all drinks *compris*. Interesting local *apéritif* called *Hipocras*, a white wine with herbs. Rooms 200f with excellent breakfast.

GANAC. 09000

8 km SW of Foix. D21 from Foix.

La Carcis (S)
Mme Piednoel. 61.02.96.54. cl. January.

High up in the mountains above Foix is this little Hansel and Gretel cottage, quite enchanting, on the edge of the village of Ganac. The only sound you will hear at night will be that of a mountain stream running beside your room. Walks straight up into the mountains or fishing on the spot.

One comfortable room for three is on the ground floor, warmly carpeted and with armchairs. Entry either by steep stairs from the salon above where you have meals, or from a little private grassy terrace right beside the stream. In fine weather meals are served on the terrace outside looking towards the surrounding peaceful mountains and forests. The room at 190f and evening meal at 65f, with regional cooking, make this very good value for such a quiet retreat.

OUST. 09110

13 km SE of St Girons.

Mme Andrieu (M)
Rue du Pouech. 61.66.92.30. cl. 16/10 to 31/12.

A small village just at the foot of the Pyrénées. Take the winding D618 from St Girons, through the Gorges de Ribaouto and you will reach Oust without climbing a hill; but afterwards the road becomes a rapid ascent to the Spanish border.

Right in the middle of the village is a large building, once a hotel with the small rear garden overlooking a swimming pool and the owners' house. At the moment only six rooms are in use as chambres d'hôtes, three on the first floor and three on the second. Every room has an identical small balcony with furniture, overlooking the terrace and pool. Downstairs is a large dining-room for breakfast and guests may use a fridge in the kitchen area. Rooms are pleasantly carpeted, but the whole place felt as if it was regretting its former days as an active hotel. Its time will come again as in three or four years Madame hopes to open up the whole hotel with all 21 rooms when her son has qualified as a chef. Meanwhile enjoy the hotel-

like rooms with fewer people to use the garden and pool. No evening meals, but two restaurants in the village. Two roads back to St Girons, one partly one-way traffic making it an easy run. Rooms 260f.

SAINT-PAUL-DE-JARRAT. 09000

8 km S of Foix. Leave Foix by the N20 going south. In 8 km turn left on to the D117, then turn right opposite the church up a small lane.

A very useful stop on the route to Spain via Andorra. Quite near Montségur; one of the last Cathar strongholds. It is possible to walk up to the castle ruins at the top; a long haul.

M. Savignol (S)
61.64.14.26.

The mountains and village make a good background to this modern Canadian-style house. M. & Mme Savignol have lived in Canada and keep their memories alive with this typical house. On the ground floor two comfortable rooms share a bathroom, small kitchen and a large sitting-room opening on to a terrace, leading to the garden with a round swimming pool. One other large room on the first floor is

quite luxurious. 210-230f. No evening meals, but there are restaurants nearby or you can self-cater. Breakfast – orange juice, croissants, more than a dozen jams, peanut butter and chocolate spread to choose from, and *crêpes*, too, on Sundays. They certainly cater for all tastes here.

SERRES-SUR-ARGET. 09000

9 km W of Foix. Take the D17 from Foix and follow the signs through the village.

Foix is about six miles away down winding roads and after a day out there seeing castle and museum, visiting the large market on Friday and fighting your way through heavy traffic, you will be glad to speed back to your mountain retreat.

➤ ### Le Poulsieu (M)
M. & Mme Brogneaux. 61.02.77.72.

Le Poulsieu

If you have always dreamt of a holiday in the mountains of the Pyrénées, this is just the place. You will think you are at the end of the world as you bump your way slowly up the last kilometre of the unmade track. Park your car out of sight and forget about it for a week.

Bob and Jenny Brogneaux will give you a splendid welcome and take you to one of their five rooms, with a choice of double or single beds, delightfully rustic with pretty windows having glorious mountain views. There are four rooms in the main house and another family room for four in a small building across the courtyard, where young early morning risers can disturb only their own parents. This room has a double bed on the ground floor, and a bathroom half way up to a mezzanine area with two beds for children.

There are sunny tables in the courtyard and an excellent, large, covered terrace where meals are taken in fine weather, with a splendid view of the wide valley and surrounding mountains. A refreshing swimming pool is on a raised terrace by the house; there are rumours of it being heated in future for the cooler months. A delightful house-party atmosphere prevails. You eat with your hosts and no one bothers about taking dinner elsewhere. It is too far to drive back and nowhere else will you find such an international menu, always of four courses, 70f including all drinks. Wine is offered as an *apéritif* and with the meal. Should you be desperate for something stronger you pay extra.

Rooms 200f. If you stay more than six nights, you will pay *demi-pension* rates of 320f for two people.

I do realise this wouldn't be everyone's idea of an ideal holiday, so tucked away from towns and shops, but if you like mountain treks, beautiful scenery, swimming and good food and wine, make haste to book, and book you must; news is spreading fast. Jenny, being Dutch, speaks excellent English. Bob is Belgian. Arrowed for special atmosphere.

AVEYRON

ASPRIÈRES. 12700

15 km SE of Figeac. One of the prettiest drives along the river Lot is from Cahors to Figeac; the road winds on both sides of the river passing many old villages, including the famous tourist attraction St Cirq-Lapopie. From Figéac take the Décazeville road (N140) and follow the signs to Asprières.

A handy place to stay for visiting places on the river Lot, especially Conques, a delightful hill village with a rich Abbey. During the Revolution when the *maire* heard the officials of the Republic were coming to seize them he distributed all the treasures to the villagers to hide in their houses and orchards. When the Republicans arrived he told them they had had their Revolution, and the citizens, like good revolutionaries, had taken everything. Later when the Terror was over, the people returned everything to the Abbey, and Conques now has some of the rarest medieval treasures in the world. There are some excellent restaurants in the village and the narrow back streets are well worth tramping round.

Le Mas de Calmouze (M)
M. & Mme Maurel. 65.63.89.89. cl. Oct. to May.
During the season only weekly stays.

Le Mas du Calmouze

Two kilometres down the road from Asprières is this lovely, old stone farmhouse nestling on land which slopes away to wooded countryside. Four rooms overlook the pool, and there are two larger ones for a family, in the main house. The tiled floors are sensible, so near the pool, but a bit chilly out of season. M. Maurel breeds horses and offers rides in his barouche (120f for two hours per person). Madame does the cooking and serves the meals. Both your hosts are from Alsace and speak German and some English, and have many regular visitors each year.

Meals are taken in a large beamed room on the first floor of the owners' house. M. and Mme Maurel eat at another table, not with their guests. The food is very good and interesting. A typical dinner was – Roquefort and walnut quiche, *blanquette à veau* with rice, cheese and strawberries and cream. The normal breakfast is served but cheese, charcuterie, paté, etc. is available at extra cost. Rooms 270f. Evening meal 85f, wine not *compris*.

SALLES-COURBATIERS. 12260

25 km S of Figéac. D922 south from Figéac; in 20 km before Villeneuve turn east on to the D545. The small village of Salles-Courbatiers, with its little pond opposite the *mairie* where two swans live all the year round is very quiet and handy for Conques (40 km) and Figeac which is a large town with all amenities plus many restaurants.

Au Marronnier (M)
M. Lagarde. Place Basse. 65.81.63.39. cl. 30/10 to 1/4.

Right in the centre of the village is a large house offering chambres d'hôtes, aptly named, with an enormous chestnut tree right by the front door. Enter by the tower up a magnificent stone staircase, a real feature. All accommodation is on the first floor. Three pleasant double rooms, two facing south overlooking the village and church tower, one facing east over the garden. There is a large wild garden behind the house with ample parking, but M. Lagarde can offer a locked garage a few steps away. No evening meal, but there is a shop with a café in the village. Rooms 200f.

GERS

AUTERIVE. 32550

On the D929 10 km S of Auch.

Poudos (M)
Mme Gerda Wieggers. 62.61.00.93.

Easy to find but not to be confused with the Auterive on the N20. Here are very fine chambres d'hôtes rooms, a caravan and camping site (six tents only). Amenities are numerous with a large area of green lawn, a round swimming pool and good parking. Your hosts are Dutch and serve good *tables d'hôtes* in the sunny dining room.

The rooms have varied accommodation, upstairs and downstairs, both double and single rooms. or family units plus shared kitchen facilities. Trust the Dutch to think of everything. Most of these rooms have tiled floors and independent entry from the garden, and face south. In a garage at the back are washing facilities for the campers and a washing machine for all. Pleasant views over the countryside.

Prices reasonable at 190/225f. Go for *demi-pension* at 170/185f which is good value. Might be a bit crowded in August.

TOURNECOUPE. 32380

35 km NE of Auch. From Fleurance about 24 km north of Auch take the D654, then almost immediately the D953 to St. Clar. In about 8 km turn right on to the D8 to Tournecoupe, drive through the village and at the far end of the square bear right and immediately left and En Bigorre is straight ahead.

The countryside of Gers is full of interest, with many small bastide towns and the traffic is light even in August. Auch is the capital of the department, the birthplace of D'Artagnan of *The Three Musketeers*. If you are visiting Auch one day and feel like a blowout at lunchtime, drive 15 km west to Barran and eat at *Chez Georgette* in the middle of the village. It is an unpretentious little restaurant packed at midday with locals. A six course meal costs 47f! Such places are becoming more and more difficult to find.

En Bigorre (M)
M. & Mme Marqué. 62.66.42.47.

This garlic farm (not a whiff of it!) is situated at the end of a hill village, with one wing allocated to guests. The five rooms are large and cool and well furnished. The garden with green lawns and swimming pool makes it an ideal place for children. Guests eat *en famille* outside on the covered terrace in good weather. Meals are of substantial local fare, with wine and Armagnac included. *Apéritifs* are

set out by the swimming pool before dinner; very civilized. Guests may use the fridge, cooker and sink, etc. on the terrace to make their own lunch. M. & Mme

Marqué are charming hosts who cannot do enough for their guests, and are very entertaining at the evening meal.

The house is dominated by a large *château d'eau* (water tower), I suspect this accounts for the very green lawns in summer. Rooms 220f. *Demi-pension* 320f for two people after three days. Possible arrow.

HAUTE-GARONNE

CINTEGABELLE. 31550

26 km S of Toulouse. Take the N20 south from Toulouse and in about 26 km turn left to Cintegabelle on the D25. From there take the D35 to Calmont and in about 2 km you will see a sign to Escautils on your left.

Escautils (M)
Mme Degrammont. 61.08.08.60.

Mme Degrammont emerged from the stables to greet us, a true château-born hostess; nothing throws these ladies, they can cope in any situation. We arrived on a night when the riding school at the house was *en fête*. Madame and her sons were rushing about preparing for a *crêpe* party. We were given a huge, very comfortable room up a polished wood staircase on the first floor of this large manor house,

with an enormous bathroom full of amenities – washing machine, hairdryer, weighing machine, you name it. I strongly suspect this is Madame's own room out of season. Two large windows looked out on lawns sloping down to the river l'Hers, where ponies peacefully grazed. Another room has toilet facilities on the landing. Young people were everywhere; we were invited to join in, but opted out for an early night with *crêpes* and more *crêpes* in the pretty little dining room Madame keeps for guests.

In the morning my husband told me a young lady had walked through our room in the night to use the bathroom! Having heard nothing, I looked at him oddly, calculated his wine consumption, even wondered about ghosts. At breakfast Madame said, 'I hear you had a *petite visite* during the night!' One young lady was keeping firmly out of our way. How lucky can you get!

The only building visible from the house is the old Abbaye Boulbonne which lies just below on the other side of the river and can be visited on occasions. Anyone keen on riding would love it here. A mount is 60f an hour. Rooms 200f. Evening meal 80f.

GAILLAC-TOULZA. 31550

40 km S of Toulouse and 24 km N of Foix.

Larra (M)
Mme Dusmesnil. Mailhol. 61.08.90.53. cl. 1/10 to 30/4.

Not really near Gaillac-Toulza at all, but coming south on the N20 from Toulouse 6 km south of Auterive at La Fourane, turn right on to the D25 and you will see signs to this lovely château-like house which is silhouetted at the end of a long drive. I felt I should have been approaching in a horse-drawn carriage rather than a mere automobile, especially when we passed the stables flanking the entrance to the courtyard in front of the house. The house has been in the family for years and is situated in extensive grounds with lawns, trees and swimming pool.

Two high rooms on the first floor have good views and share a sitting room with an adjacent kitchen. 270f. M. Dusmesnil (Madame's son), who speaks perfect English, is busy restoring the house in his spare time, so don't expect perfection yet. Come prepared to self-cater, as no evening meal here, but there is a TIMY super-market and good *boulangerie* in Saverdun only 5 km away.

HAUTES-PYRÉNÉES

LOUBAJAC. 65100

6 km N of Lourdes on the D3. Lourdes, which lies on the Gave de Pau, owes its fame to the young peasant girl Bernadette Soubirous, who at the age of fourteen claimed to have fourteen visions of the Virgin Mary at a grotto in 1858. She was told by Our Lady that the waters of the well flowing from this grotto had healing powers. Once these powers were proved to the satisfaction of the Roman Catholic authorities the Church of the Rosary was built next to the grotto where the fountain runs and in whose waters the pilgrims are bathed. Bernadette became a nun at the age of twenty, died fifteen years later and was canonised in 1933. Next to the Church of the Rosary a basilica was built in the style of the thirteenth century, with

a bell tower some 70 metres high. Inside is a small chapel reserved for private prayer when there are no services taking place. The extensive grounds also contain a huge subterranean church (completed in 1958 to mark the centenary of the visions), designed to hold 20,000 pilgrims and unadorned except for the central altar. Lourdes is an international pilgrimage centre for the sick, and of course is crowded in the holiday months of July and August. Tourist souvenir shops abound in the town and I wouldn't recommend a visit there if you can help it; parking is almost impossible and the queues to visit the grotto horrendous in the heat. By September all has cleared and the weather is usually pleasant and sunny, as it is in May and June. The Castle rises above the town and contains a Pyrennean museum. Ste Bernadette's birthplace can be seen at the foot of Castle Hill in the rue Bernadette Soubirous.

➤
Mme Vives (S)
Route de Bartres. 62.94.44.17.

There is a superb view of the Pyrénées from the Route de Bartres. Right beside the road is a small sheep farm where Mme Vives has created four delightfully beamed and warmly carpeted guest rooms on the first floor. Ask for one of the rooms which overlook the flowery garden and have views to the mountains. There is a small sitting area on the landing, and chairs in the garden for sunny days and facilities for washing clothes are thoughtfully provided. Rooms 200f.

Breakfast is served in the dining-room downstairs and evening meals at 65f, wine compris. Guests eat together but not with the family.

A really pleasant place to stay, the nearest and the best for Lourdes, and very reasonably priced. Arrowed accordingly.

PINAS. 65300

4.5 km E of Lannemezan on the N117. About 20 km to the south-east is St-Bertrand-de-Comminges which must be one of the world's smallest cities with a population of about 300. An independent city, too, for when the present French departmental system was instituted in 1790 the Deputies of Comminges refused to amalgamate with the district of Couserans in Ariège, although they had artistic and economic links; so the border of Haute-Garonne was stretched southwards to include their city. The cathedral and old town are regarded as sights surpassed only by Mont-Saint-Michel. The city was founded by Pompey in the first century BC as Lugdunum Convenarum, from which the name Comminges evolved. In the nearby village of Valcabrère there is a very chic restaurant 'le Lugdunum'. (Menus from 150f). I have not yet had a chance to try this place but I am told that as well as regional dishes you can get genuine Roman cooking based on a cookery book by Apicius, who wrote some two thousand years ago.

Magnificent is the only way to describe St. Mary's Cathedral. It was originally built in 1100 in Romanesque style, but enlarged in the fourteenth century in Gothic. The choir is completely enclosed, making it a church within a church, with 66 canons' stalls all intricately carved. However, in the cloister you will find the famous pillar of St Bertrand, which consists of the four evangelists standing back to back. The organ, again, seems to be in a church of its own with the choir completely screened off and a wide open space in front. Fifteen metres high and ten metres wide with magnificent wood carving covering the whole facade, it is the centre of the music festivals which are held here every summer. (Information from the office at Mazères-sur-Salat, Tel: 61.88.32.00.). The cathedral is open throughout the year, closing of course for lunch from noon till two, and at six in the evening in winter and seven in summer. It is open only to ticket holders when the festivals are on.

There are a few artisans' shops, good restaurants and cafés in the village, one with a delightful terrace overlooking the countryside.

Domaine de Jean-Pierre (M)
Mme Colombier. Route de Villeneuve. 62.98.15.08.

A really gracious mansion, covered with ivy, which has been in the family for many years and is well preserved. From the moment you enter the tiled hallway and climb the gently sloping stairs to the large airy rooms you will feel you could stay here for days. There are four interesting rooms with polished wood floors, and large, well furnished bathrooms almost adjoining. One is a family room for four, another for three people, and others for couples, but only one room is carpeted for winter use. 240f.

A very comfortable lounge has one wall completely lined with books. Breakfast can be taken in summer on the extensive gravel terrace. Mme Colombier (a keen golfer) is a very charming hostess who speaks some English and will look after you well. This is a true chambres d'hôtes where you really are private guests.

LOT

AUTOIRE. 46400

20 km NE of Rocamadour. From Rocamadour take the D673 (signposted St Céré) across the N140; in 14 km turn left on to the D38 to Autoire.

What a lovely part of France this is, in the Lot department, but only a spitting distance from the banks of the Dordogne. Ideal for sightseeing. Close by is Rocamadour, the famous hill village which Henry II's son pillaged. It clings precariously to the hillside, but there is a little train that will take the less energetic right into the heart of the village, and a lift to the castle at the top from where you will get a wonderful view. Numerous restaurants and cafés to choose from, all with glimpses of the valley. The quiet, little village of Autoire itself is well worth a stroll round as there are many old interesting buildings. Near at hand, too, are the Padirac caves, and Carennac where there is a striking old tower standing alone. Some say it was here that Fénélon who was prior here in 1681 wrote his novel *Télémaque*.

La Plantade (S)
Mme Gauzin. 65.38.15.61.

La Plantade

This nice, old-fashioned farmhouse beside a stream is on a road leading to the village of Autoire. You cross over a bridge to get to the house, which is rather fun for children. Modernised rooms, warm and comfortable have real linen monogrammed sheets, and excellent individual spotlamps over the bed (other chambres d'hôtes please note!). Our room overlooked the pretty garden and farmyard with distant views of the hills. Mme Gauzin who is a widow, runs the chambres d'hôtes while son looks after the farm; his schoolteacher wife livened up the conversation at dinner and ticked off her husband for trying to smoke between courses. I am sure Monsieur would appreciate a fellow smoker here! Good value for rooms and plentiful food. This is the sort of place which would be loved by many who like simple farm fare and a friendly atmosphere. Evening meal 75f, all drinks *compris*. Rooms 180f.

CASTELNAU-MONTRATIER. 46170

22 km SSW of Cahors. This small village is a bastide dating from the 13th century, replacing a village destroyed by Simon de Montfort. The church was designed by Paul Abadie, the architect of the Sacré-Cœur, but is not regarded as one of his better works.

Take the N20 south of Cahors and in 16 km turn right on to the D19 to Castelnau-Montratier. Go through the village leaving by the D659 (signposted Molières) and after passing a garage on the edge of the village you will see a small road on the left signposted to the Château de Feral which is 200 yards up this road on the left.

Château de Feral (M)
M. & Mme Parmentier. 65.21.96.08. cl. 1/10 to 31/5.

It is easy to imagine yourself in a crinoline sweeping along the wide corridor on the first floor of this old château in large rural grounds. M. & Mme Parmentier bought it about fourteen years ago and are slowly doing it up, while running a chicken farm. All a bit crumbly outside but with a lovely old terrace at the back, where breakfast is served in summer, overlooking the village, across a deep valley. There is just one enormous bedroom with a carved wooden bed and carpeted bathroom. Two windows open on to a narrow balcony above the terrace. Telephone by the bed, left from the days when it used to be a *Logis*. Madame is very down to earth, and will probably meet you in working clothes while feeding the chickens. A quiet, spacious, and easy-going place to stay. Some English spoken. Room 280f. Extra beds available.

LALBENQUE. 46230

15 km SE of Cahors. Lalbenque is a dull little town, and dies completely on Mondays when your nearest shop is 'Mammouth' at the entrance to Cahors on the N20. It is however the truffle capital of the region, and there is a market every Tuesday afternoon. The village church boasts a superb reredos dating from the seventeenth century and a gilded tabernacle.

l'Ermitage (S)
M. Pasquier. 65.31.75.91.

From Lalbenque take the D6 towards Cahors and just at the 'end of village' sign fork right by a faded sign saying *Gariottes à Louer* and you will find the most unusual chambres d'hôtes ever. In a small, wooded area are three perfect replicas of the old shepherds' stone huts, just like giant honey pots; they are known as

Gariottes here, and called *Bories* in other parts of France. Well separated from each other, they each have a gravel patio area with small, shady trees for eating outside. Inside the circular room has a double bed, a kitchen corner, and shower and toilet, tiled floors, painted cream walls; all three have a different colour scheme picked up in bedding and tiling (pink, blue or green) and a very nice, carved stone

L'Ermitage

bench and pine table and chairs, but not a lot of storage space for clothes. A mattress for a third person is on a wide shelf, a bit precarious, up a steep wooden ladder.

Really these are little studios, only 15 feet in diameter, where you have to self-cater even for breakfast; so arrive prepared. With good-sized fridge, gas rings and all china, this is no problem. All heated electrically, the thick stone walls with tiny windows and glazed front door make this a very cosy stop for one night or longer. Price per *Gariotte* for two is only 180f per night.

Ring M. Pasquier and he will be there to receive you; he doesn't live at the house nearby any longer. Very well kept little hidey-holes and worth a visit for the fun of sleeping in a *Gariotte*.

LOUBRESSAC. 46130

24 km NE of Rocamadour. Take the D673 from St. Céré to Carennac, turning right on to the D30 in about 3 km still signed Carennac and look out for a left turn to Loubressac in about 8 km. The chambres d'hôtes is at the top of the hill past the church.

Mme Mérot-Maury (M-L)
65.38.15.79. cl. 1/10 to 30/4.

In the hill village of Loubressac, situated in the Dordogne valley, this newly built house belonging to an artist, often has an *Exposition* on the ground floor while the first floor is devoted to a chambres d'hôtes. At the rear of the house is a private kitchen patio and garden for guests' use; all this is linked to the upstairs rooms. A very pleasant place to stay for self-catering, especially as the village has a *boulangerie* and other shops, and your hostess lives only a few doors away.

Possibly this location could be a little noisy during the day with people looking round the art exhibition, but would be quiet at night. I have not stayed here yet as it wasn't quite ready when I was shown round by Mme Mérot-Maury. I known Madame prefers to have met her guests before letting the rooms so there may be a little difficulty here. We met her when we were strolling round the village one after-noon and she was weeding her garden, we got into conversation and were given a tour of the new house, as easy as that. A written booking would be equally accept-able. There are good views from Loubressac over the countryside to the famous Château Castelnau outside Bretenoux, which is worth visiting; don't miss a snack at the very good crêperie in the grounds near the car park. Loubressac has its own Logis and restaurant, all within walking distance of the chambres d'hôtes.

Double room 350f with extra bed 390f. Breakfast 30f extra. No evening meal. Parking in garden. Rather expensive, but a very elegantly furnished chambres d'hôtes in a most attractive hill village. Weekly bookings preferred.

MARCILHAC-SUR-CELE. 46160

22 km WSW of Figéac.

Montredon (S)
Madame Blanc. 65.40.67.74.

Montredon

Driving from Cahors to Aurillac along a very twisty main road in the middle of March, the morning mist lifted and I realised we were in for a real summer's day. So decided to drop down into the Célé valley and take the even twistier road by the river. The Célé is a tributary of the Lot which it joins before Cahors. It is such a pretty little val-ley with tiny stone villages. We arrived at Marcilhac-sur-Célé, where the old abbey was partially destroyed in the Revolution and was reduced to the sta-tus of a parish church. You will be taken round by a deaf and dumb little man who insists that you miss nothing. He makes each of you sit in the bishop's chair and strikes the old tower bell which is now on the ground right beside you, a really deaf-ening noise, which of course he can't hear! If he spots you in the village, it's difficult to escape; he has the key to the abbey and propels you round it.

St Cirque-Lapopie and the Pêche-Merle caves, are not far away and a *bateau-mouche* based at Bouzies on the Lot is the best way of seeing the river.

At the *boulangerie* we were directed to an isolated farm on the *Causse* (plateau): Madame Blanc's cottage was built in 1772 and is adorned with climbing roses in May. A delightful, crazy-paved terrace is surrounded by a three-foot wall sheltering her little tubs and boxes of flowers. In summer it is completely roofed by vines. One delightfully old-fashioned room is sunny and warm and has low windows opening on to the terrace, wooden floor, pretty wallpaper, a double bed with antique wooden ends, and a giant wardrobe behind which, curtained off, were the shower, loo, basin facilities. When I asked if I could sit outside, a plastic white table and chairs arrived immediately. Evening meals are at her daughter's, in the other house on the farm. The meal at 80f (*apéritif* and wine *compris*) is substantial but not exciting.

Cajarc, 15 km away, would be the nearest town for eating out. The Blancs were sheep farmers but have now retired, keeping just a few as a hobby. They have two *gîtes* on their land, in converted farm buildings.

OK, so the room was old-fashioned but it had all the amenities we wanted. Not a paradise of modern plumbing, but clean, warm and homely. Breakfast with plentiful good coffee, bread, croissants and cake à la maison rather like brioche, honey and home-made jams. At 180f for two people it was well worth it. Mme Blanc can't do enough for one. At 4 p.m. she arrived with home-made *apéritif* or cold drinks. She also gives full permission to do as much washing as you like, with a nice blowy line in the field on which to hang it. Other rooms available sometimes in their gites. Same price.

SAINT-PIERRE-LAFEUILLE. 46090

8 km N of Cahors. From Cahors take the N20 north to St Pierre-Lafeuille; turn left on to the D47 and you will find Lou Castellou signed on your left, before a campsite.

Les Graves (S-M)
M. & Mme Beranger. Lou Castellou. 65.36.83.76.

If you are looking for a place to stop on a hot summer's day, then try this modern Périgord-type house complete with tower room, and cool off in the swimming pool in the large garden. Though this house is really modern, it sadly does not have even basins in the bedrooms; there is a very luxurious bathroom and a separate toilet on the landing, but shared by all 5 rooms. The rooms are very nicely furnished with matching curtains and bedspreads. One family room does boast a shower. The French are notoriously early risers if travelling, so your best bet is to hang on in bed until the coast is clear, and you will have all the washing facilities to yourself! Mme Beranger is a very good cook and the evening meal is extremely good value, with delicious soups and salads, wine *compris* at 74f. Breakfast is pleasantly served in the conservatory overlooking the garden.

With rooms at 185f, this would make a good budget stop if you don't mind the lack of facilities, as everything else is A1.

SAUX. 46800

30 km W of Cahors. On the D656 between Penne d'Agenais and Cahors.

Le Mas (M)
Mme Mahieu-Dulor. La Guilhaumeri. 65.31.91.82.

Genteel Mme Mahieu-Dulor lives in a typical Quercynoise house in a tiny hamlet surrounded by orchards, 5 km from Tournon d'Agenais. She offers one room in her house as a true guest room, sometimes another in her delightfully rustic *pigeonnier* when it is not in use as a *gîte*. Madame has lived for a long time in Gabon and her home is overflowing with interesting memorabilia in every room.

Not a good place for children; the more robust *gîte* would suit them! She is a very kind lady who does all she can to make you feel at home. All rooms are on the first floor with a good view of the surrounding, flat country, the large garden and a pleasant swimming pool. Madame makes her own *apéritif* from plums and offers elegantly served candle-lit evening meals. She is also very happy to have a guest recuperating from an illness or who just needs peace and quiet for a week or a month. If it is elegance you want, you will find it here. Evening meal 80f wine *compris*. Room 280f.

TARN

BELLEGARDE. 81430

10 km E of Albi. Take the D999 from Albi (signposted Millau) and in about 8 km at Fontcouverte you will see a sign right to Bellegarde. A strategic place to stay for visiting Albi and its imposing cathedral and the Toulouse Lautrec museum. Often a good antique market in the shopping precinct on Saturdays. North of Albi are the hill villages of Cordes and Najac. Cordes, an artisan's mecca, is more widely acclaimed, but I prefer Najac, more 'lived in', where the wide street lined with flower bedecked houses and shops and restaurants descends to the old part of the town. Just when you think you have reached the end, the road climbs up again to the church and the castle which is on the skyline. Friendly villagers chat with you as you pass by. Back at Bellegarde visit Ambialet where the river Tarn loops round the high priory making it nearly an island.

La Borie Neuve (M)
M. & Mme Richard. 63.55.33.64.

The house is on the left before the
village. It has been a chambres
d'hôtes for some time and has
lovely views from the terrace overlooking the swimming pool, surrounded by lawns. M. and Mme
Richard are a charming couple from
Paris who have recently moved here
and are building it up into quite a
large concern. There is an exercise
area and fax machines for execu-
tives.

La Borie Neuve

The rooms are extremely well furnished, with choice of bath or shower and
some with kitchenettes. 230 to 290f. Central heating full on, even in June when
chilly. Evening meals taken with your hosts, with *apéritifs* and wine *compris* at 95f,
are not to be missed.

MEZENS. 81800

30 km NE of Toulouse. Just outside Mezens on D28 turn right.

Le Cambou (S)
M. & Mme Saulle-Bulteau. 63.41.82.66.

Mezens is right in the heart of the
Gaillac vineyards in the Tarn
valley; they are reputed to be the
oldest in France.

Monsieur is a sculptor and
Madame taught maths. Now they
have converted rooms for guests in
their old farmhouse on the outskirts of the village; some of the
rooms still have *pisé* walls. The five
rooms have varying facilities;
something for everyone here.

Le Cambou

You will enjoy sipping your *apéritif* on the long wisteria-covered terrace overlooking the countryside. Delicious evening meals with all drinks *compris* at 60f
taken with your hosts and their small daughter.

Rooms 190f for a one-night stop, but if you stay longer, 160f, reducing to 150f
if staying a week or more.

ROQUEMAURE. 81800

28 km NNE of Toulouse. 4 km N of Bessières. Pretty hill villages abound in this region in all directions; Puycelsi to the north and Lautrec to the south. Make for Bessières on the D630, which has a large market on Monday mornings.

From Bessières turn north over the Tarn. Over the bridge, ignore signs to Roquemaure, turn immediately left and in 2 km turn right up a small lane where you will find the chambres d'hôtes sign; continue up hill turning right at the top and you will find Le Pendut further on, the only house in view on your right.

Le Pendut (S)
M. & Mme Aboujoid. 63.41.90.07. cl. 1/11 to 31/5.

Isolated and high on a hill above the village, this is a wonderful place to stay for a relaxing, hot summer week. The two rooms are on a terrace beside the swimming pool; each room has its own terrace area with chairs and table. The rooms themselves are rather small, and have only one cupboard; but shower rooms have vanitory units. There is a delightful little kitchenette, with fridge and electric hot-plates, all for guests' use beside the pool. Rooms 180f.

Dinner with the Aboujoids is a real treat, on the terrace of their house where on a really clear day you can see the faint outline of the Pyrénées, and at night the lights of Toulouse. If you have not exhausted yourself sight seeing and swimming during the day, join the Aboujoids for their evening stroll after dinner; their dogs and cats come, too. Evening meal 80f with apéritif and wine *compris*.

TARN-ET-GARONNE

CASTELSAGRAT. 82400

17 km NW of Moissac. West off the D953 between Valence and Lauzette.

Moissac, with its old cloisters, has a market on Saturday and Sunday, and an excellent viewpoint up at Boudou close by, overlooking the confluence of the rivers Tarn and Garonne. The tiny village of Castelsagrat is the most perfect baby bastide village I have ever seen (13th-15th centuries). A road leads off each corner of the square, all four sides of which have arched arcades, one housing a boulangerie, and the church is opposite. The walls are peeling inside but there are many lovely, old stained glass windows. The village is a nice walk from the *ferme auberge* if you feel energetic; if not there is plenty of parking.

Ferme Auberge de Pachot (M)
M. & Mme Boyer. 63.94.23.50.

What a charming couple M and Mme Boyer are. I called to see them at the unforgiveable time of 1 p.m. They were coping with a party of six and were expecting a busload of Spaniards for lunch. Luckily the Spanish coach was keeping Spanish time and arrived just after Madame had finished showing us her attractive variety of rooms, all on the first floor entered from an outside staircase. Here the priority is the *ferme auberge* dining-room, which appeared to be flourishing even in mid-March. A huge log fire, good food and jolly company in an attractive rustic setting. Rooms are 220f for two people. Evening meal from 80f (wine and *apéritifs compris*). *Demi-pension* can be arranged for over three days, which would be the best value.

CASTELSARRASIN. 82100

6 km S of Moissac. Castelsarrasin is a commercial town (market on Thursday). More than any other town in the area it was strongly Republican during the Revolution. So much so that all the main streets were renamed after republican ideals; Liberté, Egalité, etc., the rue de la Tolérance led into the Place de Raison! However all this was changed in 1812 and the old names were restored. Antoine Laumet, a knight of Lamothe-Cadillac, lived at 6 place de Lamothe-Cadillac, whence he left to seek his fortune in the New world. There he fought against the British in the War of Independence and founded the city of Detroit now home of the motor industry. In his honour General Motors named one of their most prestigious models the Cadillac.

➤ ## Dantous Sud (M)
M. & Mme Galea. 63.32.26.95.

The warmest room of our trip thanks to central heating throughout this large, restored farmhouse. Situated on the edge of the town, between the N113 and the Autoroute Des Deux-Mers (A62) it is an ideal place to stop off for a night. Many have stopped off for a night and stayed longer! Madame Galea is ready to receive

you and offer you an excellent meal at very short notice. The old farmhouse has been restored completely by Monsieur. The former stables are now a huge dining room with stairs leading to a mezzanine gallery for TV. Through a door to the old granary is a choice of five comfortable rooms with impeccable matching decor. A covered terrace, with a barbecue, overlooks the swimming pool and fields of nectarines in the Tarn and Garonne valley. So nice after being cooped up in a car all day. Both Monsieur and Madame joined us for the evening meal. We had soup, Madame's own charcuterie, roast duck, a special sauce and pasta, salad, cheese and apple pie. Wine and coffee *compris* 80f. Rooms 220f. Arrowed for all round comfort.

FAJOLLES. 82210

15 km S of Castelsarrasin. Exit 9 from the A62, then D12 to St Aigan and D63 to Angeville, signed from there. A little haven in a tiny French village within easy reach of Montauban, Albi or Moissac, or the delightful bastide villages of the Gers to the south.

Langans (M)
Mr & Mrs Callaghan. 63.95.65.31; fax 63.04.35.75.

English hosts here. This tall, terraced, typically French house would not arouse a great deal of interest in passing but on entering you will be amazed at the wonders wrought. Three delightfully pretty and cosy bedrooms overlook the long back garden and swimming pool with views to the country beyond and there is also a family suite. 265 to 290f or 310f from June to September. A dining room cum lounge and a large bar/kitchen for guests to make their own drinks, all opening on to the terrace where meals are taken in summer. Parking is opposite the house but this seems no problem in such a tiny village of only a few houses and a church.

The family join their guests for evening meals, 90f each, half a carafe of wine *compris*. Light lunch is available at 40f. Summer season weekly bookings only.

LAFRANÇAISE. 82130

17 km NW of Montauban. About 2 miles out of Lafrançaise on the D20 to Molières, turn off right at the large silo to the farm.

A good view of the Tarn from near the church of this busy little town. In the church near the Lady Chapel is a pew rather like a Royal Box with well worn cushions, presumably for the family of the Château Lafrançaise.

Trouilles (M)
M. & Mme Guffroy. 63.65.84.46.

I was delighted to find that Tarn-et-Garonne has a reputation for exceptionally good *ferme auberges*, offering a range of meals at lunchtime or in the evening from 85f to 180f. Some even offer chambres d'hôtes rooms and one of these is at Lafrançaise, east of Castelsarrasin. Six rooms, three very new on the ground floor which open on to the farm grounds just across from the swimming pool cost 270f. Nice views from the pool across undulating country-side. *Demi-pension* 420f for two people after three days.

Typical menus: *Menu Campagnard* for 85f: soup, paté, sauté of lamb or duck, salad, cheese and *patisserie de la maison*. Menu Cassoulet for 110f: Soup, *salade composée, cassoulet maison au confit du canard*, cheese and *patisserie*.

MONTESQUI. 82200

9 km N of Moissac. Take the D957 from Moissac to Montesqui; in 6 km branch right on to the D16 towards Durfort-Lacapallette and pick up signs to La Baysse on the left.

'La Baysse' (M)
M. & Mme Orsini. 63.04.54.00.

Isolated on a hilltop this farmhouse has a swimming pool overlooking rolling country-side. Expect a very nice welcome from your Spanish hostess and her French husband who produce copious evening meals beginning with Monsieur's home-made *apéritif*.

Five large well-furnished rooms, upstairs, downstairs, carpeted or tiled, cope with all weathers and make this a good base for visiting the *Bas-Quercy* area of Tarn-et-Garonne. Evening meals 90f, wine *compris*. Rooms 230/310f. *Demi-pension* after three nights is good value.

MONTPEZAT-DE-QUERCY. 82270

24 km S of Cahors. Take the N20 south from Cahors; in 22 km turn right on to the D20, signposted Montpezat de Quercy.

A delightful bastide village, unspoilt by modernisation. Go through the village and turn left about 50 m after the Post Office. Signed on the left.

➤ ### 'Le Barry' (M)
MM. Bankes & Jarros. Faubourg Saint-Roch.
63.02.05.50; fax 63.02.03.07.

On the ramparts of the village, this charming 17th century terraced house, is impeccably run, offering five spacious bedrooms, comfortably furnished, losing none of their old character. The sheltered garden, high above the road, with an inviting swimming pool overlooks the Quercy countryside. Relax on the terrace and enjoy the green lawns and flower beds, a perfect setting for evening meals in fine

weather, an alternative to the large lounge, dining room. Your English and German hosts really enjoy entertaining. Freshly squeezed orange juice for breakfast.

A great advantage here is being able to step right out into the old part of the town. The only snag is perhaps parking, which is under the wall of the garden on the roadside, but I have been assured that there has been no problem. Certainly worth a long stay here, to visit the lovely Quercy villages or even Cahors and the Lot valley where the prehistoric grotto of Pech-Merle and the hillside village of St.

Cirque-Lapopie are within easy reach. Evening meals 95f. All drinks *compris*. Rooms 310f. Worth every franc!

NEGREPELISSE. 82800

23 km ENE of Montauban. Another misleading postal address here; it is 1 km on the small, white road (D958) from Montricoux to Nègrepelisse which forks right off the D115 just outside Montricoux. A most enjoyable place to stay, just at the beginning of the Gorges d'Aveyron. There are numerous, small villages to visit such as Penne, where the perched ruined castle stands out on the horizon and a *Son et Lumière* is held on Wednesdays and Fridays. Visit the local markets at Caussade on Mondays, Nègrepelisse on Tuesdays and (very large) St. Antonin-Noble-Val on Sundays.

Les Brunis (M)
M. & Mme Antony. 63.67.24.08.

Not far from the N20 if you want a night stop; but I think you will want to stay longer.

An interesting, restored farmhouse now has four very different rooms in summertime and three from September to May. The two on the first floor are small. A family suite on the ground floor is very spacious with a huge fireplace. The 'summer only' room is up a small flight of steps and is an enormous

room with a palatial bathroom; if you land up in this room consider yourself privileged. All rooms have external access so you won't disturb anyone if you come in late. There is a pleasant garden complete with sunny swimming pool and terrace for summer meals. The very charming hosts dine with you whenever possible. Madame Antony speaks excellent English.

Evening meals are 90f with all drinks *compris*; or 120f if you want a gastronomic blowout. Rooms are 260f in high season, 220f out of season.

LANGUEDOC-ROUSSILLON

....

Départements: **Aude**   **Lozère**
                      Gard   **Pyrénées-Orientales**
                      Hérault

This is a very large region, with five departments and a coastline stretching from the Spanish border south of Perpignan almost to the Camargue at the mouth of the Rhône, about 175 km of seashore.

The name of the region signifies the north/south division of France in earlier times, and derives from the different words for 'Yes'. In the north the term 'Oui' was used, whereas in the south-west the term was 'Oc', hence *'langue d'Oc'* and this persists today in the Occitan language which is still spoken and understood by about ten million people. Towns throughout the area bear street names in both French and Occitan. When in this part of the world one should never forget the Catalan influence in the south of the region. Sovereignty passed from France to Spain and back again regularly for centuries, and although the southern part of the region is now firmly in France, most of the native inhabitants think of themselves as Catalan first and French second, and even as late as 1907 they have never neglected an opportunity to revolt or demonstrate against the northerners, especially Parisians.

The **Pyrénées Orientales**, as its departmental name implies, is the eastern end of the chain of mountains, which separate France and Spain, and which were the escape route for many of our servicemen during the Second World War. The Pic de Canigou (2,784 metres high) seems to dominate this end of the chain; it is almost an object of veneration locally. The first bonfires to celebrate the feast of St John the Baptist (Midsummer Day 24th June) are lit at the top, attended by notabilities from both sides of the frontier. Although the peak is covered in snow for most of the year, the flora and fauna are still magnificent on the lower slopes with gorges and pine forests, and as early as March the hillsides are yellow with mimosa.

The *Préfecture* of the department is at Perpignan. This department is

LANGUEDOC-ROUSSILLON

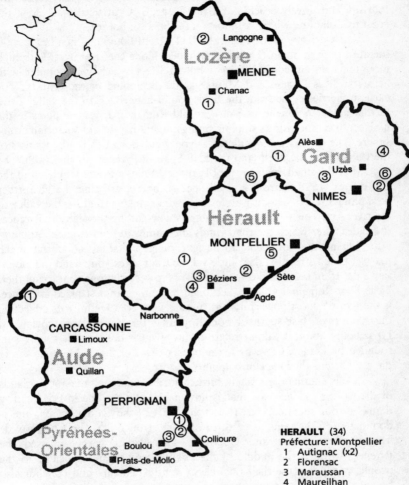

HERAULT (34)
Préfecture: Montpellier
1 Autignac (x2)
2 Florensac
3 Maraussan
4 Maureilhan
5 Saussan

LOZERE (48)
Préfecture: Mende
1 Chanac
2 Fontans

PYRENEES-ORIENTALES (66)
Préfecture: Perpignan
1 Alenya
2 Elne
3 Ortaffa

AUDE (11)
Préfecture: Carcassonne
1 Montmaur

GARD (30)
Préfecture: Nîmes
1 Anduze
2 Aramon
3 Collorgues
4 La Roque-sur-Cèze
5 Saint-Julien-de-la-Nef
6 Saze

■ Préfecture

■ Town

① Chambres d'Hôtes

mainly agricultural, with little heavy industry, and is a great centre for tourism, with lovely beaches at Canet-Plage, St Cyprien and all along the coast to Collioure, which is almost on the Spanish border.

Take a drive westerly along the D115 from Boulou, which lies just off the autoroute to Spain. The road meanders along the river Tech with high mountains on either side, turn uphill to Céret which was popular with artists such as Picasso and Matisse at the beginning of the century. The earliest cherries come from the fields round here. Back to the valley drive further along to Amélie-les-Bains, an old Roman spa, very popular in the nineteenth century for its sulphur springs. It still has an old Victorian atmosphere. The scenery is magnificent as you wind along this road, glimpses of the Canigou to the north and the high Spanish Pyrénées to the south. The road after the small, high town of Prats-de-Mollo-la-Preste winds up to the Col d'Ares (1610 metres), a small Spanish border crossing. To go further west along the Pyrénées, it is necessary to take the N116 along the valley of the river Tet. This is a wider, straighter valley cutting through the Pyrénées to Prades, after which the road winds and climbs to Font-Romeu. Stop and visit Villefranche-Confluent, an ancient village, allowing no traffic in the marble, paved streets. A dear little yellow train takes you round the mountain sides from here, used often by walkers to get from one spot to another. Near Font-Romeu at Odeillo, reckoned to be the sunniest place in France, is the world's most powerful solar furnace with concave mirrors collecting the sun's rays. Just south of Font-Romeu is the tiny Spanish enclave of Llivia, only about a kilometre from the Spanish border, but totally surrounded by France. Close by is the border town of Bourg-Madame where the road begins the long climb up into Andorra.

Aude is another department further north, containing the hot dry lands of the Corbières, the wine that is now a household name in this country thanks to our supermarkets. It was the heart of the Cathar region, and is dominated by the remains of three of their strongholds, the Châteaux de Termes, Peyrepertuse and Quéribus. The Cathar heresy crossed the Pyrénées towards the middle of the twelfth century and appealed to the people, partly because their own clergy were so corrupt and lazy but also because the Cathar preachers spoke to the people in *Occitan*, their native language. The Cathars believed that all material things were evil, only spiritual things were good, and although Jesus was good he was not divine. It was this latter point which led to their persecution and the crusade against them. They were also known as Albigensians as the first conflict with the Church took place in the diocese of Albi. The champion of the Cathars was Viscount Raymond VI of Toulouse, one of the Trenceval family, and the

Albigensian Crusade against them was perhaps as much a fight between the Kings of France and the Counts of Toulouse as a religious battle. The Crusade which lasted forty years was led, of course, by Simon de Montfort and ended when the last small group surrendered in 1229 at the Château de Quéribus. The Corbières lands eventually passed to Louis VIII.

Further west you will find the pretty little town of Limoux, whose inhabitants insist that the famous sparkling *Blanquette-de-Limoux* is not a copy of Champagne as it was first made here in the sixteenth century and so preceded Dom Pérignon.

Carcassonne in the north of Aude is the *Préfecture*, two separate towns really, with the old city a fairy-tale fort on top of a hill overlooking the new. There is a delightful legend that Carcassonne owes its name, to a foreign princess, Dame Carcas, who held the fortified city against the armies of Charlemagne. When the people had nothing left to eat but one solitary pig, she ordered the body of the pig to be thrown over the walls to show how well off for food they were. Charlemagne fell for the bluff, lifted the siege and retreated. However, history does not support this charming story as the *Cité*, one of the largest fortresses of Europe, was fortified by the Romans in the first century B.C. and given the name *Carcasso*. Situated as it is at a strategic crossroads, it was taken by the Visigoths, then the Saracens, who were chased out by the Trenceval family in the eighth century. This family also ruled over Albi, Nîmes and Béziers.

The old city of Carcassonne is well worth a full day's visit. There is adequate parking outside the walls. A good way to start is to take a trip round the outer walls in a horse-drawn coach, complete with commentary from the driver. Then wander round the fascinating old streets, visit the ancient cathedral, sit in one of the many, little shady squares and enjoy a cool drink and watch the world go by, and there's a lot of 'world' in Carcassonne in the summer! After this, a visit to the modern city hardly seems worthwhile.

37 km to the west along the N113 is the town of Castelnaudary, famous for its *cassoulet*, a pork and bean casserole, a wonderful dish on a cold day. Beware of feeling it is *obligatoire* if the weather is really hot; you might regret it.

l'Hérault to the north-east of the region is pure wine country, with no ordinary farmsteads, just vineyards. Names such as Minervois lead the way here. It is interesting that nearly all the chambres d'hôtes in this department are in the middle of small towns and not way out in the country as in other parts. This is because nearly all the agriculture is devoted to wine, and the *Viticulteurs* (vine growers) work out in the country; but as they do not own the land, they live in town. The only folk who live in the country are the large landowners, and, as yet, they are not interested in providing chambres d'hôtes facilities. The local *Faugères* wine 'Comte d'Altinhac' named after the landowner who founded the large vineyards near Autignac in 1050, is well worth trying.

The Canal du Midi is a feature of this department. Starting at Toulouse it runs for 240 km to the Bassin-de-Thau at Sète, passing through 64 locks and over 55 aqueducts. Thau is famous for its oysters. The town of Agde, founded by the Greeks and given the name of 'Agatha' is an impressive town; but the beaches near Cap d'Agde have become a boring conglomeration of characterless holiday flats and complexes, crowded in summer and deserted out of season.

Monpellier, the *Préfecture*, is a large industrial town, whose population was swollen some thirty years ago by the massive influx of repatriated French from Algeria, *les Pieds Noirs* as they are known.

l'Hérault is also well known to the pilgrims on their way to Compostella as the route starting from Arles passes through it from Saint-Guilhem-le-Desert to la Salvetat-sur-Agout, thence to the Pyrénées.

Yet further north is the department of **Gard**, rich in Roman history. The Arena at Nîmes, the *Préfecture*, is one of the best preserved in Europe. Nîmes was colonised in about 40 B.C., as it lay on the 'Via Domitia', the main route from Rome to Spain. 1480 km of road used by merchants and the Roman legions, so of course it was fortified along its length. The name derives from the Roman god 'Nemesus' (the god of rivers and fountains). Having been colonised and made a military fort and staging post, the city needed fresh drinking water. So an aqueduct 50 km long was built between Uzès and Nîmes during the first decade B.C. The most spectacular part of this aqueduct is at the *Pont du Gard* (25 km west of Avignon). Although it was built some 2000 years ago, the Pont has suffered little damage, and a thorough restoration programme is now in process. There is a 'Pay and Display' car park on both sides of the bridge, but entry is free, even though this is one of the third most popular tourist spots in France. The best view is from the right bank, and the best time to see the Pont is either early in the morning, or between 6 and 7 in the evening. In the 16th century Nîmes was a Protestant stronghold, having come under the influence of the Huguenots who came down from the Cévennes. It was consequently right in the centre of the religious wars which followed the revocation of the Edict of Nantes by Louis XIV in 1685. It could be said that 'denim' originated here as the material comes from the fabric *Serge-de-Nîmes*.

In the north-west of this region is the Grotte-des-Demoiselles, where a funicular train takes you into the mountain. Visit the curious Cirque-de-Navacelles, where the river winds so much that it leaves one bank high and dry, best seen from the hill top.

At the foot of the Cévennes we find Alès, a town which in its earlier days was again a stronghold of Protestantism. Further east do visit the hill village of La Roque-sur-Cèze. It doesn't feel it has changed much since Roman times and hopefully never will.

Further north in the region is the Lozère, a very different terrain with the sweeping, massive hills of the Cévennes covered with sheep in the summer and often snow in winter; it is a popular holiday region. Take a drive along the Corniche des Cévennes from St Jean-du-Gard to Florac. This is a real must and it will lead you to the famous Gorges du Tarn. You are now crossing the tracks of Robert Louis Stevenson in 'Travels with a Donkey'. The Gorges du Tarn is a deep ravine made by the river Tarn cutting its way through the steep cliffs on either side; it is 53 kms long and extends from Ispagnac in the north-east to Rozier in the south-west. The delightful little village of Sainte-Enimie is a very popular resort about half way along. Legend has it that a princess, suffering from leprosy, plunged into the fountain here and was cured. When she left the leprosy returned so she came back for a further cure and founded a convent. The fountain is still there near the twelfth century church.

The Gorges de la Jonte runs almost parallel with the Gorges du Tarn the other side of the Causse de Méjean, not quite as spectacular but less crowded. Do drive across these *causses* (high plateaux) especially the Causse Noir, reached from Meyrueis. It has a lot going for it, particularly in June when the wild flowers are all in bloom. It was not quite as barren on top as I expected; there were copses of small trees among the flowers and ample places to stop and picnic. Visit the *Chaos de Montpellier-le-Vieux*, a weird outcrop of rock formations which looks like a ruined village. You pay to go in and there is a little train which takes you round. Descend to the busy little town of Millau, centre of the glove trade. Because the male lambs produce no milk for the Roquefort cheese factory nearby, they finish up pretty smartly as kid gloves. That's enough to put you off buying any!

AUDE

MONTMAUR. 11320

42 km SE of Toulouse. 50 km NW of Carcassonne.

La Castagne (M)
M & Mme Martin. 68.60.00.40.

La Castagne

I was beginning to despair of ever finding a suitable chambres d'hôtes in the Aude. With lovely places to visit such as old Carcassonne, the historical Cathar châteaux and the wine of the Corbières to chase after, nothing seemed to suit, until I found Montmaur. From the small village, where the château cellars store the Corbières wine of Château-la-Toque, drive down towards the D43 and la Castagne is signed on your left. M & Mme Martin will welcome you in their beautifully restored farmhouse; part of it was once a guard-house for the Château. There is only one guest room, but others in the gîte if needed. The galleried landing looks down on a very comfortable lounge with a large fireplace where in complete luxury you may watch videos of the surrounding historic places, making your choice of what to visit much easier. A refreshing swimming pool is a big plus.

Madame Martin is a graduate in law and economics, who speaks fluent English, and runs weekly 'cordon bleu' courses, using her gîtes to accommodate her guests. Chambres d'hôtes guests may join the cookery lesson each afternoon, gratis, the results of which will be appearing on the menu each evening. Evening meal 100/120f, all drinks, from apèritif (Muscat de Rives Saltes) and wine and coffee are compris. Not just vin de pays here; the right wine for the right course! Room 270f.

If you care to take the week's course, Madame takes great care to arrange it to suit her guests. The daily routine is a morning of walking, swimming or visiting such historic sites as Albi with the Toulouse Lautrec museum and the cathedral, or Vieille-Carcassonne, churches and the Cathar châteaux, antiques or food markets, followed by lunch in a ferme auberge. Afternoons are taken up with cookery classes and everyone relaxes in the evening over a superb dinner. I take it that Madame makes sure no calamities reach the table!

A week of the course will set you back 7,000f, or 13,000f for two if you share a room, but all transport from picking up at Toulouse station or airport and ferme auberge lunches are included in the price.

GARD

ANDUZE. 30140

13 km SW of Alès. Anduze is known as the gateway to the Cévennes. The high *Corniche des Cévennes* is a well wooded road leading to Florac and the famous Gorges du Tarn.

On entering Anduze from St Ambroix there is a bridge over the river St Jean and just on the right of this is Mme Gobbo's large house.

Mme Gobbo (S-M)
Faubourg du Port. I. 66.61.77.05.

The house is beside the river, and has five rooms, two of which have a balcony overhanging the river. You'd pay a lot for this on the Thames. Breakfast is brought to your room and in summer it would be very pleasant eating it looking across the water to Anduze. The thumbs down bit is the noise of traffic on the bridge or past the other side of the house, and parking which is across the road in a small open lay-by. But if pushed for somewhere to stay for one night you could do a lot worse. Madame Gobbo is a capable lady, running a busy establishment. Rooms are 190f for two with 18f each extra for breakfast.

Take the Nîmes road out of Anduze 'Camping Veyrac' is signed up a small lane on your right. Going up the lane you will come to a stone house with a garage/office. Ring the 'Accueil' bell and charming Madame Tirfort will appear.

Quartier de Veyrac (M)
M. & Mme. Tirfort. 66.61.74.87.

A really rustic hideaway at the end of a track, two rooms are in a stone house shared with a gîte. So far away from the main house that Madame brings your breakfast but you make your own coffee or tea, everything provided in the neat little kitchen alcove in your room. Delightful rooms spacious and quiet in large wild grounds but unbelievably only 1 km from the centre of Anduze. For more elaborate self catering there is a full kitchen at the entrance and barbecue and tables in the garden. Rooms 250f.

Veyrac

ARAMON. 30390

11 km SW of Avignon. From the D2 Avignon to Aramon road turn right on to the D126 to Saze, in about 2 km fork left at sign to 'Le Rocher Pointu'. Coming from Avignon the D126 is just before the Pont de Barbentane over the Rhône. Aramon is a quaint old town almost on the banks of the Rhône, partly walled with tiny passageways and a rampart on one side.

'Le Rocher Pointu' (M)
M. & Mme Malek. Plan de Deve. 66.57.41.87; fax 66.57.01.77.

Le Rocher Pointu

If you are looking for a true old Provençale atmosphere the rooms in this huge house nestling under the Rocher Pointu are just the thing. Four cosy rooms, every one different, one with a mezzanine for one to two children. There are a few studios for two to four which are equally well furnished down to the last serviette. Rocky paths round the house and leading to the swimming pool are not for the handicapped. A high terrace extends past the pool with magnificent views to Mont Ventoux and all around. No picture does it justice. The pool is ready for use in March for the stalwarts. No shortage of plastic loungers here. A cosy covered sitting area beside the pool traps the sun; furnished with a fridge, it is an added asset. No evening meals but a nice little kitchen and barbecue for guests to cook their own meals faces a cosy terraced corner leading from a large, comfortable sitting room. The 'Trudaine', a restaurant/pizzeria as you enter Aramon, is recommended, only 3 km away. Rooms 330/380f.

COLLORGUES. 30190

25 km N of Nîmes. 10 km W of Uzès. A wee village on a hill, centrally situated for the old Roman sites of the Gard; not difficult to find the village off the D9. Climb the small hill in the centre, turn right by the fire hydrant to the *mairie*. The Place Plantane is just below and on the right a well-cared-for stone house with locked gates.

Mas du Plantane (M)
M. & Mme. Vieillot. Collorgues Saint-Chaptes. 66.81.29.04.

Don't look for any signs, there are none, this is a very discreet chambres d'hôtes. One independent room, carpeted, with entrance vestibule and terrace overlooking the pool, and pretty terraced garden is very pleasantly furnished; a second room in a separate building, not heated, is for July and August only. Peace and quiet assured, no children allowed. The car can be brought to the room for unloading but parked

in the small square below the
house. In such a tiny village with no
shops it is quite safe. Beautifully situated on the hillside, a charming
place and very pleasant hosts.
Evening meals offered with your
hosts at 100f all *compris* are not
obligatory, so this leaves you free to
visit M. Vieillot's son, who has a
charming restaurant in the nearby
village of Brignon, the *Jardin d'Eté*,
furnished in Provençale blue and

yellow with china to match. Menus from 75f/95f and à la carte. I feel the price of
320f for two people's bed and breakfast is merited here.

LA ROQUE-SUR-CEZE. 30200

31 km W of Orange. Right in the middle of the Côte-de-Viverais vineyards, just off
the D980, 12 km from Bagnols-sur-Cèze, is the charming hill village of La Roque-
sur-Cèze. Plenty to interest active antiquarians here, a veritable cluster of old houses
soaring to the skyline and no cars allowed past the first level, so you need to be fit! If
you do feel more adventuresome, Orange with its Roman theatre and lovely Arc De
Triomphe is 30 km away, and Avignon and the Pont du Gard are not much further.

La Tonelle (M)
M. & Mme Rigaud. 66.82.79.37. cl. 1/11 to Easter.

By the small carpark a tall old
house with a large garden has five
very smart bedrooms on the second
floor. All have natural stone walls
and beams, just the right mixture
of old and new. Rooms named
after flowers. I liked 'Camellia'
best. 240–280f.

It is a long climb up the stone
staircase with a black iron handrail
to the second floor, hardly worth it
for a night stop if you have a lot of
luggage, so stay a few days and enjoy the village and the company of M. & Mme
Rigaud and laze in their garden beside the swimming pool high up above the valley
and watch the grapes ripening in the fields right beside you.

There is a small kitchen for snacks in the garden and an adequate choice of
restaurants within walking distance.

SAINT-JULIEN-DE-LA-NEF. 30440

11 km SE of Le Vigan. 5 km N of Ganges. Turn at the large sign to Château d'Isis on the D999 between Ganges and Le Vigan and follow the signs along the river bank. A handy place to stay for visiting the Cirque de Navacelles just south of Le Vigan, a spectacular sight especially in spring when you are the only one looking down on to the tiny village in the basin of the surrounding hills.

Château d'Isis (M)
M. Roudier & Mme Villard. Rive Droite de l'Hérault.
67.73.56.22; fax 67.73.56.22

A peaceful setting on a wooded hill-side. First impressions were a bit shattering here as a very cross turkey and two drakes defended the rather untidy entrance to a large and many towered château, but a lot of restoration work explains it all and the two bedrooms and salon which have been redecorated are very pleasant and spacious, with tiled floors. One facing south has a modern corner bath, the other faces north with shower. 280f. There are also some gîtes in the grounds and the occupants often eat in the château, which now incorporates a *ferme auberge*. Forget the tatty approach and enjoy the rooms that are finished and the excellent evening meal at 85f (wine *compris*). Breakfast includes an unusual selection of jams – banana, fig, kiwi, orange, and honey and almonds.

SAZE. 30650

10 km W of Avignon. From Avignon take the N100 towards Pont du Gard. In about 8 km after the turn to Saze, there will be an ELF garage on your right; turn right and directly behind this garage is a lane up to La Calade which is on your right.

La Calade (M)
Mme Masquelier. 90.31.70.52.

Just off the Avignon-Nîmes road, La Calade is an ideal stop for visiting the Arena at Nîmes, the '*Palais des Papes*' at Avignon, the Pont du Gard, Les Baux, and the theatre and Arc de Triomphe at Orange.

Five well furnished rooms, three on the ground floor, open on to a terrace. Two other rooms are on the first floor. Large fridges in each room enable one to cater for cold drinks and light snacks. A plunge into the swimming pool in a dell behind the house is most refreshing after a hard day's sightseeing.

Mme Masquelier speaks good English, is an excellent cook with evening meals at 100f, wine *compris* representing good value. Rooms 320f perhaps a little pricy, but the meals and *accueil* are excellent.

HÉRAULT

AUTIGNAC. 34480

20 km N of Béziers. Take the D909 north from Béziers then turn off west on to the D16e.

Surrounded by vineyards, Autignac is quite a large village and has many useful shops, a few restaurants and a cafe, church and post office. At one time all the viticulteurs had *caves* under their houses, but now all the grapes go to a co-operative centre so the *caves* are all being made into gîtes etc. So much to see in the Hérault. It is flat round Montpellier in the east but rises slowly to the Cévennes mountains in the north-west. You have a choice of gorges, grottoes, and old villages to visit.

La Coquillade (M)
M & Mme Horter. 10 ave de Béziers. 67.90.26.79 or 67.90.24.05.

The Horter's house is named after the Pic de la Coquillade which can be seen from the village. Real *centre ville* chambres d'hôtes here. Looks nothing from outside, but enter through a small tunnel archway and you will be in a pleasant patio walled garden. Three rooms all well heated, prettily furnished and pine-cladded. Locked garage sometimes possible. A welcome cup of tea on arrival. We joined the

Horters and other guests in the *cave*, now a lounge/dining room, for *apéritifs* before dinner, which was excellent, wine *compris* for 85f. No one eats out here! Rooms 230f.

Breakfast whenever you like, orange juice, croissants and very fresh bread, the advantage of being in a village near a *boulangerie*.

FLORENSAC. 34510

16 km East of Béziers. A9. (Sortie 'Agde'). 10 km N of Cap d'Agde.

A quiet little town behind the purpose-built coastal resorts of this part of the Med. which are packed solid in summer and ghost towns in winter.

La Cruz-de-Clapié (M)
Mme Valentin. 21 Ave. de Pomerols. 67.77.91.54.

La Cruz de Clapié

What a delightfully cheerful person Mme Valentin is; just meeting her was a tonic. La Cruz de Clapié is a modern house set in a garden on the fringe of the village, with vineyards behind; but the large front lawn hidden from the road by the high wall is a real suntrap. Five comfortable rooms, all differently furnished, upstairs with independent entry, downstairs share a bathroom. Evening meal 75f wine *compris*. Rooms 200/215f.

MARAUSSAN. 34370

7 km NW of Béziers. On the D14 NW of Béziers.

M. & Mme Ramos (M)
90 rue de Crès. 67.90.00.56.

As chambres d'hôtes in Hérault are often in the centre of small towns, they don't have the attraction of a rustic French farmhouse, but they certainly make up for it by their internal decoration and this one is no exception. As soon as you step over the doormat you will be amazed at the immaculate condition of the house. Five charmingly decorated bedrooms are in a variety of colours for 190f. A dining room leads through glass doors to a delightful walled-in terrace where barbecued meals are served. It must have been a plain backyard before M. and Madame Ramos redesigned it. Madame's kitchen could rival one in the Ideal Homes Exhibition. I have not eaten here, but I am sure if her cooking is as exciting as her rooms you are in for a good time. Locked parking available. Evening meal 60f.

MAUREILHAN. 34370

9 km W of Béziers on the N112. Maureilhan is a small town just north of Béziers and on the fringe of the higher ground of the Hérault, surrounded by vineyards. Plenty of interesting places to visit, such as grottoes and hill villages.

'Les Arbousiers' (S)
Mme Marie-Andrée Fabre-Barthez. 7 rue Jean Jaurès. 67.90.52.49.

Four nicely furnished country rooms on the first floor which open on to one balcony. Again in a town house with quite a large courtyard and garden. Room for parking inside gates. Two other rooms across the courtyard, handy for wheelchairs but not so nice. Evening meal 75f, wine *compris*. Rooms 195/210f. Demi-Pension 350f for two.

Les Arbousiers

SAUSSAN. 34570

10 km SW of Montpeillier. Take the N113 from Montpellier to Fabrègues, then turn right on to the D27 to Saussan.

A small village not far from the Mediterranean beaches.

Mme. Gine (M)
6 Rue des Penitents. 67.47.81.01.

In the centre of the village just a door on the roadside leads into a most luxurious, spacious chambres d'hôtes. A large sitting room with patio doors opens into a walled garden. A superb modern kitchen is for self catering. There are four well-furnished rooms. Two are on the ground floor and a sweeping staircase leads to a landing with a billiard table and the two other rooms. 240f. Madame Gine is a charming hostess who lives next door and there is space for parking in her drive. Central heating makes this a good winter stop. A restaurant in the village.

LOZÈRE

CHANAC. 48230

14 km SW of Mende. As the Ardèche merges into the Lozère the volcanic hills disappear and the more rounded, less-wooded hills of the Cévennes are on the horizon. Lovely winding small roads leading off the D122, which is probably the highest road dividing the north from the south of the Ardèche, viewpoints everywhere. A delightful drive through St Eulalie will take you past flat fields of grass interspersed with the wild spring flowers of narcissi, tiny daffodils and violas; fields of dandelions make the biggest splash of colour, competing with the masses of wild broom, in spring. The young river Loire bubbles along beside you until the village of Rieutard when it turns north. Going south through the town of Langogne you will reach the lake and barrage of Naussac, a good holiday centre with picnic places on the lakeside. Take the N88 to Mende and you will be in the heart of the Lozère. It is the *Préfecture*, a busy town with a delightful semi-circular boulevard often cordoned off on Sundays for cycle races. The N88 goes south west to the famous Gorges du Tarn, a winding part of the R. Tarn which is an absolute 'must', but crowded in summer.

Chanac lies just off the N88; from the village follow the D32 and turn right at signs to Gazy.

Ferme Auberge Pradeilles (S)
Mme Pradeilles. Le Gazy. 66.48.21.91.

Hidden away in fields 2 km from the main road is the *ferme auberge* of the Pradeilles family. Here you will receive a warm charming welcome from Madame and her son who run the restaurant and the chambres d'hôtes. Probably the best budget stop you will find in the area judging by the number of cars here for Sunday lunch. A selection of five fairly basic rooms with showers but some shared toilets. 160f. Try great-grandma's matrimonial bed in the family room, now en suite. 220f. M. Pradeilles' grazing sheep produce milk for Roquefort cheeses. Once a

day from January to July a lorry rushes the milk to the large *fromagerie* in the caves at Roquefort. Chambres d'hôtes guests can have four courses for 55f or go for the top menu at 80f! Well worth using this as a base for visiting the Gorges du Tarn, only 25 km away.

FONTANS. 48700

36 km W of Mende. In the northern part of the Lozère, 3 km W of Fontans on the N106, turn at the Pont d'Estrets to the little village where there is a small well-cared-for church completely in natural stone with beautiful polished wooden pews. The altar frontal is a fairly new carved picture of the Last Supper. There are no shops in this village, everyone knows everyone else so you only have to ask the first person you meet where Madame Rousset lives.

➤ Les Estrets (S)
Mme Rousset. 66.31.27.74. cl. 1/11 to 28/2.

Madame Rousset has a superb couple of rooms on the ground floor, one double and one family with the car parked right outside the window, for 190f. Lovely bunches of fresh wild flowers in your room. She serves excellent five course meals for 55f, vin *compris* in the modern cosy dining room. Sit on the terrace in the setting sun or stroll round the tiny village before being called *à table*.

Les Estrets

I can't recommend this place too highly, all comforts with simplicity and great kindness shown by your hostess.

PYRÉNÉES ORIENTALES

ALENYA. 66200

10 km SE of Perpignan. A very pleasant route along the eastern Mediterranean is the coast road turning off the A9 or N9 near Caves on to the N627 to Leucate. The road takes you south, with the Mediterranean on your left and the calm waters of the Étang de Leucate on your right. At Port Leucate there is only a bridge dividing the two. Go on south, keeping to the coast past Perpignan to St Cyprien-Plage, a purpose-built holiday complex. Turn off here through Alenya, turn off again on to the D39 and the farm is on your right.

Domaine du Mas Bazan (S)
M & Mme Favier. 68.22.98.26; fax 68.22.97.37.

This is a large isolated farmhouse well off the road with simple rustic rooms on the first floor in surrounding grounds with a swimming pool. A huge salon on the first floor takes care of the children in wet weather. There is a *Ferme Auberge* dining room on the ground floor, where during the season evening meals are on offer for house guests only. Rooms with unpolished wood floors and natural stone walls all have pleasant views over flat terrain to the Pyrénées. Vineyards surround and M. Favier keeps pigs, ponies and chickens. The beach only ten minutes away is less commercial than further north. This would make a good holiday centre for a family.

Evening meals in high season, from 85f, wine, coffee *compris*. Rooms 250f.

ELNE. 66200

13 km SE of Perpignan. Elne was the ancient capital of Roussillon. Established as a bishopric in the sixth century, there is almost a Spanish atmosphere to the old town, now famous for the Cathedral of Ste Eulalie, consecrated in the eleventh century, and its cloister, which dates from the twelfth. There is a good market in Elne on Monday, Wednesday and Friday, where you can buy fresh figs as well as peaches and other local fruit.

Leave Elne by the D612 to Bages. The farm is on your right.

Mas de la Couloumine (S)
Mme. Tubert. Route de Bages. 68.22.36.07/

Swimming pool in the middle of a kiwi grove! M & Mme. Tubert have tastefully renovated an old house. Well insulated, it is warm in winter and cool in summer. There are six rooms to choose from, including a family suite. Some have views to the Pic du Canigou. M. Tubert grows his own salads all winter and Madame produces generous evening meals for her guests, preceded by aperitifs in the lounge for 65f vin *compris*.

Well worth staying a week in summer and handy for the beach or exploring the Pyrénées, or even taking a trip into Spain. So book early for the Mas de la Couloumine. Coffee *bols* for breakfast and kiwi fruits creep into all the jams.

Rooms 180f. You can have a third bed in the room for 40f extra including breakfast.

ORTAFFA. 66560

14 km S of Perpignan. Take the N114 south from Perpignan to Elne, then the D40 to Ortaffa, drive through the village bearing right up hill to the railway crossing, but turn right just before the railway and immediately left on to an estate of houses and you will see the sign on your left leading to the Mas de Gênets d'Or standing well back from the road.

Mas-des-Gênets-d'Or (M)
Mme. Chollat-Namy. 68.22.17.60.

Dr and Mme. Chollat-Namy's home, in a large garden with a swimming pool, is a delightful place for a week's holiday in this very warm part of France, near Mediterranean beaches and the Pyrénées. There are six large homely rooms, some with shared toilets, a little over-priced at 240f.

Guests congregate in the bar for aperitifs (6f each) creating an excellent house party atmosphere for the evening meal. Super food for 95f with plentiful wine. Facilities for washing and ironing and use of fridge. Breakfast, in the garden in summer, is a little bit like the Mad Hatter's tea party, coffee and hot milk on the table in large thermos flasks, piles of plates etc. plentiful jam and bread, and everyone fends for themselves, home from home!

PROVENCE

....

The accompanying guides are: French Entrée 10 – The South of France and
French Entrée 13 – Provence

Situated in the south-east corner of France, rich in history, it now has six
departments covering an area of about 32,000 square kilometres with a
population of four and a quarter million. The story of Provence stretches
back to 600 BC when the Greeks from Phocis, a state just north of Corinth,
landed and founded the trading post of 'Massilia', now Marseille. Thence
they spread along the coast and inland and their influence still shows in such
famous place-names as Nice (Nike – the Goddess of Victory) and Antibes
(Antipolis – the city opposite Nike). In 500 BC the Celts pinned the Greeks to
the coastline; but when they invaded Massilia in 121 BC the Romans came to
the rescue, chased the Celts back to the Isère, and took over the whole area
making it a Roman province. Hence the name from the Latin 'Provincia'.
Julius Caesar was governor of this province in 59 BC before he set out on his
conquest of the rest of Gaul. The modern autoroutes A8 and A9 follow the
route of the old main Roman roads, the *Via Aurelia* and the *Via Domitia*,
from Italy through Nice, Fréjus, Aix and Arles then onwards to Narbonne
and Spain. After the decline and collapse of the Roman Empire in the fourth
century the history of the region was turbulent to say the least. First there
was the conflict between the Franks, the Burgundians and the Visigoths,
with the Franks gaining the ascendancy in the end. It was a kingdom in its
own right in the 9th century, became part of France in 1481, then came
under the domination of the Italian kingdoms, and was eventually ceded to
France by Sardinia in 1860.

To most people it means the holiday resorts along the coast from
Menton to Marseille, or perhaps inland, the Vaucluse where Parisians buy
their second homes, as do quite a few British. In summer people tend to stay
close to the coast forgetting there is far more to the region; temperatures are

PROVENCE

■ Préfecture

■ Town

① Chambres d'Hôtes

ALPES-de-HAUTE-PROVENCE (04)
Préfecture: Digne-les-Bains
1 Entrevaux
2 Seyne-les-Alpes

HAUTES-ALPES (05)
Préfecture: Gap
1 Ancelle
2 Montmaur
3 Venterol

ALPES-MARITIMES (06)
Préfecture: Nice
1 Berre-les-Alpes
2 Cabris
3 Courmes
4 Gillette

BOUCHES-du-RHONE (13)
Préfecture: Marseille
1 Eygalières

VAR (83)
Préfecture: Toulon
1 Bagnoles-en-Forêt
2 Bauduen
3 Ginasservis
4 Solliès-Pont
5 Varages
6 Vidauban

VAUCLUSE (84)
Préfecture: Avignon
1 Ansouis
2 Les Beaumettes
3 Bonnieux and Buoux
4 Cabrières
5 Cairanne
6 Camaret-sur-Aigues
7 Caumont-sur-Durance
8 Entrechaux (x2)
9 Fontaine-de-Vaucluse
10 Gargas
11 Orange
12 Saignon
13 Saint-Roman-de-Malegarde
14 Saumane-de-Vaucluse (x2)
15 Seguret
16 Le Thor (x2)
17 Vacqueyras
18 Venasque

hot then but mild in winter except when the *Mistral* blows, the cold dry northerly wind which is funnelled down the Rhône valley from the Alps. It can be very fierce and sudden, lasting for hours and sometimes days.

In the north the **Hautes-Alpes** extend to Savoie, and the Italian border in the east. The *Préfecture* is Gap, a small town on the Route Napoléon N85. The enormous Parc de National Des Ecrins takes up a good part of this mountainous area, where Briançon is the highest town in Europe. Few major roads running north south, just the N94 along the valley of the river Durance, which thirty years ago was made into a very pretty lake by building an enormous dam; it is now a popular holiday resort and a delightful drive right round the lake (100 km) passing the rock formations of the *Demoiselles Coiffées*.

South-east the **Alpes-de-Haute-Provence** department is sandwiched between the Vaucluse and the Alpes Maritimes, with a small Italian border in the east. The *Préfecture* of Digne-les-Bains lies in the west of the department also on the Route Napoléon, due of course to the mountainous terrain. Roads again skirt where they can, avoiding the mountains, and running along river valleys.

The area has steep rocky mountains with narrow gorges leading to the **Alpes-Maritimes**. Menton, right against the Italian border, is still an elegant old town where many Edwardians spent their holidays and where the Russians were wise enough to buy property at the time of their Revolution; their descendants live there to this day. The stark Alpes Maritimes protect the town from the north, as they do all the towns along this coast. From Nice to Menton is one of the most famous corniches in the world, often portrayed in films with glimpses of the blue sea below. At one time there were just three roads. On the coast the *Basse Corniche*, hugging the sea, passing all the lovely, small resorts like Villefranche running into Monte-Carlo. Up above was the *Moyenne Corniche* which was a faster road skirting the towns but just as winding, passing by Èze, the tiny perched village which I think has the best views of all these villages, and above that the *Grande Corniche*, the top road on which it was safe enough to tow a caravan and which has extensive views out to sea or looking down on the coast. It is on this road that the old Roman remains of the Trophée des Alpes at La Turbie stands out white on the skyline, built in the 6th century BC to commemorate the final reduction of the 44 tribes in the area to obedience to Rome, linking Italy with Gaul and Germany. Wonderful panorama from the surrounding gardens overlooking Monaco. All these three roads meet at Cap Martin.

Now time has moved on and there is a vast motorway all the way from Nice to Italy, easier by far but lacking the excitement and the views of the three corniches. Nice, the *Préfecture*, is right on the coast with the *Prome-*

nade des Anglais overlooking the stony beach. Away from the coast the old town is still very interesting and the port is just round a corner where the ferries leave for Corsica. The major airport for this corner of France is right here on the front. Back in the mountains behind there are ski resorts in winter above St Martin-Vésubie.

Follow the coast along to Antibes where the busy covered market, the old town and large port full of pleasure craft will take a whole day to explore. Continue to Cannes where the beaches are sandy and the hinterland more flat, sweeping up to the hills again at Grasse a town on the hill perched under the mountains, for centuries the centre of scent manufacture.

All this coast is jam-packed in the summer holidays, the beaches strewn with people packed like sardines in a tin of Ambre Solaire. But venture up into the hills and you will find peace and quiet and delightful hidden villages like Courmes near the waterfall in the Valley du Loup, which I once found tourist-free in August. Higher up winding roads, Cipières and Gréolières north of Grasse are well worth the drive. Vence and St Paul de Vence are a bit too popular but you will regret not visiting them. Go further in that direction to St Jeannet.

Napoleon landed at Golfe-Juan and marched up through France along the Route Napoléon (N85) through Grasse and St Vallier-de-Thiery, a pleasant little town where in August they have an enormous *brocante* fair. Close by is the village of Cabris, perched on a hill which is littered with villas. The grottoes of St Cézaire are just above, where stalactites and stalagmites are deep underground.

In the west, the department of **Var** occupies a coastal position and stretches back into the hills as far as the Gorge du Verdon. Toulon is the *Préfecture* down on the coast, the largest naval port in France. Near the coast is the Massif Des Maures, another hilly area keeping the north winds away from the beaches; it stretches from Toulon to Fréjus where it is continued by the Massif de L'Esterel which protrudes into the sea making many lovely coves. Even the road ceases to be along the coast here. This is one of the most attractive and expensive parts of the Riviera where the rich have their villas, and the hills are covered with mimosa in the spring. Beaches for camping are good from Ste Maxime to Port Grimaud, which is a custom-built little port in the old style, fascinating to walk round where the little houses and flatlets all have a mooring and are nearly all holiday homes. Walk round the narrow streets and waterways, sit at cafés and watch the occupants messing about in small boats. Worth visiting but I had the feeling I was on a film set. Gassin is a delightful little hill village. There is a good food market at Cogolin, the town where pipes of all descriptions are made.

St Tropez needs no introduction; most people have heard of it if not been there to see the crowded port with luxury yachts stacked against the quay. Mutual entertainment for the boat people and those on shore watching each other down their *apéritifs* as the sun sets. Pretty deserted in winter though. Better beaches by far west of St Tropez along the coast to Le Lavandou, then more built-up round Toulon, but more attractive rocky coves from there west at La Ciotat and Cassis, which are in the Bouches du Rhône just round the corner from Marseille. Further north the Var is more penetrable than the eastern departments. More roads straddle the plains leading to the Lac de Ste Croix, a large man-made lake at one end of the Gorge du Verdon. It is now a holiday centre with numerous campsites beside the beaches. Nice outlook from the little village of St Croix up on the hill. The Gorge de Verdon is a massive canyon made by the River Verdon cutting a winding course through the limestone rock. The Gorge is 21 km long and varies in depth from 250 to 700 metres. It stretches from Aiguines to Rougon, with good roads on both sides. This fantastic sight has viewing points (*belvédères*) at the best parts. Paths for experienced walkers along the bottom of the canyon. All this hinterland is a popular area for expensive gîtes.

The most westerly department of **Bouches-du-Rhône** boasts the great Mediterranean port of Marseille as its *Préfecture* on the coast. The flat, salt marshy lands of the Camargues lie west of Marseille, cut by the delta of the Rhône, where the white horses roam and the flamingoes add their brilliance to the wildlife of the many lagoons.

Aix-en-Provence, north of Marseille, is a university town, probably best known for the Cours Mirabeau, a central boulevard, lined with trees and wide pavements. Restaurants, cafés on the sunny side, on the other impressive facaded *hôtels*. Cézanne lived and painted here. His studio is open to the public for guided tours; times vary, but it is closed on Tuesdays and public holidays. St-Sauveur cathedral has a famous triptych of the Burning Bush (viewing mornings and afternoons except on Tuesdays and Sundays). Spend a day or so in Aix; it is well worth it.

The **Vaucluse** geographically is a selection of mountain ranges which run from East to West interspersed with valleys and plateaux, the most northerly being the Baronnies. South of them is Mont Ventoux, the highest peak (1909 metres), where there is an observatory, covered in snow in the winter. The *Dentelles* limestone peaks at the end of the Ventoux range look higher than they are, so bare and sharp are the toothlike peaks. The Lubéron is the most southerly range in the department, a great favourite with climbers.

Avignon, the *Préfecture*, on the River Rhône is firmly tucked away in the north-west of the department. The Popes made their home there in the

14th century when lawlessness broke out in Rome. Their old palace is still there open to the public. Of course, don't forget to dance under the St Bénézet bridge which has been only half a bridge since the flooding of the Rhône washed part away in the 17th century. The dancing was never Sur le Pont d'Avignon, but on an island underneath.

The slopes of the mountains are covered with vineyards and many well known names crop up like Côtes du Ventoux, Valréas and Gigondas which all come from these hills. In the plains the perfume of the large lavender fields wafts through the air on a warm day.

There are many old Roman towns in the department. Orange with its amphitheatre and glorious Arc-de-Triomphe dating back to 6 BC simply mustn't be missed. The numerous hill villages such as Gordes, Bonnieux and La Coste are all east of Cavaillon where the largest fruit market in France is held from spring onwards.

The majority of chambres d'hôtes in this region are in the Vaucluse, with just a sprinkling in the other Departments.

ALPES-DE-HAUTE-PROVENCE

ENTREVAUX. 04320

76 km E of Digne. 6 km E of Entrevaux. The N202 is a left turn off the Route Napoléon at Barrême and continues east snaking up and down *cols*, cutting through ravines and diving through tunnels until Entrevaux where the valley widens, fruit fields line the route and the river Var flows alongside. At Plan du Puget, 1 km before Puget-Théniers, a track leads off right to La Siberie, well signed.

La Siberie (S)
Mme Gaydon. Plan du Puget. 93.05.06.91.

The tall, oblong farmhouse can be seen from the main road. Reno-vations are still going on but currently five bright well-fitted rooms for two or four people share a salon and kitchen area. No evening meals, but easy self-catering or the village of Puget close by with a choice of restaurants. The young Gaydons have a dairy farm and run a convalescent home for horses. A charming welcome,

La Siberie

a quiet spot to stay, swings for children. Rooms at 194f make this a good budget stop.

SEYNE-LES-ALPES. 04140

42 km N of Digne. Just over the border in this part of Alpes-de-Haute-Provence the scenery is much the same as the Hautes-Alpes – wide valleys with high, snow-capped mountains and a main road running through the centre of the valley.

From the D900 2 km before Seyne turn off right to Bas Chardavon and follow signs to Ferme des Clots.

Ferme des Clots (S)
Mlles De Dea-Cicorelli. 92.35.23.13.

At the end of a bumpy track between fields, on the side of a mountain this restored farmhouse is beside a stream. Lydia and Michele welcome guests to their sunny home where absolute peace is assured overlooking the valley. Rooms are for families sharing shower and toilet on two floors and one separate room *en suite* in summer only (no heating). A very nice position here. Evening meal 80f. Rooms 190/300f.

ALPES-MARITIMES

BERRE-LES-ALPES. 06390

21 km N of Nice. Take the autoroute from Nice to Menton and come off at exit 55 (La Trinité), then the D2204 to Sospel, dreary and industrial at first, then turn left on to the D215 to Berre-les-Alpes. The U bend turns eventually bring you to the clock in the centre of the village. If you think you have climbed to the top you have more in store, for Super Berre is even higher but flattens out into quite a wide residential area. A right fork by the clock will take you past the cemetery and over sleeping policemen to the villa on the right.

Villa Benoît (M)
M. & Mme Legras. Super Berre.
93.91.81.07 or 93.91.84.30; fax 93.91.85.47

An interesting village with two hotels and various shops. Magnificent views from beside the post office.

Once a recording studio (Super Bear), used by the Beatles and other groups, the house was burnt out in 1986, bought and rebuilt by the Legras. The garden is still under reconstruction but the swimming pool is intact. A very large villa with three pleasant rooms, Lavender for two people, Rose for three and Chestnuts for three. The walls of the salon/dining room are covered with exhibits from local artists changed every two months. The chambres d'hôtes guests can be *en pension* (270f each) or *demi-pension* (210f each) but Madame is extremely elastic about meals, Monsieur does the cooking and you can order full meals at 80f or snacks each evening. Accommodating and friendly hosts. Rooms 300f.

CABRIS. 06530

9 km W of Grasse. The village with the most panoramic views in the area, close to the St Cézaire caves and not far from the Route Napoléon at St Vallier de Thiey. From the D2562 from Grasse to Draguignan climb up the D11 north to Cabris.

Mme Faraut (M)
14 rue de l'Agachon. 93.60.52.36 or 93.77.24.49.

Right in the centre of the village in a narrow street this plain house has four well-furnished rooms with good private facilities, but two have their loos on the corridor. Three rooms have glorious views, one with a large balcony. A second-floor salon has equally delightful views stretching to the Med. No evening meal but a variety of restaurants within 50 yds, an interesting little village for strolling round. The only snag is that parking is in the municipal car park 100 yds away. For those who prefer the amenities and choice of restaurants, Cabris is ideal, but you have to forego private parking. No smoking in the rooms. Rooms from 270f (no view) to 290f or 300f for balcony.

COURMES. 06620

23 km NE of Grasse. Turn off at Pré-du-Lac east of Grasse and follow the road to Pont-du-Loup and just after the bridge fork back left on the D6. Follow this road past the cascade which has a viewing bridge and is part of the river Loup. Turn right at signpost Courmes, a narrow road for 4 km. Go through the village nestling against a hill (you'll be lucky if you see a soul) and turn right down a private road to the stone-built farmhouse home of the Baracco's, on a wooded hillside where they grow vegetables.

M. & Mme. Baracco (M)
93.09.65.85.

Six very pleasant new rooms on the ground floor, all with baths, three for two; three family rooms with double bed and bunks. Plenty of freedom for children. An isolated place with mountain walks from the door. Not far from Grasse or Gourdon. Madame does her shopping up at Cipières, a village well worth visiting with a château and a couple of restaurants and the ever necessary *boulangerie*. Evening meals from 75f. Wine 35f a bottle. Rooms 250/290f according to season.

GILLETTE. 06380

24 km NW of Nice. 4 km from the N202. The N202 emerges from a lengthy tunnel and runs beside the river Var and the railway to Nice with ever increasing industrialisation on either side, a latter part dual carriageway. From the N202 turn west at the Pont Charles-Albert and climb 4 km of bends to Gillette, a delightful perched village overlooking the Var valley. A unique archway crosses the road and steps ascend either side to another road and the church which has a magnificent ornate marble reredos. The most important date in the village calendar is the *Fête-Dieu* (Corpus Christi), when candles are lit and placed on the walls of all the houses in the village. There are panoramic views from the square. One km before the village fork left at a sign to Quartier St-Pierre.

Ferme Equestre Saint-Pierre (M)
Mme Le Fraper du Hellen. Quartier Saint-Pierre. 93.08.53.32.

If you survive the bends of the rough track down the hillside you will eventually arrive at a very pleasant chalet house where not only are there twenty horses and a gîte d'étape but three very well furnished chambres d'hôtes rooms with a large salon and a kitchen opening on to a sunny terrace. Not at all abashed to find us waiting for her unexpectedly when returning from a day out, Madame offered us a meal with the family and gave us a room at once, even lighting a fire in the apartment. Situated on the hillside with the Alpes Maritimes bearing down from all sides, this is a very quiet peaceful spot for a holiday even if you don't join in with the riding activities (though beginners are welcome). English spoken; Monsieur is American. Evening meal 80f, wine *compris*. Rooms 206f, including the use of the kitchen; extremely reasonable for the area.

BOUCHES-DU-RHÔNE

EYGALIÈRES. 13810

12 km E of St Rémy-de-Provence. Facing the Alpilles mountains this is a truly delightful place for a summer holiday, within walking distance of the village of Eygalières, and not far from the historic hill village of Les Baux-de-Provence. Van Gogh spent some time in hospital in St Rémy.

Drive through the village and turn off to the right for the Avenue des Molassis and the Barbier's house is on your left.

M. & Mme Barbier (M)
Avenue des Molassis. 90.95.98.13.

Now retired, M. & Mme Barbier share their lovely new home with guests. Three rooms on the ground floor have patio doors to their own patch of terrace overlooking an inviting swimming pool and large garden. No evening meals, but a good choice of restaurants and cafés in the village. Book well ahead here; such a superb position on the fringe of the Camargue and not far from Avignon or Aix-en-Provence makes this a very popular chambres d'hôtes all the summer. Rooms are 230f for two and 300f for three.

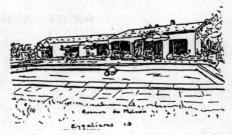

HAUTES-ALPES

ANCELLE. 05260

17 km NE of Gap. A small road off the Route Napoléon leads you up the Col de Manse, with breath-taking views of the snow-capped mountains, and brings you out on a wide plateau where there are small ski resorts with snow from 15 Dec to 1 Mar.

From Gap take the N85 north for 3 km, right on to the D944 for 6.5 km, right again on to the D13 signposted Ancelle.

Les Auches (M)
Mme Meizel. 92.50.82.39.

Drive through the village past small apartment blocks, hotels and the little church and on the left you will find the modern chalet of the Meizel's. Three colourfully furnished rooms on the first floor have independent entry up outside stairs to a sitting-room and corner kitchen. One room is for three people; two have balconies. Swings for children in the open garden. No evening meal, but plenty of restau-

rants in the village or picnic in the kitchen. Rooms 250f are good value.

MONTMAUR. 05400

26 km NE of Serres. 23 km W of Gap. From the D994 between Serres and Gap turn off on the D32.

In the centre of the village the Château of Montmaur overlooks a valley in the Hautes-Alpes. From the 14th century it has passed through many families; it was even once let to an Englishman who ran it as a vegetarian pension, with noted guests such as the King and Queen of Belgium. In 1942 Antoine Mauduit led a Resistance Group 'La Chaine' from a room in the château; it remains as a memorial to them. François Mitterand, then a junior civil servant, was connected with this group, and there is a photograph of him with the leaders taken in December 1942. As President of France he unveiled a commemorative plaque at the castle in 1988. The huge salons with enormous fireplaces and frescoes on the walls dating from the 15th century, are now used for various receptions and concerts.

Château de Montmaur (M-L)
M. & Mme Laurens. 92.58.11.42.

The present owners receive guests in the oldest part of the castle where five small rooms are richly furnished in red velvet. Virtually all are suites for three or four people, and guests are free to roam at will, perhaps even to encounter the resident ghost of Balthazar de Flotte-de-Montauban. Full of history it is a château well worth visiting. Rooms 400f.

VENTEROL. 05130

20 km S of Gap. Just east of the Route Napoléon the high valleys are most attractive surrounded by snow-capped peaks; some like Céüse have ski pistés. Close by the Lac de Serre-Ponçon has been formed by damming the powerful river Durance; there are extensive views as you drive round the lake which is well supplied with picnic sites.

From Gap take the D900B, turn left at the junction of the D942, continue for 3 km towards Barcellonnette, then fork right on the tiny D311 (signposted Venterol and Piégut and easily missed). Over a narrow bridge turn right to Venterol through the hamlet of Tournaires and keep on the Venterol road winding uphill for 8 km until you arrive in the tiny hamlet of Le Blanchet; chambres d'hôtes signed on the right.

➤ ## Le Meridienne (M)

M. & Mme Boyer. Le Blanchet. 92.54.18.51.

Panoramic mountain-top views from this chambres d'hôtes which was once an *auberge*. Lively Madame Boyer will give you an excellent welcome. She has five delightful, beamed rooms with all comforts, especially good lighting, and mezzanines for a third person in four of them. A comfortable lounge/dining room with log fire makes a winter stop a pleasure here. Mountain walks from the door, vast open garden, swings for children and delicious evening meals are well worth the climb up the hill and you will want to stay much more than one night. A very friendly place for a lone traveller. A little departing gift of lavender, honey and soap arrives on the breakfast table by courtesy of the local Chamber of Commerce.

If you want to be in the mountains, well away from towns, this is the place. Ask for a room with a valley view. Early booking is essential here in summer. Evening meal 80f. Demi-pension if you stay a week or more at 350f for two. Arrowed for excellent value. Rooms 200f.

VAR

BAGNOLS-EN-FÔRET. 83600

17 km N of Fréjus. 14 km S of Fayence. In the heart of shrubby countryside north of Fréjus this small town is the only spot of commerce. 4 km north on the D4 turn at a sign to Valoube, easy to miss. Follow the small road for nearly 1 km then turn left again and Mme Orsat is signed on the left.

Villa 'Ma Provençale' (S)

Mme Orsat. Quartier de Valoube. 98.40.63.71.

Your elderly hostess has a very pleasant house and garden with a swimming pool; just one well furnished small room facing north has all amenities including a fridge and TV. Very quiet and peaceful here, no evening meal but restaurants 4 km away at Bagnols. Excellent safe parking. Room 225f.

BAUDUEN. 83630

16 km N of Aups. At the South end of Lac-de-Sainte-Croix.

Domaine de Majastre (M)
M. Phillipe de Santis. 94.70.05.12.

So pleased with her visit here a
friend sent me the following:

*'Having driven along the
Lac-de-Sainte-Croix, we came to
the Domaine de Majastre, drove
through a small wood and emerged
before the Mansion, an 18th century
building which once belonged to the
secretary to the last kings of France.*

*'The entrance hall is large, and
alight with flowers and paintings,
and a wide staircase leads to the
bedrooms. Ours was spacious and had a bathroom en suit. Walking through the
gardens, you will come upon aviaries full of exotic birds and a very large pond full
of heartily croaking frogs!*

*'The morning room, where we breakfasted, overlooks the garden and is airy
and full of sunlight.*

*'As an evening meal is not offered, we made our way to Aups (ten minutes
down the road), a little, old town full of restaurants and charming people, all of
whom seemed intent on stopping us for a chat! Both the Domaine and Aups I shall
remember and revisit, and the whole area is ideal for those who wish to do some
horse-riding, indulge in nautical sports on the Lac-de-Sainte-Croix or simply walk
in the stunning surroundings of the Gorges de Verdon.'* M.A.

The addition of a swimming pool makes this chambres d'hôtes even more
enticing. Six rooms – 300f for two people.

GINASSERVIS. 83560

23 km SE of Manosque. 10 km NE of Rians. A farm situated in the middle of culti-
vated fields in the Var, not far from the Gorges-de-Verdon and the Lac de Saint-Croix.
Easy to find, take the D23 out of Rians in the direction of Ginasservis, then the D30 in
the direction of La Verdière. The house is on the left in 3 km just past the silos.

Domaine Espagne (M)
Mme Grech. 94.80.11.03.

A string of stone-built, typical Provençale rooms all on the ground floor are
half gîtes, half chambres d'hôtes, with parking close by. They open on to a shady

terrace with rattan armchairs overlooking a lawn surrounding by fir
trees. Baths in all rooms and electric
heaters, but not really soundproof.
A useful night stop on the way to
the Côte d'Azur. Robust evening
meals 90f, wine *compris*. Rooms
270f.

SOLLIES-PONT. 83210

15 km NE of Toulon. In a very useful position not far from the coast between
Toulon and Hyères. Coming south on the N97 branch left just before the village.

Domaine de Fontvive (M)
Mme Gandin-Chaix. Quartier-sous-les-Andues. 94.28.91.39.
I have not seen these rooms, but the house stands in large grounds near the
autoroute, and has a lot going for it, including a swimming pool. Evening meals 80f
and rooms 250f.

VIDAUBAN. 83550

17 km S of Draguignan. 27 km W of Fréjus. On the N7 traffic thunders through the
narrow one-way streets of this rather dreary town so you would hardly expect to
find one of the most promising chambres d'hôtes. 600m W of Vidauban on the
right in vineyards lying back from the N7.

➤ Le Clos Rival (M)
M. & Mme Rival. 137 Ave. Wilson. 94.73.00.32.
Quite unexpectedly we turned up at Le Clos Rival when looking for another place.
The old wall near the house was once part of a *chaix* (wine storehouse), now hiding
the water tank for irrigating the vines. The coast near St Tropez is only 35 km
south. Mme Rival's mother met us and showed us over this spacious mansion, now
being restored along with the surrounding vineyards, and we liked it so much we
abandoned our search and stayed, with the promise of an evening meal with the
family. The young Rivals have modernised five large, high-ceilinged rooms on the
first floor, losing none of their character. Sunshine pours in through the two tall
windows in each room and pretty fabrics match the bed linen. Double glazing in the
front rooms ensures no noise, though the house is well back from the main road.
Three rooms have private bathrooms, two others at the end of the corridor share a

huge bathroom, suitable for a family. Plentiful towels and even writing paper are in the rooms. There is a large lounge and dining-room downstairs and an equally large shared kitchen on the first floor, with an adjoining terrace for meals. Evening meals are on request only, but self-catering would be a pleasure in this sunny kitchen and eating out on the terrace overlooking the vineyards and the river behind, would be a peaceful end to a hot summer's day.

Le Clos Riond

Superb hospitality from this charming young family and a house, built about 1890 and still full of character, made this an unexpectedly pleasant stop. Breakfast – apricot juice, orange and fig jam and the local paper on the table. Evening meals 90f. Rooms 200/250f.

VAUCLUSE

ANSOUIS. 84240

8 km NW of Pertuis. A charming, old, but well-kept village sitting on the side of a hill only a short distance from Pertuis. An interesting castle on top has been in the Sabran family since 1160, and although they still live there it is open to the public. The last Sunday in September is the special feast day of St Eléazar and his wife Ste Delphine; it is unusual for a married coupled to be canonised and even more interesting that they were members of the Sabran family.

Le Jardin d'Ansouis (M)
Mme Rogers. Rue du Petit Portail. 90.09.89.27.

'Arlette Rogers is a charming and vivacious hostess who works long hours to ensure that her guests lack for nothing. She speaks excellent English. The two rooms are very large, with private bathrooms, one not adjoining. Both look out on to the flower-filled garden and patio where breakfast is served in summer.' P. King.

Le Jardin d'Ansouis

Dinner available on reservation in winter only; 175f includes four courses, *apéritif* and wine. Rooms 290f for two.

APT. 84400

40 km W of Manosque. 55 km N of Aix-en-Provence. Apt is a busy town on the N100, central for many of the surrounding hill villages and chambres d'hôtes. A large market is held here on Saturdays when all the villagers bring in their wares of fruit and vegetables; the production of crystallised fruit is a speciality. There is no by-pass so it is always a slow process driving through the town. Formerly a Roman colony, Apt has been a prosperous city and bishopric since the third century. The first shrine in France dedicated to Saint Anne, grandmother of Jesus, is here. Her relics, miraculously found by Charlemagne in 776, are preserved in the cathedral, scene of a traditional pilgrimage on the last Sunday in July. The present building (*Ancienne cathédrale Sainte-Anne*) was built in the eleventh century. Many fairs, especially during July and August, including antiques.

An interesting procession takes place in time of drought, when a statue of St Maur is carried through the town; if he doesn't bring rain quickly he is dunked in the fountain of St Martin and left there until the next shower.

From the centre of Apt take the Bd Nationale and past the *mairie* turn right on to the Ave des Druids, then first right (opposite the Judo Club) into the rue des Bassins where you will find signs to:

Les Mylanettes (M)
Mme Heuzard-la-Couture. Par la rue des Bassins. 90.74.67.15.

'This is a really fine example of a chambres d'hôtes. Madame is an excellent hostess, who speaks some English as she has spent time in England as an 'au pair'. There are five well fitted rooms, a large living-room, and spectacular views from the terrace, and a separate fridge available for guests. Fresh orange juice for breakfast which is often served on the terrace. No evening meals but several restaurants within reasonable reach.' Trevor and Pat Roberts.

Rooms 250f. (10% reductions after three nights).

LES BEAUMETTES. 84220

14 km E of Cavaillon. It should be called Les Baumettes and probably was at one time because the name derives from 'baumo' (grottoes). Earlier inhabitants lived in the numerous grottoes around while the N100 which goes through Les Beaumettes was once the Domitian Way, one of the great Roman roads. Festival – First Sunday in October – local fête.

Le Ralenti du Lierre (M)
Mme Marthe Deneits. Le Village. 90.72.39.22. cl. 1/11 to 1/4.

Au Ralenti du Lierre
Les Beaumettes

In the village, Madame Deneit's friendly chambres d'hôtes has a pool on the terrace, a large lounge, a living-room with a fireplace and a separate dining room.

All five rooms are furnished differently. Three of them have a private bathroom and toilet, one has a mezzanine, private bath and toilet, and the fifth has toilet and washbasin, but no bath or shower. No evening meal, but a restaurant opposite. Rooms 300–500f.

BONNIEUX. 84480

47 km SE of Avignon. 12 km SW of Apt. Not an isolated hill village, but one very much in the thick of things as it is en route to many places. Lovely views over the Lubéron from the main street which wanders through from east to west, then descends down a winding hill to the lower part where the road branches off to La Coste in one direction or Apt in the other.

Les Eydins (L)
M. & Mme Kozlowski. Route Pont Julien. 90.75.84.99. cl. 1/11 to Easter.

'This beautifully restored old Provençal farmhouse 2 km from Bonnieux on the road towards Pont Julien, the old Roman bridge, makes a welcome addition to the chambres d'hôtes accommodation in the region. Jan and Shirley have three double rooms, all with private toilet and bath. There is a common room near the pool with telephone, barbecue and kitchen and private parking. The property is extensive and there are magnificent views over the neighbouring olive groves and vineyards. A garden and a patio provide ample space for rest and relaxation while breakfast may be enjoyed on the terrace or in the vaulted dining-room. Rooms are 420f with breakfast included and Polish Jan and English Shirley will make you really feel at home.' P. King.

BUOUX. 84480

8 km S of Apt. Buoux was better known for its ancient history, from cave dwellers to medieval château and fort, until Peter Mayle discovered the *Auberge de la Loube* in his book 'A Year in Provence'; but I wonder how many know of Madame Gallardo's gîte d'étape and chambres d'hôtes which is right next door to the restaurant. Leave Apt by the D113, at the crossroads with the D232 go straight on and you will be in the tiny village of Buoux; on the left almost opposite the *mairie* you will find a chambres d'hôtes and gîte d'étape.

La Sparagoule (S)
M. & Mme Gallardo. Quartier de la Loube. 90.74.47.82.

The gîte d'étape is very popular with climbers; but not in the hot summer months, so visit in August and you will have a choice of rooms. Four very simple rooms for four or two, with a glorious view of the Lubéron, especially at night with a full moon. Plenty of shared showers and toilets and a very modern kitchen/sitting/dining room also shared with the Youth Hostellers. You can cater for yourself, but Madame will provide a very good evening meal with a litre bottle of wine for 70f. Or splash out and eat next door at the now famous restaurant. Safe parking in the grounds. Rooms 200f.

CABRIÈRES-D'AVIGNON. 84220

25 km E of Avignon. From the N100 at Coustellet take the D2 (direction Gordes) and turn left on to the D148.

The plague which originated in Marseille in 1720 swept through Provence with catastrophic effects. As nothing was known of the cause of the infection the authorities decided to keep out all strangers by building a wall round their village. Remnants of this wall can still be seen.

A good place to stay for visiting many of the historical and interesting villages in this area west of Apt. Bonnieux, La Coste and most renowned of all, the hill village of Gordes, where artists flocked in the 1930s. Partially destroyed by the Germans in the last war, it has been rebuilt. Now a Mecca for artisans with their shops in the hilly, narrow streets. The château dominates the village, where in the square coachloads of tourists arrive constantly; the most prevalent accent is American. On a hot day take refuge in the simple cool church. Nearby is the small village of *bories*, old circular stone huts looking like giant beehives; once lived in by shepherds, now restored – a great attraction. The tourist trade has driven prices sky high so you will be glad to find a resting place in the small village of Cabrières-d'Avignon, just down the hill.

Madame Truc (M)
90.76.97.03; fax 90.76.74.67.

Cabrières D'Avignon   Cours Jean Giono

'The village has a highly recommended chambres d'hôtes in a large house about 100 metres from the village itself. It has a private pool and a terrace. There is a nice balcony and a large lounge. There are five rooms on the first floor; 200–280f is good value in this region.' P. King.

No evening meal, restaurant in the village.

CAIRANNE. 84290

15 km NE of Orange.

Domaine le Plaisir (S)
Mme Pierrefeu. 90.30.82.04.

Domaine le Plaisir

'Cairanne is very much a wine-growing village keeping a low profile, but the excellent Côtes du Rhône it produces is well worth trying, heavier than Beaujolais but lighter than claret. Not a lot to attract in the village but one chambres d'hôtes at the Domaine le Plaisir is handy for visiting Orange. A pleasant quiet garden and five delightful, simple rooms in which Charlotte Pierrefeu takes great pride. Two rooms have toilet and a shower, two have bidet and bath, one has a toilet and bidet. Anyone should be able to make a choice from all these especially as the prices are 120–150f for two people including breakfast. A meal is 60f, also simple, but satisfying local fare. Demi-pension at 150f per person is another option worth considering.' P. King.

CAUMONT-SUR-DURANCE. 84510

8 km NW of Cavaillon. 6 km E of Avignon. In the heart of the village is a most unusual structure known as *La Lanterne des Morts* (the Lantern of the Dead). It is a tall chimney nearly 50 feet high and has a circular top with eight small windows in it. In earlier days the lamp inside would be lit whenever a person of note died, or when there was a threat of plague. A good pizzeria/restaurant on the main road going through the village.

M. Bernard Lefèbvre (S)
Chemin des Terre de Magues. 90.23.07.49.

Just outside in a villa on a hillside in a heavily wooded area, M. Lefèbvre has only one room on the first floor, but accessible from the garden. 180f. Another room with kitchen on the ground floor 250f. Extra bed 60f.

ENTRECHAUX. 84340

6 km SE of Vaison les Romaines. Leave Vaison-la-Romaine by the D938 by-pass. Take the first left, D75, to St Marcellin then bear right (signpost Entrechaux) and you will pass the Auberge d'Anais on your left; L'Escleriade is also on your left a few hundred metres further on.

You are spoilt for places of interest in this part of the Vaucluse. Two routes round Mont Ventoux, one taking you over the top by the observatory. There are *dégustations* all the way, especially near Bedoin, and Roman theatre remains at Vaison La Romaine and just outside, opposite the hill village of Entrechaux, two good places to stay.

Ferme Auberge d'Anais (M)
Mme Blanc. 90.36.20.06.

Although this nicely situated farmhouse is no longer a real chambres d'hôtes, it still has some of the same ambience. Mme Blanc has concentrated on the food and now runs a flourishing restaurant with rooms.

Three spacious *en suite* bedrooms on the first floor facing south with views of the Ventoux, (there are now three others which I haven't seen). A very smart pool and surrounding terraces level with the rooms, an ideal place to spend a lazy afternoon reclining on the loungers, enjoying the view and building up an appetite for Mme Blanc's evening meal. With demi-pension rates still so reasonable at 440f for two, wine and coffee *compris*, it would be a pity not to include this place. Mme Blanc is a very kind and thoughtful hostess, and a stay here is most relaxing and enjoyable.

Just along the road:

L'Escleriade (M)
M. & Mme Gallo. Route de St. Marcellin. 90.46.01.32.

Separate tables rather curtail the comradeship of this one. Madame cooks expertly while Monsieur Gallo serves at table in a very professional manner; but they find time to chat to their guests over coffee.

The modern rooms are quite superb, with choice of bath or shower, walk-in wardrobes, private patios, every convenience. It would be difficult to find a chambres d'hôtes in a nicer position, on the side of the hill, southerly views over Mont Ventoux and a swimming pool nestling below the terrace. All quite perfect, designed by M. Gallo, who is Italian; Madame is French.

Just one niggle, plastic packets of butter and jam for breakfast! Evening meal 90f. Rooms 280/330f.

FONTAINE-DE-VAUCLUSE. 84800

30 km E of Avignon. 21 km S of Carpentras. 33 km W of Apt. This village is a must when visiting the Vaucluse. It is here that a fountain of water the source of the river Sorgue, bursts through the limestone rock, and rushes down the rocky gorge. At the actual spot, surrounded by high cliffs, is a deceptively calm green pool. Quite a surprise – I was expecting a *jet d'eau* in spring. No one really knows the exact source of all this water in spite of repeated attempts to trace it with

remote-controlled mini-submarines. Certainly the water dominates the little village and many cafés have their tables right beside the fast moving stream. It attracts a million visitors a year and parking can be difficult in summer. Take the Chemin de la Fontaine from the Place de la Colonne and it is about fifteen minutes walk. The column is in memory of the 14th century poet Petrarch who lived in Fontaine-de-Vaucluse.

2 km W of Fontaine near the junction of the D24 and the D57 is the home of:

Bois Court (M)
Mme Douyere. 90.20.31.93.

This house on the edge of the village has a large shady garden, and three pleasantly furnished rooms on the first floor, of which two have balconies. A rather formal welcome, and as there is no evening meal one is left very much to one's own devices. A wide choice of restaurants in the village. Rooms 250f.

Bois Court

GARGAS. 84400

2 km N of Apt.

Les Devens Longs (S)
Mme Hélène Guigou. 90.04.73.57.

'Just off the N100 north of Apt makes this a very useful and economic chambres d'hôtes. The advantage is that there is only one room so you will be sure to be pampered. It is a very large room though with private bath and toilet and the price is a modest 210/230f for two people. There is a pool and Mme Guigou will cook you a dinner for 80f per person.' P. King.

Li Gineste

ORANGE. 84100

29 km N of Avignon. Market day in Orange on Wednesdays and plenty of room to park. Do visit the old Roman theatre right in the centre of the town, the best preserved in existence, and don't fail to drive to the edge of the town to the lovely *Arc-de-Triomphe*; easy to park near it. Considering it was built in 6 BC it is in very good condition.

La Barque aux Romarins (M)
M. Claude Monnier. Route de Roquemaure. Quartier Bois Feuillet.
90.34.55.96

If you prefer to be out of town or are looking for inexpensive accommodation, M. Monnier's chambres d'hôtes could be just the thing. There are six very small rooms and it's only about 5 km south of Orange on the road to Roquemaure. Unenclosed land surrounds it and there is a large living-room.

There is now a *ferme auberge* with simple farmhouse menus at 65f each. Rooms 180f.

SAIGNON. 84400

5 km SE of Apt.

La Pyramide (M-L)
Madame Hélène Guillaume. Quartier du Jas. 90.74.46.86.

'Hélène Guillaume is a Provençale herself and she believes in life, peace and serenity. Her approach is a holistic one and if you have any problems, she will be very happy to have you talk them out with her. There's a service you don't get at a Hilton!

Quartier du Jas La Pyramide

'Her four chambres d'hôtes are modern in a Provençal style, with a large common area for breakfast. The pool is new and there are panoramic views.' P. King. Rooms 360f.

SAINT ROMAN-DE-MALEGARDE. 84290

16 km NW of Vaison-la-Romaine. From Tulette take the D7 (Signposted St Roman); at the second crossroads you will find the chambres d'hôtes on the left.

There are many old Roman towns in the vicinity and any number of *dégustations* to visit where you can buy the local wines after a tasting session.

Le Colombier (S)
M. Arnaud. 90.28.92.21. cl. 1/10 to Easter.

A good place to stay if you want to buy wine. In the middle of vineyards at the foot of the hill village this sturdy looking, square house belongs to a *vigneron* (Domaine de la Fauconnière). Four good-sized, plain rooms on the first floor, reached by an outside staircase, have modern amenities, but are not heated. You will certainly be offered the house wine here. With prices like this you won't be disappointed. Evening meal 60f. Rooms 180f; only 200f for three; useful for a family.

SAUMANE-DE-VAUCLUSE. 84800

12 km S of Carpentras. The fortress castle in this village was bought by the uncle of the wicked Marquis de Sade in the 18th century. It is now open to the public. The chambres d'hôtes here make a good attractive budget stop for visiting the Fontaine de Vaucluse.

M. Robert Beaumet (S)
Chemin de la Tapy. 90.20.32.97.

The old stone Provençal house on a hill has a view of the village, approached by a narrow track on the side of a hill. There are three rooms, a large living-room and a fully equipped little kitchen. No evening meals, but a restaurant in the village, *Lou Clapes*, has good views and seems reasonable with menus from 69/130f. Rooms at the chambres d'hôtes are 190f.

SEGURET. 84110

9 km SW of Vaison-la-Romaine.

Domaine Saint Just (M)
Mme Jacqueline Montjean. 90.46.11.55. cl. 16/9 to 31/3.

'*A village backing on to the Dentelles mountains in the heart of the wine-growing valley near Gigondas. Much has been done to improve the village without spoiling it and it is now a most attractive place to visit. An equally attractive chambres d'hôtes offers you five rooms in an old stone building on the second floor, having fine views. A caring hostess ensures you enjoy your visit. No evening meal.*' P. King. Rooms 230f.

LE THOR. 84250

14 km W of Fontaine-de-Vaucluse. 16 km E of Avignon. A small town between Avignon and L'Isle-sur-la-Sorgue, so called because a bull once unearthed a statue of the Blessed Virgin Mary on the banks of the river Sorgue. A grotto found in the hillside here with stalagmites and stalactites is now open to the public.

Eleuthera (M)
Mme de Mazieux. Route de Saint-Saturnin. 90.33.70.26.

Drive under the arch in the centre of town, right by the church, over the bridge, and follow signs to St Saturnin at the roundabout. Eleuthera is on the left sideways on to the road about 2 km from the roundabout. Ignore other chambres d'hôtes signs. Mme de Mazieux has three comfortable rooms on the first floor; one with a bathroom and separate toilet on the landing, others *en suite* with showers, 210f.

All rooms overlooking the garden. Good parking, gates locked at night. A peaceful choice for Avignon. Madame de Mazieux, a widow, is a keen gardener but finds time to chat to her guests and she produces wholesome evening meals on reservation at 65f, wine *compris*. Should you wish to eat out, the Quatre Saisons in le Thor, a local favourite, with meals from 65f and pichets of wine from 10f is very good value. Or you could try the ever popular logis Le Pescador at la Partage des Eaux on the outskirts of L'Isle-sur-la-Sorgue, menus 75/170f.

VACQUEYRAS. 84190

12 km N of Carpentras.

Domaine l'Oustau des Lecques (M)
M. Claude Chabran. 90.65.85.51. cl. 1/11 to 28/2.

'This is another chambres d'hôtes that gives real value for money and provides a pleasing alternative to hotel accommodation. The five rooms all have TV. The setting in a domaine surrounded by vineyards and just on the edge of the village is hard to beat, with kitchen, washing machine and fridge for guests. Evening meal 100f. Rooms 210/ 240f. Demi-pension 250f each.'
P. King.

Domaine l'Oustau des Lecques

VENASQUE. 84210

12 km SE of Carpentras. 32 km N of Cavaillon. Venasque is a perched village, rare in the Vaucluse, which is well preserved but has lost none of its interesting origins. Bishops from Carpentras used to move here in time of trouble in the fifth to tenth centuries. A delightful village to wander round and if you feel like a bit of luxury stay at La Maison aux Volets Bleus.

La Maison Aux Volets Bleus (M)
M. & Mme Maret. Place des Bouviers. le Village. 90.66.03.04; fax 90.66.16.14. cl. 12/11 to 14/3.

'It is a very rare occasion when it is possible to recommend a chambres d'hôtes as being in the same quality and value category as a 700f a night hotel, but this is the case with the aptly named Maison aux Volets Bleus. La Maison is right in the heart of the old town and was once just another house. It has been transformed by Martine Maret and her husband and now Martine runs it with efficiency, style and careful

attention to her guests' needs. There are six rooms and all are different and beautifully furnished. All have TV and bathrooms. Evening meals at 8 p.m. are 120f each and well worth it. The produce and the cooking are Provençal. Lamb and trout are two of the carefully prepared and extremely tasty specialities of the region. Martine speaks English. Parking is not immediate but

La Maison aux Volets Bleus

there are several spots in the village only a couple of minutes away.' P. King. Rooms 300/370f.

Wines and spirits by John Doxat

AN INTRODUCTION TO FRENCH WINES

Bonne cuisine et bons vins, c'est le paradis sur terre. (Good cooking and good wines, that is earthly paradise.)

King Henri IV

French food positively invites accompaniment by wine, albeit only a couple of glasses because one is driving on after lunch. At dinner one can usually be self-indulgent. Then wine becomes more than a sensory pleasure: with some rich regional meals it is almost imperative digestively. Civilised drinking of wine inhibits the speedy eating that is the cause of much Anglo-Saxon dyspepsia.

The most basic French wine generically is *vin ordinaire*, and very ordinary indeed it can be. The term is seldom used nowadays: *vin de table* is a fancier description – simple blended wine of no particular provenance. *Vins de table* often come under brand-names, such as those of the ubiquitous Nicolas stores (Vieux Ceps, etc.) – and highly reliable they are. Only personal experience can lead you to your preference: in a take-away situation I would never buy the absolute cheapest just to save a franc or so.

Nearly every restaurant has its house wines. Many an owner, even of a chain of establishments, takes pride in those he has chosen to signify as *vins de la maison*, *vin du patron* or similar listing. In a wine-rich area, house wines (in carafe or bottle) are likely to be *vins de pays*, one step up from *vins de table*, since this label indicated that they come from a distinct certificated area and only that area, though they may be a blend (thus sometimes an improvement) of several wines.

Ever since they invented the useful, if frequently confusing, *Appellation d'Origine Contrôlée* (AC) the French have created qualitative sub-divisions. An AC wine, whose label will give you a good deal of information, will usually be costlier – but not necessarily better – than one that is a VDQS. To avoid excessive use of French, I translate that as 'designated (regional) wine of superior quality'. A newer, marginally lesser category is VQPRD: 'quality wine from a specified district'.

Hundreds of wines bear AC descriptions: you require knowledge and/or a wine guide to find your way around. The intention of the AC laws was to protect consumers and ensure wine was not falsely labelled – and also to prevent over-production, without noticeable reduction of the 'EEC wine lake'. Only wines of reasonable standards should achieve AC status: new ones are being regularly admitted to the list, and the hand of politics as much as the expertise of the taster can be suspected in some instances. Thus AC covers some unimportant wines as well as the rarest, vastly expensive vintages.

Advice? In wine regions, drink local wines. Do not hesitate to ask the opinion of patron or wine-waiter: they are not all venal, and most folk are flattered by being consulted. By all means refer to a vintage chart, when considering top class wines, but it cannot be an infallible guide: it has no bearing on blended wines.

Bordeaux

Divided into a score of districts, and sub-divided into very many *communes* (parishes). The big district names are Médoc, St. Emilion, Pomerol, Graves and Sauternes. Prices for the great reds (châteaux Pérus, Mouton-Rothschild, etc.) or the finest sweet whites (especially the miraculous Yquem) have become stratospheric. Yet château in itself means little and the classification of various rankings of châteaux is not easily understood. Some tiny vineyards are entitled to be called château, which has led to disputes about what have been dubbed 'phantom châteaux'. Visitors are advised, unless wine-wise, to stick to the simpler designations.

Bourgogne (Burgundy)

Topographically a large region, stretching from Chablis (on the east end of the Loire), noted for its steely dry whites, to Lyons. It is particularly associated with fairly powerful red wines and very dry whites, which tend to acidity except for the costlier styles. Almost to Bordeaux excesses, the prices for really top Burgundies have gone through the roof. For value, stick to simpler local wines.

Technically Burgundies, but often separately listed, are the Beaujolais wines. The young red Beaujolais (not necessarily the over-publicised *nouveau*) are delicious, mildly chilled. There are several rather neglected Beaujolais wines (Moulin-à-Vent, Morgon, St. Amour, for instance) that improve for several years: they represent good value as a rule. The Mâconnais and Chalonnais also produce sound Burgundies (red and white) that are usually priced within reason.

Rhône

Continuation south of Burgundy. The Rhône is particularly associated with very robust reds, notably Châteauneuf-du-Pape; also Tavel, to my mind the finest of all still *rosé* wines. Lirac *rosé* is nearly as good. Hermitage and Gigondas are names to respect for reds, whites and *rosés*. Rhône has well earned its modern reputation – no longer Burgundy's poorer brother. From the extreme south comes the newly 'smart' dessert *vin doux naturel*, ultra-sweet Muscat des Beaumes-de-Venise, once despised by British wine-drinkers. There are fashions in wine just like anything else.

Alsace

Producer of attractive, light white wines, mostly medium-dry, widely used as carafe wines in middle-range French restaurants. Alsace wines are not greatly appreciated overseas and thus remain comparatively inexpensive for their quality; they are well placed to compete with popular German varieties. Alsace wines are designated by grape – principally Sylvaner for lightest styles and, the widespread and reliable Riesling for a large part of the total, and Gerwürtztraminer for slightly fruitier wines.

Loire

Prolific producer of very reliable, if rarely great, white wines, notably Muscadet, Sancerre, Anjou (its *rosé* is famous), Vouvray (sparkling and semi-sparkling), and Saumur (particularly its 'champagne styles'). Touraine makes excellent whites and also reds of some distinction – Bourgueil and Chinon. It used to be widely believed – a rumour put out by rivals? – that Loire wines 'did not travel'; nonsense. They are a successful export.

Champagne

So important is Champagne that, alone of French wines, it carries no AC: its name is sufficient guarantee. (It shares this distinction with the brandies Cognac and Armagnac.) Vintage Champagnes from the *grandes marques* – a limited number of 'great brands' – tend to be as expensive in France as in Britain. You can find unknown brands of high quality (often off-shoots of *grandes marques*) at attractive prices, especially in the Champagne country itself. However, you need information to discover these, and there are true Champagnes for the home market that are *doux* (sweet) or *demi-sec* (medium sweet) that are pleasing to few non-French tastes. Champagne is very closely controlled as to region, quantities, grape types, and is made only by secondary fermentation in the bottle. From 1993, it is prohibited (under EEC law) to state that other wines are made by the 'champagne method' – even if they are.

Minor regions, very briefly

Jura – Virtually known outside France. Try local speciality wines such as *vin jaune* if in the region.

Jurançon – Remote area; sound, unimportant white wines, sweet styles being the better.

Cahors – Noted for its powerful *vin de pays* 'black wine', darkest red made.

Gaillac – Little known; once celebrated for dessert wines.

Savoy – Good enough table wines for local consumption. Best product of the region is delicious Chambéry vermouth: as an aperitif, do try the well distributed Chambéryzette, a unique vermouth with a hint of wild strawberries.

Bergerac – Attractive basic reds; also sweet Monbazillac, relished in France but not easily obtained outside: aged examples can be superb.

Provence – Large wine region of immense antiquity. Many and varied *vins de pays* of little distinction, usually on the sweet side, inexpensive and totally drinkable.

Midi – Stretches from Marseilles to the Spanish border. Outstandingly prolific contributor to the 'EEC wine lake' and producer of some 80 per cent of French *vins de table*, white and red. Sweet whites dominate, and there is major production of *vins doux naturels* (fortified sugary wines).

Corsica – Roughish wines of more antiquity than breeding, but by all means drink local reds – and try the wine-based aperitif Cap Corse – if visiting this remarkable island.

Paris – Yes, there is a vineyard – in Montmartre! Don't ask for a bottle: the tiny production is sold by auction, for charity, to rich collectors of curiosities.

HINTS ON SPIRITS

The great French spirit is brandy. Cognac, commercially the leader, must come from the closely controlled region of that name. Of various quality designations, the commonest is VSOP (very special old pale): it will be a cognac worth drinking neat. Remember, *champagne* in a cognac connotation has absolutely no connection with the wine. It is a topographical term, *grande champagne* being the most prestigious cognac area: *fine champagne* is a blend of brandy from the two top cognac sub-divisions.

Armagnac has become better known lately outside France, and rightly so. As a brandy it has a much longer history than cognac: some connoisseurs rate old armagnac (the quality designations are roughly similar) above cognac.

Be cautious of French brandy without a cognac or armagnac title, regardless of how many meaningless 'stars' the label carries or even the magic word 'Napoléon' (which has no legal significance).

Little appreciated in Britain is the splendid 'apple brandy', Calvados, mainly associated with Normandy but also made in Brittany and the Marne. The best is *Calvados du Pays d'Auge*. Do take well-aged Calvados, but avoid any suspiciously cheap.

Contrary to popular belief, true Calvados is not distilled from cider – but an inferior imitation is: French cider (*cidre*) is excellent.

Though most French proprietary aperitifs, like Dubonnet, are fairly low in alcohol, the extremely popular Pernod/Ricard *pastis*-style brands are highly spirituous. *Eau-de-vie* is the generic term for all spirits, but colloquially tends to refer to local, often rough, distillates. Exceptions are the better *alcohols blancs* (white spirits), which are not inexpensive, made from fresh fruits and not sweetened as *crèmes* are.

Liqueurs

Numerous travellers deem it worth allocating their allowance to bring back some of the famous French liqueurs (Bénédictine, Chartreuse, Cointreau, and so on) which are so costly in Britain. Compare 'duty free' prices with those in stores, which can vary markedly. There is a plethora of regional liqueurs, and numerous sickly *crèmes*, interesting to taste locally. The only *crème* generally meriting serious consideration as a liqueur is *crème de menthe* (preferably Cusenier), though the newish *crème de Grand Marnier* has been successful. *Crème de cassis* has a special function: see *Kir* in alphabetical list.

THE LOIRE THROUGH A WINEGLASS

The most peaceful holidays I have enjoyed in France have been spent ambling (if one can amble by car) through the tranquil Loire valley, just before or after the summer holidays. We always avoided the large towns and showed minimal interest in tourist attractions, staying at random in secluded and very comfortable country hotels, lingering over delicious meals, and quaffing much pleasing wine.

Ignoring the glamour of the fabulous châteaux – one can easily understand why they were built there – I find the great virtue of the Loire to be its understated beauty. This gentle, civilised unpretentiousness is reflected in the variety of its copious reservoir of wines. The Loire does not boast of vintage rarities about which connoisseurs rave, for which huge prices are paid, nor does it attract writers to pen those fancifully adjectival descriptions of numbing inconsequence to the generality of drinkers. It is for the wine-lover of modest experience, intelligent but not over-demanding, that the Loire offers many delights and, unlike some wine regions, it produces no utterly bad wines.

Let us briefly examine the most important.

Muscadet

This is not the most splendid Loire wine but it is the most widely known. It comes from the westerly Pays Nantais: the great city of Nantes is the regional capital. Yet until comparatively recently, Muscadet – a grape, not a place – was little drunk outside its own principal locality, Sèvre-et-Maine, which is now almost synonymous with Muscadet.

The Muscadet grape originated long ago as the 'Burgundy melon'. It made a wine renowned as a sauce base: it is still in minor cultivation in Burgundy for a handful of gourmets. Around two and a half centuries ago, the vine was planted in the Loire region and did well. It is only in the last thirty years, or less, that production has rocketed to meet demand.

Muscadet is unique amongst French wines in that, for reasons I do not know, it is the only one to have a legal maximum strength – a perfectly adequate 12.3°. Muscadet is best drunk young: if more than one vintage appears on a list, choose the most recent. All but the simplest Muscadet AC is now described – or most are – as *sur lie* (on the lees). This is not racked but is bottled from the cask after short fermentation. It is easy to appreciate the popularity of Muscadet. It is reasonably fruity, makes no demands on purse or palate. It is a perfect accompaniment to the fish in which the adjacent Atlantic remains rich.

An important town of the Muscadet area is St Fiacre-sur-Maine. I mention this only as an odd sacramental connection between drinking and driving: St Fiacre is the patron saint of cab-drivers.

Anjou

The wines of this historic region are of great antiquity. Charlemagne, first Holy Roman Emperor, owned vineyards here. Later, Anjou came under English rule. The prestige of Anjou wines was such that in 1194 they could bear a tax four times that applied to other wines imported into England. Notable French monarchs recorded a liking for Anjou's products: Louis XVI showed his appreciation by allowing the Layon river to be canalised to give Dutch vessels easier access to wine cargoes. Britain's Edward VII, a great wine-drinker, made a personal friend of his Loire vintner.

Simple Anjou Blanc, without further attribution, is an inexpensive all-purpose medium-dry wine. Anjou is particularly associated with *rosé*: Anjou *rosé* was famous before nearly every white wine producer started making this style. That said, there is nothing very exciting about Anjou *rosé*: reliable light beverage wine, highly suitable for summer.

It is with sweeter and dessert wines that Anjou really scores, and it is almost certainly these which attracted the high and mighty in times past. Our forebears did not share the modern vogue for 'dryness', or 'lightness'. They liked wines rich and strong. The best Anjou sweet wines rival all but the top Sauternes and are much less costly. They come from grapes affected by *pourriture noble* (noble rot), the curious fungus that appears to destroy over-ripe grapes: yet in practice it absorbs moisture, thus concentrating the sugar in the fruit. The *Chenin Blanc*, much grown in the Loire, is particularly susceptible to 'noble rot' which readily occurs by nature in Anjou, whereas elsewhere it may be necessary to introduce it. The affected Chenin makes fine sweet wine. Look out for Coteaux du Layon for good value, or Coteaux de L'Aubance. Costlier, but worth every franc, are more specifically named Quarts de Chaume and Bonnezeaux.

Saumur

This region is part of Anjou but has claims for separate treatment. It produces the best, though not widely distributed, Anjou reds, led by Saumur-Champigny, and amongst *premiers crus* (first growths) is Parnay: it was the Parnay proprietor who was the king's friend mentioned above. There is also an outstanding white Parnay. Abroad, Saumur is best known for its sparklers, made, for the time being, by the 'champagne method', and also semi-sparkling *pétillant* varieties. Inevitably, there are also *rosé* and *créme* sparklers. I reckon you will do best with a Saumur AC *Brut*.

Touraine

The vinous virtues of Touraine were hymned by Rabelais, Balzac and Dumas, amongst other writers. It lies in the heart of the long Loire valley and its centre is gracious Tours. This used to – still does? – enjoy the reputation of being the home of the purest spoken French: once it was almost obligatory for aspirant entrants to the Foreign Office to study there for a spell! Touraine produces sound, reliable whites from the Sauvignon grape, so a Touraine Sauvignon in itself guarantees a superior *vin de table*. It is Vouvray and Montlouis that are associated with the better whites. Touraine makes the most widely distributed reds of the Loire, notably Bourgeuil and Chinon. These can stand

considerable bottle-age. Touraine *rosé* wines are comparable to the
more celebrated Anjou *rosés*. Sparkling Vouvray, very lively, has a
considerable reputation.

Sancerre

Commercially, this district has some affinity to Muscadet. From an
ancient, not much regarded – even declining – wine area, Sancerre
has, in about a quarter-century, become not only popular but distinctly
fashionable. Prices have risen accordingly. The dominant Sauvignon
grape produces excellent, crisp whites. Look for 'Sancerre' with a
domaine designation for the better types, though you will find straight
Sancerre AC more than adequate; sometimes over-priced because of
the vogue the name enjoys. Reuilly and Quincy are place-names to
remember, plus the slightly lighter Menetou-Salon. Reuilly reds and
rosés deserve serious attention.

Pouilly

Likes to consider itself separate from Sancerre. Do not confuse its basic
Pouilly-sur-Loire with the much more special Pouilly-Fumé, a delicious,
dry, yellowish white. It must be stressed that Pouilly-Fumé has
absolutely no connection with Burgundy's Pouilly-Fuissé, a more acidic
wine. Pouilly-Fumé is usually drunk young, though it does gain with
some ageing.

A general merit of most Loire white wines is that they are as suitable
before a meal as during it.

> *If the alchemists of old had known your wines, they would
> have had no need to seek further for gold one can drink.*
> King Edward VII, to M. Crystal,
> owner of Clos-des-Murs, Parnay (Saumur)

Condensed glossary
of French wine and ancillary terminology

Abricotine – Generic apricot liqueur. Look for known brand-names.

Alcool blanc – Spirit distilled from fruit (not wine); not to be confused with fruit-flavoured cordials.

Aligoté – Burgundy wine (from grape of same name); light and dry.

Anis – Aniseed; much used in aperitifs of Pernod type.

Apéritif – Any drink taken as an appetiser (literally 'opener'). France has a huge range of proprietary aperitifs.

Appellation (d'Origine) Contrôlée – AC; see An Introduction to French Wines.

Armagnac – Superb brandy of the Gascon country, now achieving something of a rediscovery. See Hints on Spirits.

Barsac – Sweet Bordeaux wine (officially part of Sauternes); wide range from excellent to sickly boring.

Basserau – Sparkling red Burgundy; unusual if nothing else.

Beaune – Prestigious Burgundy name (red), the best very costly.

Blanc de Blancs – White wine from white grapes only. White wine is often made from black grapes, skins being removed before fermentation – as this is.

Blanc de Noirs – See immediately above: these are essentially type descriptions; some prestige accrues to *Blanc de Blancs*.

Bordeaux – See An Introduction to French Wines.

Bourgogne – Burgundy, see An Introduction to French Wines.

Brut – Very dry; particularly with good Champagne.

Cabernet – Noble grape, especially Cabernet-Sauvignon. Just its name on a label denotes a sound red wine.

Cacao – Cocoa; usually as *crème de cacao*.

Calvados – Apple brandy; see Hints on Spirits.

Cassis – Blackcurrant; *crème de cassis* widely favoured, notably in Kir (q.v.).

Cave – Cellar.

Cépage – Indication of grape variety; e.g. *cépage Sauvignon*.

Chai – Ground-level wine store, exclusively used in Cognac, frequently also in Bordeaux.

Champagne – See An Introduction to French Wines.

Clairet – Unimportant little-known Bordeaux wine, but probably origin of English word Claret (red Bordeaux).

Clos – Principally Burgundian word for vineyard enclosed, or formerly protected, by a wall.

Cognac – see Hints on Spirits.

Côte – Vineyard on a slope; no particular quality significance.

Coteau(x) – Hillside(s); much the same as *côte*.

Crème – Sweet, mildly alcoholic cordials of many flavours. Not rated as true liqueurs, but one exception is *crème de menthe* (mint). See also *cassis*.

Crémant – Sparkling wine, without lasting champagne-style effervescence.

Cru – Literally 'growth'. Somewhat complicated term. *Grand cru* only meaningful if allied to good name. *Grand cru classé* (officially classified great wine) covers greatest wines, but not all *cru classé* is *grand*.

Cuve close – Sealed vat; describes production of sparkling wine by bulk secondary fermentation as opposed to bottle fermentation of 'champagne method'.

Cuvée – Wine from one vat, unblended. Another confusing word; *cuvée spéciale* can have more than its literal meaning.

Demi-sec – Translates as 'medium dry'; in practice means sweet.

Domaine – Mainly Burgundian word; broadly equivalent to château.

Doux – Very sweet.

Eau-de-vie – Generic term for all distilled spirits.

Frappé – Drink served on finely crushed ice.

Glacé – Iced by immersion of bottle, or other refrigeration.

Goût – Taste. In some regions also describes rough local spirit.

Haut – 'High'; denotes upper part of wine district. Not necessarily a mark of quality, though Haut-Medoc produces notably better wines than its lower areas

Izarra – Ancient, Armagnac-based Basque liqueur.

Kir – Excellent, now very popular aperitif: very dry chilled white wine (properly *Bourgogne Aligoté*) with a teaspoon of *crème de cassis* (q.v.) added. Kir Royale employs champagne.

Liqueur – originally *liqueur de dessert*, denoting post-prandial digestive use. Always sweet, so to speak of a 'liqueur Cognac' is absurd.

Litre – 1.7 pints; 5 litres equals 1.1 gallons.

Méthode Champenoise – Wine made by the champagne method.

Marc – Usually roughish brandy distilled from wine residue, though a few *Marcs* (pronounced 'mar') – notably *Marc de Bourgogne* – have some status.

Marque – Brand or company name.

Mise – As in *mise en bouteilles au château* (bottled at the château) or . . . *dans nos caves* (in our own cellars), etc.

Moelleux – On the sweet side.

Mousseux – Semi-technical term for sparkling; applies to the greatest champagne and to artificially carbonated rubbish.

Nouveau – New wine, particularly Beaujolais; made for drinking within a few months of harvest.

Pastis – General description, once more specific, for strong anis/ liquorice-flavoured aperitifs originating in Marseilles; Ricard is a prime example.

Pétillant – Gently effervescent; sometimes translated as 'prickly' or 'crackling'.

Pineau – Unfermented grape juice fortified with grape spirit. Made in many regions: *Pineau des Charantes* (Cognac area) is best known. Well chilled, an attractive aperitif.

Porto – Port wine. The French are very big consumers, often using it (chilled) as an aperitif.

Primeur – Basically the same as *nouveau*. However, much fine

Bordeaux and Burgundy is sold *'en primeur'* for long maturing by buyer.

Rosé – 'Pink wine'. Made by leaving skins of black grapes briefly in contact with juice; also by addition of red wine to white.

Sauvignon – Splendid white grape.

Sec – 'Dry', but wines thus marked will be sweetish. *Extra sec* may actually mean what it says.

Sirop – Syrup; akin to non-alcoholic *crème*.

Vermout – Vermouth.

Vin de Xérès – 'Vin de 'ereth'; sherry.

Glossary of cooking terms and dishes

(It would take another book to list comprehensively French cooking terms and dishes, but here are the ones most likely to be encountered)

Aigre-doux	bittersweet
Aiguillette	thin slice (aiguille – needle)
Aile	wing
Aïoli	garlic mayonnaise
Allemande (à l')	German style, i.e. with sausages and sauerkraut
Amuses-gueule	appetisers
Anglaise (à l')	plain boiled. Crème Anglaise – egg and cream sauce
Andouille	large boiling sausage
Andouillettes	ditto but made from smaller intestines, usually served hot after grilling
Anis	aniseed
Argenteuil	with asparagus
Assiette Anglaise	plate of cold meats
Baba au Rhum	yeast-based sponge macerated in rum
Baguette	long thin loaf
Ballotine	boned, stuffed and rolled meat or poultry, usually cold
Béarnaise	sauce made from egg yolks, butter, tarragon, wine, shallots
Beurre blanc	sauce from Nantes, with butter, reduction of shallot-flavoured vinegar or wine
Béchamel	white sauce flavoured with infusion of herbs
Beignets	fritters
Bercy	sauce with white wine and shallots
Beurre noir	browned butter
Bigarade	with oranges
Billy By	mussel soup
Bisque	creamy shellfish soup
Blanquette	stew with thick white creamy sauce, usually veal
Boeuf à la mode	braised beef
Bombe	ice cream mould
Bonne femme	with root vegetables
Bordelais	Bordeaux-style, with red or white wine, marrow bone fat
Bouchée	mouthful, i.e. vol au vent
Boudin	sausage or black pudding
Bourride	thick fish soup

Braisé	braised
Brandade (de morue)	dried salt cod pounded into a mousse
Broche	spit
Brochette	skewer
Brouillade	stew, using oil
Brouillé	scrambled
Brulé	burnt, i.e. crème brulée
Campagne	country style
Cannelle	cinnamon
Carbonade	braised in beer
Cardinal	red-coloured sauce, i.e. with lobster or in pâtisserie with redcurrant
Cassolette or cassoulette	small pan
Cassoulet	rich stew with goose, pork and haricot beans
Cervelas	pork garlic sausage
Cervelles	brains
Chantilly	whipped sweetened cream
Charcuterie	cold pork-butcher's meats
Charlotte	mould, as dessert lined with sponge fingers, as savoury lined with vegetable
Chasseur	with mushrooms, shallots, wine
Chausson	pastry turnover
Chemise	covering, i.e. pastry
Chiffonade	thinly cut, i.e. lettuce
Choron	tomato Béarnaise
Choucroute	Alsatian stew with sauerkraut and sausages
Civet	stew
Clafoutis	batter desert, usually with cherries
Clamart	with peas
Cocotte	covered casserole
Compôte	cooked fruit
Concassé	i.e. tomatoes concassées – skinned, chopped, juice extracted
Confit	preserved
Confiture	jam
Consommé	clear soup
Coque (à la)	i.e. oeufs – boiled eggs
Cou	neck

Coulis	juice, purée (of vegetables or fruit)
Court-bouillon	aromatic liquor for cooking meat, fish, vegetables
Couscous	N. African dish with millet, chicken, vegetable variations
Crapaudine	involving fowl, particularly pigeon, trussed
Crécy	with carrots
Crême pâtissière	thick custard filling
Crêpe	pancake
Crépinette	little flat sausage, encased in caul
Croque Monsieur	toasted cheese and ham sandwich
Croustade	pastry or baked bread shell
Croûte	pastry crust
Croûton	cube of fried or toasted bread
Cru	raw
Crudités	raw vegetables
Demi-glâce	basic brown sauce
Doria	with cucumber
Emincé	thinly sliced
Entremets	sweets
Etuvé	stewed, i.e. vegetables in butter
Farci	stuffed
Fines herbes	parsley, thyme, bayleaf
Feuilleté	leaves of flaky pastry
Flamande	Flemish style, with beer
Flambé	flamed in spirit
Flamiche	flan
Florentine	with spinach
Flute	thinnest bread loaf
Foie gras	goose liver
Fond (d'artichaut)	heart (of artichoke)
Fondu	melted
Forestière	with mushrooms, bacon and potatoes
Four (au)	baked in the oven
Fourré	stuffed, usually sweets
Frais, fraiche	fresh and cool
Frangipane	almond crême pâtisserie
Fricadelle	Swedish meat ball
Fricandeau	veal, usually topside
Fricassée	(usually of veal) in creamy sauce
Frit	fried
Frites	chips
Friture	assorted small fish, fried in batter

Froid	cold
Fumé	smoked
Galatine	loaf-shaped chopped meat, fish or vegetable, set in natural jelly
Galette	Breton pancake, flat cake
Garbure	thick country soup
Garni	garnished, usually with vegetables
Gaufre	waffle
Gelée	aspic
Gésier	gizzard
Gibier	game
Gigôt	leg
Glacé	iced
Gougère	choux pastry, large base
Goujons	fried strips, usually of fish
Graine	seed
Gratin	baked dish of vegetables cooked in cream and eggs
Gratinée	browned under grill
Grêcque (à la)	cold vegetables served in oil
Grenouilles	frogs; cuisses de grenouill – frogs' legs
Grillé	grilled
Gros sel	coarse salt
Hachis	minced or chopped
Haricot	slow cooked stew
Hochepot	hotpot
Hollandaise	sauce with egg, butter, lemon
Hongroise	Hungarian, i.e. spiced with paprika
Hors d'oeuvres	assorted starters
Huile	oil
Île flottante	floating island – soft meringue on egg custard sauce
Indienne	Indian, i.e. with hot spices
Jambon	ham
Jardinière	from the garden, i.e. with vegetables
Jarret	shin, i.e. jarret de veau
Julienne	matchstick vegetables
Jus	natural juice
Lait	milk
Langue	tongue
Lard	bacon
Longe	loin
Macedoine	diced fruits or vegetables
Madeleine	small sponge cake

Magret	breast (of duck)
Maïs	sweetcorn
Maître d'hôtel	sauce with butter, lemon, parsley
Marchand de vin	sauce with red wine, shallot
Marengo	sauce with tomatoes, olive oil, white wine
Marinière	seamen's style, i.e. moules marinières (mussels in white wine)
Marmite	deep casserole
Matelote	fish stew, i.e. of eel
Médaillon	round slice
Mélange	mixture
Meunière	sauce with butter, lemon
Miel	honey
Mille feuille	flaky pastry, lit. 1,000 leaves
Mirepoix	cubed carrot, onion, etc. used for sauces
Moëlle	beef marrow
Mornay	cheese sauce
Mouclade	mussel stew
Mousseline	Hollandaise sauce, lightened with egg white
Moutarde	mustard
Nage (à la)	poached in flavoured liquor (fish)
Nature	plain
Navarin (d'agneau)	stew of lamb with spring vegetables
Noisette	nut-brown, burned butter
Noix de veau	nut of veal (leg)
Normande	Normandy style, with cream, apple, cider, Calvados
Nouilles	noodles
Os	bone
Paillettes	straws (of pastry)
Panaché	mixed
Panade	flour crust
Papillote (en)	cooked in paper case
Parmentier	with potatoes
Pâté	paste, of meat or fish
Pâte	pastry
Pâte brisée	rich short crust pastry
Pâtisserie	pastries
Paupiettes	paper-thin slice
Pavé	thick slice
Paysan	country style
Perigueux	with truffles
Persillade	chopped parsley and garlic topping
Petit pain	bread roll
Petits fours	tiny cakes, sweetmeats
Piperade	peppers, onions, tomatoes in scrambled egg

Poché	poached
Poëlé	fried
Poitrine	breast
Poivre	pepper
Pommade	paste
Potage	thick soup
Pot-au-four	broth with meat and vegetables
Potée	country soup with cabbage
Pralines	caramelised almonds
Primeurs	young veg
Printanièr(e)	garnished with early vegetables
Profiteroles	choux pastry balls
Provençale	with garlic, tomatoes, olive oil, peppers
Purée	mashed and sieved
Quenelle	pounded fish or meat, bound with egg, poached
Queue	tail
Quiche	pastry flan, i.e. quiche Lorraine – egg, bacon, cream
Râble	saddle, i.e. rable de lièvre
Ragoût	stew
Ramequin	little pot
Rapé	grated
Ratatouille	Provençale stew of onions, garlic, peppers, tomatoes
Ravigote	highly seasoned white sauce
Rémoulade	mayonnaise with gherkins, capers, herbs and shallot
Rillettes	potted shredded meat, usually fat pork or goose
Riz	rice
Robert	sauce with mustard, vinegar, onion
Roquefort	ewe's milk blue cheese
Rossini	garnished with foie gras and truffle
Rôti	roast
Rouelle	nugget
Rouille	hot garlicky sauce for soupe de poisson
Roulade	roll
Roux	sauce base – flour and butter
Sabayon	sweet fluffy sauce, with eggs and wine
Safran	saffron
Sagou	sago
St.-Germain	with peas
Salade niçoise	with tunny, anchovies, tomatoes, beans, black olives

Salé	salted
Salmis	dish of game or fowl, with red wine
Sang	blood
Santé	lit. healthy, i.e. with spinach and potato
Salpicon	meat, fowl, vegetables, chopped fine, bound with sauce and used as fillings
Saucisse	fresh sausage
Saucisson	dried sausage
Sauté	cooked in fat in open pan
Sauvage	wild
Savarin	ring of yeast sponge, soaked in syrup and liquor
Sel	salt
Selle	saddle
Selon	according to, i.e. selon grosseur (according to size)
Smitane	with sour cream, white wine, onion
Soissons	with dried white beans
Sorbet	water ice
Soubise	with creamed onions
Soufflé	puffed, i.e. mixed with egg white and baked
Sucre	sugar (sucré – sugared)
Suprême	fillet of poultry breast or fish
Tartare	raw minced beef, flavoured with onion etc. and bound with raw egg
Tartare (sauce)	mayonnaise with capers, herbs, onions

Tarte Tatin	upside-down apple pie
Terrine	pottery dish/baked minced, chopped meat, veg., chicken, fish or fruit
Thé	tea
Tiède	lukewarm
Timbale	steamed mould
Tisane	infusion
Tourte	pie
Tranche	thick slice
Truffes	truffles
Tuile	tile, i.e. thin biscuit
Vacherin	meringue confection
Vallée d'Auge	with cream, apple, Calvados
Vapeur (au)	steamed
Velouté	white sauce, bouillon-flavoured
Véronique	with grapes
Vert(e)	green, i.e. sauce verte with herbs
Vessie	pig's bladder
Vichyssoise	chilled creamy leek and potato soup
Vierge	prime olive oil
Vinaigre	vinegar (lit. bitter wine)
Vinaigrette	wine vinegar and oil dressing
Volaille	poultry
Vol-au-vent	puff pastry case
Xérès	sherry
Yaourt	yoghurt

FISH – Les poissons, SHELLFISH – Les coquillages

Aiglefin	haddock – also Églefin	*Langouste*	crawfish
Alose	shad	*Langoustine*	Dublin Bay prawn
Anchois	anchovy	*Lieu*	ling
Anguille	eel	*Limand*	lemon sole
Araignée de mer	spider crab	*Lotte de mer*	monkfish
Bar	sea bass	*Loup de mer*	sea bass
Barbue	brill	*Maquereau*	mackerel
Baudroie	monkfish, anglerfish	*Merlan*	whiting
Belon	oyster – flat shelled	*Mérou*	grouper
Bigorneau	winkle	*Morue*	salt cod
Blanchaille	whitebait	*Moule*	mussel
Brochet	pike	*Muge, mulet*	grey mullet
Cabillaud	cod	*Murène*	moray eel
Calmar	squid	*Nonat*	tiny fish similar to
Carrelet	plaice		whitebait
Chapon de mer	scorpion fish	*Ombre*	grayling
Claire	oyster	*Orade*	gilt-headed bream
Clovisse	large clam	*Oursin*	sea urchin
Colin	hake	*Pageot*	sea bream
Congre	conger eel	*Palourde*	clam
Coques	cockles	*Perche*	perch
Coquille	scallop	*Petoncle*	small scallop
St. Jacques		*Plie*	plaice
Crabe	crab	*Portugaise*	oyster
Crevette grise	shrimp	*Poulpe*	octopus
Crevette rose	prawn	*Praire*	small clam
Daurade	sea bream	*Raie*	skate
Donzelle or Girelle	a brightly coloured eel-	*Rascasse*	scorpion-fish
	like Mediterranean fish	*Rouget*	red mullet
Écrevisse	crayfish	*St. Pierre*	John Dory
Encornet	cuttlefish, squid	*Sauclet*	sand smelt
Éperlan	smelt	*Saumon*	salmon
Espadon	swordfish	*Saumonette*	rock salmon
Etrille	baby crab	*Scipion*	cuttlefish
Favouille	spider crab	*Seiche*	squid
Fiecas	conger eel	*Sole*	sole
Flétan	halibut	*Soupion*	inkfish
Fruits de mer	seafood	*Sourdon*	cockle
Gamba	large prawn	*Thon*	tunny
Grondin	red gurnet	*Tortue*	turtle
Hareng	herring	*Tourteau*	large crab
Homard	lobster	*Truite*	trout
Huitre	oyster	*Turbot*	turbot
Julienne	ling	*Turbotin*	chicken turbot
Laitance	soft herring roe	*Vernis*	clam
Lamproie	lamprey	*Violet*	soft-shelled shellfish

FRUITS – Les fruits, VEGETABLES – Les légumes, NUTS – Les noix
HERBS – Les herbes, SPICES – Les épices

Ail	garlic
Algue	seaweed
Amande	almond
Ananas	pineapple
Aneth	dill
Abricot	apricot
Arachide	peanut
Artichaut	globe artichoke
Asperge	asparagus
Avocat	avocado
Banane	banana
Basilic	basil
Betterave	beetroot
Blette	Swiss chard
Brugnon	nectarine
Cassis	blackcurrant
Céleri	celery
Céleri-rave	celeriac
Cèpe	edible fungus
Cerfeuil	chervil
Cérise	cherry
Champignon	mushroom
Chanterelle	edible fungus
Chatâigne	chestnut
Chicorée	endive
Chou	cabbage
Choufleur	cauliflower
Choux de Bruxelles	Brussels sprout
Ciboulette	chive
Citron	lemon
Citron vert	lime
Coing	quince
Concombre	cucumber
Coriandre	coriander
Cornichon	gherkin
Courge	marrow, pumpkin
Courgette	courgette
Cresson	watercress
Échalotte	shallot
Endive	chicory
Épinard	spinach
Escarole	salad leaves
Estragon	tarragon
Fenouil	fennel
Fève	broad bean
Flageolet	small green bean
Fraise	strawberry
Framboise	raspberry
Genièvre	juniper
Gingembre	ginger
Girofle	clove
Girolle	edible fungus
Granade	pomegranate
Griotte	bitter red cherry
Groseille à maquereau	gooseberry
Groseille noire	blackcurrant
Groseille rouge	redcurrant
Haricot	dried white bean
Haricot vert	French bean
Laitue	lettuce
Mandarine	tangerine, mandarin
Mangetout	sugar pea
Marron	chestnut
Menthe	mint
Mirabelle	tiny gold plum
Morille	dark brown crinkly edible fungus
Mûre	blackberry
Muscade	nutmeg
Myrtille	bilberry, blueberry
Navet	turnip
Noisette	hazelnut
Oignon	onion
Oseille	sorrel
Palmier	palm
Pamplemousse	grapefruit
Panais	parsnip
Passe-Pierre	seaweed
Pastèque	water melon
Pêche	peach
Persil	parsley
Petit pois	pea
Piment doux	sweet pepper
Pissenlit	dandelion
Pistache	pistachio
Pleurote	edible fungi
Poire	pear
Poireau	leek
Poivre	pepper
Poivron	green, red and yellow peppers
Pomme	apple
Pomme-de-terre	potato
Prune	plum
Pruneau	prune
Quetsch	small dark plum
Radis	radish
Raifort	horseradish
Raisin	grape
Reine Claude	greengage
Romarin	rosemary
Safran	saffron
Salisifis	salsify
Thym	thyme
Tilleul	lime blossom
Tomate	tomato
Topinambour	Jerusalem artichoke
Truffe	truffle

MEAT – Les viandes

Le Boeuf	Beef	*Jambon cru*	raw smoked ham
Charolais	is the best	*Porcelet*	suckling pig
Chateaubriand	double fillet steak		
Contrefilet	sirloin	*Le Veau*	Veal
Entrecôte	rib steak	*Escalope*	thin slice cut from fillet
Faux filet	sirloin steak		
Filet	fillet	*Les Abats*	Offal
		Cervelles	brains
L'Agneau	Lamb	*Foie*	liver
Carré	neck cutlets	*Foie gras*	goose liver
Côte	chump chop	*Langue*	tongue
Epaule	shoulder	*Ris*	sweetbreads
Gigot	leg	*Rognons*	kidneys
Pré-Salé	is the best	*Tripes*	tripe
Le Porc	Pork		
Jambon	ham		

POULTRY– Volaille, GAME – Gibier

Abatis	giblets	*Lièvre*	hare
Bécasse	woodcock	*Oie*	goose
Bécassine	snipe	*Perdreau*	partridge
Caille	quail	*Pigeon*	pigeon
Canard	duck	*Pintade*	guineafowl
Caneton	duckling	*Pluvier*	plover
Chapon	capon	*Poularde*	chicken (boiling)
Chevreuil	roe deer	*Poulet*	chicken (roasting)
Dinde	young hen turkey	*Poussin*	spring chicken
Dindon	turkey	*Sanglier*	wild boar
Dindonneau	young turkey	*Sarcelle*	teal
Faisan	pheasant	*Venaison*	venison
Grive	thrush		

Other French Entrée Guides

French Entrée 8	The Loire	£6.95
French Entrée 9	Normandy Encore	£6.95
French Entrée 10	The South of France	£6.95
French Entrée 11	Paris	£6.95
French Entrée 12	North of France	£6.95
French Entrée 13	Provence	£6.95
French Entrée 14	Brittany Encore	£6.95
French Entrée 16	Gardens of France	£9.99

Also Entrées to Majorca, Algarve, Malta, Florida, Catalunya, Halkidiki.